# UNIX®

## TEXT PROCESSING

# UNIX®
## TEXT PROCESSING

## DALE DOUGHERTY AND TIM O'REILLY
*and the staff of O'Reilly & Associates, Inc.*

CONSULTING EDITORS:
**Stephen G. Kochan and Patrick H. Wood**

## *HAYDEN BOOKS*
*A Division of Howard W. Sams & Company*
*11711 North College, Carmel, Indiana 46032 USA*

International Standard Book Number: 0-8104-6291-5
Library of Congress Catalog Card Number: 87-60537

Acquisitions Editor: *Therese Zak*
Editor: *Susan Pink Bussiere*
Cover: *Visual Graphic Services, Indianapolis*
        Design by Jerry Bates
        Illustration by Patrick Sarles
Typesetting: *O'Reilly & Associates, Inc.*

*Printed in the United States of America*

## Trademark Acknowledgements

# C O N T E N T S

# Preface

Many people think of computers primarily as "number crunchers," and think of word processors as generating form letters and boilerplate proposals. That computers can be used productively by writers, not just research scientists, accountants, and secretaries, is not so widely recognized. Today, writers not only work with words, they work with computers and the software programs, printers, and terminals that are part of a computer system.

The computer has not simply replaced a typewriter; it has become a system for integrating many other technologies. As these technologies are made available at a reasonable cost, writers may begin to find themselves in new roles as computer programmers, systems integrators, data base managers, graphic designers, typesetters, printers, and archivists.

The writer functioning in these new roles is faced with additional responsibilities. Obviously, it is one thing to have a tool available and another thing to use it skillfully. Like a craftsman, the writer must develop a number of specialized skills, gaining control over the method of production as well as the product. The writer must look for ways to improve the process by integrating new technologies and designing new tools in software.

In this book, we want to show how computers can be used effectively in the preparation of written documents, especially in the process of producing book-length documents. Surely it is important to learn the tools of the trade, and we will demonstrate the tools available in the UNIX environment. However, it is also valuable to examine text processing in terms of problems and solutions: the problems faced by a writer undertaking a large writing project and the solutions offered by using the resources and power of a computer system.

In Chapter 1, we begin by outlining the general capabilities of word-processing systems. We describe in brief the kinds of things that a computer must be able to do for a writer, regardless of whether that writer is working on a UNIX system or on an IBM PC with a word-processing package such as WordStar or MultiMate. Then, having defined basic word-processing capabilities, we look at how a text-processing system includes and extends these capabilities and benefits. Last, we introduce the set of text-processing tools in the UNIX environment. These tools, used individually or in combination, provide the basic framework for a text-processing system, one that can be custom-tailored to supply additional capabilities.

Chapter 2 gives a brief review of UNIX fundamentals. We assume you are already somewhat acquainted with UNIX, but we included this information to make sure that you are familiar with basic concepts that we will be relying on later in the book.

Chapter 3 introduces the vi editor, a basic tool for entering and editing text. Although many other editors and word-processing programs are available with UNIX, vi has the advantage that it works, without modification, on almost every UNIX system and with almost every type of terminal. If you learn vi, you can be confident that your text editing skills will be completely transferable when you sit down at someone else's terminal or use someone else's system.

Chapter 4 introduces the nroff and troff formatting programs. Because vi is a text editor, not a word-processing program, it does only rudimentary formatting of the text you enter. You can enter special formatting codes to specify how you want the document to look, then format the text using either nroff or troff. (The nroff formatter is used for formatting documents to the screen or to typewriter-like printers; troff uses much the same formatting language, but has additional constructs that allow it to produce more elaborate effects on typesetters and laser printers.)

In this chapter, we also describe the different types of output devices for printing your finished documents. With the wider availability of laser printers, you need to become familiar with many typesetting terms and concepts to get the most out of troff's capabilities.

The formatting markup language required by nroff and troff is quite complex, because it allows detailed control over the placement of every character on the page, as well as a large number of programming constructs that you can use to define custom formatting requests or macros. A number of macro packages have been developed to make the markup language easier to use. These macro packages define commonly used formatting requests for different types of documents, set up default values for page layout, and so on.

Although someone working with the macro packages does not need to know about the underlying requests in the formatting language used by nroff and troff, we believe that the reader wants to go beyond the basics. As a result, Chapter 4 introduces additional basic requests that the casual user might not need. However, your understanding of what is going on should be considerably enhanced.

There are two principal macro packages in use today, ms and mm (named for the command-line options to nroff and troff used to invoke them). Both macro packages were available with most UNIX systems; now, however, ms is chiefly available on UNIX systems derived from Berkeley 4.x BSD, and mm is chiefly available on UNIX systems derived from AT&T System V. If you are lucky enough to have both macro packages on your system, you can choose which one you want to learn. Otherwise, you should read either Chapter 5, *The ms Macros*, or Chapter 6, *The mm Macros*, depending on which version you have available.

Chapter 7 returns to vi to consider its more advanced features. In addition, it takes a look at how some of these features can support easy entry of formatting codes used by nroff and troff.

Tables and mathematical equations provide special formatting problems. The low-level nroff and troff commands for typesetting a complex table or equation are extraordinarily complex. However, no one needs to learn or type these commands, because two preprocessors, tbl and eqn, take a high-level specification of the table or equation and do the dirty work for you. They produce a "script" of nroff or troff commands that can be piped to the formatter to lay out the table or equations. The tbl and eqn preprocessors are described in Chapters 8 and 9, respectively.

More recent versions of UNIX (those that include AT&T's separate *Documenter's Workbench* software) also support a preprocessor called pic that makes it easier to create simple line drawings with troff and include them in your text. We talk about pic in Chapter 10.

Chapter 11 introduces a range of other UNIX text-processing tools—programs for sorting, comparing, and in various ways examining the contents of text files. This chapter includes a discussion of the standard UNIX spell program and the *Writer's Workbench* programs style and diction.

This concludes the first part of the book, which covers the tools that the writer finds at hand in the UNIX environment. This material is not elementary. In places, it grows quite complex. However, we believe there is a fundamental difference between learning how to use an existing tool and developing skills that extend a tool's capabilities to achieve your own goals.

That is the real beauty of the UNIX environment. Nearly all the tools it provides are extensible, either because they have built-in constructs for self-extension, like nroff and troff's macro capability, or because of the wonderful programming powers of the UNIX command interpreter, the shell.

The second part of the book begins with Chapter 12, on editing scripts. There are several editors in UNIX that allow you to write and save what essentially amount to programs for manipulating text. The ex editor can be used from within vi to make global changes or complex edits. The next step is to use ex on its own; and after you do that, it is a small step to the even more powerful global editor sed. After you have mastered these tools, you can build a library of special-purpose editing scripts that vastly extend your power over the recalcitrant words you have put down on paper and now wish to change.

Chapter 13 discusses another program—awk—that extends the concept of a text editor even further than the programs discussed in Chapter 12. The awk program is really a database programming language that is appropriate for performing certain kinds of text-processing tasks. In particular, we use it in this book to process output from troff for indexing.

The next five chapters turn to the details of writing troff macros, and show how to customize the formatting language to simplify formatting tasks. We start in Chapter 14 by looking at the basic requests used to build macros, then go on in Chapter 15 to the requests for achieving various types of special effects. In Chapters 16 and 17, we'll take a look at the basic structure of a macro package and focus on how to define the appearance/of large documents such as manuals. We'll show you how to define different styles of section headings, page headers, footers, and so on. We'll also talk about how to generate an automatic table of contents and index—two tasks that take you beyond `troff` into the world of shell programming and various UNIX text-processing utilities.

To complete these tasks, we need to return to the UNIX shell in Chapter 18 and examine in more detail the ways that it allows you to incorporate the many tools provided by UNIX into an integrated text-processing environment.

Numerous appendices summarize information that is spread throughout the text, or that couldn't be crammed into it.

* * *

Before we turn to the subject at hand, a few acknowledgements are in order. Though only two names appear on the cover of this book, it is in fact the work of many hands. In particular, Grace Todino wrote the chapters on `tbl` and `eqn` in their entirety, and the chapters on `vi` and `ex` are based on the O'Reilly & Associates' Nutshell Handbook, *Learning the Vi Editor*, written by Linda Lamb. Other members of the O'Reilly & Associates staff—Linda Mui, Valerie Quercia, and Donna Woonteiler—helped tirelessly with copyediting, proofreading, illustrations, typesetting, and indexing.

Donna was new to our staff when she took on responsibility for the job of copyfitting—that final stage in page layout made especially arduous by the many figures and examples in this book. She and Linda especially spent many long hours getting this book ready for the printer. Linda had the special job of doing the final consistency check on examples, making sure that copyediting changes or typesetting errors had not compromized the accuracy of the examples.

Special thanks go to Steve Talbott of Masscomp, who first introduced us to the power of `troff` and who wrote the first version of the extended `ms` macros, `format` shell script, and indexing mechanism described in the second half of this book. Steve's help and patience were invaluable during the long road to mastery of the UNIX text-processing environment.

We'd also like to thank Teri Zak, the acquisitions editor at Hayden Books, for her vision of the Hayden UNIX series, and this book's place in it.

In the course of this book's development, Hayden was acquired by Howard Sams, where Teri's role was taken over by Jim Hill. Thanks also to the excellent production editors at Sams, Wendy Ford, Lou Keglovitz, and especially Susan Pink Bussiere, whose copyediting was outstanding.

Through it all, we have had the help of Steve Kochan and Pat Wood of Pipeline Associates, Inc., consulting editors to the Hayden UNIX Series. We are grateful for their thoughtful and thorough review of this book for technical accuracy. (We must, of course, make the usual disclaimer: any errors that remain are our own.)

Steve and Pat also provided the macros to typeset the book. Our working drafts were printed on an HP LaserJet printer, using `ditroff` and TextWare International's `tplus` postprocessor. Final typeset output was prepared with Pipeline Associates' `devps`, which was used to convert `ditroff` output to PostScript, which was used in turn to drive a Linotronic L100 typesetter.

# From Typewriters to Word Processors

Before we consider the special tools that the UNIX environment provides for text processing, we need to think about the underlying changes in the process of writing that are inevitable when you begin to use a computer.

The most important features of a computer program for writers are the ability to remember what is typed and the ability to allow incremental changes—no more retyping from scratch each time a draft is revised. For a writer first encountering word-processing software, no other features even begin to compare. The crudest command structure, the most elementary formatting capabilities, will be forgiven because of the immense labor savings that take place.

Writing is basically an iterative process. It is a rare writer who dashes out a finished piece; most of us work in circles, returning again and again to the same piece of prose, adding or deleting words, phrases, and sentences, changing the order of thoughts, and elaborating a single sentence into pages of text.

A writer working on paper periodically needs to clear the deck—to type a clean copy, free of elaboration. As the writer reads the new copy, the process of revision continues, a word here, a sentence there, until the new draft is as obscured by changes as the first. As Joyce Carol Oates is said to have remarked: "No book is ever finished. It is abandoned."

Word processing first took hold in the office as a tool to help secretaries prepare perfect letters, memos, and reports. As dedicated word processors were replaced with low-cost personal computers, writers were quick to see the value of this new tool. In a civilization obsessed with the written word, it is no accident that WordStar, a word-processing program, was one of the first best sellers of the personal computer revolution.

As you learn to write with a word processor, your working style changes. Because it is so easy to make revisions, it is much more forgivable to think with your fingers when you write, rather than to carefully outline your thoughts beforehand and polish each sentence as you create it.

If you do work from an outline, you can enter it first, then write your first draft by filling in the outline, section by section. If you are writing a structured document such as a technical manual, your outline points become the headings in your document; if you are writing a free-flowing work, they can be subsumed gradually in the text as you flesh them out. In either case, it is easy to write in small segments that can be moved as you reorganize your ideas.

Watching a writer at work on a word processor is very different from watching a writer at work on a typewriter. A typewriter tends to enforce a linear flow—you must write a passage and then go back later to revise it. On a word processor, revisions are constant—you type a sentence, then go back to change the sentence above. Perhaps you write a few words, change your mind, and back up to take a different tack; or you decide the paragraph you just wrote would make more sense if you put it ahead of the one you wrote before, and move it on the spot.

This is not to say that a written work is created on a word processor in a single smooth flow; in fact, the writer using a word processor tends to create many more drafts than a compatriot who still uses a pen or typewriter. Instead of three or four drafts, the writer may produce ten or twenty. There is still a certain editorial distance that comes only when you read a printed copy. This is especially true when that printed copy is nicely formatted and letter perfect.

This brings us to the second major benefit of word-processing programs: they help the writer with simple formatting of a document. For example, a word processor may automatically insert carriage returns at the end of each line and adjust the space between words so that all the lines are the same length. Even more importantly, the text is automatically readjusted when you make changes. There are probably commands for centering, underlining, and boldfacing text.

The rough formatting of a document can cover a multitude of sins. As you read through your scrawled markup of a preliminary typewritten draft, it is easy to lose track of the overall flow of the document. Not so when you have a clean copy—the flaws of organization and content stand out vividly against the crisp new sheets of paper.

However, the added capability to print a clean draft after each revision also puts an added burden on the writer. Where once you had only to worry about content, you may now find yourself fussing with consistency of margins, headings, boldface, italics, and all the other formerly superfluous impedimenta that have now become integral to your task.

As the writer gets increasingly involved in the formatting of a document, it becomes essential that the tools help revise the document's appearance as easily as its content. Given these changes imposed by the evolution from typewriters to word processors, let's take a look at what a word-processing system needs to offer to the writer.

## ▪ A Workspace ▪

One of the most important capabilities of a word processor is that it provides a space in which you can create documents. In one sense, the video display screen on your terminal, which echoes the characters you type, is analogous to a sheet of paper. But the workspace of a word processor is not so unambiguous as a sheet of paper wound into a typewriter, that may be added neatly to the stack of completed work when finished, or torn out and crumpled as a false start. From the computer's point of view, your workspace is a block of memory, called a *buffer*, that is allocated when you begin a word-processing session. This buffer is a temporary holding area for storing your work and is emptied at the end of each session.

To save your work, you have to write the contents of the buffer to a file. A file is a permanent storage area on a disk (a hard disk or a floppy disk). After you have saved your work in a file, you can retrieve it for use in another session.

When you begin a session editing a document that exists on file, a copy of the file is made and its contents are read into the buffer. You actually work on the copy, making changes to *it*, not the original. The file is not changed until you save your changes during or at the end of your work session. You can also discard changes made to the buffered copy, keeping the original file intact, or save multiple versions of a document in separate files.

Particularly when working with larger documents, the management of disk files can become a major effort. If, like most writers, you save multiple drafts, it is easy to lose track of which version of a file is the latest.

An ideal text-processing environment for serious writers should provide tools for saving and managing multiple drafts on disk, not just on paper. It should allow the writer to

- work on documents of any length;
- save multiple versions of a file;
- save part of the buffer into a file for later use;
- switch easily between multiple files;
- insert the contents of an existing file into the buffer;
- summarize the differences between two versions of a document.

Most word-processing programs for personal computers seem to work best for short documents such as the letters and memos that offices churn out by the millions each day. Although it is possible to create longer documents, many features that would help organize a large document such as a book or manual are missing from these programs.

However, long before word processors became popular, programmers were using another class of programs called *text editors*. Text editors were designed chiefly for entering computer programs, not text. Furthermore, they were designed for use by computer professionals, not computer novices. As a result, a text editor can be more difficult to learn, lacking many on-screen formatting features available with most word processors.

Nonetheless, the text editors used in program development environments can provide much better facilities for managing large writing projects than their office word-processing counterparts. Large programs, like large documents, are often contained in many separate files; furthermore, it is essential to track the differences between versions of a program.

UNIX is a pre-eminent program development environment and, as such, it is also a superb document development environment. Although its text editing tools at first may appear limited in contrast to sophisticated office word processors, they are in fact considerably more powerful.

## ▪ Tools for Editing ▪

For many, the ability to retrieve a document from a file and make multiple revisions painlessly makes it impossible to write at a typewriter again. However, before you can get the benefits of word processing, there is a lot to learn.

Editing operations are performed by issuing commands. Each word-processing system has its own unique set of commands. At a minimum, there are commands to

- move to a particular position in the document;
- insert new text;
- change or replace text;
- delete text;
- copy or move text.

To make changes to a document, you must be able to move to that place in the text where you want to make your edits. Most documents are too large to be displayed in their entirety on a single terminal screen, which generally displays 24 lines of text. Usually only a portion of a document is displayed. This partial view of your document is sometimes referred to as a *window*.* If you are entering new text and reach the bottom line in the window, the text on the screen automatically scrolls (rolls up) to reveal an additional line at the bottom. A cursor (an underline or block) marks your current position in the window.

There are basically two kinds of movement:

- scrolling new text into the window
- positioning the cursor within the window

When you begin a session, the first line of text is the first line in the window, and the cursor is positioned on the first character. Scrolling commands change which lines are displayed in the window by moving forward or backward through the document. Cursor-positioning commands allow you to move up and down to individual lines, and along lines to particular characters.

After you position the cursor, you must issue a command to make the desired edit. The command you choose indicates how much text will be affected: a character, a word, a line, or a sentence.

Because the same keyboard is used to enter both text and commands, there must be some way to distinguish between the two. Some word-processing programs assume that you are entering text unless you specify otherwise; newly entered text either

---

*Some editors, such as `emacs`, can split the terminal screen into multiple windows. In addition, many high-powered UNIX workstations with large bit-mapped screens have their own windowing software that allows multiple programs to be run simultaneously in separate windows. For purposes of this book, we assume you are using the `vi` editor and an alphanumeric terminal with only a single window.

replaces existing text or pushes it over to make room for the new text. Commands are entered by pressing special keys on the keyboard, or by combining a standard key with a special key, such as the *control key* (*CTRL*).

Other programs assume that you are issuing commands; you must enter a command before you can type any text at all. There are advantages and disadvantages to each approach. Starting out in text mode is more intuitive to those coming from a typewriter, but may be slower for experienced writers, because all commands must be entered by special key combinations that are often hard to reach and slow down typing. (We'll return to this topic when we discuss `vi`, a UNIX text editor.)

Far more significant than the style of command entry is the range and speed of commands. For example, though it is heaven for someone used to a typewriter to be able to delete a word and type in a replacement, it is even better to be able to issue a command that will replace every occurrence of that word in an entire document. And, after you start making such global changes, it is essential to have some way to undo them if you make a mistake.

A word processor that substitutes ease of learning for ease of use by having fewer commands will ultimately fail the serious writer, because the investment of time spent learning complex commands can easily be repaid when they simplify complex tasks.

And when you do issue a complex command, it is important that it works as quickly as possible, so that you aren't left waiting while the computer grinds away. The extra seconds add up when you spend hours or days at the keyboard, and, once having been given a taste of freedom from drudgery, writers want as much freedom as they can get.

Text editors were developed before word processors (in the rapid evolution of computers). Many of them were originally designed for printing terminals, rather than for the CRT-based terminals used by word processors. These programs tend to have commands that work with text on a line-by-line basis. These commands are often more obscure than the equivalent office word processing commands.

However, though the commands used by text editors are sometimes more difficult to learn, they are usually very effective. (The commands designed for use with slow paper terminals were often extraordinarily powerful, to make up for the limited capabilities of the input and output device.)

There are two basic kinds of text editors, *line editors* and *screen editors*, and both are available in UNIX. The difference is simple: line editors display one line at a time, and screen editors can display approximately 24 lines or a full screen.

The line editors in UNIX include `ed`, `sed`, and `ex`. Although these line editors are obsolete for general-purpose use by writers, there are applications at which they excel, as we will see in Chapters 7 and 12.

The most common screen editor in UNIX is `vi`. Learning `vi` or some other suitable editor is the first step in mastering the UNIX text-processing environment. Most of your time will be spent using the editor.

UNIX screen editors such as `vi` and `emacs` (another editor available on many UNIX systems) lack ease-of-learning features common in many word processors—there are no menus and only primitive on-line help screens, and the commands are often complex and nonintuitive—but they are powerful and fast. What's more, UNIX line editors such as `ex` and `sed` give additional capabilities not found in word processors—the ability to write a script of editing commands that can be applied to multiple files. Such editing scripts open new ranges of capability to the writer.

## ▪ Document Formatting ▪

Text editing is wonderful, but the object of the writing process is to produce a printed document for others to read. And a printed document is more than words on paper; it is an arrangement of text on a page. For instance, the elements of a business letter are arranged in a consistent format, which helps the person reading the letter identify those elements. Reports and more complex documents, such as technical manuals or books, require even greater attention to formatting. The format of a document conveys how information is organized, assisting in the presentation of ideas to a reader.

Most word-processing programs have built-in formatting capabilities. Formatting commands are intermixed with editing commands, so that you can shape your document on the screen. Such formatting commands are simple extensions of those available to someone working with a typewriter. For example, an automatic centering command saves the trouble of manually counting characters to center a title or other text. There may also be such features as automatic pagination and printing of headers or footers.

Text editors, by contrast, usually have few formatting capabilities. Because they were designed for entering programs, their formatting capabilities tend to be oriented toward the formats required by one or more programming languages.

Even programmers write reports, however. Especially at AT&T (where UNIX was developed), there was a great emphasis on document preparation tools to help the programmers and scientists of Bell Labs produce research reports, manuals, and other documents associated with their development work.

Word processing, with its emphasis on easy-to-use programs with simple on-screen formatting, was in its infancy. Computerized phototypesetting, on the other hand, was already a developed art. Until quite recently, it was not possible to represent on a video screen the variable type styles and sizes used in typeset documents. As a result, phototypesetting has long used a markup system that indicates formatting instructions with special codes. These formatting instructions to the computerized typesetter are often direct descendants of the instructions that were formerly given to a human typesetter—center the next line, indent five spaces, boldface this heading.

The text formatter most commonly used with the UNIX system is called `nroff`. To use it, you must intersperse formatting instructions (usually one- or two-letter codes preceded by a period) within your text, then pass the file through the formatter. The `nroff` program interprets the formatting codes and reformats the document ''on the fly'' while passing it on to the printer. The `nroff` formatter prepares documents for printing on line printers, dot-matrix printers, and letter-quality printers. Another program called `troff` uses an extended version of the same markup language used by `nroff`, but prepares documents for printing on laser printers and typesetters. We'll talk more about printing in a moment.

Although formatting with a markup language may seem to be a far inferior system to the ''what you see is what you get'' (*wysiwyg*) approach of most office word-processing programs, it actually has many advantages.

First, unless you are using a very sophisticated computer, with very sophisticated software (what has come to be called an electronic publishing system, rather than a mere word processor), it is not possible to display everything on the screen just as it will appear on the printed page. For example, the screen may not be able to represent boldfacing or underlining except with special formatting codes. WordStar, one of the grandfathers of word-processing programs for personal computers, represents underlining by surrounding the word or words to be underlined with the special control character ^S (the character generated by holding down the *control* key while typing the letter *S*). For example, the following title line would be underlined when the document is printed:

```
^SWord Processing with WordStar^S
```

Is this really superior to the following nroff construct?

```
.ul
Text Processing with vi and nroff
```

It is perhaps unfair to pick on WordStar, an older word-processing program, but very few word-processing programs can complete the illusion that what you see on the screen is what you will get on paper. There is usually some mix of control codes with on-screen formatting. More to the point, though, is the fact that most word processors are oriented toward the production of short documents. When you get beyond a letter, memo, or report, you start to understand that there is more to formatting than meets the eye.

Although "what you see is what you get" is fine for laying out a single page, it is much harder to enforce consistency across a large document. The design of a large document is often determined before writing is begun, just as a set of plans for a house are drawn up before anyone starts construction. The design is a plan for organizing a document, arranging various parts so that the same types of material are handled in the same way.

The parts of a document might be chapters, sections, or subsections. For instance, a technical manual is often organized into chapters and appendices. Within each chapter, there might be numbered sections that are further divided into three or four levels of subsections.

Document design seeks to accomplish across the entire document what is accomplished by the table of contents of a book. It presents the structure of a document and helps the reader locate information.

Each of the parts must be clearly identified. The design specifies how they will look, trying to achieve consistency throughout the document. The strategy might specify that major section headings will be all uppercase, underlined, with three blank lines above and two below, and secondary headings will be in uppercase and lowercase, underlined, with two blank lines above and one below.

If you have ever tried to format a large document using a word processor, you have probably found it difficult to enforce consistency in such formatting details as these. By contrast, a markup language—especially one like nroff that allows you to define repeated command sequences, or *macros*—makes it easy: the style of a heading is defined once, and a code used to reference it. For example, a top-level heading might be specified by the code .H1, and a secondary heading by .H2.

Even more significantly, if you later decide to change the design, you simply change the definition of the relevant design elements. If you have used a word processor to format the document as it was written, it is usually a painful task to go back and change the format.

Some word-processing programs, such as Microsoft WORD, include features for defining global document formats, but these features are not as widespread as they are in markup systems.

## ▪ Printing ▪

The formatting capabilities of a word-processing system are limited by what can be output on a printer. For example, some printers cannot backspace and therefore cannot underline. For this discussion, we are considering four different classes of printers: dot matrix, letter quality, phototypesetter, and laser.

A *dot-matrix* printer composes characters as a series of dots. It is usually suitable for preparing interoffice memos and obtaining fast printouts of large files.

```
This paragraph was printed with a dot-matrix printer.  It uses a print
head containing 9 pins, which are adjusted to produce the shape of each
character.  More sophicated dot-matrix printers have print heads
containing up to 24 pins.  The greater the number of pins, the finer
the dots that are printed, and the more possible it is to fool the eye
into thinking it sees a solid character.  Dot matrix printers are also
capable of printing out graphic displays.
```

A *letter-quality* printer is more expensive and slower. Its printing mechanism operates like a typewriter and achieves a similar result.

```
This paragraph was printed with a letter-
quality printer.  It is essentially a
computer-controlled typewriter and, like a
typewriter, uses a print ball or wheel
containing fully formed characters.
```

A letter-quality printer produces clearer, easier-to-read copy than a dot-matrix printer. Letter-quality printers are generally used in offices for formal correspondence as well as for the final drafts of proposals and reports.

Until very recently, documents that needed a higher quality of printing than that available with letter-quality printers were sent out for typesetting. Even if draft copy was word-processed, the material was often re-entered by the typesetter, although many typesetting companies can read the files created by popular word-processing programs and use them as a starting point for typesetting.

This paragraph, like the rest of this book, was phototypeset. In photo-typesetting, a photographic technique is used to print characters on film or photographic paper. There is a wide choice of type styles, and the characters are much more finely formed that those produced by a letter-quality printer. Characters are produced by an arrangement of tiny dots, much like a dot-matrix printer—but there are over 1000 dots per inch.

There are several major advantages to typesetting. The high resolution allows for the design of aesthetically pleasing type. The shape of the characters is much finer. In addition, where dot-matrix and letter-quality type is usually constant width (narrow letters like *i* take up the same amount of space as wide ones like *m*), typesetters use variable-width type, in which narrow letters take up less space than wide ones. In addition, it's possible to mix styles (for example, bold and italic) and sizes of type on the same page.

Most typesetting equipment uses a markup language rather than a *wysiwyg* approach to specify point sizes, type styles, leading, and so on. Until recently, the technology didn't even exist to represent on a screen the variable-width typefaces that appear in published books and magazines.

AT&T, a company with its own extensive internal publishing operation, developed its own typesetting markup language and typesetting program—a sister to nroff called troff (*typesetter-roff*). Although troff extends the capabilities of nroff in significant ways, it is almost totally compatible with it.

Until recently, unless you had access to a typesetter, you didn't have much use for troff. The development of low-cost laser printers that can produce near typeset-quality output at a fraction of the cost has changed all that.

This paragraph was produced on a laser printer. Laser printers produce high-resolution characters—300 to 500 dots per inch—though they are not quite as finely formed as phototypeset characters. Laser printers are not only cheaper to purchase than phototypesetters, they also print on plain paper, just like Xerox machines, and are therefore much cheaper to operate. However, as is always the case with computers, you need the proper software to take advantage of improved hardware capabilities.

Word-processing software (particularly that developed for the Apple Macintosh, which has a high-resolution graphics screen capable of representing variable type fonts) is beginning to tap the capabilities of laser printers. However, most of the microcomputer-based packages still have many limitations. Nonetheless, a markup language such as that provided by troff still provides the easiest and lowest-cost access to the world of electronic publishing for many types of documents.

The point made previously, that markup languages are preferable to *wysiwyg* systems for large documents, is especially true when you begin to use variable size fonts, leading, and other advanced formatting features. It is easy to lose track of the overall format of your document and difficult to make overall changes after your formatted text is in place. Only the most expensive electronic publishing systems (most of them based on advanced UNIX workstations) give you both the capability to see what you will get on the screen and the ability to define and easily change overall document formats.

## ▪ Other UNIX Text-Processing Tools ▪

Document editing and formatting are the most important parts of text processing, but they are not the whole story. For instance, in writing many types of documents, such as technical manuals, the writer rarely starts from scratch. Something is already written, whether it be a first draft written by someone else, a product specification, or an outdated version of a manual. It would be useful to get a copy of that material to work with. If that material was produced with a word processor or has been entered on another system, UNIX's communications facilities can transfer the file from the remote system to your own.

Then you can use a number of custom-made programs to search through and extract useful information. Word-processing programs often store text in files with different internal formats. UNIX provides a number of useful analysis and translation tools that can help decipher files with nonstandard formats. Other tools allow you to "cut and paste" portions of a document into the one you are writing.

As the document is being written, there are programs to check spelling, style, and diction. The reports produced by those programs can help you see if there is any detectable pattern in syntax or structure that might make a document more difficult for the user than it needs to be.

Although many documents are written once and published or filed, there is also a large class of documents (manuals in particular) that are revised again and again. Documents such as these require special tools for managing revisions. UNIX program development tools such as SCCS (Source Code Control System) and diff can be used by writers to compare past versions with the current draft and print out reports of the differences, or generate printed copies with change bars in the margin marking the differences.

In addition to all of the individual tools it provides, UNIX is a particularly fertile environment for writers who aren't afraid of computers, because it is easy to write command files, or *shell scripts*, that combine individual programs into more complex tools to meet your specific needs. For example, automatic index generation is a complex task that is not handled by any of the standard UNIX text-processing tools. We will show you ways to perform this and other tasks by applying the tools available in the UNIX environment and a little ingenuity.

We have two different objectives in this book. The first objective is that you learn to use many of the tools available on most UNIX systems. The second objective is that you develop an understanding of how these different tools can work together in a document preparation system. We're not just presenting a UNIX user's manual, but suggesting applications for which the various programs can be used.

To take full advantage of the UNIX text-processing environment, you must do more than just learn a few programs. For the writer, the job includes establishing standards and conventions about how documents will be stored, in what format they should appear in print, and what kinds of programs are needed to help this process take place efficiently with the use of a computer. Another way of looking at it is that you have to make certain choices prior to beginning a project. We want to encourage you to make your own choices, set your own standards, and realize the many possibilities that are open to a diligent and creative person.

In the past, many of the steps in creating a finished book were out of the hands of the writer. Proofreaders and copyeditors went over the text for spelling and grammatical errors. It was generally the printer who did the typesetting (a service usually paid by the publisher). At the print shop, a typesetter (a person) retyped the text and specified the font sizes and styles. A graphic artist, performing layout and pasteup, made many of the decisions about the appearance of the printed page.

Although producing a high-quality book can still involve many people, UNIX provides the tools that allow a writer to control the process from start to finish. An analogy is the difference between an assembly worker on a production line who views only one step in the process and a craftsman who guides the product from beginning to end. The craftsman has his own system of putting together a product, whereas the assembly worker has the system imposed upon him.

After you are acquainted with the basic tools available in UNIX and have spent some time using them, you can design additional tools to perform work that you think is necessary and helpful. To create these tools, you will write shell scripts that use the resources of UNIX in special ways. We think there is a certain satisfaction that comes with accomplishing such tasks by computer. It seems to us to reward careful thought.

What programming means to us is that when we confront a problem that normally submits only to tedium or brute force, we think of a way to get the computer to solve the problem. Doing this often means looking at the problem in a more general way and solving it in a way that can be applied again and again.

One of the most important books on UNIX is *The UNIX Programming Environment* by Brian W. Kernighan and Rob Pike. They write that what makes UNIX effective "is an approach to programming, a philosophy of using the computer." At the heart of this philosophy "is the idea that the power of a system comes more from the relationships among programs than from the programs themselves."

When we talk about building a document preparation system, it is this philosophy that we are trying to apply. As a consequence, this is a system that has great flexibility and gives the builders a feeling of breaking new ground. The UNIX text-processing environment is a system that can be tailored to the specific tasks you want to accomplish. In many instances, it can let you do just what a word processor does. In many more instances, it lets you use more of the computer to do things that a word processor either can't do or can't do very well.

# 2

# UNIX Fundamentals

The UNIX operating system is a collection of programs that controls and organizes the resources and activities of a computer system. These resources consist of hardware such as the computer's memory, various peripherals such as terminals, printers, and disk drives, and software utilities that perform specific tasks on the computer system. UNIX is a multiuser, multitasking operating system that allows the computer to perform a variety of functions for many users. It also provides users with an environment in which they can access the computer's resources and utilities. This environment is characterized by its command interpreter, the shell.

In this chapter, we review a set of basic concepts for users working in the UNIX environment. As we mentioned in the preface, this book does not replace a general introduction to UNIX. A complete overview is essential to anyone not familiar with the file system, input and output redirection, pipes and filters, and many basic utilities. In addition, there are different versions of UNIX, and not all commands are identical in each version. In writing this book, we've used System V Release 2 on a Convergent Technologies' Miniframe.

These disclaimers aside, if it has been a while since you tackled a general introduction, this chapter should help refresh your memory. If you are already familiar with UNIX, you can skip or skim this chapter.

As we explain these basic concepts, using a tutorial approach, we demonstrate the broad capabilities of UNIX as an applications environment for text-processing. What you learn about UNIX in general can be applied to performing specific tasks related to text-processing.

## · The UNIX Shell ·

As an interactive computer system, UNIX provides a command interpreter called a shell. The shell accepts commands typed at your terminal, invokes a program to perform specific tasks on the computer, and handles the output or result of this program, normally directing it to the terminal's video display screen.

UNIX commands can be simple one-word entries like the `date` command:

```
$ date
Tue Apr  8 13:23:41 EST 1987
```

Or their usage can be more complex, requiring that you specify options and arguments, such as filenames. Although some commands have a peculiar syntax, many UNIX commands follow this general form:

*command option(s) argument(s)*

A *command* identifies a software program or utility. Commands are entered in lowercase letters. One typical command, `ls`, lists the files that are available in your immediate storage area, or *directory*.

An *option* modifies the way in which a command works. Usually options are indicated by a minus sign followed by a single letter. For example, `ls -l` modifies what information is displayed about a file. The set of possible options is particular to the command and generally only a few of them are regularly used. However, if you want to modify a command to perform in a special manner, be sure to consult a UNIX reference guide and examine the available options.

An *argument* can specify an expression or the name of a file on which the command is to act. Arguments may also be required when you specify certain options. In addition, if more than one filename is being specified, special *metacharacters* (such as * and ?) can be used to represent the filenames. For instance, `ls -l ch*` will display information about all files that have names beginning with `ch`.

The UNIX shell is itself a program that is invoked as part of the login process. When you have properly identified yourself by logging in, the UNIX system prompt appears on your terminal screen.

The prompt that appears on your screen may be different from the one shown in the examples in this book. There are two widely used shells: the Bourne shell and the C shell. Traditionally, the Bourne shell uses a dollar sign ($) as a system prompt, and the C shell uses a percent sign (%). The two shells differ in the features they provide and in the syntax of their programming constructs. However, they are fundamentally very similar. In this book, we use the Bourne shell.

Your prompt may be different from either of these traditional prompts. This is because the UNIX environment can be customized and the prompt may have been changed by your system administrator. Whatever the prompt looks like, when it appears, the system is ready for you to enter a command.

When you type a command from the keyboard, the characters are echoed on the screen. The shell does not interpret the command until you press the *RETURN* key. This means that you can use the *erase character* (usually the *DEL* or *BACKSPACE* key) to correct typing mistakes. After you have entered a command line, the shell tries to identify and locate the program specified on the command line. If the command line that you entered is not valid, then an error message is returned.

When a program is invoked and processing begun, the output it produces is sent to your screen, unless otherwise directed. To interrupt and cancel a program before it has completed, you can press the *interrupt character* (usually *CTRL-C* or the *DEL* key). If the output of a command scrolls by the screen too fast, you can suspend the output by pressing the *suspend character* (usually *CTRL-S*) and resume it by pressing the *resume character* (usually *CTRL-Q*).

Some commands invoke utilities that offer their own environment—with a command interpreter and a set of special "internal" commands. A text editor is one such utility, the mail facility another. In both instances, you enter commands while you are "inside" the program. In these kinds of programs, you must use a command to exit and return to the system prompt.

The return of the system prompt signals that a command is finished and that you can enter another command. Familiarity with the power and flexibility of the UNIX shell is essential to working productively in the UNIX environment.

## ▪ Output Redirection ▪

Some programs do their work in silence, but most produce some kind of result, or output. There are generally two types of output: the expected result—referred to as *standard output*—and error messages—referred to as *standard error*. Both types of output are normally sent to the screen and appear to be indistinguishable. However, they can be manipulated separately—a feature we will later put to good use.

Let's look at some examples. The echo command is a simple command that displays a string of text on the screen.

```
$ echo my name
my name
```

In this case, the input echo my name is processed and its output is my name. The name of the command—echo—refers to a program that interprets the command-line arguments as a literal expression that is sent to standard output. Let's replace echo with a different command called cat:

```
$ cat my name
cat: Cannot open my
cat: Cannot open name
```

The cat program takes its arguments to be the names of files. If these files existed, their contents would be displayed on the screen. Because the arguments were not filenames in this example, an error message was printed instead.

The output from a command can be sent to a file instead of the screen by using the output redirection operator (>). In the next example, we redirect the output of the echo command to a file named reminders.

```
$ echo Call home at 3:00 > reminders
$
```

No output is sent to the screen, and the UNIX prompt returns when the program is finished. Now the cat command should work because we have created a file.

```
$ cat reminders
Call home at 3:00
```

The cat command displays the contents of the file named reminders on the screen. If we redirect again to the same filename, we overwrite its previous contents:

```
$ echo Pick up expense voucher > reminders
$ cat reminders
Pick up expense voucher
```

We can send another line to the file, but we have to use a different redirect operator to append (>>) the new line at the end of the file:

```
$ echo Call home at 3:00 > reminders
$ echo Pick up expense voucher >> reminders
$ cat reminders
Call home at 3:00
Pick up expense voucher
```

The cat command is useful not only for printing a file on the screen, but for con-*cat*enating existing files (printing them one after the other). For example:

```
$ cat reminders todolist
Call home at 3:00
Pick up expense voucher
Proofread Chapter 2
Discuss output redirection
```

The combined output can also be redirected:

```
$ cat reminders todolist > do_now
```

The contents of both reminders and todolist are combined into do_now. The original files remain intact.

If one of the files does not exist, an error message is printed, even though standard output is redirected:

```
$ rm todolist
$ cat reminders todolist > do_now
cat: todolist: not found
```

The files we've created are stored in our *current working directory*.

## Files and Directories

The UNIX file system consists of files and directories. Because the file system can contain thousands of files, directories perform the same function as file drawers in a paper file system. They organize files into more manageable groupings. The file system is hierarchical. It can be represented as an inverted tree structure with the *root directory* at the top. The root directory contains other directories that in turn contain other directories.*

---

*In addition to subdirectories, the root directory can contain other *file systems*. A file system is the skeletal structure of a directory tree, which is built on a magnetic disk before any files or directories are stored on it. On a system containing more than one disk, or on a disk divided into several partitions, there are multiple file systems. However, this is generally invisible to the user, because the secondary file systems are *mounted* on the root directory, creating the illusion of a single file system.

On many UNIX systems, users store their files in the /usr file system. (As disk storage has become cheaper and larger, the placement of user directories is no longer standard. For example, on our system, /usr contains only UNIX software; user accounts are in a separate file system called /work.)

Fred's *home directory* is /usr/fred. It is the location of Fred's account on the system. When he logs in, his home directory is his current working directory. Your working directory is where you are currently located and changes as you move up and down the file system.

A *pathname* specifies the location of a directory or file on the UNIX file system. An *absolute pathname* specifies where a file or directory is located off the root file system. A *relative pathname* specifies the location of a file or directory in relation to the current working directory.

To find out the pathname of our current directory, enter pwd.

```
$ pwd
/usr/fred
```

The absolute pathname of the current working directory is /usr/fred. The ls command lists the contents of the current directory. Let's list the files and subdirectories in /usr/fred by entering the ls command with the −F option. This option prints a slash (/) following the names of subdirectories. In the following example, oldstuff is a directory, and notes and reminders are files.

```
$ ls −F
reminders
notes
oldstuff/
```

When you specify a filename with the ls command, it simply prints the name of the file, if the file exists. When you specify the name of directory, it prints the names of the files and subdirectories in that directory.

```
$ ls reminders
reminders
$ ls oldstuff
ch01_draft
letter.212
memo
```

In this example, a relative pathname is used to specify oldstuff. That is, its location is specified in relation to the current directory, /usr/fred. You could also enter an absolute pathname, as in the following example:

```
$ ls /usr/fred/oldstuff
ch01_draft
letter.212
memo
```

Similarly, you can use an absolute or relative pathname to change directories using the cd command. To move from /usr/fred to /usr/fred/oldstuff, you can enter a relative pathname:

```
$ cd oldstuff
$ pwd
/usr/fred/oldstuff
```

The directory `/usr/fred/oldstuff` becomes the current working directory.
The `cd` command without an argument returns you to your home directory.

```
$ cd
```

When you log in, you are positioned in your home directory, which is thus your current working directory. The name of your home directory is stored in a shell variable that is accessible by prefacing the name of the variable (HOME) with a dollar sign (`$`). Thus:

```
$ echo $HOME
/usr/fred
```

You could also use this variable in pathnames to specify a file or directory in your home directory.

```
$ ls $HOME/oldstuff/memo
/usr/fred/oldstuff/memo
```

In this tutorial, `/usr/fred` is our home directory.

The command to create a directory is `mkdir`. An absolute or relative pathname can be specified.

```
$ mkdir /usr/fred/reports
$ mkdir reports/monthly
```

Setting up directories is a convenient method of organizing your work on the system. For instance, in writing this book, we set up a directory `/work/textp` and, under that, subdirectories for each chapter in the book (`/work/textp/ch01`, `/work/textp/ch02`, etc.). In each of those subdirectories, there are files that divide the chapter into sections (`sect1`, `sect2`, etc.). There is also a subdirectory set up to hold old versions or drafts of these sections.

## Copying and Moving Files

You can copy, move, and rename files within your current working directory or (by specifying the full pathname) within other directories on the file system. The `cp` command makes a copy of a file and the `mv` command can be used to move a file to a new directory or simply rename it. If you give the name of a new or existing file as the last argument to `cp` or `mv`, the file named in the first argument is copied, and the copy given the new name. (If the target file already exists, it will be overwritten by the copy. If you give the name of a directory as the last argument to `cp` or `mv`, the file or files named first will be copied to that directory, and will keep their original names.)

Look at the following sequence of commands:

```
$ pwd                    Print working directory
/usr/fred
```

```
$ ls -F                    List contents of current directory
meeting
oldstuff/
notes
reports/
$ mv notes oldstuff        Move notes to oldstuff directory
$ ls                       List contents of current directory
meeting
oldstuff
reports/
$ mv meeting meet.306       Rename meeting
$ ls oldstuff              List contents of oldstuff subdirectory
ch01_draft
letter.212
memo
notes
```

In this example, the mv command was used to rename the file meeting and to move
the file notes from /usr/fred to /usr/fred/oldstuff. You can also
use the mv command to rename a directory itself.


## Permissions

Access to UNIX files is governed by ownership and permissions. If you create a file,
you are the owner of the file and can set the permissions for that file to give or deny
access to other users of the system. There are three different levels of permission:

r            Read permission allows users to read a file or make a copy of it.
w            Write permission allows users to make changes to that file.
x            Execute permission signifies a program file and allows other users to
             execute this program.

File permissions can be set for three different levels of ownership:

owner        The user who created the file is its owner.
group        A group to which you are assigned, usually made up of those users
             engaged in similar activities and who need to share files among them-
             selves.
other        All other users on the system, the public.

Thus, you can set read, write, and execute permissions for the three levels of ownership. This can be represented as:

```
rwxrwxrwx
 /   |   \
owner group other
```

# HOWARD W. SAMS & COMPANY

*fff*

**Bookmark**

DEAR VALUED CUSTOMER:

Howard W. Sams & Company is dedicated to bringing you timely and authoritative books for your personal and professional library. Our goal is to provide you with excellent technical books written by the most qualified authors. You can assist us in this endeavor by checking the box next to your particular areas of interest.

We appreciate your comments and will use the information to provide you with a more comprehensive selection of titles.

Thank you,

Vice President, Book Publishing
Howard W. Sams & Company

## COMPUTER TITLES:

### Hardware
- ☐ Apple 140
- ☐ Macintosh 101
- ☐ Commodore 110
- ☐ IBM & Compatibles 114

### Business Applications
- ☐ Word Processing J01
- ☐ Data Base J04
- ☐ Spreadsheets J02

### Operating Systems
- ☐ MS-DOS K05
- ☐ OS/2 K10
- ☐ CP/M K01
- ☐ UNIX K03

### Programming Languages
- ☐ C L03
- ☐ Pascal L05
- ☐ Prolog L12
- ☐ Assembly L01
- ☐ BASIC L02
- ☐ HyperTalk L14

### Troubleshooting & Repair
- ☐ Computers S05
- ☐ Peripherals S10

### Other
- ☐ Communications/Networking M03
- ☐ AI/Expert Systems T18

## ELECTRONICS TITLES:
- ☐ Amateur Radio T01
- ☐ Audio T03
- ☐ Basic Electronics T20
- ☐ Basic Electricity T21
- ☐ Electronics Design T12
- ☐ Electronics Projects T04
- ☐ Satellites T09

- ☐ Instrumentation T05
- ☐ Digital Electronics T11

### Troubleshooting & Repair
- ☐ Audio S11
- ☐ Television S04
- ☐ VCR S01
- ☐ Compact Disc S02
- ☐ Automotive S06
- ☐ Microwave Oven S03

Other interests or comments: _____

_____

_____

Name_____

Title _____

Company _____

Address _____

City _____

State/Zip _____

Daytime Telephone No. _____

*A Division of Macmillan, Inc.*

*4300 West 62nd Street  Indianapolis, Indiana 46268*

**46291**

# Bookmark

## BUSINESS REPLY CARD

FIRST CLASS     PERMIT NO. 1076     INDIANAPOLIS, IN

POSTAGE WILL BE PAID BY ADDRESSEE

**HOWARD W. SAMS & COMPANY**
ATTN: Public Relations Department
P.O. Box 7092
Indianapolis, IN 46209-9921

*fff*

HOWARD W. SAMS
& COMPANY

When you enter the command `ls  -l`, information about the status of the file is displayed on the screen. You can determine what the file permissions are, who the owner of the file is, and with what group the file is associated.

```
$ ls -l meet.306
-rw-rw-r-- 1 fred   techpubs  126  March 6  10:32  meet.306
```

This file has read and write permissions set for the user `fred` and the group `techpubs`. All others can read the file, but they cannot modify it. Because `fred` is the owner of the file, he can change the permissions, making it available to others or denying them access to it. The `chmod` command is used to set permissions. For instance, if he wanted to make the file writeable by everyone, he would enter:

```
$ chmod o+w meet.306
$ ls -l meet.306
-rw-rw-rw- 1 fred   techpubs  126  March 6  10:32  meet.306
```

This translates to "add write permission (+w) to others (o)." If he wanted to remove write permission from a file, keeping anyone but himself from accidentally modifying a finished document, he might enter:

```
$ chmod go-w meet.306
$ ls -l meet.306
-rw-r--r-- 1 fred   techpubs  126  March 6  10:32  meet.306
```

This command removes write permission (−w) from group (g) and other (o).

File permissions are important in UNIX, especially when you start using a text editor to create and modify files. They can be used to protect information you have on the system.

## ▪ Special Characters ▪

As part of the shell environment, there are a few special characters (metacharacters) that make working in UNIX much easier. We won't review all the special characters, but enough of them to make sure you see how useful they are.

The *asterisk* (*) and the *question mark* (?) are filename generation metacharacters. The asterisk matches any or all characters in a string. By itself, the asterisk expands to all the names in the specified directory.

```
$ echo *
meet.306  oldstuff reports
```

In this example, the `echo` command displays in a row the names of all the files and directories in the current directory. The asterisk can also be used as a shorthand notation for specifying one or more files.

```
$ ls meet*
meet.306
$ ls /work/textp/ch*
/work/textp/ch01
/work/textp/ch02
```

```
/work/textp/ch03
/work/textp/chapter_make
```

The question mark matches any single character.

```
$ ls /work/textp/ch01/sect?
/work/textp/ch01/sect1
/work/textp/ch01/sect2
/work/textp/ch01/sect3
```

Besides filename metacharacters, there are other characters that have special meaning when placed in a command line. The *semicolon* (`;`) separates multiple commands on the same command line. Each command is executed in sequence from left to right, one before the other.

```
$ cd oldstuff;pwd;ls
/usr/fred/oldstuff
ch01_draft
letter.212
memo
notes
```

Another special character is the *ampersand* (`&`). The ampersand signifies that a command should be processed in the background, meaning that the shell does not wait for the program to finish before returning a system prompt. When a program takes a significant amount of processing time, it is best to have it run in the background so that you can do other work at your terminal in the meantime. We will demonstrate background processing in Chapter 4 when we look at the `nroff/troff` text formatter.

## • Environment Variables •

The shell stores useful information about who you are and what you are doing in *environment variables*. Entering the `set` command will display a list of the environment variables that are currently defined in your account.

```
$ set
PATH    .:bin:/usr/bin:/usr/local/bin:/etc
argv    ()
cwd     /work/textp/ch03
home    /usr/fred
shell   /bin/sh
status 0
TERM    wy50
```

These variables can be accessed from the command line by prefacing their name with a dollar sign:

```
$ echo $TERM
wy50
```

The `TERM` variable identifies what type of terminal you are using. It is important that you correctly define the `TERM` environment variable, especially because the `vi` text editor relies upon it. Shell variables can be reassigned from the command line. Some variables, such as TERM, need to be *exported* if they are reassigned, so that they are available to all shell processes.

```
$ TERM=tvi925; export TERM    Tell UNIX I'm using a Televideo 925
```

You can also define your own environment variables for use in commands.

```
$ friends="alice ed ralph"
$ echo $friends
alice ed ralph
```

You could use this variable when sending mail.

```
$ mail $friends
A message to friends
<CTRL-D>
```

This command sends the mail message to three people whose names are defined in the friends environment variable. Pathnames can also be assigned to environment variables, shortening the amount of typing:

```
$ pwd
/usr/fred
$ book="/work/textp"
$ cd $book
$ pwd
/work/textp
```

## ▪ Pipes and Filters ▪

Earlier we demonstrated how you can redirect the output of a command to a file. Normally, command input is taken from the keyboard and command output is displayed on the terminal screen. A program can be thought of as processing a stream of input and producing a stream of output. As we have seen, this stream can be redirected to a file. In addition, it can originate from or be passed to another command.

A *pipe* is formed when the output of one command is sent as input to the next command. For example:

```
$ ls | wc
```

might produce:

```
    10      10      72
```

The ls command produces a list of filenames which is provided as input to wc. The wc command counts the number of lines, words, and characters.

Any program that takes its input from another program, performs some operation on that input, and writes the result to the standard output is referred to as a *filter*. Most UNIX programs are designed to work as filters. This is one reason why UNIX programs do not print "friendly" prompts or other extraneous information to the user.

Because all programs expect—and produce—only a data stream, that data stream can easily be processed by multiple programs in sequence.

One of the most common uses of filters is to process output from a command. Usually, the processing modifies it by rearranging it or reducing the amount of information it displays. For example:

```
$ who                          List who is on the system, and at which terminal
peter       tty001      Mar   6 17:12
walter      tty003      Mar   6 13:51
chris       tty004      Mar   6 15:53
val         tty020      Mar   6 15:48
tim         tty005      Mar   4 17:23
ruth        tty006      Mar   6 17:02
fred        tty000      Mar   6 10:34
dale        tty008      Mar   6 15:26
$ who | sort                   List the same information in alphabetic order
chris       tty004      Mar   6 15:53
dale        tty008      Mar   6 15:26
fred        tty000      Mar   6 10:34
peter       tty001      Mar   6 17:12
ruth        tty006      Mar   6 17:02
tim         tty005      Mar   4 17:23
val         tty020      Mar   6 15:48
walter      tty003      Mar   6 13:51
$
```

The sort program arranges lines of input in alphabetic or numeric order. It sorts lines alphabetically by default. Another frequently used filter, especially in text-processing environments, is grep, perhaps UNIX's most renowned program. The grep program selects lines containing a pattern:

```
$ who | grep tty001            Find out who is on terminal 1
peter       tty001      Mar   6 17:12
```

One of the beauties of UNIX is that almost any program can be used to filter the output of any other. The pipe is the master key to building command sequences that go beyond the capabilities provided by a single program and allow users to create custom ''programs'' of their own to meet specific needs.

If a command line gets too long to fit on a single screen line, simply type a backslash followed by a carriage return, or (if a pipe symbol comes at the appropriate place) a pipe symbol followed by a carriage return. Instead of executing the command, the shell will give you a secondary prompt (usually >) so you can continue the line:

```
$ echo This is a long line shown here as a demonstration |
> wc
        1      10      49
```

This feature works in the Bourne shell only.

## ▪ Shell Scripts ▪

A *shell script* is a file that contains a sequence of UNIX commands. Part of the flexibility of UNIX is that anything you enter from the terminal can be put in a file and executed. To give a simple example, we'll assume that the last command example (`grep`) has been stored in a file called `whoison`:

```
$ cat whoison
who | grep tty001
```

The permissions on this file must be changed to make it executable. After a file is made executable, its name can be entered as a command.

```
$ chmod +x whoison
$ ls -l whoison
-rwxrwxr-x   1 fred        doc          123 Mar   6 17:34 whois
$ whoison
peter          tty001       Mar   6 17:12
```

Shell scripts can do more than simply function as a batch command facility. The basic constructs of a programming language are available for use in a shell script, allowing users to perform a variety of complicated tasks with relatively simple programs.

The simple shell script shown above is not very useful because it is too specific. However, instead of specifying the name of a single terminal line in the file, we can read the name as an argument on the command line. In a shell script, `$1` represents the first argument on the command line.

```
$ cat whoison
who | grep $1
```

Now we can find who is logged on to any terminal:

```
$ whoison tty004
chris         tty004       Mar   6 15:53
```

Later in this book, we will look at shell scripts in detail. They are an important part of the writer's toolbox, because they provide the "glue" for users of the UNIX system—the mechanism by which all the other tools can be made to work together.

# 3

# Learning `vi`

UNIX has a number of editors that can process the contents of readable files, whether those files contain data, source code, or text. There are line editors, such as `ed` and `ex`, which display a line of the file on the screen, and there are screen editors, such as `vi` and `emacs`, which display a part of the file on your terminal screen.

The most useful standard text editor on your system is `vi`. Unlike `emacs`, it is available in nearly identical form on almost every UNIX system, thus providing a kind of text editing *lingua franca*. The same might be said of `ed` and `ex`, but screen editors are generally much easier to use. With a screen editor you can scroll the page, move the cursor, delete lines, insert characters, and more, while seeing the results of your edits as you make them. Screen editors are very popular because they allow you to make changes as you read a file, much as you would edit a printed copy, only faster.

To many beginners, `vi` looks unintuitive and cumbersome—instead of letting you type normally and use special control keys for word-processing functions, it uses all of the regular keyboard keys for issuing commands. You must be in a special *insert mode* before you can type. In addition, there seem to be *so many* commands.

You can't learn `vi` by memorizing every single `vi` command. Begin by learning some basic commands. As you do, be aware of the patterns of usage that commands have in common. Be on the lookout for new ways to perform tasks, experimenting with new commands and combinations of commands.

As you become more familiar with `vi`, you will find that you need fewer keystrokes to tell `vi` what to do. You will learn shortcuts that transfer more and more of the editing work to the computer—where it belongs. Not as much memorization is required as first appears from a list of `vi` commands. Like any skill, the more editing you do, the more you know about it and the more you can accomplish.

This chapter has three sections, and each one corresponds to a set of material about `vi` that you should be able to tackle in a single session. After you have finished each session, put aside the book for a while and do some experimenting. When you feel comfortable with what you have learned, continue to the next session.

### · Session 1: Basic Commands ·

The first session contains the basic knowledge you need to operate the vi editor. After a general description of vi, you are shown some simple operations. You will learn how to

- open and close a file;

- give commands and insert text;

- move the cursor;

- edit text (change, delete, and copy).

You can use vi to edit any file that contains readable text, whether it is a report, a series of shell commands, or a program. The vi editor copies the file to be edited into a buffer (an area temporarily set aside in memory), displays as much of the buffer as possible on the screen, and lets you add, delete, and move text. When you save your edits, vi copies the buffer into a permanent file, overwriting the contents of the old file.

### · Opening a File ·

The syntax for the vi command is:

> vi [*filename*]

where *filename* is the name of either an existing file or a new file. If you don't specify a filename, vi will open an unnamed buffer, and ask you to name it before you can save any edits you have made. Press *RETURN* to execute the command.

A filename must be unique inside its directory. On AT&T (System V) UNIX systems, it cannot exceed 14 characters. (Berkeley UNIX systems allow longer filenames.) A filename can include any ASCII character except /, which is reserved as the separator between files and directories in a pathname. You can even include spaces in a filename by "escaping" them with a backslash. In practice, though, filenames consist of any combination of uppercase and lowercase letters, numbers, and the characters . (dot) and _ (underscore). Remember that UNIX is case-sensitive: lowercase filenames are distinct from uppercase filenames, and, by convention, lowercase is preferred.

If you want to open a new file called notes in the current directory, enter:

> $ **vi notes**

The vi command clears the screen and displays a new buffer for you to begin work. Because notes is a new file, the screen displays a column of *tildes* (~) to indicate that there is no text in the file, not even blank lines.

```
~
~
~
~
~
~
~
~
~
~
~
~
~
"notes" [New file].
```

If you specify the name of a file that already exists, its contents will be displayed on the
screen.  For example:

    $ **vi letter**

might bring a copy of the existing file `letter` to the screen.

```
Mr. John Fust
Vice President, Research and Development
Gutenberg Galaxy Software
Waltham, Massachusetts 02154

Dear Mr. Fust:

In our conversation last Thursday, we discussed a
documentation project that would produce a user's manual
on the Alcuin product.  Yesterday, I received the product
demo and other materials that you sent me.
~
~
~
~
"letter" 11 lines, 250 characters
```

The prompt line at the bottom of the screen echoes the name and size of the file.

Sometimes when you invoke  vi, you may get either of the following messages:

```
[using open mode]
```

or:

```
Visual needs addressable cursor or upline capability
```

In both cases, there is a problem identifying the type of terminal you are using.  You can quit the editing session immediately by typing  :q.

Although  vi can run on almost any terminal, it must know what kind of terminal you are using.  The terminal type is usually set as part of the UNIX login sequence.  If you are not sure whether your terminal type is defined correctly, ask your system administrator or an experienced user to help you set up your terminal.  If you know your terminal type (wy50 for instance), you can set your  TERM environment variable with the following command:

```
TERM=wy50; export TERM
```

## vi Commands

The  vi editor has two *modes*: command mode and insert mode.  Unlike many word processors,  vi's command mode is the initial or *default* mode.  To insert lines of text, you must give a command to enter insert mode and then type away.

Most commands consist of one or two characters.  For example:

i                insert
c                change

Using letters as commands, you can edit a file quickly.  You don't have to memorize banks of function keys or stretch your fingers to reach awkward combinations of keys.

In general,  vi commands

- are case-sensitive (uppercase and lowercase keystrokes mean different things; e.g., *I* is different from *i*);

- are not echoed on the screen;

- do not require a *RETURN* after the command.

There is also a special group of commands that echo on the bottom line of the screen.  Bottom-line commands are indicated by special symbols.  The slash (/) and the question mark (?) begin search commands, which are discussed in session 2.  A colon (:) indicates an  ex command.  You are introduced to one  ex command (to quit a file without saving edits) in this chapter, and the  ex line editor is discussed in detail in Chapter 7.

To tell  vi that you want to begin insert mode, press  i.  Nothing appears on the screen, but you can now type any text at the cursor.  To tell  vi to stop inserting text, press *ESC* and you will return to command mode.

For example, suppose that you want to insert the word *introduction*. If you type the keystrokes `iintroduction`, what appears on the screen is

```
introduction
```

Because you are starting out in command mode, `vi` interprets the first keystroke (i) as the insert command. All keystrokes after that result in characters placed in the file, until you press *ESC*. If you need to correct a mistake while in insert mode, backspace and type over the error.

While you are inserting text, press *RETURN* to break the lines before the right margin. An autowrap option provides a carriage return automatically after you exceed the right margin. To move the right margin in ten spaces, for example, enter `:set wm=10`.

Sometimes you may not know if you are in insert mode or command mode. Whenever `vi` does not respond as you expect, press *ESC*. When you hear a beep, you are in command mode.

### Saving a File

You can quit working on a file at any time, save the edits, and return to the UNIX prompt. The `vi` command to quit and save edits is `ZZ`. (Note that `ZZ` is capitalized.)

Let's assume that you create a file called `letter` to practice `vi` commands and that you type in 36 lines of text. To save the file, first check that you are in command mode by pressing *ESC*, and then give the write and save command, `ZZ`. Your file is saved as a regular file. The result is:

```
"letter" [New file] 36 lines, 1331 characters
```

You return to the UNIX prompt. If you check the list of files in the directory, by typing `ls` at the prompt, the new file is listed:

```
$ ls
ch01   ch02   letter
```

You now know enough to create a new file. As an exercise, create a file called `letter` and insert the text shown in Figure 3-1. When you have finished, type `ZZ` to save the file and return to the UNIX prompt.

## ▪ Moving the Cursor ▪

Only a small percentage of time in an editing session may be spent adding new text in insert mode. Much of the time, you will be editing existing text.

In command mode, you can position the cursor anywhere in the file. You start all basic edits (changing, deleting, and copying text) by placing the cursor at the text that you want to change. Thus, you want to be able to quickly move the cursor to that place.

April 1, 1987

Mr. John Fust
Vice President, Research and Development
Gutenberg Galaxy Software
Waltham, Massachusetts 02159

Dear Mr. Fust:

In our conversation last Thursday, we discussed a
documentation project that would produce a user's
manual on the Alcuin product.  Yesterday, I received
the product demo and other materials that you sent me.

Going through a demo session gave me a much better
understanding of the product.  I confess to being
amazed by Alcuin.  Some people around here, looking
over my shoulder, were also astounded by the
illustrated manuscript I produced with Alcuin.  One
person, a student of calligraphy, was really impressed.

Today, I'll start putting together a written plan
that shows different strategies for documenting
the Alcuin product.  After I submit this plan, and
you have had time to review it, let's arrange a
meeting at your company to discuss these strategies.

Thanks again for giving us the opportunity to bid on
this documentation project.  I hope we can decide upon
a strategy and get started as soon as possible in order
to have the manual ready in time for the first customer
shipment.  I look forward to meeting with you towards
the end of next week.

                                        Sincerely,



                                        Fred Caslon


*Fig. 3-1.*  A sample letter entered with vi

There are vi commands to move

- up, down, left, or right, one *character* at a time;
- forward or backward by *blocks of text* such as words, sentences, or paragraphs;
- forward or backward through a file, one *screen* at a time.

To move the cursor, make sure you are in command mode by pressing *ESC*. Give the command for moving forward or backward in the file from the current cursor position. When you have gone as far in one direction as possible, you'll hear a beep and the cursor stops. You cannot move the cursor past the tildes (~) at the end of the file.

## Single Movements

The keys h, j, k, and l, right under your fingertips, will move the cursor:

| | |
|---|---|
| h | left one space |
| j | down one line |
| k | up one line |
| l | right one space |

You *could* use the cursor arrow keys (↑, ↓, →, ←) or the *RETURN* and *BACK-SPACE* keys, but they are out of the way and are not supported on all terminals.

You can also combine the h, j, k, and l keys with numeric arguments and other vi commands.

## Numeric Arguments

You can precede movement commands with numbers. The command 4l moves the cursor (shown as a small box around a letter) four spaces to the right, just like typing the letter l four times (llll).

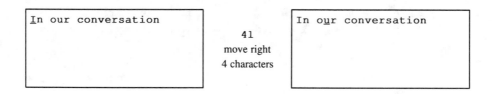

This one concept (being able to multiply commands) gives you more options (and power) for each command. Keep it in mind as you are introduced to additional commands.

## Movement by Lines

When you saved the file letter, the editor displayed a message telling you how many lines were in that file. A *line* in the file is not necessarily the same length as a physical line (limited to 80 characters) that appears on the screen. A line is any text entered between carriage returns. If you type 200 characters before pressing *RETURN*, vi regards all 200 characters as a single line (even though those 200 characters look like several physical lines on the screen).

Two useful commands in line movement are:

| 0 <zero> | move to beginning of line |
| $ | move to end of line |

In the following file, the line numbers are shown. To get line numbers on your screen, enter :set nu.

```
1   With the screen editor you can scroll the page,
2   move the cursor, delete lines, and insert characters,
    while seeing the results of edits as you make them.
3   Screen editors are very popular.
```

The number of logical lines (3) does not correspond to the number of physical lines (4) that you see on the screen. If you enter $, with the cursor positioned on the *d* in the word *delete*, the cursor would move to the period following the word *them*.

```
1   With the screen editor you can scroll the page,
2   move the cursor, delete lines, and insert characters,
    while seeing the results of edits as you make them.
3   Screen editors are very popular.
```

If you enter U (zero), the cursor would move back to the letter *t* in the word *the*, at the beginning of the line.

```
1   With the screen editor you can scroll the page,
2   move the cursor, delete lines, and insert characters,
    while seeing the results of edits as you make them.
3   Screen editors are very popular.
```

If you do not use the automatic wraparound option (:set wm=10) in vi, you must break lines with carriage returns to keep the lines of manageable length.

## Movement by Text Blocks

You can also move the cursor by blocks of text (words, sentences, or paragraphs).

The command w moves the cursor forward one word at a time, treating symbols and punctuation marks as equivalent to words. The following line shows cursor movement caused by ten successive w commands:

```
move the cursor, delete lines, and insert characters,
```

You can also move forward one word at a time, ignoring symbols and punctuation marks, using the command W (note the uppercase *W*). It causes the cursor to move to the first character following a blank space. Cursor movement using W looks like this:

```
move the cursor, delete lines, and insert characters,
```

To move backward one word at a time, use the command b. The B command allows you to move backward one word at a time, ignoring punctuation.

With either the w, W, b, or B commands, you can multiply the movement with numbers. For example, 2w moves forward two words; 5B moves back five words, ignoring punctuation. Practice using the cursor movement commands, combining them with numeric multipliers.

## ▪ Simple Edits ▪

When you enter text in your file, it is rarely perfect. You find errors or want to improve a phrase. After you enter text, you have to be able to change it.

What are the components of editing? You want to *insert* text (a forgotten word or a missing sentence). And you want to *delete* text (a stray character or an entire paragraph). You also need to *change* letters and words (correct misspellings or reflect a change of mind). You want to *move* text from one place to another part of your file. And on occasion, you want to *copy* text to duplicate it in another part of your file.

There are four basic edit commands: i for *insert* (which you have already seen), c for *change*, d for *delete*, d then p for *move* (delete and put), and y for *yank* (copy). Each type of edit is described in this section. Table 3-1 gives a few simple examples.

### TABLE 3-1. Basic Editing Commands

| Object | Change | Delete | Copy (Yank) |
|---|---|---|---|
| One word | cw | dw | yw |
| Two words | 2cW | 2dW | 2yW |
| Three words back | 3cb | 3db | 3yb |
| One line | cc | dd | yy or Y |
| To end of line | c$ or C | d$ or D | y$ |
| To beginning of line | c0 | d0 | y0 |
| Single character | r | x | yl |

### Inserting New Text

You have already used the insert command to enter text into a new file. You also use the insert command while editing existing text to add characters, words, and sentences. Suppose you have to insert Today, at the beginning of a sentence. Enter the following sequence of commands and text:

```
┌─────────────────────┐              ┌─────────────────────┐
│ I'll start putting  │              │ I'll start putting  │
│ together a written  │     3k       │ together a written  │
│ plan that shows     │  move up 3   │ plan that shows     │
│ different strategies│    lines     │ different strategies│
└─────────────────────┘              └─────────────────────┘


┌─────────────────────┐              ┌─────────────────────┐
│ I'll start putting  │              │ Today, I'll start putting │
│ together a written  │ iToday, <ESC>│ together a written  │
│ plan that shows     │   insert     │ plan that shows     │
│ different strategies│   Today,     │ different strategies│
└─────────────────────┘              └─────────────────────┘
```

In the previous example, vi moves existing text to the right as the new text is inserted. That is because we are showing vi on an "intelligent" terminal, which can adjust the screen with each character you type. An insert on a "dumb" terminal (such as an adm3a) will look different. The terminal itself cannot update the screen for each character typed (without a tremendous sacrifice of speed), so vi doesn't rewrite the screen until after you press *ESC*. Rather, when you type, the dumb terminal appears to overwrite the existing text. When you press *ESC*, the line is adjusted immediately so that the missing characters reappear. Thus, on a dumb terminal, the same insert would appear as follows:

```
┌─────────────────────┐              ┌─────────────────────┐
│ I'll start putting  │              │ Today, art putting  │
│ together a written  │   iToday     │ together a written  │
│ plan that shows     │   insert     │ plan that shows     │
│ different strategies│   Today,     │ different strategies│
└─────────────────────┘              └─────────────────────┘


┌─────────────────────┐              ┌─────────────────────┐
│ Today, art putting  │              │ Today, I'll start putting │
│ together a written  │    <ESC>     │ together a written  │
│ plan that shows     │    leave     │ plan that shows     │
│ different strategies│  insert mode │ different strategies│
└─────────────────────┘              └─────────────────────┘
```

## Changing Text

You can replace any text in your file with the change command, c. To identify the amount of text that you want replaced, combine the change command with a movement command. For example, c can be used to change text from the cursor

| cw  | to the end of a word |
|-----|----------------------|
| 2cb | back two words       |
| c$  | to the end of a line |

Then you can replace the identified text with any amount of new text: no characters at all, one word, or hundreds of lines. The c command leaves you in insert mode until you press the *ESC* key.

## Words

You can replace a word (cw) with a longer word, a shorter word, or any amount of text. The cw command can be thought of as "delete the word marked and insert new text until *ESC* is pressed."

Suppose that you have the following lines in your file letter and want to change *designing* to *putting together*. You only need to change one word.

```
I'll start                    cw           I'll start
designing a                change a        designin$ a
                             word
```

Note that the cw command places a $ at the last character of the word to be changed.

```
I'll start                  putting        I'll start
designin$ a                together        putting together a
                            <ESC>
                          enter change
```

The cw command also works on a portion of a word. For example, to change *putting* to *puts*, position the cursor on the second *t*, enter cw, then type *s* and press *ESC*. By using numeric prefixes, you can change multiple words or characters immediately. For example:

| 3cw | change three words to the right of the cursor   |
|-----|-------------------------------------------------|
| 5cl | change five letters to the right of the cursor  |

You don't need to replace the specified number of words, characters, or lines with a like amount of text. For example:

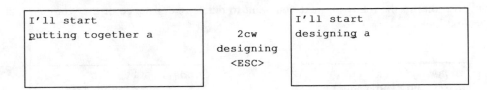

### Lines

To replace the entire current line, there is the special change command cc. This command changes an entire line, replacing that line with the text entered before an *ESC*. The cc command replaces the entire line of text, regardless of where the cursor is located on the line.

The C command replaces characters from the current cursor position to the end of the line. It has the same effect as combining c with the special end-of-line indicator, $ (as in c$).

### Characters

One other replacement edit is performed with the r command. This command replaces a single character with another single character. One of its uses is to correct misspellings. You probably don't want to use cw in such an instance, because you would have to retype the entire word. Use r to replace a single character at the cursor:

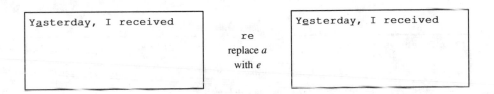

The r command makes only a single character replacement. You do *not* have to press *ESC* to finish the edit. Following an r command, you are automatically returned to command mode.

### Deleting Text

You can also delete any text in your file with the delete command, d. Like the change command, the delete command requires an argument (the amount of text to be operated on). You can delete by word (dw), by line (dd and D), or by other movement commands that you will learn later.

With all deletions, you move to where you want the edit to take place and enter the delete command (d) followed by the amount of text to be deleted (such as a text object, w for *word*).

## Words

Suppose that in the following text you want to delete one instance of the word *start* in the first line.

```
Today, I'll start
start putting together
a written plan
thatth shows different
```
dw
delete word
```
Today, I'll_
start putting together
a written plan
thatth shows different
```

The  dw command deletes from the cursor's position to the end of a word. Thus,  dw can be used to delete a portion of a word.

```
thatth shows different
```
dw
delete word
```
thatshows different
```

As you can see,  dw deleted not only the remainder of the word, but also the space before any subsequent word on the same line. To retain the space between words, use de, which will delete only to the end of the word.

```
thatth shows different
```
de
delete to
word end
```
that_shows different
```

You can also delete backwards (db) or to the end or beginning of a line (d$ or  d0).


## Lines

The  dd command deletes the entire line that the cursor is on. Using the same text as in the previous example, with the cursor positioned on the first line as shown, you can delete the first two lines:

```
Today, I'll_                              a written plan
start putting together      2dd          that shows different
a written plan           delete first
that shows different        2 lines
```

If you are using a dumb terminal or one working at less than 1200 baud, line deletions look different. The dumb or slow terminal will not redraw the screen until you scroll past the bottom of the screen. Instead the deletion appears as:

```
@
@
a written plan
that shows different
```

An @ symbol "holds the place" of the deleted line, until the terminal redraws the entire screen. (You can force vi to redraw the screen immediately by pressing either *CTRL-L* or *CTRL-R*, depending on the terminal you're using.)

The D command deletes from the cursor position to the end of the line:

```
Today, I'll start                        Today, I'll start
putting together a            D          putting together a
written plan               delete to     written plan that
that shows different       end of line   that_
```

You cannot use numeric prefixes with the D command.


## Characters

Often, while editing a file, you want to delete a single character or two. Just as r changes one character, x deletes a single character. The x command deletes any character the cursor is on. In the following line, you can delete the letter *l* by pressing x.

```
Today, I'lll start                       Today, I'll start
putting                       x          putting
                            delete
                           character
```

The X command deletes the character before the cursor. Prefix either of these commands with a number to delete that number of characters. For example, 5X will delete the five characters to the left of the cursor.

## Moving Text

You can move text by deleting it and then placing that deleted text elsewhere in the file, like a "cut and paste." Each time you delete a text block, that deletion is temporarily saved in a buffer. You can move to another position in the file and use the put command to place the text in a new position. Although you can move any block of text, this command sequence is more useful with lines than with words.

The put command, p, places saved or deleted text (in the buffer) *after* the cursor position. The uppercase version of the command, P, puts the text *before* the cursor. If you delete one or more lines, p puts the deleted text on a new line(s) below the cursor. If you delete a word, p puts the deleted text on the same line after the cursor.

Suppose that in your file letter you have the following lines and you want to move the fourth line of text. Using delete, you can make this edit. First delete the line in question:

```
Today, I'll start                  Today, I'll start
putting together a        dd       putting together a
plan for documenting   delete line plan for documenting
the Alcuin product                 that shows
that shows
```

Then use p to restore the deleted line at the next line below the cursor:

```
Today, I'll start                     Today, I'll start
putting together a           p        putting together a
plan for documenting  restore deleted plan for documenting
that shows                  line      that shows
                                      the Alcuin product
```

You can also use xp (delete character and put after cursor) to transpose two letters. For example, in the word *mvoe*, the letters *vo* are transposed (reversed). To correct this, place the cursor on *v* and press x then p.

After you delete the text, you must restore it before the next change or delete command. If you make another edit that affects the buffer, your deleted text will be lost. You can repeat the put command over and over, as long as you don't make a new edit. In the advanced vi chapter, you will learn how to retrieve text from named and numbered buffers.

## Copying Text

Often, you can save editing time (and keystrokes) by copying part of your file to another place. You can copy any amount of existing text and place that copied text elsewhere in the file with the two commands  y  *(yank)* and  p  *(put)*. The yank command is used to get a copy of text into the buffer without altering the original text. This copy can then be placed elsewhere in the file with the put command.

Yank can be combined with any movement command (for example, yw, y$, or 4yy). Yank is most frequently used with a line (or more) of text, because to yank and put a word generally takes longer than simply inserting the word. For example, to yank five lines of text:

```
on the Alcuin product.
Yesterday, I received
the product demo
and other materials
that you sent me.
~
~
~
```

       5yy
    yank 5
     lines

```
on the Alcuin product.
Yesterday, I received
the product demo
and other materials
that you sent me.
~
~
5 lines yanked
```

To place the yanked text, move the cursor to where you want to put the text, and use the  p  command to insert it below the current line, or  P  to insert it above the current line.

```
that you sent me.
~
~
~
~
~
```

         p
   place yanked
       text

```
that you sent me.
on the Alcuin product.
Yesterday, I received
the product demo
and other materials
that you sent me.

5 more lines
```

The yanked text will appear on the line below the cursor. Deleting uses the same buffer as yanking. Delete and put can be used in much the same way as yank and put. Each new deletion or yank replaces the previous contents of the yank buffer. As we'll see later, up to nine previous yanks or deletions can be recalled with put commands.

## Using Your Last Command

Each command that you give is stored in a temporary buffer until you give the next command. If you insert *the* after a word in your file, the command used to insert the text, along with the text that you entered, is temporarily saved. Anytime you are making the same editing command repeatedly, you can save time by duplicating the command with  . (dot). To duplicate a command, position the cursor anywhere on the screen, and press  . to repeat your last command (such as an insertion or deletion) in the buffer. You can also use numeric arguments (as in  2 .) to repeat the previous command more than once.

Suppose that you have the following lines in your file letter. Place the cursor on the line you want to delete:

| | | |
|---|---|---|
| Yesterday, I received<br>the product demo.<br>Yesterday, I received<br>other materials | dd<br>delete line | Yesterday, I received<br>the product demo.<br>other materials |

| | | |
|---|---|---|
| Yesterday, I received<br>the product demo.<br>other materials | .<br>repeat last<br>command (dd) | Yesterday, I received<br>the product demo. |

In some versions of vi, the command CTRL-@ (^@) repeats the last insert (or append) command. This is in contrast to the  . command, which repeats the last command that changed the text, including delete or change commands.

You can also *undo* your last command if you make an error. To undo a command, the cursor can be anywhere on the screen. Simply press u to undo the last command (such as an insertion or deletion).

To continue the previous example:

| | | |
|---|---|---|
| Yesterday, I received<br>the product demo. | u<br>undo last<br>command | Yesterday, I received<br>the product demo.<br>other materials |

The uppercase version of u (U) undoes all edits on a single line, as long as the cursor remains on that line. After you move off a line, you can no longer use U.

## Joining Two Lines with J

Sometimes while editing a file, you will end up with a series of short lines that are difficult to read. When you want to merge two lines, position the cursor anywhere on the first line and press J to join the two lines.

```
Yesterday,
I received
the product demo.
```
     J
     join lines
```
Yesterday, I received
the product demo.
```

A numeric argument joins that number of consecutive lines.

## Quitting without Saving Edits

When you are first learning vi, especially if you are an intrepid experimenter, there is one other command that is handy for getting out of any mess that you might create. You already know how to save your edits with ZZ, but what if you want to wipe out all the edits you have made in a session and return to the original file?

You can quit vi without saving edits with a special bottom-line command based on the ex line editor. The ex commands are explained fully in the advanced vi chapter, but for basic vi editing you should just memorize this command:

     :q!      <RETURN>

The q! command quits the file you are in. All edits made since the last time you saved the file are lost.

You can get by in vi using only the commands you have learned in this session. However, to harness the real power of vi (and increase your own productivity) you will want to continue to the next session.

## ▪ Session 2: Moving Around in a Hurry ▪

You use vi not only to create new files but also to edit existing files. You rarely open to the first line in the file and move through it line by line. You want to get to a specific place in a file and start work.

All edits begin with moving the cursor to where the edit begins (or, with ex line editor commands, identifying the line numbers to be edited). This chapter shows you how to think about movement in a variety of ways (by screens, text, patterns, or line numbers). There are many ways to move in vi, because editing speed depends on getting to your destination with only a few keystrokes.

In this session, you will learn how to move around in a file by

- screens;
- text blocks;
- searches for patterns;
- lines.

## ▪ Movement by Screens ▪

When you read a book you think of "places" in the book by page: the page where you stopped reading or the page number in an index. Some vi files take up only a few lines, and you can see the whole file at once. But many files have hundreds of lines.

You can think of a vi file as text on a long roll of paper. The screen is a window of (usually) 24 lines of text on that long roll. In insert mode, as you fill up the screen with text, you will end up typing on the bottom line of the screen. When you reach the end and press *RETURN*, the top line rolls out of sight, and a blank line for new text appears on the bottom of the screen. This is called *scrolling*. You can move through a file by scrolling the screen ahead or back to see any text in the file.

### Scrolling the Screen

There are vi commands to scroll forward and backward through the file by full and half screens:

| | |
|---|---|
| ^F | forward one screen |
| ^B | backward one screen |
| ^D | forward half screen |
| ^U | backward half screen |

(The ^ symbol represents the *CTRL* key. ^F means to simultaneously press the *CTRL* key and the *F* key.)

```
In our conversation last Thursday, we
discussed a documentation project that would
produce a user's manual on the Alcuin product.
Yesterday, I received the product demo and
other materials that you sent me.

Going through a demo session gave me a
much better understanding of the product.  I
confess to being amazed by Alcuin.  Some
```

If you press  ^F, the screen appears as follows:

```
better understanding of the product.   I
confess to being amazed by Alcuin.   Some
people around here, looking over my shoulder,
were also astounded by the illustrated
manuscript I produced with Alcuin.   One
person, a student of calligraphy, was really
impressed.


Today, I'll start putting together a written
```

There are also commands to scroll the screen up one line (^E) and down one line (^Y). (These commands are not available on small systems, such as the PDP-11 or Xenix for the PC-XT.)

## Movement within a Screen

You can also keep your current screen or view of the file and move around within the screen using:

| | |
|---|---|
| H | home—top line on screen |
| M | middle line on screen |
| L | last line on screen |
| *n*H | to *n* lines below top line |
| *n*L | to *n* lines above last line |

The  H  command moves the cursor from anywhere on the screen to the first, or *home*, line. The  M  command moves to the middle line,  L  to the last.  To move to the line below the first line, use  2H.

```
Today, I'll start
putting together a
written plan that
shows the different
strategies for the
```
2H
move to
second line
```
Today, I'll start
putting together a
written plan that
shows the different
strategies for the
```

These screen movement commands can also be used for editing.  For example,  dH deletes to the top line shown on the screen.

## Movement within Lines

Within the current screen there are also commands to move by line. You have already learned the line movement commands  $ and  0.

| RETURN | beginning of next line |
|---|---|
| ^ | to first character of current line |
| + | beginning of next line |
| − | beginning of previous line |

```
┌─────────────────────┐        ┌─────────────────────┐
│Going through a demo │        │Going through a demo │
│session gave me a much│   −    │session gave me a much│
│better understanding │ go to start│better understanding │
│of the product.      │ of previous│of the product.      │
└─────────────────────┘   line   └─────────────────────┘
```

The  ^ command moves to the first *character* of the line, ignoring any spaces or tabs. (0, by contrast, moves to the first *position* of the line, even if that position is blank.)

## ▪ **Movement by Text Blocks** ▪

Another way that you can think of moving through a  vi file is by text blocks—words, sentences, or paragraphs. You have already learned to move forward and backward by word (w or  b).

| e | end of word |
|---|---|
| E | end of word (ignore punctuation) |
| ( | beginning of previous sentence |
| ) | beginning of next sentence |
| { | beginning of previous paragraph |
| } | beginning of next paragraph |

The  vi program locates the end of a sentence by finding a period followed by at least two spaces, or a period as the last nonblank character on a line. If you have left only a single space following a period, the sentence won't be recognized.

A *paragraph* is defined as text up to the next blank line, or up to one of the default paragraph macros (.IP,  .P,  .PP, or  .QP) in the  mm or  ms macro packages. The macros that are recognized as paragraph separators can be customized with the  :set command, as described in Chapter 7.

```
┌─────────────────────┐        ┌─────────────────────┐
│In our conversation  │        │In our conversation  │
│last Thursday, we ...│   {    │last Thursday, we ...│
│                     │ go to start│                     │
│Going through a demo │ of previous│Going through a demo │
│session gave me ...  │ paragraph│session gave me ...  │
└─────────────────────┘        └─────────────────────┘
```

Most people find it easier to visualize moving ahead, so the forward commands are generally more useful.

Remember that you can combine numbers with movement. For example, 3) moves ahead three sentences. Also remember that you can edit using movement commands: d) deletes to the end of the current sentence, 2y} copies (yanks) two paragraphs ahead.

## ▪ **Movement by Searches** ▪

One of the most useful ways to move around quickly in a large file is by searching for text, or, more properly, for a *pattern* of characters. The pattern can include a "wildcard" shorthand that lets you match more than one character. For example, you can search for a misspelled word or each occurrence of a variable in a program.

The search command is the *slash* character (/). When you enter a slash, it appears on the bottom line of the screen; then type in the pattern (a word or other string of characters) that you want to find:

     /*text*<RETURN>    search forward for *text*

A space before or after *text* will be included in the search. As with all bottom-line commands, press *RETURN* to finish.

The search begins at the cursor and moves forward, wrapping around to the start of the file if necessary. The cursor will move to the first occurrence of the pattern (or the message "Pattern not found" will be shown on the status line if there is no match).

If you wanted to search for the pattern *shows*:

```
Today, I'll start            Today, I'll start
putting together a   /shows<CR>  putting together a
written plan that    search for  written plan that
shows the different     shows     shows the different
~                                 ~
~                                 ~
~                                 /shows
```

```
Today, I'll start            Today, I'll start
putting together a   /th<CR>     putting together a
written plan that    search for  written plan that
shows the different     th       shows the different
~                                 ~
~                                 ~
~                                 /th
```

The search proceeds forward from the present position in the file. You can give any combination of characters; a search does not have to be for a complete word.

You can also search backwards using the ? command:

*?text*<RETURN>   search backward for *text*

The last pattern that you searched for remains available throughout your editing session. After a search, instead of repeating your original keystrokes, you can use a command to search again for the last pattern.

| | |
|---|---|
| n | repeat search in same direction |
| N | repeat search in opposite direction |
| /<RETURN> | repeat search in forward direction |
| ?<RETURN> | repeat search in backward direction |

Because the last pattern remains available, you can search for a pattern, do some work, and then search again for the pattern without retyping by using n, N, /, or ?. The direction of your search (/=forwards, ?=backwards) is displayed at the bottom left of the screen.

Continuing the previous example, the pattern *th* is still available to search for:

```
Today, I'll start
putting together a
written plan that
shows the different
```
n
search for
next *th*
```
Today, I'll start
putting together a
written plan that
shows the different
```

```
Today, I'll start
putting together a
written plan that
shows the different
~
~
~
```
?<CR>
search back
for *th*
```
Today, I'll start
putting together a
written plan that
shows the different
~
~
?the
```

```
Today, I'll start
putting together a
written plan that
shows the different
```
N
repeat search
in opposite
direction
```
Today, I'll start
putting together a
written plan that
shows the different
```

This section has given only the barest introduction to searching for patterns. Chapter 7 will teach more about pattern matching and its use in making global changes to a file.

### Current Line Searches

There is also a miniature version of the search command that operates within the current line. The command  f  moves the cursor to the next instance of the character you name. Semicolons can then be used to repeat the "find." Note, however, that the  f  command will not move the cursor to the next line.

| | |
|---|---|
| f*x* | find (move cursor to) next occurrence of *x* in the line, where *x* can be any character |
| ; | repeat previous find command |

Suppose that you are editing on this line:

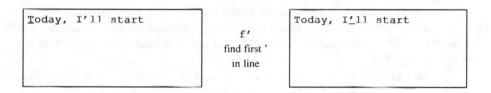

Use  df'  to delete up to and including the named character (in this instance  ' ). This command is useful in deleting or copying partial lines.

The  t  command works just like  f, except it positions the cursor just before the character searched for. As with  f  and  b, a numeric prefix will locate the *n*th occurrence. For example:

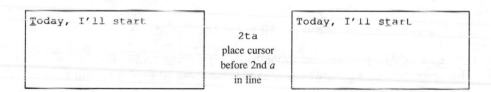

## ▪ Movement by Line Numbers ▪

A file contains sequentially numbered lines, and you can move through a file by specifying line numbers. Line numbers are useful for identifying the beginning and end of large blocks of text you want to edit. Line numbers are also useful for programmers because compiler error messages refer to line numbers. Line numbers are also used by ex commands, as you will learn in Chapter 7.

If you are going to move by line numbers, you need a way to identify line numbers. Line numbers can be displayed on the screen using the `:set nu` option described in Chapter 7. In `vi`, you can also display the current line number on the bottom of the screen.

The command `^G` displays the following on the bottom of your screen: the current line number, the total number of lines in the file, and what percentage of the total the present line number represents. For example, for the file `letter`, `^G` might display:

```
"letter" line 10 of 40 --25%--
```

`^G` is used to display the line number to use in a command, or to orient yourself if you have been distracted from your editing session.

The `G` (*go to*) command uses a line number as a numeric argument, and moves to the first position on that line. For instance, `44G` moves the cursor to the beginning of line 44. The `G` command without a line number moves the cursor to the last line of the file.

Two single quotes (´´) return you to the beginning of the line you were originally on. Two backquotes (``) return you to your original position exactly. If you have issued a search command (`/` or `?`), `` will return the cursor to its position when you started the search.

The total number of lines shown with `^G` can be used to give yourself a rough idea of how many lines to move. If you are on line 10 of a 1000-line file:

```
"ch01" line 10 of 1000 --1%--
```

and know that you want to begin editing near the end of that file, you could give an approximation of your destination with:

```
800G
```

Movement by line number can get you around quickly in a large file.

## ▪ Session 3:  Beyond the Basics  ▪

You have already been introduced to the basic `vi` editing commands, `i`, `c`, `d`, and `y`. This session expands on what you already know about editing. You will learn

- additional ways to enter `vi`;

- how to customize `vi`;

- how to combine all edits with movement commands;

- additional ways to enter insert mode;

- how to use buffers that store deletions, yanks, and your last command;

- how to mark your place in a file.

## ▪ Command-Line Options ▪

There are other options to the vi command that can be helpful. You can open a file directly to a specific line number or pattern. You can also open a file in read-only mode. Another option recovers all changes to a file that you were editing when the system crashes.

### Advancing to a Specific Place

When you begin editing an existing file, you can load the file and then move to the first occurrence of a pattern or to a specific line number. You can also combine the open command, vi, with your first movement by search or by line number. For example:

        $ **vi +***n* **letter**

opens letter at line number *n*. The following:

        $ **vi + letter**

opens letter at the last line. And:

        $ **vi +/***pattern* **letter**

opens letter at the first occurrence of *pattern*.

　　To open the file letter and advance directly to the line containing *Alcuin*, enter:

        $ **vi +/Alcuin letter**

```
    Today I'll start putting together a
    written plan that presents the different
    strategies for the Alcuin
    ~
    ~
    ~
    ~
    ~
    ~
    ~
    ~
    ~
```

There can be no spaces in the pattern because characters after a space are interpreted as filenames.

　　If you have to leave an editing session before you are finished, you can mark your place by inserting a pattern such as ZZZ or HERE. Then when you return to the file, all you have to remember is /ZZZ or /HERE.

## Read-Only Mode

There will be times that you want to look at a file, but you want to protect that file from inadvertent keystrokes and changes. (You might want to call in a lengthy file to practice `vi` movements, or you might want to scroll through a command file or program.) If you enter a file in read-only mode, you can use all the `vi` movement commands, but you cannot change the file with any edits. To look at your file `letter` in read-only mode, you can enter either:

        $ **vi -R letter**

or:

        $ **view letter**


## Recovering a Buffer

Occasionally, there will be a system failure while you are editing a file. Ordinarily, any edits made after your last write (save) are lost. However, there is an option, `-r`, which lets you recover the edited buffer at the time of a system crash. (A system program called `preserve` saves the buffer as the system is going down.)

When you first log in after the system is running again, you will receive a mail message stating that your buffer is saved. The first time that you call in the file, use the `-r` option to recover the edited buffer. For example, to recover the edited buffer of the file `letter` after a system crash, enter:

        $ **vi -r letter**

If you first call in the file *without* using the `-r` option, your buffered edits are lost.

You can force the system to preserve your buffer even when there is not a crash by using the command `:pre`. You may find this useful if you have made edits to a file, then discover you can't save your edits because you don't have write permission. (You could also just write a copy of the file out under another name or in a directory where you do have write permission.)


##                 · **Customizing `vi`** ·

A number of options that you can set as part of your editing environment affect how `vi` operates. For example, you can set a right margin that will cause `vi` to wrap lines automatically, so you don't need to insert carriage returns.

You can change options from within `vi` by using the `:set` command. In addition, `vi` reads an initialization file in your home directory called `.exrc` for further operating instructions. By placing `set` commands in this file, you can modify the way `vi` acts whenever you use it.

You can also set up `.exrc` files in local directories to initialize various options that you want to use in different environments. For example, you might define one set of options for editing text, but another set for editing source programs. The `.exrc` file in your home directory will be executed first, then the one on your current directory.

Finally, if the shell variable EXINIT is set in your environment (with the Bourne shell export command, or the C shell setenv command), any commands it contains will be executed by vi on startup. If EXINIT is set, it will be used instead of .exrc; vi will not take commands from both.

## The set Command

There are two types of options that can be changed with the set command: toggle options, which are either on or off, and options that take a numeric or string value (such as the location of a margin or the name of a file).

Toggle options may be on or off by default. To turn a toggle option on, the command is:

    :set *option*

To turn a toggle option off, the command is:

    :set no*option*

For example, to specify that pattern searches should ignore case, you type:

    :set ic

If you want vi to return to being case-sensitive in searches, give the command:

    :set noic

Some options have values. For example, the option window sets the number of lines shown in the screen "window." You set values for these options with an equals sign (=). For example:

    set window=20

During a vi session, you can check what options are available. The command:

    :set all

displays the complete list of options, including options that you have set and defaults that vi has chosen. The display will look something like this:

```
noautoindent        open               tabstop=8
autoprint           prompt             taglength=0
noautowrite         noreadonly         term=wy50
nobeautify          redraw             noterse
directory=/tmp      /remap             timeout
noedcompatible      report=5           ttytype=wy50
noerrorbells        scrolls=11         warn
hardtabs=8          sections=AhBhChDh  window=20
noignorecase        shell=/bin/csh     wrapscan
nolisp              shiftwidth=8       wrapmargin=10
nolist              noshowmatch        nowriteany
magic               noslowopen
mesg                paragraphs=IPLPPPQP LIpplpipbb
number              tags=tags /usr/lib/tags
nooptimize
```

You can also ask about the setting for any individual option by name, using the command:

    :set *option*?

The command `:set` shows options that you have specifically changed, or set, either in your `.exrc` file or during the current session. For example, the display might look like this:

    number  window=20  wrapmargin=10

See Appendix A for a description of what these options mean.

## The .exrc File

The `.exrc` file that controls the `vi` environment for you is in your home directory. Enter into this file the `set` options that you want to have in effect whenever you use `vi` or `ex`.

The `.exrc` file can be modified with the `vi` editor, like any other file. A sample `.exrc` file might look like this:

    set  wrapmargin=10  window=20

Because the file is actually read by `ex` before it enters visual mode (`vi`), commands in `.exrc` should not have a preceding colon.

## Alternate Environments

You can define alternate `vi` environments by saving option settings in an `.exrc` file that is placed in a local directory. If you enter `vi` from that directory, the local `.exrc` file will be read in. If it does not exist, the one in your home directory will be read in.

For example, you might want to have one set of options for programming:

    set number lisp autoindent sw=4 tags=/usr/lib/tags terse

and another set of options for text editing:

    set wrapmargin=15  ignorecase

Local `.exrc` files are especially useful when you define abbreviations, which are described in Chapter 7.

## Some Useful Options

As you can see when you type `:set all`, there are many options. Most options are used internally by `vi` and aren't usually changed. Others are important in certain cases, but not in others (for example, `noredraw` and `window` can be useful on a dialup line at a low baud rate). Appendix A contains a brief description of each option. We recommend that you take some time to play with option setting—if an option looks interesting, try setting it (or unsetting it) and watch what happens while you edit. You may find some surprisingly useful tools.

There is one option that is almost essential for editing nonprogram text. The wrapmargin option specifies the size of the right margin that will be used to autowrap text as you type. (This saves manually typing carriage returns.) This option is in effect if its value is set to greater than 0. A typical value is 10 or 15:

```
set  wrapmargin=15
```

There are also three options that control how vi acts in conducting a search. By default, it differentiates between uppercase and lowercase (*foo* does not match *Foo*), wraps around to the beginning of the file during a search (this means you can begin your search anywhere in the file and still find all occurrences), and recognizes wildcard characters when matching patterns. The default settings that control these options are noignorcase, wrapscan, and magic, respectively. To change any of these defaults, set the opposite toggles:  ignorecase, nowrapscan, or nomagic.

Another useful option is shiftwidth. This option was designed to help programmers properly indent their programs, but it can also be useful to writers. The >> and << commands can be used to indent (or un-indent) text by shiftwidth characters. The position of the cursor on the line doesn't matter—the entire line will be shifted. The shift.width option is set to 8 by default, but you can use :set to change this value.

Give the >> or << command a numeric prefix to affect more than on line. For example:

```
10>>
```

will indent the next 10 lines by shiftwidth.

### ▪ Edits and Movement ▪

You have learned the edit commands c, d, and y, and how to combine them with movements and numbers (such as 2cw or 4dd). Since that point, you have added many more movement commands to your repertoire. Although the fact that you can combine edit commands with movement is not a "new" concept to you, Table 3-2 gives you a feel for the many editing options you now have.

**TABLE 3-2. Combining vi Commands**

| From Cursor to | Change | Delete | Copy |
|---|---|---|---|
| Bottom of screen | cL | dL | yL |
| Next line | c+ | d+ | y+ |
| Next sentence | c) | d) | y) |
| Next paragraph | c} | d} | y} |
| Pattern | c/*pattern* | d/*pattern* | y/*pattern* |
| End of file | cG | dG | yG |
| Line number 13 | c13G | d13G | y13G |

You can also combine numbers with any of the commands in Table 3-2 to multiply them. For example, `2c)` changes the next two sentences. Although this table may seem forbidding, experiment with combinations and try to understand the patterns. When you find how much time and effort you can save, combinations of change and movement keys will no longer seem obscure, but will readily come to mind.

## ▪ More Ways to Insert Text ▪

You have inserted text before the cursor with the sequence:

    i*text* <ESC>

There are many insert commands. The difference between them is that they insert text at different positions relative to the cursor:

| | |
|---|---|
| a | append text after cursor |
| A | append text to end of current line |
| i | insert text before cursor |
| I | insert text at beginning of line |
| o | open new line below cursor for text |
| O | open new line above cursor for text |
| R | overstrike existing characters with new characters |

All these commands leave you in insert mode. After inserting text, remember to press *ESC* to escape back to command mode.

The A (*append*) and I (*insert*) commands save you from having to move the cursor to the end or beginning of the line before invoking insert mode. For example, A saves one keystroke over `$a`. Although one keystroke might not seem like a timesaver, as you become a more adept (and impatient) editor, you'll want to omit any unnecessary keystrokes.

There are other combinations of commands that work together naturally. For example, `ea` is useful for appending new text to the end of a word. (It sometimes helps to train yourself to recognize such frequent combinations so that invoking them becomes automatic.)

## ▪ Using Buffers ▪

While you are editing, you have seen that your last deletion (d or x) or yank (y) is saved in a buffer (a place in stored memory). You can access the contents of that buffer and put the saved text back in your file with the put command (p or P).

The last nine deletions are stored by `vi` in *numbered* buffers. You can access any of these numbered buffers to restore any (or all) of the last nine deletions. You can also place yanks (copied text) in buffers identified by *letters*. You can fill up to 26 buffers (*a* through *z*) with yanked text and restore that text with a put command any time in your editing session.

The vi program also saves your last edit command (insert, change, delete, or yank) in a buffer. Your last command is available to repeat or undo with a single keystroke.

## Recovering Deletions

Being able to delete large blocks of text at a single bound is all well and good, but what if you mistakenly delete 53 lines that you need? There is a way to recover any of your past nine deletions, which are saved in numbered buffers. The last deletion is saved in buffer 1; the second-to-last in buffer 2, and so on.

To recover a deletion, type " (quotation mark), identify the buffered text by number, and then give the put command. For example, to recover your second-to-last deletion from buffer 2, type:

    "2p

Sometimes it's hard to remember what's in the last nine buffers. Here's a trick that can help.

The . command (repeat last command) has a special meaning when used with p and u. The p command will print the last deletion or change, but 2p will print the last two. By combining p, . (dot), and u (undo), you can step back through the numbered buffers.

The "1p command will put the last deletion, now stored in buffer 1, back into your text. If you then type u, it will go away. But when you type the . command, instead of repeating the last command ("1p), it will show the next buffer as if you'd typed "2p. You can thus step back through the buffers. For example, the sequence:

    "1pu.u.u.u.

will show you, in sequence, the contents of the last six numbered buffers.

## Yanking to Named Buffers

With unnamed buffers, you have seen that you must put (p or P) the contents of the buffer before making any other edit, or the buffer is overwritten. You can also use y with a set of 26 named buffers (a through z), which are specifically for copying and moving text. If you name a buffer to store the yanked text, you can place the contents of the named buffer at any time during your editing session.

To yank into a named buffer, precede the yank command with a quotation mark (") and the character for the name of the buffer you want to load. For example:

| | |
|---|---|
| "dyy | yank current line into buffer *d* |
| "a6yy | yank next six lines into buffer *a* |

After loading the named buffers and moving to the new position, use p or P to put the text back.

| | |
|---|---|
| "dP | put buffer *d* before cursor |
| "ap | put buffer *a* after cursor |

```
In our conversation last         "a6yy      In our conversation last
Thursday, we discussed a       yank 6 lines  Thursday, we discussed a
documentation project           to buffer a  documentation project
that would produce a                         that would produce a
user's manual on the                         user's manual on the
Alcuin product.                              Alcuin product.


                                             6 lines yanked
```

```
Alcuin product.                    "ap       Alcuin product.
                                put buffer a  In our conversation last
                                after cursor  Thursday, we discussed a
                                             documentation project
                                             that would produce a
                                             user's manual on the
                                             Alcuin product.
```

There is no way to put part of a buffer into the text—it is all or nothing.

Named buffers allow you to make other edits before placing the buffer with `p`. After you know how to travel between files without leaving `vi`, you can use named buffers to selectively transfer text between files.

You can also delete text into named buffers, using much the same procedure. For example:

"a5dd            delete five lines into buffer *a*

If you specify the buffer name with a capital latter, yanked or deleted text will be *appended* to the current contents of the buffer. For example:

"byy            yank current line into buffer *b*
"B5dd           delete five lines and append to buffer *b*
3}              move down three paragraphs
"bP             insert the six lines from buffer *b* above the cursor

When you put text from a named buffer, a copy still remains in that buffer; you can repeat the put as often as you like until you quit your editing session or replace the text in the buffer.

For example, suppose you were preparing a document with some repetitive elements, such as the skeleton for each page of the reference section in a manual. You could store the skeleton in a named buffer, put it into your file, fill in the blanks, then put the skeleton in again each time you need it.

## ▪ **Marking Your Place** ▪

During a vi session, you can mark your place in the file with an invisible "book-mark," perform edits elsewhere, then return to your marked place. In the command mode:

| | |
|---|---|
| **m**$x$ | marks current position with $x$ ($x$ can be any letter) |
| " $´x$ | moves cursor to beginning of line marked by $x$ |
| " ` $x$ | moves cursor to character marked by $x$ |
| " ` ` | returns to previous mark or context after a move |

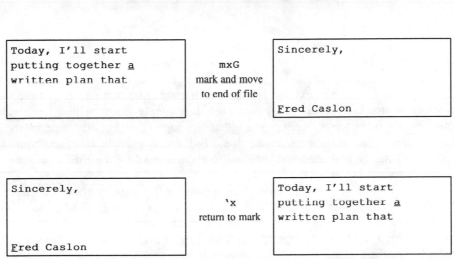

Place markers are set only during the current vi session; they are not stored in the file.

## ▪ **Other Advanced Edits** ▪

You may wonder why we haven't discussed global changes, moving text between files, or other advanced ex topics. The reason is that, to use these tools, it helps to learn more about ex and a set of UNIX pattern-matching tools that we discuss together in Chapter 7.

# 4

# nroff and troff

The `vi` editor lets you edit text, but it is not much good at formatting. A text file such as program source code might be formatted with a simple program like `pr`, which inserts a header at the top of every page and handles pagination, but otherwise prints the document exactly as it appears in the file. But for any application requiring the preparation of neatly formatted text, you will use the `nroff` ("en-roff") or `troff` ("tee-roff") formatting program.

These programs are used to process an input text file, usually coded or "marked up" with formatting instructions. When you use a *wysiwyg* program like most word processors, you use commands to lay out the text on the screen as it will be laid out on the page. With a markup language like that used by `nroff` and `troff`, you enter commands into the text that tell the formatting program what to do.

Our purpose in this chapter is twofold. We want to introduce the basic formatting codes that you will find useful. But at the same time, we want to present them in the context of what the formatter is doing and how it works. If you find this chapter rough-going—especially if this is your first exposure to `nroff/troff`—skip ahead to either Chapter 5 or Chapter 6 and become familiar with one of the macro packages, `ms` or `mm`; then come back and resume this chapter. We assume that you are reading this book because you would like more than the basics, that you intend to master the complexities of `nroff/troff`. As a result, this chapter is somewhat longer and more complex than it would be if the book were an introductory user's guide.

## Conventions

To distinguish input text and requests shown in examples from formatter output, we have adopted the convention of showing "page corners" around output from `nroff` or `troff`. Output from `nroff` is shown in the same constant-width typeface as other examples:

```
Here is an example of nroff output.
```

Output from troff is shown in the same typeface as the text, but with the size of the type reduced by one point, unless the example calls for an explicit type size:

> Here is an example of troff output.

In representing output, compromises sometimes had to be made. For example, when showing nroff output, we have processed the example separately with nroff, and read the results back into the source file. However, from there, they have been typeset in a constant-width font by troff. As a result, there might be slight differences from true nroff output, particularly in line length or page size. However, the context should always make clear just what is being demonstrated.

## ▪ **What the Formatter Does** ▪

Take a moment to think about the things you do when you format a page on a *wysiwyg* device such as a typewriter:

- You set aside part of the page as the text area. This requires setting top, bottom, left, and right margins.

- You adjust the lines that you type so they are all approximately the same length and fit into the designated text area.

- You break the text into syntactic units such as paragraphs.

- You switch to a new page when you reach the bottom of the text area.

Left to themselves, nroff or troff will do only one of these tasks: they will adjust the length of the lines in the input file so that they come out even in the output file. To do so, they make two assumptions:

- They assume that the line length is 6.5 inches.

- They assume that a blank line in the input signals the start of a new paragraph. The last line of the preceding text is not adjusted, and a blank line is placed in the output.

The process of filling and adjusting is intuitively obvious—we've all done much the same thing manually when using a typewriter or had it done for us by a *wysiwyg* word processor. However, especially when it comes to a typesetting program like troff, there are ramifications to the process of line adjustment that are not obvious. Having a clear idea of what is going on will be very useful later. For this reason, we'll examine the process in detail.

## Line Adjustment

There are three parts to line adjustment: *filling*, *justification*, and *hyphenation*.  Filling is the process of making all lines of text approximately equal in length.  When working on a typewriter, you do this automatically, simply by typing a carriage return when the line is full.  Most word-processing programs automatically insert a carriage return at the end of a line, and we have seen how to set up `vi` to do so as well.

However, `nroff` and `troff` ignore carriage returns in the input except in a special "no fill" mode.  They reformat the input text, collecting all input lines into even-length output lines, stopping only when they reach a blank line or (as we shall see shortly) a formatting instruction that tells them to stop.  Lines that begin with one or more blank spaces are not filled, but trailing blank spaces are trimmed.  Extra blank spaces between words on the input line are preserved, and the formatter adds an extra blank space after each period, question mark, or exclamation point.

Justification is a closely related feature that should not be confused with filling. Filling simply tries to keep lines approximately the same length; justification adjusts the space between words so that the ends of the lines match exactly.

By default, `nroff` and `troff` both fill and justify text.  Justification implies filling, but it is possible to have filling without justification.  Let's look at some examples.  First, we'll look at a paragraph entered in `vi`.  Here's a paragraph from the letter you entered in the last chapter, modified so that it offers to prepare not just a user's guide for the Alcuin illuminated lettering software, but a reference manual as well.  In the course of making the changes, we've left a short line in the middle of the paragraph.

```
In our conversation last Thursday, we discussed a
documentation project that would produce a user's guide
and reference manual
for the Alcuin product. Yesterday, I received the product
demo and other materials that you sent me.
```

Now, let's look at the paragraph after processing by `nroff`:

```
In our   conversation   last Thursday, we discussed   a
documentation project   that   would   produce a user's
guide and reference manual   for the Alcuin   product.
Yesterday, I   received   the   product   demo and other
materials that you sent me.
```

The paragraph has been both filled and justified.  If the formatter were told to fill, but not to justify, the paragraph would look like this:

```
In our conversation last Thursday, we discussed a
documentation project that would produce a user's guide
and reference manual for the Alcuin product. Yesterday,
I received the product demo and other materials that
you sent me.
```

As you can see, `nroff` justified the text in the first example by adding extra space between words.

Most typewritten material is filled but not justified. In printer's terms, it is typed *ragged right*. Books, magazines, and other typeset materials, by contrast, are usually *right justified*. Occasionally, you will see printed material (such as ad copy) in which the right end of each line is justified, but the left end is ragged. It is for this reason that we usually say that text is *right* or *left justified*, rather than simply *justified*.

When it is difficult to perform filling or justification or both because a long word falls at the end of a line, the formatter has another trick to fall back on (one we are all familiar with)—hyphenation.

The `nroff` and `troff` programs perform filling, justification, and hyphenation in much the same way as a human typesetter used to set cold lead type. Human typesetters used to assemble a line of type by placing individual letters in a tray until each line was filled. There were several options for filling as the typesetter reached the end of the line:

- The next word might fit exactly.

- The next word might fit if the typesetter squeezed the words a little closer together.

- The next word could be hyphenated, with part put on the current line and part on the next line.

If, in addition to being filled, the text was to be justified, there was one additional issue: after the line was approximately the right length, space needed to be added between each word so that the line length came out even.

Just like the human typesetter they replace, `nroff` and `troff` assemble one line of text at a time, measuring the length of the line and making adjustments to the spacing to make the line come out even (assuming that the line is to be justified). Input lines are collected into a temporary storage area, or *buffer*, until enough text has been collected for a single output line. Then that line is output, and the next line collected.

It is in the process of justification that you see the first significant difference between the two programs. The `nroff` program was designed for use with typewriter-like printers; `troff` was designed for use with phototypesetters.

A typewriter-style printer has characters all of the same size—an *i* takes up the same amount of space as an *m*. (Typical widths are 1/10 or 1/12 inch per character.) And although some printers (such as daisywheel printers) allow you to change the style of type by changing the daisywheel or thimble, you can usually have only one typeface at a time.

A typesetter, by contrast, uses typefaces in which each letter takes up an amount of space proportional to its outline. The space allotted for an *i* is quite definitely narrower than the space allotted for an *m*. The use of variable-width characters makes the job of filling and justification much more difficult for `troff` than for `nroff`. Where `nroff` only needs to count characters, `troff` has to add up the width of each character as it assembles the line. (Character widths are defined by a "box" around the character, rather than by its natural, somewhat irregular shape.)

The `troff` program also justifies by adding space between words, but because the variable-width fonts it uses are much more compact, it fits more on a line and generally does a much better job of justification.*

There's another difference as well. Left to itself, `nroff` will insert only full spaces between words—that is, it might put two spaces between one pair of words, and three between another, to fill the line. If you call `nroff` with the −e option, it will attempt to make all interword spaces the same size (using fractional spaces if possible). But even then, `nroff` will only succeed if the output device allows fractional spacing. The `troff` program always uses even interword spacing.

Here's the same paragraph filled and justified by `troff`:

In our conversation last Thursday, we discussed a documentation project that would produce a user's guide and reference manual for the Alcuin product. Yesterday, I received the product demo and other materials that you sent me.

To make matters still more difficult, typeset characters come in a variety of different designs, or *fonts*. A font is a set of alphabetic, numeric, and punctuation characters that share certain design elements. Typically, fonts come in families of several related typefaces. For example, this book is typeset for the most part in the Times Roman family of typefaces. There are three separate fonts:

roman
**bold**
*italic*

Typesetting allows for the use of multiple fonts on the same page, as you can see from the mixture of fonts throughout this book. Sometimes the fonts are from the same family, as with the Times Roman, Times Bold, and Times Italic just shown. However, you can see other fonts, such as Helvetica, in the running headers on each page. Bold and italic fonts are generally used for emphasis; in computer books such as this, a constant-width typewriter font is used for examples and other "computer voice" statements.

Even within the same font family, the width of the same character varies from font to font. For example, a bold "**m**" is slightly wider than a Roman "m."

To make things still more complicated, the same font comes in different sizes. If you look at this book, you will notice that the section headings within each chapter are slightly larger for emphasis. Type sizes are measured in units called *points*. We'll talk more about this later, but to get a rough idea of what type sizes mean, simply look at the current page. The body type of the book is 10-point Times Roman; the next heading is 12-point Times Bold. The spacing between lines is generally proportional to the point size, instead of fixed, as it is with `nroff`.

---

*The very best typesetting programs have the capability to adjust the space between individual characters as well. This process is called *kerning*. SoftQuad Publishing Software in Toronto sells an enhanced version of `troff` called `SQroff` that does support kerning.

The `troff` program gets information about the widths of the various characters in each font from tables stored on the system in the directory `/usr/lib/font`. These tables tell `troff` how far to move over after it has output each character on the line.

We'll talk more about `troff` later. For the moment, you should be aware that the job of the formatting program is much more complicated when typesetting than it is when preparing text for typewriter-style printers.

## ▪ Using nroff ▪

As mentioned previously, left to themselves, `nroff` and `troff` perform only rudimentary formatting. They will fill and justify the text, using a default line length of 6.5 inches, but they leave no margins, other than the implicit right margin caused by the line length. To make this clearer, let's look at the sample letter from the last chapter (including the edit we made in this chapter) as it appears after formatting with `nroff`.

First, let's look at how to invoke the formatter. The `nroff` program takes as an argument the name of a file to be formatted:

```
$ nroff letter
```

Alternatively, it can take standard input, allowing you to preprocess the text with some other program before formatting it:

```
$ tbl report | nroff
```

There are numerous options to `nroff`. They are described at various points in this book (as appropriate to the topic) and summarized in Appendix B.

One basic option is −T, which specifies the terminal (printer) type for which output should be prepared. Although `nroff` output is fairly straightforward, some differences between printers can significantly affect the output. (For example, one printer may perform underlining by backspacing and printing an underscore under each underlined letter, and another may do it by suppressing a newline and printing the underscores in a second pass over the line.) The default device is the Teletype Model 37 terminal—a fairly obsolete device. Other devices are listed in Appendix B. If you don't recognize any of the printers or terminals, the safest type is probably `lp`:

```
$ nroff -Tlp file
```

In examples in this book, we will leave off the −T option, but you may want to experiment, and use whichever type gives the best results with your equipment.

Like most UNIX programs, `nroff` prints its results on standard output. So, assuming that the text is stored in a file called `letter`, all you need to do is type:

```
$ nroff letter
```

A few moments later, you should see the results on the screen. Because the letter will scroll by quickly, you should pipe the output of `nroff` to a paging program such as `pg` or `more`:

```
$ nroff letter | pg
```

or out to a printer using `lp` or `lpr`:

```
$ nroff letter | lp
```

## ▪ Using `troff` ▪

The chief advantage of `troff` over `nroff` is that it allows different types of character sets, or fonts, and so lets you take full advantage of the higher-quality printing available with typesetters and laser printers. There are a number of requests, useful only in `troff`, for specifying fonts, type sizes, and the vertical spacing between lines. Before we describe the actual requests though, we need to look at a bit of history.

The `troff` program was originally designed for a specific typesetter, the Wang C/A/T. Later, it was modified to work with a wide range of output devices. We'll discuss the original version of `troff` (which is still in use at many sites) first, before discussing the newer versions. The C/A/T typesetter was designed in such a way that it could use only four fonts at one time.

(Early phototypesetters worked by projecting light through a film containing the outline of the various characters. The film was often mounted on a wheel that rotated to position the desired character in front of the light source as it flashed, thus photographing the character onto photographic paper or negative film. Lenses enlarged and reduced the characters to produce various type sizes. The C/A/T typesetter had a wheel divided into four quadrants, onto which one could mount four different typefaces.)

Typically, the four fonts were the standard (roman), bold, and italic fonts of the same family, plus a "special" font that contained additional punctuation characters, Greek characters (for equations), bullets, rules, and other nonstandard characters. Figure 4-1 shows the characters available in these standard fonts.

### The Coming of `ditroff`

Later, `troff` was modified to support other typesetters and, more importantly (at least from the perspective of many readers of this book), laser printers. The later version of `troff` is often called `ditroff` (for device-independent `troff`), but many UNIX systems have changed the name of the original `troff` to `otroff` and simply call `ditroff` by the original name, `troff`.

The `ditroff` program has not been universally available because, when it was developed, it was "unbundled" from the basic UNIX distribution and made part of a separate product called *Documenter's Workbench* or *DWB*. UNIX system manufacturers have the option not to include this package, although increasingly, they have been doing so. Versions of DWB are also available separately from third party vendors.

The newer version of `troff` allows you to specify any number of different fonts. (You can mount fonts at up to ten imaginary "positions" with `.fp` and can request additional fonts by name).

Times Roman

abcdefghijklmnopqrstuvwxyz
ABCDEFGHIJKLMNOPQRSTUVWXYZ
1234567890
! $ % & ( ) ' ' * + - . , / : ; = ? [ ] |
• □ — - _ ¹/₄ ¹/₂ ³/₄ fi fl     ° † ´ ¢ ® ©

*Times Italic*

*abcdefghijklmnopqrstuvwxyz*
*ABCDEFGHIJKLMNOPQRSTUVWXYZ*
*1234567890*
*! $ % & ( ) ' ' * + - . , / : ; = ? [ ] |*
 • □ — - _ ¹/₄ ¹/₂ ³/₄ fi fl     ° † ´ ¢ ® ©

**Times Bold**

**abcdefghijklmnopqrstuvwxyz**
**ABCDEFGHIJKLMNOPQRSTUVWXYZ**
**1234567890**
**! $ % & ( ) ' ' * + - . , / : ; = ? [ ] |**
**• □ — - _ ¹/₄ ¹/₂ ³/₄ fi fl     ° † ´ ¢ ® ©**

Special Mathematical Font

" ´ \ ^ _ ` ~ / < > { } # @ + - = *
α β γ δ ε ζ η θ ι κ λ μ ν ξ ο π ρ σ ς τ υ φ χ ψ ω
Γ Δ Θ Λ Ξ Π Σ Υ Φ Ψ Ω
√ ‾ > < ≡ ~ ≠ → ← ↑ ↓ × ÷ ± ∪ ∩ ⊂ ⊃ ⊆ ⊇ ∞ ∂
§ ∇ ¬ ∫ ∝ ∅ ∈ ‡ ☞ ☜ | ○ ⌈ ⌉ ⌊ ⌋ ⎰ ⎱ | ⎵ ⎴ ⎲

**Fig. 4-1.** The Four Standard Fonts

There may also be different font sizes available, and there are some additional commands for line drawing (`ditroff` can draw curves as well as straight lines). For the most part, though, `ditroff` is very similar to the original program, except in the greater flexibility it offers to use different output devices.

One way to find out which version of `troff` you have on your system (unless you have a program explicitly called `ditroff`) is to list the contents of the directory `/usr/lib/font`:

```
$ls -F /usr/lib/font
devlj/
devps/
ftB
ftI
ftR
ftS
```

If there are one or more subdirectories whose name begins with the letters dev, your system is using ditroff. Our system supports both ditroff and otroff, so we have both a device subdirectory (for ditroff) and font files (for otroff) directly in /usr/lib/font.

We'll talk more about font files later. For the moment, all you need to know is that they contain information about the widths of the characters in various fonts for a specific output device.

Contrary to what a novice might expect, font files do not contain outlines of the characters themselves. For a proper typesetter, character outlines reside in the typesetter itself. All troff sends out to the typesetter are character codes and size and position information.

However, troff has increasingly come to be used with laser printers, many of which use *downloadable fonts*. An electronic image of each character is loaded from the computer into the printer's memory, typically at the start of each printing job. There may be additional "font files" containing character outlines in this case, but these files are used by the software that controls the printer, and have nothing to do with troff itself. In other cases, font images are stored in ROM (read-only memory) in the printer.

If you are using a laser printer, it is important to remember that troff itself has nothing to do with the actual drawing of characters or images on the printed page. In a case like this, troff simply formats the page, using tables describing the widths of the characters used by the printer, and generates instructions about page layout, spacing, and so on. The actual job of driving the printer is handled by another program, generally referred to as a *printer driver* or troff *postprocessor*.

To use troff with such a postprocessor, you will generally need to pipe the output of troff to the postprocessor and from there to the print spooler:

$ **troff** *file* | *postprocessor* | **lp**

If you are using the old version of troff, which expects to send its output directly to the C/A/T typesetter, you need to specify the −t option, which tells troff to use standard output. If you don't, you will get the message:

```
Typesetter busy.
```

(Of course, if by any chance you *are* connected to a C/A/T typesetter, you don't need this option. There are several other options listed in Appendix B that you may find useful.) When you use ditroff, on the other hand, you will need to specify the −T command-line option that tells it what device you are using. The postprocessor will then translate the device-independent troff output into instructions for that particular type of laser printer or typesetter. For example, at our site, we use troff with an

postprocessor, which translates
ne looks something like this:

oly by changing the  −T option and
on a laser printer, then switch to a
changes to your files.  (To actually
ve to specify a printer name as an
e, we simply use  lp without any
ected as the *default* printer.)

sy as it sounds.  Because the fonts
dths even when the nominal font
breaks may be different when you

iety of output devices is becoming
-wide *page description languages*
and Imagen's DDL.  These page
st computer, and provide a device-
s and graphics on the page.

each output device, you can now
ut to the desired page description
s' TranScript postprocessor (or an
e Associates) to convert troff
output to any one of a number of

, we are generally referring to
discuss nroff as it differs from
n.  It is our opinion that the grow-
e program of choice for almost all

troff to nroff with entirely
quests that cannot be handled by
locuments coded for nroff to
y of the characteristics that make

## age

called *requests*) typically consist
of one or two lowercase letters and stand on their own line, following a period or apostrophe in column one.  Most requests are reasonably mnemonic.  For example, the request to leave space is:

```
.sp
```

There are also requests that can be embedded anywhere in the text.  These requests are commonly called *escape sequences*.  Escape sequences usually begin with a backslash

(\). For example, the escape sequence \l will draw a horizontal line. Especially in troff, escape sequences are used for line drawing or for printing various special characters that do not appear in the standard ASCII character set. For instance, you enter \ (bu to get •, a bullet.

There are three classes of formatting instructions:

- Instructions that have an immediate one-time effect, such as a request to space down an inch before outputting the next line of text.

- Instructions that have a persistent effect, such as requests to set the line length or to enable or disable justification.

- Instructions that are useful for writing *macros*. There is a "programming language" built into the formatter that allows you to build up complex requests from sequences of simpler ones. As part of this language there are requests for storing values into variables called *strings* and *number registers*, for testing conditions and acting on the result, and so on.

For the most part, we will discuss the requests used to define macros, strings, and number registers later in this book.

At this point, we want to focus on understanding the basic requests that control the basic actions of the formatter. We will also learn many of the most useful requests with immediate, one-time effects. Table 4-1 summarizes the requests that you will use most often.

### TABLE 4-1. Basic nroff/troff Requests

| Request | Meaning | Request | Meaning |
|---------|---------|---------|---------|
| .ad | Enable line adjustment | .na | No justification of lines |
| .br | Line break | .ne | Need lines to end of page |
| .bp | Page break | .nf | No filling of lines |
| .ce | Center next line | .nr | Define and set number register |
| .de | Define macro | .po | Set page offset |
| .ds | Define string | .ps | Set point size |
| .fi | Fill output lines | .so | Switch to source file and return |
| .ft | Set current font | .sp | Space |
| .in | Set indent | .ta | Set tab stop positions |
| .ls | Set double or triple spacing | .ti | Set temporary indent |
| .ll | Specify line length | .vs | Set vertical line spacing |

## Looking at nroff Output

When we discussed the basic operations of the text formatter, we saw that nroff and troff perform rudimentary formatting. They will fill and justify the text, using a default line length of 6.5 inches, but they leave no margins, other than the implicit right margin caused by the line length.

To make this clearer, let's look at the sample letter from the last chapter as it appears after formatting with nroff, without any embedded requests, and without using any macro package. From Figure 4-2, you can see immediately that the formatter has adjusted all of the lines, so that they are all the same length—even in the address block of the letter, where we would have preferred them to be left as they were. Blank lines in the input produce blank lines in the output, and the partial lines at the ends of paragraphs are not adjusted.

The most noticeable aspect of the raw formatting is a little difficult to reproduce here, though we've tried. No top or left margin is automatically allocated by nroff.

## · Turning Filling On and Off ·

Even though filling of uneven text lines resulting from editing is probably the most basic action we want from the formatter, it is not always desirable. For example, in our letter, we don't want the address block to be filled. There are two requests we could use to correct the problem: .br (*break*) and .nf (*no fill*).

A .br request following a line outputs the current contents of the line buffer and starts the next line, even though the buffer is not yet full. To produce a properly formatted address block, we could enter the following requests in the file:

```
Mr. John Fust
.br
Vice President, Research and Development
.br
Gutenberg Galaxy Software
.br
Waltham, Massachusetts 02159
```

Each individual input line will be output without filling or justification. We could also use the .nf request, which tells nroff to stop filling altogether. Text following this request will be printed by the formatter exactly as it appears in the input file. Use this request when you want text to be laid out as it was typed in.

Because we do want the body of the letter to be filled, we must turn filling back on with the .fi (*fill*) request:

```
                                        April 1, 1987

.nf
Mr. John Fust
Vice President, Research and Development
Gutenberg Galaxy Software
Waltham, Massachusetts 02159
.fi
Dear Mr. Fust:
```

April 1, 1987

Mr. John Fust Vice President, Research and
Development Gutenberg Galaxy Software Waltham,
Massachusetts 02159

Dear Mr. Fust:

In our conversation last Thursday, we discussed a
documentation project that would produce a user's
guide and reference manual for the Alcuin product.
Yesterday, I received the product demo and other
materials that you sent me. After studying them,
I want to clarify a couple of points:

Going through a demo session gave me a much better
understanding of the product. I confess to being
amazed by Alcuin. Some people around here,
looking over my shoulder, were also astounded by
the illustrated manuscript I produced with Alcuin.
One person, a student of calligraphy, was really
impressed.

Tomorrow, I'll start putting together a written
plan that presents different strategies for
documenting the Alcuin product. After I submit
this plan, and you have had time to review it,
let's arrange a meeting at your company to discuss
these stratgies.

Thanks again for giving us the opportunity to bid
on this documentation project. I hope we can
decide upon a strategy and get started as soon as
possible in order to have the manual ready in time
for first customer ship. I look forward to meeting
with you towards the end of next week.

                              Sincerely,



                              Fred Caslon

*Fig. 4-2.* A Raw nroff-formatted File

If you look carefully at the previous example, you will probably notice that we entered the two formatting requests on blank lines in the letter. If we were to format the letter now, here is what we'd get:

```
                                                      April 1, 1987

Mr. John Fust
Vice President, Research and Development
Gutenberg Galaxy Software
Waltham, Massachusetts 02159
Dear Mr. Fust:
```

As you may notice, we've lost the blank lines that used to separate the date from the address block, and the address block from the salutation. Lines containing formatting requests do not result in any space being output (unless they are spacing requests), so you should be sure not to inadvertently replace blank lines when entering formatting codes.

## ▪ Controlling Justification ▪

Justification can be controlled separately from filling by the `.ad` (*adjust*) request. (However, filling must be on for justification to work at all.) You can adjust text at either margin or at both margins.

Unlike the `.br` and `.nf` requests introduced, `.ad` takes an *argument*, which specifies the type of justification you want:

| | |
|---|---|
| l | adjust left margin only |
| r | adjust right margin only |
| b | adjust both margins |
| c | center filled line between margins |

There is another related request, `.na` (*no adjust*). Because the text entered in a file is usually left justified to begin with, turning justification off entirely with `.na` produces similar results to `.ad l` in most cases.

However, there is an important difference. Normally, if no argument is given to the `.ad` request, both margins will be adjusted. That is, `.ad` is the same as `.ad b`. However, following an `.na` request, `.ad` reverts to the value last specified. That is, the sequence:

```
.ad r
Some text
.ad l
Some text
.ad
Some text
```

will adjust both margins in the third block of text. However, the sequence:

```
.ad r
Some text
.na
Some text
.ad
Some text
```

will adjust only the right margin in the third block of text.

It's easy to see where you would use `.ad b` or `.ad l`. Let's suppose that you would like a ragged margin for the body of your letter, to make it look more like it was prepared on a typewriter. Simply follow the `.fi` request we entered previously with `.ad l`.

Right-only justification may seem a little harder to find a use for. Occasionally, you've probably seen ragged-left copy in advertising, but that's about it. However, if you think for a moment, you'll realize that it is also a good way to get a single line over to the right margin.

For example, in our sample letter, instead of typing all those leading spaces before the date (and having it fail to come out flush with the margin anyway), we could enter the lines:

```
.ad r
April 1, 1987
.ad b
```

As it turns out, this construct won't *quite* work. If you remember, when filling is enabled, `nroff` and `troff` collect input in a one-line buffer and only output the saved text when the line has been filled. There are some non-obvious consequences of this that will ripple all through your use of `nroff` and `troff`. If you issue a request that temporarily sets a formatting condition, then reset it before the line is output, your original setting may have no effect. *The result will be controlled by the request that is in effect at the time the line is output, not at the time that it is first collected in the line buffer.*

Certain requests cause implicit line breaks (the equivalent of carriage returns on a typewriter) in the output, but others do not. The `.ad` request does not cause a break. Therefore, a construction like:

```
.ad r
April 1, 1987
.ad b
Mr. John Fust
```

will result in the following output:

```
    April 1, 1987 Mr. John Fust
```

and not:

```
                                        April 1, 1987

    Mr. John Fust
```

To make sure that you get the desired result from a temporary setting like this, be sure to follow the line to be affected with a condition that will cause a break.* For instance, in the previous example, you would probably follow the date with a blank line or an `.sp` request, either of which will normally cause a break. If you don't, you should put in an explicit break, as follows:

```
.ad r
April 1, 1987
.br
.ad b
Mr. John Fust
```

A final point about justification: the formatter adjusts a line by widening the blank space between words. If you do not want the space between two words adjusted or split across output lines, precede the space with a backslash. This is called an *unpaddable space*.

There are many obscure applications for unpaddable spaces; we will mention them as appropriate. Here's a simple one that may come in handy: `nroff` and `troff` normally add two blank spaces after a period, question mark, or exclamation point. The formatter can't distinguish between the end of a sentence and an abbreviation, so if you find the extra spacing unaesthetic, you might follow an abbreviation like Mr. with an unpaddable space: `Mr.\ John Fust`.

## ▪ **Hyphenation** ▪

As pointed out previously, hyphenation is closely related to filling and justification, in that it gives `nroff` and `troff` some additional power to produce filled and justified lines without large gaps.

The `nroff` and `troff` programs perform hyphenation according to a general set of rules. Occasionally, you need to control the hyphenation of particular words. You can specify either that a word not be hyphenated or that it be hyphenated in a certain way. You can also turn hyphenation off entirely.

### Specifying Hyphenation for Individual Words

There are two ways to specify that a word be hyphenated a specific way: with the `.hw` request and with the special hyphenation indicator `\%`.

The `.hw` (*hyphenate word*) request allows you to specify a small list of words that should be hyphenated a specific way. The space available for the word list is small (about 128 characters), so you should use this request only for words you use frequently, and that `nroff` and `troff` hyphenate badly.

---

*The following requests cause a break:

.bp .br .ce .fi .nf .sp .in .ti

All other requests can be interspersed with text without causing a break. In addition, as discussed later, even these requests can be introduced with a special "no break" control character (′ instead of .) so that they too will not cause a break.

To use .hw, simply specify the word or words that constitute the exception list, typing a hyphen at the point or points in the word where you would like it to be hyphenated:

```
.hw hy-phen-a-tion
```

You can specify multiple words with one .hw request, or you can issue multiple .hw requests as you need them.

However, if it is just a matter of making sure that a particular instance of a word is hyphenated the way you want, you can use the hyphenation indication character sequence \%. As you type the word in your text, simply type the two characters \% at each acceptable hyphenation point, or at the front of the word if you don't want the word to be hyphenated at all:

```
\%acknowledge          the word acknowledge will not be hyphenated
ac\%know\%ledge        the word acknowledge can be hyphenated only
                       at the specified points
```

This character sequence is the first instance we have seen of a formatting request that does not consist of a request name following a period in column one. We will see many more of these later. This sequence is embedded right in the text but does not print out.

In general, nroff and troff do a reasonable job with hyphenation. You will need to set specific hyphenation points only in rare instances. In general, you shouldn't even worry about hyphenation points, unless you notice a bad break. Then use either .hw or \% to correct it.

The UNIX hyphen command can be used to print out all of the hyphenation points in a file formatted with nroff or troff -a.

```
$ nroff options files | hyphen
```

or:

```
$ troff options -a files | hyphen
```

If your system doesn't have the hyphen command, you can use grep instead:

```
$ nroff options files | grep '-$'
```

(The single quotation marks are important because they keep grep from interpreting the – as the beginning of an option.)

## Turning Hyphenation Off and On

If you don't want any hyphenation, use the .nh (*no hyphenation*) request. Even if you do this, though, you should be aware that words already containing embedded hyphens, em dashes (—), or hyphen indication characters (\%) will still be subject to hyphenation.

After you've turned hyphenation off, you can turn it back on with the .hy (*hyphenate*) request. This request has a few twists. Not only does it allow you to turn hyphenation on, it also allows you to adjust the hyphenation rules that nroff and troff use. It takes the following numeric arguments:

| 0 | turn hyphenation off |
|---|---|
| 1 | turn hyphenation on |
| 2 | do not hyphenate the last line on a page |
| 4 | do not hyphenate after the first two characters of a word |
| 8 | do not hyphenate before the last two characters of a word |

Specifying `.hy` with no argument is the same as specifying `.hy 1`. The other numeric values are additive. For example, `.hy 12` (`.hy 4` plus `.hy 8`) will keep `nroff` and `troff` from breaking short syllables at the beginning or end of words, and `.hy 14` will put all three hyphenation restrictions into effect.

## ▪ Page Layout ▪

Apart from the adjusted address block, the biggest formatting drawback that you probably noticed when we formatted the sample letter is that there was no left or top margin. Furthermore, though it is not apparent from our one-page example, there is no bottom margin either. If there were enough text in the input file to run onto a second page, you would see that the text ran continuously across the page boundary.

In normal use, these layout problems would be handled automatically by either the ms or mm macro packages (described later). Here, though, we want to understand how the formatter itself works.

Let's continue our investigation of the `nroff` and `troff` markup language with some basic page layout commands. These commands allow you to affect the placement of text on the page. Some of them (those whose descriptions begin with the word *set*) specify conditions that will remain in effect until they are explicitly changed by another instance of the same request. Others have a one-time effect.

As shown in Table 4-2, there are two groups of page layout commands, those that affect horizontal placement of text on the page and those that affect vertical placement. A moment's glance at these requests will tell you that, before anything else, we need to talk about units.

**TABLE 4-2. Layout Commands**

| | | |
|---|---|---|
| Horizontal Layout | `.ll` *n* | Set the line length to *n* |
| | `.po` *n* | Set the left margin (page offset) to *n* |
| | `.in` *n* | Indent the left margin to *n* |
| | `.ti` *n* | Temporarily indent the left margin to *n* |
| | `.ce` *n* | Center the following *n* lines |
| Vertical Layout | `.pl` *n* | Set the page length to *n* |
| | `.sp` *n* | Insert *n* spaces |
| | `.bp` *n* | Start a new page |
| | `.wh` *n* | Specify *wh*en (at what vertical position on the page) to execute a command |

## Units of Measure

By default, most `nroff` and `troff` commands that measure vertical distance (such as `.sp`) do so in terms of a number of "lines" (also referred to as vertical spaces, or vs). The `nroff` program has constant, device-dependent line spacing; `troff` has variable line spacing, which is generally proportional to the point size. However, both programs do allow you to use a variety of other units as well. You can specify spacing in terms of inches and centimeters, as well as the standard printer's measures *picas* and *points*. (A pica is 1/6 of an inch; a point is about 1/72 of an inch. These units were originally developed to measure the size of type, and the relationship between these two units is not as arbitrary as it might seem. A standard 12-point type is 1 pica high.)

Horizontal measures, such as the depth of an indent, can also be specified using any of these measures, as well as the printer's measures *ems* and *ens*. These are relative measures, originally based on the size of the letters *m* and *n* in the current type size and typeface. By default, horizontal measures are always taken to be in ems.

There is also a relationship between these units and points and picas. An em is always equivalent in width to the height of the character specified by the point size. In other words, an em in a 12-point type is 12 points wide. An en is always half the size of an em, or half of the current point size. The advantage of using these units is that they are relative to the size of the type being used. This is unimportant in `nroff`, but using these units in `troff` gives increased flexiblility to change the appearance of the document without recoding.

The `nroff` and `troff` programs measure not in any of these units, but in device-dependent basic units. Any measures you specify are converted to basic units before they are used. Typically, `nroff` measures in horizontal units of 1/240 of an inch and `otroff` uses a unit of 1/432 inch. These units too are not as arbitrary as they may seem. According to Joseph Osanna's *Nroff/Troff User's Manual*—the original, dense, and authoritative documentation on `troff` published by AT&T as part of the *UNIX Programmer's Manual*—the `nroff` units were chosen as "the least common multiple of the horizontal and vertical resolutions of various typewriter-like output devices." The units for `otroff` were based on the C/A/T typesetter (the device for which `troff` was originally designed), which could move in horizontal increments of 1/432 of an inch and in vertical increments of exactly one-third that, or 1/144 inch. Units for `ditroff` depend on the resolution of the output device. For example, units for a 300 dot-per-inch (dpi) laser printer will be 1/300 of an inch in either a vertical or a horizontal direction. See Appendix D for more information on `ditroff` device units.

You don't need to remember the details of all these measures now. You can generally use the units that are most familiar to you, and we'll come back to the others when we need them.

To specify units, you simply need to add the appropriate scale indicator from Table 4-3 to the numeric value you supply to a formatting request. For example, to space down 3 inches rather than 3 lines, enter the request:

```
.sp 3i
```

The numeric part of any scale indicator can include decimal fractions. Before the specified value is used, `nroff` and `troff` will round the value to the nearest number of device units.

**TABLE 4-3. Units of Measure**

| Indicator | Units |
|:---:|:---|
| c | Centimeters |
| i | Inches |
| m | Ems |
| n | Ens |
| p | Points |
| P | Picas |
| u | Device Units |
| v | Vertical spaces (lines) |
| none | Default |

In fact, you can use any reasonable numeric expression with any request that expects a numeric argument. However, when using arithmetic expressions, you have to be careful about what units you specify. All of the horizontally oriented requests— .ll, .in, .ti, .ta, .po, .lt, and .mc—assume you mean ems unless you specify otherwise.

Vertically oriented requests like .sp assume v's unless otherwise specified. The only exceptions to this rule are .ps and .vs, which assume points by default— but these are not really motion requests anyway.

As a result, if you make a request like:

    .ll 7i/2

what you are really requesting is:

    .ll 7i/2m

The request:

    .ll 7i/2i

is not what you want either. In performing arithmetic, as with fractions, the formatter converts scaled values to device units. In otroff, this means the previous expression is really evaluated as:

    .ll (7*432u)/(2*432u)

If you really want half of 7 inches, you should specify the expression like this:

    .ll 7i/2u

You could easily divide 7 by 2 yourself and simply specify 3.5i. The point of this example is that when you are doing arithmetic—usually with values stored in variables called number registers (more on these later)—you will need to pay attention to the interaction between units. Furthermore, because fractional device units are always rounded down, you should avoid expressions like 7i/2.5u because this is equivalent to 7i/2u.

In addition to absolute values, many `nroff` and `troff` requests allow you to specify relative values, by adding a + or a − before the value. For example:

```
.ll −.5i
```

will subtract ½ inch from the current line length, whatever it is.

## Setting Margins

In `nroff` and `troff`, margins are set by the combination of the `.po` (*page offset*) and `.ll` (*line length*) requests. The `.po` request defines the left margin. The `.ll` request defines how long each line will be after filling, and so implicitly defines the right margin:

| po | ll | *right margin* |
|---|---|---|

The `nroff` program's default line length of 6.5 inches is fairly standard for an 8½-by-11 page—it allows for 1-inch margins on either side.

Assuming that we'd like 1¼-inch margins on either side of the page, we would issue the following requests:

```
.ll 6i
.po 1.25i
```

This will give us 1¼ inches for both the right and left margins. The `.po` request specifies a left margin, or page offset, of 1¼ inches. When the 6-inch line length is added to this, it will leave a similar margin on the right side of the page.

Let's take a look at how our sample letter will format now. One paragraph of the output should give you the idea.

```
In   our   conversation   last   Thursday,   we
discussed   a   documentation   project   that would
produce a user's guide and reference   manual   for
the   Alcuin   product.   Yesterday,   I received the
product demo and other materials that you sent me.
```

As we saw earlier, `nroff` assumes a default page offset of 0. Either you or the macro package you are using must set the page offset. In `troff`, though, there is a default page offset of 26/27 inch, so you can get away without setting this value.

(Keep in mind that all `nroff` output examples are actually simulated with `troff`, and are reduced to fit on our own 5-inch wide printed page. As a result, the widths shown in our example output are not exact, but are suggestive of what the actual result would be on an 8½-by-11 inch page.)

## Setting Indents

In addition to the basic page offset, or left margin, you may want to set an indent, either for a single line or an entire block of text. You may also want to center one or more lines of text.

To do a single-line indent, as is commonly used to introduce a paragraph, use the `.ti` (*temporary indent*) request. For example, if you followed the blank lines between paragraphs in the sample letter with the request `.ti 5`, you'd get a result like this from `nroff`:

```
      ...Yesterday, I received the product demo and other
      materials that you sent me.

           Going  through  a  demo  session  gave  me  a
      much  better  understanding  of  the  product.   I
      confess  to being  amazed by  Alcuin...
```

The `.in` request, by contrast, sets an indent that remains in effect until it is changed. For example, if you had entered the line `.in 5` between the paragraphs, (instead of `.ti 5`), the result would have looked like this:

```
      ...Yesterday, I received the product demo and other
      materials that you sent me.

           Going  through  a  demo  session  gave  me  a
      much better  understanding  of  the  product.
      I confess  to being  amazed by  Alcuin...
```

All succeeding paragraphs will continue to be indented, until the indent is reset. The default indent (the value at the left margin) is 0.

These two indent requests can be combined to give a "hanging indent." Remember that you can specify negative values to many requests that take numeric arguments. Here is the first case where this makes sense. Let's say we would like to modify the letter so that it numbers the points and indents the body of the numbered paragraph:

```
...Yesterday, I received the product demo and other materials
that you sent me.  After studying them, I want to clarify
a couple of points:

.in 4
.ti -4
1.  Going through a demo session gave me a much better
understanding of the product.  I confess to being amazed by
Alcuin...
```

The first line will start at the margin, and subsequent lines will be indented:

```
...Yesterday, I received the product demo and other
materials that you sent me.    After studying them,
I want to clarify a couple of points:

1.   Going through  a demo session  gave  me  a much
     better understanding of the product.  I confess
     to  being  amazed  by  Alcuin...
```

To line up an indented paragraph like this in `nroff`, just count the number of characters you want to space over, then use that number as the size of the indent.  But this
trick is not so simple in `troff`.  Because characters, and even spaces, are not of constant width, it is more difficult to create a hanging indent.  Ens are a good unit to use
for indents.  Like ems, they are relative to the point size, but they are much closer to the
average character width than an em.  As a result, they are relatively intuitive to work
with.  An indent of `5n` is about where you expect a 5-character indent to be from familiarity with a typewriter.

## Centering Output Lines

Centering is another useful layout tool.  To center the next line, use the `.ce` request:

```
.ce
This line will be centered.
```

Here's the result:

```
                    This line will be centered.
```

Centering takes into account any indents that are in effect.  That is, if you have used
`.in` to specify an indent of 1 inch, and the line length is 5 inches, text will be centered
within the 4-inch span following the indent.

To center multiple lines, specify a number as an argument to the request:

```
.ce 3
Documentation for the Alcuin Product

A Proposal Prepared by
Fred Caslon
```

Here's the result:

```
        Documentation for the Alcuin Product

             A Proposal Prepared by
                 Fred Caslon
```

Notice that `.ce` centered all three *text* lines, ignoring the blank line between.

To center an indeterminately large number of lines, specify a very large number with the `.ce` request, then turn it off by entering `.ce 0`:

```
.ce 1000
Many lines of text here.
.ce 0
```

In looking at the examples, you probably noticed that centering automatically disables filling and justification. Each line is centered individually. However, there is also the case in which you would like to center an entire filled and justified paragraph. (This paragraph style is often used to set off quoted material in a book or paper.) You can do this by using both the `.in` and `.ll` requests:

```
I was particularly interested by one comment that I
read in your company literature:

.in +5n
.ll -5n
The development of Alcuin can be traced back to our
founder's early interest in medieval manuscripts.
He spent several years in the seminary before
becoming interested in computers.  After he became
an expert on typesetting software, he resolved to
put his two interests together.
.in -5n
.ll +5n
```

Here's the result:

```
I was particularly interested by one comment that I
read in your company literature:

    The development of Alcuin can be traced back to
    our  founder's  early  interest  in  medieval
    manuscripts.  He  spent  several  years  in  the
    seminary before becoming interested in comput-
    ers.  After he became an expert on typesetting
    software,  he  resolved  to  put  his  two interests
    together.
```

Remember that a line centered with `.ce` takes into account any indents in effect at the time. You can visualize the relationship between page offset, line length, indents, and centering as follows:

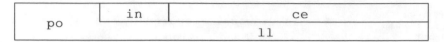

## Setting Tabs

No discussion of how to align text would be complete without a discussion of tabs. A tab, as anyone who has used a typewriter well knows, is a horizontal motion to a predefined position on the line.

The problem with using tabs in `nroff` and `troff` is that what you see on the screen is very different from what you get on the page. Unlike a typewriter or a *wysiwyg* word processor, the editor/formatter combination presents you with two different tab settings. You can set tabs in `vi`, and you can set them in `nroff` and `troff`, but the settings are likely to be different, and the results on the screen definitely unaesthetic.

However, after you get used to the fact that tabs will not line up on the screen in the same way as they will on the printed page, you can use tabs quite effectively.

By default, tab stops are set every .8 inches in `nroff` and every .5 inches in `troff`. To set your own tab stops in `nroff` or `troff`, use the `.ta` request. For example:

```
.ta 1i 2.5i 3i
```

will set three tab stops, at 1 inch, $2^1/_2$ inches, and 3 inches, respectively. Any previous or default settings are now no longer in effect.

You can also set incremental tab stops. The request:

```
.ta 1i +1.5i +.5i
```

will set tabs at the same positions as the previous example. Values preceded with a plus sign are added to the value of the last tab stop.

You can also specify the alignment of text at a tab stop. Settings made with a numeric value alone are left adjusted, just as they are on a typewriter. However, by adding either the letter `R` or `C` to the definition of a tab stop, you can make text right adjusted or centered on the stop.

For example, the following input lines (where a tab character is shown by the symbol |————|):

```
.nf
.ta 1i 2.5i 3.5i
|———|First|———|Second|———|Third
.fi
```

will produce the following output:

```
                 First              Second      Third
```

But:

```
    .nf
    .ta 1i 2.5iR 3.5iC
    |──────|First|──────|Second|──────|Third
    .fi
```

will produce:

```
                 First        Second        Third
```

Right-adjusted tabs can be useful for aligning numeric data.  This is especially true in troff, where all characters (including blank spaces) have different sizes, and, as a result, you can't just line things up by eye.  If the numbers you want to align have an uneven number of decimal positions, you can manually force right adjustment of numeric data using the special escape sequence \0, which will produce a blank space exactly the same width as a digit.  For example:

```
    .ta 1iR
    |──────|500.2\0
    |──────|125.35
    |──────|50.\0\0
```

will produce:

```
        500.2
        125.35
         50.
```

As on a typewriter, if you have already spaced past a tab position (either by printing characters, or with an indent or other horizontal motion), a tab in the input will push text over to the next available tab stop.  If you have passed the last tab stop, any tabs present in the input will be ignored.

You must be in no-fill mode for tabs to work correctly.  This is not just because filling will override the effect of the tabs.  Using .nf when specifying tabs is an important rule of thumb; we'll look at the reasoning behind it in Chapter 15.

## Underlining

We haven't yet described how to underline text, a primary type of emphasis in nroff, which lacks the troff ability to switch fonts for emphasis.

There are two underlining requests: .ul (*underline*) and .cu (*continuous underline*).  The .ul request underlines only printable characters (the words, but not the spaces), and .cu underlines the entire text string.

These requests are used just like `.ce`. Without an argument, they underline the text on the following input line. You can use a numeric argument to specify that more than one line should be underlined.

Both of these requests produce italics instead of underlines in `troff`. Although there is a request, `.uf`, that allows you to reset the underline font to some other font than italics,* there is no way to have these requests produce underlining even in `troff`. (The `ms` and `mm` macro packages both include a *macro* to do underlining in `troff`, but this uses an entirely different mechanism, which is not explained until Chapter 15.)

## Inserting Vertical Space

As you have seen, a blank line in the input text results in a blank line in the output. You can leave blank space on the page (for example, between the closing of a letter and the signature) by inserting a number of blank lines in the input text.

However, particularly when you are entering formatting codes as you write, rather than going back to code an existing file like our sample letter, it is often more convenient to specify the spacing with the `.sp` request.

For example, you could type:

```
Sincerely,
.sp 3
Fred Caslon
```

In `troff`, the `.sp` request is even more important, because `troff` can space in much finer increments.

For example, if we were formatting the letter with `troff`, a full space between paragraphs would look like this:

In our conversation last Thursday, we discussed a documentation project that would produce a user's guide and reference manual for the Alcuin product. Yesterday, I received the product demo and other materials that you sent me.

Going through a demo session gave me a better understanding of the product. I confess to being amazed by Alcuin. Some people around here, looking over my shoulder, were also astounded by the illuminated manuscript I produced with Alcuin. One person, a student of calligraphy, was really impressed.

The output would probably look better if there was a smaller amount of space between the lines. If we replace the line between the paragraphs with the request `.sp .5`, here is what we will get:

---

*This request is generally used when the document is being typeset in a font family other than Times Roman. It might be used to set the "underline font" to Helvetica Italic, rather than the standard Italic.

> In our conversation last Thursday, we discussed a documentation project that would produce a user's guide and reference manual for the Alcuin product. Yesterday, I received the product demo and other materials that you sent me.
>
> Going through a demo session gave me a much better understanding of the product. I confess to being amazed by Alcuin. Some people around here, looking over my shoulder, were also astounded by the illuminated manuscript I produced with Alcuin. One person, a student of calligraphy, was really impressed.

Although it may not yet be apparent how this will be useful, you can also space to an absolute position on the page, by inserting a vertical bar before the distance. The following:

```
.sp |3i
```

will space down to a position 3 inches from the top of the page, rather than 3 inches from the current position.

You can also use negative values with ordinary relative spacing requests. For example:

```
.sp -3
```

will move back up the page three lines. Of course, when you use any of these requests, you have to know what you are doing. If you tell nroff or troff to put one line on top of another, that's exactly what you'll get. For example:

```
This is the first line.
.sp -2
This is the second line.
.br
This is the third line.
```

will result in:

```
This is the second line.
This is the thrsu lluei
```

Sure enough, the second line is printed above the first, but because we haven't restored the original position, the third line is then printed on top of the first.

When you make negative vertical motions, you should always make compensatory positive motions, so that you end up at the correct position for future output. The previous example would have avoided disaster if it had been coded:

```
This is the first line.
.sp -2
This is the second line.
.sp
This is the third line.
```

(Notice that you need to space down one less line than you have spaced up because, in this case, printing the second line "uses up" one of the spaces you went back on.)

These kind of vertical motions are generally used for line drawing (e.g., for drawing boxes around tables), in which all of the text is output, and the formatter then goes back up the page to draw in the lines. At this stage, it is unlikely that you will find an immediate use for this capability. Nonetheless, we are sure that a creative person, knowing that it is there, will find it just the right tool for a job. (We'll show a few creative uses of our own later.)

You probably aren't surprised that a typesetter can go back up the page. But you may wonder how a typewriter-like printer can go back up the page like this. The answer is that it can't. If you do any reverse line motions (and you do when you use certain macros in the standard packages, or the `tbl` and `eqn` preprocessors), you must pass the `nroff` output through a special filter program called `col` to get all of the motions sorted out beforehand, so that the page will be printed in the desired order:

```
$   nroff files | col | lp
```

## Double or Triple Spacing

Both `nroff` and `troff` provide a request to produce double- or triple-spaced output without individually adjusting the space between each line. For example:

```
.ls 2
```

Putting this at the top of the file produces double-spaced lines. An argument of 3 specifies triple-spaced lines.

## · Page Transitions ·

If we want space at the top of our one-page letter, it is easy enough to insert the command:

```
.sp 1i
```

before the first line of the text. However, `nroff` and `troff` do not provide an easy way of handling page transitions in multipage documents.

By default, `nroff` and `troff` assume that the page length is 11 inches. However, neither program makes immediate use of this information. There is no default top and bottom margin, so text output begins on the first line, and goes to the end of the page.

The `.bp` (*break page*) request allows you to force a page break. If you do this, the remainder of the current page will be filled with blank lines, and output will start again at the top of the second page. If you care to test this, insert a `.bp` anywhere in the text of our sample letter, then process the letter with `nroff`. If you save the resulting output in a file:

```
$ nroff letter > letter.out
```

you will find that the text following the `.bp` begins on line 67 (11 inches at 6 lines per inch equals 66 lines per page).

To automatically leave space at the top and bottom of each page, you need to use the `.wh` (*when*) request. In `nroff` and `troff` parlance, this request sets a *trap*—a position on the page at which a given macro will be executed.

You'll notice that we said *macro*, not *request*. There's the rub. To use `.wh`, you need to know how to define a macro. It doesn't work with single requests.

There's not all that much to defining macros, though. A macro is simply a sequence of stored requests that can be executed all at once with a single command. We'll come back to this later, after we've looked at the process of macro definition.

For the moment, let's assume that we've defined two macros, one containing the commands that will handle the top margin, and another for the bottom margin. The first macro will be called `.TM`, and the second `.BM`. (By convention, macros are often given names consisting of uppercase letters, to distinguish them from the basic `nroff` and `troff` requests. However, this is a convention only, and one that is not always followed.)

To set traps that will execute these macros, we would use the `.wh` request as follows:

```
.wh 0 TM
.wh -1i BM
```

The first argument to `.wh` specifies the vertical position on the page at which to execute the macro. An argument of 0 always stands for the top of the page, and a negative value is always counted from the bottom of the page, as defined by the page length.

In its simplest form, the `.TM` macro need only contain the single request to space down 1 inch, and `.BM` need only contain the single request to break to a new page. If `.wh` allowed you to specify a single request rather than a macro, this would be equivalent to:

```
.wh 0 .sp 1i
.wh -1i .bp
```

With an 11-inch page length, this would result in an effective 9 inch text area, because on every page, the formatter's first act would be to space down 1 inch, and it would break to a new page when it reached 1 inch from the bottom.

You might wonder why `nroff` and `troff` have made the business of page transition more complicated than any of the other essential page layout tasks. There are two reasons:

- The `nroff` and `troff` programs were designed with the typesetting heritage in mind. Until fairly recently, most typesetters produced continuous output on rolls of photographic paper or film. This output was manually cut and pasted up onto pages.

- Especially in `troff`, page transition is inherently more complex than the other tasks we've described. For example, books often contain headers and footers that are set in different type sizes or styles. At every page transition, the software must automatically save information about the current type style, switch to the style used by the header or footer, and then revert to the original style when it returns to the main text. Or consider the matter of footnotes—the position at which the page ends is different when a footnote is on the page. The page transition trap must make some allowance for this.

In short, what you might like the formatter to do during page transitions can vary. For this reason, the developers of `nroff` and `troff` have allowed users to define their own macros for handling this area.

When you start out with `nroff` or `troff`, we advise you to use one of the ready-made macro packages, `ms` or `mm`. The standard macro package for UNIX systems based on System V is `mm`; the standard on Berkeley UNIX systems is `ms`. Berkeley UNIX systems also support a third macro package called `me`. In addition, there are specialized macro packages for formatting viewgraphs, standard UNIX reference manual pages (`man`), and UNIX permuted indexes (`mptx`). Only the `ms` and `mm` packages are described in this book. The macro packages have already taken into account many of the complexities in page transition (and other advanced formatting problems), and provide many capabilities that would take considerable time and effort to design yourself.

Of course, it is quite possible to design your own macro package, and we will go into all of the details later. (In fact, this book is coded with neither of the standard macro packages, but with one developed by Steve Kochan and Pat Wood of Pipeline Associates, the consulting editors of this series, for use specifically with the Hayden UNIX library.)

## Page Length Revisited

Before we take a closer look at macros, let's take a moment to make a few more points about page length, page breaks, and the like.

Assuming that some provision has been made for handling page transitions, there are several wrinkles to the requests we have already introduced, plus several new requests that you will probably find useful.

First, let's talk about page length. It's important to remember that the printing area is defined by the interaction of the page length and the location of the traps you define. For example, you could define a text area 7.5 inches high (as we did in preparing copy for this book) either by

- changing the page length to 9.5 inches, and setting 1-inch margins at the top and bottom;

- leaving the page length at 11 inches, and setting 1.75-inch margins at the top and bottom.

In general, we prefer to think of `.pl` as setting the *paper length*, and use the page transition traps to set larger or smaller margins.

However, there are cases where you really are working with a different paper size. A good example of this is printing addresses on envelopes: the physical paper height is about 4 inches (24 lines on a typewriter-like printer printing 6 lines per inch), and we want to print in a narrow window consisting of four or five lines. A good set of definitions for this case would be:

```
.pl 4i
.wh 0 TM
.wh -9v BM
```

with `.TM` containing the request `.sp 9v`, and with `.BM`, as before, containing `.bp`.

There is more to say about traps, but it will make more sense later, so we'll leave the subject for now.

## Page Breaks without Line Breaks

Page breaks—we've talked about their use in page transition traps, but they also have a common use on their own. Often, you will want to break a page before it would normally end. For example, if the page breaks right after the first line of a paragraph, you will probably want to force the line onto the next page, rather than leaving an "orphaned" line. Or you might want to leave blank space at the bottom of a page for an illustration. To do this, simply enter a `.bp` at the desired point. A new page will be started immediately.

However, consider the case in which you need to force a break in the middle of a paragraph to prevent a "widowed" line at the top of the next page. If you do this:

```
The medieval masters of calligraphy and illumination
are largely unknown to us.  We thankfully have examples
of their work, and even
.bp
marginal notes by the copyists of some manuscripts,
but the men who produced these minute masterpieces
are anonymous.
```

the `.bp` request will also cause a line break, and the text will not be filled properly:

```
The medieval masters of  calligraphy  and  illumination
are largely unknown to us.  We thankfully have examples
of their work, and even
```

*New page begins here*

```
marginal notes by the copyists of some manuscripts, but
the  men  who  produced  these  minute  masterpieces  are
anonymous.
```

Fortunately, there is a way around this problem. If you begin a request with an apostrophe instead of a period, the request will not cause a break.

```
     The medieval masters of calligraphy and illumination
     are largely unknown to us.  We thankfully have examples
     of their work, and even
     'bp
     marginal notes by the copyists of some manuscripts,
     but the men who produced these minute masterpieces
     are anonymous.
```

Now we have the desired result:

```
     The  medieval  masters  of  calligraphy  and  illumination
     are  largely  unknown  to  us.   We  thankfully  have  examples
```

*New page begins here*

```
     of their work, and even marginal notes by the copyists
     of  some  manuscripts,  but  the  men  who  produced  these
     minute masterpieces are anonymous.
```

(In fact, most page transition macros use this feature to make paragraphs continue across page boundaries. We'll take a closer look at this in later chapters.)

Another very useful request is the conditional page break, or `.ne` (*need*) request. If you want to make sure an entire block of text appears on the same page, you can use this request to force a page break if there isn't enough space left. If there is sufficient space, the request is ignored.

For example, the two requests:

```
.ne 3.2i
.sp 3i
```

might be used to reserve blank space to paste in an illustration that is 3 inches high.

The `.ne` request does not cause a break, so you should be sure to precede it with `.br` or another request that causes a break if you don't want the remnants of the current line buffer carried to the next page if the `.ne` is triggered.

It is often better to use `.ne` instead of `.bp`, unless you're absolutely sure that you will *always* want a page break at a particular point. If, in the course of editing, an `.ne` request moves away from the bottom of the page, it will have no effect. But a `.bp` will always start a new page, sometimes leaving a page nearly blank when the text in a file has been changed significantly.

There are other special spacing requests that can be used for this purpose. (Depending on the macro package, these may have to be used.) For example, `.sv` (*save space*) requests a block of contiguous space. If the remainder of the page does not contain the requested amount of space, no space is output. Instead, the amount of space requested is remembered and is output when an `.os` (*output saved space*) request is encountered.

These are advanced requests, but you may need to know about them because most macro packages include two other spacing requests in their page transition macros: `.ns` (*no space*) and `.rs` (*restore space*). An `.ns` inhibits the effect of spacing requests; `.rs` restores the effectiveness of such requests.

Both the `ms` and `mm` macros include an `.ns` request in their page transition macros. As a result, if you issue a request like:

    .sp 3i

with 1 inch remaining before the bottom of the page, you will not get 1 inch at the bottom, plus 2 inches at the top of the next page, but only whatever remains at the bottom. The next page will start right at the top. However, both macro packages also include an `.os` request in their page top macro, so if you truly want 3 inches, use `.sv 3i`, and you will get the expected result.

However, if you use `.sv`, you will also have another unexpected result: text following the spacing request will "float" ahead of it to fill up the remainder of the current page.

We'll talk more about this later. We introduced it now to prevent confusion when spacing requests don't always act the way you expect.

## Page Numbering

The `nroff` and `troff` programs keep track of page numbers and make the current page number available to be printed out (usually by a page transition macro). You can artificially set the page number with the `.pn` request:

| | |
|---|---|
| `.pn 5` | Set the current page number to 5 |
| `.pn +5` | Increment the current page number by 5 |
| `.pn -5` | Decrement the current page number by 5 |

You can also artificially set the number for the *next* page whenever you issue a `.bp` request, simply by adding a numeric argument:

| | |
|---|---|
| `.bp 5` | Break the page and set the next page number to 5 |
| `.bp +5` | Break the page and increment the next page number by 5 |
| `.bp -5` | Break the page and decrement the next page number by 5 |

In addition to inhibiting `.sp`, the `.ns` request inhibits the action of `.bp`, *unless* a page number is specified. This means (at least in the existing macro packages), that the sequence:

    .bp
    .bp

will not result in a blank page being output. You will get the same effect as if you had specified only a simple `.bp`. Instead, you should specify:

    .bp +1

The starting page number (usually 1) can also be set from the command line, using the −n option. For example:

```
$ nroff -ms -n10 file
```

will start numbering *file* at page number 10. In addition, there is a command-line option to print only selected pages of the output. The −o option takes a list of page numbers as its argument. The entire file (up to the last page number in the list) is processed, but only the specified pages are output. The list can include single pages separated by commas, or a range of pages separated by a hyphen, or both. A number followed by a trailing hyphen means to output from that page to the end. For example:

```
$ nroff -ms -o1,5,7-9,13- file
```

will output pages 1, 5, 7 through 9, and from 13 to the end of the file. There should be no spaces anywhere in the list.

## ▪  Changing Fonts  ▪

In old troff (otroff), you were limited to four fonts at a time, because the fonts had to be physically mounted on the C/A/T typesetter. With ditroff and a laser printer or a modem typesetter, you can use a virtually unlimited number of fonts in the same document.

In otroff you needed to specify the basic fonts that are in use with the .fp (*font position*) request. Normally, at the front of a file (or, more likely, in the macro package), you would use this request to specify which fonts are mounted in each of the four quadrants (positions) of the typesetter wheel. By default, the roman font is mounted in position 1, the italic font in position 2, the bold font in position 3, and the special font in position 4. That is, troff acts as though you had included the lines:

```
.fp 1 R
.fp 2 I
.fp 3 B
.fp 4 S
```

In ditroff, up to ten fonts are automatically mounted, with the special font in position 10. Which fonts are mounted, and in which positions, depends on the output device. See Appendix D for details. The font that is mounted in position 1 will be used for the body type of the text—it is the font that will be used if no other specification is given. The special font is also used without any intervention on your part when a character not in the normal character set is requested.

To request one of the other fonts, you can use either the .ft request, or the inline font-switch escape sequence \f.

For example:

```
.ft B
This line will be set in bold type.
.br
.ft R
This line will again be set in roman type.
```

will produce:

> **This line will be set in bold type.**
> This line will again be set in roman type.

You can also change fonts using an inline font *escape sequence*. For example, the preceding sentence was coded like this:

```
...an inline font \fIescape sequence\fP.
```

You may wonder at the `\fP` at the end, rather than `\fR`. The `P` command is a special code that can be used with either the `.ft` request or the `\f` escape sequence. It means "return to the previous font, whatever it was." This is often preferable to an explicit font request, because it is more general.

All of this begs the question of fonts different than Times Roman, Bold, and Italic. There are two issues: first, which fonts are available on the output device, and second, which fonts does `troff` have width tables for. (As described previously, `troff` uses these tables to determine how far to space over after it outputs each character.) For `otroff` these width tables are in the directory `/usr/lib/font`, in files whose names begin with `ft`. If you list the contents of this directory, you might see something like this for `otroff`:

```
$ ls /usr/lib/font
ftB     ftBC    ftC     ftCE    ftCI
ftCK    ftCS    ftCW    ftFD    ftG
ftGI    ftGM    ftGR    ftH     ftHB
ftHI    ftI     ftL     ftLI    ftPA
ftPB    ftPI    ftR     ftS     ftSB
ftSI    ftSM    ftUD
```

You can pick out the familiar R, I, B, and S fonts, and may guess that `ftH`, `ftHI`, and `ftHB` refer to Helvetica, Helvetica Italic, and Helvetica Bold fonts. However, unless you are familiar with typesetting, the other names might as well be Greek to you. In any event, these width tables, normally supplied with `troff`, are for fonts that are commonly used with the C/A/T typesetter. *If you are using a different device, they may be of no use to you.*

The point is that if you are using a different typesetting device, you will need to get information about the font names for your system from whoever set up the equipment to work with `troff`. The contents of `/usr/lib/font` will vary from installation to installation, depending on what fonts are supported.

For `ditroff`, there is a separate subdirectory in `/usr/lib/font` for each supported output device. For example:

```
$ ls /usr/lib/font
devlj       devps
$ ls /usr/lib/font/devps
B.out     BI.out    CB.out    CI.out    CW.out    CX.out
DESC.out  H.out     HB.out    HI.out    HK.out    HO.out
HX.out    I.out     LI.out    PA.out    PB.out    PI.out
PX.out    R.out     O.out     RS.out    S.out     S1.out
```

Here, the font name is followed by the string `.out`.

Again, the font names themselves are probably Greek to you. However, with `ditroff`, you can actually use any of these names, and see what results they give you, because all fonts should be available at any time.

For the sake of argument, let's assume that your typesetter or other `troff`-compatible equipment supports the Helvetica font family shown in Figure 4-3, with the names `H`, `HI`, and `HB`. (This is a fairly reasonable assumption, because Helvetica is probably the most widely available font family after Times.)

Helvetica

abcdefghijklmnopqrstuvwxyz
ABCDEFGHIJKLMNOPQRSTUVWXYZ
1234567890
! $ % & ( ) ' ' * + - . , / : ; = ? [ ] |
• □ — - _ ¼ ½ ¾ fi fl      ° † ´ ® ©

*Helvetica Italic*

*abcdefghijklmnopqrstuvwxyz*
*ABCDEFGHIJKLMNOPQRSTUVWXYZ*
*1234567890*
*! $ % & ( ) ' ' * + - . , / : ; = ? [ ] |*
*• □ — - _ ¼ ½ ¾ fi fl      ° † ´ ® ©*

**Helvetica    Bold**

**abcdefghijklmnopqrstuvwxyz**
**ABCDEFGHIJKLMNOPQRSTUVWXYZ**
**1234567890**
**! $ % & ( ) ' ' * + - . , / : ; = ? [ ] |**
**• □ — - _ ¼ ½ ¾ fi fl      ° † ´ ® ©**

Special Mathematical Font

" ´ \ ^ _ ` ~ / < > { } # @ + − = *
α β γ δ ε ζ η θ ι κ λ μ ν ξ ο π ρ σ ς τ υ φ χ ψ ω
Γ Δ Θ Λ Ξ Π Σ Υ Φ Ψ Ω
√ ≥ ≤ ≡ ~ ≠ → ← ↑ ↓ × ÷ ± ∪ ∩ ⊂ ⊆ ⊃ ⊇ ∞ ∂
§ ∇ ¬ ∫ ∝ ∅ ∈ ‡ ▬ ▬ | ○ ⌈ ⌊ ⌋ ⌉ ⌈ ⌋ | ⊔ ⊓ |

**Fig. 4-3.** Helvetica Fonts

When specifying two-character font names with the `\f` escape sequence, you must add the `(` prefix as well. For example, you would specify Helvetica Italic by the inline sequence `\f(HI`, and Helvetica Bold by `\f(HB`.

There is another issue when you are using fonts other than the Times Roman family. Assume that you decide to typeset your document in Helvetica rather than Roman. You reset your initial font position settings to read:

```
.fp 1 H
.fp 2 HI
.fp 3 HB
.fp 4 S
```

However, throughout the text, you have requests of the form:

```
.ft B
```

or:

```
\fB
```

You will need to make a set of global replacements throughout your file. To insulate yourself in a broader way from overall font change decisions, troff allows you to specify fonts by position, even within .ft and \f requests:

| .ft 1 | or | \f1 | Use the font mounted in position 1 |
| .ft 2 | or | \f2 | Use the font mounted in position 2 |
| .ft 3 | or | \f3 | Use the font mounted in position 3 |
| .ft 4 | or | \f4 | Use the font mounted in position 4 |

Because you don't need to use the .fp request to set font positions with ditroff, and the range of fonts is much greater, you may have a problem knowing which fonts are mounted in which positions. A quick way to find out which fonts are mounted is to run ditroff on a short file, sending the output to the screen. For example:

```
$ ditroff -Tps junk | more
x T ps
x res 720 1 1
x init
x font 1 R
x font 2 I
x font 3 B
x font 4 BI
x font 5 CW
x font 6 CB
x font 7 H
x font 8 HB
x font 9 HI
x font 10 S
...
```

The font positions should appear at the top of the file. In this example, you see the following fonts: (Times) Roman, (Times) Bold, (Times) Italic, (Times) Bold Italic, Constant Width, Constant Bold, Helvetica, Helvetica Bold, Helvetica Italic, and Special. Which font is mounted in which position is controlled by the file DESC.out in the device subdirectory of /usr/lib/font. See Appendix D for details.

## Special Characters

A variety of special characters that are not part of the standard ASCII character set are supported by `nroff` and `troff`. These include Greek letters, mathematical symbols, and graphic characters. Some of these characters are part of the font referred to earlier as the *special font*. Others are part of the standard typesetter fonts.

Regardless of the font in which they are contained, special characters are included in a file by means of special four-character escape sequences beginning with \ (.

Appendix B gives a complete list of special characters. However, some of the most useful are listed in Table 4-4, because even as a beginner you may want to include them in your text. Although `nroff` makes a valiant effort to produce some of these characters, they are really best suited for `troff`.

**TABLE 4-4. Special Characters**

| Name | Escape Sequence | Output Character |
| --- | --- | --- |
| em dash | \(em | — |
| bullet | \(bu | • |
| square | \(sq | □ |
| baseline rule | \(ru | — |
| underrule | \(ul | _ |
| 1/4 | \(14 | ¹/₄ |
| 1/2 | \(12 | ¹/₂ |
| 3/4 | \(34 | ³/₄ |
| degrees | \(de | ° |
| dagger | \(dg | † |
| double dagger | \(dd | ‡ |
| registered mark | \rg | ® |
| copyright symbol | \(co | © |
| section mark | \(sc | § |
| square root | \(sq | √ |
| greater than or equal | \(>= | ≥ |
| less than or equal | \(<= | ≤ |
| not equal | \(!= | ≠ |
| multiply | \(mu | × |
| divide | \(di | ÷ |
| plus or minus | \(+- | ± |
| right arrow | \(-> | → |
| left arrow | \(<- | ← |
| up arrow | \(ua | ↑ |
| down arrow | \(da | ↓ |

We'll talk more about some of these special characters as we use them. Some are used internally by `eqn` for producing mathematical equations. The use of symbols such as the copyright, registered trademark, and dagger is fairly obvious.

However, you shouldn't limit yourself to the obvious. Many of these special characters can be put to innovative use. For example, the square root symbol can be used to simulate a check mark, and the square can become an alternate type of bullet. As we'll show in Chapter 15, you can create additional, effective character combinations, such as a checkmark in a box, with overstriking.

The point is to add these symbols to your repertoire, where they can wait until need and imagination provide a use for them.

### Type Size Specification

Typesetting also allows for different overall sizes of characters. Typesetting character sizes are described by units called *points*. A point is approximately 1/72 of an inch. Typical type sizes range from 6 to 72 points. A few different sizes follow:

This line is set in 6-point type.

This line is set in 8-point type.

This line is set in 10-point type.

This line is set in 12-point type.

This line is set in 14-point type.

## This line is set in 18-point type.

(The exact size of a typeface does not always match its official size designation.. For example, 12-point type is not always 1/6 inch high, nor is 72-point type 1 inch high. The precise size will vary with the typeface.)

As with font changes, there are two ways to make size changes: with a request and with an inline escape sequence. The `.ps` request sets the point size. For example:

```
.ps 10          Set the point size to 10 points
```

A `.ps` request that does not specify any point size reverts to the previous point size setting, whatever it was:

```
.ps 10
```

*Some text here*

```
.ps             Revert to the point size before we changed it
```

To switch point size in the middle of the line, use the `\s` escape sequence. For example, many books reduce the point size when they print the word UNIX in the middle of a line. The preceding sentence was produced by these input lines:

```
For example, many books reduce the point size when
they print the word \s8UNIX\s0 in the middle of a line.
```

As you can probably guess from the example, \s0 does not mean to use a point size of 0, but to revert to the previous size.

In addition, you can use relative values when specifying point sizes. Knowing that the body of the book is set in 10-point type, we could have achieved the same result by entering:

```
For example, many books reduce the point size when
they print the word \s-2UNIX\s0 in the middle of a line.
```

You can increment or decrement point sizes only using a single digit; that is, you can't increment or decrement the size by more than 9 points.

Only certain sizes may be available on the typesetter. (Legal point sizes in otroff are 6, 7, 8, 9, 10, 11, 12, 14, 16, 18, 20, 22, 24, 28, and 36. Legal point sizes in ditroff depend upon the output device, but there will generally be more sizes available.) If you request a point size between two legal sizes, otroff will round up to the next legal point size; ditroff will round to the nearest available size.


## Vertical Spacing

In addition to its ability to change typefaces and type sizes on the same page, a typesetter allows you to change the amount of vertical space between lines. This spacing is sometimes referred to as the *baseline spacing* because it is the distance between the base of characters on successive lines. (The difference between the point size and the baseline spacing is referred to as *leading*, from the old days when a human compositor inserted thin strips of lead between successive lines of type.)

A typewriter or typewriter-style printer usually spaces vertically in 1/6-inch increments (i.e., 6 lines per inch). A typesetter usually adjusts the space according to the point size. For example, the type samples shown previously were all set with 20 points of vertical space. More typically, the vertical space will vary along with the type size, like this:

This line is set in 6-point type and 8-point spacing.
This line is set in 8-point type and 10-point spacing.
This line is set in 10-point type and 12-point spacing.
This line is set in 12-point type and 14-point spacing.
This line is set in 14-point type and 16-point spacing.
This line is set in 18-point type and 20-poi

Typically, the body of a book is set with a single size of type (usually 9 or 10 point, with vertical spacing set to 11 or 12 points, respectively). Larger sizes are used occasionally for emphasis, for example, in chapter or section headings. When the type size is changed, the vertical spacing needs to be changed too, or the type will overrun the previous line, as follows, where 14-point type is shown with only 10-point spacing.

Here is type larger than
the space allotted for it.

Vertical spacing is changed with the `.vs` request. A vertical space request will typically be paired with a point size request:

```
.ps 10
.vs 12
```

After you set the vertical spacing with `.vs`, this becomes the basis of the `v` unit for `troff`. For example, if you enter `.vs 12`, the request `.sp` will space down 12 points; the request:

```
.sp 0.5v
```

will space down 6 points, or half the current vertical line spacing. However, if you change the baseline vertical spacing to 16, the `.sp` request will space down 16 points. Spacing specified in any other units will be unaffected. What all this adds up to is the commonsense observation that a blank line takes up the same amount of space as one containing text.

When you use double and triple spacing, it applies a multiplication factor to the baseline spacing. The request `.ls 2` will double the baseline spacing. You can specify any multiplication factor you like, though 2 and 3 are the most reasonable values.

The `.ls` request will only affect the spacing between output lines of text. It does not change the definition of `v` or affect vertical spacing requests.

## ▪ A First Look at Macros ▪

Although we won't go into all the details of macro design until we have discussed the existing macro packages in the next two chapters, we'll cover some of the basic concepts here. This will help you understand what the macro packages are doing and how they work.

To define a macro, you use the `.de` request, followed by the sequence of requests that you want to execute when the macro is invoked. The macro definition is terminated by the request `..` (two dots). The name to be assigned to the macro is given as an argument to the `.de` request.

You should consider defining a macro whenever you find yourself issuing a repetitive sequence of requests. If you are not using one of the existing macro packages (which have already taken care of this kind of thing), paragraphing is a good example of the kind of formatting that lends itself to macros.

Although it is certainly adequate to separate paragraphs simply by a blank line, you might instead want to separate them with a blank line and a temporary indent. What's more, to prevent "orphaned" lines, you would like to be sure that at least two lines of each paragraph appear at the bottom of the page. So you might define the following macro:

```
.de P
.sp
.ne 2
.ti 5n
..
```

This is the simplest kind of macro—a straightforward sequence of stored commands. However, macros can take arguments, take different actions depending on the presence or absence of various conditions, and do many other interesting and wonderful things.

We'll talk more about the enormous range of potential in macros in later chapters. For the moment, let's just consider one or two points that you will need to understand in order to use the existing macro packages.

## Macro Arguments

Most basic `troff` requests take simple arguments—single characters or letters. Many macros take more complex arguments, such as character strings. There are a few simple pointers you need to keep in mind through the discussion of macro packages in the next two chapters.

First, a space is taken by default as the separator between arguments. If a single macro argument is a string that contains spaces, you need to quote the entire string to keep it from being treated as a series of separate arguments.

For example, imagine a macro to print the title of a chapter in this book. The macro call looks like this:

```
.CH 4 "Nroff and Troff"
```

A second point: to skip an argument that you want to ignore, supply a null string (`""`). For example:

```
.CH "" "Preface"
```

As you can see, it does no harm to quote a string argument that doesn't contain spaces (`"Preface"`), and it is probably a good habit to quote all strings.

## Number Registers

When you use a specific value in a macro definition, you are limited to that value when you use the macro. For example, in the paragraph macro definition shown previously, the space will always be 1, and the indent always `5n`.

However, `nroff` and `troff` allow you to save numeric values in special variables known as *number registers*. If you use the value of a register in a macro definition, the action of the macro can be changed just by placing a new value in the register. For example, in `ms`, the size of the top and bottom margins is not specified with an absolute value, but with a number register. As a result, you don't need to change the macro definition to change these margins; you simply reset the value of the appropriate number register. Just as importantly, the contents of number registers can be used as *flags* (a kind of message between macros). There are conditional statements in the markup language of `nroff` and `troff`, so that a macro can say: "If number register

*Y* has the value *x*, then do thus-and-so. Otherwise, do this.'' For example, in the mm macros, hyphenation is turned off by default. To turn it on, you set the value of a certain number register to 1. Various macros test the value of this register, and use it as a signal to re-enable hyphenation.

To store a value into a number register, use the `.nr` request. This request takes two arguments: the name of a number register,* and the value to be placed into it.

For example, in the ms macros, the size of the top and bottom margins is stored in the registers HM (*header margin*) and FM (*footer margin*). To reset these margins from their default value of 1 inch to 1.75 inches (thus producing a shorter page like the one used in this book), all you would need to do is to issue the requests:

```
.nr HM 1.75i
.nr FM 1.75i
```

You can also set number registers with single-character names from the command line by using the −r option. (The mm macros make heavy use of this capability.) For example:

```
$ nroff −mm −rN1 file
```

will format *file* using the mm macros, with number register N set to the value 1. We will talk more about using number registers later, when we describe how to write your own macros. For the moment, all you need to know is how to put new values into existing registers. The next two chapters will describe the particular number registers that you may find useful with the mm and ms macro packages.

## Predefined Strings

The mm and ms macro packages also make use of some predefined text strings. The nroff and troff programs allow you to associate a text string with a one- or two-character string name. When the formatter encounters a special escape sequence including the string name, the complete string is substituted in the output.

To define a string, use the `.ds` request. This request takes two arguments, the string name and the string itself. For example:

```
.ds nt Nroff and Troff
```

The string should *not* be quoted. It can optionally begin with a quotation mark, but it should not end with one, or the concluding quotation mark will appear in the output. If you want to *start* a string with one or more blank spaces, though, you should begin the definition with a quotation mark. Even in this case, there is no concluding quotation mark. As always, the string is terminated by a newline.

---

*Number register names can consist of either one or two characters, just like macro names. However, they are distinct—that is, a number register and a macro can be given the same name without conflict.

You can define a multiline string by hiding the newlines with a backslash. For example:

```
.ds LS This is a very long string that goes over \
more than one line.
```

When the string is interpolated, it will be subject to filling (unless no-fill mode is in effect) and may not be broken into lines at the same points as you've specified in the definition. To interpolate the string in the output, you use one of the following escape sequences:

```
\*a
\*(ab
```

where *a* is a one-character string name, and *ab* is a two-character string name.

To use the *nt* string we defined earlier, you would type:

```
\*(nt
```

It would be replaced in the output by the words *Nroff and Troff*.

Strings use the same pool of names as macros. Defining a string with the same name as an existing macro will make the macro inoperable, so it is not advisable to go around wildly defining shorthand strings. The vi editor's abbreviation facility (described in Chapter 7) is a more effective way to save yourself work typing.

Strings are useful in macro design in much the same way number registers are— they allow a macro to be defined in a more general way. For example, consider this book, which prints the title of the chapter in the header on each odd-numbered page. The chapter title is not coded into the page top macro. Instead, a predefined string is interpolated there. The same macro that describes the format of the chapter title on the first page of the chapter also defines the string that will appear in the header.

In using each of the existing macro packages, you may be asked to define or interpolate the contents of an existing string. For the most part, though, string definitions are hidden inside macro definitions, so you may not run across them. However, there are a couple of handy predefined strings you may find yourself using, such as:

```
\*(DY
```

which always contains the current date in the ms macro package. (The equivalent string in mm is \*(DT.) For example, if you wanted a form letter to contain the date that it was formatted and printed rather than the date it was written, you could interpolate this string.

## Just What Is a Macro Package?

Before leaving the topic of macros, we ought to take a moment to treat a subject we have skirted up to this point: just what is a macro package?

As the name suggests, a macro package is simply a collection of macro definitions. The fact that there are command-line options for using the existing packages may seem to give them a special status, but they are text files that you can read and modify (assuming that your system has the UNIX file permissions set up so you can do so).

There is no magic to the options −ms and −mm. The actual option to nroff and troff is −m*x*, which tells the program to look in the directory /usr/lib/tmac for a file with a name of the form tmac.*x*. As you might expect, this means that there is a file in that directory called tmac.s or tmac.m (depending on which package you have on your system). It also means that you can invoke a macro package of your own from the command line simply by storing the macro definitions in a file with the appropriate pathname. This file will be added to any other files in the formatting run. This means that if you are using the ms macros you could achieve the same result by including the line:

```
.so /usr/lib/tmac/tmac.s
```

at the start of each source file, and omitting the command-line switch −ms. (The .so request reads another file into the input stream, and when its contents have been exhausted, returns to the current file. Multiple .so requests can be nested, not just to read in macro definitions, but also to read in additional text files.)

The macros in the standard macro packages are no different (other than in complexity) than the macros you might write yourself. In fact, you can print out and study the contents of the existing macro packages to learn how they work. We'll be looking in detail at the actions of the existing macro packages, but for copyright reasons we can't actually show their internal design. We'll come back to all this later. For now, all you need to know is that macros aren't magic—just an assemblage of simple commands working together.

# 5

# The ms Macros

The UNIX shell is a user interface for the kernel, the actual heart of the operating system. You can choose the C shell or Korn shell instead of the Bourne shell, without worrying about its effects on the low-level operations of the kernel. Likewise, a macro package is a user interface for accessing the capabilities of the `nroff/troff` formatter. Users can select either the `ms` or `mm` macro packages (as well as other packages that are available on some systems) to use with `nroff/troff`.

The `ms` package was the original Bell Labs macro package, and is available on many UNIX systems, but it is no longer officially supported by AT&T. Our main reason for giving `ms` equal time is that many Berkeley UNIX systems ship `ms` instead of `mm`. In addition, it is a less complex package, so it is much easier to learn the principles of macro design by studying `ms` than by studying `mm`.

A third general-purpose package, called `me`, is also distributed with Berkeley UNIX systems. It was written by Eric Allman and is comparable to `ms` and `mm`. (Mark Horton writes us: I think of `ms` as the FORTRAN of `nroff`, `mm` as the PL/I, and `me` as the Pascal.) The `me` package is not described in this book.

In addition, there are specialized packages—`mv`, for formatting viewgraphs, `mptx`, for formatting the permuted index found in the *UNIX Reference Manual*, and `man`, for formatting the reference pages in that same manual. These packages are simple and are covered in the standard UNIX documentation.

Regardless of which macro package you choose, the formatter knows only to replace each call of a macro with its definition. The macro definition contains the set of requests that the formatter executes. Whether a definition is supplied with the text in the input file or found in a macro package is irrelevant to `nroff/troff`. The formatter can be said to be oblivious to the idea of a macro package.

You might not expect this rather freely structured arrangement between a macro package and `nroff/troff`. Macros are application programs of sorts. They organize the types of functions that you need to be able to do. However, the actual work is accomplished by `nroff/troff` requests.

In other words, the basic formatting capabilities are inherent in `nroff` and `troff`; the user implementation of these capabilities to achieve particular formats is accomplished with a macro package. If a macro doesn't work the way you expect, its definition may have been modified. It doesn't mean that `nroff/troff` works differently on your system. It is one thing to say "nroff/troff won't let me do it," and another to say "I don't have the macro to do it (but I could do it, perhaps)."

A general-purpose macro package like ms provides a way of describing the format of various kinds of documents. Each document presents its own specific problems, and macros help to provide a simple and flexible solution. The ms macro package is designed to help you format letters, proposals, memos, technical papers, and reports.

For simple documents such as letters, ms offers few advantages to the basic format requests described in Chapter 4. But as you begin to format more complex documents, you will quickly see the advantage of working with a macro package, which provides specialized tools for so many of the formatting tasks you will encounter.

A text file that contains ms macros can be processed by either `nroff` or `troff`, and the output can be displayed on a terminal screen or printed on a line printer, a laser printer, or a typesetter.

## • Formatting a Text File with ms •

If you want to format an ms document for a line printer or for a terminal screen, enter this command line:

```
$ nroff −ms file(s)
```

To format for a laser printer or typesetter, enter this command line:

```
$ troff −ms file(s) | device postprocessor
```

Be sure to redirect the output to a file or pipe it to the printer; if you do not, the output will be sent to your terminal screen.

### Problems in Getting Formatted Output

There are two ways for a program to handle errors. One is to have the program terminate and issue an error message. The other way is to have it keep going in hopes that the problems won't affect the rest of the output. The ms macros take this second approach.

In general, ms does its best to carry on no matter how scrambled the output looks. Sometimes the problems do get corrected within a page or two; other times the problem continues, making the remaining pages worthless. Usually, this is because the formatter had a problem executing the codes as they were entered in the input file. Most of the time input errors are caused by not including one of the macros that must be used in pairs.

Because ms allows formatting to continue unless the error is a "fatal" one, error correction is characteristic of the ms macro definitions. Apart from the main function of the macro, some of them, such as the paragraph macro, also invoke another macro called .RT to restore certain default values.

Thus, if you forget to reset the point size or indentation, you might notice that the problem continues for a while and then stops.

## ▪ **Page Layout** ▪

As suggested in the last chapter, one of the most important functions of a macro package is that it provides basic page layout defaults. This feature makes it worthwhile to use a macro package even if you don't enter a single macro into your source file.

At the beginning of Chapter 4, we showed how `nroff` alone formatted a sample letter. If we format the same letter with `ms`, the text will be adjusted on a page that has a default top and bottom margin of 1 inch, a default left margin, or page offset, of about 1 inch, and a default line length of 6 inches.

All of these default values are stored in number registers so that you can easily change them:

| | |
|---|---|
| LL | Line Length |
| HM | Header (top) Margin |
| FM | Footer (bottom) Margin |
| PO | Page offset (left margin) |

For example, if you like larger top and bottom margins, all you need to do is insert the following requests at the top of your file:

```
.nr HM 1.5i
.nr FM 1.5i
```

Registers such as these are used internally by a number of `ms` macros to reset the formatter to its default state. They will not take effect until one of those "reset" macros is encountered. In the case of HM and FM, they will not take effect until the next page unless they are specified at the very beginning of the file.*

## ▪ **Paragraphs** ▪

As we saw in the last chapter, paragraph transitions are natural candidates for macros because each paragraph generally will require several requests (spacing, indentation,) for proper formatting.

There are four paragraph macros in `ms`:

---

*These "reset" macros (those that call the internal macro `.RT`) include `.LP`, `.PP`, `.IP`, `.QP`, `.SH`, `.NH`, `.RS`, `.RE`, `.TS`, and `.TE`. The very first reset macro calls a special initialization macro called `.BG` that is used only once, on the first page. This macro prints the cover sheet, if any (see "Cover Sheet Macros" later in this chapter), as well as performing some special first-page initialization.

```
.LP        Block paragraph
.PP        First line of paragraph indented
.QP        Paragraph indented from both margins
.IP        Paragraph with hanging indent (list item)
```

The `.LP` macro produces a justified, block paragraph. This is the type of paragraph used for most technical documentation. The `.PP` macro produces a paragraph with a temporary indent for the first line. This paragraph type is commonly used in published books and magazines, as well as in typewritten correspondence.

Let's use the same letter to illustrate the use of these macros. In the original example (in Chapter 4), we left blank lines between paragraphs, producing an effect similar to that produced by the `.LP` macro.

In contrast, `.PP` produces a standard indented paragraph. Let's code the letter using `.PP` macros. Because this is a letter, let's also disable justification with an `.na` request. And of course, we want to print the address block in no-fill mode, as shown in Chapter 4. Figure 5-1 shows the coded letter and Figure 5-2 shows the formatted output.

## Spacing between Paragraphs

With `nroff`, all of the paragraph macros produce a full space between paragraphs. However, with `troff`, the paragraph macros output a blank space of 0.3v. Basically, this means that a blank line will output one full space and the paragraph macros will output about a third of that space.

The amount of spacing between paragraphs is contained in the number register PD (*paragraph distance*). If you want to change the amount of space generated by any of the paragraph macros, simply change the contents of this register.

For example, if you don't want to leave any space between paragraphs in the letter, you could put the following line at the start of your file:

```
.nr PD 0
```

This flexibility afforded by macro packages is a major advantage. It is often possible to completely change the appearance of a coded document by resetting only a few number registers at the start of a file. (As we'll see, this statement is even more true of of mm than of ms.)

## Quoted Paragraphs

A paragraph that is indented equally from the left and right margins is typically used to display quoted material. It is produced by `.QP`. For example:

```
.QP
In the next couple of days, I'll be putting together a ...
```

```
.ad r
April 1, 1987
.sp 2
.ad
.nf
Mr. John Fust
Vice President, Research and Development
Gutenberg Galaxy Software
Waltham, Massachusetts 02159
.fi
.sp
.na
Dear Mr. Fust:
.PP
```
In our conversation last Thursday, we discussed a documentation
project that would produce a user's manual on the Alcuin
product.  Yesterday, I received the product demo and other
materials that you sent me.
```
.PP
```
Going through a demo session gave me a much better understanding
of the product.  I confess to being amazed by Alcuin.
Some people around here, looking over my shoulder, were also
astounded by the illustrated manuscript I produced with Alcuin.
One person, a student of calligraphy, was really impressed.
```
.PP
```
In the next couple of days, I'll be putting together a written
plan that presents different strategies for documenting the
Alcuin product. After I submit this plan, and you have had time
to review it, let's arrange a meeting at your company to discuss
these strategies.
```
.PP
```
Thanks again for giving us the opportunity to bid on this
documentation project.  I hope we can decide upon a strategy
and get started as soon as possible in order to have the manual
ready in time for the first customer shipment. I look forward to
meeting with you towards the end of next week.
```
.sp
Sincerely,
.sp 3
Fred Caslon
```

*Fig. 5-1.* Letter Coded with ms Macros

April 1, 1987

Mr. John Fust
Vice President, Research and Development
Gutenberg Galaxy Software
Waltham, Massachusetts 02159

Dear Mr. Fust:

In our conversation last Thursday, we discussed a documentation project that would produce a user's manual on the Alcuin product. Yesterday, I received the product demo and other materials that you sent me.

Going through a demo session gave me a much better understanding of the product. I confess to being amazed by Alcuin. Some people around here, looking over my shoulder, were also astounded by the illustrated manuscript I produced with Alcuin. One person, a student of calligraphy, was really impressed.

In the next couple of days, I'll be putting together a written plan that presents different strategies for documenting the Alcuin product. After I submit this plan, and you have had time to review it, let's arrange a meeting at your company to discuss these strategies.

Thanks again for giving us the opportunity to bid on this documentation project. I hope we can decide upon a strategy and get started as soon as possible in order to have the manual ready in time for the first customer shipment. I look forward to meeting with you towards the end of next week.

Sincerely,

Fred Caslon

*Fig. 5-2.* Formatted Output

The .QP macro produces a paragraph indented on both sides. The pair of macros .QS and .QE can be used to mark a section longer than one paragraph that is indented. This is useful in reports and proposals that quote at length from another source.

```
.LP
I was particularly interested in the following comment
found in the product specification:
.QS
Users first need a brief introduction to what
the product does.  Sometimes this is more for the
benefit of people who haven't yet bought the
product, and are just looking at the manual.
However, it also serves to put the rest of the
manual, and the product itself, in
the proper context.
.QE
```

The result of formatting is:

```
I was particularly interested in the following comment
found in the product specification:

    Users first need a brief introduction to what the
    product does.  Sometimes this is more for the bene-
    fit of people who haven't yet bought the product,
    and are just looking at the manual.  However, it
    also serves to put the rest of the manual, and the
    product itself, in the proper context.
```

Use the .QP macro inside a .QS/.QE block to break up paragraphs.

## Indented Paragraphs

The .IP macro produces an entire paragraph indented from the left margin. This is especially useful for constructing lists, in which a mark of some kind (e.g., a letter or number) extends into the left margin. We call these *labeled item lists*.

The .IP macro takes three arguments. The first argument is a text label; if the label contains spaces, it should be enclosed within quotation marks. The second argument is optional and specifies the amount of indentation; a default of 5 is used if the second argument is not specified. A third argument of 0 inhibits spacing before the indented paragraph.

Item lists are useful in preparing command reference pages that describe various syntax items, and in glossaries that present a term in one column and its definition in the other. The following example shows a portion of the input file for a reference page:

```
.IP figure 10
is the name of a cataloged figure.  If
a figure has not been cataloged, you need to use
the LOCATE command.
.IP f:p 10
is the scale of the
figure in relation to the page.
.IP font 10
is the two-character abbreviation or
full name of one of the available fonts
from the Alcuin library.
```

The following item list is produced:

```
figure      is the name of a cataloged figure.  If a figure
            has not been  cataloged,  you  need  to use the
            LOCATE command.

f:p         is the scale of the figure in relation  to  the
            page.

font        is the two-character abbreviation or full  name
            of one of the available fonts from  the  Alcuin
            library.
```

An .LP or .PP should be specified after the last item so that the text following the
list is not also indented.

   If you want to indent the label as well as the paragraph, you can use the .in
request around the list.  The following example:

```
.in 10
.IP figure 10
is the name of a cataloged figure.  If
a figure has not been cataloged, you need to use
the LOCATE command.
.in 0
```

will produce:

```
        figure      is the name of a  cataloged  figure.   If a
                    figure has not been cataloged,  you need to
                    use the LOCATE command.
```

You can specify an absolute or relative indent.  To achieve the effect of a nested list,
you can use the .RS (you can think of this as either *relative start* or *right shift*) and
.RE (*relative end* or *retreat*) macros:

```
.IP font 10
is the two-character abbreviation or
full name of one of the available fonts
from the Alcuin library.
.RS
.IP CU
Cursive
.IP RS
Slanted
.RS
.IP LH 5 0
Left handed
.IP RH 5 0
Right handed
.RE
.IP BL
Block
.RE
```

The labels on the second level are aligned with the indented left margin of paragraphs
on the first level.

```
font    is the two-character abbreviation or full name  of
        one   of  the  available  fonts  from  the  Alcuin
        library.

        CU   Cursive

        RS   Slanted

             LH   Left handed
             RH   Right handed

        BL   Block
```

One thing you need to watch out for in using the `.IP` macro is not to include space in
the label argument.  Because of the way the macro is coded, the space may be expanded
when the finished line is adjusted.  The first line will not be aligned with the rest.  For
example:

```
.IP "font name" 10
is the two-character abbreviation or full name . . .
```

might produce the following:

```
font name    is the two-character  abbreviation  or full
             name of one of the available  fonts from the
             Alcuin library.
```

To avoid this problem, always use an unpaddable space (a backslash followed by a space) to separate words in the label argument to `.IP`. This caution applies to many other formatting situations as well.

Automatically numbered and alphabetized lists are not provided for in `ms`. (Chapter 16 shows how to write your own macros for this.) However, by specifying the number or letter as a label, you can make do with the `.IP` macro. For example:

```
User-oriented documentation recognizes three things:
.in +3n
.IP 1) 5n
that a new user needs
to learn the system in stages, getting a sense of the
system as a whole while becoming proficient in performing
particular tasks;
.IP 2) 5n
that there are different levels of users, and not
every user needs to learn all the capabilities
of the system in order to be productive;
.IP 3) 5n
that an experienced user must be able to rely on
the documentation for accurate and thorough reference
information.
.in -3n
```

This produces:

```
User-oriented documentation recognizes three things:

    1)    that a new  user  needs to  learn the  system in
          stages, getting  a  sense  of  the  system  as a
          whole  while  becoming  proficient in performing
          particular tasks;

    2)    that there are different levels  of  users,  and
          not every user needs to  learn  all the capabil
          ities of the system in  order  to be productive;

    3)    that an experienced user must be able to rely on
          the  documentation  for  accurate  and  thorough
          reference information.
```

The number is indented three ens and the text is indented five more ens. (Note: If you are using `nroff`, you don't need to specify units on the indents. However, if you are using `troff`, the default scaling for both the `.IP` macro and the `.in` requests shown in the previous example is ems. Remember that you can append a scaling indicator to the numeric arguments of most macros and `troff` requests.)

### ▪ Changing Font and Point Size ▪

When you format with `nroff` and print on a line printer, you can put emphasis on individual words or phrases by underlining or overstriking. When you are use `troff` and send your output to a laser printer or typesetter, you can specify variations of type, font, and point size based on the capabilities of the output devices.

### Roman, Italic, and Bold Fonts

Most typefaces have at least three fonts available: roman, **bold**, and *italic*. Normal body copy is printed in the roman font. You can change temporarily to a bold or italic font for emphasis. In Chapter 4, you learned how to specify font changes using the `.ft` request and inline `\f` requests. The `ms` package provides a set of mnemonic macros for changing fonts:

```
.B        bold
.I        italic
.R        roman
```

Each macro prints a single argument in a particular font. You might code a single sentence as follows:

```
.B Alcuin
revitalizes an
.I age-old
tradition.
```

The printed sentence has one word in bold and one in italic.

---
**Alcuin** revitalizes an *age-old* tradition.

---

If no argument is specified, the selected font is current until it is explicitly changed:

```
The art of
.B
calligraphy
.R
is, quite simply,
.I
beautiful
.R
handwriting;
```

The example produces:

---
The art of **calligraphy** is, quite simply, *beautiful* handwriting;

You've already seen that the first argument is changed to the selected font. If you supply a second argument, it is printed in the previous font. (You are limited to two arguments, set off by a space; a phrase must be enclosed within quotation marks to be taken as a single argument.) A good use for the alternate argument is to supply punctuation, especially because of the restriction that you cannot begin a line with a period.

```
its opposite is
.B cacography .
```

This example produces:

its opposite is **cacography**.

If the second argument is a word or phrase, you must supply the spacing:

```
The ink pen has been replaced by a
.I light " pen."
```

This produces:

The ink pen has been replaced by a *light* pen.

If you are using nroff, specifying a bold font results in character overstrike; specifying an italic font results in an underline for each character (not a continuous rule). Overstriking and underlining can cause problems on some printers and terminals.

The chief advantage of these macros over the corresponding troff constructs is the ease of entry. It is easier to type:

```
.B calligraphy
```

than:

```
\fBcalligraphy\fP
```

However, you'll notice that using these macros changes the style of your input considerably. As shown in the examples on the preceding pages, these macros require you to code your input file using short lines that do not resemble the resulting filled output text.

This style, which clearly divorces the form of the input from the form of the output, is recommended by many nroff and troff users. They recommend that you use macros like these rather than inline codes, and that you begin each sentence or clause on a new line. There are advantages in speed of editing. However, there are others (one of the authors included) who find this style of input unreadable on the screen, and prefer to use inline codes, and to keep the input file as readable as possible. (There is no difference in the output file.)

## Underlining

If you want to underline a single word, regardless of whether you are using `nroff` or `troff`, use the `.UL` macro:

```
the
.UL art
of calligraphy.
```

It will print a continuous rule beneath the word. You cannot specify more than a single word with this macro.

## Changing Point Size

As discussed in Chapter 4, you can change the point size and vertical spacing with the `.ps` and `.vs` requests. However, if you do this in `ms`, you will find that the point size and vertical spacing revert to 10 and 12 points, respectively, after the next paragraph macro. This is because the paragraph macro, in addition to other tasks, resets the point size and vertical spacing (along with various other values) to default values stored in number registers.

The default point size and vertical spacing for a document are kept in the registers `PS` and `VS`, respectively. If you want to change the overall point size or vertical spacing, change the value in these registers. (The default values are 10 and 12, respectively.) For example, to change the body type to 8 points and the spacing to 10 points, enter the following requests at the top of your document:

```
.nr PS 8
.nr VS 12
```

At the top of a document, these settings will take effect immediately. Otherwise, you must wait for the next paragraph macro for the new values to be recognized. If you need both immediate and long-lasting effects, you may need a construct like:

```
.ps 8
.nr PS 8
.vs 12
.nr VS 12
```

There are also several macros for making local point size changes. The `.LG` macro increases the current point size by 2 points; the `.SM` macro decreases the point size by 2 points. The new point size remains in effect until you change it. The `.NL` macro changes the point size back to its default or normal setting. For example:

```
.LG
Alcuin
.NL
is a graphic arts product for
.SM
UNIX
.NL
systems.
```

The following line is produced:

---

**Alcuin** is a graphic arts product for UNIX systems.

---

The `.LG` and `.SM` macros simply increment or decrement the current point size by 2 points. Because you change the point size relative to the current setting, repeating a macro adds or subtracts 2 more points. If you are going to change the point size by more than 2, it makes more sense to use the `.ps` request. The `.NL` macro uses the value of the number register `PS` to reset the normal point size. Its default value is 10.

In the following example, the `.ps` request changes the point size to 12. The `.LG` and `.SM` macros increase and decrease the point size relative to 12 points. The `.NL` macro is not used until the end because it changes the point size back to 10.

```
.ps 12
.LG
Alcuin
.SM
is a graphic arts product for
.SM
UNIX
.LG
systems.
.NL
```

It produces the following line:

---

**Alcuin** is a graphic arts product for UNIX systems.

A change in the point size affects how much vertical space is needed for the larger or smaller characters. Vertical spacing is usually 2 points larger than the point size (10 on 12). Use the vertical spacing request to temporarily change the vertical spacing, if necessary.

## ▪ Displays ▪

A document often includes material—such as tables, figures, or equations—that are not a part of the running text, and must be kept together on the page. In ms and mm, such document elements are referred to generically as *displays*.

The macros `.DS`, `.DE`, `.ID`, `.CD`, and `.LD` are used to handle displays in ms. The display macros can be relied upon to provide

- adequate spacing before and after the display;

- horizontal positioning of the display as a left-justified, indented, or centered block;

- proper page breaks, keeping the entire display together.

The default action of the .DS macro is to indent the block of text without filling lines:

```
Some of the typefaces that are currently available are:
.DS
Roman
Caslon
Baskerville
Helvetica
.DE
```

This produces:

```
Some of the typefaces that are currently available are:

    Roman
    Caslon
    Baskerville
    Helvetica
```

You can select a different format for a display by specifying a left-justified or centered display with one of the following arguments:

| | |
|---|---|
| I | Indented (default) |
| L | Left-justified |
| C | Center each line |
| B | Block (center entire display) |

The L argument can be used for formatting an address block in a letter:

```
.DS L
Mr. John Fust
Vice President, Research and Development
Gutenberg Galaxy Software
Waltham, Massachusetts 02154
.DE
```

The display macro prevents these lines from being filled; it "protects" the carriage returns as they were entered in the file.

A display can be centered in two ways: either each individual line in the display is centered (C), or the entire display is centered as a block (B) based on the longest line of the display.

The use of tabs often presents a problem outside of displays. Material that has been entered with tabs in the input file should be formatted in no-fill mode, the default setting of the display macros. The following table was designed using tabs to provide the spacing.

```
.DS L
Dates              Description of Task

June 30            Submit audience analysis
July 2             Meeting to review audience analysis
July 15            Submit detailed outline
August 1           Submit first draft
August 5           Return of first draft
August 8           Meeting to review comments
                   and establish revisions
.DE
```

This table appears in the output just as it looks in the file. If this material had not been processed inside a display, the columns would be improperly aligned.

## Static and Floating Displays

One of the basic functions of a display is to make sure the displayed material stays together on one page. If the display is longer than the distance to the bottom of the page, there is a page break.

If the display is large, causing a page break can leave a large block of white space at the bottom of the page. To avoid this problem, ms provides a set of macros for *floating displays*, as well as macros for the *static displays* we've already discussed. If a floating display doesn't fit on the page, the formatter doesn't force a page break. Instead, it simply holds the displayed text in reserve while it fills up the remainder of the page with the text following the display. It prints the display at the top of the next page, then continues where it left off.

We have already used .DS and .DE to mark the beginning and end of a static display. To specify a floating display, the closing mark is the same but the beginning is marked by a different macro:

```
.ID        Same as .DS I (indented) but floating
.LD        Same as .DS L (left justified) but floating
.CD        Same as .DS C (center each line) but floating
.BD        Same as .DS B (center display) but floating
```

In the following example of an input file, numbers are used instead of actual lines of text to make the placement of the display more obvious:

```
1
2
3
4
5
.LD
Long Display
.DE
6
```

```
7
8
9
10
```

The following two formatted pages might be produced, assuming that there are a sufficient number of lines to cause a page break:

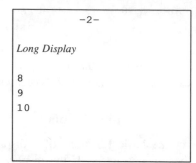

If there had been room on page 1 to fit the display, it would have been placed there, and lines 6 and 7 would have followed the display, as they did in the input file.

If a static display had been specified in the previous example, the display would be placed in the same position on the second page, and lines 6 and 7 would have followed it, leaving extra space at the bottom of page 1. A floating display attempts to make the best use of the available space on a page.

The formatter maintains a queue to hold floating displays that it has not yet output. When the top of a page is encountered, the next display in the queue is output. The queue is emptied in the order in which it was filled (first in, first out).

The macros called by the display macros to control output of a block of text are available for other uses. They are known as "keep and release" macros. The pair .KS/.KE keep a block together and output it on the next available page. The pair .KF/.KE specify a floating keep; the block saved by the keep can float and lines of text following the block may appear before it in the text.

## ▪ **Headings** ▪

In ms, you can have numbered and unnumbered headings. There are two heading macros: .NH for numbered headings and .SH for unnumbered section headings.

Let's first look at how to produce numbered headings. The syntax for the .NH macro is:

```
.NH  [level]
[heading text]
.LP
```

(The brackets indicate optional arguments.) You can supply a numerical value indicating the *level* of the heading. If no value is provided for *level*, then a top-level heading is assumed. The *heading text* begins on the line following the macro and can extend over several lines. You have to use one of the paragraph macros, either `.LP` or `.PP`, after the last line of the heading. For example:

```
.NH
Quick Tour of Alcuin
.LP
```

The result is a heading preceded by a first-level heading number:

```
1.   Quick Tour of Alcuin
```

The next time you use this macro the heading number will be incremented to 2, and after that, to 3.

You can add levels by specifying a numeric argument. A second-level heading is indicated by 2:

```
.NH 2
Introduction to Calligraphy
.LP
```

The first second-level heading number is printed:

```
1.1   Introduction to Calligraphy
```

When another heading is specified at the same level, the heading number is automatically incremented. If the next heading is at the second level:

```
.NH 2
Digest of Alcuin Commands
.LP
```

ms produces:

```
1.2   Digest of Alcuin Commands
```

Each time you go to a new level, `.1` is appended to the number representing the existing level. That number is incremented for each call at the same level. When you back out of a level (for instance, when you go from level 5 to 4) the counter for the level (in this case level 5) is reset to 0.

The macro for unnumbered headings is `.SH`:

```
.SH
Introduction to Calligraphy
.LP
```

Unnumbered headings and numbered headings can be intermixed without affecting the numbering scheme:

```
1.  Quick Tour of Alcuin

Introduction to Calligraphy

1.1  Digest of Alcuin Commands
```

Headings are visible keys to your document's structure. Their appearance can contribute significantly to a reader recognizing that organization. If you are using unnumbered headings, it becomes even more important to make headings stand out. A simple thing you can do is use uppercase letters for a first-level heading.

## ▪ Cover Sheet Macros ▪

In their original incarnation at Bell Laboratories, the `ms` macros were called on to format many internal AT&T documents. Accordingly, it is not surprising that there were quite a few macros that controlled the format of specific internal document types. What is surprising is that these macros are still present in copies of the `ms` macros distributed outside of AT&T.

You have the option of specifying that your document contains Engineer's Notes (`.EG`), an Internal Memorandum (`.IM`), a Memorandum for Record (`.MR`), a Memorandum for File (`.MF`), a Released Paper (`.RP`), a Technical Reprint (`.TR`), or a letter (`.LT`).

Many of these formats are quite useless outside of AT&T, unless you customize them heavily for other institutions. We prefer simply to ignore them.

In general, what these document type macros control is the appearance of the document's cover sheet. The content of that cover sheet is specified using the following macros:

| | |
|---|---|
| `.TL` | Title |
| `.AU` | Author |
| `.AI` | Author's Institution |
| `.AB` | Abstract Start |
| `.AE` | Abstract End |

These macros are general enough that you can still use them even if you aren't from Bell Laboratories.

Each macro takes its data from the following line(s) rather than from an argument. They are typically used together. For example:

```
.TL
UNIX Text Processing
.AU
Dale Dougherty
.AU
Tim O'Reilly
```

```
.AI
O'Reilly & Associates, Inc.
.AB
This book provides a comprehensive introduction to the major
UNIX text-processing tools.  It includes a discussion of
vi, ex, nroff, and troff, as
well as many other text-processing programs.
.AE
.LP
```

Exactly how the output will look depends on which document types you have selected. If you don't specify any of the formats, you will get something like this:

---

# UNIX Text Processing

*Dale Dougherty*

*Tim O'Reilly*

O'Reilly & Associates, Inc.

*ABSTRACT*

This book provides a comprehensive introduction to the major UNIX text-processing tools.  It includes a discussion of `vi`, `ex`, `nroff`, and `troff`, as well as many other text-processing programs.

---

You can specify as many title lines as you want following `.TL`. The macro will be terminated by any of the other cover sheet macros, or by any paragraph macro. For multiple authors, `.AU` and `.AI` can be repeated up to nine times.

The cover sheet isn't actually printed until a reset (such as that caused by any of the paragraph macros) is encountered, so if you want to print only a cover page, you should conclude it with a paragraph macro even if there is no following text.

In addition, if you use these macros without one of the overall document type macros like `.RP`, the cover sheet will not be printed separately. Instead, the text will immediately follow. Insert a `.bp` if you want a separate cover sheet.

## ▪ Miscellaneous Features ▪

### Putting Information in a Box

Another way of handling special information is to place it in a box. Individual words can be boxed for emphasis using the `.BX` command:

```
To move to the next menu, press the
.BX RETURN
key.
```

This draws a box around the word RETURN.

```
To move to the next menu, press the
RETURN
key.
```

As you can see, it might be a good idea to reduce the point size of the boxed word.

You can enclose a block of material within a box by using the pair of macros `.B1` and `.B2`:

```
.B1
.B
.ce
Note to Reviewers
.R
.LP
Can you get a copy of a manuscript without annotations?
It seems to me that you should be
able to mark up a page with comments or
other scribbles while in Annotation Mode and
still obtain a printed copy without these marks.
Any ideas?
.sp
.B2
```

This example produces the following boxed section in `troff`:

---

**Note to Reviewers**

Can you get a copy of a manuscript without annotations?  It seems to me that you should be able to mark up a page with comments or other scribbles while in Annotation Mode and still obtain a printed copy without these marks.  Any ideas?

---

You may want to place boxed information inside a pair of keep or display macros.  This will prevent the box macro from breaking if it crosses a page boundary.  If you use these macros with `nroff`, you must also pipe your output through the `col` postprocessor as described in Chapter 4.

## Footnotes

Footnotes present special problems—the main is printing the text at the bottom of the page.  The `.FS` macro indicates the start of the text for the footnote, and `.FE` indicates the end of the text for the footnote.  These macros surround the footnote text that will appear at the bottom of the page.  The `.FS` macro is put on the line immediately following some kind of marker, such as an asterisk, that you supply in the text and in the footnote.

```
... in an article on desktop publishing.*
.FS
* "Publish or Perish: Start-up grabs early page language
lead," Computerworld, April 21, 1986, p. 1.
.FE
```

All the footnotes are collected and output at the bottom of each page underneath a short rule. The footnote text is printed in smaller type, with a slightly shorter line length then the body text. However, you can change these if you want.

Footnotes in ms use an nroff/troff feature called *environments* (see Chapter 14), so that parameters like line length or font that are set inside a footnote are saved independently of the body text. So, for example, if you issued the requests:

```
.FS
.ft B
.ll -5n
.in +5n
Some text
~
..

~
.FE
```

the text within the footnote would be printed in boldface, with a 5-en indent, and the line length would be shortened by 5 ens. The text following the footnote would be unaffected by those formatting requests. However, the next time a footnote was called, that special formatting would again be in effect.

----

**\*"Publish or Perish: Start-up grabs early page language
lead,"** *Computerworld***, April 21, 1986, p. 1.**

If a footnote is too long to fit on one page, it will be continued at the bottom of the next page.

## Two-Column Processing

One of the nice features of the ms macros is the ease with which you can create multiple columns and format documents, such as newsletters or data sheets, that are best suited to a multicolumn format.

To switch to two-column mode, simply insert the .2C macro. To return to single-column mode, use .1C. Because of the way two-column processing works in ms, you can switch to two-column mode in the middle of a page, but switching back to a single column forces a page break. (You'll understand the reason for this when we return to two-column processing in Chapter 16.)

The default column width for two-column processing is 7/15th of the line length. It is stored in the register CW (*column width*). The gutter between the columns is

1/15th of the line length, and is stored in the register GW (*gutter width*). By changing the values in these registers, you can change the column and gutter width.

For more than two columns, you can use the .MC macro. This macro takes two arguments, the column width and the gutter width, and creates as many columns as will fit in the line length. For example, if the line lengths are 7 inches, the request:

```
.MC 2i .3i
```

would create three columns 2 inches wide, with a gutter of .3 inches between the columns.

Again, .1C can be used to return to single-column mode. In some versions of ms, the .RC macro can be used to break columns. If you are in the left column, following text will go to the top of the next column. If you are in the right column, .RC will start a new page.

## ▪ Page Headers and Footers ▪

When you format a page with ms, the formatter is instructed to provide several lines at the top and the bottom of the page for a header and a footer. Beginning with the second page, a page number appears on a single line in the header and only blank lines are printed for the footer.

The ms package allows you to define strings that appear in the header or footer. You can place text in three locations in the header or footer: left justified, centered, and right justified. For example, we could place the name of the client, the title of the document, and the date in the page header and we could place the page number in the footer.

```
.ds LH GGS
.ds CH Alcuin Project Proposal
.ds RH \*(DY
.ds CF Page %
```

You may notice that we use the string DY to supply today's date in the header. In the footer, we use a special symbol (%) to access the current page number. Here are the resulting header and footer:

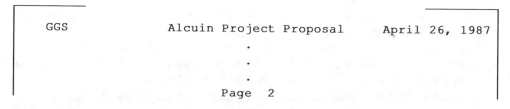

```
GGS             Alcuin Project Proposal     April 26, 1987
                            .
                            .
                            .
                        Page  2
```

Normally, you would define the header and footer strings at the start of the document, so they would take effect throughout. However, note that there is nothing to prevent you from changing one or more of them from page to page. (Changes to a footer string will take effect on the same page; changes to a header string will take effect at the top of the next page.)

## ▪ **Problems on the First Page** ▪

Because ms was originally designed to work with the cover sheet macros and one of the standard Bell document types, there are a number of problems that can occur on the first page of a document that doesn't use these macros.*

First, headers are not printed on the first page, nor is it apparent how to get them printed there if you want them. The trick is to invoke the internal .NP (*new page*) macro at the top of your text. This will not actually start a new page, but will execute the various internal goings-on that normally take place at the top of a page.

Second, it is not evident how to space down from the top if you want to start your text at some distance down the page. For example, if you want to create your own title page, the sequence:

```
.sp 3i
.ce
\s16The Invention of Movable Type\s0
```

will not work.

The page top macro includes an .ns request, designed to ensure that all leftover space from the bottom of one page doesn't carry over to the next, so that all pages start evenly. To circumvent this on all pages after the first one, precede your spacing request with an .rs (*restore spacing*) request. On the first page, a .fl request must precede a .rs request.

## ▪ **Extensions to ms** ▪

In many ways, ms can be used to give you a head start on defining your own macro package. Many of the features that are missing in ms can be supplied by user-defined macros. Many of these features are covered in Chapters 14 through 18, where, for example, we show macros for formatting numbered lists.

---

*This problem actually can occur on any page, but is most frequently encountered on the first page.

# 6

# The mm Macros

A macro package provides a way of describing the format of various kinds of documents. Each document presents its own specific problems, and macros help to provide a simple and flexible solution. The mm macro package is designed to help you format letters, proposals, memos, technical papers, and reports. A text file that contains mm macros can be processed by either `nroff` or `troff`, the two text formatting programs in UNIX. The output from these programs can be displayed on a terminal screen or printed on a line printer, a laser printer, or a typesetter.

Some users of the mm macro package learn only a few macros and work productively. Others choose from a variety of macros to produce a number of different formats. More advanced users modify the macro definitions and extend the capabilities of the package by defining their own special-purpose macros.

Macros are the *words* that make up a format description language. Like words, the result of a macro is often determined by context. That is, you may not always understand your output by looking up an individual macro, just like you may not understand the meaning of an entire sentence by looking up a particular word. Without examining the macro definition, you may find it hard to figure out which macro is causing a particular result. Macros are interrelated; some macros call other macros, like a subroutine in a program, to perform a particular function.

After finding out what the macro package allows you to do, you will probably decide upon a particular format that you like (or one that has evolved according to the decisions of a group of people). To describe that format, you are likely to use only a few of the macros, those that do the job. In everyday use, you want to minimize the number of codes you need to format documents in a consistent manner.

## · Formatting a Text File ·

To figure out the role of a macro package such as mm, it may help to consider the distinction between *formatting* and *format*. Formatting is an operation, a process of supplying and executing instructions. You can achieve a variety of results, some pleasing, some not, by any combination of formatting instructions. A format is a consistent product, achieved by a selected set of formatting instructions. A macro package makes it possible for a format to be recreated again and again with minimal difficulty. It encourages the user to concentrate more on the requirements of a document and less on the operations of the text formatter.

Working with a macro package will help reduce the number of formatting instructions you need to supply. This means that a macro package will take care of many things automatically. However, you should gradually become familiar with the operations of the nroff/troff formatter and the additional flexibility it offers to define new formats. If you have a basic understanding of how the formatter works, as described in Chapter 4, you will find it easier to learn the intricacies of a macro package.

## Invoking nroff/troff with mm

The mm command is a shell script that invokes the nroff formatter and reads in the files that contain the mm macro definitions before processing the text file(s) specified on the command line.

$ mm *option(s) filename(s)*

If more than one file is specified on the command line, the files are concatenated before processing. There are a variety of *options* for invoking preprocessors and postprocessors, naming an output device, and setting various number registers to alter default values for a document. Using the mm command is the same as invoking nroff explicitly with the −mm option.

Unless you specify otherwise, the mm command sets nroff's −T option to the terminal type set in your login environment. By default, output is sent to the terminal screen. If you have problems viewing your output, or if you have a graphics terminal, you may want to specify another device name using the −T option. For a list of available devices, see Appendix B. The mm command also has a −c option, which invokes the col filter to remove reverse linefeeds, and options to invoke tbl (−t) and eqn (−e).

When you format a file to the screen, the output usually streams by too swiftly to read, just as when you cat a file to the screen. Pipe the output of the mm command through either of the paging programs, pg or more, to view one screenful at a time. This will give you a general indication that the formatting commands achieved the results you had expected. To print a file formatted with mm, simply pipe the output to the print spooler (e.g., lp) instead of to a screen paging program.

Many of the actions that a text formatter performs are dependent upon how the document is going to be printed. If you want your document to be formatted with troff instead of nroff, use the mmt command (another shell script) or invoke troff directly, using the −mm option. The mmt command prepares output for laser printers and typesetters. The formatted output should be piped directly to the print spooler (e.g., lp) or directed to a file and printed separately. You will probably need to check at your site for the proper invocation of mmt if your site supports more than one type of laser printer or typesetter.

If you are using `otroff`, be sure you don't let `troff` send the output to your terminal because, in all probability, it will cause your terminal to hang, or at least to scream and holler.

In this chapter, we will generally show the results of the `mm` command, rather than `mmt`—that is, we'll be showing `nroff` rather than `troff`. Where the subject under discussion is better demonstrated by `troff`, we will show `troff` output instead. We assume that by now, you will be able to tell which of the programs has been used, without our mentioning the actual commands.

## Problems in Getting Formatted Output

When you format an `mm`-coded document, you may only get a portion of your formatted document. Or you may get none of it. Usually, this is because the formatter has had a problem executing the codes as they were entered in the input file. Most of the time it is caused by omitting one of the macros that must be used in pairs.

When formatting stops like this, one or more error messages might appear on your screen, helping you to diagnose the problems. These messages refer to the line numbers in the input file where the problems appear to be, and try to tell you what is missing:

**ERROR**:(*filename*) *line number*
   *Error message*

Sometimes, you won't get error messages, but your output will break midway. Generally, you have to go in the file at the point where it broke, or before that point, and examine the macros or a sequence of macros. You can also run a program on the input file to examine the code you have entered. This program, available at most sites, is called `checkmm`.

## Default Formatting

In Chapter 4, we looked at a sample letter formatted by `nroff`. It might be interesting, before putting any macros in the file, to see what happens if we format `letter` as it is, this time using the `mm` command to read in the `mm` macro package.

Refer to Figure 6-1 and note that

- a page number appears in a header at the top of the page;

- the address block still forms two long lines;

- lines of input text have been filled, forming block paragraphs;

- the right margin is ragged, not justified as with `nroff`;

- the text is not hyphenated;

- space has been allocated for a page with top, bottom, left, and right margins.

```
                        - 1 -


                                  April 1, 1987

Mr. John Fust Vice President, Research and
Development Gutenberg Galaxy Software Waltham,
Massachusetts 02159

Dear Mr. Fust:

In our conversation last Thursday, we discussed a
documentation project that would produce a user's
manual on the Alcuin product. Yesterday, I
received the product demo and other materials that
you sent me.

Going through a demo session gave me a much better
understanding of the product.  I confess to being
amazed by Alcuin.  Some people around here,
looking over my shoulder, were also astounded by
the illustrated manuscript I produced with Alcuin.
One person, a student of calligraphy, was really
impressed.

In the next couple of days, I'll be putting
together a written plan that presents different
strategies for documenting the Alcuin product.
After I submit this plan, and you have had time to
review it, let's arrange a meeting at your company
to discuss these strategies.

Thanks again for giving us the opportunity to bid
on this documentation project.  I hope we can
decide upon a strategy and get started as soon as
possible in order to have the manual ready in time
for the first customer shipment. I look forward to
meeting with you towards the end of next week.

                            Sincerely,


                            Fred Caslon
```

*Fig. 6-1.* A Raw mm-formatted File

## ▪ Page Layout ▪

When you format a page with mm, the formatter is instructed to provide several lines at the top and the bottom of the page for a header and a footer. By default, a page number appears on a single line in the header and only blank lines are printed for the footer.

There are basically two different ways to change the default header and footer. The first way is to specify a command-line parameter with the mm or mmt commands to set the number register N. This allows you to affect how pages are numbered and where the page number appears. The second way is to specify in the input file a macro that places text in the header or footer. Let's look at both of these techniques.

### Setting Page Numbering Style

When you format a document, pages are numbered in sequence up to the end of the document. This page number is usually printed in the header, set off by dashes.

    –1–

Another style of page numbering, used in documents such as technical manuals, numbers pages specific to a section. The first page of the second section would be printed as:

    2–1

The other type of change affects whether or not the page number is printed in the header at the top of the first page.

The number register N controls these actions. This register has a default setting of 0 and can take values from 0 through 5. Table 6-1 shows the effect of these values.

**TABLE 6-1.  Page Number Styles, Register N**

| Value | Action |
|-------|--------|
| 0 | The page number prints in the header on all pages. This is the default page numbering style. |
| 1 | On page 1, the page number is printed in place of the footer. |
| 2 | On page 1, the page number in not printed. |
| 3 | All pages are numbered by section, and the page number appears in the footer. This setting affects the defaults of several section-related registers and macros. It causes a page break for a top-level heading (Ej=1), and invokes both the .FD and .RP macros to reset footnote and reference numbering. |

**TABLE 6-1. —(Cont'd)**

| Value | Action |
|---|---|
| 4 | The default header containing the page number is suppressed, but it has no effect on a header supplied by a page header macro. |
| 5 | All pages are numbered by section, and the page number appears in the footer. In addition, labeled displays (.FC, .TB, .EX, and .EC) are also numbered by section. |

The register N can be set from the command line using the −r option. If we set it to 2, no page number will appear at the top of page 1 when we print the sample letter:

```
$ mm -rN2 letter | lp
```

## Header and Footer Macros

The mm package has a pair of macros for defining what should appear in a page header (.PH) and a page footer (.PF). There is also a set of related macros for specifying page headers and footers for odd-numbered pages (.OH and .OF) or for even-numbered pages (.EH and .EF). All of these macros have the same form, allowing you to place text in three places in the header or footer: left justified, centered, and right justified. This is specified as a single argument in double quotation marks, consisting of three parts delimited by single quotation marks.

*' left' center' right'*

For example, we could place the name of a client, the title of the document, and the date in the page header, and we could place the page number in the footer:

```
.PH "'GGS'Alcuin Project Proposal'\*(DT'"
.PF "''Page % ''"
```

You may notice that we use the string DT to supply today's date in the header. The following header appears at the top of the page.

```
GGS          Alcuin Project Proposal    April 26, 1987
```

In the footer, we use a special symbol (%) to access the current page number. Only text to be centered was specified; however, the four delimiters were still required to place the text correctly. This footer appears at the bottom of the page:

```
                              ⋮

              Page   2
```

The header and footer macros override the default header and footer.

## Setting Other Page Control Registers

The mm package uses number registers to supply the values that control line length, page offset, point size, and page length, as shown in Table 6-2.

**TABLE 6-2. Number Registers**

| Register | Contains | `troff` Default | `nroff` Default |
|---|---|---|---|
| O | Page offset (left margin) | .75i | .5i |
| N | Page numbering style | 0 | 0 |
| P | Page length | 66v | 66 lines |
| S | Point size (`troff` only) | 10 | NA |
| W | Line length or width | 6i | 60 |

These registers must be defined before the mm macro package is read by `nroff` or `troff`. Thus, they can be set from the command line using the −r option, as we showed when we gave a new value for register N. Values of registers O and W for `nroff` must be given in character positions (depending on the character size of the output device for `nroff`, .5i might translate as either 5 or 6 character positions), but `troff` can accept any of the units descibed in Chapter 4. For example:

$ **mm −rN2 −rW65 −rO10** *file*

but:

$ **mmt −rN2 −rW6.5i −rO1i** *file*

Or the page control registers can be set at the top of your file, using the .so request to read in the mm macro package, as follows:

```
.nr N 2
.nr W 65
.nr O 10
.so /usr/lib/tmac/tmac.m
```

If you do it this way, you cannot use the mm command. Use `nroff` or `troff` without the −mm option. Specifying −mm would cause the mm macro package to be read twice; mm would trap that error and bail out.

## Paragraphs

The `.P` macro marks the beginning of a paragraph.

```
.P
In our conversation last Thursday, we discussed a
```

This macro produces a left-justified, block paragraph. A blank line in the input file also results in a left-justified, block paragraph, as you saw when we formatted an uncoded file.

However, the paragraph macro controls a number of actions in the formatter, many of which can be changed by overriding the default values of several number registers. The `.P` macro takes a numeric argument that overrides the default paragraph type, which is a block paragraph. Specifying 1 results in an indented paragraph:

```
.P 1
Going through a demo session gave me a much better
```

The first three paragraphs formatted for the screen follow:

```
    In our conversation last Thursday, we discussed a
    documentation project that would produce a user's manual
    on the Alcuin product.  Yesterday, I received the product
    demo and other materials that you sent me.

        Going through a demo session gave me a much better
    understanding of the product.  I confess to being amazed
    by Alcuin.  Some people around here, looking over my
    shoulder, were also astounded by the illustrated
    manuscript I produced with Alcuin.  One person, a student
    of calligraphy, was really impressed.

    In the next couple of days, I'll be putting together a
    written plan that presents different strategies for
    documenting the Alcuin product. After I submit this plan,
    and you have had time to review it, let's arrange a
    meeting at your company to discuss these strategies.
```

The first line of the second paragraph is indented five spaces. (In `troff` the default indent is three ens.) Notice that the paragraph type specification changes only the second paragraph. The third paragraph, which is preceded in the input file by `.P` without an argument, is a block paragraph.

If you want to create a document in which all the paragraphs are indented, you can change the number register that specifies the default paragraph type. The value of `Pt` is 0 by default, producing block paragraphs. For indented paragraphs, set the value of `Pt` to 1. Now the `.P` macro will produce indented paragraphs.

```
.nr Pt 1
```

If you want to obtain a block paragraph after you have changed the default type, specify an argument of 0:

```
.P  0
```

When you specify a type argument, it overrides whatever paragraph type is in effect.

There is a third paragraph type that produces an indented paragraph with some exceptions. If `Pt` is set to 2, paragraphs are indented except those following section headings, lists, and displays. It is the paragraph type used in this book.

The following list summarizes the three default paragraph types:

| | |
|---|---|
| 0 | Block |
| 1 | Indented |
| 2 | Indented with exceptions |

## Vertical Spacing

The paragraph macro also controls the spacing between paragraphs. The amount of space is specified in the number register `Ps`. This amount differs between `nroff` and `troff`.

With `nroff`, the `.P` macro has the same effect as a blank line, producing a full space between paragraphs. However, with `troff`, the `.P` macro outputs a blank space that is equal to one-half of the current vertical spacing setting. Basically, this means that a blank line will cause one full space to be output, and the `.P` macro will output half that space.

The `.P` macro invokes the `.SP` macro for vertical spacing. This macro take a numeric argument requesting that many lines of space.

```
Sincerely,
.SP  3
Fred Caslon
```

Three lines of space will be provided between the salutation and the signature lines.

You do not achieve the same effect if you enter `.SP` macros on three consecutive lines. The vertical space does not accumulate and one line of space is output, not three.

Two or more consecutive `.SP` macros with numeric arguments results in the spacing specified by the greatest argument. The other arguments are ignored.

```
.SP  5
.SP
.SP  2
```

In this example, five lines are output, not eight.

Because the `.P` macro calls the `.SP` macro, it means that two or more consecutive paragraph macros will have the same effect as one.

### The `.SP` Macro versus the `.sp` Request

There are several differences between the `.SP` macro and the `.sp` request. A series of `.sp` requests does cause vertical spacing to accumulate. The following three requests produce eight blank lines:

```
.sp 5
.sp
.sp 2
```

The argument specified with the `.SP` macro cannot be scaled nor can it be a negative number. The `.SP` macro automatically works in the scale (v) of the current vertical spacing. However, both `.SP` and `.sp` accept fractions, so that each of the following codes has the same result:

```
.sp .3v    .SP .3    .sp .3
```

## ▪ Justification ▪

A document formatted by `nroff` with mm produces, by default, unjustified text (an uneven or ragged-right margin). When formatted by `troff`, the same document is automatically justified (the right margin is even).

If you are using both `nroff` and `troff`, it is probably a good idea to explicitly set justification on or off rather than depend upon the default chosen by the formatter. Use the `.SA` macro (*set adjustment*) to set document-wide justification. An argument of 0 specifies no justification; 1 specifies justification.

If you insert this macro at the top of your file:

```
.SA 1
```

both `nroff` and `troff` will produce right-justified paragraphs like the following:

```
     In   our  conversation  last  Thursday,  we  discussed
a documentation  project  that  would  produce  a  user's
manual on the Alquin product.  Yesterday, I received the
product demo and other materials that you sent me.
```

## ▪ Word Hyphenation ▪

One way to achieve better line breaks and more evenly filled lines is to instruct the formatter to perform word hyphenation.

Hyphenation is turned off in the mm macro package. This means that the formatter does not try to hyphenate words to make them fit on a line unless you request it by setting the number register `Hy` to 1. If you want the formatter to automatically hyphenate words, insert the following line at the top of your file:

```
.nr Hy 1
```

Most of the time, the formatter breaks up a word correctly when hyphenating. Some-times, however, it does not and you have to explicitly tell the formatter either how to split a word (using the `.hy` request) or not to hyphenate at all (using the `.nh` request).

## ▪ Displays ▪

When we format a text file, the line breaks caused by carriage returns are ignored by `nroff/troff`. How text is entered on lines in the input file does not affect how lines are formed in the output. It doesn't really matter whether information is typed on three lines or four; it appears the same after formatting.

You probably noticed that the name and address at the beginning of our sample file did not come out in block form. The four lines of input ran together and produced two filled lines of output:

```
Mr. John Fust Vice President, Research and Development
Gutenberg Galaxy Software Waltham, Massachusetts 02159
```

The formatter, instead of paying attention to carriage returns, acts on specific macros or requests that cause a break, such as `.P`, `.SP`, or a blank line. The formatter request `.br` is probably the simplest way to break a line:

```
Mr. John Fust
.br
Vice President, Research and Development
```

The `.br` request is most appropriate when you are forcing a break of a single line. For larger blocks of text, the mm macro package provides a pair of macros for indicat-ing that a block of text should be output just as it was entered in the input file. The `.DS` (*display start*) macro is placed at the start of the text, and the `.DE` (*display end*) macro is placed at the end:

```
.DS
Mr. John Fust
Vice President, Research and Development
Gutenberg Galaxy Software
Waltham, Massachusetts 02159
.DE
```

The formatter does not fill these lines, so the address block is output on four lines, just as it was typed. In addition, the `.DE` macro provides a line of space following the display.

## Our Coding Efforts, So Far

We have pretty much exhausted what we can do using the sample letter. Before going on to larger documents, you may want to compare the coded file in Figure 6-2 with the `nroff`-formatted output in Figure 6-3. Look them over and make sure you understand what the different macros are accomplishing.

```
.nr Pt 1
.SA 1
```
                                          April 1, 1987
```
.SP 2
.DS
```
Mr. John Fust
Vice President, Research and Development
Gutenberg Galaxy Software
Waltham, Massachusetts 02159
```
.DE
```
Dear Mr. Fust:
```
.P
```
In our conversation last Thursday, we discussed a
documentation project that would produce a user's manual
on the Alcuin product.  Yesterday, I received the product
demo and other materials that you sent me.
```
.P
```
Going through a demo session gave me a much better
understanding of the product.  I confess to being amazed
by Alcuin.  Some people around here, looking over my
shoulder, were also astounded by the illustrated
manuscript I produced with Alcuin. One person, a student
of calligraphy, was really impressed.
```
.P
```
In the next couple of days, I'll be putting together a
written plan that presents different strategies for
documenting the Alcuin product. After I submit this plan,
and you have had time to review it, let's arrange a
meeting at your company to discuss these strategies.
```
.P
```
Thanks again for giving us the opportunity to bid on this
documentation project.  I hope we can decide upon a
strategy and get started as soon as possible in order to
have the manual ready in time for the first customer
shipment.  I look forward to meeting with you towards the
end of next week.
```
.SP
```
                                          Sincerely,
```
.SP 2
```
                                          Fred Caslon

*Fig. 6-2.* Coded File

```
                           - 1 -


                                        April 1, 1987


    Mr. John Fust
    Vice President, Research and Development
    Gutenberg Galaxy Software
    Waltham, Massachusetts 02159

    Dear Mr. Fust:

        In  our  conversation  last  Thursday,  we
    discussed  a  documentation  project  that  would
    produce a user's manual  on  the  Alcuin  product.
    Yesterday,  I  received the product demo and other
    materials that you sent me.

        Going through a demo session gave me  a  much
    better understanding of the product.  I confess to
    being amazed by Alcuin.  Some people around  here,
    looking  over  my shoulder, were also astounded by
    the illustrated manuscript I produced with Alcuin.
    One  person,  a student of calligraphy, was really
    impressed.

        In the next couple of days, I'll  be  putting
    together  a  written  plan that presents different
    strategies for  documenting  the  Alcuin  product.
    After I submit this plan, and you have had time to
    review it, let's arrange a meeting at your company
    to discuss these strategies.

        Thanks again for giving us the opportunity to
    bid  on this documentation project.  I hope we can
    decide upon a strategy and get started as soon  as
    possible in order to have the manual ready in time
    for the first customer shipment. I look forward to
    meeting with you towards the end of next week.

                                    Sincerely,


                                    Fred Caslon
```

*Fig. 6-3.* Formatted Output

We have worked through some of the problems presented by a very simple one-page letter. As we move on, we will be describing specialized macros that address the problems of multiple page documents, such as proposals and reports. In many ways, the macros for more complex documents are the feature performers in a macro package, the ones that really convince you that a markup language is worth learning.

## ▪ Changing Font and Point Size ▪

When you format with `nroff` and print on a line printer, you can put emphasis on individual words or phrases by underlining or overstriking. When you are using `troff` and send your output to a laser printer or typesetter, you can specify variations of type, font, and point size based on the capabilities of the output device.

### Roman, Italic, and Bold Fonts

Most typefaces have at least three fonts available: roman, **bold**, and *italic*. Normal body copy is printed in the roman font. You can change temporarily to a bold or italic font for emphasis. In Chapter 4, you learned how to specify font changes using the `.ft` request and inline `\f` requests. The mm package provides a set of mnemonic macros for changing fonts:

|       |        |
|-------|--------|
| `.B`  | Bold   |
| `.I`  | Italic |
| `.R`  | Roman  |

Each macro prints a single argument in a particular font. You might code a single sentence as follows:

```
.B Alcuin
revitalizes an
.I age-old
tradition.
```

The printed sentence has a word in bold and one in italic. (In `nroff`, bold space is simulated by overstriking, and italics by underlining.)

> **Alcuin** revitalizes an *age-old* tradition.

If no argument is specified, the selected font is current until it is explicitly changed:

```
The art of
.B
calligraphy
.R
is, quite simply,
.I
beautiful
.R
handwriting;
```

The previous example produces:

---

The art of **calligraphy** is, quite simply, *beautiful* handwriting;

---

You've already seen that the first argument is changed to the selected font. If you supply a second argument, it is printed in the previous font. Each macro takes up to six arguments for alternating font changes. (An argument is set off by a space; a phrase must be enclosed within quotation marks to be taken as a single argument.) A good use for the alternate argument is to supply punctuation, especially because of the restriction that you cannot begin an input line with a period.

```
its opposite is
.B cacography .
```

This example produces:

---

its opposite is **cacography**.

---

If you specify alternate arguments consisting of words or phrases, you must supply the spacing:

```
The ink pen has been replaced by a
.I light " pen."
```

This produces:

---

The ink pen has been replaced by a *light* pen.

---

Here's an example using all six arguments:

```
Alcuin uses three input devices, a
.B "light pen" ", a " "mouse" ", and a " "graphics tablet."
```

This produces:

---

Alcuin uses three input devices, a **light pen**, a **mouse**, and a **graphics tablet**.

---

There are additional macros for selecting other main and alternate fonts. These macros also take up to six arguments, displayed in alternate fonts:

| | |
|---|---|
| .BR | Alternate bold and roman |
| .IB | Alternate italic and bold |
| .RI | Alternate roman and italic |
| .BI | Alternate bold and italic |
| .IR | Alternate italic and roman |
| .RB | Alternate roman and bold |

If you are using `nroff`, specifying a bold font results in character overstrike; specifying an italic font results in an underline for each character (not a continuous rule). Overstriking and underlining can cause problems on some printers and terminals.

## Changing Point Size

When formatting with `troff`, you can request a larger or smaller point size for the type. A change in the point size affects how much vertical space is needed for the larger or smaller characters. Normal body copy is set in 10-point type with the vertical spacing 2 points larger.

You learned about the `.ps` (*point size*) and `.vs` (*vertical spacing*) requests in Chapter 4. These will work in mm; however, mm also has a single macro for changing both the point size and vertical space:

    `.S` [*point size*] [*vertical spacing*]

The values for *point size* and *vertical spacing* can be set in relation to the current setting: + increments and − decrements the current value. For example, you could specify relative point size changes:

    `.S +2 +2`

or absolute ones:

    `.S 12 14`

By default, if you don't specify vertical spacing, a relation of 2 points greater than the point size will be maintained. A null value ("") does not change the current setting.

The new point size and vertical spacing remain in effect until you change them. Simply entering the `.S` macro without arguments restores the previous settings:

    `.S`

The mm package keeps track of the default, previous, and current values, making it easy to switch between different settings using one of these three arguments:

| | |
|---|---|
| D | Default |
| P | Previous |
| C | Current |

To restore the default values, enter:

```
.S D
```

The point size returns to 10 points and the vertical spacing is automatically reset to 12 points.  To increase the vertical space to 16 points while keeping the point size the same, enter:

```
.S C 16
```

In the following example for a letterhead, the company name is specified in 18-point type and a tag line in 12-point type; then the default settings are restored:

```
.S 18
Caslon Inc.
.S 12
Communicating Expertise
.S D
```

The result is:

# Caslon Inc.
## Communicating Expertise

You can also change the font along with the point size, using the  .I macro described previously.  Following is the tag line in 12-point italic.

### *Communicating Expertise*

A special-purpose macro in  mm reduces by 1 point the point size of a specified string. The  .SM macro can be followed by one, two, or three strings.  Only one argument is reduced; which one depends upon how many arguments are given.  If you specify one or two arguments, the first argument will be reduced by 1 point:

```
using
.SM UNIX ,
you will find
```

The second argument is concatenated to the first argument, so that the comma immediately follows the word *UNIX*:

    using UNIX, you will find

If you specify three arguments:

```
.SM [ UNIX ]
```

The second argument is reduced by one point, but the first and third arguments are printed in the current point size, and all three are concatenated:

[UNIX]

# ▪ **More about Displays** ▪

Broadly speaking, a display is any kind of information in the body of a document that cannot be set as a normal paragraph. Displays can be figures, quotations, examples, tables, lists, equations, or diagrams.

The display macros position the display on the page. Inside the display, you might use other macros or preprocessors such as `tbl` or `eqn`. You might simply have a block of text that deserves special treatment.

The display macros can be relied upon to provide

- adequate spacing before and after the display;

- horizontal positioning of the display as a left justified, indented, or centered block;

- proper page breaks by keeping the entire display together.

The default action of the `.DS` macro is to left justify the text block in no-fill mode. It provides no indentation from the current margins.

You can specify a different format for a display by specifying up to three arguments with the `.DS` macro. The syntax is:

`.DS` [*format*] [*fill mode*] [*right indent*]

The *format* argument allows you to specify an indented or centered display. The argument can be set by a numeric value or a letter corresponding to the following options:

| | | |
|---|---|---|
| 0 | L | No indent (default) |
| 1 | I | Indented |
| 2 | C | Center each line |
| 3 | CB | Center entire display |

For consistency, the indent of displays is initially set to be the same as indented paragraphs (five spaces in `nroff` and three ens in `troff`), although these values are maintained independently in two different number registers, `Pi` and `Si`. (To change the defaults, simply use the `.nr` request to put the desired value in the appropriate register.)

A display can be centered in two ways: either each individual line in the display is centered (C) or the entire display is centered as a block based on the longest line of the display (CB).

For instance, the preceding list was formatted using `tbl`, but its placement was controlled by the display macro.

```
.DS CB
.TS
```
*table specifications*
```
.TE
.DE
```

The *fill mode* argument is represented by either a number or a letter.

| 0 | N | No-fill mode (default) |
|---|---|---|
| 1 | F | Fill mode |

The *right indent* argument is a numeric value that is subtracted from the right margin. In nroff, this value is automatically scaled in ens. In troff, you can specify a scaled number; otherwise, the default is ems.

The use of fill mode, along with other indented display options, can provide a paragraph indented on both sides. This is often used in reports and proposals that quote at length from another source. For example:

```
.P
I was particularly interested in the following comment
found in the product specification:
.DS I F 5
Users first need a brief introduction to what the product
does.  Sometimes this is more for the benefit of people
who haven't yet bought the product, and
are just looking at the manual.
However, it also serves to put the rest of
the manual, and the product itself, in the proper context.
.DE
```

The result of formatting is:

```
I was particularly interested in the following comment
found in the the product specification:

    Users first  need  a  brief  introduction to
    what the product  does.   Sometimes  this is
    more for the  benefit of people  who haven't
    yet bought the product, and are just looking
    at the manual.  However, it  also  serves to
    put the rest of the manual,  and the product
    itself, in the proper context.
```

The use of tabs often presents a problem outside of displays.  Material that has been entered with tabs in the input file should be formatted in no-fill mode, the default setting of the display macros.  The following table was designed using tabs to provide the spacing:

```
.DF I
Dates                   Description of Task

June 30                 Submit audience analysis
July 2                  Meeting to review audience analysis
July 15                 Submit detailed outline
August 1                Submit first draft
August 5                Return of first draft
August 8                Meeting to review comments
.DE
```

This table appears in the output just as it looks in the file. If this material had not been processed inside a display in no-fill mode, the columns would be improperly aligned.

## Static and Floating Displays

There are two types of displays, *static* and *floating*. The difference between them has to do with what happens when a display cannot fit in its entirety on the current page. Both the static and the floating display output the block at the top of the next page if it doesn't fit on the current page; however, only the floating display allows text that follows the display to be used to fill up the preceding page. A static display maintains the order in which a display was placed in the input file.

We have already used .DS and .DE to mark the beginning and end of a static display. To specify a floating display, the closing mark is the same, but the beginning is marked by the .DF macro. The options are the same as for the .DS macro.

In the following example of an input file, numbers are used instead of actual lines of text:

```
1
2
3
4
5
.DF
Long Display
.DE
6
7
8
9
10
```

The following two formatted pages might be produced, assuming that there are a sufficient number of lines in the display to cause a page break:

```
 _____          _____
|         -1-            |        |          -2-           |
|                        |        |                        |
| 1                      |        |  Long Display          |
| 2                      |        |                        |
| 3                      |        |  8                     |
| 4                      |        |  9                     |
| 5                      |        |  10                    |
| 6                      |        |                        |
| 7                      |        |                        |
|_____|        |_____|
```

If there had been room on page 1 to fit the display, it would have been placed there, and lines 6 and 7 would have followed the display, as they did in the input file.

If a static display had been specified, the display would be placed in the same position on page 2, and lines 6 and 7 would have to follow it, leaving extra space at the bottom of page 1. A floating display attempts to make the best use of the available space on a page.

The formatter maintains a queue to hold floating displays that it has not yet output. When the top of a page is encountered, the next display in the queue is output. The queue is emptied in the order in which it was filled, (first in, first out). Two number registers, De and Df, allow you to control when displays are removed from the queue and placed in position.

At the end of a section, as indicated by the section macros .H and .HU (which we will see shortly), or at the end of the input file, any floating displays that remain in the queue will be placed in the document.

## Display Labels

You can provide a title or caption for tables, equations, exhibits, and figures. In addition, the display can be labeled and numbered in sequence, as well as printed in a table of contents at the end of the file. The following group of macros are available:

| | |
|---|---|
| .EC | Equation |
| .EX | Exhibit |
| .FG | Figure |

All of these macros work the same way and are usually specified within a pair of .DS/.DE macros, so that the title and the display appear on the same page. Each macro can be followed by a title. If the title contains spaces, it should be enclosed within quotation marks. The title of a table usually appears at the top of a table, so it must be specified before the .TS macro that signals to tbl the presence of a table (see Chapter 8).

```
     .TB "List of Required Resources"
     .TS
```

The label is centered:

---

**Table 1.** List of Required Resources

---

If the title exceeds the line length, then it will be broken onto several lines. Additional lines are indented and begin at the first character of the title.

---

**Table 1.** List of Required Resources
Provided by Gutenberg Galaxy
Software

---

The label for equations, exhibits, and figures usually follows the display. The following:

```
     .FG "Drawing with a Light Pen"
```

produces a centered line:

---

**Figure 1.** Drawing with a Light Pen

---

The default format of the label can be changed slightly by setting the number register Of to 1. This replaces the period with a dash.

---

**Figure 1** — Drawing with a Light Pen

---

Second and third arguments, specified with the label macros, can be used to modify or override the default numbering of displays. Basically, the second argument is a literal and the third argument a numeric value that specifies what the literal means.
If the third argument is

0    then the second argument will be treated as a prefix;

1    then the second argument will be treated as a suffix;

2    then the second argument replaces the normal table number.

Thus, a pair of related tables could be specified as 1a and 1b using the following labels:

```
     .TB "Estimated Hours: June, July, and August" a 1
     .TB "Estimated Hours: September and November," 1b 2
```

(These labels show two different uses of the third argument. Usually, you would consistently use one technique or the other for a given set of tables.)
For tbl, the delimiters for tables are .TS/.TE. For eqn, the delimiters for equations are .EQ/.EN. For pic, the delimiters for pictures or diagrams are .PS/.PE. These pairs of delimiters indicate a block to be processed by a specific

preprocessor. You will find the information about each of the preprocessors in Chapters 8 through 10. As mentioned, the preprocessor creates the display, the display macros position it, and the label macros add titles and a number.

Although it may seem a minor point, each of these steps is independent, and because they are not fully integrated, there is some overlap.

The label macros, being independent of the preprocessors, do not make sure that a display exists or check whether a table has been created with tbl. You can create a two-column table using tabs or create a figure using character symbols and still give it a label. Or you can create a table heading as the first line of your table and let tbl process it (tbl won't provide a number and the table won't be collected for the table of contents).

In tbl, you can specify a centered table and not use the .DS/.DE macros. But, as a consequence, nroff/troff won't make a very good attempt at keeping the table together on one page, and you may have to manually break the page. It is recommended that you use the display macros throughout a document, regardless of whether you can get the same effect another way, because if nothing else you will achieve consistency.

## ▪ Forcing a Page Break ▪

Occasionally, you may want to force a page break, whether to ensure that a block of related material is kept together or to allow several pages for material that will be manually pasted in, such as a figure. The .SK (*skip*) macro forces a page break. The text following this macro is output at the top of the next page. If supplied with an argument greater than 0, it causes that number of pages to be skipped before resuming the output of text. The ''blank'' pages are printed, and they have the normal header and footer.

```
On the next page, you will find a sample page from an
Alcuin manuscript printed with a 16-color plotter.
.SK 1
```

## ▪ Formatting Lists ▪

The mm macro package provides a variety of different formats for presenting a list of items. You can select from four standard list types:

- bulleted
- dashed
- numbered
- alphabetized

In addition, you have the flexibility to create lists with nonstandard marks or text labels. The list macros can also be used to produce paragraphs with a hanging indent.

Each list item consists of a special mark, letter, number, or label in a left-hand column with a paragraph of text indented in a right-hand column.

## Structuring a List

The list macros help to simplify what could be a much larger and tedious formatting task. Here's the coding for the bulleted list just shown:

```
.BL
.LI
bulleted
.LI
dashed
.LI
numbered
.LI
alphabetized
.LE
```

The structure of text in the input file has three parts: a list-initialization macro (`.BL`), an item-mark macro (`.LI`), and a list-end macro (`.LE`).

First, you initialize the list, specifying the particular macro for the type of list that you want. For instance, `BL` initializes a bulleted list.

You can specify arguments with the list-initialization macro that change the indentation of the text and turn off the automatic spacing between items in the list. We will examine these arguments when we look at the list-initialization macros in more detail later.

Next, you specify each of the items in the list. The item-mark macro, `.LI`, is placed before each item. You can enter one or more lines of text following the macro.

```
.BL
.LI
Item 1
.LI
Item 2
.LI
Item 3
```

When the list is formatted, the `.LI` macro provides a line of space before each item. (This line can be omitted through an argument to the list-initialization macro if you want to produce a more compact list. We'll be talking more about this in a moment.)

The `.LI` macro can also be used to override or prefix the current mark. If a mark is supplied as the only argument, it replaces the current mark. For example:

```
.LI o
Item 4
```

If a mark is supplied as the first argument, followed by a second argument of 1 , then the specified mark is prefixed to the current mark. The following:

```
.LI - 1
Item 5
```

would produce:

-•     Item 5

A text label can also be supplied in place of the mark, but it presents some additional problems for the proper alignment of the list. We will look at text labels for variable-item lists.

The  .LI macro does not automatically provide spacing after each list item. An argument of 1 can be specified if a line of space is desired.

The end of the list is marked by the list-end macro  .LE. It restores page formatting settings that were in effect prior to the invocation of the last list-initialization macro. The  .LE macro does not output any space following the list unless you specify an argument of 1. (Don't specify this argument when the list is immediately followed by a macro that outputs space, such as the paragraph macro.)

Be sure you are familiar with the basic structure of a list. A common problem is not closing the list with  .LE. Most of the time, this error causes the formatter to quit at this point in the file. A less serious, but nonetheless frequent, oversight is omitting the first  .LI between the list-initialization macro and the first item in the list. The list is output but the first item will be askew.

Here is a sample list:

```
.BL
.LI
Item 1
.LI
Item 2
.LI
Item 3
.LI o
Item 4
.LI - 1
Item 5
.LE
```

The `troff` output produced by the sample list is:

---

- • Item 1
- • Item 2
- • Item 3
- o Item 4
- -• Item 5

---

Complete list structures can be nested within other lists up to six levels. Different types of lists can be nested, making it possible to produce indented outline structures. But, like nested if-then structures in a program, make sure you know which level you are at and remember to close each list.

For instance, we could nest the bulleted list inside a numbered list. The list initialization macro `.AL` generates alphabetized and numbered lists.

```
.AL
.LI
Don't worry, we'll get to the list-initialization macro .AL.
You can specify five different variations of
alphabetic and numbered lists.
.BL
.LI
Item 1
.LI
Item 2
.LI
item 3
.LE
.LI
We'll also look at variable-item lists.
.LE
```

This input produces the following formatted list from `troff`:

1.              Don't worry, we'll get to the list-initialization macro  `.AL`.
                You can specify five different variations of alphabetic and
                numbered lists.

        •       Item 1

        •       Item 2

        •       Item 3

2.              We'll also look at variable-item lists.

You may already realize the ease with which you can make changes to a list. The items in a list can be easily put in a new order. New items can be added to a numbered list without readjusting the numbering scheme. A bulleted list can be changed to an alphabetized list by simply changing the list-initialization macro. And you normally don't have to be concerned with a variety of specific formatting requests, such as setting indentation levels or specifying spacing between items.

On the other hand, because the structure of the list is not as easy to recognize in the input file as it is in the formatted output, you may find it difficult to interpret complicated lists, in particular ones that have been nested to several levels. The code-checking program, `checkmm`, can help; in addition, you may want to format and print repeatedly to examine and correct problems with lists.

## Marked Lists

Long a standby of technical documents, a marked list clearly organizes a group of related items and sets them apart for easy reading. A list of items marked by a bullet (•) is perhaps the most common type of list. Another type of marked list uses a dash (—). A third type of list allows the user to specify a mark, such as a square ( □ ). The list-initialization macros for these lists are:

```
.BL        [text indent] [1]
.DL        [text indent] [1]
.ML        [mark] [text indent] [1]
```

With the  `.BL` macro, the text is indented the same amount as the first line of an indented paragraph. A single space is maintained between the bullet and the text. The bullet is right justified, causing an indent of several spaces from the left margin.

As you can see from this  `nroff`-formatted output, the bullet is simulated in `nroff` by a  + overstriking an  `o`:

```
        Currently, the following internal documentation is
    available on the Alcuin product:

        ⚭ GGS Technical Memo 3200

        ⚭ GGS Product Marketing Spec

        ⚭ Alcuin/UNIX interface definition

        ⚭ Programmer's documentation for Alcuin
```

If you specify a *text indent*, the first character of the text will start at that position. The position of the bullet is relative to the text, always one space to its left.

If the last argument is 1, the blank line of space separating items is omitted. If you want to specify only this argument, you must specify either a value or a null value ("") for a *text indent*.

```
.BL "" 1
```

It produces a much more compact list:

```
        ⚭ GGS Technical Memo 3200
        ⚭ GGS Product Marketing Spec
        ⚭ Alcuin/UNIX interface definition
        ⚭ Programmer's documentation for Alcuin
```

Because the bullets produced by nroff are not always appropriate due to the overstriking, a dashed list provides a suitable alternative. With the .DL macro, the dash is placed in the same position as a bullet in a bulleted list. A single space is maintained between the dash and the text, which, like the text with a bulleted list, is indented by the amount specified in the number register for indented paragraphs (Pi).

The nroff formatter supplies a dash that is a single hyphen, and troff supplies an em dash. Because the em dash is longer, and the dash is right justified, the alignment with the left margin is noticeably different. It appears left justified in troff; in nroff, the dash appears indented several spaces because it is smaller.

```
        The third chapter on the principles of computerized
    font design should cover the following topics:

        - Building a Font Dictionary

        - Loading a Font

        - Scaling a Font
```

You can specify a *text indent* and a second argument of 1 to inhibit spacing between items.

With the .ML macro, you have to supply the mark for the list. Some possible candidates are the square (enter \(sq to get □), the square root (enter \(sr to get √), which resembles a check mark, and the gradient symbol (enter \(gr to get ∇). The user-specified mark is the first argument.

```
.ML \(sq
```

Not all of the characters or symbols that you can use in troff will have the same effect in nroff.

Unlike bulleted and dashed lists, text is not automatically indented after a user-specified mark. However, a space is added after the mark. The following example of an indented paragraph and a list, which specifies a square as a mark, has been formatted using nroff. The square appears as a pair of brackets.

```
[] Remove old initialization files.

[] Run install program.

[] Exit to main menu and choose selection 3.
```

The user-supplied mark can be followed by a second argument that specifies a *text indent* and a third argument of 1 to omit spacing between items.

The following example was produced using the list-initialization command:

```
.ML \(sq 5 1
```

The specified indent of 5 aligns the text with an indented paragraph:

```
        Check to see that you have completed the following
steps:

    [] Remove old initialization files.
    [] Run install program.
    [] Exit to main menu and choose selection 3.
```

## Numbered and Alphabetic Lists

The .AL macro is used to initialize automatically numbered or alphabetized lists. The syntax for this macro is:

```
.AL    [type] [text indent] [1]
```

If no arguments are specified, the .AL macro produces a numbered list. For instance, we can code the following paragraph with the list-initialization macro .AL:

```
User-oriented documentation recognizes three things:
.AL
.LI
that a new user needs to learn the system in stages,
getting a sense of the system as a whole while becoming
proficient in performing particular tasks;
.LI
that there are different levels of users, and not every
user needs to learn all the capabilities of the system
in order to be productive;
.LI
that an experienced user must be able to rely on the
documentation for accurate and thorough reference
information.
.LE
```

to produce a numbered list:

---

User-oriented documentation recognizes three things:

1.   that a new user needs to learn the system in stages,
     getting a sense of the system as a whole while
     becoming proficient in performing particular tasks;

2.   that there are different levels of users, and not
     every user needs to learn all the capabilities of
     the system in order to be productive;

3.   that an experienced user must be able to rely on the
     documentation for accurate and thorough reference
     information.

---

The number is followed by a period, and two spaces are maintained between the period and the first character of text.

The level of *text indent*, specified in the number register `Li`, is 6 in `nroff` and 5 in `troff`. This value is added to the current indent. If a *text indent* is specified, that value is added to the current indent, but it does not change the value of `Li`.

The third argument inhibits spacing between items in the list. Additionally, the number register `Ls` can be set to a value from 0 to 6 indicating a nesting level. Lists after this level will not have spacing between items. The default is 6, the maximum nesting depth. If `Ls` were set to 2, lists only up to the second level would have a blank line of space between items.

Other types of lists can be specified with `.AL`, using the first argument to specify the list type, as follows:

| Value | Sequence | Description |
|-------|----------|-------------|
| 1 | 1, 2, 3 | Numbered |
| A | A, B, C | Alphabetic (uppercase) |
| a | a, b, c | Alphabetic (lowercase) |
| I | I, II, III | Roman numerals (uppercase) |
| i | i, ii, iii | Roman numerals (lowercase) |

You can produce various list types by simply changing the *type* argument. You can create a very useful outline format by nesting different types of lists. The example we show of such an outline is one that is nested to four levels using I, A, 1, and a, in that order. The rather complicated looking input file is shown in Figure 6-4 (indented for easier viewing of each list, although it could not be formatted this way), and the nroff-formatted output is shown in Figure 6-5.

Another list-initialization macro that produces a numbered list is .RL (*reference list*). The only difference is that the reference number is surrounded by brackets ([ ]).

.RL [*text indent*] [1]

The arguments have the same effect as those specified with the .AL macro. To initialize a reference list with no spacing between items, use:

.RL "" 1

It produces the following reference list:

```
[1]   The Main Menu
[2]   Menus or Commands?
[3]   Error Handling
[4]   Getting Help
[5]   Escaping to UNIX
```

## Variable-Item Lists

With a variable-item list, you do not supply a mark; instead, you specify a text label with each .LI. One or more lines of text following .LI are used to form a block paragraph indented from the label. If no label is specified, a paragraph with a hanging indent is produced. The syntax is:

.VL *text indent* [*label indent*] [1]

Unlike the other list-initialization macros, a *text indent* is required. By default, the label is left justified, unless a *label indent* is given. If you specify both a *text indent* and a *label indent*, the indent for the text will be added to the *label indent*.

```
.AL I
.LI
Quick Tour of Alcuin
      .AL A
      .LI
      Introduction to Calligraphy
      .LI
      Digest of Alcuin Commands
            .AL 1
            .LI
            Three Methods of Command Entry
                  .AL a
                  .LI
                  Mouse
                  .LI
                  Keyboard
                  .LI
                  Light Pen
                  .LE
            .LI
            Starting a Page
            .LI
            Drawing Characters
                  .AL a
                  .LI
                  Choosing a Font
                  .LI
                  Switching Fonts
                  .LE
            .LI
            Creating Figures
            .LI
            Printing
            .LE
      .LI
      Sample Illuminated Manuscripts
      .LE
.LI
Using Graphic Characters
      .AL A
      .LI
      Modifying Font Style
      .LI
      Drawing Your Own Font
      .LE
.LI
Library of Hand-Lettered Fonts
.LE
```

***Fig. 6-4.*** Input for a Complex List

– 1 –

I. Quick Tour of Alcuin

   A. Introduction to Calligraphy

   B. Digest of Alcuin Commands

      1. Three Methods of Command Entry

         a. Mouse

         b. Keyboard

         c. Light Pen

      2. Starting a Page

      3. Drawing Characters

         a. Choosing a Font

         b. Switching Fonts

      4. Creating Figures

      5. Printing

   C. Sample Illuminated Manuscripts

II. Using Graphic Characters

   A. Modifying Font Style

   B. Drawing Your Own Font

III. Library of Hand-Lettered Fonts

**Fig. 6-5.** Output of a Complex List

Variable-item lists are useful in preparing command reference pages, which describe various syntax items, and glossaries, which present a term in one column and its definition in the other. The text label should be a single word or phrase. The following example shows a portion of the input file for a reference page:

```
.VL 15 5
.LI figure
is the name of a cataloged figure.  If
a figure has not been cataloged, you need to use
the LOCATE command.
.LI f:p
is the scale of the
figure in relation to the page.
.LI font
is the two-character abbreviation or
full name of one of the available fonts
from the Alcuin library.
.LE
```

The following variable-item list is produced:

```
        figure     is the name of a cataloged figure.  If a
                   figure has not been cataloged, you need to
                   use the LOCATE command.


        f:p        is the scale of the figure in relation to
                   the page.


        font       is the two-character abbreviation or full
                   name of one of the available fonts from the
                   Alcuin library.
```

If you don't provide a text label with `.LI` or give a null argument (`""`), you will get a paragraph with a hanging indent. If you want to print an item without a label, specify a backslash followed by a space (\ ) or \0 after `.LI`. Similarly, if you want to specify a label that contains a space, you should also precede the space with a backslash and enclose the label within quotation marks:

```
.LI "point\ size"
```

or simply substitute a `\0` for a space:

```
.LI point\0size
```

The first line of text is left justified (or indented by the amount specified in *label indent*) and the remaining lines will be indented by the amount specified by *text indent*. This produces a paragraph with a hanging indent:

```
.VL 15
.LI
There are currently 16 font dictionaries in the Alcuin
library.  Any application may have up to 12 dictionaries
resident in memory at the same time.
.LE
```

When formatted, this item has a hanging indent of 15:

```
There are currently 16 font dictionaries in the Alcuin
                library.  Any application may have up to
                12 dictionaries resident in memory at the
                same time.
```

## ▪ Headings ▪

Earlier we used the list macros to produce an indented outline. That outline, indented to four levels, is a visual representation of the structure of a document. Headings perform a related function, showing how the document is organized into sections and subsections. In technical documentation and book-length manuscripts, having a structure that is easily recognized by the reader is very important.

### Numbered and Unnumbered Headings

Using mm, you can have up to seven levels of numbered and unnumbered headings, with variable styles. There are two heading macros: .H for numbered headings and .HU for unnumbered headings. A different style for each level of heading can be specified by setting various number registers and defining strings.

Let's first look at how to produce numbered headings. The syntax for the .H macro is:

.H    *level* [*heading text*] [*heading suffix*]

The simplest use of the .H macro is to specify the *level* as a number between 1 and 7 followed by the text that is printed as a heading. If the *heading text* contains spaces, you should enclose it within quotation marks. A heading that is longer than a single line will be wrapped on to the next line. A multiline heading will be kept together in case of a page break.

If you specify a *heading suffix*, this text or mark will appear in the heading but will not be collected for a table of contents.

A top-level heading is indicated by an argument of 1:

```
.H 1 "Quick Tour of Alcuin"
```

The result is a heading preceded by a heading-level number. The first-level heading has the number 1.

```
1.  Quick Tour of Alcuin
```

A second-level heading is indicated by an argument of 2:

```
.H 2 "Introduction to Calligraphy"
```

The first second-level heading number is printed:

```
1.1  Introduction to Calligraphy
```

When another heading is specified at the same level, the heading-level number is automatically incremented. If the next heading is at the second level:

```
.H 2 "Digest of Alcuin Commands"
```

it produces:

```
1.2  Digest of Alcuin Commands
```

Each time you go to a new (higher-numbered) level, .1 is appended to the number representing the existing level. That number is incremented for each call at the same level. When you back out of a level (for instance, from level 5 to 4), the counter for the level (in this case level 5), is reset to 0.

An unnumbered heading is really a zero-level heading:

```
.H 0 "Introduction to Calligraphy"
```

A separate macro, .HU, has been developed for unnumbered headings, although its effect is the same.

```
.HU "Introduction to Calligraphy"
```

Even though an unnumbered heading does not display a number, it increments the counter for second-level headings. Thus, in the following example, the heading ''Introduction to Calligraphy'' is unnumbered, but it has the same effect on the numbering scheme as if it had been a second-level heading (1.1).

```
1.  Quick Tour of Alcuin

Introduction to Calligraphy

1.2  Digest of Alcuin Commands
```

If you are going to intermix numbered and unnumbered headings, you can change the number register Hu to the lowest-level heading that is in the document. By changing Hu from 2 to a higher number:

```
.nr Hu 5
.H 1 "Quick Tour of Alcuin"
.HU "Introduction to Calligraphy"
.H 2 "Digest of Alcuin Commands"
```

the numbering sequence is preserved for the numbered heading following an unnumbered heading:

```
1.   Quick Tour of Alcuin

Introduction to Calligraphy

1.1   Digest of Alcuin Commands
```

Headings are meant to be visible keys to your document's structure. If you are using unnumbered headings, it becomes even more important to make headings stand out. A simple thing you can do is use uppercase letters for a first-level heading.

Here is a list of some of the other things you can do to affect the appearance of headings, although some of the items depend upon whether you are formatting with `nroff` or `troff`:

- change to roman, italic, or bold font

- change the point size of the heading

- adjust spacing after the heading

- center or left justify the heading

- change the numbering scheme

- select a different heading mark

The basic issue in designing a heading style is to help the reader distinguish between different levels of headings. For instance, in an outline form, different levels of indent show whether a topic is a section or subsection. Using numbered headings is an effective way to accomplish this. If you use unnumbered headings, you probably want to vary the heading style for each level, although, for practical purposes, you should limit yourself to two or three levels.

First, let's look at what happens if we use the default heading style.

The first two levels of headings are set up to produce italicized text in `troff` and underlined text in `nroff`. After the heading, there is a blank line before the first paragraph of text. In addition, a top-level heading has two blank lines before the heading; all the other levels have a single line of space.

### 1.2 *Introduction to Calligraphy*

Alcuin revitalizes an age-old tradition. Calligraphy, quite simply, is the art of beautiful handwriting.

Levels three through seven all have the same appearance. The text is italicized or underlined and no line break occurs. Two blank lines are maintained before and after the text of the heading. For example:

1.2.1.3   *Light Pen*   The copyist's pen and ink has been replaced by a light pen.

To change the normal appearance of headings in a document, you specify new values for the two strings:

HF        Heading font
HP        Heading point size

You can specify individual settings for each level, up to seven values.

The font for each level of heading can be set by the string HF. The following codes are used to select a font:

1        Roman
2        Italic
3        Bold

By default, the arguments for all seven levels are set to 2, resulting in italicized headings in troff and underlining in nroff. Here the .HF string specifies bold for the top three levels followed by two italic levels:

```
.ds HF 3 3 3 2 2
```

If you do not specify a level, it defaults to 1. Thus, in the previous example, level 6 and 7 headings would be printed in a roman font.

The point size is set by the string HP. Normally, headings are printed in the same size as the body copy, except for bold headings. A bold heading is reduced by 1 point when it is a standalone heading, as are the top-level headings. The HP string can take up to seven arguments, setting the point size for each level.

```
.ds HP 14 14 12
```

If an argument is not given, or a null value or 0 is given, the default setting of 10 points is used for that level. Point size can also be given relative to the current point size:

```
.ds HP +4 +4 +2
```

A group of number registers control other default formats of headings:

Ej        Eject page
Hb        Break follows heading
Hc        Center headings
Hi        Align text after heading
Hs        Vertical spacing after heading

For each of these number registers, you specify the number of the level at which some action is to be turned on or off.

The Ej register is set to the highest-level heading, usually 1, that should start on a new page. Its default setting is 0. This ensures that the major sections of a document will begin on their own page.

```
.nr Ej 1
```

The Hb register determines if a line break occurs after the heading. The Hs register determines if a blank line is output after the heading. Both are set to 2 by default. Settings of 2 mean that, for levels 1 and 2, the section heading is printed, followed by a line break and a blank line separating the heading from the first paragraph of text. For lower-level headings (an argument greater than 2), the first paragraph follows immediately on the same line.

The Hc register is set to the highest-level heading that you want centered. Normally, this is not used with numbered headings and its default value is 0. However, unnumbered heads are often centered. A setting of 2 will center first- and second-level headings:

```
.nr Hc 2
```

With unnumbered headings, you also have to keep in mind that the value of Hc must be greater than or equal to Hb and Hu. The heading must be on a line by itself; therefore a break must be set in Hb for that level. The Hu register sets the level of an unnumbered heading to 2, requiring that Hc be at least 2 to have an effect on unnumbered headings.

There really is no way, using these registers, to get the first and second levels left justified and have the rest of the headings centered.

The number register Hi determines the paragraph type for a heading that causes a line break (Hb). It can be set to one of three values:

| | |
|---|---|
| 0 | Left justified |
| 1 | Paragraph type determined by Pt |
| 2 | Indented to align with first character in heading |

If you want to improve the visibility of numbered headings, set Hi to 2:

```
.nr Hi 2
```

It produces the following results:

```
4.1  Generating Output

An  Alcuin manuscript  is a computer  representation
that has to be converted for output on various kinds
of devices, including plotters and laser printers.
```

## Changing the Heading Mark

Remember how the list-initialization macro `.AL` allowed you to change the mark used for a list, producing an alphabetic list instead of a numbered list? These same options are available for headings using the `.HM` macro.

The `.HM` macro takes up to seven arguments specifying the mark for each level. The following codes can be specified:

| | |
|---|---|
| 1 | Arabic |
| 001 | Arabic with leading zeros |
| A | Uppercase alphabetic |
| a | Lowercase alphabetic |
| I | Uppercase roman |
| i | Lowercase roman |

If no mark is specified, the default numbering system (arabic) is used. Uppercase alphabetic marks can be used in putting together a series of appendices. You can specify A for the top level:

```
.HM A
```

and retain the default section numbering for the rest of the headings. This could produce sections in the following series:

A, A.1, A.2, A.2.1, etc.

Marks can be mixed for an outline style similar to the one we produced using the list macros:

```
.HM I A 1 a i
```

Roman numerals can be used to indicate sections or parts. If you specify:

```
.HM I i
```

the headings for the first two levels are marked by roman numerals. A third-level heading is shown to demonstrate that the heading mark reverted to arabic by default:

```
I.   Quick Tour of Alcuin

I.i   Introduction to Calligraphy

I.ii   Digest of Alcuin Commands

I.ii.1   Three Methods of Command Entry
```

When you use marks consisting of roman numerals or alphabetic characters, you might not want the mark of the current level to be concatenated to the mark of the previous level. Concatenation can be suppressed by setting the number register Ht to 1:

```
.HM I i
.nr Ht 1
```

Now, each heading in the list has only the mark representing that level:

```
I.    Quick Tour of Alcuin

i.    Introduction to Calligraphy

ii.   Digest of Alcuin Commands

1.    Three Methods of Command Entry
```

## ▪ Table of Contents ▪

Getting a table of contents easily and automatically is almost reason enough to justify all the energy, yours and the computer's, that goes into text processing. You realize that this is something that the computer was really meant to do.

When the table of contents page comes out of the printer, a writer attains a state of happiness known only to a statistician who can give the computer a simple instruction to tabulate vast amounts of data and, in an instant, get a single piece of paper listing the results.

The reason that producing a table of contents seems so easy is that most of the work is performed in coding the document. That means entering codes to mark each level of heading and all the figures, tables, exhibits, and equations. Processing a table of contents is simply a matter of telling the formatter to collect the information that's already in the file.

There are only two simple codes to put in a file, one at the beginning and one at the end, to generate a table of contents automatically.

At the beginning of the file, you have to set the number register Cl to the level of headings that you want collected for a table of contents. For example, setting Cl to 2 saves first- and second-level headings.

Place the .TC macro at the end of the file. This macro actually does the processing and formatting of the table of contents. The table of contents page is output at the end of a document.

A sample table of contents page follows. The header "CONTENTS" is printed at the top of the page. At the bottom of the page, lowercase roman numerals are used as page numbers.

CONTENTS

- i -

One blank line is output before each first-level heading. All first-level headings are left justified. Lower-level headings are indented so that they line up with the start of text for the previous level.

If you have included various displays in your document, and used the macros .FG, .TB, and .EX to specify captions and headings for the displays, this information is collected and output when the .TC macro is invoked. A separate page is printed for each accumulated list of figures, tables, and exhibits. For example:

LIST OF TABLES

TABLE 1. List of Required Resources.................... 7

TABLE 2. List of Available Resources.................... 16

If you want the lists of displays to be printed immediately following the table of contents (no page breaks), you can set the number register Cp to 1.

If you want to suppress the printing of individual lists, you can set the following number registers to 0:

Lf        If 0, no figures
Lt        If 0, no tables
Lx       If 0, no exhibits

In addition, there is a number register for equations that is set to 0 by default. If you want equations marked by .EC to be listed, specify:

```
.nr Le 1
```

There are a set of strings, using the same names as the number registers, that define the titles used for the top of the lists:

```
Lf          LIST OF FIGURES
Lt          LIST OF TABLES
Lx          LIST OF EXHIBITS
Le          LIST OF EQUATIONS
```

You can redefine a string using the .ds (*define string*) request. For instance, we can redefine the title for figures as follows:

```
.ds Lf LIST OF ALCUIN DRAWINGS
```

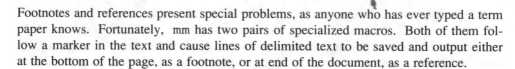

## ▪ Footnotes and References

Footnotes and references present special problems, as anyone who has ever typed a term paper knows. Fortunately, mm has two pairs of specialized macros. Both of them follow a marker in the text and cause lines of delimited text to be saved and output either at the bottom of the page, as a footnote, or at end of the document, as a reference.

### Footnotes

A footnote is marked in the body of a document by the string \*F. It follows immediately after the text (no spaces).

```
in an article on desktop publishing.\*F
```

The string F supplies the number for the footnote. It is printed (using troff) as a superscript in the text and its value is incremented with each use.

The .FS macro indicates the start, and .FE the end, of the text for the footnote. These macros surround the footnote text that will appear at the bottom of the page. The .FS macro is put on the line immediately following the marker.

```
.FS
"Publish or Perish: Start-up grabs early page language lead,"
\fIComputerworld\fR, April 21, 1986, p. 1.
.FE
```

You can use labels instead of numbers to mark footnotes. The label must be specified as a mark in the text and as an argument with .FS.

```
...in accord with the internal specs.[APS]
.FS [APS]
"Alcuin Product Specification," March 1986
.FE
```

You can use both numbered and labeled footnotes in the same document. All the foot-notes are collected and output at the bottom of each page underneath a short line rule. If you are using troff, the footnote text will be set in a type size 2 points less than the body copy.

If you want to change the standard format of footnotes, you can specify the .FD macro. It controls hyphenation, text adjustment, indentation, and justification of the label.

Normally, the text of a footnote is indented from the left margin and the mark or label is left justified in relation to the start of the text. It is possible that a long footnote could run over to the next page. Hyphenation is turned off so that a word will not be broken at a page break. These specifications can be changed by giving a value between 0 and 11 as the first argument with .FD, as shown in Table 6-3.

**TABLE 6-3. .FD Argument Values**

| Argument | Hyphenation | Adjust | Text Indent | Label Justification |
|:---:|:---:|:---:|:---:|:---:|
| 0 | no | yes | yes | left |
| 1 | yes | yes | yes | left |
| 2 | no | no | yes | left |
| 3 | yes | no | yes | left |
| 4 | no | yes | no | left |
| 5 | yes | yes | no | left |
| 6 | no | no | no | left |
| 7 | yes | no | no | left |
| 8 | no | yes | yes | right |
| 9 | yes | yes | yes | right |
| 10 | no | no | yes | right |
| 11 | yes | no | yes | right |

The second argument for .FD, if 1, resets the footnote numbering counter to 1. This can be invoked at the end of a section or paragraph to initiate a new numbering sequence. If specified by itself, the first argument must be null:

```
.FD "" 1
```

## References

A reference differs from a footnote in that all references are collected and printed on a single page at the end of the document. In addition, you can label a reference so that you can refer to it later.

A reference is marked where it occurs in the text with \*(Rf. The formatter converts the string into a value printed in brackets, such as [1]. The mark is followed by a pair of macros surrounding the reference text. The .RS macro indicates the start, and .RF the end, of the text for the reference.

```
You will find information on this page description language
in their reference manual, which has been published
as a book.\*(Rf
.RS
Adobe Systems, Inc. PostScript Reference Manual.
Reading, Massachusetts: Addison-Wesley; 1985.
.RF
```

You can also give as a *string label* argument to .RS the name of a string that will be assigned the current reference number. This string can be referenced later in the document. For instance, if we had specified a *string label* in the previous example:

```
.RS As
```

We could refer back to the first reference in another place:

```
The output itself is a readable file which you can interpret
with the aid of the PostScript manual.\*(As
```

At the end of the document, a reference page is printed. The title printed on the reference page is defined in the string Rp. You can replace "REFERENCES" with another title simply by redefining this string with .ds.

*REFERENCES*

1. Adobe Systems, Inc.; PostScript Reference Manual.
   Reading, Massachusetts: Addison-Wesley; 1985.

In a large document, you might want to print a list of references at the end of a chapter or a long section. You can invoke the .RP macro anywhere in a document.

```
.RP
.H 1 "Detailed Outline of User Guide"
```

It will print the list of references on a separate page and reset the reference counter to 0. A *reset* argument and a *paging* argument can be supplied to change these actions. The *reset* argument is the first value specified with the .RP macro. It is normally 0, resetting the reference counter to 1 so that each section is numbered independently. If reference numbering should be maintained in sequence for the entire document, specify a value of 1.

The *paging* argument is the second value specified. It controls whether or not a page break occurs before and after the list. It is normally set to 0, putting the list on a new page. Specifying a value of 3 suppresses the page break before and after the list; the result is that the list of references is printed following the end of the section and the next section begins immediately after the list. A value of 1 will suppress only the page break that occurs after the list and a value of 2 will suppress only the page break that occurs before the list.

If you want an effect opposite that of the default settings, specify:

```
.RP  1  3
```

The first argument of 1 saves the current reference number for use in the next section or chapter. The second argument of 3 inhibits page breaks before and after the list of references.

## ▪ Extensions to mm ▪

So far, we have covered most but not all of the features of the mm macro package.

We have not covered the Technical Memorandum macros, a set of specialized macros for formatting technical memos and reports. Like the ones in the ms macro package, these macros were designed for internal use at AT&T's Bell Laboratories, reflecting a company-wide set of standards. Anyone outside of Bell Labs will want to make some modifications to the macros before using them. The Technical Memorandum macros are a good example of employing a limited set of user macros to produce a standard format. Seeing how they work will be especially important to those who are responsible for implementing documentation standards for a group of people, some of whom understand the basics of formatting and some of whom do not.

Writing or rewriting macros is only one part of the process of customizing mm. The mm macros were designed as a comprehensive formatting system. As we've seen, there are even macros to replace common primitive requests, like .sp. The developers of mm recommend, in fact, that you not use nroff or troff requests unless absolutely necessary, lest you interfere with the action of the macros.

Furthermore, as you will see if you print out the mm macros, the internal code of mm is extraordinarily dense, and uses extremely un-mnemonic register names. This makes it very difficult for all but the most experienced user to modify the basic structure of the package. You can always add your own macros, as long as they don't conflict with existing macro and number register names, but you can't easily go in and change the basic macros that make up the mm package.

At the same time, the developers of mm have made it possible for the user to make selective modifications—those which mm has allowed mechanisms for in advance. There are two such mechanisms:

- mm's use of number registers to control all aspects of document formatting

- mm's invocation of undefined (and therefore user-definable) macros at various places in the mm code

The mm package is very heavily parameterized. Almost every feature of the formatting system—from the fonts in which different levels of heading are printed to the size of indents and the amount of space above and below displays—is controlled by values in number registers. By learning and modifying these number registers, you can make significant changes to the overall appearance of your documents.

In addition, there are a number of values stored in strings. These strings are used like number registers to supply default values to various macros.

The registers you are most likely to want to change follow. Registers marked with a dagger can only be changed on the comand line with the −r option (e.g., −rN4).

| | |
|---|---|
| Cl | Level of headings saved for table of contents. See .TC macro. Default is 2. |
| Cp | If set to 1, lists of figures and tables appear on same page as table of contents. Otherwise, they start on a new page. Default is 1. |
| Ds | Sets the pre- and post-space used for static displays. |
| Fs | Vertical spacing between footnotes. |
| Hb | Level of heading for which break occurs before output of body text. Default is 2 lines. |
| Hc | Level of heading for which centering occurs. Default is 0. |
| Hi | Indent type after heading. Default is 1 (paragraph indent). Legal values are: 0=left justified (default); 1=indented; 2=indented except after .H, .LC, .DE. |
| Hs | Level of heading for which space after heading occurs. Default is 2, i.e., space will occur after first- and second-level headings. |
| Hy | Sets hyphenation. If set to 1, enables hyphenation. Default is 0. |
| L† | Sets length of page. Default is 66v. |
| Li | Default indent of lists. Default is 5. |
| Ls | List spacing between items by level. Default is 6, which is spacing between all levels of list. |
| N† | Page numbering style. 0=all pages get header; 1=header printed as footer on page 1; 2=no header on page 1; 3=section page as footer; 4=no header unless .PH defined; 5=section page and section figure as footer. Default is 0. |
| Np | Numbering style for paragraphs. 0=unnumbered; 1=numbered. |
| O | Offset of page. For nroff, this value is an unscaled number representing character positions. (Default is 9 characters; about .75i.) For troff, this value is scaled (.5i). |

Of  Figure caption style. 0=period separator; 1=hyphen separator. Default is 0.

Pi  Amount of indent for paragraph. Default is 5 for `nroff`, 3n for `troff`.

Ps  Amount of spacing between paragraphs. Default is 3v.

Pt  Paragraph type. Default is 0.

S†  Default point size for `troff`. Default is 10. Vertical spacing is \nS+2.

Si  Standard indent for displays. Default is 5 for `nroff`, 3 for `troff`.

W  Width of page (line and title length). Default is 6 in `troff`, 60 characters in `nroff`.

There are also some values that you would expect to be kept in number registers that are actually kept in strings:

HF  Fonts used for each level of heading (1=roman, 2=italic, 3=bold)
HP  Point size used for each level of heading

For example, placing the following register settings at the start of your document:

```
.nr Hc 1
.nr Hs 3
.nr Hb 4
.nr Hi 2
.ds HF 3 3 3 3 2 2 2
.ds HP 16 14 12 10 10 10 10
```

will have the following effects:

- Top-level headings (generated by `.H1`) will be centered.

- The first three levels of heading will be followed by a blank line.

- The fourth-level heading will be followed by a break.

- Fifth- through seventh-level headings will be run-in with the text.

- All headings will have the following text indented under the first word of the heading, so that the section number hangs in the margin.

- The first five levels of heading will be in bold type; the sixth and seventh will be italic.

- A first-level heading will be printed in 16-point type; a second-level heading in 14-point type; a third-level heading in 12-point type; and all subsequent levels in 10-point type.

There isn't space in this book for a comprehensive discussion of this topic. However, a complete list of user-settable mm number registers is given in Appendix B. Study this list, along with the discussion of the relevant macros, and you will begin to get a picture of just how many facets of mm you can modify by changing the values in number registers and strings.

The second feature—the provision of so-called "user exit macros" at various points—is almost as ingenious. The following macros are available for user definition:

```
.HX    .HY    .HZ    .PX    .TX    .TY
```

The .HX, .HY, and .HZ macros are associated with headings. The .HX macro is executed at the start of each heading macro, .HY in the middle (to allow you to respecify any settings, such as temporary indents, that were lost because of mm's own processing), and .HZ at the end.

By default, these macros are undefined. And, when troff encounters an undefined macro name, it simply ignores it. These macros thus lie hidden in the code until you define them. By defining these macros, you can supplement the processing of headings without actually modifying the mm code. Before you define these macros, be sure to study the mm documentation for details of how to use them.

Similarly, .PX is executed at the top of each page, just after .PH. Accordingly, it allows you to perform additional top-of-page processing. (In addition, you can redefine the .TP macro, which prints the standard header, because this macro is relatively self-contained.)

There is a slightly different mechanism for generalized bottom-of-page processing. The .BS/.BE macro pair can be used to enclose text that will be printed at the bottom of each page, after any footnotes but before the footer. To remove this text after you have defined it, simply specify an empty block.

The .VM (*vertical margins*) macro allows you to specify additional space at the top of the page, bottom of the page, or both. For example:

```
.VM 3 3
```

will add three lines each to the top and bottom margins. The arguments to this macro should be unscaled. The first argument applies to the top margin, the second to the bottom.

The .TX and .TY macros allow you to control the appearance of the table of contents pages. The .TX macro is executed at the top of the first page of the table of contents, above the title; .TY is executed in place of the standard title ("CONTENTS").

In Chapter 14, you will learn about writing macro definitions, which should give you the information you need to write these supplementary "user exit macros."

# 7

# Advanced Editing

Sometimes, in order to advance, you have to go backward. In this chapter, we are going to demonstrate how you can improve your text-editing skills by understanding how line editors work. This doesn't mean you'll have to abandon full-screen editing. The vi editor was constructed on top of a line editor named ex, which was an improved version of another line editor named ed. So in one sense we'll be looking at the ancestors of vi. We'll look at many of the ways line editors attack certain problems and how that applies to those of us who use full-screen editors.

Line editors came into existence for use on "paper terminals," which were basically printers. This was before the time of video display terminals. A programmer, or some other person of great patience, worked somewhat interactively on a printer. Typically, you saw a line of your file by printing it out on paper; you entered commands that would affect just that line; then you printed out the edited line again. Line editors were designed for this kind of process, editing one line at a time.

People rarely edit files on paper terminals any more, but there are diehards who still prefer line editors. For one thing, it imposes less of a burden on the computer. Line editors display the current line; they don't update the entire screen.

On some occasions, a line editor is simpler and faster than a full-screen editor. Sometimes, a system's response can be so slow that it is less frustrating to work if you switch to a line editor. Or you may have occasion to work remotely over a dial-up line operating at a baud rate that is too slow to work productively with a full-screen editor. In these situations, a line editor can be a way to improve your efficiency. It can reduce the amount of time you are waiting for the computer to respond to your commands.

The truth is, however, that after you switch from a screen editor to a line editor, you are likely to feel deprived. But you shouldn't skip this chapter just because you won't be using a line editor. The purpose of learning ex is to extend what you can do in vi.

## ■ The **ex** Editor ■

The ex editor is a line editor with its own complete set of editing commands. Although it is simpler to make most edits with vi, the line orientation of ex is an advantage when you are making large-scale changes to more than one part of a file. With ex, you can move easily between files and transfer text from one file to another in a variety of ways. You can search and replace text on a line-by-line basis, or globally. You can also save a series of editing commands as a macro and access them with a single keystroke.

Seeing how ex works when it is invoked directly will help take some of the "mystery" out of line editors and make it more apparent to you how many ex commands work.

Let's open a file and try a few ex commands. After you invoke ex on a file, you will see a message about the total number of lines in the file, and a colon command prompt. For example:

```
$ ex intro
  "intro" 20 lines, 731 characters
:
```

You won't see any lines in the file, unless you give an ex command that causes one or more lines to be printed.

All ex commands consist of a line address, which can simply be a line number, and a command. You complete the command with a carriage return. A line number by itself is equivalent to a print command for that line. So, for example, if you type the numeral 1 at the prompt, you will see the first line of the file:

```
:1
Sometimes, to advance,
:
```

To print more than one line, you can specify a range of lines. Two line numbers are specified, separated by commas, with no spaces in between them:

```
:1,3
Sometimes, to advance,
you have to go backward.
Alcuin is a computer graphics tool
```

The current line is the last line affected by a command. For instance, before we issued the command 1,3, line 1 was the current line; after that command, line 3 became the current line. It can be represented by a special symbol, a dot (.).

```
:.,+3
that lets you design and create hand-lettered, illuminated
manuscripts, such as were created in the Middle Ages.
```

The previous command results in three more lines being printed, starting with the current line. A + or − specifies a positive or negative offset from the current line.

The  ex editor has a command mode and an insert mode.  To put text in a file, you can enter the  append or  a command to place text on the line following the current line.  The  insert or  i command places text on the line above the current line.  Type in your text and when you are finished, enter a dot ( . ) on a line by itself:

```
:a
Monks, skilled in calligraphy,
labored to make copies of ancient
documents and preserve in a
library the works of many Greek and
Roman authors.
.
:
```

Entering the dot takes you out of insert mode and puts you back in command mode.

A line editor does not have a cursor, and you cannot move along a line of text to a particular word.  Apart from not seeing more of your file, the lack of a cursor (and therefore cursor motion keys) is probably the most difficult thing to get used to.  After using a line editor, you long to get back to using the  cw command in  vi.

If you want to change a word, you have to move to the line that contains the word, tell the editor which word on the line you want to change, and then provide its replacement.  You have to think this way to use the  substitute or  s command. It allows you to substitute one word for another.

We can change the last word on the first line from *tool* to *environment*:

```
:1
Alcuin is a computer graphics tool
:s/tool/environment/
Alcuin is a computer graphics environment
:
```

The word you want to change and its replacement are separated by slashes (/).  As a result of the substitute command, the line you changed is printed.

With a line editor, the commands that you enter affect the current line.  Thus, we made sure that the first line was our current line.  We could also make the same change by specifying the line number with the command:

```
:1s/environment/tool/
Alcuin is a computer graphics tool
```

If you specify an *address*, such as a range of line numbers, then the command will affect the lines that you specify:

```
:1,20s/Alcuin/ALCUIN/
ALCUIN is named after an English scholar
```

The last line on which a substitution was made is printed.

Remember, when using a line editor, you have to tell the editor which line (or lines) to work on as well as which command to execute.

Another reason that knowing  ex  is useful is that sometimes when you are working in  vi, you might unexpectedly find yourself using "open mode." For instance, if
you press  Q  while in  vi, you will be dropped into the  ex  editor. You can switch to
vi  by entering the command  vi  at the colon prompt:

    :vi

After you are in  vi, you can execute any  ex  command by first typing a  :
(colon).  The colon appears on the bottom of the screen and what you type will be
echoed there. Enter an  ex  command and press *RETURN* to execute it.


## ▪  Using ex Commands in vi  ▪

Many  ex  commands that perform normal editing operations have equivalent  vi  commands that do the job in a simpler manner. Obviously, you will use  dw  or  dd  to
delete a single word or line rather than using the  delete  command in  ex. However, when you want to make changes that affect numerous lines, you will find that the
ex  commands are very useful. They allow you to modify large blocks of text with a
single command.

Some of these commands and their abbreviations follow. You can use the full
command name or the abbreviation, whichever is easier to remember.

| | | |
|---|---|---|
| delete | d | Delete lines |
| move | m | Move lines |
| copy | co | Copy lines |
| substitute | s | Substitute one string for another |

The substitute command best exemplifies the  ex  editor's ability to make editing easier.
It gives you the ability to change any string of text every place it occurs in the file. To
perform edits on a global replacement basis requires a good deal of confidence in, as
well as full knowledge of, the use of pattern matching or "regular expressions."
Although somewhat arcane, learning to do global replacements can be one of the most
rewarding experiences of working in the UNIX text-processing environment.

Other  ex  commands give you additional editing capabilities. For all practical
purposes, they can be seen as an integrated part of  vi. Examples of these capabilities
are the commands for editing multiple files and executing UNIX commands. We will
look at these after we look at pattern-matching and global replacements.


## ▪  Write Locally, Edit Globally  ▪

Sometimes, halfway through a document or at the end of a draft, you recognize inconsistencies in the way that you refer to certain things. Or, in a manual, some product
that you called by name is suddenly renamed (marketing!). Often enough, you have to
go back and change what you've already written in several places.

The way to make these changes is with the search and replace commands in ex. You can automatically replace a word (or string of characters) wherever it occurs in the file. You have already seen one example of this use of the substitute command, when we replaced *Alcuin* with *ALCUIN*:

```
:1,20s/Alcuin/ALCUIN/
```

There are really two steps in using a search and replace command. The first step is to define the area in which a search will take place. The search can be specified locally to cover a block of text or globally to cover the entire file. The second step is to specify, using the substitute command, the text that will be removed and the text that will replace it.

At first, the syntax for specifying a search and replace command may strike you as difficult to learn, especially when we introduce pattern matching. Try to keep in mind that this is a very powerful tool, one that can save you a lot of drudgery. Besides, you will congratulate yourself when you succeed, and everyone else will think you are very clever.

## Searching Text Blocks

To define a search area, you need to be more familiar with how line addressing works in ex. A line address simply indicates which line or range of lines an ex command will operate on. If you don't specify a line address, the command only affects the current line. You already know that you can indicate any individual line by specifying its number. What we want to look at now are the various ways of indicating a block of text in a file.

You can use absolute or relative line numbers to define a range of lines. Identify the line number of the start of a block of text and the line number of the end of the block. In vi, you can use ^G to find the current line number.

There are also special symbols for addressing particular places in the file:

| | |
|---|---|
| . | Current line |
| $ | Last line |
| % | All lines (same as 1,$) |

The following are examples that define the block of text that the substitute command will act upon:

| | |
|---|---|
| :.,$s | Search from the current line to the end of the file |
| :20,.s | Search from line 20 through the current line |
| :.,.+20s | Search from the current line through the next 20 lines |
| :100,$s | Search from line 100 through the end of the file |
| :%s | Search all lines in the file |

Within the search area, as defined in these examples, the substitute command will look for one string of text and replace it with another string.

You can also use pattern matching to specify a place in the text. A pattern is delimited by a slash both *before* and *after* it.

| | |
|---|---|
| /*pattern1*/,/*pattern2*/ s | Search from the first line containing *pattern1* through the first line containing *pattern2* |
| :.,/*pattern*/ s | Search from the current line through the line containing *pattern* |

It is important to note that the action takes place on the entire line containing the pattern, not simply the text up to the pattern.

## Search and Replace

You've already seen the substitute command used to replace one string with another one. A slash is used as a delimiter separating the old string and the new. By prefixing the s command with an address, you can extend its range beyond a single line:

```
:1,20s/Alcuin/ALCUIN/
```

Combined with a line address, this command searches all the lines within the block of text. But it only replaces the first occurrence of the pattern on each line. For instance, if we specified a substitute command replacing *roman* with *Roman* in the following line:

```
after the roman hand.  In teaching the roman script
```

only the first, not the second, occurrence of the word would be changed.

To specify each occurrence on the line, you have to add a g at the end of the command:

```
:s/roman/Roman/g
```

This command changes *every* occurrence of *roman* to *Roman* on the current line.

Using search and replace is much faster than finding each instance of a string and replacing it individually. It has many applications, especially if you are a poor speller.

So far, we have replaced one word with another word. Usually, it's not that easy. A word may have a prefix or suffix that throws things off. In a while, we will look at pattern matching. This will really expand what you are able to do. But first, we want to look at how to specify that a search and replace take place globally in a file.

## Confirming Substitutions

It is understandable if you are over-careful when using a search and replace command. It does happen that what you get is not what you expected. You can undo any search and replacement command by entering u. But you don't always catch undesired changes until it is too late to undo them. Another way to protect your edited file is to save the file with :w before performing a replacement. Then, at least you can quit the file without saving your edits and go back to where you were before the change was made. You can also use :e! to read in the previous version of the buffer.

It may be best to be cautious and know exactly what is going to be changed in your file. If you'd like to see what the search turns up and confirm each replacement before it is made, add a  c at the end of the substitute command:

```
:1,30s/his/the/gc
```

It will display the entire line where the string has been located and the string itself will be marked by a series of carets (^^^).

```
copyists at his school
           ^^^
```

If you want to make the replacement, you must enter  y and press *RETURN*.
     If you don't want to make a change, simply press *RETURN*.

```
this can be used for invitations, signs, and menus.
    ^^^
```

The combination of the  vi commands // (repeat last search) and  . (repeat last command) is also an extraordinarily useful (and quick) way to page through a file and make repetitive changes that require a judgment call rather than an absolute global replacement.

## Global Search and Replace

When we looked at line addressing symbols, the percent symbol,  %, was introduced. If you specify it with the substitute command, the search and replace command will affect all lines in the file:

```
:%s/Alcuin/ALCUIN/g
```

This command searches all lines and replaces each occurrence on a line.
     There is another way to do this, which is slightly more complex but has other benefits. The pattern is specified as part of the address, preceded by a  g indicating that the search is global:

```
:g/Alcuin/s//ALCUIN/g
```

It selects all lines containing the pattern *Alcuin* and replaces every occurrence of that pattern with *ALCUIN*. Because the search pattern is the same as the word you want to change, you don't have to repeat it in the  substitute command.
     The extra benefit that this gives is the ability to search for a pattern and then make a different substitution. We call this context-sensitive replacement.
     The gist of this command is globally search for a pattern:

```
:g/pattern/
```

Replace it:

```
:g/pattern/s//
```

or replace another string on that line:

:g/*pattern*/s/*string*/

with a new string:

:g/*pattern*/s/*string*/*new*/

and do this for every occurrence on the line:

:g/*pattern*/s/*string*/*new*/g

For example, we use the macro .BX to draw a box around the name of a special key. To show an *ESCAPE* key in a manual, we enter:

.BX Esc

Suppose we had to change *Esc* to *ESC*, but we didn't want to change any references to *Escape* in the text. We could use the following command to make the change:

:g/BX/s/Esc/ESC/

This command might be phrased: "Globally search for each instance of BX and on those lines substitute the Esc with ESC". We didn't specify g at the end of the command because we would not expect more than one occurrence per line.

Actually, after you get used to this syntax, and admit that it is a little awkward, you may begin to like it.

## ▪ **Pattern Matching** ▪

If you are familiar with grep, then you know something about regular expressions. In making global replacements, you can search not just for fixed strings of characters, but also for patterns of words, referred to as *regular expressions*.

When you specify a literal string of characters, the search might turn up other occurrences that you didn't want to match. The problem with searching for words in a file is that a word can be used in many different ways. Regular expressions help you conduct a search for words in context.

Regular expressions are made up by combining normal characters with a number of special characters. The special characters and their use follow.*

.        Matches any single character except newline.

*        Matches any number (including 0) of the single character (including a character specified by a regular expression) that immediately precedes it. For example, because . (dot) means any character, .* means match any number of any character.

---

*\( and \), and \{*n,m*\} are not supported in all versions of vi. \<, \>, \u, \U, \l, and \L are supported only in vi/ex, and not in other programs using regular expressions.

**[...]**     Matches any one of the characters enclosed between the brackets. For example, [*AB*] matches either *A* or *B*. A range of consecutive characters can be specified by separating the first and last characters in the range with a hyphen. For example, [A-Z] will match any uppercase letter from *A* to *Z* and [0-9] will match any digit from *0* to *9*.

**\{*n,m*}\**     Matches a range of occurrences of the single character (including a character specified by a regular expression) that immediately precedes it. The *n* and *m* are integers between 0 and 256 that specify how many occurrences to match. \{*n*\} will match exactly *n* occurrences, \{*n*,\} will match at least *n* occurrences, and \{*n,m*\} will match any number of occurrences between *n* and *m*. For example, A\{2,3\} will match either *AA* (as in *AARDVARK* or *AAA* but will not match the single letter *A*).

**^**     Requires that the following regular expression be found at the beginning of the line.

**$**     Requires that the preceding regular expression be found at the end of the line.

**\\**     Treats the following special character as an ordinary character. For example, \. stands for a period and \* for an asterisk.

**\(**     Saves the pattern enclosed between \( and \) in a special holding space. Up to nine patterns can be saved in this way on a single line. They can be "replayed" in substitutions by the escape sequences \1 to \9.

**\n**     Matches the *n*th pattern previously saved by \( and \), where *n* is a number from 0 to 9 and previously saved patterns are counted from the left on the line.

**\< \>**     Matches characters at the beginning (\<) or at the end (\>) of a word. The expression \<ac would only match words that begin with *ac*, such as *action* but not *react*.

**&**     Prints the entire search pattern when used in a replacement string.

**\u**     Converts the first character of the replacement string to uppercase.

**\U**     Converts the replacement string to uppercase as in :/Unix/\U&/.

**\l**     Converts the first character of the replacement string to lowercase, as in :s/ Act/\l&/.

**\L**     Converts the replacement string to lowercase.

Unless you are already familiar with UNIX's wildcard characters, this list of special characters probably looks complex. A few examples should make things clearer. In the examples that follow, a square (□) is used to mark a blank space.

Let's follow how you might use some special characters in a replacement.  Suppose you have a long file and you want to substitute the word *balls* for the word *ball* throughout that file.  You first save the edited buffer with  `:w`, then try the global replacement:

```
:g/ball/s//balls/g
```

When you continue editing, you notice occurrences of words such as *ballsoon*, *globallsy*, and *ballss*.  Returning to the last saved buffer with  `:e!`, you now try specifying a space after *ball* to limit the search:

```
:g/ball□/s//balls□/g
```

But this command misses the occurrences *ball.*, *ball,*, *ball:*, and so on.

```
:g/\<ball\>/s//balls/g
```

By surrounding the search pattern with  `\<` and  `\>`, we specify that the pattern should only match entire words, with or without a subsequent punctuation mark.  Thus, it does not match the word *balls* if it already exists.

Because the  `\<` and  `\>` are only available in  `ex` (and thus  `vi`), you may have occasions to use a longer form:

```
:g/ball\([□,.;:!?]\)/s//balls\1/g
```

This searches for and replaces *ball* followed by either a space (indicated by  □) or any one of the punctuation characters  `,.;:!?`.  Additionally, the character that is matched is saved using  `\(` and  `\)` and restored on the right-hand side with  `\1`.  The syntax may seem complicated, but this command sequence can save you a lot of work in a similar replacement situation.

## Search for General Classes of Words

The special character  `&` is used in the replacement portion of a substitution command to represent the pattern that was matched.  It can be useful in searching for and changing similar but different words and phrases.

For instance, a manufacturer decides to make a minor change to the names of their computer models, necessitating a change in a marketing brochure.  The *HX5000* model has been renamed the *Series HX5000*, along with the *HX6000* and *HX8500* models.  Here's a way to do this using the  `&` character:

```
:g/HX[568][05]00/s//Series &/g
```

This changes *HX8500* to *Series HX8500*.  The  `&` character is useful when you want to replay the entire search pattern and add to it.  If you want to capture only part of the search pattern, you must use  `\(` and  `\)` and replay the saved pattern with  `\1 . . . \n`.)

For instance, the same computer manufacturer decides to drop the *HX* from the model numbers and place *Series* after that number.  We could make the change using the following command:

10. Delete all leading blanks on a line:

    `:g/^□□*\(.*\)/s//\1/g`

Search for one or more blanks at the beginning of a line; save the rest of the line and replace it without any leading blanks.

11. Delete all trailing blanks:

    `:g/□□*$/s///`

12. Remove manual numbering from section headings (e.g., *1.1 Introduction*) in a document:

    `:g/[1-9]\.[1-9]*\(.*\)/s//\1/g`

A hyphen-separated pair of letters or digits enclosed in square brackets (e.g, `[1-9]`) specifies a range of characters.

13. Change manually numbered section heads (e.g., *1.1, 1.2*) to a `troff` macro (e.g., `.Ah` for an *A-level heading*):

    `:g/^[1-9]\.[1-9]/s//\.Ah/`

14. Show macros in the output by protecting them from interpretation. Putting `\&` in front of a macro prevents `troff` from expanding them. This command was used frequently throughout this book to print an example that contained macros. Three backslashes are needed in the replacement pattern: two to print a backslash and one to have the first ampersand interpreted literally.

    `:g/^\./s//\\\&&/`

### • Writing and Quitting Files •

You have learned the `vi` command `ZZ` to quit and write (save) your file. But you will usually want to exit a file using `ex` commands, because these commands give you greater control.

`:w`  Writes (saves) the buffer to the file but does not exit. You can use `:w` throughout your editing session to protect your edits against system failure or a major editing error.

`:q`  Quits the file (and returns to the UNIX prompt).

`:wq`  Both writes and quits the file.

The `vi` editor protects existing files and your edits in the buffer. For example, if you want to write your buffer to an existing file, `vi` will give you a warning, because s would delete the original file. Likewise, if you have invoked `vi` on a file, made

`:g/\(Series\) HX\([568])[05]00\)/s//\2 \1/g`

This command replaces *Series HX8500* with *8500 Series*.

Suppose you have subroutine names beginning with the prefixes `mgi`, `mgr`, and `mga`.

```
mgibox routine
mgrbox routine
mgabox routine
```

If you want to save the prefixes, but want to change the name *box* to *square*, either of the following replacement commands will do the trick:

    `:g/mg([iar])box/s//mg\1square/`

The global replacement keeps track of whether an `i`, `a`, or `r` is saved, so that only *box* is changed to *square*. This has the same effect as the previous command:

    `:g/mg[iar]box/s/box/square/g`

The result is:

```
mgisquare routine
mgrsquare routine
mgasquare routine
```

### Block Move by Patterns

You can edit blocks of text delimited by patterns. For example, assume you have a 150 page reference manual. All references pages are organized in the same way: a paragraph with the heading *SYNTAX*, followed by *DESCRIPTION*, followed by *PARAMETERS*. A sample of one reference page follows:

```
.Rh 0 "Get status of named file" "STAT"
.Rh "SYNTAX"
.nf
integer*4 stat, retval
integer*4 status(11)
character*123 filename
...
retval = stat (filename, status)
.fi
.Rh "DESCRIPTION"
Writes the fields of a system data structure into the
status array.  These fields contain (among other
things) information about the file's location, access
privileges, owner, and time of last modification.
.Rh "PARAMETERS"
.IP "filename" 15n
```

```
A character string variable or constant containing
the UNIX pathname for the file whose status you want
to retrieve.  You can give the...
```

Suppose that you decide to move *DESCRIPTION* above the *SYNTAX* paragraph. With pattern matching, you can move blocks of text on all 150 pages with one command!

```
:g/SYNTAX/,/DESCRIPTION/-1,mo/PARAMETERS/-1
```

This command moves the block of text between the line containing the word *SYNTAX* and the line just before the word *DESCRIPTION* (/DESCRIPTION/-1) to the line just before *PARAMETERS*. In a case like this, one command literally saves hours of work.

This applies equally well to other ex commands. For example, if you wanted to delete all *DESCRIPTION* paragraphs in the reference chapter, you could enter:

```
:g/SYNTAX/,/DESCRIPTION/-1,d
```

This very powerful kind of change is implicit in the ex editor's line addressing syntax, but is not readily apparent. For this reason, whenever you are faced with a complex, repetitive editing task, take the time to analyze the problem and find out if you can apply pattern-matching tools to do the job.

## More Examples

Because the best way to learn pattern matching is by example, the following section gives a list of examples with brief explanations. Study the syntax carefully, so that you understand the principles at work. You should then be able to adapt them to your situation.

1. Delete all blank lines:

    ```
    :g/^$/d
    ```

    What you are matching is the beginning of the line followed by the end of the line, with nothing in between.

2. Put troff italic codes around the word *RETURN*:

    ```
    :g/RETURN/s//\\fIRETURN\\fR/g
    ```

    Notice that two backslashes (\\) are needed in the replacement, because the backslash in the troff italic code will be interpreted as a special character. (\fI alone would be interpreted as fI; it takes \\fI to get \fI.)

3. Modify a list of pathnames in a file:

    ```
    :g/\/usr\/tim/s//\/usr\/linda/g
    ```

    A slash (used as a delimiter in the global replacement sequence) must be escaped with a backslash when it is part of the pattern or replacement; use \/ to get /. Another way to achieve this same effect is to use a different

character as the pattern delimiter. For example, you could make the previous replacement as follows:

```
:g:/usr/tim:s::/usr/linda:g
```

4. Change all periods to semicolons in lines 1 to 10:

    ```
    :1,10g/\./s//;/g
    ```

    A period is a special character and must be escaped with a backslash.

5. Reverse the order of all hyphen-separated items in a list:

    ```
    :g/\(.*\)□-□\(.*\)/s//\2□-□\1/
    ```

    The effect of this command on several items is:

    ```
    more-display files becomes display files-more
    lp-print files becomes print files-lp
    ```

6. Standardize various uses of a word or heading:

    ```
    :g/^Example[□s:]/s//Examples:□/g
    ```

    Note that the brackets enclose three characters: a space (represented in the example by □), a colon, and the letter s. Therefore, this command searches for *Example□*, *Examples*, or *Example:* at the beginning of a line and replaces it with *Examples:*. (If you don't include the space, *Examples* would be replaced with *Exampless:*.)

    As another similar example, change all occurrences of the word *help* (o *Help*) to *HELP*:

    ```
    :g/[Hh]elp/s//HELP/g
    ```

7. Replace *one or more* spaces with a single space:

    ```
    :g/□□*/s//□/g
    ```

    Make sure you understand how the asterisk works as a special
    An asterisk following any character (or any regular expression t
    a single character, such as . or [a-z]) matches *zero or m*
    of that character. Therefore, you must specify *two* spaces f
    asterisk to match one or more spaces (one plus zero or more

8. Replace one or more spaces following a colon with two sp

    ```
    :g/:□□*/s//:□□/g
    ```

9. Replace one or more spaces following a period *or* a c

    ```
    :g/\([:.]\)□□*/s//\1□□/g
    ```

    Either of the two characters within brackets can b
    is saved, using parentheses, and restored on the
    that a special character such as a period does
    brackets.

edits, and want to quit *without* saving the edits, `vi` will give you an error message such as:

        No write since last change.

These warnings can prevent costly mistakes, but sometimes you want to proceed with the command anyway. An exclamation mark (!) after your command overrides this warning:

        :w! *filename*
        :q!

The `:q!` command is an essential editing command that allows you to quit without affecting the original file, regardless of any changes you made in the session. The contents of the buffer are discarded.

## Renaming the Buffer

You can also use `:w` to save the entire buffer (the copy of the file you are editing) under a new filename.

Suppose that you have a file `letter` that contains 600 lines. You call in a copy and make extensive edits. You want to quit and save *both* the old version of `letter` and your new edits for comparison. To rename your buffer `letter.new`, give the command:

        .wq letter.new

## Saving Part of a File

In an editing session, you will sometimes want to save just part of your file as a separate, new file. For example, you might have entered formatting codes and text that you want to use as a header for several files.

You can combine `ex` line addressing with the write command, `w`, to save part of a file. For example, if you are in the file `letter` and want to save part of `letter` as the file `newfile`, you could enter:

        :230,$w newfile

which saves from line 230 to the end of the file, or:

        :.,600w newfile

which saves from the current line to line 600 in `newfile`.

## Appending to a Saved File

You can use the UNIX redirect and append operator (>>) with `w` to append the contents of the buffer to an existing file. For example:

```
:1,10w newfile
:340,$w>>newfile
```

The existing file, `newfile`, will contain lines 1 through 10, and from line 340 to the end of the buffer.

## ▪ Reading In a File ▪

Sometimes you want to copy text or data already entered on the system into the file you are editing. In `vi`, you can read in the contents of another file with the `ex` command:

> :read *filename*

or:

> :r *filename*

This reads in the contents of *filename* on the line after the cursor position in the file.

Let's suppose that you are editing the file `letter`, and want to read in data from a file in another directory called `/work/alcuin/ch01`. Position the cursor just above the line where you want the new data inserted, and enter:

> :r /work/alcuin/ch01

The entire contents of `/work/alcuin/ch01` are read into `letter`, beginning below your cursor position.

## ▪ Executing UNIX Commands ▪

You can also display or read in the results of any UNIX command while you are editing in `vi`. An exclamation mark (`!`) tells `ex` to create a shell and regard what follows as a UNIX command.

> :!*command*

So, if you are editing and want to check the time or date without exiting `vi`, you can enter:

> :!date

The time and date will appear on your screen; press *RETURN* to continue editing at the same place in your file. If you want to give several UNIX commands in a row, without returning to `vi` in between, you can create a shell with the `ex` command:

> :sh

When you want to exit the shell and return to `vi`, press `^D`.

You can combine `:read` with a call to UNIX, to read the results of a UNIX command into your file. As a very simple example:

```
:r !date
```

This will read in the system's date information into the text of your file.

Suppose that you are editing a file, and want to read in four phone numbers from a file called `phone`, but in alphabetical order. The `phone` file is in the following order:

```
Willing, Sue  333-4444
Walsh, Linda  555-6666
Quercia, Valerie  777-8888
Dougherty, Nancy  999-0000
```

The command:

```
:r !sort phone
```

reads in the contents of `phone` after they have been passed through the `sort` filter:

```
Dougherty, Nancy  999-0000
Quercia, Valerie  777-8888
Walsh, Linda  555-6666
Willing, Sue  333-4444
```

Suppose that you are editing a file and want to insert text from another file in the directory, but you can't remember the new file's name.

You *could* perform this task the long way: exit your file, give the `ls` command, note the correct filename, reenter your file, and search for your place.

Or, you could do the task in fewer steps. The command `:!ls` will display a list of files in the directory. Note the correct filename. Press *RETURN* to continue editing.

```
file1
file2
letter
newfile
```

The command:

```
:r newfile
```

will read in the new file:

```
"newfile" 35 lines, 949 characters
```

## Filtering Text through a Command

You can also send a block of text as standard input to a UNIX command. The output from this command replaces the block of text in the buffer. Filtering text through a command can be done either from `ex` or `vi`. The main difference between the two methods is that the block of text is indicated with line addresses in `ex` and with text objects in `vi`.

The first example demonstrates how to do this with `ex`. Assume that instead of being contained in a separate file called `phone`, the list of names in the preceding example was already contained in the current file, on lines 96 to 99.

You simply type the addresses of the lines you want affected, followed by an exclamation mark and the UNIX command line to be executed. For example, the command:

```
:96,99!sort
```

will pass lines 96 to 99 through the `sort` filter, and replace those lines with the output of `sort`.

In `vi`, this sequence is invoked by typing an exclamation mark followed by any `vi` objects that indicate a block of text, and then the UNIX command line to be executed. For example:

```
!)command
```

will pass the next sentence through *command*.

There are some unusual features about how `vi` acts when you use this feature. First, the exclamation mark that you type is not echoed right away. When you type the symbol for the text object to be affected, the exclamation mark appears at the bottom of the screen, *but the symbol you type to reference the object does not.*

Second, only objects that refer to more than one line of text (G, { }, (), [ ]) can be used. A number may precede either the exclamation mark or the object to repeat the effect. Objects such as `w` do not not work unless enough of them are specified so as to exceed a single line. A slash (/) followed by a pattern and a *RETURN* can also be specified, taking the text up to the pattern as input to the command.

Third, there is a special object that is used only with this command syntax. The current line can be specified by entering a second exclamation mark:

```
!!command
```

Either the entire sequence or the text object can be preceded by a number to repeat the effect. For instance, to change the same lines as in the previous example, you could position the cursor on line 96, and enter:

```
4!!sort
```

or:

```
!4!sort
```

As another example, assume you have a portion of text in a file that you want to change from lowercase to uppercase letters. You could process that portion with the `tr` command. In these examples, the second sentence is the block of text that will be filtered to the command. An exclamation mark appears on the last line to prompt you for the UNIX command:

```
:g/\(Series\) HX\([568])[05]00\)/s//\2 \1/g
```

This command replaces *Series HX8500* with *8500 Series*.

Suppose you have subroutine names beginning with the prefixes `mgi`, `mgr`, and `mga`.

```
mgibox routine
mgrbox routine
mgabox routine
```

If you want to save the prefixes, but want to change the name *box* to *square*, either of the following replacement commands will do the trick:

```
:g/mg([iar])box/s//mg\1square/
```

The global replacement keeps track of whether an `i`, `a`, or `r` is saved, so that only *box* is changed to *square*. This has the same effect as the previous command:

```
:g/mg[iar]box/s/box/square/g
```

The result is:

```
mgisquare routine
mgrsquare routine
mgasquare routine
```

## Block Move by Patterns

You can edit blocks of text delimited by patterns. For example, assume you have a 150 page reference manual. All references pages are organized in the same way: a paragraph with the heading *SYNTAX*, followed by *DESCRIPTION*, followed by *PARAMETERS*. A sample of one reference page follows:

```
.Rh 0 "Get status of named file" "STAT"
.Rh "SYNTAX"
.nf
integer*4 stat, retval
integer*4 status(11)
character*123 filename
...
retval = stat (filename, status)
.fi
.Rh "DESCRIPTION"
Writes the fields of a system data structure into the
status array.  These fields contain (among other
things) information about the file's location, access
privileges, owner, and time of last modification.
.Rh "PARAMETERS"
.IP "filename" 15n
```

```
A character string variable or constant containing
the UNIX pathname for the file whose status you want
to retrieve.  You can give the...
```

Suppose that you decide to move *DESCRIPTION* above the *SYNTAX* paragraph. With pattern matching, you can move blocks of text on all 150 pages with one command!

```
:g/SYNTAX/,/DESCRIPTION/-1,mo/PARAMETERS/-1
```

This command moves the block of text between the line containing the word *SYNTAX* and the line just before the word *DESCRIPTION* (/DESCRIPTION/-1) to the line just before *PARAMETERS*.  In a case like this, one command literally saves hours of work.

This applies equally well to other  ex commands.  For example, if you wanted to delete all *DESCRIPTION* paragraphs in the reference chapter, you could enter:

```
:g/SYNTAX/,/DESCRIPTION/-1,d
```

This very powerful kind of change is implicit in the  ex editor's line addressing syntax, but is not readily apparent.  For this reason, whenever you are faced with a complex, repetitive editing task, take the time to analyze the problem and find out if you can apply pattern-matching tools to do the job.

## More Examples

Because the best way to learn pattern matching is by example, the following section gives a list of examples with brief explanations.  Study the syntax carefully, so that you understand the principles at work.  You should then be able to adapt them to your situation.

1.   Delete all blank lines:

```
:g/^$/d
```

What you are matching is the beginning of the line followed by the end of the line, with nothing in between.

2.   Put  troff italic codes around the word *RETURN*:

```
:g/RETURN/s//\\fIRETURN\\fR/g
```

Notice that two backslashes (\\) are needed in the replacement, because the backslash in the  troff italic code will be interpreted as a special character. (\fI alone would be interpreted as  fI; it takes  \\fI to get \fI.)

3.   Modify a list of pathnames in a file:

```
:g/\/usr\/tim/s//\/usr\/linda/g
```

A slash (used as a delimiter in the global replacement sequence) must be escaped with a backslash when it is part of the pattern or replacement; use \/ to get /.  Another way to achieve this same effect is to use a different character as the pattern delimiter. For example, you could make the previous replacement as follows:

```
:g:/usr/tim:s::/usr/linda:g
```

4. Change all periods to semicolons in lines 1 to 10:

```
:1,10g/\./s//;/g
```

A period is a special character and must be escaped with a backslash.

5. Reverse the order of all hyphen-separated items in a list:

```
:g/\(.*\)□-□\(.*\)/s//\2□-□\1/
```

The effect of this command on several items is:

```
more-display files becomes display files-more
lp-print files becomes print files-lp
```

6. Standardize various uses of a word or heading:

```
:g/^Example[□s:]/s//Examples:□/g
```

Note that the brackets enclose three characters: a space (represented in the example by □), a colon, and the letter s. Therefore, this command searches for *Example□*, *Examples*, or *Example:* at the beginning of a line and replaces it with *Examples:*. (If you don't include the space, *Examples* would be replaced with *Exampless:*.)

As another similar example, change all occurrences of the word *help* (or *Help*) to *HELP*:

```
:g/[Hh]elp/s//HELP/g
```

7. Replace *one or more* spaces with a single space:

```
:g/□□*/s//□/g
```

Make sure you understand how the asterisk works as a special character. An asterisk following any character (or any regular expression that matches a single character, such as . or [a-z]) matches *zero or more* instances of that character. Therefore, you must specify *two* spaces followed by an asterisk to match one or more spaces (one plus zero or more).

8. Replace one or more spaces following a colon with two spaces:

```
:g/:□□*/s//:□□/g
```

9. Replace one or more spaces following a period *or* a colon with two spaces:

```
:g/\([:.]\)□□*/s//\1□□/g
```

Either of the two characters within brackets can be matched. This character is saved, using parentheses, and restored on the right-hand side as 1. Note that a special character such as a period does not need to be escaped within brackets.

10.  Delete all leading blanks on a line:

    `:g/^□□*\(.*\)/s//\1/g`

Search for one or more blanks at the beginning of a line; save the rest of the line and replace it without any leading blanks.

11.  Delete all trailing blanks:

    `:g/□□*$/s///`

12.  Remove manual numbering from section headings (e.g., *1.1 Introduction*) in a document:

    `:g/[1-9]\.[1-9]*\(.*\)/s//\1/g`

A hyphen-separated pair of letters or digits enclosed in square brackets (e.g, `[1-9]`) specifies a range of characters.

13.  Change manually numbered section heads (e.g., *1.1, 1.2*) to a `troff` macro (e.g., `.Ah` for an *A-level heading*):

    `:g/^[1-9]\.[1-9]/s//\.Ah/`

14.  Show macros in the output by protecting them from interpretation. Putting `\&` in front of a macro prevents `troff` from expanding them. This command was used frequently throughout this book to print an example that contained macros. Three backslashes are needed in the replacement pattern: two to print a backslash and one to have the first ampersand interpreted literally.

    `:g/^\./s//\\\&&/`

## · Writing and Quitting Files ·

You have learned the `vi` command `ZZ` to quit and write (save) your file. But you will usually want to exit a file using `ex` commands, because these commands give you greater control.

`:w`    Writes (saves) the buffer to the file but does not exit. You can use `:w` throughout your editing session to protect your edits against system failure or a major editing error.

`:q`    Quits the file (and returns to the UNIX prompt).

`:wq`    Both writes and quits the file.

The `vi` editor protects existing files and your edits in the buffer. For example, if you want to write your buffer to an existing file, `vi` will give you a warning, because this would delete the original file. Likewise, if you have invoked `vi` on a file, made

```
of the product.
I confess to being
amazed by Alcuin.
Some people around
```
                        !)
                   ! appears on
                     last line
```
of the product.
I confess to being
amazed by Alcuin.
Some people around
!_
```

Enter the UNIX command and press *RETURN*.  The input is replaced by the output.

```
of the product.
I confess to being
amazed by Alcuin.
Some people around
```
                   Lr'[a-z]'
                    '[A-Z]'
                 input replaced
                   by output
```
of the product.
I CONFESS TO BEING
AMAZED BY ALCUIN.
Some people around
```

To repeat the previous command, the syntax is:

> ! *block* !

It is sometimes useful to send sections of a coded document to `nroff` to be replaced by formatted output.  However, remember that the "original" input is replaced by the output.

If there is a mistake, such as an error message being sent instead of the expected output, you can undo the command and restore the lines.

## ▪ Editing Multiple Files ▪

The `ex` commands enable you to edit multiple files.  The advantage to editing multiple files is speed.  When you are sharing the system with other users, it takes time to exit and reenter `vi` for each file you want to edit.  Staying in the same editing session and traveling between files is not only faster in access time:  you save abbreviations and command sequences you have defined and keep named buffers so that you can copy text from one file to another.

### Invoking `vi` on Multiple Files

When you first invoke `vi`, you can name more than one file to edit files sequentially, and then use `ex` commands to travel between the files.  The following:

```
$ vi file1 file2
```

invokes *file1* first. After you have finished editing the first file, the `ex` command `:w` writes (saves) *file1*, and `:n` calls in the next file (*file2*).

Suppose that you know you want to edit two files, `letter` and `note`. Open the two files by typing:

```
$ vi letter note
```

The message:

```
Two files to edit
```

appears on the screen. The first named file, `letter`, appears. Perform your edits to `letter`, and then save it with the `ex` command `:w`. Call in the next file, `note`, with the `ex` command `:n` and press *RETURN*. Perform any edits and use `:wq` to quit the editing session.

There is no practical limit to the number of files you can invoke `vi` on at one time. You can use any of the shell's pattern-matching characters, or even more complex constructions. Suppose you were writing a program, and wanted to change the name of a function call, for example, `getcursor`. The command:

```
$ vi `grep -l getcursor *`
```

would invoke `vi` on all of the files in the current directory containing the string `getcursor`. The command:

```
$ grep -l
```

prints the names of all files containing a string; using a command enclosed in backquotes (```) as an argument to another command causes the shell to use the *output* of the command in backquotes as the argument list for the first command.

The `vi` editor will print a message similar to:

```
5 files to edit
```

before displaying the first file.

If you try to quit without editing all of the files, `vi` will issue a warning message:

```
4 more files to edit
```

You must type `:q!` if you want to exit without editing all of the files.

## Calling In New Files

You don't have to call in multiple files at the beginning of your editing session. Any time in `vi`, you can switch to another file with the `ex` command `:e`. If you want to edit another file within `vi`, first save your current file (:w), then give the command:

```
:e filename
```

Suppose that you are editing the file `letter`, and want to edit the file `note` and then return to `letter`.

Save `letter` with `w` and press *RETURN*. The file `letter` is saved and remains on the screen. You can now switch to another file, because your edits are saved. Call in the file `letter` with `:e` and press *RETURN*.

The `vi` editor ''remembers'' two filenames at a time as the current and alternate filenames. These can be referred to by the symbols `%` (current filename) and `#` (alternate filename). The `#` symbol is particularly useful with `:e`, because it allows you to switch easily back and forth between files. In the example just given, you could return to the first file, `letter`, by typing the command `:e#`.

If you have not first saved the current file, `vi` will not allow you to switch files with `:e` or `:n` unless you tell it imperatively to do so by adding an exclamation mark after the command. For example, if after making some edits to `note`, you wanted to discard the edits and return to `letter`, you could type `:e!#`.

The command:

    e!

is also useful. It discards your edits and returns to the last saved version of the current file. The `%` symbol, by contrast, is useful mainly when writing out the contents of the buffer to a new file. For example, a few pages earlier we showed how to save a second version of the file `letter` with the command:

    :w letter.new

This could also have been typed:

    :w %.new

## Edits between Files

Named buffers provide one convenient way to move text from one file to another. Named buffers are not cleared when a new file is loaded into the `vi` buffer with the `:e` command. Thus, by yanking text in one file (into multiple named buffers if necessary), reading in a new file with `:e`, and putting the named buffer into the new file, material can be transferred selectively between files.

The following example illustrates transferring text from one file to another.

| | | |
|---|---|---|
| In our conversation<br>last Thursday, we<br>discussed a<br>documentation project<br>that would produce a<br>user's manual on the . . . | `"f6yy`<br>yank 6 lines<br>to buffer *f* | In our conversation<br>last Thursday, we<br>discussed a<br>documentation project<br>that would produce a<br>user's manual on the . . .<br><br>6 lines yanked |

Save the file with the `:w` command. Enter the file `note` with `:e`, and move the cursor to where the copied text will be placed.

```
┌─────────────────────────┐                ┌─────────────────────────┐
│ Dear Mr. Caslon,        │                │ Dear Mr. Caslon,        │
│ Thank you for . . .     │     "fp        │ In our conversation     │
│                         │ put yanked text│ last Thursday, we dis-  │
│                         │ below cursor   │ cussed a documentation  │
│                         │                │ project that would      │
│                         │                │ produce a user's        │
│                         │                │ manual on the . . .     │
│                         │                │ Thank you for . . .     │
└─────────────────────────┘                └─────────────────────────┘
```

### ▪ Word Abbreviation ▪

Often, you will type the same long phrases over and over in a file. You can define abbreviations that `vi` will automatically expand into the full text whenever you type the abbreviation in insert mode. To define an abbreviation, use the `ex` command:

> :ab *abbr phrase*

Where *abbr* is an abbreviation for the specified *phrase*. The sequence of characters that make up the abbreviation will be expanded in insert mode only if you type it as a full word; *abbr* will not be expanded within a word.

Suppose that in the file `letter` you want to enter text that contains a frequently recurring phrase, such as a difficult product or company name. The command:

> :ab IMRC International Materials Research Center

abbreviates *International Materials Research Center* to the initials IMRC.

Now when you type IMRC in insert mode:

> i the IMRC

IMRC expands to the full text:

> the International Materials Research Center

When you are choosing abbreviations, select combinations of characters that don't ordinarily occur while you are typing text.

### ▪ Saving Commands with map ▪

While you are editing, you may use a particular command sequence frequently, or you may occasionally use a very complex command sequence. To save keystrokes, or the time that it takes to remember the sequence, you can assign the sequence to an unused key.

The `map` command acts a lot like `ab` except that you define a macro for command mode instead of insert mode.

| | |
|---|---|
| :map x *sequence* | Define character x as a *sequence* of editing commands |
| :unmap x | Disable the *sequence* defined for x |
| :map | List the characters that are currently mapped |

Before you can start creating your own maps, you need to know the keys not used in command mode that are available for user-defined commands:

```
^A        g       K       ^K
^O        q       ^T      v
V         ^W      ^X      ^Z
*         \       _  (underscore)
```

Depending on your terminal, you may also be able to associate map sequences with special function keys. With maps, you can create simple or complex command sequences. As a simple example, you could define a command to reverse the order of words. In vi, with the cursor as shown:

```
you can the scroll page
```

the sequence to put *the* after *scroll* would be dwelp: delete word, dw; move to the end of next word, e; move one space to the right, 1; put the deleted word there, p. Saving this sequence:

```
:map v dwelp
```

enables you to reverse the order of two words anytime in the editing session with the single keystroke v.

Note that when defining a map, you cannot simply type certain keys, such as *RETURN*, *ESC*, *TAB*, *BACKSPACE*, and *DELETE*, as part of the map command. If you want to include one of these keys as part of the command sequence, preface that key with a ^V. The keystroke ^V appears in the map as the ^ character. Characters following the ^V also do not appear as you expect. For example, a carriage return appears as ^M, escape as ^[, tab as ^I, and so on.

You can undo the effect of any map sequence with the u command. Fortunately, the undo restores the file as it was before you executed the map sequence, treating the series of commands as though it were a single vi command.

Unless you use unmap to remove a mapped key, its special meaning is in effect for as long as your current session, even if you move between files. It can therefore be a convenient way of making the same edits in a number of files.

All the vi and ex commands can be used in map sequences, with the exception that the p or put command cannot be used to replace entire lines yanked in the same mapping. If you try to yank and then put back a deleted line within a map, you will get the error message:

```
Cannot put inside global macro.
```

If you want to move lines from one place to another within a mapping, you can usually get around this restriction using the ex editor's copy or co command.

## Complex Mapping Example

Assume that you have a glossary with entries like this:

```
map - an ex command that allows you to associate
a complex command sequence with a single key.
```

You would like to convert this glossary list to `nroff` format, so that it looks like this:

```
.IP "map" 10n
An ex command...
```

The best way to do this is to perform the edit on one of the entries and write down the sequence of commands. You want to:

1.   Insert the macro for an indented paragraph at the beginning of the line.

2.   Press *ESC* to terminate insert mode.

3.   Move to the end of the word and add the size of the indent.

4.   Press *RETURN* to insert a new line.

5.   Press *ESC* to terminate insert mode.

6.   Remove the hyphen and capitalize the next word.

That's quite an editing chore if you have to repeat it more than a few times! With `:map`, you can save the entire sequence so that it can be re-executed with a single key-stroke:

```
:map z I.IP "^[ea" 10n^M^[3x~
```

The sequence `^[` appears when you type `^V` followed by *ESC*. The sequence `^M` is shown when you type `^V` *RETURN*.

Now, simply typing `z` will perform the entire series of edits. On a slow terminal, you can actually see the edits happening individually. On a fast terminal, it will seem to happen by magic.

Don't be discouraged if your first attempt at key mapping fails. A small error in defining the map can give you very different results than you expect. Simply type `u` to undo the edit, and try again.

Remember, the best way to define a complex map is to do the edit once manually, writing down each keystroke that you must type.

## Mapping Keys for Insert Mode

Normally, maps apply only to command mode—after all, in insert mode, keys stand for themselves, and shouldn't be mapped as commands.

However, by adding an exclamation mark (!) to the `map` command, you can force it to override the ordinary meaning of a key and produce the map in insert mode. You may find this feature appropriate for tying character strings to special keys that you wouldn't otherwise use. It is especially useful with programmable function keys, as we'll see in a minute. Many terminals have programmable function keys. You can usually set up these keys to print whatever character or characters you want using a special setup mode on the terminal. But this will limit you to a particular terminal, and may limit the actions of programs that want to set up those function keys themselves.

The `ex` editor allows you to map function keys by number, using the syntax:

```
:map #1 commands
```

for function key number 1, and so on. (It can do this because the editor has access to the entry for that terminal found in either the `termcap` or `terminfo` database and knows the escape sequence normally output by the function key. )

As with other keys, maps apply by default to command mode, but by using the `map!` commands as well, you can define two separate values for a function key—one to use in command mode, the other in insert mode. For example, if you are a `troff` user, you might want to put font-switch codes on function keys. For example:

```
:map #1 i\f(CW^[
:map! #1 \fI
```

If you are in command mode, the first function key will enter insert mode, type in the three characters `\fI`, and return to command mode. If you are already in insert mode, the key will simply type the three-character `troff` code.

Note: If function keys have been redefined in the terminal's setup mode, the *#n* syntax might not work because the function keys no longer put out the expected control or escape sequence as described in the terminal database entry. You will need to examine the `termcap` entry (or `terminfo` source) for your terminal and check the definitions for the function keys. The terminal capabilties `k1`, `k2` through `k9`, `k0` describe the first ten function keys. The capabilities `l1` ,`l2` through `l9`, `l0` describe the remaining function keys. Using your terminal's setup mode, you can change the control or escape sequence output by the function key to correspond with the `termcap` or `terminfo` entry. (If the sequence contains `^M`, which is a carriage return, press `^M`, not the *RETURN* key.) For instance, to have function key 1 available for mapping, the terminal database entry for your terminal must have a definition of `k1`, such as `k1=^A@`. In turn, the definition `^A@` must be what is output when you press that key. To test what the function key puts out, press the key at the UNIX prompt, followed by a *RETURN* if necessary. The shell should display the sequence output by the function key after trying unsuccessfully to execute it as a command.

## @ Functions

Named buffers provide yet another way to create macros—complex command sequences that you can repeat with only a few keystrokes.

If you type a command line in your text (either a `vi` sequence or an `ex` command *preceded by a colon*), then yank or delete it into a named buffer, you can execute the contents of that buffer with the `@` command. It works in the same way as a `map` sequence, except that you enter the command line in the file instead of at the colon prompt; this is helpful if the command sequence is long and might need editing to work properly. Let's look at a simple but not very useful example of an `@` function. In your file, enter this key sequence:

```
cw\fIgadfly\fR^VESC
```

This will appear on your screen as:

```
cw\fIgadfly\fR^[
```

Then delete your command line into buffer *g* by typing `"gdd`. Now, whenever you place the cursor at the beginning of a word and type `@g`, that word in your text will be changed to *gadfly*. Because `@` is interpreted as a `vi` command, `.` will repeat the entire sequence, even if it is an `ex` command. The command `@@` repeats the last `@`, and `u` or `U` can be used to undo the effect of `@`. The `@` function is useful because you can create very specific commands. It is especially useful when you are making specific editing commands between files, because you can store the commands in named buffers and access them in any file you edit.

# 8

# Formatting with `tbl`

Some information is best presented in tabular format, that is, displayed in rows and columns. You can structure data in columns using tabs, but that can be difficult, especially if the table consists of long lines of text. The `tbl` preprocessor was designed to make it easier to prepare complicated tables, such as the following.

| Production of Audio Equipment (units: 1000 scts) | | |
|---|---|---|
| Product | 1984 | 1985 |
| General radio | 8,895 | 8,770 |
| Clock radio | 5,467 | 6,500 |
| Radio/cassette | 29,734 | 27,523 |
| Tape deck | 11,788 | 14,300 |
| Car radio | 9,450 | 10,398 |
| Car stereo | 15,670 | 17,456 |

With `tbl`, you can center, left justify, and right justify columns of data or align numeric data within a column. You can put headings that span one or more columns or rows, and draw horizontal and vertical lines to box individual entries or the whole table. An entry may contain equations or consist of several lines of text, as is usually the case with descriptive tables. A table can have as many as 35 columns and essentially an unlimited number of rows.

When you use `tbl`, you should have an idea or, better still, a written design of the table. Then, using a few `tbl` specifications, you can define how a formatted table should look. The data is entered row by row; each column is separated by ordinary tabs.

For example, the `tbl` description for the previous table looks like this:

```
.TS
center,box;
c s s
c s s
c c c
l r r.
Production of Audio Equipment
(units:1000 sets)
_
Product              1984           1985
_
General radio        8,895          8,770
Clock radio          5,467          6,500
Radio/cassette       29,734 27,523
Tape deck            11,788 14,300
Car radio            9,450          10,398
Car stereo           15,670 17,456
.TE
```

When `tbl` processes the specifications, it calculates all the values needed to produce the table and passes these values to `nroff` or `troff`, which formats or outputs the final table.

In this chapter, we will show you how to use `tbl` to specify the general appearance of a table. We begin with some very simple examples, then gradually work up to more complicated ones to show all of `tbl`'s capabilities.

## ▪ Using `tbl` ▪

The `tbl` description can be written in a file or as part of a larger file that contains other tables and text. You can format a table in a file using the `tbl` command as in the following:

```
$ tbl file | troff
$ tbl file | nroff
```

The `tbl` command writes its results to standard output. Because you will probably not be interested in the generated formatting requests, you would normally pipe the output to `nroff` or `troff` and then to a printer.

The `tbl` command also accepts a list of filenames as input and processes them one by one in the order in which they are named on the command line. If you don't give any filenames, `tbl` reads from standard input. The standard input may also be read in the middle of a list of files by typing a minus sign at the desired place.

If you're using a line printer that doesn't have fractional or reverse line motions, use the `−T` option of `nroff` and give the type of output device you're using. This is important when you're using `nroff` together with `tbl` to create boxed tables. For example, if you're using a regular line printer, the option should read `−Tlp`. You must also pipe the nroff output to a program called col, which filters the reverse linefeeds. The command line for a table with boxes would then read:

```
$ tbl file | nroff -Tlp | col
```

## tbl with eqn

When you have equations within your table and you use the eqn preprocessor to format them, invoke tbl before eqn. The tbl command usually executes faster because eqn normally produces a larger amount of output. To use eqn with tbl, use the following command line:

```
$ tbl file | eqn | troff
```

There is a possible complication that can occur with any of the preprocessors (tbl, eqn, or pic). If you read in subsidiary files with the .so request, those files will never be passed through the preprocessor, since the .so request has not been encountered yet by the preprocessor. Some UNIX systems support a program called soelim, which works just like cat, except that it reads in files called by .so requests. If any subsidiary files contain data that must be processed, start your command line with soelim:

```
$ soelim file | tbl | eqn ... | nroff
```

## ▪ Specifying Tables ▪

A table is always indicated by a .TS (*table start*) at the beginning of the table description and a .TE (*table end*) at the end. The general format of each table looks like this:

```
.TS
global options line;
format section.
data
.TE
```

These delimiters serve two functions. First, they signal to tbl the beginning and end of the table description. The tbl program processes the table, and enables formatting requests into the text of the table. The .TS and .TE lines remain after processing by tbl. This allows them to be used as macro calls by nroff and troff. Both ms and mm define these macros; however, an enterprising user can redefine them, and surround a table with consistent formatting effects. If the macros are undefined, tbl will not suffer in any way because the use of .TS/.TE as delimiters is separate from their secondary use as macros.

As you can see from the general format, tbl sees a table in terms of three distinct parts:

1.  The overall layout of the table described in the *global options line*. For example, this line describes whether the table is to be centered on the page or made as wide as the rest of the document. The global options line is optional.

2.  The layout of each column in the table described in the *format section*. For example, in this section, you specify whether a column is to be left or right justified. The format section is required and may contain one or more format lines.

3.  The actual text or numbers, *data*, to be entered in the table.

### ▪ A Simple Table Example ▪

Let's start with a simple table like the following to show the different parts of the `tbl` description:

```
1   User console
2   Monochromatic graphics terminal
3   Color graphics terminal
4   Line printer
5   Digitizer
6   Laser printer
7   Unallocated
```

You can lay out this table using the following `tbl` requests:

```
.TS                                 Table Start macro
tab (@);                            Options line
c l.                                Format line
1@User console
2@Monochromatic graphics terminal
3@Color graphics terminal
4@Line printer
5@Digitizer                         Table entries
6@Laser printer
7@Unallocated
.TE                                 Table End macro
```

Now let's see what these lines mean:

1.  The `.TS` at the beginning says that a table follows.

2.  The options line applies to the layout of the table as a whole. The option `tab(@)` means that you will be using the @ character as a tab character when you input data to the table. Normally, `tbl` expects the columns in

the table to be separated by actual tabs. But it is much easier to figure out whether you have the right number of columns if you use a visible character that is not part of the data. This is useful in debugging a table error when the formatted data doesn't appear in the proper columns. The options line *always* ends with a semicolon (;).

3.     The format section applies to the lines of data in the table. Each format line contains a *key letter* for each column of the table. The layout of the key letters resembles the layout of actual data in the table.

Each format line corresponds to a single line in the table. However, you can have fewer format lines than lines in the table. In this case, the *last* line of the description applies to all remaining lines of data. In our example, we have only one format line, so all lines in the table will follow this format. For example:

```
c l.
```

means that there are two columns in each line. The first column will be centered (c), and the second left justified (l). The format section ends with a period at the end of the last format line.

4.     The data itself. Each line of data corresponds to one line in the table. If you have very long input lines, they can be broken into smaller line segments. A backslash (\) at the end of a line segment means that it continues to the next line and is part of a longer input line. Each of the columns in our table is separated by an @ sign, which we are using in place of a tab character, as we have specified in the options line.

5.     A `.TE` signals the end of the table description.

## ▪ Laying Out a Table ▪

The global options line is an optional line that controls the overall appearance of the table. Normally, a table is positioned on the left-hand side of the page. Because the table is probably part of a larger document, you may want to center the table and enclose it in a box to make it stand out. Let's modify the options line in our example to produce this new layout:

```
.TS
center,box,tab(@);   New options line
c l.
1@User console
2@Monochromatic graphics terminal
3@Color graphics terminal
     etc.
```

When formatted, the table looks like this:

| | |
|---|---|
| 1 | User console |
| 2 | Monochromatic graphics terminal |
| 3 | Color graphics terminal |
| 4 | Line printer |
| 5 | Digitizer |
| 6 | Laser printer |
| 7 | Unallocated |
| 8 | Pen plotter |
| 9 | Raster plotter |
| 10, 11, 12 | Unallocated |

Now you know how to use three of the option names: `center`, `box`, and `tab()`. If you use one or more option names, they must be separated by spaces, tabs, or commas. The options line, if present, must *immediately follow* the `.TS` line. There are other options that you can use:

| | |
|---|---|
| `expand` | Make the table as wide as the current line length |
| `allbox` | Enclose each item in the table in a box |
| `doublebox` | Box the whole table with a double line |
| `linesize` *(n)* | Set lines (for `box`, `allbox`, and `doublebox`) in *n*-point type |
| `delim` *(xy)* | Set *x* and *y* as `eqn` delimiters. See Chapter 9 for information on the equation preprocessor `eqn`. |

The difference between a table that is centered or left justified and one that is expanded is the amount of space between columns. If you specify `center` or the default, the width between columns will be three ens. If you specify `expand`, `tbl` will expand the width of the overall columns until the table is as wide as the current margins.

If the overall width of the table calculated by `tbl` is greater than the width of the text, `nroff/troff` will ignore any positioning option you specify. The table will be printed as is necessary to fit everything, even if the table runs to the edge of the paper.

The `linesize` option changes the width of the lines used in enclosing tables to a given point size. Normally, the lines are 10 point. You can specify an absolute line size, such as `linesize (24)`, to print thicker box lines, or a relative size, such as `linesize (+14)`, to produce the same effect.

Let's try one more example by enclosing all the data entries in boxes. The options line for the table now reads:

```
center,allbox,tab(@);
```

The new table would look like this:

| 1 | User console |
|---|---|
| 2 | Monochromatic graphics terminal |
| 3 | Color graphics terminal |
| 4 | Line printer |
| 5 | Digitizer |
| 6 | Laser printer |
| 7 | Unallocated |
| 8 | Pen plotter |
| 9 | Raster plotter |
| 10, 11, 12 | Unallocated |

The `tbl` program isn't very good at keeping boxed tables on one page. If you have a long table, `tbl` may break it up at an awkward point (for example, placing the last line of a table on another page). To keep a boxed table together on one page, enclose it in a `.DS/.DE` macro pair (in either `ms` or `mm`). Alternatively, you can give `tbl` the latitude to split a table and print each section with its own table heading using the `.TS H` macro, as you will see later.

## ▪  **Describing Column Formats**   ▪

Each column in the table is described by a key letter in the format section. Key letters are separated from each other by spaces or tabs for readability. The basic set of key letters includes:

L or l           Left justify the data within a column.

R or r           Right justify the data within a column.

C or c           Center the data within a column.

S or s           Extend data in the previous column to this column (horizontal span).

N or n           Align numbers by their decimal points. If there are no decimal points, align them by the units digit.

A or a           Indent characters in the column from the standard left alignment by one em.

^           Extend entry from previous row down through this row (vertical span). Text will be centered between the specified rows.

T or t           Also vertical span, but text will appear at the top of the column instead of midway within the specified area.

If all columns of the table follow the same format, you need only one format line for the entire table. However, not all tables contain the same number of columns throughout. For example, you might have a table where the upper half consists of three columns, and the lower half contains only two.

The rule in writing format lines is to specify key letters for the largest number of columns in the table and carry that number for all format lines. That way, if you specify three columns, and you're using only two, you can use two consecutive tab characters (with nothing in between) to denote an empty field for the unused column. The longest format line defines the number of columns in the table.

Suppose you defined four columns in the first format line, and then defined only three columns in the succeeding lines. The tbl program will still format your table, but it assumes that the undefined column is left justified.

In the following sections, we will show some typical applications of these and other key letters to format table headings and columns of data.

## Tables with Headers

You can think of a table header as an extra row of data that may or may not have the same format as the actual data. If the format of the header is different, you must add another line at the beginning of your format section to describe the header.

For example, we'll change the first column in the previous table to have the header *Port* and the second to have the header *Device*, so that we get the following table.

| Port | Device |
|---|---|
| 1 | User console |
| 2 | Monochromatic graphics terminal |
| 3 | Color graphics terminal |
| 4 | Line printer |
| 5 | Digitizer |
| 6 | Laser printer |
| 7 | Unallocated |
| 8 | Pen plotter |
| 9 | Raster plotter |
| 10, 11, 12 | Unallocated |

The relevant lines that produced this table follow:

```
.TS
center, box, tab(@);
c c
c l.
Port@Device
.sp
1@User console
```

```
2@Monochromatic graphics terminal
```
        *etc.*

The first line of the format description (c  c) says that there are two columns of data, each one centered within each column. (Note that there is no period at the end of this line.)  Because this is the first line of the format description, it applies to the first line of our data, which happens to be the table heading. This means that the words *Port* and *Device* will be centered in each column. The second (and last) format line is the same as in the previous example and applies to the rest of the table. Note the period at the end of this line.

We used  `.sp` to produce a blank line after the table header. The  `tbl` command assumes that any non-numeric string preceded by a dot is a  `troff` or  `nroff` request and passes it unchanged to the formatter. Thus, you can vary spacing between rows, or use other  `nroff/troff` commands within a table.

## Tables with Spanned Headers

Our previous table now contains a header for each column. We now want to have an overall title or header that spans the width of the table. As before, you can think of the spanned header as an extra data line with its own format description.

We want the header to be only one column, centered across the whole table like the following.

| Output Device Configuration | |
|---|---|
| Port | Device |
| 1 | User console |
| 2 | Monochromatic graphics terminal |
| 3 | Color graphics terminal |
| 4 | Line printer |
| 5 | Digitizer |
| 6 | Laser printer |
| 7 | Unallocated |
| 8 | Pen plotter |
| 9 | Raster plotter |
| 10, 11, 12 | Unallocated |

Because we should keep the number of columns the same throughout the table, we use the *span* format option (s) to tell  `tbl` that the entry in a preceding column continues on to the other columns. The relevant portion of our table description contains the following lines:

```
.TS
center, box, tab (@);
c s
c c
c l.
```

```
Output Device Configuration
.sp .5v
Port@Device
.sp .5v
1@User console
       etc.
```

We now have three format lines: the first describes the main header, the second describes each column header, and the third applies to the rest of the data in the table.

## Numeric and Alphabetic Columns

You can align numeric data by the decimal point or the units digit using the key letter n in the format line. When you use n, numbers in a column will be aligned as follows:

$$
\begin{array}{r}
23.6 \\
155 \\
98.08.6 \\
5.26 \\
12798 \\
0.2365 \\
980.
\end{array}
$$

You should never enter non-numeric data in a column that is designated as n. On the other hand, you can enter numbers in columns that are aligned using any of the other key letters. The numbers will just be treated as if they were ordinary alphabetic characters. Thus, a column of numbers might also be centered, left justified, or right justified.

You should also avoid putting equations in numeric columns because tbl attempts to split numeric format items into two parts. To prevent this from happening, use the delim *(xy)* global option. For example, if the eqn delimiters are $$, a delim ($$) option causes a numeric column such as:

```
79.909 $+- .157$
```

to be divided after 79.909 and not after .157.

Columns designated as a are always slightly indented relative to left-justified columns. If necessary, tbl increases the column width to force this. Data in an a format is positioned so that the widest entry is centered within the column.

A note about n and a: when you have several command lines, do not use both n and a to format different rows in the same column. For example, the format lines:

```
r n r
r a r
```

are not allowed. This is because n and a share the same number register location in nroff/troff's memory.

The special nonprinting character string `\&` may be used to override the normal alignment of numeric or alphabetic data. For example, if you use `\&` before a digit, then the digit will line up with the decimal point and `\&` will not appear in the output. The effect of `\&` is as follows.

| Input Form | Output |
|---|---|
| 9.65 | 9.65 |
| 12.4.8 | 12.4.8 |
| 15.\&7.32 | 15.7.32 |
| 2\&0.9.19 | 20.9.19 |
| processor | processor |
| half | half |
| half\& | half |

## Vertically Spanned Columns

Let's see how the vertical span key (^) is used in a table like the following.

| Fuel | Substance | kcal/ gram mol. wt. |
|---|---|---|
| | Hydrogen | 68.4 |
| Gases | Methane | 211 |
| | Butane | 680 |
| | Ethane | 368 |
| | Benzene | 782 |
| Liquids | Ethyl alcohol | 328 |
| | Methyl alcohol | 171 |

The `tbl` description for this table is:

```
.TS
tab(@);
c c c
^ ^ c
l l n.
Fuel@Substance@kcal/
@@gram mol. wt.
.sp
Gases@Hydrogen@68.4
\^@Methane@211
\^@Butane@680
\^@Ethane@368
.sp
```

```
Liquids@Benzene@82
\^@Ethyl alcohol@328
\^@Methyl alcohol@171
.TE
```

There are three lines in the format section: the first two describe the column headings, and the last describes the format of the data.

We can imagine the first line of the header as consisting of the words *Fuel Substance kcal/* and the second line as *Fuel Substance gram mol. wt.* The words *Fuel Substance* don't actually appear twice, but are centered relative to the two lines that form the third column header. We use the caret key (^) in the second format line to tell tbl that these two column names vertically span their respective columns. Note the first two data lines that correspond to the first two format lines.

. We could have also used the same approach to describe the rest of the data, but this would mean writing seven more format lines, one for each of the lines of data. The table really has three columns with the same format throughout, so you can use just one format line to describe all of them. Then you can enter the characters \^ in place of a column entry to tell tbl that the entry in the previous row for that column vertically spans this row also.

You can use the ^ key letter in the format section and at the same time enter \^ in the data section as we did previously. You don't lose anything by doing this and tbl doesn't complain.

Another way of describing a vertically spanned column is by using the key letter t (or T) in the format line. Any corresponding vertically spanned item will begin at the top of its range. Thus, if we specify t instead of ^ in the format line, the words *Fuel and Substance* will be in line with *kcal/*.

## Drawing Lines in Tables

Horizontal rules are specified by underscores and by equal signs entered between the appropriate lines of data. An underscore on a line by itself entered between two rows of data produces a single rule running the whole width of the table. An equal sign on a line by itself produces a double rule.

If you want a horizontal rule to be only as wide as the contents of the column, enter an underscore or equal sign in that column as part of the data. The underscore or equal sign must be separated from the other columns by tabs or the tab character we've specified in the options line. To print these characters explicitly, they should be preceded by a \& or followed by a space before the usual tab or newline character.

You can also use these two characters in place of a key letter in the format line. If an adjacent column contains a horizontal or vertical line, the horizontal line is extended to meet nearby lines. If you enter any data in this column, the data will be ignored and you will get a warning message. The following table has a fairly complicated heading:

| 1984 (Jan.-July) | | |
|---|---|---|
| Items | Units | 1984/1983 (%) |
| TV | 3,889,543 | 145.7 |
| Color | 2,766,004 | 110.7 |
| B/W | 1,123,539 | 12.5 |

The `tbl` description for this table looks like this:

```
.TS
center,box,tab(@);
c s s
c c _
^ ^ | c
^ ^ | c
l r n.
1984 (Jan.-July)
Items@Units
@@1984/1983
@@(%)

TV@3,889,543@145.7
Color@2,766,004@110.7
B/W@1,123,539@12.5
.TE
```

As you can see from the preceding description, vertical lines are drawn by specifying bars *within the format lines*. A single vertical bar between two key letters draws a single vertical line between those two columns in the table. You can enter the bar after the first key letter or before the second key letter. A vertical bar to the left of the first key letter or to the right of the last one produces a vertical line at the edge of the table. Two vertical bars (| |) draw a double rule.

These characters are really more useful for drawing lines inside the table rather than for manually enclosing a table in a box because there are global options that automatically do this. To draw vertical and horizontal lines in our table "Fuels," we modify the relevant format and data lines as follows:

```
c  | |c  |c
^  | |^  |c
l  | |l  |n.
Fuel@Substance@kcal/
@@gram mol. wt.
=
Gases@Hydrogen@68.4
        etc.
```

```
Liquids@Benzene@782
```
*etc.*

This input produces the following table:

| Fuel | Substance | kcal/ gram mol. wt. |
|---|---|---|
| Gases | Hydrogen | 68.4 |
| | Methane | 211 |
| | Butane | 680 |
| | Ethane | 368 |
| Liquids | Benzene | 782 |
| | Ethyl alcohol | 328 |
| | Methyl alcohol | 171 |

## Changing Fonts and Sizes

The `tbl` program assumes that the table is always set in roman type. However, you can always change the typeface of all entries in a column to italic or boldface. You can add one of the following letters after the column key letter:

| | | | | |
|---|---|---|---|---|
| fb | fB | b | B | Boldface |
| fi | fI | i | I | Italic |
| fcw | fCW | cw | CW | Constant width |

If you want to change the font of only some of the entries, you should use explicit `nroff/troff` requests rather than specifying the font in the format line. For example, let's change the headers in the previous table to boldface and the words *Gases* and *Liquids* to italic. The format lines would look like this:

```
c  |  |cB  |cB
^  |  |^   |cB
l  |  |l   |n.
```

*Gases* will be written as `\fIGases\fR` and *Liquids* as `\fILiquids\fR`. The effect would be as follows:

| Fuel | Substance | kcal/<br>gram mol. wt. |
|------|-----------|------------------------|
| *Gases* | Hydrogen | 68.4 |
| | Methane | 211 |
| | Butane | 680 |
| | Ethane | 368 |
| *Liquids* | Benzene | 782 |
| | Ethyl alcohol | 328 |
| | Methyl alcohol | 171 |

The type size in which headings and data are printed is normally 10 points. You can also change the size of the type by using the key letter p and an absolute or relative point size. To specify a change in size relative to the existing point size, use a + or − before the value. For example, a column specification of cp12 or cp+2 will both result in a centered column using 12-point type.

## Changing the Column Width

When you're not using the expand option, the normal spacing between any two columns is three ens. You can change the spacing by specifying a numeric value between the key letters representing those columns. The number specifies the separation in ens. When you're using the expand option and you specify a column space, the number is multiplied by a constant such that the table is as wide as the current line length.

If you don't want any spaces between the columns, simply write 0, as in:

```
r0 l
```

which yields:

Hydrogen68.4<br>
Methane211<br>
Butane680

These spacings are only nominal spacings. The data may be so irregular in length that no two columns will actually appear to be separated by the specified distance. However, varying the amount of separation between two columns still leaves tbl free to make each column as wide or as narrow as is necessary.

You can specify a minimum width for any column by entering the letter w (or W) after the key letter, followed by the desired width in parentheses. You can use any unit of measurement recognized by nroff/troff when specifying a width dimension. You can also enter a value without a unit of measurement, in which case tbl assumes the value is in ens. Thus, the format:

```
rw(15)
```

specifies a column that is 15 ens wide with the text right justified within the column, and:

```
lw(2.25i)
```

specifies a left-justified column that is 2.25 inches wide.

You can also force `tbl` to make the width of particular columns equal by using the letter `e` (or `E`) after the key letter for those columns. This allows a group of regularly spaced columns.

To show that `tbl` can be used for any text that needs to be laid out in columns (as opposed to tables), we can print the following text:

| Signature | | |
| --- | --- | --- |
| August 31, 1987 | J. White | K. Kimura |

using this `tbl` description:

```
.TS
expand, tab(@);
c c c
cew(1.3i) ce ce.
Signature@@
\_@\_@\_
August 31,@J. White@K. Kimura
1987@@
.TE
```

In the last format line, we specified that all three columns be 1.3 inches wide. Because all columns will be of equal width, we need to specify the width only once.

## Other Key Letters

We already showed you some of the more widely used key letters. Additional features that can be used with the basic set of key letters are:

V or v
: Used with a number to indicate the vertical line spacing used within a table entry. Used only with text blocks (discussed in a later section).

U or u
: Move the corresponding entry up by one-half line to produce staggered columns. This doesn't work with the `allbox` global option.

Z or z    Ignore the data entry in calculating column width. This is useful in allowing headings to run across adjacent columns where spanned headings might be inappropriate.

Key letters for a column can be written in any order. They do not need to be separated, except when you specify both a point size (p) and a column separation number. Thus, a numeric column entered in bold 18-point type with a minimum column width of 1.5 inches and separated from the next column by 12 ens can be written as:

```
np18w(1.5i)B 12
```

Two or more format lines can also be written on one line by separating them with commas. For example, the format lines:

```
c c c
l l n.
```

can be written as:

```
c c c, l l n.
```

## ▪ Changing the Format within a Table ▪

All our examples so far have shown tables that consist of somewhat complicated headings followed by identical rows of data. Thus, we can keep the number of format lines comparatively small. This may not be the case when a table is divided into sections, each of which has its own heading. Let's look at the following table (from AT&T's *Documenter's Workbench Text Formatter's Reference*):

| Horizontal Local Motions | | |
|---|---|---|
| **Function** | **Effect in** | |
| | *troff* | *nroff* |
| \h'N'<br>\(space)<br>\0 | Move distance N<br>Unpaddable space-size space<br>Digit-size space | |
| \|<br>\^ | 1/6 em space<br>1/12 em space | ignored<br>ignored |

It has both a main header and column headers. The body of the table is divided into two parts. The upper part contains two columns, and the lower part contains three. To format each part correctly, we must enter a command line for each row of data so that `tbl` can keep track of which rows of the table have which format. This process is tedious and prone to error. Fortunately, `tbl` has a way around this.

To change the format of columns within a table, `tbl` has the table continue request `.T&`. We can change the format of a table at any time by entering `.T&` fol-

lowed by the new format line(s) and the additional data. The general format for the
`tbl` description is as follows:

```
.TS
option line;
format section.
data
.T&
new format section.
data
.T&
another new format section.
data
.TE
```

There are two things we cannot change after a `.T&` request: the global options line
and the number of columns specified. Our original options line holds for the entire
table.

Let's see how we can use the `.T&` request to produce the previous table:

```
.TS
center,box,linesize (6),tab(@);
cB s s.
Horizontal Local Motions
_
.T&
cI | cI s
cI | cI s
cI | cI | cI
c | l s.
Function@Effect in
\e^@_
\e^@troff@nroff
_
\eh'N'@Move distance N
\e(space)@Unpaddable space-size space
\e0@Digit-size space
_
.T&
c | l | l.
\e|@1/6 em space@ignored
\e^@1/12 em space@ignored
.TE
```

We take the largest number of columns in the table, which is three. We have two `.T&`
requests to break up the table into three parts with their own format sections. The first
part applies to the main header only. The second describes the column headers and the

three-column segment of the table. Finally, the lower part applies to the last part of the table.

Although you can have hundreds of lines in a table, `tbl` uses only the first 200 lines to set up the table. Any format changes you make after the 200th column will not be processed by `tbl`. In this case, you should break up the table into smaller table segments.

Should you specify `.TS H` but forget to follow it with `.TH`, some strange things will happen. One recent instance of this caused the table to be output in a nearly endless succession of pages. (In `troff` terms, a diversion created to capture the table heading filled up with the table instead; this caused the first page break that triggered the output of the diversion at the top of the next page; each time the diversion was output, it caused a new page break and the diversion was output again.)

## ▪ Putting Text Blocks in a Column ▪

Some tables consist of column entries that cannot be conveniently typed as a simple string between tabs. Descriptive tables, for example, require ordinary flowing text justified between the margins of the specific column in which it appears in the table. These sections of flowing text are called *text blocks*.

Each block of text is preceded by a `T{` and followed by a `T}`. The `T{` marker must be at the end of a line, and the `T}` must be at the start of a line:

```
...T{
Block of
text
T}...
```

When a text block is included in a row that contains other columns of data or text, the `T{` that marks the beginning of the text block must appear at the end of the line in the text. Even a single blank space following the `T{` will cause the table to fail. Likewise, the `T}` symbol must always begin the line:

```
... Data@T{
Block of
text
T}@data ...
```

This makes it easy for you to revise text when necessary and also allows you to insert any special `nroff/troff` commands before or after the text block.

Let's lay out the following table:

| Some Pattern-Matching Characters in *vi* | |
|---|---|
| *Special Characters* | *Usage* |
| . | Matches any single character except *newline*. |
| * | Matches any number (including zero) of the single character (including a character specified by a regular expression) that immediately precedes it. |
| [ . . . ] | Matches any *one* of the characters enclosed between the brackets. A range of consecutive characters can be specified by separating the first and last characters in the range with a hyphen. |
| $ | Requires that the preceding regular expression be found at the end of the line. |
| \{*n,m*\} | Matches a range of occurrences of the single character (including a character specified by a regular expression) that immediately precedes it. *n* and *m* are integers between 0 and 256 that specify how many occurrences to match. |

The `tbl` description of this table is:

```
.TS
box,tab(@);
cb s
cI| cI
cw(1.25i)| lw(3.25i).
Some Pattern-Matching Characters in \fIvi\fR
_
Special Characters@Usage
_
\fI.\fR@Matches any single character\
except \fInewline\fR.

*@T{
Matches any number (including zero) of the
single character (including
a character specified by a regular expression)
that immediately precedes it.
T}
```

```
[...]@T{
Matches any \fIone\fR of the characters enclosed
between the brackets.
A range of consecutive characters can be
specified by separating the
first and last characters in the range with a hyphen.
T}

$@T{
Requires that the preceding regular
expression be found at the end of the line.
T}

\{\fIn,m\fR\}@T{
Matches a range of occurrences of the
single character (including a
character specified by a regular expression)
that immediately precedes
it.  n and m are integers between
0 and 256 that specify how many occurrences to match.
T}
.TE
```

What might confuse you about this source text is that each block of text occupies two or more lines. Just think of everything that comes between a `T{` and a `T}` as a single entry that occupies a single column in that row. It is separated from its neighbors by tabs. If you keep track of the tabs, you will be able to sort out quite easily the sequence of columns.

In the previous description, we specified a minimum width for each column. If a width is not given, `tbl` uses the default:

$$L * C / (N+1)$$

where $L$ is the current line length, $C$ is the number of table columns spanned by the text, and $N$ is the total number of columns in the table. It is sometimes better to define a column width because `tbl` might make the table too narrow by default.

You can also use the `nroff/troff` commands `.na` and `.ad` to left justify text blocks if the output doesn't come out fully justified. The `tbl` description would be:

```
... T{
.na
Block of
text
.ad
T}
```

The `nroff` and `troff` formatters can accept only about twenty or thirty small text blocks in a table without exceeding certain internal limits. If the limits are exceeded, you will get error messages like "too many string/macro names" or "too many number registers."

In this case, you should divide the table into two or more independent tables, each with its own `.TS` and `.TE` requests. The final formatted sections can be "joined" and made to appear as one table by inserting minus `.sp` requests (such as `.sp -12p`) between the sections. This will cause the formatter to draw them together.

You can also change the vertical line spacing within a text block using a key letter followed by `v` (or `V`) and a number. The number may be a signed digit and is taken as an increase or decrease from the current vertical spacing.

### ▪ Breaking Up Long Tables ▪

If you have a very long table that will fill many pages, it might be helpful to break up the table into several smaller ones, with the main heading reproduced at the top of each page. Then the reader doesn't have to keep returning to the first page to see what the columns indicate. The `tbl` program also automatically breaks a boxed table if it runs over one page.

You can use the `.TS H` and `.TH` macros to reproduce the original heading at the top of each page of the table:

```
.TS H
options;
format section.
main header
.TH
data
.TE
```

The `.TH` (*table header*) macro is a feature of the `ms` macro package (not `tbl`). This macro can take the letter `N` as an argument; this causes the table header to be printed *only if it is the first table header on a page*. This is useful when you have to build a long table from smaller `.TS H`/`.TE` segments. For example:

```
.TS  H
```
*global options;*
*format section.*
*main header*
```
.TH
```
*data*
```
.TE
.TS  H
```
*global options;*
*format section.*
*main header*
```
.TH  N
```
*data*
```
.TE
```

This causes the table header to appear at the top of the first table segment. The header will not appear on top of the second segment when both segments appear on the same page. If the table continues to another page, the heading will still appear at the top of the new page. This feature is useful when breaking a long complex table into segments.

### ▪ **Putting Titles on Tables** ▪

The mm macro `.TB` can be used to automatically number and title a table. All tables with `.TB` are numbered consecutively. The title is centered above the table if it can fit on one line. If the title is longer than one line, all succeeding lines of the title are indented to line up with the first character of the title. The `.TB` macro is normally used inside a `.DS/.DE` pair.

The `.TB` macro is not part of `tbl`. Thus, it can be used to generate titles or headers for tables that are created using only tabs and none of the `tbl` commands. The general format of the `.TB` macro is:

    `.TB` [*title*] [*n*] [*flag*]

where *n* is used to override the normal numbering. The *flag* option can take one of the following values:

0    *n* is used as a prefix to the normal table number

1    *n* is used as a suffix to the normal table number

2    *n* replaces the normal table number

If you put the `.TB` macro before the `.TS` macro, the title is placed above the table. You can also put the title below the table by using the `.TB` macro after `.TE`.

For example, we can modify one of our tables by adding a title and labeling it as *Table 5*. We add the following lines before the `.TS`:

```
.DS
.TB "Horizontal Local Motions" "5" "2"
.sp
```

And we add a `.DE` after the `.TE`. The table now looks like this.

**Table 5.** Horizontal Local Motions

| Function | Effect in | |
|---|---|---|
| | troff | nroff |
| \h'N' | Move distance N | |
| \(space) | Unpaddable space-size space | |
| \0 | Digit-size space | |
| \| | 1/6 em space | ignored |
| \^ | 1/12 em space | ignored |

Another useful mm macro is the `.TC` macro. The `.TC` macro is placed at the end of the file. When the file is formatted, `.TC` collects the titles of tables that were generated using `.TB` for the table of contents. Thus, if we had used `.TB` to put headers in our examples, the table of contents might look like this:

## LIST OF TABLES

## ▪ A **tbl** Checklist ▪

Most table formatting errors come from specifying too few columns in the format section, forgetting a tab character between column entries in a table, or omitting one or more of the characters that `tbl` expects in a table description. After you've finished laying out a table, check that you have the following:

- a `.TS` with a `.TE`
- a `.TH` with a `.TS H`
- a semicolon at the end of the options line (if there is one)

- a period at the end of the last format line (including format sections with a `.T&`)

- in the format section, an item for each column and a format line for each line of the table

- a tab symbol for each column in each line of the table, except for the first column when horizontally spanning, and within text blocks

- for text blocks, a `T{` with every `T}`

- no extra blanks after:

    any `.TS`, `.TE`, `.TS H`, `.TH`, or `.T&`

    the end of the options and format lines

    any `T{` or `T}`

- no periods at the beginning of any "data" text lines (add a `\&` before the period, if necessary)

- a space after each table entry of `_` and `=` unless you want the lines to extend across the column

## ▪ Some Complex Tables ▪

Surely, the best way to learn more about `tbl` is to study tables of greater complexity than the ones we've look at so far. The `tbl` article by M.E. Lesk in the *UNIX Programmer's Manual* provides many fine examples of difficult tables. Look at the formatted tables and try to "break" the code that produced them. In this section, you'll find two complicated tables followed by the `tbl` input for you to decipher.

The weight table shown in Figure 8-1 is taken from a manual that describes the safe operation of mobile cranes. This table was coded by an associate, Daniel Gilly, over several hours. The code is listed in Figure 8-2. Look at how the vertical line indicator (|) is used between entries to draw a line at the end of each column. Note also the use of the alphabetic (a) format specification to produce indented text.

The financial table shown in Figure 8-3 is adapted from a prospectus prepared by `troff` users at a large New York law firm. The code for this table is listed in Figure 8-4. Note the use of a leader character (\a) in the first entry, coupled with a fixed width specification for the first column, to produce leaders that fill out the column. Also, notice how the table headings are printed in a smaller point size than the rest of the table, using the format specification (p8).

| WEIGHTS OF MATERIALS (Based On Volume) | | | |
|---|---|---|---|
| Material | Approx. Weight, Lbs. Per Cubic Foot | Material | Approx. Weight, Lbs. Per Cubic Foot |
| **METALS** | | **TIMBER, AIR-DRY** | |
| Aluminum | 165 | Cedar | 22 |
| Brass | 535 | Fir, Douglas, seasoned | 34 |
| Bronze | 500 | Fir, Douglas, unseasoned | 40 |
| Copper | 560 | Fir, Douglas, wet | 50 |
| Iron | 480 | Fir, Douglas, glue | |
| Lead | 710 | laminated | 34 |
| Steel | 490 | Hemlock | 30 |
| Tin | 460 | Pine | 30 |
| **MASONRY** | | Poplar | 30 |
| Ashlar masonry | 140-160 | Spruce | 28 |
| Brick masonry, soft | 110 | **LIQUIDS** | |
| Brick masonry, com- | | Alcohol, pure | 49 |
| mon (about 3 tons | | Gasoline | 42 |
| per thousand) | 125 | Oil | 58 |
| Brick masonry, pressed | 140 | Water | 62 |
| Clay tile masonry, | | **EARTH** | |
| average | 60 | Earth, wet | 100 |
| Rubble masonry | 130-155 | Earth, dry (about 2050 | |
| Concrete, cinder, | | lbs. per cu. yd.) | 75 |
| haydite | 100-110 | Sand and gravel, wet | 120 |
| Concrete, slag | 130 | Sand and gravel, dry | 105 |
| Concrete, stone | 144 | River sand (about 3240 | |
| Concrete, stone, | | lbs. per cu. yd.) | 120 |
| reinforced (4050 lbs. | | **VARIOUS BUILDING** | |
| per cu. yd.) | 150 | **MATERIALS** | |
| **ICE AND SNOW** | | Cement, Portland, loose | 94 |
| Ice | 56 | Cement, Portland, set | 183 |
| Snow, dry, fresh fallen | 8 | Lime, gypsum, loose | 53-64 |
| Snow, dry, packed | 12-25 | Mortar, cement-lime, | |
| Snow, wet | 27-40 | set | 103 |
| **MISCELLANEOUS** | | Crushed rock (about | |
| Asphalt | 80 | 2565 lbs. per | |
| Tar | 75 | cu. yd.) | 90-110 |
| Glass | 160 | | |
| Paper | 60 | | |

*Fig. 8-1.* A Complex Table

```
.ps 8
.vs 10
.TS
center,box,tab(@);
cb s s s
c|c|c|c
^|c|^|c
^|c|^|c
^|c|^|c.
WEIGHTS OF MATERIALS (Based On Volume)
_
Material@Approx.@Material@Approx.
@Weight,@@Weight,
@Lbs. Per@@Lbs. Per
@Cubic Foot@@Cubic Foot
_
.sp .5
.T&
lb|c|lb|c.
METALS@@TIMBER, AIR-DRY@
.T&
a|c|a|c.
Aluminum@165@Cedar@\022
Brass@535@Fir, Douglas, seasoned@\034
Bronze@500@Fir, Douglas, unseasoned@\040
Copper@560@Fir, Douglas, wet@\050
Iron@480@Fir, Douglas, glue@
Lead@710@\0\0laminated@\034
Steel@490@Hemlock@\030
Tin@460@Pine@\030
.T&
lb|c|a|c.
MASONRY@@Poplar@\030
.T&
a|c|a|c.
Ashlar masonry@140-160@Spruce@\028
.T&
a|c|lb|c.
Brick masonry, soft@110@LIQUIDS@
.T&
a|c|a|c.
Brick masonry, com-@@Alcohol, pure@\049
\0\0mon (about 3 tons@@Gasoline@\042
\0\0per thousand)@125@Oil@\058
Brick masonry, pressed@140@Water@\062
.T&
a|c|lb|a.
Clay tile masonry,@@EARTH@
.T&
a|c|a|c.
\0\0average@\060@Earth, wet@100
Rubble masonry@130-155@Earth, dry (about 2050@
```

**Fig. 8-2.** Input for Figure 8-1

```
Concrete, cinder,@@\0\0lbs. per cu. yd.)@\075
\0\0haydite@100-110@Sand and gravel, wet@120
Concrete, slag@130@Sand and gravel, dry@105
Concrete, stone@144@River sand (about 3240@
Concrete, stone,@@\0\0lbs. per cu. yd.)@120
.T&
a|c|lb|c.
\0\0reinforced (4050 lbs.@@VARIOUS BUILDING@
\0\0per cu. yd.)@150@\0\0MATERIALS@
.T&
lb|c|a|c.
ICE AND SNOW@@Cement, Portland, loose@\094
.T&
a|c|a|c.
Ice@\056@Cement, Portland, set@183
Snow, dry, fresh fallen@\0\08@Lime, gypsum, loose@53-64
Snow, dry, packed@12-25@Mortar, cement-lime,@
Snow, wet@27-40@\0\0set@103
.T&
lb|c|a|c.
MISCELLANEOUS@@Crushed rock (about@
.T&
a|c|a|c.
Asphalt@\080@\0\02565 lbs. per@
Tar@\075@\0\0cu. yd.)@90-110
Glass@160@@
Paper@\060@@
.sp .5
.TE
```

*Fig. 8-2.* —(Cont'd)

| | Year Ending December 31 | | | |
|---|---|---|---|---|
| | 1986 | 1985 | 1984 | 1983 |
| | | (Dollars in millions) | | |
| Premiums............................................. | $ 10,922.7 | $ 10,330.7 | $ 9,252.4 | $ 9,071.8 |
| Investment income ............................. | 3,671.7 | 3,146.0 | 2,749.7 | 2,308.9 |
| Federal income taxes........................... | 24.4 | 91.6 | 71.9 | 20.8 |
| Operating income ................................ | 359.8 | 346.1 | 342.6 | 309.6 |
| Realized gains (losses)........................ | 15.4 | 27.0 | (30.2) | (15.2) |
| Net income ......................................... | 375.2 | 373.1 | 312.4 | 295.8 |
| Cash provided by operations ............... | 4,123.2 | 3,560.8 | 3,514.9 | 3,067.4 |
| Assets ................................................. | 41,645.8 | 34,434.7 | 32,876.6 | 27,987.6 |

*Fig. 8-3.* Financial Table

```
.TS
expand, tab(@);
lw(13P) cbp8 s s s
lw(13P) c s s s
lw(13P) cbp8 cbp8 cbp8 cbp8
lw(13P) cbp8 s s s
lw(13P) n n n n.
@Year Ending December 31
.sp .2v
@_
@1986@1985@1984@1983
@(Dollars in millions)
.sp .5v
Premiums\a@$\010,922.7@$\010,330.7@$\0\09,252.4@$\0\09,071.8
Investment income\a@3,671.7@3,146.0@2,749.7@2,308.9
Federal income taxes\a@24.4@91.6@71.9@20.8
Operating income\a@359.8@346.1@342.6@309.6
Realized gains (losses)\a@15.4@27.0@(30.2)@(15.2)
Net income\a@375.2@373.1@312.4@295.8
Cash provided by operations\a@4,123.2@3,560.8@3,514.9@3,067.4
Assets\a@41,645.8@34,434.7@32,876.6@27,987.6
.TE
```

*Fig. 8-4.* Input for Figure 8-3

# Typesetting Equations with eqn

Typesetting mathematical equations has always been a problem for users who have a limited knowledge of mathematics or typesetting. This is because mathematical expressions are often a mixture of standard text and special characters in different point sizes. For example, the equation:

$$\sum_{i=0}^{\infty} c^i = \lim_{m \to \infty} \sum_{i=0}^{m} c^i$$

requires three special characters ($\Sigma$, $\infty$, and $\to$) and roman and italic characters in two different sizes. Expressions also may require horizontal and vertical printing motions (as in subscripts and superscripts).

You could code this example using `troff` requests, but the syntax for describing the printing motions, sizes, and fonts are difficult to learn and difficult to type in correctly. UNIX has formatting tools specifically designed for documents containing mathematical symbols—the programs `eqn` and `neqn`. The `eqn` program is a preprocessor for `troff`; `neqn` is a preprocessor for `nroff`.

With `eqn` you can typeset both inline equations and equations that are set off from the body of the text like the example shown. It takes an English-like description of a mathematical equation and generates a `troff` script. You don't need to understand what you are typing.

The `eqn` preprocessor was designed to be easy to learn and even easier to use. This implies that normal mathematical conventions such as operator precedence and parentheses cannot be used. Nor does `eqn` assume that parentheses are always balanced, or that an expression is better written in another form. There are only a few rules, keywords, special symbols, and operators to remember. If something works in one situation, it should work everywhere.

This section shows you how to typeset mathematical equations using a set of special words that belong to the `eqn` vocabulary. With `eqn`, you can format the following quite easily:

- the Greek alphabet

- special symbols, such as summations ($\Sigma$), products ($\Pi$) integrals ($\int$), and square roots ($\sqrt{\phantom{x}}$)

- positional notation, such as subscripts and superscripts, fractions, matrices, and vertical piles

- diacritical marks

- sizes and fonts

- horizontal and vertical spacing

You can even define a string that appears repeatedly throughout the document so that you do not need to type it in each time it appears.

## · A Simple eqn Example ·

To best illustrate how eqn works and how easy it is to learn the syntax, let's take a simple example:

$$\frac{a_2}{b}$$

If you were to read this mathematical expression aloud to another person, you might say "a sub 2 over b." This is exactly how you would describe the expression to eqn. The word sub denotes a *sub*script; the word over denotes a fraction. You will see the other words that eqn treats as special (i.e., that belong to the eqn vocabulary) as we move along in this section.

When you use eqn, it assumes that you have a two-dimensional picture of how the equation should appear in the document. The key in writing the eqn decription is to familiarize yourself with the special words used by eqn in printing mathematical characters. Then, describe the equation as if you were reading it aloud to another person.

The eqn preprocessor takes care of the standard things that you would expect to happen automatically, such as printing superscripts and subscripts in an appropriately smaller size, and adjusting the length and size of fraction bars. Following mathematical convention, variables are made italic, parentheses, operators, and digits are made roman, and normal spacing is automatically adjusted to make the expression look better.

## · Using eqn ·

The eqn preprocessor is used not only for typesetting equations, but also for typesetting nontechnical documents. For example, many documents contain subscripted or superscripted words. Using eqn can be easier than formatting the subscript or superscript using troff commands.

To format a document with `eqn`, you would enter:

```
$ eqn /usr/pub/eqnchar files | troff [options]
```

You can then pipe the output to the desired printer. The file `/usr/pub/eqnchar` contains definitions of additional special characters that can be used by `eqn`. It is not essential that you use it, but you may get better results with certain equations if you do.

If you use `eqn` with the `tbl` preprocessor to print tables containing mathematical expressions, invoke `tbl` before `eqn` to mimimize the data passed through the pipe:

```
$ tbl /usr/pub/eqnchar file | eqn | troff
```

If you are using `nroff` instead of `troff`, you can get a reasonable approximation of `eqn` output by using `neqn`. However, printers used with `nroff` may be unable to print many of the special characters used in equations.

## ▪ Specifying Equations ▪

Mathematical documents contain both displayed equations and standard text mixed with mathematical expressions. The `eqn` preprocessor allows you to typeset both forms.

### Displayed Equations

For equations that appear outside the body of the text, mark the beginning of each equation with an `.EQ` and the end with an `.EN`. Note that these delimiters may or may not also be defined as macros. They are recognized by `eqn` as flags to begin and end processing.

If they are not defined as macros by the package you are using, you can define them yourself, or can simply supplement them with `troff` requests (such as `.ce` to center the equation) as desired.

If you are using the `ms` macro package, `.EQ` and `.EN` are defined as macros, and the equation is centered by default. Thus, if you type:

```
.EQ
C=Ax+By
.EN
```

the output will be:

$$C = Ax + By$$

In `ms`, you can also left justify the equation using `.EQ L` or indent it using `.EQ I`. You can further specify an arbitrary equation number or label that will be printed at the right margin. For example, the lines:

```
.EQ I (13a)
C=Ax+By
.EN
```

produce the following:

$$C=Ax+By \hspace{6cm} \text{(13a)}$$

The mathematical symbols +, −, =, and ( ) are typed in just as they appear in the equation.

If you're using the mm macro package, put the `.EQ`/`.EN` pair inside a `.DS`/`.DE` pair so that the format looks like this:

```
.DS
.EQ
equation
.EN
.DE
```

This automatically centers the displayed equation. You can also use a break producing request (such as `.br` or `.sp`) immediately following the `.DS` macro but before the `.EQ` macro to display the equation at the left margin of the text.

## Inline Expressions

If you are using ms or mm, `.EQ` and `.EN` imply a displayed equation and so cannot be used for short inline expressions. But eqn provides a shorthand notation for displaying this type of expression. You can define any two characters as delimiters to mark the beginning and end of an inline equation, and then type the expression right in the middle of the text. To do this, define the equation delimiters within an `.EQ` and an `.EN` at the beginning of your file.

For example, to set both delimiters to #, add the following lines:

```
.EQ
delim ##
.EN
```

If you're using mm, do not use the `.DS`/`.DE` pair to enclose a `.EQ`/`.EN` pair that only defines the delimiters for inline equations. If you do, extra blank lines will appear in the output.

Do *not* use braces ({ }), a circumflex (^), a tilde (~), or double quotation marks ('') as delimiters because these have a special meaning to eqn. Choose characters that you are unlikely to use within any equation in the document. After you have defined your delimiter, you can begin using it within a line of text as in the following example:

```
The possible prices of an ice cream cone in cents are
#y sub 1 = 75#, #y sub 2 = 85#, and #y sub 3 = 95#.
```

This produces the line:

Assume that the possible prices of an ice cream cone in cents are $y_1=76$, $y_2=85$, and $y_3=95$.

The eqn program leaves enough room before and after a line containing inline expressions with fractions or large characters so that they don't interfere with the surrounding lines.

To turn off the delimiters, use:

```
.EQ
delim off
.EN
```

Throughout this section, we will use the delimiters ## in our eqn examples. However, we will typically show the results as a displayed equation.

### ▪ Spaces in Equations ▪

You may have noticed in the previous example that the word sub is surrounded by blanks, and the subscript is separated from the = sign with a blank. Spaces and new lines are used to tell eqn that certain words belong to the eqn vocabulary and deserve special treatment. The spaces and new lines that you type in the input equation do *not* appear in the printed output.

For example, all of the following equations:

```
#C=Ax+By#
#C = Ax + By#
#C= A x +
     By#
```

produce the same output:

$$C = Ax + By$$

Note that the spaces and newlines were ignored by eqn.

You should use spaces as freely as possible to break up more complex equations and make your input more readable and easier to edit. Remember that any spaces or newlines you enter within an equation are *not* printed out. This is often a point of confusion for new users. If your equation doesn't turn out the way it should, chances are you missed typing in a space somewhere. A useful rule of thumb is: when in doubt, use a space.

### Printing Spaces in the Output

You may want to fine-tune the printed appearance of an equation by adding spaces between groups of terms. If you want to print spaces in the output, use a tilde (~) for each space. A circumflex (^) gives a space half the width of a tilde. For example:

```
#C~=~Ax~+~By#
```

yields:

$$C = Ax + By$$

and:

```
#C^=^Ax^+^By#
```

yields:

$$C = Ax + By$$

You can also use tabs to separate parts of an equation, but the tab stops must set by the troff .ta request. For example:

```
.ta 1i 1.5i 2i 2.5i
.EQ
x sub 1
+x sub 2
+s sub 1
=10
.EN
.EQ
-2x sub 1
+s sub 1
=42
.EN
```

yields:

$$x_1 \qquad\qquad +x_2 \qquad +s_1 \qquad =10$$
$$-2x_1 \qquad\qquad\qquad +s_1 \qquad =42$$

(Note that each equation must have its own pair of .EQ/.EN delimiters.) Another way of aligning equations uses the eqn words mark and lineup, as you will see later.

## Subscripts and Superscripts: A Common Use

Perhaps the most common application of eqn is in generating subscripts and superscripts within a line of text or a table. As you have seen in previous examples, subscripts are denoted by the word sub. Superscripts are designated by sup. For example:

```
#y sub 1 = x sup 2^+^1#
```

yields:

$$y_1 = x^2 + 1$$

There are two simple rules to remember in writing subscripts and superscripts:

1. Put at least one space or space delimiter (such as ^ or ~) before *and* after the words sup and sub.

2. Leave at least one space or space delimiter after the subscript or superscript.

Let's see the effect on the output when you omit necessary spaces. For example:

```
#y sub 1 =x sup2^+^1#
```

yields:

$$y_{1=x} \, sup \, 2 + 1$$

and:

```
#y sub 1 =x sup 2+^1#
```

yields:

$$y\,_{1=x}^{2+}\,1$$

If you don't leave a space after `sub` or `sup` (as in the first example), `eqn` will not recognize them as special words, and so will not produce a subscript or superscript. Also, if you don't leave a space after the subscript or superscript, `eqn` thinks that the character(s) following it are still part of the subscript or superscript. This is a very common mistake made by new users.

You can also write subscripted subscripts and superscripted superscripts. If a superscript and subscript both appear for the same item, `sub` should come before `sup`. Therefore:

```
#a sub k sup 2#
```

yields:

$$a_k^{\,2}$$

Reversing the order of the words:

```
#a sup 2 sub k#
```

yields:

$$a^{2_k}$$

Some equations also require you to type chemical symbols like:

$$2He_4$$

Because `sup` technically means a superscript on something, you must use a place-holder (a pair of double quotation marks) before the word `sup` and write this expression as:

```
#"" sup 2 He sub 4#
```

## ▪  Using Braces for Grouping  ▪

Normally, you would use a blank or a space delimiter to signal the end of a subscript or superscript. But if your subscript or superscript consists of two or more characters or words separated by blanks, or if you are writing nested subscripts or superscripts, this will not work. In this case, use braces to mark the beginning and end of your subscript or superscript.

For example, the line:

```
#r sub {i=5;t=10^years}#
```

yields:

$r_{i=5;t=10\,years}$

In contrast, this line without the braces:

```
#r sub i=5;t=10^years#
```

yields:

$r_{i=5;t=10}\,years$

In the first example, we used braces to force eqn to treat the string:

```
i=5;t=10 years
```

as a subscript. Use braces to make your intent perfectly clear whenever you are unsure of how eqn will treat the equation. You can also use braces within braces, as in the line:

```
#e sup {i sup {k+1}}#
```

which yields:

$e^{i^{k+1}}$

Make sure that a left brace always has a corresponding right brace.

If you have to print braces in your document, enclose them in double quotation marks like "{" and "}".

## ▪ Special Character Names ▪

In many mathematical equations, you use the Greek alphabet to define variables. To print Greek letters, spell them out in the case that you want. For example, delta produces δ, and DELTA gives Δ. Thus, you only need to spell out the character π, as in:

```
#pi r sup 2#
```

to print:

$\pi r^2$

Note that special names don't exist for all uppercase Greek letters, such as ALPHA or ETA, because they are identical to the equivalent English letters. See Table 9-1 for a list of Greek letters.

**TABLE 9-1. Names for Greek Letters**

| Name | Character | Name | Character |
|---|---|---|---|
| DELTA | Δ | iota | ι |
| GAMMA | Γ | kappa | κ |
| LAMBDA | Λ | lambda | λ |
| OMEGA | Ω | mu | μ |
| PHI | Φ | nu | ν |
| PI | Π | omega | ω |
| PSI | Ψ | omicron | o |
| SIGMA | Σ | phi | φ |
| THETA | Θ | pi | π |
| UPSILON | Υ | psi | ψ |
| XI | Ξ | rho | ρ |
| alpha | α | sigma | σ |
| beta | β | tau | τ |
| chi | χ | theta | θ |
| delta | δ | upsilon | υ |
| epsilon | ε | xi | ξ |
| eta | η | zeta | ζ |
| gamma | γ | | |

A common mistake is to forget to put a space around the Greek name. For example, typing:

```
#f(theta)#
```

yields:

$f(theta)$

and not:

$f(\theta)$

which is what we want. Because there are no spaces surrounding the word `theta`, eqn doesn't recognize it as a special word.

You can also use `troff` four-character names for characters, as in the description:

```
#c = a \(pl b#
```

which yields:

$c = a + b$

## · Special Symbols ·

The eqn program recognizes the sequences in Table 9-2 as belonging to the eqn vocabulary, and translates them to the appropriate symbols.

**TABLE 9-2. eqn Special Symbols**

| Sequence | Symbol | Sequence | Symbol |
|----------|--------|----------|--------|
| >= | ≥ | approx | ≈ |
| <= | ≤ | nothing | |
| == | ≡ | cdot | · |
| != | ≠ | times | × |
| +- | ± | del | ∇ |
| -> | → | grad | ∇ |
| w<- | ← | ... | ... |
| << | ≪ | ,..., | ,...., |
| >> | ≫ | sum | Σ |
| inf | ∞ | int | ∫ |
| partial | ∂ | prod | ∏ |
| half | ½ | union | ∪ |
| prime | ′ | inter | ∩ |

The following examples illustrate the use of these character sequences.

```
#C sub O prime
```

yields:

$C_O{}'$

and:

```
#0 <= a <= 1#
```

yields:

$0 \leq a \leq 1$

and:

```
#del y / del x#
```

yields:

$\nabla y / \nabla x$

and:

```
#partial x / partial t#
```

yields:

$\partial x / \partial t$

Digits, parentheses, brackets, punctuation marks, and the following mathematical words are converted into roman font instead of the italic font used for other text:

```
sin   cos   tan   sinh  cosh  tanh  arc
max   min   lim   log   ln    exp
Re    Im    and   if    for   det
```

### Summations, Integrals, Products, and Limits

Summations, integrals, products, and limits often require an upper and lower part around the symbol. The word `from` indicates the character sequence to be entered at the lower part; the word `to` indicates the upper part. These parts are both optional, but if they are used, they should appear in that order. For example, you would type:

```
#Expected~Value~=~sum from {i=1} to inf pi sub 1 X sub i#
```

to print the following expression:

$$Expected\ Value = \sum_{i=1}^{\infty} \pi_i X_i$$

Notice that we used braces around the `from` part although this was not neccessary because there were no imbedded blanks in the string `i=1`. But if the `from` and `to` parts contain any blanks to separate special words, you must use braces around them.

A `from` does not necessarily need an accompanying `to`, as you will see in the following example:

```
#lim from {m -> inf} sum from i=0 to m c sup i#
```

which yields:

$$\lim_{m \to \infty} \sum_{i=0}^{m} c^i$$

### Square Root Signs

To draw a square root sign, use the word `sqrt`. For example:

```
#sqrt {b sup 2 - 4ac}#
```

yields:

$$\sqrt{b^2-4ac}$$

Square roots of tall quantities appear too dark and heavy. Big square root quantities are better written to the power $1/2$, as in:

$$2C_O/D^{1/2}$$

Creating a cube root or a higher root sign requires a little imagination. You can think of a cube root sign, for example, as consisting of two parts: a superscript 3 (with nothing before it) and a square root sign. However, you can't type:

```
#sup 3 sqrt x#
```

because a `sup` is a superscript on something. You must use a pair of double quotation marks as a placeholder for `sup`. For example:

```
#"" sup 3 sqrt x#
```

yields:

$$\sqrt[3]{x}$$

## Enclosing Braces and Brackets

You can generate big brackets [], braces {}, parentheses (), and bars | around quantities by using the words `left` and `right`, followed by the desired character. For example:

```
#P~=~R~left [ 1^-^{1+i sup n } over i right ]#
```

yields:

$$P = R \left[ \frac{1 - 1 + i^n}{i} \right]$$

The resulting brackets (and any character you specify) are made big enough to enclose the quantity. (Braces are typically bigger than brackets and parentheses.) Note the spaces surrounding the words `left` and `right` and the character to be expanded.

Two other characters that you can use are the `floor` and `ceiling` characters shown in the following example:

```
#left floor a over b right floor !=
left ceiling x over y right ceiling#
```

which yields:

$$\left\lfloor \frac{a}{b} \right\rfloor \neq \left\lceil \frac{x}{y} \right\rceil$$

A `left` does not need a corresponding `right`. If the `right` part is omitted, use braces to enclose the quantity that you want the left bracket to cover. This is useful when you are making piles, as you will see in the next section.

You can also omit the `left` part, although technically you can't have a `right` without an accompanying `left`. To get around this, you must type:

```
#left "" expression right )#
```

The `left` `""` in this equation means a "left nothing."

## ▪ Other Positional Notation ▪

In addition to subscripts and superscripts, eqn lets you format expressions containing fractions, matrices, and vertical piles.

### Fractions

Making a fraction, such as one-third, is as simple as typing "1 over 3." For more complex fractions, eqn automatically positions the fraction bar and adjusts its length. Thus, the line:

```
#Income over Capital~=~Income over Sales~times~Sales
over Capital#
```

yields:

$$\frac{Income}{Capital} = \frac{Income}{Sales} \times \frac{Sales}{Capital}$$

When you have both a sup and an over in the same equation, eqn does sup before over. However, you can always use braces to tell eqn what part goes with what. For example, you would type:

```
#e sup {k over t}#
```

to yield:

$$e^{\frac{k}{t}}$$

You would *not* type:

```
#e sup k over t#
```

The latter form produces:

$$\frac{e^k}{t}$$

which is not what we want.

### Arrays and Matrices

To make an array or a matrix, use the word matrix , and the words lcol, ccol, and rcol to denote the position of the columns. For example:

```
.EQ
matrix {
  lcol {1 above 0}
  rcol {half above -1}
}
.EN
```

yields:

$$1 \quad \frac{1}{2}$$
$$0 \quad -1$$

This produces a matrix with the first column left justified and the second column right justified. Each item is separated from the item below it by the word `above`. You can also center the columns using `ccol`. You can adjust each column separately and use as many columns as you like. However, each column must have the *same* number of items in it as the other columns.

A matrix should be used when the items in the columns don't all have the same height (for example, when you have fractions mixed with whole numbers). This forces the items to line up because `matrix` looks at the entire structure before deciding what spacing to use.

## Vertical Piles

To make vertical piles or columns of items, use the word `pile` before the equation description and the keyword `above` to separate the items. You can also enclose the piles in big braces or big brackets. For example:

```
.EQ
P~=~left [
   pile { nu sub 1 above nu sub 2 above cdot
   above cdot above cdot above nu sub N }
right ]
.EN
```

yields:

$$P = \begin{bmatrix} v_1 \\ v_2 \\ \cdot \\ \cdot \\ \cdot \\ v_N \end{bmatrix}$$

The items are centered one above the other and separated by the word `above`. Braces enclose the entire pile list. The items in the pile can themselves contain piles.

You can left justify (`lpile`), right justify (`rpile`), or center (`cpile`) the elements of the pile. (A `cpile` is the same as a regular pile.) However, the vertical spacing you get using these three forms will be somewhat larger than the normal pile. For example:

```
.EQ
f sub X (x)^=^left {
   rpile { 0 above 2x above 0 }
   ~~lpile { x < 0 above 0 <= x <= 1 above x > 1}
.EN
```

yields:

$$f_X(x) = \begin{cases} 0 & x<0 \\ 2x & 0 \le x \le 1 \\ 0 & x>1 \end{cases}$$

Note that in this example, we have a left brace without a corresponding right brace.

## · Diacritical Marks ·

With eqn, writing diacritical marks on top of letters is straightforward. The words known by eqn follow, with examples of how they appear on top of the letter $x$:

```
bar       x̄
under     x
dot       ẋ
dotdot    ẍ
hat       x̂
tilde     x̃
vec       x⃗
dyad      x⃡
```

The following examples show how these keywords are used:

```
#cr e hat pes#
```

yields:

$cr\hat{e}pes$

and:

```
#Citr o dotdot en#
```

yields:

$Citr\ddot{o}en$

and:

```
#a vec + b vec#
```

yields:

$\vec{a}+\vec{b}$

and:

```
#X bar sub st#
```

yields:

$\bar{X}_{st}$

The eqn program positions the diacritical marks at the appropriate height. It also makes bar and under the right length to cover the entire item. Other marks are centered above the character(s).

Typing words with diacritical marks may seem confusing at first because you have to leave spaces around the letter and its corresponding mark. Just remember that eqn doesn't print the spaces you type in.

## ▪ Defining Terms ▪

In some documents, you type a string of characters often, either within the text or within several equations. If you notice a string that is frequently used, you can name it using a define statement within an .EQ and .EN. Then you can use the name within an expression instead of typing the whole string.

Suppose you notice that the string 2 sup i appears repeatedly in equations. You can avoid retyping by naming it 2i, for example, as in the following commands:

```
.EQ
define 2i '2 sup i'
.EN
```

You should enclose the string between single quotation marks or between any two characters that don't appear inside the definition. After you've defined a term, you can use it as a convenient shorthand in other equations, just as if it were one of eqn's special keywords.

A note about using definitions: although a definition can use a previous definition, do *not* define something in terms of itself. Thus:

```
.EQ
define 2i '2 sup i'
define 1/2i '1 over 2i'
.EN
```

is acceptable, but:

```
.EQ
define X 'X bar'
.EN
```

is not because X is defined in terms of itself. If you want to do this, protect the X in the definition with double quotation marks, as in:

```
.EQ
define X ' "X" bar '
.EN
```

You can also redefine eqn keywords. For example, you can make / mean over by typing:

```
.EQ
define / 'over'
.EN
```

## ▪ Quoted Text ▪

You have seen the use of double quotation marks as placeholders (in the `sup`, `sqrt`, and `define` examples) when `eqn` needs something grammatically but you don't want anything in the output. Quotation marks are also used to get braces and other `eqn` keywords printed in the output. For example:

```
#"{ size beta }"#
```

prints the words:

*{ size beta }*

instead of looking up the two words `size` and `beta` in the `eqn` vocabulary and converting them. (The word `size` is used to change the size of the characters from the 10-point default.)

Any string entirely within quotation marks is not subject to font changes and spacing adjustments normally done by `troff` or `nroff` on the equation. This provides for individual spacing and adjusting, if needed. Thus, the line:

```
#italic "cos(x)" + cos (x)#
```

yields:

*cos(x)* +cos(*x* )

To print a literal quotation mark, you must escape it with a backslash character in the form \".

## ▪ Fine-Tuning the Document ▪

Typesetting a technical document is not only a matter of getting the `eqn` vocabulary right so you can print the appropriate mathematical expressions. Although `eqn` tries to make some actions automatic and puts items in the proper places, some fine-tuning is occasionally needed. With `eqn`, you can line up equations, define font sizes and types, and vary horizontal and vertical spacing.

### Lining Up Equations

Earlier we showed you how to line up pieces of an equation using tabs. Another method of doing this is to use the commands `mark` and `lineup`. This is useful when you have to line up a series of equations at some horizontal position, often at an equal sign.

For example, you would type in:

```
.EQ
mu~mark =~lambda t
.EN
.EQ
lineup =~int from 0 to t lambda dz
.EN
```

to line up the two equations:

$$\mu = \lambda t$$

$$= \int_0^t \lambda dz$$

The word `mark` can appear *only once* at any place in an equation. Successive equations should also contain `lineup` only once. Thus, when you have a series of equations that require you to line up items in more than one position, like the following:

| $a_1 + a_2$ | $+ x_1 + x_2$ | $= 34$ |
| $2a_1$ | $+ 4a_2$ | $= 28$ |
| $3a_1$ | $+4x_2$ | $= 56$ |

it might be better to line up the pieces of the equation on the left-hand side using tabs, and those on the right-hand side using `mark` and `lineup`.

If at all possible, you should type in the longest expression first to serve as the marking point. If you type in shorter expressions first, `mark` will not have enough room to line up successive longer expressions.

## Changing Fonts and Sizes

In `eqn`, equations are automatically set in 10-point type, with standard mathematical conventions to write some characters as roman or italic. To change sizes and fonts, use the following keywords:

| | |
|---|---|
| `size` | Change to any of the following legal sizes: |
| | 12, 14, 16, 18, 20, 22, 24, 28, 36 |
| | You can also change the size by a relative amount, such as `size +2` to make a character 2 points bigger, or `size -2` to make it 2 points smaller. |
| `bold` | Change to bold. |
| `fat` | Widen the current font by overstriking. |

italic          Change to italic.

roman           Change to roman.

Like `sup` and `sub`, these keywords only apply to the character(s) immediately following them, and revert to the original size and font at the next space. To affect more complex or longer strings (such as a whole equation), use braces. Consider the following examples:

```
#bold qP#              qP
#roman alpha~beta#     α β
#fat half#             ½
#size +3 x =y#         x=y
#size 8 {A + B}#       A+B
```

If the entire paper is to be typeset in a nonstandard size or format, you can avoid redefining each and every character sequence by setting a global size (`gsize`) or font (`gfont`) that will affect the whole document. You can set this up at the top of your file (or wherever the font and size changes begin) within an `.EQ` and `.EN`.

For example, to change the fonts to roman and the size to 12, you could enter:

```
.EQ
gfont R
gsize 12
.EN
```

The rest of the equations in the document (up to another `gfont` or `gsize`) will be set in 12-point roman type. You can use any other `troff` font names in place of `R`.

## Horizontal and Vertical Motions

You have already learned how to obtain small extra horizontal spaces in the output using ~ and ^. To move terms at some arbitrary length backward or forward, use the commands `back` *n* and `fwd` *n*, where *n* denotes how far you want to move, in 1/100s of an em. (An em is about the width of the letter *m*).

You can also move items up or down using `up` *n* or `down` *n*, where *n* is the same unit of measure as described. These local horizontal and vertical motions affect only the character(s) next to the keyword. To move larger strings or whole expressions, enclose them in braces.

## ▪ Keywords and Precedence ▪

Braces are used to group items or change the precedence of operations if you are unsure of how `eqn` will treat multiple keywords in a single expression. If you don't use braces, `eqn` performs the operations in the following order:

```
dyad vec under bar tilde hat dot dotdot
fwd back down up
fat roman italic bold size
sub sup sqrt over
from to
```

All operations group to the right, except for the following, which group to the left:

```
over sqrt left right
```

## ▪ Problem Checklist ▪

The eqn program usually displays self-explanatory messages when it encounters a syntax error or any other formatting error. To check a document before printing, type:

$ **eqn** *files* **> /dev/null**

This discards the output but prints the error message. Some of the error messages you might encounter are:

```
eqn: syntax error between lines 14 and 42, file book
```

A syntax error (such as leaving out a brace, having one too many braces, having a sup with nothing before it, or using a wrong delimiter) has occurred between lines 14 and 42, approximately, in the file book. These line numbers are not accurate, so you have to look at nearby lines as well. If the following message is displayed:

```
word overflow
```

you have exceeded the limits of troff's internal buffer. If you print the equation as a displayed equation, this message will usually go away. If the message is line overflow, the only solution is to break up the equation across multiple lines, marking each with a separate .EQ and .EN. The eqn program does not warn about equations that are too long for one line. If the following message is displayed:

```
eqn: fatal error: Unexpected end of input at 2 sub a
```

you forgot to put a closing quotation mark after the string 2 sub a when you named it in the define statement.

It is also easy to leave out an ending delimiter in an equation. In this case, eqn thinks that successive character sequences (which may run to hundreds of lines) are still part of the inline expression. You may then get an overflow error or a garbled document. The checkeq program checks for misplaced or missing inline delimiters and similar problems.

For example, when run on a draft of this chapter, checkeq produced the following report:

```
$ checkeq sect1
sect1:
    New delims ##, line 6
    2 line ##, lines 618-619
```

```
2 line ##, lines 619-620
2 line ##, lines 620-621

            .

            .

            .

EQ in ##, line 689
EN in ##, line 691
13 line ##, lines 709-721

            .

            .

            .

2 line ##, lines 1300-1301
2 line ##, lines 1301-1302
Unfinished ##
```

This report (which ran to 66 lines) was telling us that somewhere before line 618 there was an unclosed inline equation using the delimeter #.  Sure enough, the following error was found:

```
B#f( theta )
```

Because there was only one delimiter,  eqn gets "out of phase" and all subsequent delimiters are misplaced.  After we fixed this one error,  checkeq printed the following "null" report:

```
$ checkeq sect1
sect1:
```

Because a simple problem like the one shown here can cause every subsequent equation in the file to be garbled, and can waste an entire formatting run, it makes sense to run checkeq before you format any files containing equations.

# 10

# Drawing Pictures

If you are one of those who can't draw a straight line, let alone a decent picture or graph, you probably replace pictures with verbal descriptions. Perhaps you know what it is like to describe a drawing to a person who knows how to draw. The `pic` preprocessor requires you to follow the process of using "words" to describe something pictorial.

The `pic` preprocessor has a dual purpose. The first is to provide a "natural language" method of describing simple pictures and graphs in your documents. The second is to offer a "programming language" for generating pictures and graphs with minimal user input. Learning `pic` is an iterative process: describe what you want and then look at what you get. We have included many examples that show both the description and the resulting picture or graph. Take the time to create variations of these descriptions, making modifications and improvements.

The `pic` preprocessor was designed to produce output on a typesetter, which makes `pic` expensive and difficult to learn. Fortunately, some graphics terminals and most laser printers can be set up to display or print `pic` drawings. Access to one or the other is essential if you are going to get enough practice to know how `pic` responds.

As a preprocessor, `pic` is a program that processes a specific portion of an input file before the whole document goes to the `troff` formatter. (The `nroff` formatter cannot produce `pic` output for terminals or line printers.) The preprocessors translate your description into low-level formatter requests for `troff`.

Just like with `tbl` and `eqn`, a pair of macros in the input file mark the beginning and end of input to be processed by `pic`. The delimiters for `pic` are:

```
.PS
pic description
.PE
```

When you format a document that contains `pic` descriptions, you must invoke the `pic` preprocessor as follows:

```
$ pic file | troff | device
```

### ▪ The pic Preprocessor ▪

Imagine that you have to describe over the telephone the following picture:

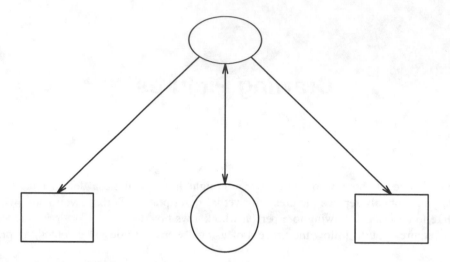

You might say: "There's an ellipse at the top. Arrows are connected to two boxes and a circle below it." Now, think about describing this picture to someone who is attempting to draw it. No matter how careful you are, you realize that it is difficult to translate a drawing into words.

> "First, draw an ellipse. Move down and draw a circle below it. Then draw one box to the left and draw another box of the same size to the right. Then draw an arrow from the bottom of the ellipse to the top of the left-hand box. Then draw a line from the bottom of the ellipse to the top of the right-hand box. The last thing to do is draw a line between the circle and the ellipse and put arrowheads on both ends."

Here's what the actual pic description looks like:

```
.PS
down
ellipse
move down 1.25
circle radius .35
move left 1i from left of last circle; box
move right 1i from right of last circle; box
arrow from lower left of last ellipse to top of 1st box
arrow from lower right of last ellipse to top of 2nd box
arrow <-> from bottom of last ellipse to top of last circle
.PE
```

Even though you may know nothing about pic, you should be able to make some sense out of this description. It names several objects: an ellipse, two boxes, a circle, and three arrows. It specifies motion in inches as well as changes in direction. It also arranges some objects in relation to others, locating the boxes to the left and right of the circle and drawing arrows between the ellipse and the circle.

Having seen a full description of a `pic` drawing in this example, you should be able to get something of the flavor of `pic`. The simpler the drawing, the less explaining you have to do. We won't go into any more detail about this `pic` description right now. We'll look at it later in this chapter after we've covered the basics of the `pic` language.

## Naming Objects

The `pic` program is easy to use if you are describing only a single box or a circle. To draw a circle, you name that object within the `.PS`/`.PE` macros:

```
.PS
circle
.PE
```

When this description is processed by `pic` it produces:

There are seven graphics primitives: `arc`, `arrow`, `box`, `circle`, `ellipse`, `line`, and `spline`. We will show these primitives in examples that present additional aspects of `pic`.

In using a computer language, you have to be precise, using as few words as possible to get the picture you want. This means that you allow the program to make as many of the decisions about the drawing as is practical. After you understand `pic`'s normal behavior, you will know what `pic` will do on its own.

For instance, we didn't specify the size of the circle in the last example. By default, `pic` draws a circle with a diameter of ½ inch (or a radius of .25 inch). You can get a circle of a different size, but you have to specify the size.

```
.PS
circle radius .5
.PE
```

The `pic` program understands any number to be in inches. You specify the size of a circle by giving its `radius`, which can be abbreviated as `rad`, or its `diameter`, which can be abbreviated as `diam`. The previous input produces a circle twice the size of the standard circle:

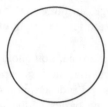

Similarly, if you specify `box`, you will get a box with a height of .5 inch and a width of .75 inch. You can get a larger or smaller box by changing its dimensions:

```
.PS
box height 1i width .5
.PE
```

The output for this example is a box twice as high as it is wide:

You can also use the abbreviations `ht` and `wid` for these attributes. The order in which you specify the dimensions does not matter, and you can change one attribute without changing the other. That is how we can draw a square:

```
.PS
box ht .75
.PE
```

The default width is already .75 inch, so this `pic` description produces:

With the attribute `same`, you can reuse the dimensions specified for a previous object of the same type. For instance, after you had described the square box, `box same` would duplicate a square of the same size.

## Labeling Objects

To provide a label for any object, specify the text within double quotation marks after the name of the object. The label is placed at the center of the object.

```
.PS
box ht .75 "Square One"
.PE
```

This `pic` description produces:

Square One

Even if a label does not contain blank spaces, you must enclose it within double quotation marks. Each individually quoted item will be output on a new line.

```
box wid .5 "Second" "Square"
```

This description produces:

Second
Square

Because `troff`, not `pic`, actually handles the text, `pic` doesn't really try to fit a label inside an object. You must determine the amount of text that will fit. The `pic` program ignores lines beginning with a period, permitting you to use `troff` requests to change the point size, font, or typeface. It is best to avoid spacing requests, and be sure to reset any change in point size.

When you specify a single text label with a `line`, `pic` centers it on the line. For instance, inline `troff` requests can be used to print a label in 14-point italic (i.e., 4 points larger than the current point size).

```
.PS
line "\fI\s14pic\s10\fR"
.PE
```

It produces:

~~pic~~

Because the standard placement of labels is not always useful, you can specify the attributes `above` or `below`. In the following example, the point size is specified using the following `.ps` request:

```
.ps +2
line "\fIPIC\fR" above
.ps -2
```

It produces:

<u>*PIC*</u>

If you supply two quoted arguments with line, the first will be printed above the line and the second printed below.

You can also select a line or box that is dotted or dashed, as you can see in the next example:

```
box dotted "\f(CWbox dotted\fP" above
```

Note the inline request to invoke the constant-width font for the label. The above keyword places the label above the center line of the box. This description produces:

The box, composed of dots, contains a label printed in constant-width font. It is obvious here that pic made no attempt to fit the label "inside" the box. The above attribute does not place text above the box, but rather above the center of the box. The description:

```
line dashed "sign here" below
```

produces a dashed line:

sign here

If the attributes of texture are followed by a value, pic will try to keep that amount of spacing between the dashes or dots. The description dashed .1 will result in dashes spaced .1 inch apart.

## pic's Drawing Motion

After you have named an object and determined its size, you have to think about where pic is going to draw it. (Indentation and other matters concerning the placement of the drawing on the page are supplied by either the .PS/.PE or .DS/.DE macros. The pic program places a single object at the left margin. If you name three objects in the same description, where will pic draw them?

```
.PS
circle "A"
line "1" "2"
box "B"
.PE
```

The following output is produced:

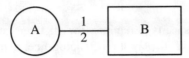

Objects are placed one after another from left to right. The `pic` program assumes that objects should be connected, as in the following example:

```
.PS
box ht 1.25
box ht 1
box ht .75
box ht .5
.PE
```

This description produces a row of boxes of decreasing size:

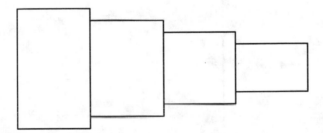

If you don't want objects to be connected, you can `move` before specifying the next object. In the next example, `move` places a `box` to the right of a `circle`:

```
.PS
circle "A" ; move; box "B"
.PE
```

As shown in this example, `pic` commands can be entered on the same line, separated by semicolons, instead of on separate lines. This description produces:

## Changing Direction

As you have seen, pic places objects in a continuous motion from left to right. You can also get pic to change direction using the attributes left, right, up, or down. We'll see examples of their use shortly.

The distance of a move is the same length as a line (.5 inch). If you want to change the distance of a move or the length of a line, then the change must be accompanied by an attribute of direction. Although it seems natural to write:

```
line 2; move 1; arrow 1    Wrong
```

pic does not accept this command unless you specify directions for all three cases. When pic objects to your choice of words, it will display the offending line, using a caret (^) to mark the error.

```
pic: syntax error near line 1, file test
  context is
        line 2 ^; move 1
```

Only the first error on the line is marked. (It is acceptable to write line; move, using the standard length and distance.) The next example shows how to draw a line of a specified length and how to move a specified distance. The pic program assumes that any value is in inches; thus you can say 2i or simply 2 to indicate 2 inches.

```
line up 2; move down 1; arrow right 1
```

Note that the attribute of direction precedes the distance. The preceding description produces:

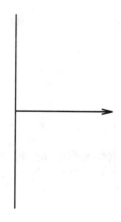

You cannot specify down 1 or right 1 without also specifying either a line or move. These attributes change the direction of the motion used to draw objects. They do not cause movement. The attributes of direction affect the position of the objects that follow it, as shown in the next example.

```
.PS
down; circle "A"; line; box "B"
.PE
```

These objects are drawn from top to bottom:

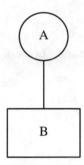

If you describe a change of motion, it affects the points where objects are connected. Look what happens if we specify the attribute down *after* the circle:

```
.PS
circle "A"; down; line; box "B"
.PE
```

Now the line begins at a different position:

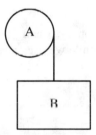

The pic program keeps track of the start and end points for each object, and their relationship to the direction in which objects are being drawn. The next object is drawn from the exit point of the previous object. Entry and exit points may seem obvious for a line, but not so obvious with circles. When the motion is from left to right, a circle's entry point is at 9 o'clock and its exit point is at 3 o'clock. When we specified down after the circle in the first example, the exit point of the circle did not change; only the direction in which the line was drawn from that point changed. Entry and exit points are reversed when the motion is from right to left, as specified by the left attribute.

```
       left; arrow; circle "A"; arrow; box "B"
```

This description produces:

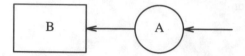

You can draw a diagonal line by applying two changes in direction. Look at how we describe a right triangle:

```
.PS
line down 1i
line right 1i
line up 1i left 1i
.PE
```

This description produces:

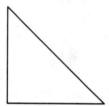

The diagonal line is drawn by combining two attributes of direction, `up` and `left`. You can describe a continuous line using `then`. In the next example we use `arrow` to demonstrate that we are describing a single object.

```
.PS
arrow down 1i then right 1i then up 1i left 1i
.PE
```

When using `then`, you have to define the motion on a single line or escape the end of the line with a backslash (\). It produces:

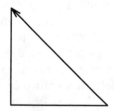

If the description ended with:

```
then up 1i then left 1i
```

we would have a 1-inch square instead of a right triangle.

    An `arc` is a portion of a circle. Naming four arcs consecutively will draw a circle. An arc is drawn counterclockwise from the current position (from 6 o'clock to 3 o'clock, for instance). The next example uses arcs to produce a box with rounded corners:

```
line right 1; arc; line up ; arc
line left 1; arc; line down; arc
```

This description starts with the bottom line of the curved box. The motion is counterclockwise.

The attribute `cw` draws an arc in a clockwise direction:

```
arc "A"; arc "B" cw
```

This description produces:

Note that text is placed at what `pic` considers to be the center of the arc, which is the center of the corresponding circle.

    A `spline` is a cross between an `arc` and a `line`. It is used to draw smoothed curves. In this example, a spline traces a path between two circles.

```
circle rad .25
spline right 1 then down .5 left 1 then right 1
circle same
```

This description produces:

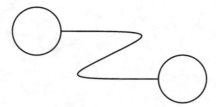

A `spline` is used in the same way as a `line`. When drawn continuously using `then`, a `spline` that changes direction draws a curve. (Similarly, a `line` would produce an angle.) We'll see more examples of `spline` later.

## Placing Objects

It isn't always useful to place objects in a continuous motion. Look at the following example, which seems like it ought to work but doesn't:

```
.PS
down; arrow; box
right; arrow; ellipse; arrow
.PE
```

This `pic` description produces:

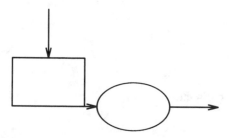

Note the short arrow, drawn from the box to the circle. What happened? The end point of the box was not on the right, but on the bottom, because the motion in effect where the box is drawn is `down`. Changing direction (`right`) affects only the direction in which the arrow is drawn; it does not change where the arrow begins. Thus, the arrow is drawn along the bottom line of the box.

Sometimes, it is best to place an object in relation to previously placed objects. The `pic` program provides a natural way to locate objects that have been drawn. For example, the attribute `first` locates the first occurrence of an object, and the attribute `from` specifies that the object serves as a starting point for the next object drawn.

```
.PS
circle ; move; circle ; arrow up from first circle
.PE
```

It produces:

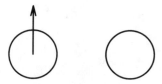

You can reference each type of object using an ordinal number. Referring to the order in which an object is drawn, you can say `first box` (`1st box` is also acceptable) or `2nd circle`. You can also work back from the last object, specifying the `last box` or `2nd last box`.

The center of each object is used as the reference point. In the last example, the arrow was drawn from the center of the circle. The attribute `chop` can be used to chop off the part of the line that would extend to the center of each circle. In the next example, a chopped line is drawn between the first and third circles:

```
.PS
circle "1" ; move down from last circle
circle "2"; move right from last circle; circle "3"
line from 1st circle to last circle chop
.PE
```

This description produces:

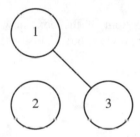

The amount that is chopped is by default equal to the radius of the circle. You can specify how much of the line is chopped, for use with other objects or text, by supplying either one or two values after the attribute. If a single value is given, then both ends of the line are chopped by that amount. If two values are given, the start of the line is chopped by the first amount and the end of the line chopped by the second amount.

It is important to remember that movement `from` a referenced object is measured from its center, unless otherwise specified. Look at these four circles:

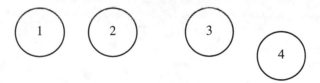

The second circle is produced by the description:

```
move right from last circle; circle "2"
```

Because the distance (.5 inch by default) is measured from the center of the circle, there is only .25 inch between the two circles. The third circle is produced by the description:

```
move right from right of last circle; circle "3"
```

Now the distance is measured from the right of the second circle. There is twice as much space between the second and third circle as between the first and second. The fourth circle is produced by the description:

```
move right from bottom of last circle; circle "4"
```

The starting point of the fourth circle (its left "side") is .5 inch right from the bottom of the previous circle.

Using bottom, top, right, and left, you can locate specific points on any object. In the next example, we solve the problem of turning a corner by specifying the place from which the arrow will be drawn:

```
.PS
down; arrow; box
right; arrow from right of last box; ellipse; arrow ; box
up; arrow from top of last box
.PE
```

In our earlier example, the arrow was drawn from the bottom of the box; now we change the starting point of the arrow to the right of the previous box. This description produces:

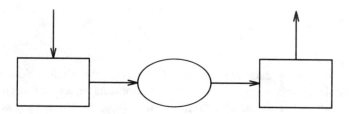

With boxes and ellipses, you can refer to an upper or lower position:

```
.PS
box; arrow from upper right of last box;
arrow down from lower left of last box
.PE
```

This description produces:

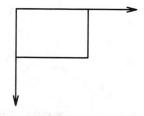

With objects like lines and arcs, it is more useful to refer to the start and end of the object. For example, here's another way to draw a triangle:

```
.PS
line down 1i
line right
line from start of 1st line to end of 2nd line
.PE
```

The last line could also be written:

```
line to start of 1st line
```

The pic description produces:

You now know enough of the basic features of pic to benefit from a second look at the pic description shown at the beginning of this chapter. The only thing we haven't covered is how to get a double-headed arrow. Because an arrow can also be specified as line -> or line <-, you can get a double-headed arrow with line <->.

```
.PS
1    down
2    ellipse
3    move down 1.25
4    circle radius .35
5    move left 1i from left of last circle; box
6    move right 1i from right of last circle; box
7    arrow from lower left of last ellipse to top of \
     1st box
8    arrow from lower right of last ellipse to top of \
     2nd box
9    line <-> from bottom of last ellipse to top of last \
     circle
.PE
```

The lines in this description are numbered for easy reference in the following exercise.

As is true with almost anything you describe, a pic description could be written in several different ways. In fact, you will learn a lot about pic by making even minor changes and checking the results. See if you can answer these questions:

- Why is `down` specified before the `ellipse`? If you removed `down`, would the circle be centered underneath the ellipse?

- `down` changes direction of movement. Does `pic` allow you to say `move 1.25` as well as `move down 1.25`?

- Where is the exit point of the `circle` when it is drawn with a downward motion in effect? If lines 5 and 6 were replaced by:

      move left 1i; box
      move right 2i; box

  where would the boxes be drawn?

- There is 1 inch between the circle and each box. How much space would there be if lines 5 and 6 were replaced by:

      move left from last circle; box
      move right from last circle; box

  Hint: The distance of a move is .5 inch, and this would be measured from the center of the circle, which has a radius of .35 inch.

- Line 8 draws an arrow from the lower right of the ellipse to the top of the right-hand box. If it were simplified to:

      arrow from last ellipse to 2nd box

  where would the beginning and ending of the arrow be?

- This drawing can present an interesting problem if the circle is omitted. How would you draw the two boxes if the circle was not there as a reference point?

Fortunately, there is a simple way to deal with the problem presented in the last question. Lacking a reference object, you can create an invisible one using the `invis` attribute. This lets you specify a circle that is not drawn but still holds a place that you can reference.

```
.PS
down
ellipse
move down 1.25
circle radius .35 invis
move left 1i from left of last circle; box
move right 1i from right of last circle; box
arrow from lower left of last ellipse to top of 1st box
arrow from lower right of last ellipse to top of 2nd box
.PE
```

This `pic` description produces:

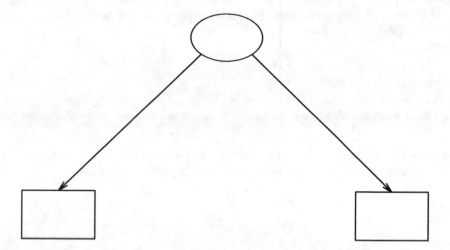

One thing that seems hard to get used to is that your current position always changes after an object is drawn, based on the motion in effect. This means you have to keep in mind the location of the starting point for the next object that you are going to draw.

You can use braces to enclose an object (or a series of objects or motions) so that the starting point is unchanged. In the last drawing, if the `invis` attribute didn't solve the problem so easily, we could have used braces to maintain a central point below the ellipse from which you can move to draw the boxes. Here's a different example that illustrates how braces can be used to control your position:

```
.PS
{arrow down}
{arrow up}
{arrow left}
arrow right
.PE
```

Each object, except the last, is enclosed in braces; all objects share the same starting point. This description produces:

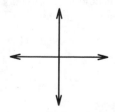

## Placing Text

Text can be placed in a drawing just like an object. You have to take care in placing text, as in the next example, where we specify a move so that the compass points are not drawn on top of the arrowheads:

```
.PS
{arrow down; move; "S" }
{arrow up; move; "N" }
{arrow left; move; "W" }
{arrow right; move; "E" }
.PE
```

Notice that the attributes of direction cause the object to be drawn in that direction and establish a new motion for successive objects. This description produces:

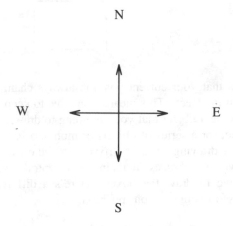

As mentioned, `pic` does not really handle text, allowing `troff` to do the work. In some ways, this is unfortunate. The thing to remember is that `pic` does not know where the text begins or ends. (You can use the attributes `ljust` or `rjust` to have the text left justified—the first character is positioned at that point—or right justified—the last character is at that point. These attributes can also be used with text labels.)

The `pic` program does not keep track of the start and the end of a text object. It only knows a single point which is the point where `troff` centers the text. In other words, a text item does not cause a change in position. Two consecutive quoted items of text (not used as labels to another object) will overwrite one another. Objects are drawn without regard to where the text item is, as shown in the next example:

```
"Start"; line;arrow;line; "Finish"
```

This description produces:

Start——————————→——————Finish

This example can be improved by right justifying the first text item (`"Start"` `rjust`) and left justifying the last text item (`"Finish"`  `ljust`). As you'll notice, though, the picture starts at the margin, and the label is forced out where it doesn't belong.

StartFinish

The location of the point that `pic` knows about is unchanged. Most of the time, you will have to use the `move` command before and after inserting text.

Because `pic` works better with objects than text, the `invis` attribute can be used to disguise the object behind the text, and give you a way to place text where you can point to it.

```
.PS
down
ellipse invis "DECISION?"
move down 1.25
circle rad .35 invis "Maybe"
move left 1i from left of last circle; box invis "Yes"
move right 1i from right of last circle; box invis "No"
arrow from lower left of last ellipse to top of 1st box
arrow from lower right of last ellipse to top of 2nd box
line <-> from bottom of last ellipse to top of last circle
.PE
```

This description produces:

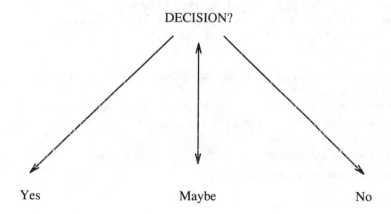

You may have recognized that the description for this drawing is basically the same one that produced the drawing at the beginning of this chapter. The `invis` attribute makes text labels, not objects, the subject of this picture. This should lead you to the idea that `pic` descriptions can be reused. Try to think of the form of a drawing separately from its content. Most drawings contain forms that can be reworked in the service of new material.

## Place and Position Notation

Can you locate the starting points of the arrows on this ellipse?

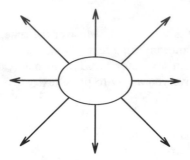

To write the description for this example is a test of patience and thoroughness, if nothing else. We start at the `upper left` of the ellipse and move clockwise around the ellipse.

```
.PS
ellipse
arrow up left from upper left of last ellipse
arrow up from top of last ellipse
arrow up right from upper right of last ellipse
arrow right from right of last ellipse
arrow right down from lower right of last ellipse
arrow down from bottom of last ellipse
arrow left down from lower left of last ellipse
arrow left from left of last ellipse
.PE
```

Although you can say `upper left` or `lower left`, you cannot say `top left` or `bottom right`.

Sometimes `pic`'s English-like input can get to be cumbersome. Fortunately, `pic` supports several different kinds of place and position notations that shorten descriptions.

You can reduce the phrase:

```
from bottom of last ellipse
```

to either of the following:

```
from .b of last ellipse
from last ellipse.b
```

You can use this notation for the primary points of any object. You can also refer to the compass points of an object, which provides a way to specify corners. Table 10-1 lists the placename notations.

**TABLE 10-1. `pic` Placename Notation**

| Value | Position |
|-------|-----------|
| t | Top |
| b | Bottom |
| l | Left |
| r | Right |
| n | North |
| e | East |
| w | West |
| s | South |
| nw | Northwest |
| sw | Southwest |
| ne | Northeast |
| se | Southeast |

Instead of writing:

```
from lower left of last ellipse
```

you might write:

```
from last ellipse.sw
```

Another simple way to shorten a description is to give an object its own name. The name must begin with an uppercase letter. If we assign the placename `Elp` to the ellipse:

```
Elp: ellipse
```

then we have either of the following ways to refer to specific points:

```
arrow up left from upper left of Elp
arrow up left from Elp.nw
```

Here's the condensed version of the description for the previous example:

```
.PS
Elp: ellipse
arrow up left from Elp.nw
arrow up from Elp.n
arrow up right from Elp.ne
arrow right from Elp.e
arrow right down from Elp.se
arrow down from Elp.s
arrow left down from Elp.sw
arrow left from Elp.w
.PE
```

At least it helps to keep you from confusing the placement of the arrow with the drawing motion.

If you want to specify a point that is not at one of the compass points, you can indicate a point somewhere in between two places. You can use the following kind of construction:

*fraction* of the way between *first.position* and *second.position*

or use the following notation:

*fraction* < *first.position, second.position* >

The following example shows both forms:

```
box
arrow down left from 1/2 of the way between last box.sw \
and last box.w
arrow down right from 1/2 < last box.se, last box.e >
```

Although you may not want to intermix different forms for the sake of someone reading the description, pic does allow it. The preceding description produces:

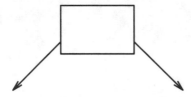

The at attribute can be used to position objects in a drawing.

```
box "A"; box with .se at last box.nw "B"
box with .sw at last box.ne "C"
```

This description produces:

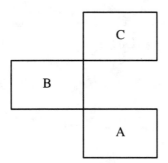

The next example illustrates again the problem of placing text. This time we want to position callouts above and below the text.

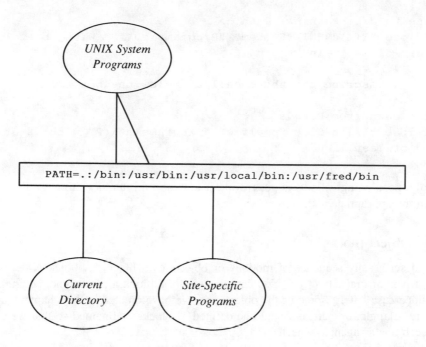

We position the text inside a long box. Because the callout lines will point to the box that surrounds the text rather than to the text itself, we try to specify approximately where to draw the lines.

```
.PS
        #       "#" introduces a comment
        #
        # Describe box; escape end of line to include
        # text on separate line
        #
Path: box ht .25 wid 4 \
"\f(CWPATH=.:/bin:/usr/bin:/usr/local/bin:/usr/fred/bin\fR"
        #
        # Describe line down from box and put top of ellipse
        # at end of last line; label will be printed
        # in 9-point italic.
        #
line down from 1/3 <Path.sw, Path.s>
ellipse "\fI\s9Current" "Directory\s0\fP" with .t at \
end of last line
        #
        # Describe two lines, one up from box
        # and a second down to the point right of it.
        #
line up from 1/2 <Path.nw, Path.n>
```

```
line to 2/3 <Path.nw, Path.n>
ellipse "\fI\s9UNIX System" "Programs\s0\fP" with .b at \
start of last line
     #
     # Describe the third callout below the box.
     #
line down from Path.s
ellipse "\fI\s9Site-Specific" "Programs\s0\fP" with .t at \
end of last line
.PE
```

Admittedly, positioning callouts is guesswork; it took several iterations to align the callouts with the appropriate text.

## Defining Object Blocks

You can describe any sequence of motions or objects as a block. A block is defined between a pair of brackets ([ ]). You can also give the block a placename, beginning with an uppercase letter. Some of the objects that we have created in this chapter, such as a square, triangle, or compass, could be defined as blocks and named so that we can refer to each one as a single object.

```
Rtriangle: [
     linewid = 1
     line down then right then up left
     ]
.ps 18
.ft I
"1" at Rtriangle.w
"2" at Rtriangle.s
"3" at Rtriangle
.ft R
.ps 10
```

This description produces:

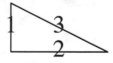

We are able to refer to the compass points of the block, although these points may not always be where you expect. The number 3 is printed at the center of Rtriangle according to pic. But in fact its position is the side opposite the right angle. The "center" of this block is at the center of a box that shares the bottom and left sides of the right triangle.

You can also refer to positions for a single block using brackets. The reference [ ].w is a position at the west end of the block.

In this example, instead of specifying individual line lengths, we redefined the variable linewid. This is the variable that pic accesses to determine how long a line should be. Shortly, we'll look at all the variables preset by pic. Generally, what you describe within a block remains local to the block. Thus, linewid would not affect other lines outside the block. Otherwise, resetting a variable has an effect not only on other objects in that drawing but also on other drawings in that file.

The best use of blocks in a drawing is to define significant portions so that you can position them accurately. Blocks usually relate to the content of a drawing. In the next example, we describe a two-dimensional box to represent a modem.

```
MOD: [
BOXA: box wid 1 ht .25 " \(bu    \(bu    \(bu    \(bu    \(bu "
line from BOXA.nw up 1 right .5 x
then right 1 then down 1 left .5 to BOXA.ne
line from BOXA.se up 1 right .5 then up .25
]
```

The block, named MOD, consists of a box followed by a series of lines. The box is given a name, BOXA. The special character sequence \(bu represents a bullet (interpreted by troff, not pic). This description produces:

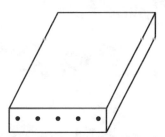

The next block, named WALL, describes a drawing of a telephone wall socket. It contains two objects, a box named BOXB and a circle inside the box named CIR.

```
WALL: [
BOXB: box wid .25 ht .5
CIR: circle at center of BOXB radius .05
]  with .s at MOD.ne + (.5,1)
```

To position this block in relation to MOD, we describe a position 1 inch up and .5 inch to the left of the top right-hand corner of MOD. Then we draw a spline from the modem to the wall socket. This introduces us to the fact that no matter how we specify an object, pic locates that object in a Cartesian coordinate system. We'll look at this in more detail in a later section. For now, it is sufficent to note how we change position by adding or subtracting from the position on the x-axis and y-axis. MOD.ne+(.5,1) adds .5 to the x-axis (moving to the right) and 1 to the y-axis (moving up) from the coordinates of MOD.ne.

```
spline from MOD.n up .25 right .5 then right 1 to center \
of WALL.CIR
```

Notice that we can refer to objects inside a block. If we had not named the circle, we could still refer to it as `WALL.circle`.

The last thing to do is to position the text:

```
move right 1 from WALL.e; " Telephone Line"
move down .5 from MOD.s "Modem"
```

This entire description produces the following drawing:

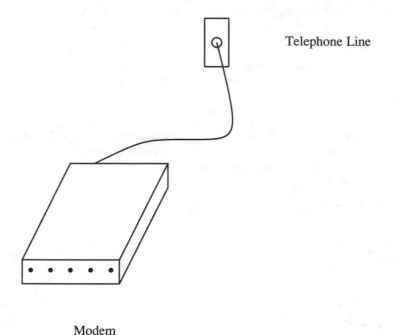

Telephone Line

Modem

## Resetting Standard Dimensions

The `pic` program has a number of built-in variables that define the values used to draw standard `pic` objects.

Refer to Table 10-2. You can redefine these variables anywhere in a `pic` description. A variable set inside one `pic` description will remain in effect for other descriptions within the same file. One exception is a variable defined within a block; that definition is local to the block.

**TABLE 10-2. `pic` System Variables**

| Variable | Default Value | Meaning |
|---|---|---|
| arcrad | .25 | Radius of arc |
| arrowwid | .05 | Width or thickness of arrowhead |
| arrowht | .1 | Height or length of arrowhead |
| boxwid | .75 | Width of box |
| boxht | .5 | Height of box |
| circlerad | .25 | Radius of circle |
| dashwid | .05 | Width of dash |
| ellipseht | .5 | Height of ellipse |
| linewid | .5 | Length of horizontal line |
| lineht | .5 | Length of vertical line |
| movewid | .5 | Distance of horizontal motion |
| moveht | .5 | Distance of vertical motion |
| scale | 1 | Scale dimensions |
| textwid | 0 | Width of area used for drawing |
| textht | 0 | Height of area used for drawing |

For instance, we can specify an oversize arrow by changing the following variables:

```
arrowwid = 1
arrowht = 1
linewid = 2
arrow
```

It produces the following `pic` drawing:

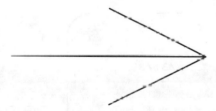

## Controlling the Dimensions of a Drawing

The `textwid` and `textht` variables control the width and height respectively, of the area used by `pic` on a page. (It doesn't refer to the amount of space occupied by an item of text .) These values can also be set as arguments to the `.PS` macro.

    .PS *width height*

When you specify the width or height or both, `pic` scales the drawing to that size regardless of the absolute dimensions that are specified within the drawing. The only thing it doesn't scale adequately is text. It can be easier to describe a drawing with simple units and have them scaled more precisely to fit on the page than to work with exact sizes.

A good example of scaling is turning the rounded box described previously in this chapter into a representation of a terminal screen.

```
.PS 2 4
line right 1; arc; line up ; arc
line left 1; arc; line down; arc
.PE
```

Although the `pic` description is made up of 1-inch lines, the actual screen produced by `pic` will be 4 inches wide and 2 inches high.

Normally, you want `troff` to output the regular lines of text on lines that follow the `pic` drawing. If the `.PF` (*F* for *flyback*) macro is used in place of `.PE`, `troff` will return to the position it held before the `pic` drawing was output. This feature is useful if we want to put formatted text within our large screen.

```
.PS 2 4
line right 1; arc; line up ; arc
line left 1; arc; line down; arc
.PE
.ft CW
.sp 2
Alcuin Development System        5/31/87
.sp
Please login:
.sp 6
```

This description produces:

```
Alcuin Development System        5/31/87

Please login:
```

You have to remember to provide the space after the text to push the current position past the end of the screen. Otherwise subsequent text will also appear within the box.

## Debugging `pic` Descriptions

You can invoke the `pic` preprocessor on its own to have it check through your file and report any syntax errors. This can save a lot of time, especially if your file contains other text that will be sent to `troff`, assuming that you wouldn't want the file processed unless the `pic` descriptions succeeded. If you have the file `circles`, for example, that contains a `pic` description, you can invoke `pic` as:

```
$ pic circles
```

If processing is successful, `pic` output will stream past on your terminal screen. If `pic` finds an error in your description, it will print the error message.

If you have several `pic` descriptions in a file, or you have regular text surrounding a `pic` description, you can send the output to `/dev/null`, and only the error messages will be displayed on your screen.

You may want to invoke `pic` on its own simply to look at the output `pic` produces. For a discussion of the output that `pic` sends to `troff`, read about line drawing in Chapter 14.

## ▪ From Describing to Programming Drawings ▪

As we look at more advanced examples of `pic`, you may begin to question the amount of description that is required to produce a drawing. You may be amazed that drawings that look so simple require so many words. After you realize that you are approaching the limits of what can be described using an English-like syntax, you may want to look at `pic` from another perspective. You can view `pic` as a programming language for generating graphics.

Looking at this other side of `pic`, you will find that the descriptions are perhaps more difficult to read but much easier to write. The purpose of a "programmed" `pic` description is not to imitate a verbal description, but to minimize user input, to provide structures that can be used to produce several kinds of drawings, and to make it easier to change a drawing.

The focus of the rest of this chapter will be to introduce many of these special features of `pic`, including variables, expressions, and macros. But there are more possibilities than we can attempt to describe. The `pic` program follows the general UNIX philosophy that any program should be able to accept input from any program and direct its output to another program, `troff`. Thus, `pic` descriptions can be built by other UNIX utilities. For instance, you might develop an `awk` program specifically designed for creating flow charts.

## Locating Objects Using Cartesian Coordinates

For more exact positioning of objects and text, pic uses a standard Cartesian coordinate system. The first object drawn, including a move, starts at position 0,0. The $x$ and $y$ position of a circle, an ellipse, or a box is at the center of the object. For lines, this position refers to the beginning. For arcs, this position is at the center point of the related circle. You can position objects using the at attribute:

```
circle "0,0" at 0,0
circle "1,1" at 1,1
circle "1,0" at 1,0
circle "2,1" at 2,1
```

This description produces:

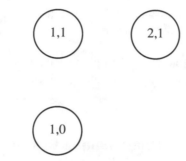

The center of the circle is placed at the specified coordinates. You could also write:

```
circle with .t at 1,1
```

and it would place the top of the circle at that position. A reference to last circle would still locate the center of the circle, but a line drawn from 1,1 would begin at the top of the circle.

Note that the position of 0,0 will not always be the same place on the page. The first object drawn is the point of reference; movement to the left of that point will cause 0,0 to be moved over towards the center of the page.

```
box ht 0.3 wid 0.3 "0,0"
move to 1,0
box "1,0" same
move to -1,0
box "-1,0" same
```

This description produces:

It may be helpful to sketch a drawing on graph paper and then translate it into a pic description. Standard graph paper is divided into quarter-inch squares. When you use

graph paper, you might find it useful to set the `scale` variable to 4. All dimensions
and positions will be divided by the value of `scale`, which is 1 by default.

It is much easier to describe a drawing in full units rather than fractions. Look at
the following description:

```
scale=4
line from 0,0 to 0,3 then to 6,3 then to 6,0 then to 0,0
line from 6,0 to 8,1 then to 8,4 then to 2,4 then to 0,3
line from 6,3 to 8,4
```

The distance between 0 and 1 is normally 1 inch. Because we are scaling this drawing
by 4, the actual distance is $^1/_4$ inch. It seems easier to describe a point as 2,3 rather than
5,.75. This description produces a two-dimensional box:

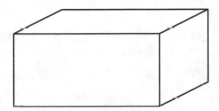

Although `pic` scales the location of text, it is your responsibility to reduce the
size of the text to fit a scaled object. You can also use `scale` to change the basic
unit of measurement from inches to any other unit. For instance, setting `scale` to 6
will cause all dimensions and coordinates to be interpreted in picas (6 picas to the inch).

Splines and arcs are much easier to draw using coordinates. In the following
example, we use a spline to draw a smooth curve between several points on a crude
graph.

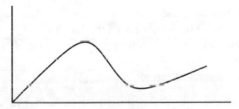

This graph is produced by the following description:

```
scale=4
line from 0,0 to 0,4
line from 0,0 to 9,0
spline from 0,0 to 3,3 then to 5,.25 then to 8,1.5
```

You can also specify relative coordinates as an expression within parentheses. It
has the effect of adding or subtracting from the absolute coordinates of a particular
place.

```
circle rad .5
circle same at last circle+(.25,0)
```

The `same` attribute allows us to duplicate the size of a previous object. The expression `circle same` means "the same size as the last circle." This description produces:

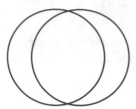

Similarly, you can achieve finer control over positioning by moving from a compass point:

```
box with .sw at last box.ne+(.05,-.05)
```

## Expressions and User-Defined Variables

An expression can be used to supply the dimensions or the position of an object. Any of the following operators can be used in an expression: +, −, *, /, and % (modulo)." Expressions can be used to manipulate the built-in variables as follows:

```
circle rad circlerad/2
```

This will draw a circle with a radius that is half the size of the default radius. An expression can also refer to the value of placenames. The coordinates of any object can be specified as `.x` and `.y`. Here's a list of some of the possibilities:

| | |
|---|---|
| `BoxA.x` | The x-coordinate of the center of `BoxA` |
| `last box.y` | The y-coordinate of the center of the last box |
| `BoxA.s.y` | The y-coordinate of the southern compass point of `BoxA` |
| `BoxA.wid` | The width of `BoxA` |
| `last circle.rad` | The radius of the last circle |

The next description defines a box and then divides the specified height and width of that box to produce a second box half that size.

```
Boxa: box ht 2 wid 3; arrow
box ht Boxa.ht/2 wid Boxa.wid/2
```

The `pic` program also has a number of functions that can be evaluated in an expression, as shown in Table 10-3:

**TABLE 10-3. `pic` Functions**

| Function | Description |
|---|---|
| `sin` (*a*) | Sine of *a* |
| `cos` (*a*) | Cosine of *a* |
| `atan2` (*a,b*) | Arctangent of *a*/*b* |
| `log` (*a*) | Natural logarithm of *a* |
| `sqrt` (*a*) | Square root of *a* |
| `int` (*a*) | Integer *a* |
| `max` (*a,b*) | Maximum value of *a,b* |
| `min` (*a,b*) | Minimum value of *a,b* |
| `rand` (*a*) | Random number generator |

In giving the size or length of an object, you can name and define your own variables. A variable is any lowercase name that is not reserved as part of the `pic` language. A variable can be defined as a constant or an expression.

```
a=ellipsewid*3
b=ellipseht/2
ellipse wid a ht b
```

This description produces:

## Defining Macros

With macros, you can predefine a series of objects or motions that will be included in the description each time you refer to the macro by name.

```
define name %
    definition
         %
```

A percent sign (%) is used here as the delimiter but any character not in the definition can be used. The format of the `define` statement is shown on three lines for readability only; a simple macro could be put on a single line. The definition can extend across as many lines as necessary.

When you refer to *name* in your description, The `pic` program will replace it with the definition.

Macros can also take arguments. These arguments are specified in the definition as $1 thru $9. They will be replaced by the arguments supplied when the macro is invoked.

```
name(arg1, arg2, arg3)
```

A macro does not exist as a place or position as far as `pic` is concerned. The `pic` program simply replaces the macro name with the lines defined in the macro. You cannot refer to the macro as you would refer to a block. However, you can set positions from within a macro.

In the following example, the "tail" hanging down from the box and the list of items drawn to the right of it were produced by a macro.

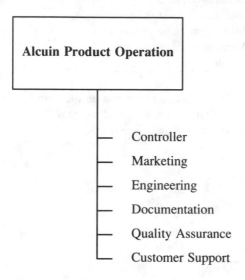

In the `pic` description that produced this drawing, the box is drawn explicitly and a short line is started down from the bottom of the box. Then a macro named `dept` is invoked to produce each item on the list.

```
define dept %
        line down .25
        { line right .15; move right .2; "$1" ljust }
        %
```

In this macro, after a line down is described, the rest of the description is put within braces to reserve the starting position for the next macro call. A short line is drawn, followed by a move to place the text in the correct position. Quotation marks are placed around the argument because the argument will contain a text label.

This macro is invoked for the first item as:

```
dept(Controller)
```

`Controller` is supplied as the first argument, which the macro inserts as a text object. Notice that the argument in the definition is quoted (`"$1"`) so that the actual text when specified does not have to be quoted.

The previous drawing was modeled after an example shown in *Estimating Illustration Costs: A Guide* published by the Society for Technical Communication. The guide considered this drawing to be of medium difficulty and estimated that it would require an hour of an illustrator's time. It took ten to fifteen minutes to design and execute this description for `pic`, including correcting some syntax errors and formatting for the laser printer. Here's the complete description of the drawing:

```
.PS
box ht .75 wid 1.75 "Alcuin Product Operation"
line down .25 from bottom of last box
define dept %
            line down .25
            { line right .15; move right .2; "$1" ljust }
            %
dept(Controller)
dept(Marketing)
dept(Engineering)
dept(Documentation)
dept(Quality Assurance)
dept(Customer Support)
.PE
```

The second example of macro use is probably harder to read than it is to write. Let's look at it in portions. The purpose of the drawing is to represent a network of computers. We decided to use three types of objects to represent each type of computer: a square, a triangle, and small circle. These objects will appear in a hierarchy and lines will be drawn to connect an object on one level with an object on the level below it. Before starting to describe it in `pic` terms, we prepared a rough sketch of the drawing on graph paper. This made us realize that we could easily determine the coordinate points of objects; thus, all the macros are set up to accept coordinate positions.

Comments, beginning with `#`, describe the user-supplied arguments. Following are the definitions for three macros: `backbone` (a box), `local` (a triangle), and `endpt` (a small circle).

```
scale = 4
top = 10
define backbone %
        # $1 = x coordinate ; $2 = label
        ycoord = top-2
        BB$1: box wid 1 ht 1 with .sw at $1,ycoord
        "$2" at ($1,ycoord)+(2,1) ljust
        %
define local %
        # $1 = x coordinate; $2 = label
        ycoord = top-5
        LO$1: move to $1,ycoord
        line down 1 left 1 then right 2 then up 1 left 1
```

```
           "$2" at ($1,ycoord)-(0,.7)
           %
define endpt %
           # $1 = x coordinate
           ycoord = top-8
           circle rad .125 with .n at $1,ycoord
           EP$1: last circle.n
           %
```

Because each type of object maintained the same height (or position on the y-axis), a variable `ycoord` was set up to supply that position from the `top` of the drawing. (The top of the drawing is defined by another variable.)

Each of these macros requires that you supply an x-axis coordinate as the first argument. This argument is also used to assign a unique placename that is used later when we draw lines between objects.

The `backbone` and `local` macros also take a second argument for a label. Handling text inside a macro definition is especially convenient if you are going to change the font and point size.

The next task is to connect the backbone systems to the local systems and the local systems to endpoints. Although we know which types of objects are connected, not all objects are connected in the same way. We decided that the macros require two arguments to supply the x-coordinate for each of the two objects.

```
define BtoL %
           # $1 = x coord of backbone; $2 = x coord of
           # local
           line from BB$1-(0,.5) to LO$2
           %
define LtoE %
           # $1 = x coord of local; $2 = x coord of endpt
           line from LO$1-(0,1) to EP$2
           %
```

The `BtoL` and `LtoE` macros draw lines between the placenames set up by the `backbone`, `local`, and `endpt` macros.

Here are the actual macro calls:

```
backbone(10,IBM/370)
backbone(18,DEC VAX)
local(8,68K-1)
local(13,68K-2)
local(17,68K-3)
endpt(7)
endpt(9)
endpt(12)
endpt(13)
endpt(14)
endpt(16)
endpt(18)
```

```
BtoL(10,8)
BtoL(10,13)
BtoL(18,17)
LtoE(8,7); LtoE(8,9)
LtoE(13,12); LtoE(13,13); LtoE(13,14)
LtoE(17,16); LtoE(17,18)
line from LO13 to LO17
"\s8Personal Computers\s0" at 13,1
"\s12\fBA Network of Computers\s0\fR" ljust at 10,top
```

Notice that arguments supplied to a macro are separated by commas and that an argument may contain a space.  Here's what the description produces:

**A Network of Computers**

Personal Computers

Twelve objects are specified and eleven lines are drawn between the objects.  One line is explicitly drawn connecting the second triangle to the third triangle.  It didn't make sense to define a macro for this single instance.  But if you were setting this up for others to use, such a macro would be necessary.

Shortly, we will be looking at several relatively new features that make pic even more powerful for generating pictures.  In particular, these features allow us to improve our effort to generate a diagram of a computer network.

### pic's Copy Facility

The pic program provides an interesting copy facility that has two different uses: it allows you to read a pic description from a remote file, and it allows you to read lines of data and pass them as individual arguments to a macro.

If you are going to use pic regularly, you should think about maintaining a macro library.  You might define frequently used objects, such as triangles, and place them in their own file. You can include the file in your description with the following line:

```
copy "usr/lib/macros/pic/triangles"
```

Putting the filename in double quotation marks is required. Any .PS/.PE macros that are found in the remote file are ignored.

You might also define a set of related macros for a particular type of drawing, such as an organizational chart or a flow diagram. After you have taken the time to create and test a description, you should consider structuring it so that the forms can be easily used in other drawings.

This copy facility replaces an older construct that allowed you to redirect input from another file through the .PS macro.

```
.PS < triangles
```

A second use of the copy facility is to read data through a macro. We'll show how the endpt macro from our last example can be designed to use this facility. In a file where we had already defined a macro named endpt, we could invoke this macro with the following command:

```
copy thru endpt
7
9
12
13
14
16
18
```

The pic program reads each line of data up to the .PE and replaces each argument in the macro definition with the corresponding field from each line. In this example, the macro is executed seven times, once for each line of data.

We could put the data in a separate file, named endpt.d, for example. Then you enter this version of the copy command:

```
copy "endpt.d" thru endpt
```

The double quotation marks are required. Now the endpt macro will be executed for each line in the file endpt.d. (The filename suffix .d is optional and signifies that the file contains data for a macro call.)

You can specify a string that pic will recognize in the remote file as a signal to stop reading input. Used with copy thru, until is followed by the string. In the following example, the word *STOP* is used as the string:

```
copy "endpt.d" thru endpt until STOP
```

You can also use until when you are taking input from the same file:

```
copy thru local until STOP
8 68K-1
13 68K-2
```

```
17 68K-3
STOP
```

In both cases, `pic` will read lines of data until it comes across the string *STOP*.

Another way to use `copy thru` is to supply the macro definition. This is a compact, single-step method:

```
copy "endpt.d" thru %
        # $1 = x coordinate
        ycoord = top-8
        circle rad .125 with .n at $1,ycoord
        EP$1: last circle.n
                %
```

Although the percent sign is used as the delimiter, any character not found in the definition could be used. The `copy thru` statement with the macro definition can be put on a single line, which is helpful for short definitions.

```
copy thru % box at $1,$2 %
1 1
1 2
1 3
1 4
```

Because you can get a description down to this level, basically consisting of functions, you could have a standard description file associated with independent data files. You could write a program to build the data files from user input or from some other source.

## Executing UNIX Commands

You can execute any UNIX command from `pic`, using the following syntax:

```
sh % command %
```

Again, the percent sign represents any valid delimiter character. The `pic` program submits this command to the shell for execution and then returns to interpret the next line of the description. You could issue a command to obtain data from another file:

```
sh % awk -F: {print$1} /etc/passwd %
```

## ▪ `pic` Enhancements ▪

Most of the enhancements found in new versions of `pic` are aimed at developing `pic` as a graphics programming language. Additional capabilities include `for` loops and `if` conditional statements. A `for` loop allows one or more `pic` commands to be executed as long as a condition is met.

```
for i=1 to 3 by .05
do%
box ht i;move
%
```

Each time through the loop the value of the variable `i` is incremented by .05, producing five boxes of increasing height. The `by` clause specifies the amount that the variable is incremented each time through the loop. If the `by` clause is omitted, then the variable is incremented by 1. The % is used as the delimiter marking the commands to be executed on each pass.

The `if` statement evaluates an expression to determine if it is true or false. If true, `then` specified `pic` commands are executed. If false, the `then` clause is not acted upon; instead, an `else` clause, if specified, is read and commands specified inside it are executed.

```
if x > y then % x = y % else % x = x + 1%
```

This conditional statement evaluates the expression `x > y`. If true, `x` is set to `y`; if false, the value of `x` is incremented by 1. The % is a delimiter marking the beginning and end of the commands specified for both `then` and `else` clauses. The expression inside an `if` statement can use any of the relational operators that are shown in Table 10-4.

**TABLE 10-4. `pic` Relational Operators**

| Operator | Meaning |
|----------|---------|
| ==       | Equal to |
| !=       | Not equal to |
| >        | Greater than |
| >=       | Greater than or equal to |
| <        | Less than |
| <=       | Less than or equal to |
| &&       | And |
| \|       | Or |
| !        | Not |

In addition to enhancements that add more graphics programming features to `pic`, progress has been made in allowing input to be taken from bit-mapped graphic terminals and translated into `pic` output. A separate program called `cip`, available on some systems, allows users to create drawings using a mouse (a la MacDraw for the Macintosh). The `cip` program generates a `pic` description of a drawing that can be included in any file to be processed by `troff`.

# A Miscellany of UNIX Commands

In this chapter, we present a miscellany of UNIX programs with text-processing applications. In addition, we introduce several UNIX utilities for communications and for reading and writing to tapes and floppy disks. These utilities are not specifically designed for text processing, but we have found them necessary for working in the UNIX environment. Although you can find more detailed information on these utilities in books aimed at a general audience, we've included brief discussions of them to encourage you to learn them.

UNIX has many standard programs, as a run-down of the table of contents for the *UNIX Reference Manual* will demonstrate. The challenge of UNIX is knowing which programs are appropriate for a specific situation. No one learns all the commands, but becoming familiar with a great number of them can be helpful. It is rather like those of us who collect far more books on our shelves than are "needed," knowing the reward of finding the right book for the right occasion.

At times, you will be surprised when you discover a program with rather unusual or specialized capabilities; at other times, you may be frustrated by a demanding program or confused by inconsistencies from one program to the next. These qualities seem to originate from the open design of UNIX, and serve to distinguish this text-processing environment from the closed systems of most word processors.

In some ways, what we are trying to do in this chapter is to address problems that arise in typical documentation projects and show how one or more UNIX programs can be applied as solutions to these problems. The emphasis is on the interactive use of these programs, although many of them can be used effectively in shell scripts or as parts of other programs. (In the next chapter, we go into more detail about shell scripts.) The commands are presented in sections, grouped by function.

## · Managing Your Files ·

One of the realities of using a computer is that you begin to think of a document in terms of files, rather than chapters or sections. You edit and print files; create and copy files; delete files accidentally and lose your edits; and look through files to find the information that is contained in them. Increasingly, files contain the goods that you trade. You exchange not only printed copies of documents, but using floppy disks, tapes, or modems, you take files off one system and put them on another system. Learning to organize and maintain files is essential to working on a computer.

## Using the File System to Your Advantage

One obvious feature of UNIX that makes it easy to handle large numbers of files is the hierarchical file system. With carefully named files and directories, the pathname, which specifies a file's unique place in the file system hierarchy, can tell a lot about not only how to get at the file, but its contents as well.

For example, on our system, we keep all source files for various books in progress on a file system called `/work`; work for a given client is kept in a directory named for the client, with a subdirectory for each separate manual. Within each manual's sub-directory, individual chapters are named consistently, `ch01`, `ch02`, and so on. As a result, it is easy both to locate a file (Chapter 1 of the FORTRAN manual for ABC Corp. can predictably be found in `/work/abc/fortran/ch01`) and to guess its contents.

If you are using the C shell, you can create an `alias` that provides a shorthand way of entering a command. In the following example, the alias allows you to think in terms of manuals instead of directories:

```
% alias fortran "cd /work/abc/fortran; pwd"
% pwd
  /work/fred
% fortran
  /work/abc/fortran
```

You can place an `alias` definition in your `.cshrc` file so that it becomes part of your environment.

In the Bourne shell, you achieve a similar result by using an environment variable called `CDPATH` to define a search path for the `cd` command. For example:

```
$ CDPATH=/work/abc:/work/textp:/usr
$ cd fortran
/work/abc/fortran
$ cd jane
/usr/jane
$ cd ch03
/work/textp/ch03
```

When you issue a `cd` command, the shell searches for a subdirectory with that name under any of the directories in the path, changes to it, and prints the full directory name.

The search directories in `CDPATH` are specified between colons. Directories listed in `CDPATH` are searched in order from left to right.

## Shell Filename Metacharacters

Even with files organized into directories, you can still accumulate a lot of files. Developing some consistent naming conventions that take advantage of shell metacharacters (wildcards) can save you a lot of trouble. Most users are familiar with metacharacters but many don't make full use of them.

In UNIX, you can match any part of a filename with a wildcard. Remember that * matches *zero* or more characters. This gives you more power to select a specific group of files out of a directory. In the following example, assume that you want to delete the files `lock`, `filelocks`, and `lock.release`, but ignore the files `filelist`, `lecture`, and `stocks.c`.

```
$ ls
filelist
filelocks
lecture
lock
lock.release
stocks.c
$ rm *lock*
```

Because * can match zero characters, `*lock*` will match `lock` as well as `filelocks`.

The shell interprets the pattern-matching character ? to match any single character, and the construct [m-n] to match a range of consecutive characters.

If you name your files consistently, you can use these characters to select groups of files. For example, in a directory containing a BASIC manual, you might have the following list of files:

```
$ ls
appa
appb
changes
ch01
ch01.old
ch02
ch03
ch03.examples
ch03.out
ch04
ch04.examples
ch05
letter.613
```

As usual in any directory, there are a number of auxiliary files. Some of these files apply to the work on this project, but they are not actually part of the book. If you've carefully chosen the names of related files, you can use metacharacters to select only the files in a particular group. For example:

```
$ ls ch0?
ch01
ch02
ch03
ch04
ch05
```

You could select a range of files, using brackets:

```
$ ls ch0[3-5]
ch03
ch04
ch05
```

If you had entered ch0*, miscellaneous files such as ch01.old would have been included. (Note that whenever you use numbers in filenames, as shown here, to consistently name a group of related files, you should begin the numbering sequence with 01, 02 . . . rather than 1, 2. . . . This will cause ls to list the files in proper alphabetical order. Otherwise, ls will list ch1, then ch11, ch12 . . . ch2, ch20 . . . and so on.)

Metacharacters have broader applications than for simply listing files. Look at this example of running spell on an entire book:

```
$ spell ch0? app? > spell.out
```

(We'll be looking at the spell command later in the section "Proofing Documents.") This command is run on the seven files that match one of the two patterns specified on the command line.

Metacharacters are also useful in moving and copying files from one directory to another:

```
$ cp basic/ch0? /work/backup
```

## Locating Files

Although a hierarchical file system with consistent naming conventions helps a lot, it is still easy to lose track of files, or just to have difficulty specifying the ones you want to manipulate. The number of files contained on even a small hard disk can be enormous, and complex directory hierarchies can be difficult to work with.

It is possible to lose a file on the file system when you have forgotten in which directory you put it. To look through an entire file system or a large directory hierarchy, you need a utility called find. The find utility looks at the external characteristics of a file—who created it, when it was last accessed, its name, and so on.

The find utility probably wins top honors for having the most cumbersome command-line syntax in UNIX. It's not that find is a difficult command; its syntax is simply difficult to recall. You might expect that all you have to enter is find and the name of the file that you want to look for. This is not the way it works, however, which is a nuisance to new users. The find command requires repeated trips to the *UNIX Reference Manual* before you grasp its atypical format.

To use find, specify the pathnames of the directories that you want to search; then place one or more conditions upon the search. The name of a particular file that you want to search for is considered one of these conditions. It is expressed as:

−name *filename*

To obtain a listing of the pathnames of files that are found, you have to specify the −print condition as well (−name must precede −print).

If you wanted to find any file named notes on the /work file system, here's the command to enter:

```
$ find /work -name notes -print
/work/alcuin/notes
/work/textp/ch02/notes
```

The output is the pathname (starting with the specified file system or directory) of each file that is found. More than one pathname can be supplied. A slash (/) represents the root directory and thus is used if you want to search the entire file system. Note that the search can take some time, and that if you do not have read permissions to a directory you will get a message saying that it cannot be opened.

In the next example, we add another condition, −user, and limit the search to files named memo that are owned by the user fred. This is helpful when you are searching for a file that has a fairly common name and might exist in several users' accounts. Filename metacharacters can be used but they must be protected from the shell using backslashes or single quotation marks. (If you don't do this, the metacharacters will be interpreted by the shell as referring to files in the current directory, and will not be passed to the find command.)

```
$ find /work /usr -name 'memo*' -user fred -print
/usr/fred/alcuin/memo
/work/alcuin/memo.523
/work/caslon/memo.214
```

Two directory hierarchies are searched, /work and /usr. If you did not specify the −name condition, this command would locate all the files owned by fred in these two file systems.

Many find conditions have uses for other tasks besides locating files. For instance, it can be useful to descend a directory hierarchy, using find to print the complete pathname of each file, as in the following example:

```
$ find /work/alcuin -print
/work/alcuin
/work/alcuin/ch01
/work/alcuin/ch01.old
/work/alcuin/commands/open
/work/alcuin/commands/stop
    ...
```

This usage provides a kind of super ls that will list all files under a given directory, not just those at the current directory level. As you'll see, this becomes very useful when it comes time to back up your files.

The longer you work with a UNIX system, the more you will come to appreciate `find`. Don't be put off by its awkward syntax and many options. The time you spend studying this command will be well repaid.

## File Characteristics

Most of us are concerned only with the contents of a file. However, to look at files from UNIX's point of view, files are labeled containers that are retrieved from storage and soon put back in the same place. It might be said that the operating system reads (and writes) the label but doesn't really care to look inside the container. The label describes a set of physical or external characteristics for each file. This information is displayed when the `ls` command produces a long listing.

```
$ ls -l /work/textp/ch01
total 20
-rw-rw-r--    1 fred    doc    9496 Jun 10 15:18 ch01
```

To the operating system, the file (`ch01`) contains a certain number of *bytes* (9496), each representing a character. The date and time (`Jun 10 15:18`) refer to the last time the file was modified. The file has an *owner* (`fred`), who is usually the person who created the file. The owner belongs to a *group* of users (`doc`) who can be given different permissions from all *other* users. The operating system keeps track of the file permissions (`-rw-rw-r--`) for the owner, group, and other users—determining who can read, write, or execute the file.

All of these characteristics can be modified either by use of the file or by commands such `chmod` (change permissions) and `chown` (change owner). You may need to become a super-user to change these characteristics.

There are some options for `ls` that allow you to make use of this information. For instance, if you had recently made some changes to a set of files, but couldn't remember which ones, you could use the `-t` option to sort a list of files with the most recently modified files first. The `-r` option reverses that order, so that `ls -rt` produces a list with the oldest files first.

In addition, `find` has a number of options that make use of external file characteristics. As we've seen, you can look for files that belong to a particular user. You can also look for files that are larger than a particular size, or have been modified more recently than a certain date.

Don't get stuck thinking that the only handle you can pick a file up with is the file's name.

## ▪ Viewing the Contents of a File ▪

You are probably familiar with a number of UNIX commands that let you view the contents of a file. The `cat` command streams a file to the screen at a rate that is usually too swift. The `pg` and `more` commands display a file one page at a time. They are frequently used as *filters*, for instance, to supply paging for `nroff` output.

```
$ nroff -mm ch01 | pg
```

You can also use these commands to examine unformatted files, proofing formatting codes as well as text. Although these are frequently used commands, not everyone is aware that they have interactive subcommands, too. You can search for a pattern; execute a UNIX command; move to another file specified on the command line; or go to the end of the file.

    You can list these subcommands by entering  h  when the program pauses at the bottom of a page. Here's the help screen  pg  provides:

```
----------------------------------------------------------
    h                   help
    q or Q              quit
    <blank> or \n       next page
    l                   next line
    d or ^D             display half a page more
    . or ^L             redisplay current page
    f                   skip the next page forward
    n                   next file
    p                   previous file
    $                   last page
    w or z              set window size and display next page
    s savefile          save current file in savefile
    /pattern/           search forward for pattern
    ?pattern? or
    ^pattern^           search backward for pattern
    !command            execute command
Most commands can be preceded by a number, as in:
+1\n (next page); -1\n (previous page); 1\n (page 1).
See the manual page for more detail.
----------------------------------------------------------
```

One advantage of  pg  is that you can move backward as well as forward when going through a file. A special feature of  more  is the ability to invoke  vi  at the current point in the file. When you quit  vi,  more  resumes paging through the rest of the file.

    Another command used for examining a file is  pr.  Its most common use is to perform minor page formatting for a file on the way to a line printer. It breaks the input file into pages (66 lines to a page) and supplies a header that contains the date, the name of the file, and the current page number. Top, bottom, and side margins are also added.

    The  pr  command also has many options that can be used to perform some oddball tasks. For example, the  -n  option adds line numbers:

```
$ pr -n test
```

The following is displayed:

```
Jul  4 14:27 1987  test Page 1
```

```
1    apples
2    oranges
3    walnuts
4    chestnuts
```

You can adjust the page length using the −l option. If you are printing to a terminal, the −p option specifies a pause at the beginning of each page. You can also display an input file in *-n* columns.

The −m option simultaneously merges two or more files and prints each of them, one per column:

```
$ pr -m -t test*
```

In this example, we display four files side-by-side:

```
apples        apples        apples        oranges
oranges       oranges       oranges       walnuts
walnuts       walnuts       grapes        chestnuts
chestnuts
```

The `test*` file specification is expanded to four filenames: `test`, `test1`, `test2`, and `test3`. The −t option suppresses the heading and does not print linefeeds to fill a page, which is especially useful when you are sending the output of `pr` to a file or the terminal.

We found a use for `pr` when working on this book. We wanted to include `nroff`-formatted examples in the text. We had difficulty because `nroff` inserts tabs, instead of spaces, to optimize horizontal positioning on printers. To remove the tabs, we used `pr` with the −e option to expand the tabs to their equivalent in blank spaces. The following shell script implements this process so that it can be invoked as a single command:

```
$ nroff -mm -rO0 examples/$1 | pr -e -t
```

The `pr` command works as a filter for `nroff`. The −r option is used with `nroff` to set register O (page offset or left margin) to zero.

Sometimes it can be useful to examine just the beginning or the end of a file. Two commands, `head` and `tail`, print the first or last ten lines of a file. The `head` command can be used to look at the initial settings of number registers and strings that are often set at the top of a file.

```
$ head ch02
.nr W 65
.nr P 3
.nr L 60
.so /usr/lib/tmac/tmac.m
.nr Pt 2
.ds Ux \s-2UNIX\s0
.ds HP 3321
```

```
.H1 "Product Overview"
.ds HM 11A
.
```

This output could be redirected to a file as a way of starting a new chapter. The `tail` command has the same syntax; it can save time when you want to check the end of a large file.

## ▪ **Searching for Information in a File** ▪

The many benefits provided by `grep` to the user who doesn't remember what his or her files contain are well known. Even users of non-UNIX systems who make fun of its obscure name wish they had a utility with its power to search through a set of files for an arbitrary text pattern, known as a *regular expression*. We have already discussed regular expressions and their use in search and replace commands in `vi` (see Chapter 7). In this section, we show some of the ways to perform pattern-matching searches using `grep` and its siblings, `egrep` and `fgrep`.

The main function of `grep` is to look for strings matching a regular expression and print only those lines that are found. Use `grep` when you want to look at how a particular word is used in one or more files.

```
$ grep "run[- ]time" ch04
This procedure avoids run-time errors for not-assigned
and a run-time error message is produced.
run-time error message is produced.
program aborts and a run-time error message is produced.
DIMENSION statement in  BASIC is executable at run time.
This means that arrays can be redimensioned at run time.
accessible or not open, the program aborts and a run-time
```

This example lists the lines in the file `ch04` that contain either `run-time` or `run time`.

Another common use is to look for a specific macro in a file. In a file coded with mm macros, the following command will list top level and second level headings:

```
$ grep "^\.H[12]" ch0[12]
ch01:.H1 "Introduction"
ch01:.H1 "Windows, Screens, and Images"
ch01:.H2 "The Standard Screen-stdscr"
ch01:.H2 "Adding Characters"
...
ch02:.H1 "Introduction"
ch02:.H1 "What Is Terminal Independence?"
ch02:.H2 "Termcap"
ch02:.H2 "Terminfo"
```

In effect, it produces a quick outline of the contents of these files. When more than one file is specified, the name of the file appears with each line. Note that we use brackets as metacharacters both in the regular expression and when specifying the filename. Because metacharacters (and spaces) have meaning to the shell, they will be interpreted as such unless the regular expression is placed within quotation marks.

There are several options commonly used with grep. The −i option specifies that the search ignore the distinction between uppercase and lowercase. The −c option tells grep to return only a count of the number of lines matched. The −l option returns only the name of the file when grep finds a match. This can be used to prepare a list of files for another command.

The shell construct *command1* `command2` causes the output of *command2* to be used as an argument to *command1*. For example, assume that you wanted to edit any file that has a reference to a function call named getcursor. The command:

```
$ vi `grep −l getcursor *`
```

would invoke vi on all of the files in the current directory containing the string getcursor. Because the grep command is enclosed in single backquotes (` `), its output becomes the list of files to be edited.

The grep command can work on the results of a find command. You can use find to supply a list of filenames and grep to search for a pattern in those files. For example, consider the following command, which uses find to look for all files in the specified directory hierarchy and passes the resulting names to grep to scan for a particular pattern:

```
$ find /work/docbook −exec grep "[aA]lcuin" {} \;
Alcuin product. Yesterday, I received the product   demo
Alcuin.  Some people around here, looking over my shoulder,
with Alcuin. One  person,  a  student  of  calligraphy,
presents different strategies for documenting the Alcuin
The development of Alcuin can be traced to our founder's
the installation file "alcuin.install"> and the font
configuration file "alcuin.ftables."
```

The −exec condition allows you to specify a command that is executed upon each file that is found ({} indicates the pathname of the file). The command must end with an escaped semicolon.

Although this is a good way to introduce the very useful −exec option to find, it is actually not the best way to solve the problem. You'll notice that even though grep is working on more than one file, the filenames are not printed because the data is actually passed to grep from a pipe. The reason is that grep is being invoked many times (once for each file that is found), and is not really working on many files at once. If you wanted to produce a list of the selected files, you could use the −l option with grep. But more to the point, this is a very inefficient way to do the job.

In this case, it would be preferable to write:

```
$ grep "[aA]lcuin" `find /work/docbook −print`
```

Because grep is invoked only once, this command will run much faster.

There is a potential danger in this approach. If the list of files is long, you may exceed the total allowable length of a command line. The best approach uses a command we haven't shown yet—xargs. This command provides an extended version of the same function the shell provides with backquotes. It converts its input into a form that can be used as an argument list by another command. The command to which the argument list is passed is specified as the first argument to xargs. So, you would write:

```
$ find /work/docbook -print | xargs grep "[aA]lcuin"
```

Or you could generalize this useful tool and save it as the following shell script, which could be called mfgrep (*multifile* grep). This script takes the pathname for find as the first argument and the pattern for grep as the second. The list of files found is passed to grep by xargs:

```
find $1 | xargs grep "$2"
```

The fgrep (*fast* grep)* command performs the same function as grep, except it searches for a fixed string rather than a regular expression. Because it doesn't interpret metacharacters, it often does a search faster than grep. For interactive use, you may not find enough difference to keep this command in your active repertoire. However, it may be of more benefit inside shell scripts.

The egrep command is yet another version of grep, one that extends the syntax of regular expressions. A + following a regular expression matches one or more occurrences of the regular expression; a ? matches zero or one occurrences. In addition, regular expressions can be nested within parentheses.

```
$ egrep "Lab(oratorie)?s" name.list
AT&T Bell Laboratories
AT&T Bell Labs
```

Parentheses surround a second regular expression and ? modifies this expression. The nesting helps to eliminate unwanted matches; for instance, the word *Labors* or *oratories* would not be matched.

Another special feature of egrep is the vertical bar (|), which serves as an *or* operator between two expressions. Lines matching either expression are printed, as in the next example:

```
$ egrep "stdscr|curscr" ch03
into the stdscr, a character array.
When stdscr is refreshed, the
stdscr is refreshed.
curscr.
initscr() creates two windows: stdscr
and curscr.
```

---

*Despite what the documentation says, egrep is usually the fastest of the three grep programs.

Remember to put the expression inside quotation marks to protect the vertical bar from being interpreted by the shell as a pipe symbol. Look at the next example:

```
$ egrep "Alcuin (User|Programmer)('s)? Guide" docguide
Alcuin Programmer's Guide is a thorough
refer to the Alcuin User Guide.
Alcuin User's Guide introduces new users to
```

You can see the flexibility that `egrep`'s syntax can give you, matching either *User* or *Programmer* and matching them if they had an *'s* or not.

Both `egrep` and `fgrep` can read search patterns from a file using the `-f` option.

## · Proofing Documents ·

There are no computer tools that completely replace the close examination of final printed copy by the human eye. However, UNIX does include a number of proofing aids, ranging from a simple spelling checker to programs for checking style and diction, and even sexist usage.

We'll look at some of these programs in this section. Not all of the programs we'll discuss are available on all UNIX systems. Keep in mind, though, that `grep` is also a very powerful proofing aid, which you can use to check for consistent usage of words and phrases.

### Looking for Spelling Errors

The `spell` command reads one or more files and prints a list of words that are possibly misspelled. You can redirect the output to a file, then use `grep` to locate each of the words, and `vi` or `ex` to make the edits. In the next chapter, though, we introduce a shell script named `proof` for running `spell` interactively and correcting spelling errors in place in a file. You will probably prefer to use `spell` in that manner rather than invoking it manually.

Even if you do build that script, you can use `spell` on its own if you are unsure about which of two possible spellings is right. Type the name of the command, followed by a *RETURN*, then type the alternative spellings you are considering. Press `^D` (on a line by itself) to end the list. The `spell` command will echo back the word(s) in the list that it considers to be in error.

```
$ spell
misspelling
mispelling
^D
mispelling
```

You can invoke `spell` in this way from within `vi`, by typing the `ex` colon prompt, an exclamation point, and the name of the `spell` command.

When you run `spell` on a file, the list of words it produces usually includes a number of legitimate words or terms that the program does not recognize. You must cull out the proper nouns and other words `spell` doesn't know about to arrive at a list of true misspellings. For instance, look at the results on this sample sentence:

```
$ cat sample
Alcuin uses TranScript to convert ditroff into
PostScript output for the LaserWriter printerr.
$ spell sample
Alcuin
ditroff
printerr
LaserWriter
PostScript
TranScript
```

Only one word in this list is actually misspelled.

On many UNIX systems, you can supply a local dictionary file so that `spell` recognizes special words and terms specific to your site or application. After you have run `spell` and looked through the word list, you can create a file containing the words that were not actual misspellings. The `spell` command will check this list after it has gone through its own dictionary.

If you added the special terms in a file named `dict`, you could specify that file on the command line using the + option:

```
$ spell +dict sample
printerr
```

The output is reduced to the single misspelling.

The `spell` command will also miss words specified as arguments to `nroff` or `troff` macros, and, like any spelling checker, will make some errors based on incorrect derivation of spellings from the root words contained in its dictionary. If you understand how `spell` works, you may be less surprised by some of these errors.

The directory `/usr/lib/spell` contains the main program invoked by the `spell` command along with auxiliary programs and data files.

```
$ ls -l /usr/lib/spell
total 604
-rwxr-xr-x   1 bin    bin     20176 Mar  9 1985 hashcheck
-rwxr-xr-x   1 bin    bin     14352 Mar  9 1985 hashmake
-rw-r--r--   1 bin    bin     53872 Mar  9 1985 hlista
-rw-r--r--   1 bin    bin     53840 Mar  9 1985 hlistb
-rw-r--r--   1 bin    bin      6328 Mar  9 1985 hstop
-rw-rw-rw-   1 root   root   102892 Jul 12 16:10 spellhist
-rwxr-xr-x   1 bin    bin     23498 Mar  9 1985 spellin
-rwxr-xr-x   1 bin    bin     27064 Mar  9 1985 spellprog
```

The `spell` command pipes its input through `deroff -w` and `sort -u` to remove formatting codes and prepare a sorted word list, one word per line. (The `deroff` and `sort` commands are discussed later in this chapter.) Two separate spelling lists are maintained, one for American usage and one for British usage (invoked with the −b option to spell). These lists, hlista and hlistb, cannot be read or updated directly. They are compressed files, compiled from a list of words represented as nine-digit hash codes. (Hash-coding is a special technique for quick search of information.)

The main program invoked by spell is spellprog. It loads the list of hash codes from either hlista or hlistb into a table, and looks for the hash code corresponding to each word on the sorted word list. This eliminates all words (or hash codes) actually found in the spelling list. For the remaining words, spellprog tries to see if it can derive a recognizable word by performing various operations on the word stem, based on suffix and prefix rules. A few of these manipulations follow:

```
-y+iness
+ness
-y+i+less
+less
-y+ies
-t+ce
-t+cy
```

The new words created as a result of these manipulations will be checked once more against the spell table. However, before the stem-derivative rules are applied, the remaining words are checked against a table of hash codes built from the file hstop. The stop list contains typical misspellings that stem-derivative operations might allow to pass. For instance, the misspelled word *thier* would be converted into *thy* using the suffix rule -y+ier. The hstop file accounts for as many cases of this type of error as possible.

The final output consists of words not found in the spell list, even after the program tried to search for their stems, and words that were found in the stop list.

You can get a better sense of these rules in action by using the −v or −x option.

The −v option eliminates the last lookup in the table, and produces a list of words that are not actually in the spelling list along with possible derivatives. It allows you to see which words were found as a result of stem-derivative operations, and prints the rule used.

```
$ spell -v sample
Alcuin
ditroff
LaserWriter
PostScript
printerr
TranScript
+out    output
+s      uses
```

The −x option makes spell begin at the stem-derivative stage, and prints the various attempts it makes to find the word stem of each word.

```
$ spell -x sample
...
=into
=LaserWriter
=LaserWrite
=LaserWrit
=laserWriter
=laserWrite
=laserWrit
=output
=put
...
LaserWriter
...
```

The stem is preceded by an equals sign. At the end of the output are the words whose stem does not appear in the spell list.

One other file you should know about is spellhist. Each time you run spell, the output is appended through a command called tee into spellhist, in effect creating a list of all the misspelled or unrecognized words for your site. The spellhist file is something of a "garbage" file that keeps on growing. You will want to reduce it or remove it periodically. To extract useful information from this spellhist, you might use the sort and uniq -c commands shown later in this chapter to compile a list of misspelled words or special terms that occur most frequently. It is possible to add these words back into the basic spelling dictionary, but this is too complex a process to describe here.

## Checking Hyphenation

The hyphen command is used on nroff-formatted files to print a list of words that have been hyphenated at the end of a line. You can check that nroff has correctly hyphenated words.

```
$ hyphen ch03.out
ch03.out:
applica-tion
pro-gram
charac-ter
```

If you disagree with the hyphenation of a word, you can go back into your source file and use either the .hw request to specify hyphenation points or the .nh request to inhibit hyphenation of the word.

If you don't have the hyphen command on your system, you can print the lines ending in hyphens using grep:

```
$ grep '-$' ch03.out
```

This will not display the second half of the hyphenated word on the following line, but it should give you enough of an idea. Alternatively, you could use awk or sed, described in the next chapter, to create a version of this command that would print both lines.

## Counting Words

In the past, writers were paid by the word. The `wc` command will count words for you:

```
$ wc ch01
   180    1529    9496 ch01
```

The three numbers printed represent the number of lines, words, and characters, respectively. (The presence of formatting commands in the input file will make this measurement somewhat inaccurate.)

## Writer's Workbench

No book on UNIX text processing can avoid some discussion of Writer's Workbench (WWB), a collection of programs for the analysis of writing style.

Unfortunately, unlike most of the programs described in this book, the Writer's Workbench is not available on all UNIX systems. It was originally developed for internal use at Bell Labs, and was available in early releases of UNIX to the academic community. But it was made into a separate product when UNIX was commercially released.

The three original programs, `style`, `diction`, and `explain`, are available in Berkeley UNIX systems and in Xenix, but not in System V.

AT&T has released a greatly improved and expanded version, including additional programs for proofreading, that is controlled from a master program called `wwb`. However, this version is only available as a separately priced package for 3B2 and 3B5 computers. The unfortunate result is that one of UNIX's most unusual contributions to text processing is not officially part of UNIX and has never been ported to many UNIX systems.

In this section, we'll describe the original `style` and `diction` programs, with a brief discussion of `wwb`.

The `style` program analyzes a document's style and computes readability indexes based on several algorithms widely accepted in the academic community. For example, when run on a draft of this section, `style` gave the following report:

```
readability grades:
        (Kincaid) 11.1  (auto) 11.6  (Coleman-Liau) 11.0
        (Flesch) 11.5 (52.7)
sentence info:
        no. sent 53 no. wds 1110
        av sent leng 20.9 av word leng 4.79
        no. questions 0 no. imperatives 0
        no. nonfunc wds 624   56.2%   av leng 6.25
        short sent (<16) 34% (18) long sent (>31)  17% (9)
        longest sent 46 wds at sent 4;
```

```
        shortest sent 5 wds at sent 47
sentence types:
        simple  32% (17) complex  47% (25)
        compound  4% (2) compound-complex  17% (9)
word usage:
        verb types as % of total verbs
        tobe  29% (33) aux  28% (32) inf  15% (17)
        passives as % of non-inf verbs   9% (9)
        types as % of total
        prep 12.0% (133) conj 3.6% (40) adv 5.0% (56)
        noun 26.8% (298) adj 15.5% (172) pron 7.3% (81)
        nominalizations   3 % (30)
sentence beginnings:
        subject opener: noun (22) pron (5) pos (1) adj (2)
                              art (4) tot  64%
        prep  17% (9) adv   9% (5)
        verb   0% (0)  sub_conj   6% (3) conj   0% (0)
        expletives   4% (2)
```

Even if you aren't an English teacher and don't know the Kincaid algorithm from the Flesch, this report can be very useful.

First, regardless of the differences between the algorithms, they all give you a general idea of the required reading level for what you have written. It is up to you to adjust your style according to the audience level you want to reach. This may not be a trivial task; however, it may be a vital one if you are writing a book for a specific audience. For example, if you were writing an instruction manual for heavy equipment to be used by people reading at the sixth-grade level, a style report like the one shown would be a dire warning that the manual would not be successful.

In general, to lower the reading level of a document, use shorter sentences and simpler constructions. (Incidentally, most writing in newspapers and general circulation magazines is at the sixth-grade level. But you shouldn't get the impression that text written for a lower reading level is *better*. Writing can be clear and effective at any level of complexity. At the same time, each of us must recognize, and adjust for, the skills of our intended reader.)

The analysis of reading level is only a small part of what style offers. The detailed analysis of sentence length and type, word usage, and sentence beginnings can give you considerable insight into your writing. If you take the time to read the report carefully at the same time as you reread your text, you will begin to see patterns and can make intelligent decisions about editorial changes.

As an exercise, run style on a short passage you have written, read the report carefully, then rewrite your work based on the report. See what difference this makes to the style report. You will eventually get a feel for what the program provides.

In some cases, diction, the other major program in the Writer's Workbench, can also help you find areas to change.

The diction program relies on a library of frequently misused words and phrases. It relentlessly searches out these words and flags them as inappropriate by enclosing them in brackets. For example, when run on a previous draft of this section, diction made the following recommendations:

```
wwb
  style performs stylistic analysis of a document  and
  computes readability indexes based on a[ number of ]
  algorithms widely accepted in the academic community.

  this may not be a trivial  task  however it may be a
  [ vital ] one if you are writing a book  with a specific
  target audience.

  for example  if you were  writing an instruction manual
  for heavy equipment to be used by  people reading at the
  sixth grade level a style report like the one shown above
  would be a dire warning that the manual would not be
  [ very ]successful.

  [ in some cases ] diction  the other  major program in the
  writer s workbench can help you  to find possible areas to
  change.

  in the latest official release of wwb there are a
  [ number of ] additional programs  including  .

  morestyle  which looks for abstract words as well as
  listing the  frequency with which each word is used
  and the word diversity the[ number of ]different words
  divided by the total[ number of ] words .

  morestyle also gives a count of the[ number of ]negative
  constructions contained in your writing.

  spellwwb  which lists possible spelling errors in a
  slightly more  usable format than the standard spell
  program  and spelladd   which allows you to build a local
  dictionary word of spelling  exceptions  words that spell
  regards as errors  but[ which ]you  know to be correct .

  you can run these programs individually  or using one of
  several [ overall ]control programs.

  running wwb will run[ all of ]these programs.

  number of sentences 37 number of hits 10
```

The diction program lists ''problem'' sentences from your source file, with words or phrases it has taken exception to enclosed in brackets. You can redirect this output to a file, or page through it on the screen. Punctuation and macros are first stripped by the `deroff` program, which explains the odd appearance of the text.

We find that we ignore `diction`'s advice much of the time—the exception list is applied across the board, without regard for context. For example, you'll notice that it flagged the phrase *number of* several times, though that was exactly what we meant in all but one case. However, the twenty percent of its recommendations that we agree with are worth the effort of running the program.

If you don't understand why `diction` complains about a phrase, you can use `explain` to ask for help. For example:

```
$ explain
phrase?
which
use "that" when clause is restrictive" for "which"
use "when" for "at which time"
phrase?
number of
use "many" for "a large number of"
use "several, many, some" for "a number of"
use "usually" for "except in a small number of cases"
use "some" for "in a number of cases"
use "enough" for "sufficient number of"
use "often" for "in a considerable number of cases"
phrase?
perform
use "do" for "perform"
use "measure" for "perform a measurement"
phrase?
^D
```

The official release of WWB for 3B computers contains improved versions of `style` and `diction`, as well as many additional programs. These programs include

- `abst`, which evaluates the abstractness of your writing.

- `acro`, which looks for acronyms (any word printed in all capital letters) so you can check that they have been properly defined.

- `dictadd`, which allows you to add to the dictionaries used by `diction`, `spell`, and `sexist`.

- `double`, which looks for double words.

- `findbe`, which looks for syntax that may be difficult to understand.

- `morestyle`, which looks for abstract words and lists the frequency with which each word is used and the word diversity (the number of different words divided by the total number of words). The `morestyle` program also gives a count of the number of negative constructions contained in your writing.

- **org**, which prints the first and last sentence of each paragraph, so you can analyze paragraph transitions and the flow of ideas within your writing.

- **punct**, which checks punctuation (e.g., the placement of commas and periods with quotation marks).

- **sexist**, which checks your writing against a dictionary of sexist words and phrases.

- **spellwwb**, which lists possible spelling errors in a slightly more usable format than the standard spell program, and **spelladd**, which allows you to build a local dictionary of spelling exceptions (words that **spell** regards as errors, but that you know to be correct).

- **splitrules**, which finds split infinitives.

- **syl**, which prints the average number of syllables in the words you use.

You can run these programs individually or use one of several control programs. The **wwb** program will run just about everything. The **proofr** program will run those programs that help you proofread (such as **spell**, **double**, **punct**, and **diction**). The **prose** program will run those that analyze style (such as **style** and **sexist**).

There is also an interactive version of **proofr** called **proofvi**, which stores its output in a temporary file and then allows you to edit your original, stepping through each flagged problem.

## · Comparing Versions of the Same Document ·

UNIX provides a number of useful programs for keeping track of different versions of documents contained in two or more files:

- the **diff** family of programs, which print out lines that are different between two or more files

- the SCCS system, which lets you keep a compact history of differences between files, so that you can go back and reconstruct any previous version

- the **make** program, which keeps track of a predefined list of dependencies between files

### Checking Differences

The **diff** command displays different versions of lines that are found when comparing two files. It prints a message that uses ed-like notation (**a** for append, **c** for change, and **d** for delete) to describe how a set of lines has changed. This is followed by the lines themselves. The < character precedes lines from the first file and > precedes lines from the second file.

Let's create an example to explain the output produced by `diff`. Look at the contents of three sample files:

| **TEST1** | **TEST2** | **TEST3** |
|-----------|-----------|-----------|
| apples    | apples    | oranges   |
| oranges   | oranges   | walnuts   |
| walnuts   | grapes    | chestnuts |

When you run `diff` on these files, the following output is produced:

```
$ diff test1 test2
3c3
< walnuts
---
> grapes
```

The `diff` command displays the only line that differs between the two files. To understand the report, remember that `diff` is prescriptive, describing what changes need to made to the first file to make it the same as the second file. This report specifies that only the third line is affected, exchanging walnuts for grapes. This is more apparent if you use the −e option, which produces an editing script that can be submitted to `ed`, the UNIX line editor. (You must redirect standard output to capture this script in a file.)

```
$ diff -e test1 test2
3c
grapes
.
```

This script, if run on `test1`, will bring `test1` into agreement with `test2`. (Later in this section, we'll look at how to get `ed` to execute this script.) If you compare the first and third files, you find more differences:

```
$ diff test1 test3
1d0
< apples
3a3
> chestnuts
```

To make `test1` the same as `test3`, you'd have to delete the first line (*apples*) and append the third line from `test3` after the third line in `test1`. Again, this can be seen more clearly in the editing script produced by the −e option. Notice that the script specifies editing lines in reverse order; otherwise, changing the first line would alter all succeeding line numbers.

```
$ diff -e test1 test3
3a
chestnuts
.
1d
```

You can use the `diff3` command to look at differences between three files. For each set of differences, it displays a row of equals signs (====) followed by 1, 2, or 3, indicating which file is different; if no number is specified, then all three files differ. Then, using `ed`-like notation, the differences are described for each file.

```
$ diff3 test1 test2 test3
====3
1:1c
2:1c
  apples
3:0a
====3
1:3c
2:3c
  grapes
3:2,3c
  walnuts
  chestnuts
```

With the output of `diff3`, it is easy to keep track of which file is which; however, the prescription given is a little harder to decipher. To bring these files into agreement, you would have to add apples at the beginning of the third file; change line 3 of the second file to line 3 of the first file; and change lines 2 and 3 of the third file, effectively dropping the last line.

The `diff3` command also has a `-e` option for creating an editing script for `ed`. It doesn't quite work the way you might think. Basically, it creates a script for building the first file from the second and third files.

```
$ diff3 -e test1 test2 test3
3c
walnuts
chestnuts
.
1c
.
w
q
```

If you reverse the second and third files, a different script is produced:

```
$ diff3 -e test1 test3 test2
3c
grapes
.
```

```
     w
     q
```

As you might guess, this is basically the same output as doing
a diff on the first and third files. (The only difference in the output is the result of a
rather errant inconsistency between diff and diff3. The latter produces an ed
script that ends with the commands that save the edited version of the file; diff
requires that you supply them.)

Another useful program is sdiff (*side-by-side* diff). Its most straightforward use is to display two files in two columns on the screen. In a gutter between the
two columns, the program displays a < if the line is unique to the first file, a > if the
line is unique to the second file, and a | if the line is different in both files. Because
the default line length of this program (130 characters) is too wide for most terminals, it
is best to use the −w option to specify a smaller width. Here are the results of running
sdiff on two different pairs of files:

```
$ sdiff -w60 test1 test2
apples                                  apples
oranges                                 oranges
walnuts                         |       grapes
$ sdiff -w60 test1 test3
apples                          <
oranges                                 oranges
walnuts                                 walnuts
                                >       chestnuts
```

The −s option to the sdiff command only shows the differences between the two
files. Identical lines are suppressed. One of the most powerful uses of sdiff is
interactive, building an output file by choosing between different versions of two files.
You have to specify the −o option and the name of an output file to be created. The
sdiff command then displays a % prompt after each set of differences. You can
compare the different versions and select the one that will be sent to the output file.
Some of the possible responses are l to choose the left column, r to choose the right
column, and q to exit the program.

```
$ sdiff -w60 -o test test1 test3
apples                          <
% l
oranges                                 oranges
walnuts                                 walnuts
                                >       chestnuts

% r
$ cat test
apples
oranges
walnuts
chestnuts
```

Having looked at these commands in simplified examples, let's now consider some practical applications for comparing documents.

When working on a document, it is not an uncommon practice to make a copy of a file and edit the copy rather than the original. This might be done, for example, if someone other than the writer is inputting edits from a written copy. The `diff` command can be used to compare the two versions of a document. A writer could use it to proof an edited copy against the original.

```
$ diff brochure brochure.edits
49c43,44
< environment for program development and communications,
---
> environment for multiprocessing, program development
> and communications, programmers
56c51
< offering even more power and productivity for commericial
---
> offering even more power and productivity for commercial
76c69
< Languages such as FORTRAN, COBOL, Pascal, and C can be
---
> Additional languages such as FORTRAN, COBOL, Pascal, and
```

Using `diff` in this manner is a simple way for a writer to examine changes without reading the entire document. By capturing `diff` output in a file, you can keep a record of changes made to any document.

As another example, suppose a company has a number of text files that comprise its help facility. These files are shipped with the product and maintained online by the customer. When there is a documentation update, these files also need to be updated. One way to accomplish this is to replace each text file in its entirety, but that involves distributing a lot of material that remains unchanged. Another way is to use `diff` and simply send a record of changes between the old and the new. The −e option creates an editing script for `ed` that can be used to recreate the second file from the first.

```
$ diff -e help.txt help.new > help.chgs
$ cat help.chgs
153,199d
65c
$INCLUDE {filename} program.name
.
56a
.Rh 0 "" "$CHAIN Statement"
.Rh "Syntax"
.in 5n
.nf
$CHAIN {filename} program.name
.fi
.in 0
```

```
.Rh "Description"
Use the $CHAIN statement to direct the compiler to read
source code from program.name and compile it along
....
```

The company could ship the file `help.chgs` with instructions on how to input this editing script to `ed`. You'd want to create a shell script to automate this process, but that is really an extension of knowing how it might be done from the command line. The following command pipes the editing script to `ed`:

```
$ (cat help.chgs; echo 'w' ) | ed - help.txt
```

To save the changes, a `w` command is submitted through `echo`. (In fact, if you have any concern about sparing the original file, you could change the `w` to `1,$p`, which will cause the edited contents to be printed to standard output, but not saved in the file. Redirect standard output to a new file to keep both copies.)

As a further example, let's take the instance where two people have made copies of a file and made changes to their own copies, and now you want to compare them both against the original. In this example, `ch01` is the original; `ch01.tom` contains edits made by Tom; and `ch01.ann` contains changes made by Ann.

```
$ diff3 ch01 ch01.ann ch01.tom
----3
1:56a
2:56a
3:57,103c
  .mc |
  .Rh 0 "" "$CHAIN Statement"
  .XX "BASIC statements, $CHAIN"
  .XX "$CHAIN statement"
  .Rh "Syntax"
  .UN
  .in 5n
  .nf
  $CHAIN {file} program.name
  .fi
  .in 0
  .Rh "Description"
  Use the $CHAIN statement to direct the compiler to read
  source code from program.name and compile it along
  ....
====3
1:65c
2:65c
  $INCLUDE {file}
3:112c
  $INCLUDE {file} program.name
====2
1:136c
```

```
2:136c
  Nesting of $INSERT statements is not permitted.
3:183c
  Nesting of $INSERT statements is permitted.
====
1:143,144c
  program.name is converted to a valid UNIX filename.
  .LP
2:143,152c
  program.name is converted to a valid UNIX filename using
  the following conversion rules:
  .TS
  center, tab(@);
  c l c.
  /@is converted to@?
  ?@is converted to@??
  Null@is converted to@?0
  An initial .@is converted to@?.
  .TE
3:190,191c
  program.name is converted to a valid UNIX filename using
  a set of conversion rules.
```

You often find that one version has some things right and another version has other things right. What if you wanted to compile a single version of this document that reflects the changes made to each copy? You want to select which version is correct for each set of differences. One effective way to do this would be to use sdiff.

We'll use the −s option to suppress the printing of identical lines. To make the example fit on the printed page, we specify a 45-character line length. (You would generally use an 80-character line length for the screen.) Because the total line length is limited to 45 characters, sdiff will be able to display only the first 15 or so characters of the line for each file; the rest of the line will be truncated.

```
$ sdiff −w45 −s −o ch01.new ch01.ann ch01.tom
56a57,103
                              >  .Rh 0 "" "$CHAIN Statement"
                              >  .XX "BASIC statements, $CHAIN"
                              >  .XX "$CHAIN statement"
                              >  .Rh "Syntax"
                              >  .UN
                              >  .in 5n
                              >  .nf
                              >  $CHAIN {\fIfile\fP} \fI
                              >  .fi
                              >  .in 0
                              >  .Rh "Description"
                              >  Use the $CHAIN statement to de
```

```
                              >   code from \fIprogram.name\fP
                      .......
   % r
   65c112
   $ INCLUDE {\fIfile\fP}    |   $INCLUDE {\fIfile\fP}
   % r
   % 143,152c190,191
   \fIprogram.name\fP is     |   \fIprogram.name\fP is
   following rules.          |   following rules.
   .TS                       <
   center, tab(@);           <
   c l c.                    <
   /@is converted to@?       <
   ?@is converted to@??      <
   Null@is converted to@?0   <
   An initial .@is converted<
   .TE                       <
   % l
```

The file `ch01.new` contains the portions of each file that were selected along with all the lines that both files have in common.

Another program worth mentioning is `bdiff` (*big file* `diff`). It is used on files too large for `diff`. This program breaks up a large file into smaller segments and then passes each one through `diff`. It maintains line numbering as though `diff` were operating on one large file.


## SCCS

We've shown an example using `diff` to produce a file that described the changes made to a text file for a help facility. It allowed the distribution of a smaller file describing changes instead of a wholly new version of the file. This indicates a potential application for `diff`, which is fully realized in the Source Code Control System or SCCS. SCCS is a facility for keeping track of the changes to files that take place at different stages of a software development or documentation project.

Suppose you have a first draft of a manual. (This is referred to as a *delta* when it is saved in a special SCCS format.) The second draft, of course, is based on changes to the first draft.

When you make the delta for the second draft, SCCS, instead of keeping a separate copy for each draft, uses `diff` to record the changes to the first draft that resulted in the second draft. Only the changes, and the instructions for having an editor make them, need to be maintained. SCCS allows you to regenerate earlier drafts, which saves disk space.

SCCS is quite complex—too complex to describe here—but we seriously suggest that you investigate it if you are working on a large, frequently-revised or multiple-author writing project.

## Using make

The make program is a UNIX facility for describing dependencies among a group of related files, usually ones that are part of the same project. This facility has enjoyed widespread use in software development projects. Programmers use make to describe how to "make" a program—what source files need to be compiled, what libraries must be included, and which object files need to be linked. By keeping track of these relationships in a single place, individual members of a software development team can make changes to a single module, run make, and be assured that the program reflects the latest changes made by others on the team.

We group make with the other commands for keeping track of differences between files only by a leap of the imagination. However, although it does not compare two versions of the same source file, it can be used to compare versions such as a source file and the formatted output.

Part of what makes UNIX a productive environment for text processing is discovering other uses for standard programs. The make utility has many possible applications for a documentation project. One such use is to maintain up-to-date copies of formatted files that make up a single manual and provide users with a way of obtaining a printed copy of the entire manual without having to know which preprocessors or nroff/troff options need to be invoked.

The basic operation that make performs is to compare two sets of files, for example, formatted files and unformatted files, and determine if any members of one set, the unformatted files, are more recent than their counterpart in the other set, the formatted files. This is accomplished by simply comparing the date or time stamp of pairs of files. If the unformatted source file has been modified since the formatted file was made, make executes the specified command to "remake" the formatted file.

To use make, you have to write a description file, usually named makefile (or Makefile), that resides in the working directory for the project. The makefile specifies a hierarchy of dependencies among individual files, called *components*. At the top of this hierarchy is a *target*. For our purposes, you can think of the target as a printed copy of a book; the components are formatted files generated by processing an unformatted file with nroff.

Here's the makefile that reflects these dependencies.

```
manual: ch01.fmt ch02.fmt ch03.fmt
        lp ch0[1-3].fmt
ch01.fmt: ch01
        nroff -mm ch01 > ch01.fmt
ch02.fmt: ch02
        tbl ch02 | nroff -mm > ch01.fmt
ch03.fmt: ch03a ch03b ch03c
        nroff -mm ch03? > ch03.fmt
```

This hierarchy can be represented in a diagram:

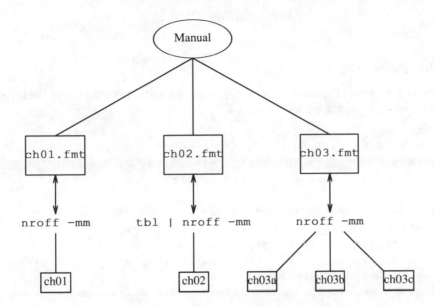

The target is `manual` and it is made up of three formatted files whose names appear after the colon. Each of these components has its own dependency line. For instance, `ch01.fmt` is dependent upon a coded file named `ch01`. Underneath the dependency line is the command that generates `ch01.fmt`. Each command line *must* begin with a tab.

When you enter the command `make`, the end result is that the three formatted files are spooled to the printer. However, a sequence of operations is performed before this final action. The dependency line for each component is evaluated, determining if the coded file has been modified since the last time the formatted file was made. The formatting command will be executed only if the coded file is more recent. After all the components are made, the `lp` command is executed.

As an example of this process, we'll assume that all the formatted files are up-to-date. Then by editing the source file `ch03a`, we change the modification time. When you execute the `make` command, any output files dependent on `ch03a` are reformatted.

```
$ make
nroff -mm ch03? > ch03.fmt
lp ch0[1-3].fmt
```

Only `ch03.fmt` needs to be remade. As soon as that formatting command finishes, the command underneath the target `manual` is executed, spooling the files to the printer.

Although this example has actually made only limited use of `make`'s facilities, we hope it suggests more ways to use `make` in a documentation project. You can keep your `makefiles` just this simple, or you can go on to learn additional notation, such as internal macros and suffixes, in an effort to generalize the description file for increased usefulness. We'll return to `make` in Chapter 18.

## · Manipulating Data ·

### Removing Formatting Codes

The `deroff` command removes `nroff/troff` requests, macros, inline backslash
sequences, and `eqn` and `tbl` specifications.

```
$ cat temp
.CH 11 "A Miscellany of UNIX Commands"
In this chapter, we present a miscellany of \s-2UNIX\s0
programs with text-processing applications.
.P
In addition, we introduce several \s-2UNIX\s0 utilities
$ deroff temp
    Miscellany  UNIX Programs
In this chapter, we present a miscellany of UNIX programs
with text-processing applications.
In addition, we introduce several UNIX utilities
```

Special rules are applied to text specified as arguments to a macro so that they are not
passed through `deroff`. A word in a macro call must contain at least three letters.
Thus, *A* and *of* are omitted.

The `deroff -w` command is used by `spell` to remove `troff` requests
and place each word on a separate line. You can use `deroff` in a similar manner to
prepare a word list.

```
$ deroff -w temp
Miscellany
UNIX
Programs
In
this
chapter
we
present
miscellany
of
UNIX
programs
with
text
processing
applications
In
addition
```

Again, not all "words" are recognized as words. The `deroff` command requires
that a word consist of at least two characters, which may be letters, numerals,

ampersands, or apostrophes. (As mentioned above, it applies slightly different rules to text specified as an argument to a macro.)

We had hoped `deroff` might be useful for our clients who wanted online copies of a document but used a word processor. Because `deroff` drops words, it was not practical for stripping out `troff`-specific constructs. Perhaps the best way to do this is to use `nroff` to process the file, and then use a combination of terminal filters to strip out tabs, backspaces (overstrikes), and reverse linefeeds.

## The `sort` and `uniq` Commands

The `sort` command puts lines of a file in alphabetic or numeric order. The `uniq` command eliminates duplicate lines in a file.

The `sort` command works on each line of a text file. Normally, it is used to order the contents of files containing data such as names, addresses, and phone numbers. In the following example, we use `grep` to search for index entries, coded with the macro `.XX` or `.XN`, and sort the output in alphabetic order.

```
$ grep ".X[XN]" ch04 | sort -df
.XX "ABORT statement"
.XX "ASSIGNMENT statement"
.XX "BASIC statements, ABORT"
.XX "BASIC statements, ASSIGNMENT"
.XX "BASIC statements, BEGIN CASE"
```

The −f option folds uppercase and lowercase words together (that is, it ignores case when performing the sort). The −d option sorts in dictionary order, ignoring any special characters.

The `uniq` command works only on sorted files, comparing each adjacent line. The `sort` command has a −u option for removing all but one indentical set of lines. Usually this is sufficient, but `uniq` does have several options, which gives you additional flexibility. For example, here's the sorted output of four files:

```
$ sort test*
apples
apples
apples
chestnuts
chestnuts
grapes
oranges
oranges
oranges
oranges
walnuts
walnuts
walnuts
```

The −d option prints one line for each duplicate line, but does not print lines that are unique.

```
$ sort test* | uniq -d
apples
chestnuts
oranges
walnuts
```

In this example, *grapes* has been filtered out. The −u option prints only unique lines. If we used the −u option, only *grapes* would appear.

You wouldn't expect sort to be useful on a document containing long lines of text. However, if you bothered to start sentences on a new line when creating the input file (as we recommended in Chapter 3), scanning a sorted file can produce some interesting things. The following command sorts the contents of ch03 and pipes the output through pg:

```
$ sort -u ch03 | pg
```

Looking at the results gives you a slightly turned about view of your document. For instance, you might notice inconsistencies among arguments to formatter requests:

```
.sp
.sp .2i
.sp .3v
.sp .5
```

Or you could check the frequency with which sentences begin in the same manner:

```
It is dangerous to use mvcur()
It is designed so that each piece of code
It is possible that some programs
```

In the next example, we use deroff to create a word list. Then we sort it and use uniq to remove duplicates. The −c option with uniq provides a count of the occurrences of identical lines. (It overrides −u and −d.)

```
$ deroff -w ch03 | sort -fd | uniq -c
   1 abort
   1 aborted
   3 about
   4 above
   1 absolute
   1 absorb
   1 accepting
   1 accomplishes
   1 active
   2 actual
   5 actually
   2 Add
   7 add
 ...
  68 you
   3 Your
```

```
 13 your
  2 zero
```

In the next example, we repeat the previous command, this time adding another sort at the end to order the words by frequency. The −r option is used to *reverse* the comparison, putting the greatest number first.

```
$ deroff -w ch03 | sort -fd | uniq -c | sort -rfd
666 the
234 to
219 is
158 window
156 of
148 and
114 in
111 screen
105 that
 83 character
 76 are
. . .
  1 aborted
  1 abort
```

You will find other examples of sort in the next section, where we look at sorting particular fields. Be sure to read the UNIX command pages for sort and uniq and experiment using different options.

## The join Command

The join command compares lines contained in separate files and joins lines that have the same key. (When you use sort or join, each line is separated into *fields* by blanks or tabs. Normally, the first field is the key field, on which the sort or join is performed. However, there are options that allow you to change the key field.) The file must be sorted in ascending ASCII sequence before being processed by join.

```
$ cat 85
jan    19
feb    05
mar    14
apr    15
may    15
jun    18
jul    19
aug    20
sep    19
nov    18
dec    18
$ cat 86
```

```
        jan     09
        feb     15
        mar     04
        apr     06
        may     14
        jun     13
        jul     13
        aug     10
        sep     14
        nov     13
        dec     12
$ sort 85 > 85.temp; sort 86 > 86.temp
```

First we sort both of these files, creating temporary files. Then we perform the  join,
followed by a  sort  with the  −M  option, to reorder them by month.

```
$ join 85.temp 86.temp | sort −M > joiner
$ cat joiner
jan 19 09
feb 05 15
mar 14 04
apr 15 06
may 15 14
jun 18 13
jul 19 13
aug 20 10
sep 19 14
nov 18 13
dec 18 12
$
```

After the data is joined in this manner, it can be sorted by field.  Fields are separated by
blank spaces or tabs.  The sort can be performed on specific fields, using + to indicate
the first sort field and - to indicate the last sort field.  The first field is  +0.  To sort on
the second field, use  +1.

```
$ sort +1 joiner
feb 05 15
mar 14 04
apr 15 06
may 15 14
dec 18 12
jun 18 13
nov 18 13
jan 19 09
jul 19 13
sep 19 14
aug 20 10
```

## The comm Command

The comm command reads the contents of two sorted files and produces for output a three-column listing of lines that are found

- only in the first file;
- only in the second file;
- in both the first and second files.

For example, let's suppose that we had generated a list of UNIX commands found in Berkeley 4.2 and another list of commands found in AT&T System V.2. We can use comm to produce a compact listing of commands found exclusively in one version and commands common to both. For obvious reasons, this example uses only the beginning of the list.

```
$ cat bsd4.2
adb
addbib
apply
apropos
ar
as
at
awk

$ cat attV.2
adb
admin
ar
as
asa
at
awk
```

Note that both files have already been sorted.

```
$ comm bsd4.2 attV.2
                                adb
addbib
                admin
apply
apropos
                                ar
                                as
                asa
                                at
                                awk
```

Commands found only on systems running Berkeley 4.2 are in the left-hand column, and those found only on AT&T System V.2 are in the center column. Commands found in both versions are listed in the right-hand column.

You can also suppress the display of one or more columns. For instance, if you wanted to display only the commands that were found on both systems, you'd enter:

```
$ comm -12 bsd4.2 attV.2
```

Only the third column would be shown.

By specifying − instead of a filename, you can also use standard input. In the next example, we produce a listing of filenames from two directories on the system, sort them, and compare them against the commands named in the `bsd4.2` file. This allows us to compare commands found on our system with those on the list of Berkeley commands.

```
$ ( cd /bin ; ls ; cd /usr/bin ; ls ) | sort | comm - bsd4.2
acctcom
                adb
                addbib
admin
apnum
                apply
                apropos
                                ar
                                as
asa
                at
                                awk
```

Parentheses are used to group a series of commands, combining their output into a single stream; we want a list of command names without pathnames from several directories. Because a new shell is created to execute these commands, notice that we do not change our current working directory when the commands in parentheses have finished executing.

## The cut and paste Commands

The `cut` and `paste` commands modify a table or any other data in fields or columns. You can extract specific columns of data using `cut`, and join them horizontally using `paste`.

For our examples, we'll make use of a portion of a table of ASCII characters that specifies their decimal and hexadecimal values. (This example is probably unnecessarily complex; you can use cut and paste for much simpler jobs than this!) Here's what the table looks like to begin with:

```
$ cat appc
.TS
center, box;
cb cb cb
```

```
n n l.
Decimal      Hexadecimal  ASCII
=
000   00     NUL
001   01     SO
002   02     STX
003   03     ETX
004   04     EOT
005   05     ENQ
006   06     ACK
007   07     BEL
008   08     BS
009   09     HT
.TE
```

Each column is separated by a tab. A tab is the default field delimiter for cut; the −d option can be used to change it. The −c option allows you to specify character positions or ranges. The command cut −c6−80 would print characters beginning at position 6 through 80, truncating the first five characters. The −f option is used to specify one or more fields that are passed to standard output. (Given the name of the command, one might reasonably think you'd specify the fields or column position you wanted *cut* out, but . . . )

In the next example we extract the third field, which contains the ASCII names:

```
$ cut −f3 −s appc
ASCII
NUL
SO
STX
ETX
EOT
ENQ
ACK
BEL
BS
HT
```

We use the −s option to remove all lines that do not have any delimiters, thus dropping the tbl constructs from the output. Normally, cut passes lines without delimiters straight through, and that is what we really want for our next feat. We are going to reorder the table so that it can be referenced by the ASCII name rather than by decimal number. All of this can be done from the command line, with only a brief entry into the editor at the end.

We'll look at this in stages. First, we extract the third column and send it along to paste:

```
$ cut -f3 appc | paste - appc
.TS     .TS
center, box; center, box;
cb cb cb     cb cb cb
n n l.n n l.
ASCII Decimal     Hexadecimal ASCII
=       =
NUL   000   00    NUL
SO    001   01    SO
STX   002   02    STX
ETX   003   03    ETX
EOT   004   04    EOT
ENQ   005   05    ENQ
ACK   006   06    ACK
BEL   007   07    BEL
BS    008   08    BS
HT    009   09    HT
.TE     .TE
```

The paste command reads one or more files or standard input (the − option) and replaces the newline with a tab in all but the last file. This gives us four columns. (Yes, it doubled the tbl specifications, but we have an editor.) Now, all we have to do is extract the first three columns from the output. Only cut −f1,2,3 has been added to the previous command, and the output is redirected to a file.

```
$ cut -f3 appc | paste - appc | cut -f1,2,3 > ascii.table
$ cat ascii.table
.TS     .TS
center, box; center, box;
cb cb cb     cb cb cb
n n l.n n l.
ASCII Decimal     Hexadecimal
=       =
NUL   000   00
SO    001   01
STX   002   02
ETX   003   03
EOT   004   04
ENQ   005   05
ACK   006   06
BEL   007   07
BS    008   08
HT    009   09
.TE     .TE
```

This gives us three columns in the correct order. We can go into vi to rearrange the tbl constructs and execute a sort command on just the data portion of the table to bring it all together.

```
$ cat ascii.table
.TS
center, box;
cb cb cb
n n l.
ASCII  Decimal       Hexadecimal
=
ACK    006    06
BEL    007    07
BS     008    08
ENQ    005    05
EOT    004    04
ETX    003    03
HT     009    09
NUL    000    00
SO     001    01
STX    002    02
.TE
```

The `paste` command can be used in several interesting ways. Normally, in order to merge two files, `paste` replaces the newline in the first file with a tab. The −d option allows you to specify a substitute for the tab. This can be any single character or a list of characters. Special characters can be represented as follows: newline (\n), tab (\t), backslash (\\), and empty string (\0). Each character in the list is assigned in sequence to replace a newline, and the list is recycled as many times as necessary. We can use `paste` to present our three-column table in six columns:

```
$ paste -s -d"\t\n" appci
.TS    center, box;
cb cb cb       n n l.
Decimal        Hexadecimal ASCII  =
000    00      NUL    001    01    SO
002    02      STX    003    03    ETX
004    04      EOT    005    05    ENQ
006    06      ACK    007    07    BEL
008    08      BS     009    09    HT
.TE
```

The −s option is used when only a single file is specified. It tells `paste` to merge subsequent lines in the same file rather than to merge one line at a time from several files. In this example, the first line's newline is replaced by a tab while the second line retains the newline. To get nine columns out of three-column input, you'd specify −d"\t\t\n".

A little work needs to be done to the `tbl` specifications. You could also execute the `paste` command from within `vi` so that it only affects the data portion.

You would probably want to go to this much trouble for a large table (or many small tables) rather than the small examples shown here. A more practical example that uses `paste` alone would be to construct a multi-column table from a single long list of words. Simply split the list into equal-sized chunks, then paste them together side by side.

## The tr Command

The tr command is a character translation filter, reading standard input and either deleting specific characters or substituting one character for another.

The most common use of tr is to change each character in one string to the corresponding character in a second string. (A string of consecutive ASCII characters can be represented as a hyphen-separated range.)

For example, the command:

```
$ tr "A-Z" "a-z" < file
```

will convert all uppercase characters in *file* to the equivalent lowercase characters. The result is printed on standard output.

As described in Chapter 7, this translation (and the reverse) can be useful from within vi for changing the case of a string. You can also delete specific characters. The -d option deletes from the input each occurrence of one or more characters specified in a string (special characters should be placed within quotation marks to protect them from the shell). For instance, the following command passes to standard output the contents of *file* with all punctuation deleted:

```
$ cat file | tr -d ",.!?;:"
```

The -s (*squeeze*) option of tr removes multiple consecutive occurrences of the same character. For example, the command:

```
$ tr -s " " < file
```

will print on standard output a copy of *file* in which multiple spaces in sequence have been replaced with a single space.

We've also found tr useful when converting documents created on other systems for use under UNIX. For example, one of our writers created some files using an IBM PC word processor. When we uploaded the files to our system, and tried to edit them with vi, we got the message:

```
Not an ascii file
```

and a blank screen. The vi editor could not read the file. However, using a programming utility that lists the actual binary values that make up the contents of a file (od, or *octal dump*), we were able to determine that the word processor used nulls (octal 000) instead of newlines (octal 012) to terminate each line.

The tr command allows you to specify characters as octal values by preceding the value with a backslash, so the command:

```
$ tr '\000' '\012'
```

was what we needed to convert the file into a form that could be edited with vi.

## Splitting Large Files

Splitting a single large file into smaller files can be done out of necessity—when you come across a program that can't handle a large file—or as a matter of preference—when you find it easier to work with smaller files. UNIX offers two different programs for breaking up files, split and csplit.

The split command divides a file into chunks, consisting of the same number of lines. This is 1000 lines, unless specified differently. In the following example of split, we break up a 1700-line file into 500-line chunks. The wc command supplies a summary of the number of lines, words, and characters in a text file.

```
$ wc ch03
1708    8962   59815 ch03
$ split -500 ch03
$ wc ch03*
500     2462   16918 ch03aa
500     2501   16731 ch03ab
500     2976   19350 ch03ac
208     1023    6816 ch03ad
1708    8962   59815 ch03
```

The split command created four files. It appended aa, ab, ac, etc. to the end of the original filename to create a unique filename for each file. You can also specify, as a third argument, a different filename to be used instead of the original filename.

Look at the end of one of these files:

```
$ tail ch03ac
.Bh "Miscellaneous Functions"
.in 5n
.TS
tab(@);
l l l.
```

Unfortunately, the file breaks in the middle of a table. The split command pays no attention to content, making it inadequate for breaking a file into manageable, but complete, sections.

The csplit command offers an alternative, allowing you to break a file in context. There are two ways to use it. The first is to supply one or more line numbers. You could enter the following command:

```
$ csplit ch03 100 145 200
```

Four files would be created (0-99, 100-144, 145-199, 200-end). The naming convention for files created by csplit is different than split. Files are named xx00, xx01, xx02, and so on. If you want to specify a prefix that is different than xx, you can do so with the −f option.

Because we do not know in advance which line numbers to specify, we can use grep to get this information. The −n option to grep causes line numbers to be returned. In this example, we specify a pattern to match the section header macros, Ah and Bh:

```
$ grep -n ".[AB]h" ch03
```

It produces the following listing:

```
   5:.Ah "Introduction"
  30:.Ah "Using the Curses Library"
 175:.Ah "The Curses Functions"
 398:.Bh "Adding Characters to the Screen Image"
 638:.Bh "Standout Mode"
 702:.Bh "Getting Characters from the Terminal"
 777:.Bh "Input Modes"
 958:.Bh "Erasing and Clearing"
1133:.Bh "Creating and Removing Multiple Windows"
1255:.Bh "Window-Specific Functions"
1301:.Bh "Manipulating Multiple Windows"
1654:.Bh "Terminal Manipulation"
```

From this listing, we select the appropriate places at which to split the file and supply these numbers to split. The −f option is used to supply a filename prefix.

```
$ csplit -f ch03. ch03 175 1133
6803                        Number of bytes in each segment
32544
20468
$ ls ch03.*
ch03.00
ch03.01
ch03.02
```

The csplit command prints a character count for each of the three files it created. (This count can be suppressed using the −s option.)

The second way to use csplit is to supply a list of patterns. For instance, if you had prepared an outline that you wanted to break into files correponding to sections I, II, and III, you could specify:

```
$ csplit -s -f sect. outline /I./ /II./ /III./
$ ls sect.*
sect.01
sect.02
sect.03
```

You can also repeat a pattern. In one project we were working on, one large file contained a number of commands in reference page format. We decided it would be easier if we put each command in its own file. The beginning of a reference header was marked by the macro .Rh 0. First, we used grep to determine the number of times this macro occurred.

```
$ grep -c ".Rh 0" ch04
43
```

We reduce this number by 1 and surround it with braces:

```
$ csplit -s -f ch04. ch04 "/.Rh 0/" {42}
```

The pattern is enclosed within double quotation marks because it contains a space. (If you use the C shell, you must protect the braces from being interpreted by placing them in double quotation marks as well.) This command creates 43 files:

```
$ ls ch04*
ch04
ch04.00
ch04.01
ch04.02
ch04.03
...
ch04.39
ch04.40
ch04.41
ch04.42
ch04.43
```

The only task remaining is to rename the files, using the name of the command listed as the first argument to the .Rh macro. (We'd have to write an awk or shell script to do this automatically.)

After you have divided a large file into a number of smaller files, you might organize them in a subdirectory. Let's look at a small example of this:

```
$ mkdir ch04.files
$ mv ch04.?? ch04.files
```

Again, the usefulness of filename metacharacters is apparent, giving us the ability to move 43 files without typing 43 filenames.

## Encryption

The cloak-and-dagger set and the security conscious will find uses for the encryption facilities of UNIX. (These facilities are not available on UNIX systems sold outside the United States.) The crypt command reads a file from standard input, asks you to supply a *key* for encoding the file, and passes to standard output an encrypted version of the file. You should redirect standard output to a new file because the encrypted file is not readable text.

```
$ cat message | crypt > encrypted.msg
Enter key:alabaster
```

Just as when you enter a password, the key does not appear on the screen as you enter it. If you prefer, you can enter the key as an argument to crypt. To decode an encrypted file, you simply cat the file to crypt and supply the key.

The UNIX editors ed, ex, and vi, can be invoked with the -x option to read or edit an encrypted file. (Some versions of these programs recognize this option but do not support the encryption feature.) Of course, you have to supply the correct key.

## ▪ Cleaning Up and Backing Up ▪

In this section, we show some procedures for backing up active files to some other medium such as tape or floppy disk. At many sites, backups are the responsibility of one person, who performs these tasks on a regular basis to ensure that users can recover much of their data in case there is a serious system crash. At other sites, individual users might be responsible for doing their own backups, especially if there are only a few users on the system. Whoever does it must ensure that backups of important files are made periodically.

A second reason for learning a backup procedure is to enable you to store files on an off-line medium. For users of PCs, this is the standard method of operation (and therefore much simpler to do), but all UNIX systems have hard disks as the primary storage medium. No matter how large a disk drive is, sooner or later, users will fill it to capacity. Frequently, there are useless files that can be deleted. Other inactive files, such as an early draft of a document, might be removed from the system after you have made a copy on floppy disk or tape. After a project is finished, you probably want to make several copies of all important files. At a later time, should you need files that have been stored off-line, you can easily restore them to the system.

We are going to describe how to use the `cpio` command for backing up one or more working directories. There are other UNIX commands that might be used as well (`tar` and `dd`, for instance). At your site, you may even have simpler shell scripts that prevent you from having to deal with `cpio` directly. Ask an expert user at your site about backup procedures and go through it once or twice. Apart from learning about `cpio`, you will need:

1.  The UNIX filename of the device (/dev/*xxxx*) to which you are directing the output of the `cpio` command.

2.  Familiarity with operating the device, such as being able to load a tape in the tape drive and knowing how to format a floppy disk prior to use.

You can use `cpio` in two basic ways, either to back up or to restore files. You use `cpio` with the `-o` option and `>` to redirect output to the device for backup, or with the `-i` option and `<` to redirect input from the device to restore files.

Unlike many of the commands we've looked at, `cpio` depends exclusively on reading a list of filenames from standard input. This list identifies the files that will be backed up. For practical purposes, this involves doing an `ls` command on the directory you want backed up and piping the results to `cpio`.

You need to know the UNIX filename for the backup device. This name is site specific, so you need to check with a knowledgeable user. At our site, we have a floppy disk drive named `/dev/rfp021`. A tape drive might be named `/dev/mt0`.

After you have loaded the tape in the tape drive or placed the floppy disk in the disk drive, you can perform the backup using your own version of this command:

```
$ ls /work/docbook/ch13 | cpio -ov > /dev/rfp021
sect3
dict
shellstuff
...
384 blocks
```

The −v (*verbose*) option prints a list of filenames on the screen.

The −i option to cpio reads or restores files from a tape or floppy disk device. Sometimes, before you actually restore files, you want to list the contents of the tape or disk. The −t option prints a table of contents but does not actually read these files onto the system.

```
$ cpio -it < /dev/rfp021
384 blocks
sect3
dict
shellstuff
...
```

Using the −v option along with the −t option produces a long (verbose) listing of files, as if you had entered ls −l.

You don't have to extract all the files from disk or tape. You can specify certain files, using filename metacharacters to specify a pattern.

```
$ cpio -iv "sect?" < /dev/rfp021
No match.
```

Remember to refer to the full pathname if the files were saved using a complete pathname, and to put pathnames that include metacharacters within double quotation marks.

```
$ cpio -i "/work/docbook/ch13/sect?" < /dev/rfp021
384 blocks
sect3
sect2
sect1
```

Before restoring a file, cpio checks to see that it won't overwrite an existing file of the same name that has been modified more recently than the file being read.

You can also use the find command with the −cpio condition to do a back up. The advantage of using find is that it descends all the way down a directory hierarchy.

```
$ find /work/docbook/ch13 -cpio /dev/rfp021
```

To restore a directory hierarchy, use the −d option to cpio. Administrators frequently use find to generate a list of files that have been modified within a certain time period. The conditions −mtime (*modification time*) and −atime (*access time*) can be followed by a number indicating a number of days. This number can be preceded by a plus sign, indicating *more than* that number of days, or a minus sign, indicating *less than* that many days. If there is no sign, the condition indicates exactly that number of days.

This example uses `find` to produce a list of files that have been modified within the last seven days. These active files are good candidates for backups.

```
$ find /work/docbook -mtime -7 -print
/work/docbook
/work/docbook/oshell
/work/docbook/ch01
...
```

Don't forget you have to specify `-print` to see the results of a `find` command.

You could work up your own version of this command to look for your own files that have not been accessed in the last 21 days. Add the option `-atime` with an argument of `+21` to list the files and directories that have not been accessed in over 21 days. Add the `-user` option to look only for your own files, the `-cpio` option to backup these files, and the `-ok` option to execute an `rm` command to delete them from the system after they've been backed up.

```
$ find /work -atime +21 -user -cpio /dev/rfp021 -ok rm {} \;
```

The `-ok` option is the same as the `-exec` option; however, instead of executing the command specified within parentheses on all files selected by `find`, it prompts you first to approve the command for each file.

### ▪ Compressing Files ▪

You can conserve the amount of disk space that text files take up by storing some of your files in a compressed form. The `pack` command can be used to compress a file. It generally reduces a text file by 25 to 40 percent.

```
$ ls -l ch04/sect1
-rw-rw-rw-   1 fred    doc    29350 Jun 10 15:22 ch04/sect1
$ pack ch04/sect1
pack: ch04/sect1: 39.9% Compression
```

The original file is replaced by a packed file with a `.z` appended to the original filename.

```
$ ls -l ch04/sect1.z
-rw-rw-rw-   1 fred    doc    17648 Jun 10 15:29 ch04/sect1.z
```

The `pack` command reduced the size of this file from 29K to 17K bytes. If used system-wide, it could save a significant amount of disk space, although the amount of compression will vary from file to file. Obviously, there is less benefit in packing small files.

To expand a packed file, use the `unpack` command. You can specify the name of the file with or without the `.z` suffix.

```
$ unpack ch04/sect1
unpack: ch04/sect1: unpacked
```

Another way to temporarily unpack a file is to use a special version of `cat` for packed files, called `pcat`. Use this command to view a packed file (pipe it through `more` or `pg`) or send it as input to another command, as in the following example:

```
$ pcat ch04/sect1 | nroff -mm
```

## ▪ Communications ▪

More and more, we find that our projects require us to work on several different computer systems, some of them UNIX systems, some not. Given this situation, the ability to work remotely on other systems and to transfer files has been essential. Fortunately, a number of useful communications programs are part of the standard UNIX shipment.

Two basic types of connections between computer systems are a *dial-up* line, using a modem to communicate across phone lines, and a *direct* line, when two computer systems are in close proximity and can be connected by a single cable. The `uucp` and `cu` commands establish communication links using both types of connections.

The `cu` command (Berkeley's version is called `tip`,  ... UNIX program for conducting a login session on a remote computer system. UUCP (UNIX-to-UNIX copy) is a series of related programs for transferring files between UNIX systems. Its main program is called `uucp`.

We cannot provide full descriptions of these facilities here. A good way to learn is to ask an expert user to help you transfer files or begin a remote login session. Keep notes on the procedure and when following it, if things don't work as expected, get more help.

The UUCP programs are quite straightforward and easy to use after you are accustomed to the conventions. Each system on the UUCP network has a file that describes the other systems linked to it and what types of links are available. This file is created by the system administrator of each system. You can find out the names of these remote systems by entering the `uuname` command. If your system is properly configured and you have a login on a remote system, such as `boston`, you can begin a remote session by entering:

```
$ cu boston
```

After you are connected to the remote system, you should get a login message. To quit a remote session, log out and then enter `~.` (tilde dot) to return to your own machine.

There are a number of commands you can enter while under the control of `cu`, permitting, for instance, the execution of commands on the local system while you are still logged in to the remote system. Check the reference page in your UNIX documentation.

You can also *dial direct* to a non-UNIX system by specifying a telephone number on the command line (providing, of course, that the files accessed by these communications programs have been properly configured by the system administrator).

You can send mail to users on these remote systems and transfer files. Generally, file transfers take place between *public directories* on both systems, usually /usr/spool/uucppublic. File transfers between other directories will contend with file and directory access permissions as well as uucp permissions set by the system administrator. The character ~ serves as a shorthand for the public directory.

For instance, when working on site for a client, we often create files that we want to send to our own system. If we are logged in on their system, we can send the file outline to our system named ora by entering:

```
$ uucp -m outline ora!~/fred/
```

The UUCP facility is batch oriented, accepting requests and acting upon them in the order in which they are received. Although it may execute your request immediately, if it is busy or encounters difficulty making the connection, UUCP will carry out the request at a later time.

The -m option is used so that we are sent mail when the copy is actually completed. The system name is followed by an exclamation mark (if you use the C shell, escape ! with a backslash). Then you specify a tilde (~) followed by the user's name. Putting a slash after the user name (fred) ensures that the user name will be interpreted as a directory (or a directory will be created if one does not exist).

Occasionally, you will need to transfer a large number of files or, perhaps, an entire directory hierarchy. There are some simple tricks you can use to combine multiple files into a single file, making it easier to transmit to another system. They are especially helpful when you transfer between public directories.

You must first create a list of the files to be included. (You can do this either manually or with a command like ls or find.) Then use cpio to create what we can call a file *archive* on standard output rather than on a backup device. Redirect standard output to a file, then use UUCP to send the archive. Use the same backup program on the target system to restore the archive. For example, if you had a book made up of files ch01, ch02, etc., you could "package" that book for transfer to another system using cpio:

```
boston$ cd /usr/proj/book
boston$ find . -name 'ch0?' -print | cpio -oc > book.archive
```

or using a manually generated list of filenames:

```
boston$ ls ch0? > filelist
boston$ cpio -oc < filelist > book.archive
```

Then, after transferring book.archive (instead of numerous individual files) to the remote system with UUCP, a user can restore the archive:

```
calif$ mkdir /usr/proj/book
calif$ mv /usr/spool/uucppublic/book.archive /usr/proj/book
calif$ cd /usr/proj/book
calif$ cpio -icd < book.archive
```

(The -c option of cpio writes header information in ASCII for portability; -d tells cpio to create directories if needed when doing the restore.)

(On Berkeley UNIX systems, you can do something similar with `tar`. See your UNIX manual for details.)

## ▪ Scripts of UNIX Sessions ▪

Throughout this chapter, we have provided examples of UNIX commands. These examples were made using a command called `script` (which is not a standard System V command). The `script` command allows you to make a file copy of a UNIX session. Without this facility, we'd have to simulate the examples by hand.

After you invoke `script`, your input and output is copied to a file. By default, the name of this file is `typescript`, but you can supply a different name on the command line.

```
$ script
Script started on Thu Jul 10 12:49:57 1987
$ echo hello
hello
$
```

To quit, you enter *CTRL-D*.

```
$ cat typescript
Script started on Thu Jul 10 12:49:57 1987
$ echo hello
hello
$
script done on Thu Jul 10 12:50:11 1987
```

After we make a script, we simply read the file into our text using `vi`.

Keeping a script of a procedure is also a good start for building a shell script that performs a routine task automatically.

# 12

# Let the Computer Do the Dirty Work

Computers are very good at doing the same thing repeatedly, or doing a series of very similar things one after another. These are just the kinds of things that people hate to do, so it makes sense to learn how to let the computer do the dirty work.

As we discussed in Chapter 7, you can save  ex  commands in a *script*, and execute the script from within  vi  with the  :so  command.  It is also possible to apply such a script to a file from the outside—without opening the file with  vi.  As you can imagine, when you apply the same series of edits to many different files, you can work very quickly using a script.

In addition, there is a special UNIX editor, called  sed  (*stream editor*), that *only* works with scripts.  Although  sed  can be used to edit files (and we will show many useful applications in this chapter), it has a unique place in the UNIX editing pantheon not as a file editor, but as a filter that performs editing operations on the fly, while data is passed from one program to another through a pipe.

The  sed  editor uses an editing syntax that is similar to that used by  ex, so it should not be difficult to learn the basics.

The  awk  program, which is discussed in the next chapter, is yet another text-processing program.  It is similar to  sed, in that it works from the outside and can be used as a filter, but there the resemblance ends.  It is really not an editor at all, but a database manipulation program that can be turned into an editor.  Its syntax goes beyond the global substitution/regular expression syntax we've already seen, and so  awk  may be the last thing that many writers learn.  Nonetheless, it has some important capabilities that you may want to be familiar with.

Finally, to make best use of these tools, you need to know a bit about shell programming.  In fact, because the shell provides a framework that you can use to put all these other tools together, we need to discuss it first.

If you are a programmer, and have already worked with the shell, this discussion may be too elementary; however, we are assuming that many of our readers are writers with only minimal exposure to programming.  They, like us when we started working with UNIX, need encouragement to branch out into these untried waters that have so little apparent connection to the task at hand.

This chapter is different from those in the first part of the book in that it not only teaches the basics of some new programs, but also puts them to work building some useful text-processing tools. At times, material is organized according to what is needed to build the tools, rather than as a comprehensive attempt to teach the program itself. As a result, the material presented on sed, for example, is less complete than our earlier treatment of vi. We cover the most important points, but in many ways this chapter is suggestive. If you come away with a sense of possibility, it has done its job.

## ▪ Shell Programming ▪

A shell script, or shell program, can be no more than a sequence of stored commands, entered in a file just as you would type them yourself to the shell.

There are two shells in common use in the UNIX system, the Bourne shell (sh), championed by AT&T, and the C shell (csh), developed at the University of California at Berkeley. Although the C shell has many features that make it preferable for interactive use, the Bourne shell is much faster, so it is the tool of choice for writing shell scripts. (Even if you use the C shell, scripts written using Bourne shell syntax will be executed in the Bourne shell.)

We discuss the Bourne shell exclusively in this chapter, although we make reference to differences from the C shell on occasion. This should pose no problem to C shell users, however, because the basic method of issuing commands is identical. The differences lie in more advanced programming constructs, which we will not introduce in detail here.

### Stored Commands

The .profile (or .login if you use the C shell) file in your home directory is a good example of a shell program consisting only of stored commands. A simple .profile might look like this:

```
stty erase '^H' echoe kill '^X' intr '^C'
PATH=/bin:/usr/bin:/usr/local/bin:.;export PATH
umask 2
date
mail
```

This file does some automatic housekeeping to set up your account environment every time you log in. Even if you aren't familiar with the commands it contains, you can get the basic idea. The commands are executed one line at a time; it is a tremendous time-saving to be able to type one command instead of five.

You can probably think of many other repetitive sequences of commands that you'd rather not type one at a time. For example, let's suppose you were accustomed to working on an MS-DOS system, and wanted to create a dir command that would print out the current directory and the names and sizes of all of your files, rather than just the names. You could save the following two commands in a file called dir:

```
pwd
ls -l
```

To execute the commands saved in a file, you can simply give its name as an argument
to the sh command. For example:

```
$ sh dir
/work/docbook/ch13
total 21
-rw-rw-r--   3 fred       doc          263 Apr 12 09:17 abbrevs
-rw-rw-r--   1 fred       doc           10 May  1 14:01 dir
-rw-rw-r--   1 fred       doc         6430 Apr 12 15:00 sect1
-rw-rw-r--   1 fred       doc        14509 Apr 15 16:29 sect2
-rw-rw-r--   1 fred       doc         1024 Apr 28 10:35 stuff
-rw-rw-r--   1 fred       doc         1758 Apr 28 10:00 tmp
```

Or you can make a file *executable* by changing its file permissions with the chmod
command:

```
$ ls -l dir
-rw-rw-r--   1 fred       doc           10 May  1 14:01 dir
$ chmod +x dir
$ ls -l dir
-rwxrwxr-x   1 fred       doc           10 May  1 14:01 dir
```

After a file has executable permission, all you need to do to execute the commands it
contains is to type the file's name:

```
$ dir
/work/docbook/ch13
total 21
-rw-rw-r--   3 fred       doc          263 Apr 12 09:17 abbrevs
-rwxrwxr-x   1 fred       doc           10 May  1 14:01 dir
-rw-rw-r--   1 fred       doc         6430 Apr 12 15:00 sect1
-rw-rw-r--   1 fred       doc        14509 Apr 15 16:29 sect2
-rw-rw-r--   1 fred       doc         1024 Apr 28 10:35 stuff
-rw-rw-r--   1 fred       doc         1758 Apr 28 10:00 tmp
```

The next step is to make the shell script accessible from whatever directory you happen
to be working in. The Bourne shell maintains a variable called PATH, which is set up
during the login process, and contains a list of directories in which the shell should look
for executable commands. This list is usually referred to as your *search path*.

To use the value of a variable, simply precede its name with a dollar sign ($).
This makes it easy to check the value of a variable like PATH—simply use the echo
command:

```
$ echo $PATH
/bin:/usr/bin:/usr/local/bin:.
```

The Bourne shell expects the list of directory names contained in the PATH variable to
be separated by colons. If your search path is defined as shown, the following directories will be searched, in order, whenever you type the name of a command:

The syntax of if...then...else clauses can get confusing. One trick is to think of each keyword (if, then, and else) as a separate command that can take other commands as its argument. The else clause is optional. (That is, you can say, "if the condition is met, do this," and give no alternatives. If the condition is not met, the script will simply go on to the next line, or exit if there is no next line.) The entire sequence is terminated with the fi keyword.

After you realize that each part of the sequence is really just a separate command, like other UNIX commands, the abbreviated form, which uses semicolons rather than newlines to separate the commands, will also make sense:

```
if condition; then command; fi
```

An if...then...else clause allows you to make a choice between at most two options. There is also an elif statement that allows you to create a sequence of if clauses to deal with more conditions. For example, suppose your system supports a third macro package—one you've written yourself, and called mS because it's a superset of ms. (More on this in Chapter 17!) You could write the script like this:

```
if [ "$1" = "-mm" ]
then tbl $2 | eqn | nroff -mm | col | lp
elif [ "$1" = "-ms" ]
then tbl $2 | eqn | nroff -ms | col | lp
elif [ "$1" = "-mS" ]
then tbl $2 | eqn | nroff -mS | col | lp
fi
```

This syntax can get awkward for more than a few conditions. Fortunately, the shell provides a more compact way to handle multiple conditions: the case statement. The syntax of this statement looks complex (even in the slightly simplified form given here):

```
case value in
pattern) command;;
..
pattern) command;;
esac
```

In fact, the statement is quite easy to use, and is most easily shown by example. We could rewrite the previous script as follows:

```
case $1 in
    -mm) tbl $2 | eqn | nroff -mm | col | lp;;
    -ms) tbl $2 | eqn | nroff -ms | col | lp;;
    -mS) tbl $2 | eqn | nroff -mS | col | lp;;
esac
```

This form is considerably more compact, especially as the number of conditions grows. (Be sure to note the ;; at the end of each line. This is an important part of the syntax.)

```
/bin
/usr/bin
/usr/local/bin
. (shorthand for the current directory)
```

The allocation of system commands to the three bin directories is historical and somewhat arbitrary, although /usr/local/bin tends to contain commands that are local to a specific implementation of UNIX. It is sometimes called /usr/lbin or some other name.

To ensure that any shell scripts you create are automatically found whenever you type their names, you can do one of two things:

1. You can add shell scripts to one of the directories already in your search path. However, in most cases, these directories are only writable by the super-user, so this option is not available to all users.

2. You can create a special "tools" directory of your own, and add the name of that directory to your search path. This directory might be a subdirectory of your own home directory, or could be a more globally available directory used by a group of people.

For example, you could put the following line in your .profile:

```
PATH=/usr/fred/tools:.:/bin:/usr/bin:/usr/local/bin:
```

The /usr/fred/tools directory would be searched before any of the standard search directories. (This means that you can define an alternate command with the same name as an existing command. The version found first in the search path is executed, and the search is stopped at that point. You should not put local directories before the standard directories if you are concerned at all with system security, because doing so creates a loophole that can be exploited by an intruder.)

If you are using the C shell, the search path is stored in a variable called path, and has a different format; see your UNIX documentation for details. In addition, you must use the rehash command whenever you add a command to one of the search directories.

## Passing Arguments to Shell Scripts

The previous example is very simple; the commands it used took no arguments. In contrast, consider a case in which you want to save a single complex command line in a file. For example, if you use tbl and eqn with nroff, your typical command line might look like this:

```
$ tbl file | eqn | nroff -ms | col | lp
```

How much easier it would be to save that whole line in a single file called format, and simply type:

```
$ format file
```

The question then becomes: how do you tell your `format` script where in the command line to insert the *file* argument?

Because all of the programs in the script are designed to read standard input as well as take a filename argument, we could avoid the problem by writing the script thus:

```
tbl | eqn | nroff -ms | col | lp
```

and using it like this:

```
$ cat file | format
```

or like this:

```
$ format < file
```

But this still begs the question of how to pass an argument to a shell script.

Up to nine arguments can be represented by positional notation. The first argument is represented in the shell script by the symbol `$1`, the second by `$2`, and so on.

So, for example, we could write our script:

```
tbl $1 | eqn | nroff -ms | col | lp
```

When specified as an argument to the `format` command:

```
$ format ch01
```

the filename would be substituted in the script for the symbol `$1`.

But what if you want to specify several files at once? The symbol `$*` means "use all arguments," so the script:

```
tbl $* | eqn | nroff -ms | col | lp
```

will allow us to write:

```
$ format file1 file2...
```

Now consider the slightly more complex case in which you'd like to support either the `ms` or the `mm` macros. You could write the script like this:

```
tbl $2 | eqn | nroff $1 | col | lp
```

The first argument will now follow the invocation of `nroff`, and the second will represent the filename:

```
$ format -ms file
```

However, at this point we have lost the ability to specify "all arguments," because the first argument is used differently than all the rest. There are several ways to handle this situation, but we need to learn a few things first.

## Conditional Execution

Commands in a shell script can be executed conditionally using either the `if...then...else` or `case` command built into the shell. However, any conditional commands require the ability to test a value and make a choice based on the result. As its name might suggest, the `test` command does the trick.

There are different kinds of things you can test, using various options to the command. The general form of the command is:

```
$ test condition
```

*Condition* is constructed from one or more options; some of the most useful are listed in Table 12-1.

**TABLE 12-1.  Useful `test` Options**

| Option | Meaning |
|---|---|
| -d *file* | True if *file* exists and is a directory |
| -f *file* | True if *file* exists and is a regular file |
| -n *s1* | True if the length of string *s1* is nonzero |
| -r *file* | True if *file* exists and is readable |
| -s *file* | True if *file* exists and has a size greater than zero |
| -w *file* | True if *file* exists and is writable |
| -x *file* | True if *file* exists and is executable |
| -z *s1* | True if the length of string *s1* is zero |
| *str1* = *str2* | True if strings *str1* and *str2* are identical |
| *str1* != *str2* | True if strings *str1* and *str2* are not identical |
| *str1* | True if string *str1* is not the null string |
| *n1* -eq *n2* | True if the integers *n1* and *n2* are algebraically equal (any of the comparisons -ne, -gt, -ge, -lt, and -le may be used in place of -eq) |

The `test` command has a special form just for use in shell scripts. Instead of using the word *test*, you can simply enclose *condition* in square brackets. The expression must be separated from the enclosing brackets by spaces.

So, for example, to return to our `format` script, we could write:

```
if [ "$1" = "-mm" ]
then
    tbl $2 | eqn | nroff -mm | col | lp
else
    tbl $2 | eqn | nroff -ms | col | lp
fi
```

We've simply used the `test` command to compare the value of two strings—the ~ argument, and the string `"-mm"`—and executed the appropriate command line result. If the strings are equal, the first command line is executed; if they are not ~ the second line is executed instead. (Notice that there are spaces surrounding the ~ sign in the test.)

Here's how the `case` statement works. Each *value* in turn is compared (using standard shell metacharacters like * and ?, if present) against the *pattern* before the close parenthesis at the start of each line. If the pattern matches, the line is executed. If not, the script tries again with the next line in the `case` statement. After the value has been compared against each case, the process starts over with the next value (if more than one has been specified).

## Discarding Used Arguments

All of the conditions we've tested for so far are mutually exclusive. What if you want to include more than one potentially true condition in your script? The trick to dealing with this situation requires two more shell commands: `while` and `shift`.

Consider the following example. You realize that it is inefficient to pass your files through `eqn` every time you use `format`. In addition, you sometimes use `pic`. You want to add options to your `format` shell script to handle these cases as well.

You could decree that the macro package will always be the first argument to your script, the name of the preprocessor the second, and the file to be formatted the third. To delay execution of the command until all of the options have been assembled, you can use the `case` statement to set shell variables, which are evaluated later to make up the actual command line. Here's a script that makes these assumptions:

```
case $1 in
    -mm) macros="-mm";;
    -ms) macros="-ms";;
    -mS) macros="-mS";;
esac
case $2 in
    -E) pre="| eqn"
    -P) pre="| pic"
esac
tbl $3 $pre | nroff $macros | col | lp
```

But what if you don't want either preprocessor, or want both `eqn` and `pic`? The whole system breaks down. We need a more general approach.

There are several ways to deal with this. For example, there is a program called `getopt` that can be used for interpreting command-line options. However, we will use another technique—discarding an argument after it is used, and *shifting* the remaining arguments. This is the function of the `shift` command.

This command finds its most elementary use when a command needs to take more than nine arguments. There is no `$10`, so a script to echo ten arguments might be written:

```
echo The first nine arguments: $1 $2 $3 $4 $5 $6 $7 $8 $9
shift
echo The tenth argument: $9
```

After the `shift` command, the old `$1` has disappeared, as far as the shell is concerned, and the remaining arguments are all shifted one position to the left. (The old `$2` is the current `$1`, and so on.) Take a moment to experiment with this if you want.

Shifting works well with conditional statements, because it allows you to test for a condition, discard the first argument, and go on to test the next argument, without requiring the arguments to be in a specific order. However, we still can't quite get the job done, because we have to establish a *loop*, and repeat the `case` statement until all of the arguments are used up.

## Repetitive Execution

As we suggested at the start of this chapter, the real secret of programming is to get the computer to do all the repetitive, boring tasks. The basic mechanism for doing this is the loop—an instruction or series of instructions that cause a program to do the same thing over and over again as long as some condition is true.

The `while` command is used like this:

```
while condition
do
commands
done
```

In the script we're trying to write, we want to repeatedly test for command-line arguments *as long as there are arguments*, build up a command line using shell variables, and then go ahead and issue the command. Here's how:

```
while [ $# -gt 0 ]
do
   case $1 in
     -E) eqn="| eqn";;
     -P) pic="| pic";;
     -*) options="$options $1";;
     *)  files="$files $1";;
   esac
   shift
done
tbl $files $eqn $pic | nroff $options | col | lp
```

The special shell variable `$#` always contains the number of arguments given to a command. What this script is saying in English is: As long as there is at least one argument

- test the first argument against the following list of possibilities; if there is a match, set the variable as instructed;

- throw away the argument now that you've used it, and shift the remaining arguments over one place;

- decrement the shell variable $#, which contains the number of arguments;

- go back to the first line following the do statement, and start over.

The loop will continue as long as the condition specified in the while statement is met—that is, until all the arguments have been used up and shifted out of existence.

As you've no doubt noticed, to make this work, we had to account for *all* of the arguments. We couldn't leave any to be interpreted in the command line because we had to use them all up to satisfy the while statement. That meant we needed to think about what other kinds of arguments there might be and include them in the case statement. We came up with two possibilities: additional nroff options and files.

In addition, because of the pattern-matching flexibility in the case statement, we don't need to call out each of the macro packages separately, but can just treat them as part of a more general case. Any argument beginning with a minus sign is simply assumed to be an nroff option.

You'll notice that we used a somewhat different syntax for assigning these last two potential groups of arguments to variables:

*variable="$variable additional_value"*

Or, as shown in the script:

```
options="$options $1"
files="$files $1"
```

This syntax is used to *add* a value to a variable. We know that we can expect at least one option to nroff, so we simply add any other options to the same variable. Similarly, there may be more than one filename argument. The *) case can be executed any number of times, each time adding one more filename to the variable.

If you want to become more familiar with how this works, you can simulate it on the command line:

```
$ files=sect1
$ files="$files sect2"
$ echo $files
sect1 sect2
```

As you've seen, in the script we used the standard shell metacharacter *, which means "any number of any characters," right in the pattern-matching part of the case statement. You can use any of the shell metacharacters that you can type on the command line equally well in a shell script. However, be sure you realize that when you do this, you're making *assumptions*—that any option not explicitly tested for in the case statement is an nroff option, and that any argument not beginning with a minus sign is a filename.

This last assumption may not be a safe one—for example, one of the filenames may be mistyped, or you may not be in the directory you expect, and the file will not be found. We may therefore want to do a little defensive programming, using another of the capabilities provided by the test command:

```
*) if [ -f $1 ]
   then
   files="$files $1"
   else echo "format: $1: file not found"; exit
   fi;;
```

The [-f] test checks to see whether the argument is the name of an existing file. If it is not, the script prints an informative message and exits. (The exit command is used to break out of a script. After this error occurs, we don't want to continue with the loop, or go on to execute any commands.)

This example is also instructive in that it shows how each element in the case statement's condition list does not need to be on a single line. A line can contain a complex sequence of commands, separated by semicolons or newlines or both, and is not terminated till the concluding ;; is encountered.

## Setting Default Values

We've considered the case where multiple values are stored in the same variable. What about the other extreme, where no value is stored?

If an option, such as -E for eqn, is not specified on the command line, the variable will not be defined. That is, the variable will have no value, and the variable substitution $eqn on the final line of the script will have no effect—it is as if it isn't there at all.

On the other hand, it is possible to export a variable, so that it will be recognized not just in the shell that created it, but in any subshell. This means that the commands:

```
$ eqn="| eqn"; export eqn
$ format -ms myfile
```

will have the same effect as:

```
$ format -ms -E myfile
```

Although there are occasions where you might want to do this sort of thing, you don't want it to happen unexpectedly. For this reason, it is considered good programming practice to *initialize* your variables—that is, to set them to a predefined value (or in many cases, a null value) to minimize random effects due to interaction with other programs.

To set a shell variable to a null value, simply equate it to a pair of quotation marks with nothing in between. For example, it would be a good idea to start off the format script with the line:

```
eqn="";pic="";options=""
```

In addition to setting arguments to null values, we can also set them to *default values*—that is, we can give them values that will be used unless the user explicitly requests otherwise. Let's suppose that we want the script to invoke troff by default, but also provide an option to select nroff. We could rewrite the entire script like this:

```
eqn="";pic="";roff="ditroff -Tps";post="| devps"
lp="lp -dlaser"
while [ $# -gt 0 ]
do
    case $1 in
      -E) eqn="| eqn";;
      -P) pic="| pic";;
      -N) roff="nroff"; post="| col";lp="lp -dline";;
      -*) options="$options $1";;
       *) if [ -f $1 ]; then
          files="$files $1"
          else echo "format: $1: file not found"; exit
          fi;;
    esac
    shift
done
eval "tbl $files $eqn $pic | $roff $options $post | $lp"
```

The troff output needs to be passed through a postprocessor before it can be sent to a printer. (We use devps, but there are almost as many different postprocessors as there are possible output devices.) The nroff output, for some printers, needs to be passed through col, which is a special filter used to remove reverse linefeeds. Likewise, the lp command will need a "destination" option. We're assuming that the system has a printer called laser for troff output, and one called line for line-printer output from nroff. The default case (troff) for both the postprocessor and destination printer is set in the variables at the start of the file. The -N option resets them to alternate values if nroff is being used. The eval command is necessary in order for the pipes to be evaluated correctly inside a variable substitution.

## What We've Accomplished

You might wonder if this script really saved you any time. After all, it took a while to write, and it seems almost as complex to use as just typing the appropriate command line. After all, was it worth all that work, just so that we can type:

```
$ format -ms -E -P -N myfile
```

instead of:

```
$ tbl myfile | eqn | pic | nroff -ms | lp
```

There are two answers to that question. First, many of the programs used to format a file may take options of their own—options that are always the same, but always need to be specified—and, especially if you're using troff, a postprocessor may also be involved. So your actual command line might work out to be something like this:

```
$ tbl myfile | eqn | pic -T720 -D | ditroff -ms -Tps |
> devps | lp
```

That's considerably more to type! You could just save your most frequently used combinations of commands into individual shell scripts. But if you build a general tool, you'll find that it gives you a base to build from, and opens up additional possibilities as you go on. For example, later in this book we'll show how to incorporate some fairly complex indexing scripts into `format`—something that would be very difficult to do from the command line. That is the far more important second reason for taking the time to build a solid shell script when the occasion warrants.

As this chapter goes on, we'll show you many other useful tools you can build for yourself using shell scripts. Many of them will use the features of the shell we introduced in this section, although a few will rely on additional features we've yet to learn.

## ▪ ex Scripts ▪

We've discussed `ex` already in Chapter 7. As we pointed out, any command, or sequence of commands, that you can type at `ex`'s colon prompt can also be saved in a file and executed with `ex`'s `:so` command.

This section discusses a further extension of this concept—how to execute `ex` scripts from outside a file and on multiple files. There are certain `ex` commands that you might save in scripts for use from within `vi` that will be of no use from the outside—maps, abbreviations, and so on. For the most part, you'll be using substitute commands in external scripts.

A very useful application of editing scripts for a writer is to ensure consistency of terminology—or even of spelling—across a document set. For the sake of example, let's assume that you've run `spell`, and it has printed out the following list of misspellings:

```
$ spell sect1 sect2
chmod
ditroff
myfile
thier
writeable
```

As is often the case, `spell` has flagged a few technical terms and special cases it doesn't recognize, but it has also identified two genuine spelling errors.

Because we checked two files at once, we don't know which files the errors occurred in, or where in the files they are. Although there are ways to find this out, and the job wouldn't be too hard for only two errors in two files, you can easily imagine how the job could grow time consuming for a poor speller or typist proofing many files at once.

We can write an `ex` script containing the following commands:

```
g/thier/s//their/g
g/writeable/s//writable/g
wq
```

Then we can edit the files as follows:

```
$ ex - sect1 < exscript
$ ex - sect2 < exscript
```

(The minus sign following the invocation of `ex` tells it to accept its commands from standard input.)

If the script were longer than the one in our simple example, we would already have saved a fair amount of time. However, given our earlier remarks about letting the computer do the dirty work, you might wonder if there isn't some way to avoid repeating the process for each file to be edited. Sure enough, we can write a shell script that includes the invocation of `ex`, but generalizes it, so that it can be used on any number of files.

## Looping in a Shell Script

One piece of shell programming we haven't discussed yet is the `for` loop. This command sequence allows you to apply a sequence of commands for each argument given to the script. (And, even though we aren't introducing it until this late in the game, it is probably the single most useful piece of shell programming for beginners. You will want to remember it even if you don't write any other shell programs.)

Here's the syntax of a `for` loop:

```
for variable in list
do
commands
done
```

For example:

```
for file in $*
do
    ex - $file < exscript
done
```

(The command doesn't need to be indented; we indented for clarity.) Now (assuming this shell script is saved in a file called `correct`), we can simply type:

```
$ correct sect1 sect2
```

The `for` loop in `correct` will assign each argument (each `file` in `$*`) to the variable `file` and execute the `ex` script on the contents of that variable.

It may be easier to grasp how the `for` loop works with an example whose output is more visible. Let's look at a script to rename files:

```
for file in $*
do
  mv $file $file.x
done
```

Assuming this script is in an executable file called `move`, here's what we can do:

```
$ ls
ch01     ch02     ch03     move
$ move ch??
$ ls
ch01.x    ch02.x    ch03.x    move
```

With a little creativity, you could rewrite the script to rename the files more specifically:

```
for nn in $*
do
   mv ch$nn sect$nn
done
```

With the script written this way, you'd specify numbers instead of filenames on the
command line:

```
$ ls
ch01     ch02     ch03     move
$ move 01 02 03
$ ls
sect01    sect02    sect03    move
```

The  for loop need not take  $* (all arguments) as the list of values to be substituted.
You can specify an explicit list as well, or substitute the output of a command.  For
example:

```
for variable in a b c d
```

will assign  variable to  a,  b,  c, and  d in turn.  And:

```
for variable in `grep -l "Alcuin"`
```

will assign  variable in turn to the name of each file in which  grep finds the
string *Alcuin.*

If no list is specified:

```
for variable
```

the variable will be assigned to each command-line argument in turn, much as it was in
our initial example.  This is actually not equivalent to  for variable in $* but
to  for variable in $@, which has a slightly different meaning.  The symbols
$* expand to  $1, $2, $3, etc., but  $@ expands to  "$1", "$2", "$3", etc.
Quotation marks prevent further interpretation of special characters.

Let's return to our main point, and our original script:

```
for file in $*
do
   ex - $file < exscript
done
```

It may seem a little inelegant to have to use two scripts—the shell script and the ex script. And in fact, the shell does provide a way to include an editing script directly into a shell script.

## Here Documents

The operator << means to take the following lines, up to a specified string, as input to a command. (This is often called a *here document*.) Using this syntax, we could include our editing commands in correct like this:

```
for file in $*
do
ex - $file << end-of-script
g/thier/s//their/g
g/writeable/s//writable/g
wq
end-of-script
done
```

The string end-of-script is entirely arbitrary—it just needs to be a string that won't otherwise appear in the input and can be used by the shell to recognize when the here document is finished. By convention, many users specify the end of a here document with the string EOF, or E-O-F, to indicate *end of file*.

There are advantages and disadvantages to each approach shown. If you want to make a one-time series of edits and don't mind rewriting the script each time, the here document provides an effective way to do the job.

However, writing the editing commands in a separate file from the shell script is more general. For example, you could establish the convention that you will always put editing commands in a file called exscript. Then, you only need to write the correct script once. You can store it away in your personal "tools" directory (which you've added to your search path), and use it whenever you like.

## ex Scripts Built by diff

A further example of the use of ex scripts is built into a program we've already looked at—diff. The -e option to diff produces an editing script usable with either ed or ex, instead of the usual output. This script consists of a sequence of a (add), c (change), and d (delete) commands necessary to recreate *file1* from *file2* (the first and second files specified on the diff command line).

Obviously, there is no need to completely recreate the first file from the second, because you could do that easily with cp. However, by editing the script produced by diff, you can come up with some desired combination of the two versions.

It might take you a moment to think of a case in which you might have use for this feature. Consider this one: two people have unknowingly made edits to different copies of a file, and you need the two versions merged. (This can happen especially easily in a networked environment, in which people copy files between machines. Poor coordination can easily result in this kind of problem.)

To make this situation concrete, let's take a look at two versions of the same paragraph, which we want to combine:

*Version 1:*

```
The Book of Kells, now one of the treasures of the Trinity
College Library in Dublin, was found in the ancient
monastery at Ceannanus Mor, now called Kells.  It is a
beautifully illustrated manuscript of the Latin Gospels,
and also contains notes on local history.
It was written in the eighth century.
The manuscript is generally regarded as the finest example
of Celtic illumination.
```

*Version 2:*

```
The Book of Kells was found in the ancient
monastery at Ceannanus Mor, now called Kells.  It is a
beautifully illustrated manuscript of the Latin Gospels,
and also contains notes on local history.
It is believed to have been written in the eighth century.
The manuscript is generally regarded as the finest example
of Celtic illumination.
```

As you can see, there is one additional phrase in each of the two files. We would like to merge them into one file that incorporates both edits.

Typing:

```
$ diff -e version1 version2 > exscript
```

will yield the following output in the file `exscript`:

```
6c
It is believed to have been written in the eighth century.
.
1,2c
The Book of Kells was found in the ancient
.
```

You'll notice that the script appears in reverse order, with the changes later in the file appearing first. This is essential whenever you're making changes based on line numbers; otherwise, changes made earlier in the file may change the numbering, rendering the later parts of the script ineffective.

You'll also notice that, as mentioned, this script will simply recreate version 1, which is not what we want. We want the change to line 5, but not the change to lines 1 and 2. We want to edit the script so that it looks like this:

```
6c
It is believed to have been written in the eighth century.
.
w
```

(Notice that we had to add the w command to write the results of the edit back into the file.) Now we can type:

```
$ ex - version1 < exscript
```

to get the resulting merged file:

```
The Book of Kells, now one of the treasures of the Trinity
College Library in Dublin, was found in the ancient
monastery at Ceannanus Mor, now called Kells.  It is a
beautifully illustrated manuscript of the Latin Gospels,
and also contains notes on local history.
It is believed to have been written in the eighth century.
The manuscript is generally regarded as the finest example
of Celtic illumination.
```

Using diff like this can get confusing, especially when there are many changes. It is very easy to get the direction of changes confused, or to make the wrong edits. Just remember to do the following:

- Specify the file that is closest in content to your eventual target as the first file on the diff command line. This will minimize the size of the editing script that is produced.

- After you have corrected the editing script so that it makes only the changes that you want, apply it to that same file (the first file).

Nonetheless, because there is so much room for error, it is better not to have your script write the changes back directly into one of your source files. Instead of adding a w command at the end of the script, add the command 1, $p to write the results to standard output. This is almost always preferable when you are using a complex editing script.

If we use this command in the editing script, the command line to actually make the edits would look like this:

```
$ ex - version1 < exscript > version3
```

The diff manual page also points out another application of this feature of the program. Often, as a writer, you find yourself making extensive changes, and then wishing you could go back and recover some part of an earlier version. Obviously, frequent backups will help. However, if backup storage space is at a premium, it is possible (though a little awkward) to save only some older version of a file, and then keep incremental diff -e scripts to mark the differences between each successive version.

To apply multiple scripts to a single file, you can simply pipe them to ex rather than redirecting input:

```
cat script1 script2 script3 | ex - oldfile
```

But wait! How do you get your w (or 1, $p) command into the pipeline? You could edit the last script to include one of these commands. But, there's another trick that we ought to look at because it illustrates another useful feature of the shell that many people are unaware of.

If you enclose a semicolon-separated list of commands in parentheses, the standard output of all of the commands are combined, and can be redirected together. The immediate application is that, if you type:

```
cat script1 script2 script3; echo '1,$p' | ex - oldfile
```

the results of the `cat` command will be sent, as usual, to standard output, and only the results of `echo` will be piped to `ex`. However, if you type:

```
(cat script1 script2 script3; echo '1,$p') | ex - oldfile
```

the output of the entire sequence will make it into the pipeline, which is what we want.

## ▪ Stream Editing ▪

We haven't seen the `sed` program yet. Not only is it a line editor rather than a screen editor, but it takes the process one step further: it is a "noninteractive" line editor. It can only be used with editing scripts. It was developed in 1978 as an extension to `ed` for three specific cases (according to the original documentation):

- to edit files too large for comfortable interactive editing

- to edit any size file when the sequence of editing commands is too complicated to be comfortably typed in interactive mode

- to perform multiple "global" editing functions efficiently in one pass through the input

All of these are still good reasons for using `sed`. But these cases can be solved by the scripting ability of `ex` that we have already looked at. Why learn yet another editor?

One answer lies in the third point. Because it was specifically designed to work with scripts, `sed` is considerably faster than `ex` when used with a comparable script.

The other answer lies in `sed`'s unique capability to be used as an editing *filter*—a program that makes edits on the fly as data is being passed through a pipe on its way to other programs.

The `sed` program uses a syntax that is very similar to that used by `ex`, so it is not very difficult to learn. However, there are some critical differences, which make it inadvisable for an experienced `ed` or `ex` user to just blindly jump in.

We're going to take a close look at `sed`, not as a general-purpose editor, but as a tool to accomplish specific tasks. As a result, we won't cover every command, but only those that differ significantly from their `ex` equivalents or offer specific benefits that we want to utilize.

First, a brief note on usage. The `sed` command has two forms:

```
sed -e  command editfiles
sed -f  scriptfile editfiles
```

The first form, using `-e`, allows you to specify an editing command right on the command line. Multiple `-e` options can be specified on the same line.

The second form, using −f, takes the name of a script containing editing commands. We prefer this form for using sed.

In addition, you can specify an entire multiline editing script as an argument to sed, like this:

```
sed '
```
*Editing script begins here*

    .

    .

    .

*Editing script ends here' editfiles*

This last form is especially useful in shell scripts, as we shall see shortly. However, it can also be used interactively. The Bourne shell will prompt for continuation lines after it sees the first single quotation mark.

You can also combine several commands on the same line, separating them with semicolons:

sed −e *'command1; command2; . . .' editfiles*

One last point: when using sed −e, you should enclose the expression in quotation marks. Although this is not absolutely essential, it can save you from serious trouble later.

Consider the following example:

```
$ sed -e s/thier/their own/g myfile
```

The expression s/thier/their own/g will work correctly in a sed script used with the −f option. But from the command line it will result in the message "Command garbled," because the shell interprets the space as a separator between arguments, and will parse the command expression as s/thier/their and treat the remainder of the line as two filenames, own/g and myfile. Lacking a closing / for the s command, sed will complain and quit.


## Differences between ex and sed

The first difference between sed and interactive line editors like ed and ex is the way lines are addressed. In ex, the default is to affect only a specifically addressed line; therefore, commands like g exist to address multiple lines. The sed program, on the other hand, works by default on all lines, so it needs commands that allow it to bypass selected lines. The sed program is implicitly global. In ex, the default is to edit the current line, and you must explicitly request global edits, or address particular lines that you want to have edited. In sed, the default is to edit every line, and line addresses are used to restrict the operation of the edit.

For example, consider the difference between ex and sed in how they interpret a command of the form:

*/pattern/s/oldstring/newstring/*

In ex, this means to locate the first line matching *pattern* and, on that line, perform the specified substitution. In sed, the same command matches every line containing *pattern*, and makes the specified edits. In other words, this command in sed works the same as ex's global flag:

g/*pattern*/s/*oldstring*/*newstring*/

In both sed and ex, a command of the form:

/*pattern1*/,/*pattern2*/*command*

means to make the specified edits on all lines between *pattern1* and *pattern2*.

Although you can use absolute line number addresses in sed scripts, you have to remember that sed has the capability to edit multiple files at once in a stream. And in such cases, line numbers are consecutive throughout the entire stream, rather than restarted with each new file.

Besides its addressing peculiarities, you also need to get used to the fact that sed automatically writes to standard output. You don't need to issue any special commands to make it print the results of its edits; in fact, you need to use a command-line option to make it stop.

To make this point clear, let's consider the following admittedly artificial example. Your file contains the following three lines:

```
The files were writeable by thier owner, not by all.
The files were writeable by thier owner, not by all.
The files were writeable by thier owner, not by all.
```

You use the following editing script (in a file called edscript):

```
/thier/s//their/
/writeable/s//writable/
1,$p
```

Here are the very different results with ex and sed:

```
$ ex - junk < edscript
The files were writeable by their owner, not by all.
The files were writable by thier owner, not by all.
The files were writeable by thier owner, not by all.
```

```
$ sed -f edscript junk
The files were writable by their owner, not by all.
The files were writable by their owner, not by all.
The files were writable by their owner, not by all.
The files were writable by their owner, not by all.
The files were writable by their owner, not by all.
The files were writable by their owner, not by all.
```

The ex command, lacking the g prefix to make the edits global, applies the first line in the script to the first line in the file, and then goes to the second line, to which it applies the second line in the script. No edits are performed on the third line. The contents of the buffer are printed to standard output by the final line in the script. This is analogous to what would happen if you issued the same commands manually in `ex`.

The `sed` command, in contrast, applies each line in the script to every line in the file, and then sends the results to standard output. A second copy of the input is printed to standard output by the final line in the script.

Although the same script almost works for `ex` and `sed`, the `sed` script can be written more simply as:

```
s/thier/their/
s/writeable/writable/
```

Because edits are applied by default to every line, we can skip the initial pattern address and simply give the `s` command. And we want to omit the print command, which gave us the annoying second copy of the input.

There are also some special added commands that support `sed`'s noninteractive operation. We will get to these commands in due course. However, in some ways, the special commands are easier to learn than the familiar ones. The cautionary example shown was intended to underline the fact that there is a potential for confusion when commands that look identical produce very different results.

## Some Shell Scripts Using `sed`

The `sed` command you are most likely to start with is `s` (or substitute) because you can put it to work without knowing anything about `sed`'s advanced control structures. Even if you learn no other `sed` commands, you should read this section, because this command is easy to learn and will greatly extend your editing power.

Within the constraints just outlined, the `s` command works similarly to its `ex` equivalent. Let's look at several shell scripts that use `sed`.

First, because speed is definitely a factor when you're making large edits to a lot of files, we might want to rewrite the `correct` script shown previously with `ex` as follows:

```
for file in $*
do
    sed -f sedscr $file > $file.tmp
    mv $file.tmp $file
done
```

This script will always look for a local editing script called `sedscr`, and will apply its edits to each file in the argument list given to `correct`. Because `sed` sends the result of its work to standard output, we capture that output in a temporary file, then move it back to the original file.

As it turns out, there is a real danger in this approach! If there is an error in the sed script, `sed` will abort without producing any output. As a result, the temporary file will be empty and, when copied back onto the original file, will effectively delete the original.

To avoid this problem, we need to include a test in the `correct` shell script:

```
for file in $*
do
    sed -f sedscr $file > $file.tmp
    if [ -s $file.tmp ]
    then
        mv $file.tmp $file
    else
        echo "Sed produced an empty file."
    fi
done
```

The [-s] test checks to see whether or not a file is empty—a very useful thing indeed when you are using editing scripts.

You might want to create another simple shell script that uses sed to correct simple errors. We'll call this one change:

```
sed -e "s/$1/$2/g" $3 > $3.tmp
if [ -s $3.tmp ]
then
    mv $3.tmp $3
else
    echo "Possible error using regular expression syntax."
```

This script will simply change the first argument to the second in the file specified by the third argument:

$ **change mispeling misspelling myfile**

(Because we control the actual editing script, the most likely errors could come from faulty regular expression syntax in one of the first two arguments; thus, we changed the wording of the error message.)

## Integrating sed into format

Let's consider a brief application that shows sed in its role as a true stream editor, making edits in a pipeline—edits that are never written back into a file.

To set the stage for this script, we need to turn back briefly to typesetting. On a typewriter-like device (including a CRT), an em dash is typically typed as a pair of hyphens (--). In typesetting, it is printed as a single, long dash (—). The troff program provides a special character name for the em dash, but it is inconvenient to type \(em in your file whenever you want an em dash.

Suppose we create a sed script like this:

```
s/--/\\(em/g
```

and incorporate it directly into our format script? We would never need to worry about em dashes—sed would automatically insert them for us. (Note that we need to double the backslash in the string \(em because the backslash has meaning to sed as well at to troff, and will be stripped off by sed.)

The `format` script might now look like this:

```
eqn="";pic="";macros="ms";col="";roff="ditroff -Tlj"
sed="| sed -e 's/--/\\(em/g'"
while [ $# -gt 0 ]
do
    case $1 in
        -E) eqn="| eqn";;
        -P) pic="| pic";;
        -N) roff="nroff";col="| col";sed="";;
        -*) options="$options $1";;
         *) if [ -f $1 ]; then
            files="$files $1"
            else echo "format: $1: file not found"; exit
            fi;;
    esac
    shift
done
eval "cat $files $sed|tbl $eqn $pic|$roff $options $col|lp"
```

(Notice that we've set up the −N option for `nroff` so that it sets the `sed` variable to null, because we only want to make this change if we are using `troff`.)

## Excluding Lines from Editing

Before we go any further, let's take a moment to be sure the script is complete.

What about the case in which someone is using hyphens to draw a horizontal line? We want to exclude from the edit any lines containing three or more hyphens together. To do this, we use the `!` (*don't!*) command:

```
/---/!s/--/\(em/g
```

It may take a moment to understand this syntax. It says, simply, "If you find a line containing three hyphens together, don't make the edit." The `sed` program will treat all other lines as fair game. (It's important to realize that the `!` command applies to the pattern match, not to the `s` command itself. Although, in this case, the effect might seem to be the same whether you read the command as "Don't match a line containing `---`" or "Match a line containing `---`, and don't substitute it," there are other cases in which it will be very confusing if you don't read the line the same way that `sed` does.)

We might also take the opportunity to improve the aesthetics even further, by putting in a very small space between the ends of the dash and the preceding and following words, using the `troff` construct `\^`, which produces a 1/12-em space:

```
/---/!s/--/\\^\\(em\\^/g
```

As it turns out, changing hyphens to em dashes is not the only "prettying up" edit we might want to make when typesetting. For example, some laser printers do not have a true typeset quotation mark (" and " as opposed to " and "). If you are using an output device with this limitation, you could use `sed` to change each double quotation mark character to a pair of single open or close quotation marks (depending on context), which, when typeset, will produce the appearance of a proper double quotation mark.

This is a considerably more difficult edit to make because there are many separate cases that we need to account for using regular expression syntax. Our script might need to look like this:

```
s/^"/``/
s/"$/´´/
s/"? /´´? /g
s/"?$/´´?/g
s/ "/ ``/g
s/" /´´ /g
s/|———|"/|———|``/g
s/"|———|/´´|———|/g
s/")/´´)/g
s/"]/´´]/g
s/("/(``/g
s/\["/\[``/g
s/";/´´;/g
s/":/´´:/g
s/,"/,´´/g
s/",/´´,/g
s/\."/.\\\&´´/g
s/"\./´´.\\\&/g
s/"\\^\\(em/´´\\(em/g
s/\\(em\\^"/\\(em``/g
s/"\\(em/´´\\(em/g
s/\\(em"/\\(em``/g
```

(This list could be shortened by judicious application of \([ ... ]\) regular expression syntax, but it is shown in its long form for effect. Note that the symbol |———| represents a tab.)

## Branching to Selective Parts of a Script

In technical books like this, it is usually desirable to show examples in a constant-width font that clearly shows each character as it actually appears. A pair of single quotation marks in a constant-width font will not appear at all similar to a proper typeset double quotation mark in a variable-width font. In short, it is not always desirable to make the substitutions shown previously.

However, we can assume that examples will be set off by some sort of macro pair (in this book, we used .ES and .EE, for *example start* and *example end*), and we can use those as the basis for exclusion. There are two ways to do this:

- Use the ! command, as we did before.

- Use the b (*branch*) command to skip portions of the editing script.

Let's look at how we'd use the ! command first.

We could apply the ! command to each individual line:

```
/^\.ES/,/^\.EE/!s/^"/`\`/
/^\.ES/,/^\.EE/!s/"$/''/
/^\.ES/,/^\.EE/!s/"? /''? /g
        .
        .
        .
```

But there has to be a better way, and there is. The sed program supports the flow control symbols { and } for grouping commands. So we simply need to write:

```
/^\.ES/,/^\.EE/!{
s/^"/`\`/
s/"$/''/
s/"? /''? /g
        .
        .
        .
s/\\(em\\^"/\\(em`\`/g
s/"\\(em/''\\(em/g
s/\\(em"/\\(em`\`/g
}
```

All commands enclosed in braces will be subject to the initial pattern address.

There is another way we can do the same thing. The sed program's b (*branch*) command allows you to transfer control to another line in the script that is marked with an optional label. Using this feature, we could write the previous script like this:

```
/^\.ES/,/^\.EE/bend
s/^"/`\`/
s/"$/''/
s/"? /''? /g
        .
        .
        .
s/\\(em\\^"/\\(em`\`/g
s/"\\(em/''\\(em/g
s/\\(em"/\\(em`\`/g
:end
```

A label consists of a colon, followed by up to eight characters. If the label is missing, the b command branches to the end of the script. (Because we don't have anything past this point at the moment, we don't actually need the label in this case. That is the form we will use from now on.)

The b command is designed for flow control within the script. It allows you to create subscripts that will only be applied to lines matching certain patterns and will not be applied elsewhere. However, as in this case, it also gives you a powerful way to exempt part of the text from the action of a single-level script.

The advantage of b over ! for our application is that we can more easily specify multiple conditions to avoid. The ! symbol can apply to a single command, or can apply to a set of commands enclosed in braces that immediately follows. The b command, on the other hand, gives you almost unlimited control over movement around the script.

For example, if we are using multiple macro packages, there may be other macro pairs besides .ES and .EE that enclose text that we don't want to apply the sed script to. So, for example, we can write:

```
/^.ES/,/^.EE/b
/^.PS/,/^.PE/b
/^.G1/,/^.G2/b
```

In addition, the quotation mark is used as part of troff's own comment syntax (\" begins a comment), so we don't want to change quotation marks on lines beginning with either a . or a ':

```
/^[.']/b
```

It may be a little difficult to grasp how these branches work unless you keep in mind how sed does its work:

1. It reads each line in the file into its buffer one line at a time.

2. It then applies all commands in the script to that one line, then goes to the next line.

When a branch dependent on a pattern match is encountered, it means that if a line that matches the pattern is read into the buffer, the branch command will cause the relevant portion of the script to be skipped *for that line*. If a label is used, the script will continue at the label; if no label is used, the script is effectively finished for that line. The next line is read into the buffer, and the script starts over.

The previous example shows how to exempt a small, clearly delineated portion of a file from the action of a sed script. To achieve the opposite effect—that is, to make a sed script affect only a small part of a file and ignore the rest—we can simply anchor the desired edits to the enclosing pattern.

For example, if there were some edits we wanted to make only within the confines of our .ES and .EE macros, and not elsewhere, we could do it like this:

```
/^\.ES/,/^\.EE/{
Editing commands here
}
```

If the script is sufficiently complex that you'd rather have a more global method of exclusion, you can reverse the sense of a branch by combining it with `!`:

```
/^\.ES/,/^\.EE/!b
```

When the first line in the script is applied to each line in the input, it says: "Does the line match the pattern? No? Branch to the end of the script. (That is, start over on the next line of the input.) Yes? Go on to the next line in the script, and make the edits."

## Back to `format`

The edits we've shown using `sed` are very useful, so we want to be sure to properly integrate them with `format`. Because we are now making a large series of edits rather than just one, we need to use `sed` with a script file rather than a single-line script using `-e`. As a result, we'll change the variable assignment in `format` to:

```
sed="| sed -f /usr/local/cleanup.sed"
```

where `cleanup.sed` is the name of the script containing the editing commands, and `/usr/local` could be any generally accessible directory. We'll add additional formatting cleanup commands to this file later.

## Inserting Lines of Text

The `sed` program, like `ex` and `vi`, has commands for inserting new lines of text. The `i` (insert) command adds text before the current line; `a` (append) adds text *after* the current line. In `ex`, after you enter insert mode, you can type as long as you like, breaking lines with carriage returns.* Insert mode is terminated by typing a period at the start of a line, followed immediately by a carriage return. In `sed`, you must instead type a backslash at the end of each inserted line. Insert mode is terminated by the first newline that is not "escaped" with a backslash in this way. For example, the `sed` script:

```
1a\
The backslash is a ubiquitous escape character used by\
many UNIX programs.  Perhaps its most confusing appearance\
is at the end of a line, when it is used to "hide a\
newline." It appears to stand alone, when in fact it is\
followed by a nonprinting character—a newline.
```

---

*The terms "carriage return" and "newline" are used somewhat loosely here. They are actually distinct characters in the ASCII character set—equivalent to ^M (carriage return) and ^J (linefeed). The confusion arises because UNIX changes the carriage return (^M) generated by the carriage return key to a linefeed (^J) on input. (That is, when you type a carriage return when editing a file, what is actually stored is a linefeed.) On output, the linefeed is mapped to both characters—that is, a ^J in a file actually is output to the terminal as a carriage return/linefeed pair (^M^J).

will append the five lines shown in the example following line 1 in the file to which the
sed script is applied.  The insert ends on the fifth line, when  sed encounters a newline that is not preceded by a backslash.

## A  sed Script for Extracting Information from a File

The  −n option to  sed suppresses normal output and causes  sed to print only the
output you explicitly ask for using the  p command.
 There are two forms of the  p command:

- As an absolute print command.  For example:

    /*pattern*/p

  will always print the line(s) matched by *pattern*.

- In combination with a substitute command, in which case the line will only be
  printed if a substitution is actually made.  For example:

    /*pattern*/s/*oldstring*/newstring/gp

  will not be printed if a line containing *pattern* is found but *oldstring* was not
  replaced with *newstring*.

This becomes much clearer if you realize that a line of the form:

 s/*oldstring*/*newstring*/p

is unrestricted—it matches every line in the file—but you only want to print the result
of successful substitutions.
 Using  sed −n with the  p command gives you a  grep-like facility with the
ability to select not just single lines but larger blocks of text.
 For example, you could create a simple online quick-reference document, in
which topics are delineated by an initial heading and a distinct terminating string, as in
the following abbreviated example:

```
$ cat alcuin_online
   .
   .
   .

Output Devices

Alcuin requires the use of a graphics device with at least
300 dpi resolution, and the ability to store at least
one-half page of graphics at that resolution...
%%%%
   .
   .
   .

Type Styles
```

> There are a number of ornamental type styles available on
> many typesetters. For example, many have an Old English
> font. But no typesetter currently on the market has the
> capability of Alcuin to create unique characters in the
> style of medieval illuminated manuscripts.
> %%%%
>
>       .
>       .
>       .
>
> $

A shell program like the following is all you need to display entries from this ''full text database'':

```
pattern=$*
sed -n "/$pattern/,/%%%%/p" alcuin_online
```

(The entire argument list supplied to the command ($*) is assigned to the variable pattern, so that the user can type a string including spaces without having to type quotation marks.)

We'll give an example that is perhaps a bit more realistic. Consider that when you are developing macros for use with an existing package, you may often need to consult macros in the package you are either using or worried about affecting. Of course, you can simply read in the entire file with the editor. However, to make things easier, you can use a simple shell script that uses sed to print out the definition of the desired macro. We use a version of this script on our own system, where we call it getmac:

```
mac="$2"
case $1 in
 -ms) file="/usr/lib/macros/tmac.s";;
 -mm) file="/usr/lib/macros/mmt";;
 -man) file="/usr/lib/macros/an";;
esac
sed -n -e "/^\.de *$mac/,/^\.\.$/p" $file
done
```

There are a couple of things about this script that bear mention. First, the name of a macro does not need to be separated from the .de request by a space. The ms package uses a space, but mm and man do not. This is the reason the search pattern includes a space followed by an asterisk (this pattern matches zero or more spaces).

Second, we use the −n option of sed to keep it from printing out the entire file. It will now print out only the lines that match: the lines from the start of the specified macro definition (.de *$mac) to the .. that ends the definition.

(If you are new to regular expressions, it may be a little difficult to separate the regular expression syntax from troff and shell special characters, but do make the effort, because this is a good application of sed and you should add it to your repertoire.)

The script prints the result on standard output, but it can easily be redirected into a file, where it can become the basis for your own redefinition. We'll find good use for this script in later chapters.

Yet another example of how we can use `sed` to extract (and manipulate) information from a file is provided by the following script, which we use to check the structure of documents we are writing.

The script assumes that `troff` macros (in this case, the macros used to format this book) are used to delineate sections, and prints out the headings. To make the structure more apparent, the script removes the section macros themselves, and prints the headings in an indented outline format.

There are three things that `sed` must accomplish:

1. Find lines that begin with the macro for chapter (`.CH`) or section headings (`.H1` or `.H2`).

2. Make substitutions on those lines, replacing macros with text.

3. Print only those lines.

The `sed` command, `do.outline`, operates on all files specified on the command line (`$*`). It prints the result to standard output (without making any changes within the files themselves).

```
sed -n  '/^\.[CH][H12]/ {
    s/"//g
    s/^\.CH /\
CHAPTER  /
    s/^\.H1/      A. /
    s/^\.H2/          B. /
    p
}' $*
```

The `sed` command is invoked with the `-n` option, which suppresses the automatic printing of lines. Then we specify a pattern that selects the lines we want to operate on, followed by an opening brace (`{`). This signifies that the group of commands up to the closing brace (`}`) are applied only to lines matching the pattern. This construct isn't as unfamiliar as it may look. The global regular expression of `ex` could work here if we only wanted to make one substitution (`g/^\.[CH][H12]/s/"//g`). The `sed` command performs several operations:

1. It removes double quotation marks.

2. It replaces the macro for chapter headings with a newline (to create a blank line) followed by the word *CHAPTER*.

3. It replaces the section heading with an appropriate letter and tabbed indent.

4. It prints the line.

The result of do.outline is as follows:

```
$ do.outline ch13/sect1
CHAPTER  13 Let the Computer Do the Dirty Work
       A.  Shell Programming
          B.   Stored Commands
          B.   Passing Arguments to Shell Scripts
          B.   Conditional Execution
          B.   Discarding Used Arguments
          B.   Repetitive Execution
          B.   Setting Default Values
          B.   What We've Accomplished
```

Because the command can be run on a series of files or ''chapters,'' an outline for an entire book can be produced in a matter of seconds. We could easily adapt this script for ms or mm section heading macros, or to include a C-level heading.

## The Quit Command

The q command causes sed to stop reading new input lines (and to stop sending them to the output). So, for example, if you only want some initial portion of your file to be edited, you can select a pattern that uniquely matches the last line you want affected, and include the following command as the last line of your script:

/pattern/q

After the line matching *pattern* is reached, the script will be terminated.*

This command is not really useful for protecting portions of a file. But, when used with a complex sed script, it is useful for improving the performance of the script. Even though sed is quite fast, in an application like getmac there is some inefficiency in continuing to scan through a large file after sed has found what it is looking for.

So, for example, we could rewrite getmac as follows:

```
mac="$2"
case $1 in
 -ms) file="/usr/lib/macros/tmac.s";;
 -mm) file="/usr/lib/macros/mmt";;
 -man) file="/usr/lib/macros/an";;
esac
shift
sed -n "
/^\.de *$mac/,/^\.\./{
```

---

*You need to be very careful not to use q in any program that writes its edits back to the original file (like our correct shell script shown previously). After q is executed, no further output is produced. It should not be used in any case where you want to edit the front of the file and pass the remainder through unchanged. Using q in this case is a very dangerous beginner's mistake.

```
p
/^\.\./q
}" $file
done
```

The grouping of commands keeps the line:

```
/^\.\./q
```

from being executed until sed reaches the end of the macro we're looking for. (This line by itself would terminate the script at the conclusion of the first macro definition.) The sed program quits on the spot, and doesn't continue through the rest of the file looking for other possible matches.

Because the macro definition files are not that long, and the script itself not that complex, the actual time saved from this version of the script is negligible. However, with a very large file, or a complex, multiline script that needs to be applied to only a small part of the file, this script could be a significant timesaver.

For example, the following simple shell program uses sed to print out the top ten lines of a file (much like the standard UNIX head program):

```
for file
do
sed 10q $file
done
```

This example shows a dramatic performance gain over the same script written as follows:

```
for file
do
sed -n 1,10p $file
done
```

## Matching Patterns across Two Lines

One of the great weaknesses of line-oriented editors is their helplessness in the face of global changes in which the pattern to be affected crosses more than one line.

Let me give you an example from a recent manual one of our writers was working on. He was using the ms .BX macro (incorrectly, it turns out) to box the first letter in a menu item, thus graphically highlighting the sequence of menu selections a user would select to reach a given command. For example:

M̲ain menu
   P̲ortfolio commands
      E̲valuate portfolios
      S̲hock factors

He had created a menu reference divided into numerous files, with hundreds of commands coded like this:

```
.in 5n
.BX "\s-2M\s0"\c
ain menu
.in +5n
.BX "\s-2P\s0"\c
ortfolio commands
.in +5n
.BX "\s-2E\s0"\c
valuate portfolios
.in +5n
.BX "\s-2S\s0"\c
hock factors
.in 0
```

Suddenly, the writer realized that the *M* in *Main Menu* should not be boxed because the user did not need to press this key. He needed a way to remove the box around the *M* if—and only if—the next line contained the string *ain menu*.

(A `troff` aside: The `\c` escape sequence brings text from the following line onto the current line. You would use this, for example, when you don't want the argument to a macro to be separated from the first word on the next line by the space that would normally be introduced by the process of filling. The fact that the `.BX` macro already makes provision for this case, and allows you to supply continued text in a second optional argument, is somewhat irrelevant to this example. The files had been coded as shown here, the mistake had been made, and there were hundreds, perhaps thousands, of instances to correct.)

The `N` command allows you to deal with this kind of problem using `sed`. This command temporarily "joins" the current line with the next for purposes of a pattern match. The position of the newline in the combined line can be indicated by the escape sequence `\n`. In this case, then, we could solve the problem with the following two-line `sed` script:

```
/.BX "\s-2M\s0"/N
s/.BX "\s-2M\s0"\c\nain Menu/Main Menu/
```

We search for a particular pattern and, after we find it, "add on" the next line using `N`. The next substitution will now apply to the combined line.

Useful as this solution was, the number of cases in which you know exactly where in the input a newline will fall are limited. Fortunately, `sed` goes even further, providing commands that allow you to manipulate multiline patterns in which the newline may occur at any point. Let's take a look at these commands.

## The Hold Space and the Pattern Space

The next set of commands—hold (h or H), get (g or G), and exchange (x)—can be difficult to understand, especially if you have read the obscure documentation provided with most UNIX systems. It may help to provide an analogy that reviews some of the points we've already made about how `sed` works.

The operations of `sed` can be explained, somewhat fancifully, in terms of an extremely deliberate scrivener or amanuensis toiling to make a copy of a manuscript. His work is bound by several spacial restrictions: the original manuscript is displayed in one room; the set of instructions for copying the manuscript are stored in a middle room; and the quill, ink, and folio are set up in yet another room. The original manuscript as well as the set of instructions are written in stone and cannot be moved about. The dutiful scrivener, being sounder of body than mind, is able to make a copy by going from room to room, working on only one line at a time. Entering the room where the original manuscript is, he removes from his robes a scrap of paper to take down the first line of the manuscript. Then he moves to the room containing the list of editing instructions. He reads each instruction to see if it applies to the single line he has scribbled down.

Each instruction, written in special notation, consists of two parts: a *pattern* and a *procedure*. The scrivener reads the first instruction and checks the pattern against his line. If there is no match, he doesn't have to worry about the procedure, so he goes to the next instruction. If he finds a match, then the scrivener follows the action or actions specified in the *procedure*.

He makes the edit on his piece of paper before trying to match the pattern in the next instruction. Remember, the scrivener has to read through a series of instructions, and he reads all of them, not just the first instruction that matches the pattern. Because he makes his edits as he goes, he is always trying to match the latest version against the next pattern; he doesn't remember the original line.

When he gets to the bottom of the list of instructions, and has made any edits that were necessary on his piece of paper, he goes into the next room to copy out the line. (He doesn't need to be told to print out the line.) After that is done, he returns to the first room and takes down the next line on a new scrap of paper. When he goes to the second room, once again he reads every instruction from first to last before leaving.

This is what he normally does, that is, unless he is told otherwise. For instance, before he starts, he can be told *not* to write out every line (the −n option). In this case, he must wait for an instruction that tells him to print (p). If he does not get that instruction, he throws away his piece of paper and starts over. By the way, regardless of whether or not he is told to write out the line, he always gets to the last instruction on the list.

Let's look at other kinds of instructions the scrivener has to interpret. First of all, an instruction can have zero, one, or two patterns specified:

- If no pattern is specified, then the same procedure is followed for each line.

- If there is only one pattern, he will follow the procedure for any line matching the pattern.

- If a pattern is followed by a !, then the procedure is followed for all lines that do *not* match the pattern.

- If two patterns are specified, the actions described in the procedure are performed on the first matching line and all succeeding lines until a line matches the second pattern.

The scrivener can work only one line at a time, so you might wonder how he handles a range of lines. Each time he goes through the instructions, he only tries to match the first of two patterns. Now, after he has found a line that matches the first pattern, each time through with a new line he tries to match the second pattern. He interprets the second pattern as pattern!, so that the procedure is followed only if there is no match. When the second pattern is matched, he starts looking again for the first pattern.

Each procedure contains one or more commands or *actions*. Remember, if a pattern is specified with a procedure, the pattern must be matched before the procedure is executed. We have already shown many of the usual commands that are similar to other editing commands. However, there are several highly unusual commands.

For instance, the N command tells the scrivener to go, right now, and get another line, adding it to the same piece of paper. The scrivener can be instructed to "hold" onto a single piece of scrap paper. The h command tells him to make a copy of the line on another piece of paper and put it in his pocket. The x command tells him to exchange the extra piece of paper in his pocket with the one in his hand. The g command tells him to throw out the paper in his hand and replace it with the one in his pocket. The G command tells him to append the line he is holding to the paper in front of him. If he encounters a d command, he throws out the scrap of paper and begins again at the top of the list of instructions. A D command has effect when he has been instructed to append two lines on his piece of paper. The D command tells him to delete the first of those lines.

If you want the analogy converted back to computers, the first and last rooms in this medieval manor are standard input and standard output. Thus, the original file is never changed. The line on the scrivener's piece of scrap paper is in the *pattern space*; the line on the piece of paper that he holds in his pocket is in the *hold space*. The hold space allows you to retain a duplicate of a line while you change the original in the pattern space. Let's look at a practical application, a sed program that searches for a particular phrase that might be split across two lines.

As powerful as regular expressions are, there is a limitation: a phrase split across two lines will not be matched. As we've shown, even though you can specify a newline, you have to know between which two words the newline might be found. Using sed, we can write instructions for general-purpose pattern matching across two lines.

```
N
h
s/ *\n/ /
/pattern-matching syntax/{
g
p
d
}
g
D
```

This sed script will recognize the phrase *pattern-matching syntax* even when it's in the input file on two lines. Let's see how the pattern space and hold space allow this to be done.

At the start, there is one line in the pattern space. The first action (N) is to get another line and append it to the first. This gives us two lines to examine, but there is an embedded newline that we have to remove (otherwise we'd have to know where the newline would fall in the pattern). Before that, we copy (h) the contents of the pattern space into the hold space so that we can have a copy that retains the newline. Then we replace the embedded newline (\n), and any blank spaces that might precede it, with a single blank. (The sed command does not remove a newline when it terminates the line in the pattern space.) Now we try to match the phrase against the contents of the pattern space. If there is a match, the duplicate copy that still contains the newline is retrieved from the hold space (g) and printed (p). The d command sends control back to the top of the list of instructions so that another line is read into the pattern space, because no further editing is attempted ''on the corpse of a deleted line'' (to use the phrasing of the original sed documentation). If, on the other hand, there is no match, then the contents of the hold buffer are replaced (g) with the contents of the pattern space. Now we have our original two lines in the pattern space, separated by a newline. We want to discard the first of these lines, and retain the second in order to pair it up with the next line. The D command deletes the pattern space up to the newline and sends us back to the top to append the next line.

This script demonstrates the limits of flow control in sed. After the first line of input is read, the action N is responsible for all input. And, using d and D to avoid ever reaching the bottom of the instruction list, sed does not print the line automatically or clear the pattern space (regardless of the −n option). To return to our analogy, after the scrivener enters the second room, an instruction is always telling him which room to go to next and whether to get another line or to write it out, for as long as there are lines to be read from the manuscript.

As we have emphasized, you can always refine a script, perfecting the way it behaves or adding features. There are three problems with the way this script works. First and most important, it is not general enough because it has been set up to search for a specific string. Building a shell script around this sed program will take care of that. Second, the program does not ''go with the flow'' of sed. We can rewrite it, using the b (*branch*) command, to make use of sed's default action when it reaches the bottom of its instruction list. Last, this program always prints matching lines in pairs, even when the search string is found in its entirety on a single line of input. We need to match the pattern before each new line of input is paired with the previous line.

Here's a generalized version of this sed script, called phrase, which allows you to specify the search string as a quoted first argument. Additional command-line arguments represent filenames.

```
search=$1
shift
for file
do
    sed '
    /'"$search"'/b
    N
    h
    s/.*\n//
```

```
            /'"$search"'/b
            g
            s/ *\n/ /
            /'"$search"'/{
            g
            b
            }
            g
            D' $file
      done
```

A shell variable defines the search string as the first argument on the command line. Now the sed program tries to match the search string at three different points. If the search string is found in a new line read from standard input, that line is printed. We use the b command to drop to the bottom of the list; sed prints the line and clears the pattern space. If the single line does not contain the pattern, the next input line is appended to the pattern space. Now it is possible that this line, by itself, matches the search string. We test this (after copying the pattern space to the hold space) by removing the previous line up to the embedded newline. If we find a match, control drops to the bottom of the list and the line is printed. If no match is made, then we get a copy of the duplicate that was put in the hold space. Now, just as in the earlier version, we remove the embedded newline and test for the pattern. If the match is made, we want to print the pair of lines. So we get another copy of the duplicate because it has the newline, and control passes to the bottom of the script. If no match is found, we also retrieve the duplicate and remove the first portion of it. The delete action causes control to be passed back to the top, where the N command causes the next line to be appended to the previous line.

Here's the result when the program is run on this section:

```
$ phrase "the procedure is followed" sect3
If a pattern is followed by a \f(CW!\fP, then the procedure
is followed for all lines that do \fInot\fP match the
so that the procedure is followed only if there is
```

## In Conclusion

The examples given here only begin to touch on the power of sed's advanced commands. For example, a variant of the hold command (H) appends matched lines to the hold space, rather than overwriting the initial contents of the hold space. Likewise, the G variant of the get command appends the contents of the hold space to the current line, instead of replacing it. The X command swaps the contents of the pattern space with the contents of the hold space. As you can imagine, these commands give you a great deal of power to make complex edits.

However, it's important to remember that you don't need to understand everything about sed to use it. As we've shown, it is a versatile editor, fast enough to recommend to beginners for making simple global edits to a large set of files, yet complex enough to tackle tasks that you'd never think to accomplish with an editor.

Although the syntax is convoluted even for experienced computer users, sed does have flow control mechanisms that, given some thought and experimentation, allow you to devise editing programs. It is easy to imagine (though more difficult to execute) a sed script that contains editing "subroutines," branched to by label, that perform different actions on parts of a file and quit when some condition has been met.

Few of us will go that far, but it is important to understand the scope of the tool. You never know when, faced with some thorny task that would take endless repetitive hours to accomplish, you'll find yourself saying: "Wait! I bet I could do that with sed."*

## · A Proofreading Tool You Can Build ·

Now let's look at a more complex script that makes minimal use of sed but extensive use of shell programming. It is the first example of a full-fledged tool built with the shell that offers significantly greater functionality than any of the individual tools that make it up.

We call this script proof. It uses spell to check for misspelled words in a file, shows the offending lines in context, and then uses sed to make the corrections. Because many documents contain technical terms, proper names, and so on that will be flagged as errors, the script also creates and maintains a local dictionary file of exceptions that should not be flagged as spelling errors.

This script was originally published with the name spellproofer in Rebecca Thomas's column in the June 1985 issue of *UNIX World*, to which it was submitted by Mike Elola. The script as originally published contained several errors, for which we submitted corrections. The following script, which incorporates those corrections, was published in the January 1986 issue, and is reprinted with permission of *UNIX World*. (Actually, we've added a few further refinements since then, so the script is not exactly as published.)

Because the contents of the script will become clearer after you see it in action, let's work backward this time, and show you the results of the script before we look at what it contains. The following example shows a sample run on an early draft of Chapter 2. In this example, <CR> indicates that the user has typed a carriage return in response to a prompt.

```
$ proof sect1
Do you want to use a local dictionary?  If so, enter
the name or press RETURN for the default dictionary: <CR>

Using local dictionary file dict
working ...
```

---

*The preceding sections have not covered all sed commands. See Appendix A for a complete list of sed commands.

The word Calisthentics appears to be misspelled.
Do you want to see it in context (y or n)?
**n**

Press RETURN for no change or replace "Calisthentics" with:
Calisthenics

.H1 "UNIX Calisthenics"
Save corrections in "sect1" file (y or n)?
**y**

The word metachacters appears to be misspelled.
Do you want to see it in context (y or n)?
**n**

Press RETURN for no change or replace "metachacters" with:
metacharacters

generation metacharacters.  The asterisk matches any or all
Save corrections in "sect1" file (y or n)?
**y**

The word textp appears to be misspelled.
Do you want to see it in context (y or n)?
**y**
a directory "/work/textp" and under that directories for
each of the chapters in the book, "/work/textp/ch01",
$ cp notes /work/textp/ch01
name in the directory /work/textp/ch01.
$ ls /work/textp/ch*
$ ls /work/textp/ch01/sect?
cwd   /work/textp/ch03
$ book="/work/textp"
/work/textp

Press RETURN for no change or replace 'textp' with: **<CR>**

You left the following words unchanged
textp

Do you wish to have any of the above words entered
into a local dictionary file (y/n)?
**y**
Append to dict (y/n)?
**y**

```
Do you wish to be selective (y/n)?
y
Include textp (y/n)?
y


Done.
$
```

Now let's look at the script. Because it is more complex than anything we have looked at so far, we have printed line numbers in the margin. These numbers are not part of the script but are used as a reference in the commentary that follows. You will find that the indentation of nested loops and so forth will make the program much easier to read.

```
1   echo "Do you want to use a local dictionary? If so, enter"
2   echo "the name or press RETURN for the default dictionary: "
3   read localfile
4   if [ -z "$localfile" ]; then
5     localfile=dict
6     echo Using local dictionary file $localfile
7   fi
8   echo "working ..."
9   touch $localfile
10  filelist="$*"; excused=""
11  if [ -z "$filelist" ]; then
12    echo 'Usage: proof file...'
13    exit 1
14  fi
15  for word in `spell $filelist`
16  do
17    found=`grep "^$word$" $localfile`
18    if [ -z "$found" ] ; then
19      echo
20      echo "The word $word appears to be misspelled."
21      echo "Do you want to see it in context (y or n)? "
22      read context
23      if [ "$context" = y ]; then
24        grep $word $filelist
25      fi
26      echo
27      echo "Press RETURN for no change or replace \"$word\" with:"
28      read correction
29      if [ -n "$correction" ]; then
30        hitlist="`grep -l $word $filelist`"
31        for file in $hitlist
32        do
33          echo
```

```
34              sed -n -e "s/$word/$correction/gp" <$file
35              echo "Save corrections in \"$file\" file (y or n)? "
36              read response
37              if [ "$response" = y ]; then
38                sed -e "s/$word/$correction/g" <$file>/usr/tmp/$file
39                if test -s /usr/tmp/$file; then
40                 mv /usr/tmp/$file $file
41                fi
42              fi
43          done
44        else
45          excused="$excused $word"
46        fi
47    fi
48 done
49 echo;echo;echo
50 if [ -n "$excused" ]; then
51   echo "You left the following words unchanged"
52   echo $excused | tr "\ " "\012" | pr -5 -t
53   echo
54   echo "Do you wish to have any of the above words entered"
55   echo "into a local dictionary file (y/n)? "
56   read response
57   if [ "$response" = "y" ]; then
58     if [ -n "$localfile" ]; then
59        echo "Append to $localfile (y/n)? "
60        read response
61        if [ "$response" != y ]; then
62        echo "Enter new/alternate local dictionary file: "
63        read localfile
64        fi
65     fi
66     echo
67     echo "Do you wish to be selective (y/n)? "
68     read select
69     for word in $excused
70     do
71       if [ "$select" = y ]; then
72         echo "Include $word (y/n)? "
73         read response
74         if test "$response" = y; then
75            echo $word >>$localfile
76         fi
77       else
78         echo $word >>$localfile
79       fi
```

```
80      done
81    fi
82  fi
83  echo
84  echo "Done."
```

1-8     The UNIX programming philosophy is to create small programs as
        general-purpose tools that can be joined in pipelines. Because of this,
        programs generally don't do prompting, or other "user-friendly" things
        that will limit the program to interactive operation. However, there are
        times, even in UNIX (!), when this is appropriate.

        The shell has commands to handle prompting and reading the resulting
        responses into the file, as demonstrated here. The `echo` command
        prints the prompt, and `read` assigns whatever is typed in response (up
        to a carriage return) to a variable. This variable can then be used in the
        script.

        The lines shown here prompt for the name of the local dictionary file,
        and, if none is supplied, use a default dictionary in the current directory
        called `dict`. In the sample run, we simply typed a carriage return, so
        the variable `localfile` is set to `dict`.

9       If this is the first time the script has been run, there is probably no local
        dictionary file, and one must be created. The `touch` command is a
        good way to do this because if a file already exists, it will merely
        update the access time that is associated with the file (as listed by `ls`
        `-l`). If the file does not exist, however, the `touch` command will
        create one.

        Although this line is included in the script as a sanity check, so that the
        script will work correctly the first time, it is preferable to create the
        local dictionary manually, at least for large files. The `spell` program
        tends to flag as errors many words that you want to use in your docu-
        ment. The `proof` script handles the job of adding these words to a
        local dictionary, but doing this interactively can be quite time-
        consuming. It is much quicker to create a base dictionary for a docu-
        ment by redirecting the output of `spell` to the dictionary, then editing
        the dictionary to *remove* authentic spelling errors and leave only the
        exception list. The errors can then be corrected with `proof` without
        the tedium of endlessly repeating `n` for words that are really not errors.

        If you use this script, you should run `spell` rather than `proof` on
        the first draft of a document, and create the dictionary at that time. Sub-
        sequent runs of `proof` for later drafts will be short and to the point.

10-14   In these lines, the script sets up some variables, in much the same way
        as we've seen before. The lines:

```
filelist="$*"
if [ -z "$filelist" ]; then
    echo "Usage:  proof file..."
    exit 1
fi
```

have much the same effect as the test of the number of arguments greater than zero that we used in earlier scripts. If `filelist` is a null string, no arguments have been specified, and so it is time to display an error message and end the program, using the shell's `exit` command.

15     This line shows a feature of the shell we've seen before, but it is still worthy of note because it may take a while to remember. The output of a command enclosed in backquotes (``` `` ```) can be substituted for the argument list of another command. That is what is happening here; the output of the `spell` command is used as the pattern list of a `for` loop.

17-18     You'll notice that `spell` still flags all of the words it finds as errors. But the `for` loop then uses `grep` to compare each word in the list generated by `spell` with the contents of the dictionary. Only those words *not* found in the dictionary are submitted for correction.

The pattern given to `grep` is ''anchored'' by the special pattern-matching characters `^` and `$` (beginning and end of line, respectively), so that only whole words in the dictionary are matched. Without these anchors, the presence of the word `ditroff` in the list would prevent the discovery of misspellings like `trof`.

20-25     Sometimes it is difficult to tell beforehand whether an apparent misspelling is really an error, or if it is correct in context. For example, in our sample run, the word `textp` appeared to be an error, but was in fact part of a pathname, and so correct. Accordingly, `proof` (again using `grep`) gives you the opportunity to look at each line containing the error before you decide to change it or not.

As an aside, you'll notice a limitation of the script. If, as is the case in our example, there are multiple occurrences of a string, they must all be changed or left alone as a set. There is no provision for making individual edits.

26-48     After a word is offered as an error, you have the option to correct it or leave it alone. The script needs to keep track of which words fall into each category, because words that are not corrected may need to be added to the dictionary.

If you do want to make a correction, you type it in. The variable `correction` will now be nonzero and can be used as the basis of a test (`test -n`). If you've typed in a correction, `proof` first checks the files on the command line to see which ones (there can be more than one) can be corrected. (grep −1 just gives the names of files in which the string is found into the variable hitlist, and the script stores the names.) The edit is then applied to each one of these files.

35      Just to be on the safe side, the script prints the correction first, rather than making any edits. (The −n option causes sed not to print the entire file on standard output, but only to print lines that are explicitly requested for printing with a p command. Used like this, sed performs much the same function as grep, only we are making an edit at the same time.

37-42      If the user approves the correction, sed is used once again, this time to actually make the edit. You should recognize this part of the script. Remember, it is essential in this application to enclose the expression used by sed in quotation marks.

50-84      If you've understood the previous part of the shell script, you should be able to decipher this part, which adds words to the local dictionary. The tr command converts the spaces separating each word in the excused list into carriage returns. They can then be printed in five tab-separated columns by pr. Study this section of the program until you do, because it is an excellent example of how UNIX programs that appear to have a single, cut-and-dry function (or no clear function at all to the uninitiated) can be used in unexpected but effective ways.

# 13

# The awk Programming Language

A program is a solution to a problem, formulated in the syntax of a particular language. It is a small step from writing complex editing scripts with sed to writing programs with awk, but it is a step that many writers may fear to take. "Script" is less loaded a term than "program" for many people, but an editing script is still a program.

Each programming language has its own "style" that lends itself to performing certain tasks better than other languages. Anyone can scan a reference page and quickly learn a language's syntax, but a close examination of programs written in that language is usually required before you understand how to apply this knowledge. In this sense, a programming language is simply another tool; you need to know not only how to use it but also when and why it is used.

We recommend that you learn more than one programming language. We have already looked at a number of different programs or scripts written for and executed by the shell, ex, and sed. As you learn the awk programming language, you will notice similarities and differences. Not insignificantly, an awk script looks different from a shell script. The awk language shares many of the same basic constructs as the shell's programming language, yet awk requires a slightly different syntax. The awk program's basic operations are not much different from sed's: reading standard input one line at a time, executing instructions that consist of two parts, *pattern* and *procedure*, and writing to standard output.

More importantly, awk has capabilities that make it the tool of choice for certain tasks. A programming language is itself a program that was written to solve certain kinds of problems for which adequate tools did not exist. The awk program was designed for text-processing applications, particularly those in which information is structured in records and fields. The major capabilities of awk that we will demonstrate in upcoming pages are as follows:

- definable record and field structure
- conditional and looping constructs

- assignment, arithmetic, relational, and logical operators
- numeric and associative arrays
- formatted print statements
- built-in functions

A quick comparison of a single feature will show you how one programming language can differ from another. You will find it much easier to perform arithmetic operations in awk than in the shell. To increment the value of x by 1 using the shell, you'd use the following line:

```
x=`expr $x + 1`
```

The expr command is a UNIX program that is executed as a separate process returning the value of its arguments. In awk, you only have to write:

```
++x
```

This is the same as x = x + 1. (This form could also be used in awk.)

## ▪ Invoking awk ▪

The awk program itself is a program that, like sed, runs a specified program on lines of input. You can enter awk from the command line, or from inside a shell script.

$ **awk** '*program*' *files*

Input is read a line at a time from one or more *files*. The *program*, enclosed in single quotation marks to protect it from the shell, consists of *pattern* and *procedure* sections. If the pattern is missing, the procedure is performed on all input lines:

$ **awk '{print}' sample**           *Prints all lines in* sample *file*

The procedure is placed within braces. If the procedure is missing, lines matching the pattern are printed:

$ **awk '/programmer's guide/' sample**   *Prints lines matching pattern*
                                          *in* sample *file*

The awk program allows you to specify zero, one, or two pattern addresses, just like sed. Regular expressions are placed inside a pair of slashes (/). In awk, patterns can also be made up of expressions. An expression (or a primary expression so as not to confuse it with a regular expression) can be a string or numeric constant (for example, *red* or *1*), a variable (whose value is a string or numeric), or a function (which we'll look at later).

You can associate a pattern with a specific procedure as follows:

```
/pattern1/ {
            procedure 1
        }
/pattern2/ {
```

```
                    procedure 2
            }
   { procedure 3 }
```

Like `sed`, only the lines matching the particular pattern are the object of a procedure, and a line can match more than one pattern. In this example, the third procedure is performed on all input lines. Usually, multiline `awk` scripts are placed in a separate file and invoked using the `-f` option:

```
$ awk -f awkscript sample
```

## ▪ Records and Fields ▪

Perhaps the most important feature of `awk` is that it divides each line of input into fields. In the simplest case, each field contains a single word, delimited by a blank space. The `awk` program allows you to reference these fields by their position in the input line, either in patterns or procedures. The symbol `$0` represents the entire input line. `$1`, `$2`,... refer, by their position in the input line, to individual fields.

We'll demonstrate some of these capabilities by building an `awk` program to search through a list of acronyms in a file. Each acronym is listed along with its meaning. If we print the first field of each line, we'll get the name of the acronym:

```
$ awk '{print $1}' sample
BASIC
CICS
COBOL
DBMS
GIGO
GIRL
```

We can construct a useful program that would allow you to specify an acronym and get its description. We could use `awk` just like `grep`:

```
$ awk '/BASIC/' sample
BASIC Beginner's All-Purpose Symbolic Instruction Code
```

However, there are three things we'd like to do to improve this program and make better use of `awk`'s capabilities:

1. Limit the pattern-matching search.

2. Make the program more general and not dependent on the particular acronym that is the subject of the search.

3. Print only the description.

## ▪ Testing Fields ▪

The pattern as specified will match the word *BASIC* anywhere on the line. That is, it might match *BASIC* used in a description. To see if the first field ($1) matches the pattern, we write:

```
$1 == "BASIC"
```

The symbol == is a relational operator meaning "equal to" and is used to compare the first field of each line with the string *BASIC*. You could also construct this test using a given regular expression that looks for the acronym at the beginning of the line.

```
$1 ~ /^BASIC/
```

The pattern-matching operator ~ evaluates as true if an expression ($1) matches a regular expression. Its opposite, !~, evaluates true if the expression does not match the regular expression.

Although these two examples look very similar, they achieve very different results. The relational operator == evaluates true if the first field is *BASIC* but false if the first field is *BASIC,* (note the comma). The pattern-matching operator ~ locates both occurrences.

Pattern-matching operations must be performed on a regular expression (a string surrounded by slashes). Variables cannot be used inside a regular expression with the exception of shell variables, as shown in the next section. Constants cannot be evaluated using the pattern-matching operator.

## ▪ Passing Parameters from a Shell Script ▪

Our program is too specific and requires too much typing. We can put the awk script in a file and invoke it with the −f option. Or we can put the command inside a shell script, named for the function it performs. This shell script should be able to read the first argument from the command line (the name of the acronym) and pass it as a parameter to awk. We'll call the shell script awkronym and set it up to read a file named acronyms. Here's the simplest way to pass an argument into an awk procedure:

```
$ cat awkronym
awk '$1 == search' search=$1 acronyms
```

Parameters passed to an awk program are specified *after* the program. The search variable is set up to pass the first argument on the command line to the awk program. Even this gets confusing, because $1 inside the awk program represents the first field of each input line, while $1 in the shell represents the first argument supplied on the command line. Here's how this version of the program works:

```
$ awkronym CICS
CICS Customer Information Control System
```

By replacing the search string BASIC with a variable (which could be set to the string CICS or BASIC), we have a program that is fairly generalized.

Notice that we had to test the parameter as a string (`$1 == search`). This is because we can't pass the parameter inside a regular expression. Thus, the expressions "`$1 ~ /search/`" or "`$1 ~ search`" will produce syntax errors.

As an aside, let's look at another way to import a shell variable into an awk program that even works inside a regular expression. However, it looks complicated:

```
search=$1
awk '$1 ~ /'"$search"'/' acronyms
```

This program works the same as the prior version (with the exception that the argument is evaluated inside a regular expression.) Note that the first line of the script makes the variable assignment before awk is invoked. In the awk program, the shell variable is enclosed within single, then double, quotation marks. These quotes cause the shell to insert the value of `$search` inside the regular expression before it is interpreted by awk. Therefore, awk never sees the shell variable and evaluates it as a constant string.

You will come upon situations when you wish it were possible to place awk variables within regular expressions. As mentioned in the previous section, pattern matching allows us to search for a variety of occurences. For instance, a field might also include incidental punctuation marks and would not match a fixed string unless the string included the specific punctuation mark. Perhaps there is some undocumented way of getting an awk variable interpreted inside a regular expression, or maybe there is a convoluted work-around waiting to be figured out.

### ▪ Changing the Field Separator ▪

The awk program is oriented toward data arranged in fields and records. A record is normally a single line of input, consisting of one or more fields. The field separator is a blank space or tab and the record separator is a newline. For example, here's one record with five fields:

```
CICS Customer Information Control System
```

Field three or `$3` is the string *Information*. In our program, we like to be able to print the description as a field. It is obvious that we can't just say `print $2` and get the entire description. But that is what we'd like to be able to do.

This will require that we change the input file using another character (other than a blank) to delimit fields. A tab is frequently used as a field separator. We'll have to insert a tab between the first and second fields:

```
$ cat acronyms
awk    Aho, Weinstein & Kernighan
BASIC  Beginner's All-Purpose Symbolic Instruction Code
CICS   Customer Information Control System
COBOL  Common Business Orientated Language
DBMS   Data Base Management System
GIGO   Garbage In, Garbage Out
GIRL   Generalized Information Retrieval Language
```

You can change the field separator from the command line using the −F option:

```
$ awk −F"|———|" '$1 == search {print $2}' search=$1 acronyms
```

Note that |———| is entered by typing a double quotation mark, pressing the *TAB* key, and typing a double quotation mark. This makes the tab character (represented in the example as |———|) the exclusive field separator; spaces no longer serve to separate fields. Now that we've implemented all three enhancements, let's see how the program works:

```
$ awkronym GIGO
Garbage In, Garbage Out
```

### ▪ System Variables ▪

The awk program defines a number of special variables that can be referenced or reset inside a program. See Table 13-1.

**TABLE 13-1. awk System Variables**

| System Variable | Meaning |
| --- | --- |
| FILENAME | Current filename |
| FS | Field separator (a blank) |
| NF | Number of fields in the current record |
| NR | Number of the current record |
| OFS | Output field separator (a blank) |
| ORS | Output record separator (a newline) |
| RS | Record separator (a newline) |

The system variable FS defines the field separator used by awk. You can set FS inside the program as well as from the command line.

Typically, if you redefine the field or record separator, it is done as part of a BEGIN procedure. The BEGIN procedure allows you to specify an action that is performed before the first input line is read.

```
BEGIN { FS = "|———|" }
```

You can also specify actions that are performed after all input is read by defining an END procedure.

The awk command sets the variable NF to the number of fields on the current line. Try running the following awk command on any text file:

```
$ awk '{print $NF}' test
```

If there are five fields in the current record, NF will be set to five; $NF refers to the fifth and last field. Shortly, we'll look at a program, double, that makes good use of this variable.

## · Looping ·

The awkronym program can print field two because we restructured the input file and redefined the field separator. Sometimes, this isn't practical, and you need another method to read or print a number of fields for each record. If the field separator is a blank or tab, the two records would have six and five fields, respectively.

```
BASIC Beginner's All-Purpose Symbolic Instruction Code
CICS Customer Information Control System
```

It is not unusual for records to have a variable number of fields. To print all but the first field, our program would require a loop that would be repeated as many times as there are fields remaining. In many awk programs, a loop is a commonly used procedure.

The while statement can be employed to build a loop. For instance, if we want to perform a procedure three times, we keep track of how many times we go through the loop by incrementing a variable at the bottom of the loop, then we check at the top of the loop to see if that variable is greater than 3. Let's take an example in which we print the input line three times.

```
{       i = 1
        while(i <= 3) {
                print
                ++i
                }
        }
```

Braces are required inside the loop to describe a procedure consisting of more than a single action. Three operators are used in this program: = assigns the value 1 to the variable i; <= compares the value of i to the constant 3; and ++ increments the variable by 1. The first time the while statement is encountered, i is equal to 1. Because the expression i <= 3 is true, the procedure is performed. The last action of the procedure is to increment the variable i. The while expression is true after the end of the second loop has incremented i to 3. However, the end of the third loop increments i to 4 and the expression evaluates as false.

A for loop serves the same purpose as a while loop, but its syntax is more compact and easier to remember and use. Here's how the previous while statement is restructured as a for loop:

```
for (i = 1; i <= 3; i++)
        print
```

The for statement consists of three expressions within parentheses. The first expression, i = 1, sets the initial value for the counter variable. The second expression states a condition that is tested at the top of the loop. (The while statement tested the condition at the bottom of the loop.) The third expression increments the counter.

Now, to loop through remaining fields on the line, we have to determine how many times we need to execute the loop. The system variable NF contains the number of fields on the current input record. If we compare our counter (i) against NF each time through the loop, we'll be able to tell when all fields have been read:

```
     for (i = 1;  i <= NF;  i++)
```

We will print out each field ($i), one to a line. Just to show how awk works, we'll print the record and field number before each field.

```
awk '{ for (i = 1;  i <= NF;  i++)
       print NR":"i, $i } ' $*
```

Notice that the print statement concatenates NR, a colon, and i. The comma produces an output field separator, which is a blank by default.

This program produces the following results on a sample file:

```
1:1 awk
1:2 Aho,
1:3 Weinstein
1:4 &
1:5 Kernighan
2:1 BASIC
2:2 Beginner's
2:3 All-Purpose
2:4 Symbolic
2:5 Instruction
2:6 Code
```

Symbolic is the fourth field of the second record. You might note that the sample file is acronyms, the one in which we inserted a tab character between the first and second fields. Because we did not change the default field separator, awk interpreted the tab or blank as a field separator. This allows you to write programs in which the special value of the tab is ignored.

## Conditional Statements

Now let's change our example so that when given an argument, the program returns the record and field number where that argument appears.

Essentially, we want to test each field to see if it matches the argument; if it does, we want to print the record and field number. We need to introduce another flow control construct, the if statement. The if statement evaluates an expression—if true, it performs the procedure; if false, it does not.

In the next example, we use the if statement to test whether the current field is equal to the argument. If it is, the current record and field number are printed.

```
awk '{ for (i = 1;  i <= NF;  i++){
       if ($i == search) {
               print NR":"i
               }
       }
} ' search=$1 acronyms
```

This new procedure prints *2:1* or *3:4* and isn't very useful by itself, but it demonstrates that you can retrieve and test any single field from any record.

The next program, double, checks if the first word on a line is a duplicate of the last word on the previous line. We use double in proofing documents and it catches a surprisingly common typing mistake.

```
awk '
NF > 0 {
        if ($1 == lastword){
                print NR ": double " $1
                }
                lastword = $NF
}' $1
```

When the first line of input is read, if the number of fields is greater than 0, then the expression in the if statement is evaluated. Because the variable lastword has not been set, it evaluates to false. The final action assigns the value of $NF to the variable lastword. ($NF refers to the last field; the value of NF is the number of the last field.) When the next input line is read, the first word is compared against the value of lastword. If they are the same, a message is printed.

```
double sect1
15: double the
32: double a
```

This version of double is based on the program presented by Kernighan and Pike in *The UNIX Programming Environment*. (Writer's Workbench now includes this program.) Kernighan and Pike's program also checks for duplicate words, side-by-side, in the same line. You might try implementing this enhancement, using a for loop and checking the current field against the previous field. Another feature of Kernighan and Pike's double is that you can run the program on more than one file. To allow for additional files, you can change the shell variable from $1 to $* but the record or line number printed by NR will correspond to consecutive input lines. Can you write a procedure to reset NR to 0 before reading input from a new file?

## Arrays

The double program shows us how we can retain data by assigning it to a variable. In awk, unlike several other programming languages, variables do not have to be initialized before they are referenced in a program. In the previous program, we evaluated lastword at the top, although it was not actually assigned a value until the bottom of the program. The awk program initialized the variable, setting it to the null string or 0, depending upon whether the variable is referenced as a string or numeric value.

An array is a variable that allows you to store a list of items or elements. An array is analogous to a restaurant menu. Each item on this menu is numbered:

#1    tuna noodle casserole

#2    roast beef and gravy

#3    pork and beans

One way of ordering roast beef is to say simply "Number 2." Using ordinary variables, you would have had to define a variable *two* and assign it the value *roast beef and gravy*. An array is a way of referencing a group of related values. This might be written:

```
menu[choice]
```

where `menu` is the name of the array and `choice` is the *subscript* used to reference items in the array. Thus, `menu[1]` is equal to *tuna noodle casserole*. In `awk`, you don't have to declare the size of the array; you only have to load the array (before referencing it). If we put our three menu choices on separate lines in a file, we could load the array with the following statement:

```
menu[NR] = $0
```

The variable `NR`, or record number, is used as the subscript for the array. Each input line is read into the next element in the array. We can print an individual element by referring to the value of the subscript (not the variable that set this value).

```
print menu[3]
```

This statement prints the third element in the array, which is *pork and beans*. If we want to refer to all the elements of this array, we can use a special version of the `for` loop. It has the following syntax:

```
for (element in array)
```

This statement can be used to descend the array to print all of the elements:

```
for (choice in menu)
        print menu[choice]
```

Each time through the loop, the variable `choice` is set to the next element in the array. The `menu` array is an example of an array that uses a numeric subscript as an index to the elements.

Now, let's use arrays to increase the functionality of `awkronym`. Our new version will read acronyms from a file and load them into an array; then we'll read a second file and search for the acronyms. Basically, we're reading one input file and defining keywords that we want to search for in other files. A similar program that reads a list of terms in a glossary might show where the words appear in a chapter. Let's see how it works first:

```
$ awkronym sect1
exposure to BASIC programming.
in COBOL and take advantage of a DBMS environment.
in COBOL and take advantage of a DBMS environment.
Of the high-level languages, BASIC is probably
```

Let's look at the program carefully.

```
awk ' {
if ( FILENAME == "acronyms" ){
     acro_desc[NR] = $1
     next
     }
for ( name in acro_desc )
        for (i = 1; i <= NF; i++)
             if ($i == acro_desc[name]) {
                  print $0
             }
}' acronyms $*
```

The current filename is stored in the system variable FILENAME. The procedure within the first conditional statement is only performed while input is taken from acronyms. The next statement ends this procedure by reading the next line of input from the file. Thus, the program does not advance beyond this procedure until input is taken from a different file.

The purpose of the first procedure is to assign each acronym ($1) to an element of the array acro_desc; the record number (NR) indexes the array.

In the second half of the program, we start comparing each element in the array to each field of every record. This requires two for loops, one to cycle through the array for each input line, and one to read each field on that line for as many times as there are elements in the array. An if statement compares the current field to the current element of the array; if they are equal, then the line is printed.

The line is printed each time an acronym is found. In our test example, because there were two acronyms on a single line, the one line is duplicated. To change this, we could add next after the print statement.

What if we changed awkronym so that it not only scanned the file for the acronym, but printed the acronym with the description as well? If a line refers to *BASIC*, we'd like to add the description (*Beginner's All-Purpose Symbolic Instruction Code*). We can design such a program for use as a *filter* that prints all lines, regardless of whether or not a change has been made. To change the previous version, we simply move the print statement outside the conditional statement. However, there are other changes we must make as well. Here's the first part of the new version.

```
awk ' {
        if ( FILENAME == "acronyms" ){
        split($0,fields,"|———|")
        acro_desc[fields[1]]=fields[2]
        next
        }
```

The records in acronyms use a tab as a field separator. Rather than change the field separator, we use the split function (we'll look at the syntax of this function later on) to give us an array named fields that has two elements, the name of the acronym and its description. This numeric array is then used in creating an associative array named acro_desc. An associative array lets us use a string as a subscript to the elements of an array. That is, given the name of the acronym, we can locate the element corresponding to the description. Thus the expression `acro_desc[GIGO]` will access `Garbage In, Garbage Out`.

Now let's look at the second half of the program:

```
for ( name in acro_desc )
        for (i = 1; i <= NF; i++)
            if ($i == name) {
                    $i = $i " ("acro_desc[name]")"
            }
print $0
```

Just like the previous version, we loop through the elements of the array and the fields for each record. At the heart of this section is the conditional statement that tests if the current field (`$i`) is equal to the subscript of the array (`name`). If the value of the field and the subscript are equal, we concatenate the field and the array element. In addition, we place the description in parentheses.

It should be clear why we make the comparison between `$i` and `name`, and not `acro_desc[name]`; the latter refers to an element, while the former refers to the subscript, the name of the acronym.

If the current field (`$i`) equals `BASIC` and the index of the array (`name`) is the string *BASIC*, then the value of the field is set to:

```
BASIC (Beginner's All-Purpose Symbolic Instruction Code)
```

For this program to be practical, the description should be inserted for the first occurrence of an acronym, not each time. (After we've inserted the description of the acronym, we don't need the description any more.) We could redefine that element in the array after we've used it:

```
acro_desc[name] = name
```

In this instance, we simply make the element equal to the subscript. Thus, `acro_desc[BASIC]` is equal to *Beginner's All-Purpose Symbolic Instruction Code* at the beginning of the procedure, and equal to *BASIC* if a match has been made. There are two places where we test the element against the subscript with the expression "`(acro_desc[name] != name)`." The first place is after the `for` loop has read in a new element from `acro_desc`; a conditional statement ensures that we don't scan the next input record for an acronym that has already been found. The second place is when we test `$i` to see if it matches `name`; this test ensures that we don't make another match for the same acronym on that line.

```
if ($i == name && acro_desc[name] != name)
```

This conditional statement evaluates a compound expression. The `&&` (and) boolean operator states a condition that both expressions have to be true for the compound expression to be true.

Another problem that we can anticipate is that we might produce lines that exceed 80 characters. After all, the descriptions are quite long. We can find out how many characters are in a string, using a built-in `awk` function, `length`. For instance, to evaluate the length of the current input record, we specify:

```
length($0)
```

The value of a function can be assigned to a variable or put inside an expression and evaluated.

```
if (length($0) > 70){
     if (i > 2)
             $i = "\n" $i
     if (i+1 < NF )
             $(i+1) = "\n" $(i+1)
     }
```

The length of the current input record is evaluated after the description has been concatenated. If it is greater than 70 characters, then two conditions test where to put the newline. The first procedure concatenates a newline and the current field; thus we only want to perform this action when we are not near the beginning of a line (field greater than 2). The second procedure concatenates the newline and the next field (i+1) so that we check that we are not near the end of the line. The newline precedes the field in each of these operations. Putting it at the end of the field would result in a new line that begins with a space output with the next field.

Another way to handle the line break, perhaps more efficiently, is to use the length function to return a value for each field. By accumulating that value, we could specify a line break when a new field causes the total to exceed a certain number. We'll look at arithmetic operations in a later section.

Here's the full version of awkronyms:

```
awk '   {
   if ( FILENAME == "acronyms" ){
   split($0,fields,"|———|")
   acro_desc[fields[1]]=fields[2]
   next
   }
for ( name in acro desc )
   if (acro_desc[name] !~ name)
      for (i = 1; i <= NF; i++)
         if ($i == name && acro_desc[name] != name) {
            $i =   $i " ("acro_desc[name]")"
            acro_desc[name] = name
            if (length($0) > 70){
               if (i > 2)
                  $i = "\n" $i
               if (i+1 < NF)
                  $(i+1) = "\n" $(i+1)
            }
         }
print $0
}' acronyms $*
```

And here's one proof that it works:

```
$ cat sect1
Most users of microcomputers have had some
exposure to BASIC programming.
Many data-processing applications are written
in COBOL and take advantage of a DBMS environment.
C, the language of the UNIX environment,
is used by systems programmers.
Of the high-level languages, BASIC is probably
the easiest to learn, and C is the most difficult.
Nonetheless, you will find the fundamental programming
constructs common to most languages.

$ awkronym sect1
Most users of microcomputers have had some
exposure to
BASIC (Beginner's All-Purpose Symbolic Instruction Code)
programming.  Many data-processing applications are
written in COBOL (Common Business Orientated Language)
and take advantage of a
DBMS (Data Base Management System) environment.
C, the language of the UNIX environment,
is used by systems programmers.
Of the high-level languages, BASIC is probably
the easiest to learn, and C is the most difficult.
Nonetheless, you will find the fundamental programming
constructs common to most languages.
```

Notice that the second reference to BASIC has not been changed.  There are other features we might add to this program.  For instance, we could use awk's pattern-matching capabilities so that we don't make the change on lines containing macros, or on lines within pairs of certain macros, such as .DS/.DE.

Another version of this program could trademark certain terms or phrases in a document.  For instance, you'd want to locate the first occurrence of UNIX and place \(rg after it.


## ▪ awk Applications ▪


A shell program is an excellent way to gather data interactively and write it into a file in a format that can be read by awk.  We're going to be looking at a series of programs for maintaining a project log.  A shell script collects the name of a project and the number of hours worked on the project.  An awk program totals the hours for each project and prints a report.

The file day is the shell script for collecting information and appending it to a file named daily in the user's home directory.

```
$ cat /usr/local/bin/day
case $# in
0) echo "Project: \c";read proj;echo "Hours: \c";read hrs;;
1) proj=$1; echo "Hours: \c"; read hrs;;
2) proj=$1;hrs=$2;;
esac
set 'who am i'; name=$1; month=$3; day=$4;
echo $name"\t"$month $day"\t"$hrs"\t"$proj>>$HOME/daily
```

The `case` statement checks how many arguments are entered on the command line. If an argument is missing, the user is prompted to enter a value. Prompting is done through a pair of statements: `echo` and `read`. The `echo` command displays the prompt on the user's terminal; `\c` suppresses the carriage return at the end of the prompt. The `read` command waits for user input, terminated by a carriage return, and assigns it to a variable. Thus, the variables `proj` and `hrs` are defined by the end of the `case` statement.

The `set` command can be used to divide the output of a command into separate arguments (`$1`, `$2`, `$3`...). By executing the command `who am i` from within `set`, we supply the user's name and the day's date automatically. The `echo` command is used to write the information to the file. There are four fields, separated by tabs. (In the Bourne shell, the escape sequence `\t` produces a tab; you must use quotation marks to keep the backslash from being stripped off by the shell.)

Here's what `daily` contains for one user at the end of a week:

```
$ cat /usr/fred/daily
fred    Aug 4 7        Course Development
fred    Aug 5 4        Training class
fred    Aug 5 4        Programmer's Guide
fred    Aug 6 2        Administrative
fred    Aug 6 6        Text-processing book
fred    Aug 7 4        Course Development
fred    Aug 7 4        Text-processing book
fred    Aug 8 4        Training class
fred    Aug 8 3        Programmer's Guide
```

There are nine records in this file. Obviously, our input program does not enforce consistency in naming projects by the user.

Given this input, we'd like an `awk` program that reports the total number of hours for the week and gives us a breakdown of hours by project. At first pass, we need only be concerned with reading fields three and four. We can total the number of hours by accumulating the value of the third field.

```
total += $3
```

The `+=` operator performs two functions: it adds `$3` to the current value of `total` and then assigns this value to `total`. It is the same as the statement:

```
total = total + $3
```

We can use an associative array to accumulate hours ($3) by project ($4).

```
hours[$4] += $3
```

Each time a record is read, the value of the third field is added to the accumulated value of `project[$4]`.

We don't want to print anything until all input records have been read. An END procedure prints the accumulated results. Here's the first version of `tot`:

```
awk '
        BEGIN { FS="|———|" }
{

                total += $3
                hours[$4] += $3
}
        END    {
               for (project in hours)
               print project, hours[project]
               print
               print "Total Hours:", total
} ' $HOME/daily
```

Let's test the program:

```
$ tot
Course Development 11
Administrative 2
Programmer's Guide 7
Training class 8
Text-processing book 10

Total Hours: 38
```

The program performs the arithmetic tasks well, but the report lacks an orderly format. It would help to change the output field separator (OFS) to a tab. But the variable lengths of the project names prevent the project hours from being aligned in a single column. The awk program offers an alternative print statement, `printf`, which is borrowed from the C programming language.

## Formatted Print Statements

The `printf` statement has two parts: the first is a quoted expression that describes the format specifications; the second is a sequence of arguments such as variable names. The two main format specifications are `%s` for strings and `%d` for decimals. (There are additional specifications for octal, hexadecimal, and noninteger numbers.) Unlike the regular print statement, `printf` does not automatically supply a newline. This can be specified as `\n`. A tab is specified as `\t`.

A simple `printf` statement containing string and decimal specifications is:

```
printf "%s\t%d\n", project, hours[project]
```

First `project` is output, then a tab (\t), the number of hours, and a newline (\n). For each format specification, you must supply a corresponding argument.

Unfortunately, such a simple statement does not solve our formatting problem. Here are sample lines that it produces:

```
Course Development 11
Administrative  2
Programmer's Guide 7
```

We need to specify a minimum field width so that the tab begins at the same position. The `printf` statement allows you to place this specification between the `%` and the conversion specification. You would use `%-20s` to specify a minimum field width of 20 characters in which the value is left justified. Without the minus sign, the value would be right justified, which is what we want for a decimal value.

```
END     {
        for (project in hours)
        printf "%-20s\t%2d\n", project, hours[project]
        printf "\n\tTotal Hours:\t%2d\n", total
        }
```

Notice that literals, such as the string `Total Hours`, are placed in the first part, with the format specification.

Just as we use the `END` procedure to print the report, we can include a `BEGIN` procedure to print a header for the report:

```
BEGIN { FS="|————|"
        printf "%20s%s\n\n","PROJECT     ", " HOURS"
        }
```

This shows an alternative way to handle strings. The following formatted report is displayed:

```
            PROJECT       HOURS

Course Development     11
Administrative          2
Programmer's Guide      7
Training class          8
Text-processing book   10

        Total Hours:    38
```

## Defensive Techniques

After you have accomplished the basic task of a program—and the code at this point is fairly easy to understand—it is often a good idea to surround this core with "defensive" procedures designed to trap inconsistent input records and prevent the program from failing. For instance, in the tot program, we might want to check that the number of hours is greater than 0 and that the project description is not null for each input record. We can use a conditional expression, using the logical operator &&.

```
$3 > 0 && $4 != ""{
                procedure
        }
```

Both conditions must be true for the procedure to be executed. The logical operator && signifies that if both conditions are true, the expression is true.

Another aspect of incorporating defensive techniques is error handling. In other words, what do we want to have happen after the program detects an error? The previous condition is set up so that if the procedure is not executed, the next line of input is read. In this example the program keeps going, but in other cases you might want the program to print an error message and halt if such an error is encountered.

However, a distinction between "professional" and "amateur" programmers might be useful. We are definitely in the latter camp, and we do not always feel compelled to write 100% user-proof programs. For one thing, defensive programming is quite time consuming and frequently tedious. Second, an amateur is at liberty to write programs that perform the way he or she expects them to; a professional has to write for an audience and must account for their expectations. Consider the possible uses and users of any program you write.

## awk and nroff/troff

It is fairly easy to have an awk program generate the necessary codes for form reports. For instance, we enhanced the tot program to produce a troff-formatted report:

```
awk ' BEGIN { FS = "|———|"
print ".ce"
print ".B "
print "PROJECT ACTIVITY REPORT"
print ".R"
print ".sp 2"
        }
NR == 1 {
        begday = $2
        }
$3 > 0 && $4 != "" {
                hours[$4] += $3
                total += $3
                endday = $2
                logname = $1
        }
```

```
        END   {
printf "Writer: %s\n", logname
print ".sp"
printf "Period: %s to %s\n",begday, endday
print ".sp"
printf "%20s%s\n\n","PROJECT     ", " HOURS"
print ".sp"
print ".nf"
print ".na"
        for (project in hours)
printf "%-20s\t%2d\n", project, hours[project]
print ".sp"
printf "Total Hours:\t %2d\n", total
print ".sp"
}' $HOME/daily
```

We incorporated one additional procedure in this version to determine the weekly period. The start date of the week is taken from the first record (NR == 1). The last record provides the final day of the week.

As you can see, awk doesn't mind if you mix print and printf statements. The regular print command is more convenient for specifying literals, such as formatting codes, because the newline is automatically provided. Because this program writes to standard output, you could pipe the output directly to nroff/troff.

You can use awk to generate input to tbl and other troff preprocessors such as pic.

## Multiline Records

In this section, we are going to take a look at a set of programs for order tracking. We developed these programs to help operate a small, mail-order publishing business. These programs could be easily adapted to track documents in a technical publications department.

Once again, we used a shell program, take.orders, for data entry. The program has two purposes: The first is to enter the customer's name and mailing address for later use in building a mailing list. The second is to display seven titles and prompt the user to enter the title number, the number of copies, and the price per copy. The data collected for the mailing list and the customer order are written to separate files.

Two sample customer order records follow:

```
Charlotte Smith
P.O  N61331 87 Y 045     Date: 03/14/87
#1 3   7.50
#2 3   7.50
#3 1   7.50
#4 1   7.50
#7 1   7.50
```

```
Martin S. Rossi
P.O  NONE     Date: 03/14/87
#1 2   7.50
#2 5   6.75
```

These are multiline records, that is, a newline is used as the field separator. A blank line separates individual records. For most programs, this will require that we redefine the default field separator and record separator. The field separator becomes a newline, and the record separator is null.

```
BEGIN { FS = "\n"; RS = "" }
```

Let's write a simple program that multiplies the number of copies by the price. We want to ignore the first two lines of each record, which supply the customer's name, a purchase order number, and the date of the order. We only want to read the lines that specify a title. There are a few ways to do this. With awk's pattern-matching capabilities, we could select lines beginning with a hash (#) and treat them as individual records, with fields separated by spaces.

```
awk '/^#/ {
                amount = $2 * $3
                printf "%s %6.2f\n", $0, amount
                next
         }
      {print}' $*
```

The main procedure only affects lines that match the pattern. It multiplies the second field by the third field, assigning the value to the variable amount. The printf conversion %f prints a floating-point number; 2 specifies a minimum field width of 6 and a precision of 2. Precision is the number of digits to the right of the decimal point; the default for %f is 6. We print the current record along with the value of the variable amount. If a line is printed within this procedure, the next line is read from standard input. Lines not matching the pattern are simply passed through. Let's look at how addem works:

```
$ addem orders
Charlotte Smith
P.O  N61331 87 Y 045    Date: 03/14/87
#1 3   7.50   22.50
#2 3   7.50   22.50
#3 1   7.50    7.50
#4 1   7.50    7.50
#7 1   7.50    7.50

Martin S. Rossi
P.O  NONE    Date: 03/14/87
#1 2   7.50   15.00
#2 5   6.75   33.75
```

Now, let's design a program that reads multiline records and accumulates order information for a report. This report should display the total number of copies and the total amount for each title. We also want totals reflecting all copies ordered and the sum of all orders.

We know that we will not be using the information in the first two fields of each record. However, each record has a variable number of fields, depending upon how many titles have been ordered. First, we check that the input record has at least three fields. Then a `for` loop reads all of the fields beginning with the third field:

```
NF >= 3 {
    for (i = 3; i <= NF; ++i)
```

In database terms, each field has a value and each value can be further broken up into subvalues. That is, if the value of a field in a multiline record is a single line, subvalues are the words on that line. You have already seen the `split` function used to break up an input record; now we'll see it used to subdivide a field. The `split` function loads any *string* into an *array*, using a specified character as the subvalue separator.

> `split` (*string*, *array*, *separator*)

The default subvalue separator is a blank. The `split` function returns the number of elements loaded into the array. The *string* can be a literal (in quotation marks) or a variable. For instance, let's digress a minute and look at an isolated use of `split`. Here's a person's name and title with each part separated by a comma:

```
title-"George Travers, Research/Development, Alcuin Inc."
```

We can use `split` to divide this string and print it on three lines.

```
need = split(title, name, ",")
    print ".ne ", need
    for ( part in name)
        print name[part]
```

This procedure prints each part on a separate line. The number of elements in the array (3) is saved in the variable `need`. This variable is passed as an argument to an `.ne` request, which tells `troff` to make sure there are at least three lines available at the bottom of the page before outputting the first line.

The awk program has twelve built-in functions, as shown in Table 13-2. Four of these are specialized arithmetic functions for cosine, sine, logarithm, and square root. The rest of these functions manipulate strings. (You have already seen how the `length` function works.) See Appendix A for the syntax of these functions.

Going back to our report generator, we need to split each field into subvalues. The variable `$i` will supply the value of the current field, subdivided as elements in the array `order`.

```
sv = split($i, order)
    if (sv == 3) {
                procedure
    }
    else print "Incomplete Record"
```

**TABLE 13-2. awk Built-in Functions**

| Function | Description |
|----------|-------------|
| cos | Cosine |
| exp | Exponent |
| getline | Read input line |
| index | Return position of substring in string |
| int | Integer |
| length | Length of string |
| log | Logarithm |
| sin | Sine |
| split | Subdivide string into array |
| sprintf | Format string like printf |
| sqrt | Square root |
| substr | Substring extraction |

The number of elements returned by the function is saved in the sv variable. This allows us to test that there are three subvalues. If there are not, the else statement is executed, printing the error message to the screen.

Next, we assign the individual elements of the array to a specific variable. This is mainly to make it easier to remember what each element represents.

```
title = order[1]
copies = order[2]
price = order[3]
```

Then a group of arithmetic operations are performed on these values.

```
amount = copies * price
total_vol += copies
total_amt += amount
vol[title] += copies
amt[title] += amount
```

These values are accumulated until the last input record is read. The END procedure prints the report.

Here's the complete program:

```
awk ' BEGIN { FS = "\n"; RS = "" }
NF >= 3 {
for (i = 3; i <= NF; ++i){
   sv = split($i, order)
     if (sv == 3){
        title = order[1]
        copies = order[2]
        price = order[3]
        amount = copies * price
        total_vol += copies
```

```
            total_amt += amount
            vol[title] += copies
            amt[title] += amount
            }
        else print "Incomplete Record"
        }
    }
    END {
        printf "%5s\t%10s\t%6s\n\n", "TITLE", \
        "COPIES SOLD", "TOTAL"
        for (title in vol)
    printf "%5s\t%10d\t$%7.2f\n", title, vol[title],\
        amt[title]
            "printf" " "%s\n", "-------------"
    printf "\t%s%4d\t$%7.2f\n","Total ",total_vol,total_amt}'
    $*
```

In awk, arrays are one dimensional; a two-dimensional array stores two elements indexed by the same subscript. You can get a pseudo two-dimensional array in awk by defining two arrays that have the same subscript. We only need one for loop to read both arrays.

The addemup file, an order report generator, produces the following output:

```
$ addemup orders.today
TITLE  COPIES SOLD    TOTAL

    #1           5  $   37.50
    #2           8  $   56.25
    #3           1  $    7.50
    #4           1  $    7.50
    #7           1  $    7.50
-------------
        Total   16  $  116.25
```

After you solve a programming problem, you will find that you can re-use that approach in other programs. For instance, the method used in the awkronym program to load acronyms into an array could be applied in the current example to read the book titles from a file and print them in the report. Similarly, you can use variations of the same program to print different reports. The construction of the next program is similar to the previous program. Yet the content of the report is quite different.

```
awk ' BEGIN { FS = "\n"; RS = ""
printf "%-15s\t%10s\t%6s\n\n", "CUSTOMER", "COPIES SOLD", \
    "TOTAL"
    }
NF >= 3 {
customer = $1
    total_vol = 0
    total_amt = 0
```

```
for (i = 3; i <= NF; ++i){
   split($i, order)
   title = order[1]
   copies = order[2]
   price = order[3]
   amount = copies * price
   total_vol += copies
   total_amt += amount
}
printf "\t%s%4d\t$%7.2f\n","Total ",total_vol,total_amt}'
}' $*
```

In this program, named `summary`, we print totals for each customer order. Notice that the variables `total_vol` and `total_amt` are reset to 0 whenever a new record is read. In the previous program, these values accumulated from one record to the next.

The `summary` program, reading a multiline record, produces a report that lists each record on a single line:

```
$ summary orders
CUSTOMER      COPIES SOLD    TOTAL

J. Andrews              7 $   52.50
John Peterson           4 $   30.00
Charlotte Miller       11 $   82.50
Dan Aspromonte        105 $  787.50
Valerie S. Rossi        4 $   30.00
Timothy P. Justice      4 $   30.00
Emma  Fleming          25 $  187.50
Antonio Pollan          5 $   37.50
Hugh Blair             15 $  112.50
```

## ▪ Testing Programs ▪

Part of writing a program is designing one or more test cases. Usually this means creating a sample input file. It is a good idea to test a program at various stages of development. Each time you add a function, test it. For instance, if you implement a conditional procedure, test that the procedure is executed when the expression is true; test what happens when it is false. Program testing involves making sure that the syntax is correct *and* that the problem has been solved.

When `awk` encounters syntax errors it will tell you that it is "bailing out." Usually it will print the line number associated with the error. Syntax errors can be caused by a variety of mistakes, such as forgetting to quote strings or to close a procedure with a brace. Sometimes, it can be as minor as an extra blank space. The `awk` program's error messages are seldom helpful, and a persistent effort is often required to uncover the fault.

You might even see a UNIX system error message, such as the dreadful declaration:

```
Segmentation fault—core dumped.
```

Not to worry. Although your program has failed badly, you have not caused an earthquake or a meltdown. An image of "core" memory at the time of the error is saved or dumped in a file named `core`. Advanced programmers can use a debugging program to examine this image and determine where in memory the fault occurred. We just delete `core` and re-examine our code.

Again, check each construct as you add it to the program. If you wait until you have a large program, and it fails, you will often have difficulty finding the error. Not only that, but you are likely to make unnecessary changes, fixing what's not broken in an attempt to find out what is.

Checking that you have solved the problem you set out to tackle is a much larger issue. After you begin testing your program on larger samples, you will undoubtedly uncover "exceptions," otherwise known as *bugs*. In testing the awkronym program, we discovered an exception where an acronym appeared as the last word in the sentence. It was not "found" because of the period ending the sentence. That is, awk found that *BASIC* and *BASIC.* were not equal. This would not be a problem if we could test the search string as a regular expression but we have to test the array variable as a literal string.

Programming is chiefly pragmatic in its aims. You must judge whether or not specific problems merit writing a program or if certain exceptions are important enough to adapt the general program to account for them. Sometimes, in large public programs as well as small private ones, bugs just become part of the program's known behavior, which the user is left to cope with as best as he or she can. The bug found in awkronym is a common enough problem, so it is necessary to implement a fix.

The fix for the awkronym bug does not involve awk at all. We run a a sed script before the awkronym program to separate punctuation marks from any word. It converts a punctuation mark to a field containing garbage characters. Another script processes the awkronym output and strips out these garbage characters. The example below shows how both scripts are used as bookends for the awkronym program.

```
sed 's/\(..*\)\([.,!;]\)/\1 @@@\2/g' $* |
awk ' {
        program lines
}' acronyms - |
sed 's/ @@@\([.,!;]\)/\1/g'
```

# 14

# Writing `nroff` and `troff` Macros

The `nroff` and `troff` formatters include a powerful macro definition and substitution capability.  As we suggested when macros were first discussed in Chapter 4, they are a good way to combine frequently used sequences of formatting requests into a single instruction.  But after working with the `ms` and `mm` macro packages, you must know that macros are more than that.

Macros are an essential part of `nroff` and `troff`—you cannot escape them if you want to make serious use of the formatter.  Precisely because macros are so essential, many users never learn to fully use them.  The most obviously useful macros are already included in the existing macro packages, whose complex internal control structures make them difficult to understand and modify.

The purpose of this chapter is to introduce the fundamental `nroff` and `troff` requests that are used for creating macros. You'll learn the basics in this chapter.  Then, in later chapters we can examine how to write macros for specific purposes, without having to make continual asides to introduce a new request.

Chapter 15 describes additional requests for creating special effects (such as pictures) with your macros, and Chapters 16 through 18 discuss how to go beyond writing individual macros and how to develop or extend an entire macro package.

## · Comments ·

Before we start, we'll introduce the syntax for inserting comments into your macro definitions.  Macros can get quite confusing, so we advise you to put in comments that explain what you are doing.  This will help immensely when you go back weeks or months later to modify a macro you have written.

A line beginning with the sequence:

```
.\"
```

will not be interpreted or printed by the formatter. Any part of a line following the sequence `\"` will be treated the same way. For example:

```
.\" O'Reilly & Associates, Inc. custom macro set
.\" Last modified 4/25/87
.de IZ \" Initialization macro
     .
     .
     .
```

Note that there is an important difference between:

```
.\" A full line comment
```

and:

```
\" A partial line comment
```

If you simply start the sequence `\"` at the margin, the formatter will insert a blank line into the output, because this sequence by itself does not suppress newline generation.

(Note that comments can be used at any time, not just in macros. You can write notes to yourself in your input file and they will never appear in the output. But if you accidentally type the sequence `\"` in your file, the remainder of the line on which it appears will disappear from the output.)

## ▪ Defining Macros ▪

As we've already discussed, use the `.de` request to define a macro:

```
.de AB     \" Define macro AB
Requests and/or text of macro here
..
```

There are also requests to remove or add to existing macros. The `.rm` request removes a macro:

```
.rm PQ  \" Remove macro PQ
```

You may sometimes want to define a macro for local use, and remove it when you are done. In general, though, this is an advanced request you will not use often.

The `.am` request appends to the end of an existing macro. It works just like `.de` but does not overwrite the existing contents:

```
.am DS  \" Append to the existing definition of DS
.ft CW
..
```

At first, you may think that this request has only limited usefulness. However, as you work more with macros, you will find unexpected uses for it. We'll mention a few of these in later chapters.

## ▪ Macro Names ▪

A macro name can be one or two characters, and can consist of any character(s), not just alphanumeric characters. For example:

```
.de ^(    \" Macro used internally whose name, we hope,
          \" never has to be remembered
```

You can even use control characters in macro names. Names can be uppercase or lowercase, or any combination of the two, and uppercase and lowercase are distinct. For example, the four names .gm, .GM, .gM, and .Gm can all be used without conflict.

If you are starting from scratch, you can use whatever macro or number register names you like except for the names of existing formatter requests. However, if you are adding macros to an existing package, you have to work around the existing names, because creating a new macro with the same name as an old one will discard the previously read-in definition.

This is not as easy as it sounds, because macro packages include internal macro, string, and number register definitions that are not visible to the casual user. You may be surprised when your new macro makes some other part of the package go haywire. (In an attempt to forestall this problem, most macro developers give odd, unmnemonic names to internally called macros. However, collisions still can and do occur.)

### Finding the Names of Existing Macros

Before you start adding macros to an existing package, it's a good idea to print the names of all existing macros.

There are two ways to do this. The .pm request will print (in blocks of 128 characters) the names and sizes of all macros defined in a given run of the formatter. So, for example, creating a file containing the single request:

```
.pm
```

and formatting it like this:

```
$ nroff -ms pmfile
```

will print on the screen a list of all the macros defined in the ms macro package. (The output could also be redirected to a file or printer.)

However, macro names are drawn from the same pool as string names (see the next example), so it might be better to search for macro or string definitions using grep *et al*, like this:

```
$ grep '^\.d[esia]' macrofiles | cut -f1,2 -d' ' | sort | uniq
```

(grep will select all lines beginning with either .de, .ds, .di, or .da; cut will select only the first two space-separated fields on each of those lines; sort and uniq together will produce a sorted list consisting of only one copy of each line. Note that for -mm, which does not use a space before the macro name, you would need to specify cut -f1 only. You will also need to substitute for *macrofiles* the actual filenames containing the macros of interest.)

You should do the same for number registers:

```
$ sed -n -e 's/.*.nr *\(..\).*/\1/p' macrofiles | sort | uniq
```

here, because we can't rely on number registers being set at the start of a line, as we can with macro definitions. The one-line `sed` script included here saves the first two nonspace characters (`..`) following the string `.nr`, and substitutes them for the rest of the line (i.e., it throws away the rest of the line).

You could also just `grep` for an individual macro, string, or number register name before you use it! Or you could take the easy way, and check Appendix B, where we've listed all the names in each of the packages.

In addition to looking for conflicting names, you may also need to look for conflicting usage, or to understand in detail the operation of a macro you are intending to call within a new macro you are writing.

To do this, you can simply read in the entire macro definition file with the editor and search for what you want. However, to make things easier, we use the `getmac` shell script described in Chapter 12 to print out the definition of the desired macro. The script prints the result on standard output, which can easily be redirected into a file, where it can become the basis for your own redefinition.

### Renaming a Macro

If you do find a conflict, you can rename macros that have already been defined. The `.rn` macro renames an existing macro:

```
.rn ^( H1      \" Rename ^( to H1; easier to remember
```

The old name will no longer work. You must use the new name to invoke the macro.

A good trick that you can *sometimes* pull off with `.rn` is to temporarily redefine a macro (without ever modifying its contents). For example, the ms macros include a macro to draw a box around a paragraph; however, these macros do not leave any space above or below the box. We can add some like this:

```
.rn B1 b1      \" Rename B1 to b1
.de B1         \" Now redefine B1
.sp .5         \" Add some space before the box is drawn
.b1            \" Execute the old definition
..

.rn B2 b2      \" Rename B2 to b2
.de B2         \" Now redefine B2
.b2            \" Execute the old definition
.sp .5         \" Add some space after the box is drawn
..
```

This only works for adding extra control lines before or after the current contents of the macro. Remember it, though, because this trick may come in handy if you don't want to (or can't) directly modify a macro in one of the existing packages, but do want a slightly different effect.

## · Macro Arguments ·

The simplest kind of macro is a sequence of stored commands, starting with a `.de` request and ending with the two dots (..) at the beginning of a line.

However, as you've seen when you've used `mm` and `ms`, macros can take arguments, and can act differently depending on various conditions. It's also possible for a macro to save information and pass it to other macros to affect their operation. An understanding of how to do these things is essential if you plan any serious macro design.

A macro can take up to nine arguments and can use them in any way. Arguments are described positionally by the character sequences `\\$1` through `\\$9`[*].

For example, we could define a very simple `.B` macro to boldface a single argument:

```
.de B              \"  Macro to boldface first argument
\fB\\$1\fP
..
```

Or, we could write a simple paragraph macro that, instead of having a fixed indent, might take a numeric argument to specify the depth of the indent:

```
.de PI             \"  Simple paragraph macro
.sp
.ne 2              \"  Prevent widows
.ti \\$1           \"  Indent to the depth specified by first
..                 \"  argument
```

As you can see in the first example, you can print an argument in your text. Or, shown in the second example, you can use it inside the macro as an argument to one or more of the requests that make up the macro.

Notice that there is nothing intrinsic about a macro that causes a break. The `.B` macro, for instance, can be placed in the input file as in the following example:

```
There are a number of ways to
.B embolden
text.
```

As long as filling is in effect, it will produce exactly the same output as:

```
There are a number of ways to \fBembolden\fP text.
```

Macro arguments are separated by spaces. If you want to include an explicit space in an argument, you should enclose the entire string in quotation marks, like this:

---

[*]Actually, the sequences are `\$1` through `\$9`, with only a single backslash. But for reasons to be described shortly, you always need at least two backslashes.

```
There are a number of ways to
.B "make text stand out."
```

If you didn't enclose the phrase *make text stand out* in quotation marks, a single word, *make*, would have been interpreted as the first argument, the next word, *text*, as the second argument, and so on. This wouldn't cause a program error—there is no requirement that arguments to a macro be used by that macro—but the unused arguments would simply disappear from the output. As shown here, the entire phrase is treated as a single argument.

To actually print a quotation mark inside a macro argument, double it. For example:

```
.B "The Quote ("") Character"
```

will produce:

---

**The Quote (") Character**

---

You've probably recognized that the syntax for specifying arguments by position is very similar to that used with shell scripts. You might wonder, though, about backslashes, which are used in the shell to prevent interpretation of a special character. In fact, they serve the same function in `troff`.

The `nroff` and `troff` formatters always read a macro at least twice: once when they read the definition (and store it away for later use), and once when they encounter it in the text. At the time the macro is defined, *there are no arguments*, so it is essential to prevent the formatter from doing any argument substitution.

When the macro definition is read, the formatter operates in what is referred to (in the *Nroff/Troff User's Manual*) as *copy mode*. That is, none of the requests are executed; they are simply copied (in this case, presumably into memory) without interpretation. The exception is that various escape sequences that may have a different value at macro definition time than at macro execution time (most notably \n, for interpolating number registers, \*, for interpolating strings, and \$, for interpolating arguments) are executed, unless you suppress interpretation with a preceding backslash. (Other escape sequences are also interpreted, but because they have fixed values, this makes no difference to the action of the macro.)

A backslash prevents interpretation of the character that follows it by sacrificing itself. The backslash tells the formatter: "Take me but let the next guy go." Each time the character sequence is read, the backslash is stripped off—that is, \\ is actually stored as \. (You can think of \ as saying "I really mean . . . ." So in the shell, for example, if you want to use an asterisk literally, rather than as a filename expansion metacharacter, you write \*—that is, "I really mean *." In a similar way, \\ says "I really mean backslash.")

When macro definitions are nested inside one another, you will need to add additional backslashes to get what you want. The true argument interpolation escape sequence is \$n, rather than \\$n; the extra backslash is needed because the first one is stripped when the macro is interpreted in copy mode. The same rule applies when you want to interpolate the value of a number register or a string in a macro definition. Think through the number of times the definition will be read before it is executed, and specify the appropriate number of backslashes, so that you get the actual value used at the point where you need it. A failure to understand this will cause more frustration than almost any other error when you are writing macros.

In the example of the `.B` macro, the sequences `\fB` and `\fP` did not need to be escaped, because `troff` could just as easily interpret them at the time the macro is defined. However, the macro would also work if they were specified with double backslashes—it is just that the interpretation of the codes would take place when the macro was used.

### ▪ Nested Macro Definitions ▪

We said previously that a macro definition begins with a `.de` request and ends with two dots (`..`). This is a simplification. The `.de` request takes an alternate terminator as an optional second argument. This feature allows you to create nested macro definitions.

```
.de M1              \" Start first macro
.de M2 !!           \" Start second macro
.!!                 \" End second macro
..                  \" End first macro
```

You can also nest macros by delaying interpretation of the `..` on the second macro:

```
.de M1              \" Start first macro
.de M2              \" Start second macro
\\..                \" End second macro
...                 \" End first macro
```

For example, a group of related macros for producing a certain type of document might be nested inside a "master" macro. A user would have to invoke the master macro, indicating document type, to make the other macros available for use. Nested macros could be used to provide alternate versions of the same set of macros within a single macro package.

### ▪ Conditional Execution ▪

One of the most powerful features of `nroff` and `troff`'s macro programming language is its facility for conditional execution. There are three conditional execution requests: `.if`, `.ie` (*if else*), and `.el` (*else*). The `.if` request is used for a single condition. ("If the condition is met, do this; otherwise, simply go to the next line.") The `.ie` and `.el` requests are used as a pair, testing a condition and then performing either one action or the other. ("If the condition is met, do this; otherwise, do that.")

## Predefined Conditions

There are a number of different conditions that can be tested with `.if` and `.ie`. The simplest looks to see if a predefined condition is true or false. There are four predefined conditions, as listed in Table 14-1.

**TABLE 14-1. Built-in Conditions**

| Condition | True if |
|:---:|:---|
| o | Current page number is odd |
| e | Current page number is even |
| n | The file is being formatted by `nroff` |
| t | The file is being formatted by `troff` |

For example, in a page bottom macro, to print the page number in the outside corner, you might write:

```
.if o .tl '''%' \" If odd, put page number in right corner
.if e .tl '%''' \" If even, put page number in left corner
```

(The `.tl` request prints three-part titles, at the left, center, and right of the page. And, within this request, the `%` character always prints the current page number. We'll explain these two items in detail later, when we look at how to write a complete page transition macro. For right now, we just want to understand how the conditions themselves work.)

Because the two conditions, odd and even, are mutually exclusive, you could also write:

```
.ie o .tl '''%' \" If odd, put page number in right corner
.el .tl '%'''    \" Otherwise, put it in left corner
```

Notice that you do not specify a condition to be tested in the `.el` request.

## Arithmetic and Logical Expressions

A closely related condition simply tests for a nonzero number or a true arithmetic expression. This is generally used with number registers, but it could also be used to test the value of numeric arguments to a macro. For example, we could write a paragraph macro that was either indented or flush left, depending on the value of its argument:

```
.de P
.sp
.ne 2
.if \\$1 .ti \\$1  \" If there is an arg, use it for indent
..
```

That is, if there is a nonzero numeric argument, do a temporary indent to the distance specified by the value of the argument.

Rather than using the simple presence of a numeric argument to satisfy the condition, you could also use an arithmetic expression to test for a value. Used in this way, the argument can simply be a *flag* telling the macro what to do.

```
.de P
.sp
.ne 2
.if \\$1=1 .ti 5n      \" If first arg = 1, indent 5 ens
..
```

The operators shown in Table 14-2 can be used in constructing an expression.

**TABLE 14-2. Expression Operators**

| Operator | Description |
|---|---|
| +, -, /, * | Standard arithmetic operators |
| % | Modulo |
| >, < | Greater than, less than |
| >=, <= | Greater than or equal, less than or equal |
| =, == | Equal |
| & | AND |
| : | OR |

Expressions are evaluated from left to right, except where indicated otherwise by the presence of parentheses. There is no precedence of operators.

Frequently, you will see numeric conditions involving number registers. Here are a few simple examples:

```
.if \\nb
.if \\nb>1
.if \\nb<\\nc
.if \\nb+\\nc>1
```

(Be sure to note the double backslash before each number register invocation: we are assuming that these requests are made within a macro definition. If they were made outside a macro, you would use only a single backslash.) The first of these conditions is commonly used in the existing macro packages. It takes a little getting used to—it is not always obvious to new users what is being tested in an expression like:

```
.if \\nb
```

A condition of this form simply tests that the specified expression (the number register b in this case) has a value greater than 0. A more complex expression that does the same thing might be:

```
.if \\nb-1
```

## Comparing Strings

Another frequent test that you can use as the basis of a condition is whether or not two strings are equal—for example, whether an argument contains a particular string. The syntax is simply:

```
.if "string1"string2"
```

(Note that there are a total of three quotation marks—either single or double will do—and no equals sign. A frequent error among beginners is to use an equals sign to compare string arguments, which will not work.)

For example, suppose you are writing a macro to center the output if the second argument is the letter C. You could write:

```
.if "\\$2"C" .ce  \" If 2nd arg is C, center the next line
```

You can also test for a null argument in this way:

```
.if "\\$1"" do something
```

Use of this condition or its inverse, the test for a non-null argument (described in the next section), allows the user to skip over an argument by supplying a null string (**" "**).

## Executing Multiple Requests as a Result of a Condition

All of the examples we've shown so far consist of a single request executed on the basis of a condition. But often you'll want to execute more than one command when a condition is met. To do so, you enclose the sequence to be executed in backslashes and braces, as in this example:

```
.if o \{\
.po +.25i
.tl '''%'\}
```

The initial sequence is terminated with an additional backslash to "hide the newline." You could also type:

```
.if o \{ .po +.25i
.tl '''%'\}
```

However, the syntax shown in the first example is almost always used, because it is easier to read. There is one caveat! You can't put any other characters, even a comment, following the slash. For example, if you type:

```
.if o \{\    \" If odd...
```

you won't be escaping the newline, you'll be escaping the spaces that precede the comment. If you want to include a comment on a condition like this, use the alternate syntax, and follow the brace with a dot, just like you would if the comment started on a line of its own:

```
.if o \{.    \" If odd...
```

The concluding \} can appear on the same line as most requests. However, we have found a problem when it immediately follows a string definition or a .tm request. For some reason:

```
.ds string \}
```

appends a ^Q character to the end of the string, at least in our version of troff. The concluding \} should be put on the next line, after an initial . to suppress newline generation in the output:

```
.\}
```

Another convention followed in multiple-line execution is to separate the initial request control character (. or ') from the body of the request with a tab. This greatly enhances readability, and can be used to show nesting of conditions:

```
.if o \{\
.        po +.25i
.        tl '''\\n%'\}
```

Conditions can be nested within each other using this syntax. However, you might wonder if a nested condition could instead be expressed using one of the logical operators & or : in an expression. Suppose, as described previously, you want to put page numbers on the outside corners of each page, except on the first page, where you want it in the center. You might put the following requests in the page bottom macro:

```
.ie \\n%>1 \{\             \"If pageno > 1
.        if o .tl '''%'
.        if e .tl '%'''\}
.el .tl ''%''
```

You might think to achieve the same result with the following requests:

```
.if \\n%>1&o .tl '''%'    \"If pageno > 1 and odd
.if \\n%>1&e .tl '%'''    \"If pageno > 1 and even
.if \\n%=1 .tl ''%''      \"If pageno = 1
```

Unfortunately, however, this example will not work. The & and : operators can only be used to construct arithmetic expressions. For example, in the case of:

```
.if \\nX&\\nY do something
```

*something* will be done only if both register X and register Y are non-zero. (Notice that there are no spaces surrounding the & operator.)

You can construct an else if clause by following an .el with another .if, and then the request to be executed if the condition is met.

```
.ie condition          do something
.el .if condition      do something else if
```

## Inverse Conditions

The meaning of any of the condition types described can be reversed by preceding them with an exclamation point (!). For example:

```
.if !e        \" If the page number is not even
.if !\\nc=1   \" If number register c is not equal to 1
.if !"\\$1""  \" If the first argument is non-null
```

It may not be immediately obvious what this adds to your repertoire. However, we will encounter many cases in which it is easier to detect when a condition is not met than when it is. In particular, negative conditions can be more comprehensive than equivalent positive conditions. For example, the condition:

```
.if !\\nc=1
```

tests not only for the cases in which number register c has been set to some number larger than 0, or explicitly to 0, but the case in which it has never been set at all.

The test for a non-null argument is also useful. For example, in the sequence:

```
.if !"\\$3"" \{\    \"  If there is a third argument
.ce                 \"  center it
\\$3\}
```

you only want the .ce request to be executed if there is an argument to be centered. Otherwise, the request will cause unexpected results, perhaps centering the line of text following the macro. Saying "If the third argument is non-null, then it exists" may be the inverse of the way you think, and will take some getting used to.

If you are reading through the definitions for the ms or mm macros, you may also encounter a construct like this:

```
.if \\n(.$-2
```

The .$ is a special predefined number register (more on this topic in a moment) that contains the number of arguments that have been given to a macro. If there are two or fewer arguments, the value of the conditional expression shown will be 0. However, it will evaluate true if there are more than two arguments. It is used in mm's .SM macro because a different action is taken on the second argument if there are three arguments instead of two.

```
.if \\n(.$-3 \\$1\s-2\\$2\s+2\\$3
.if \\n(.$-2 \s-2\\$1\s+2\\$2
```

## ▪ Interrupted Lines ▪

Occasionally, when writing a complex macro—especially one with multiple conditions—you may find yourself writing a request that is too long to fit on a single 80-character line.

You could simply let the line wrap on your screen—UNIX recognizes lines much longer than the 80 columns usually available on a terminal screen. However, you need not do this. Simply putting a backslash at the end of a line will "hide the newline" and cause the next line to be interpreted as a continuation of the first.

## ▪ Number Registers ▪

To set a number register, you use the `.nr` request. Like macros, number registers can have either one- or two-character names consisting of any character(s), not just alphanumeric characters. For example:

```
.nr ^( 1
```

sets a number register called `^(` to 1. Number register names are stored separately from macro names, so there is no conflict in having a number register with the same name as a macro. Thus, you can create mnemonic number register names, which helps to make macros that use those number registers more readable.

(If you are writing your own macro package, you can name registers from scratch. If you are adding to an existing package, check the number registers used by that package.)

To use the value stored in a number register, use the escape sequence `\n`*x* for a one-character number register name, and `\n`(*xx* for a two-character name. (In the standard `nroff` and `troff` documentation, this is referred to as "interpolating" the value of the number register.) The point made previously, about using backslashes to delay the interpretation of an argument, applies equally to number registers. In macros, you will usually see the invocation of number registers preceded by a double backslash, because you don't want to interpolate the value until the macro is executed.

The values stored in number registers can be literal numeric values (with or without scaling indicators), values from other number registers (whose value can be interpolated at a later time), or expressions. You can also increment or decrement the value placed in a number register by preceding the value with a plus or minus sign. For example:

```
.nr PN 1     \" Set number register PN to 1
.nr PN +1    \" Add 1 to the contents of number register PN
```

When you add scaling indicators to the value supplied to a number register, be aware that values are converted to basic units before they are stored, and that when you increment the value of a number register, it is incremented in basic units. So, in the previous example, in which no units were specified, the value of `PN` after incrementing is 2, but in the following case:

```
.nr LL 6.5i
.nr LL +1
```

the value initially stored into `LL` is converted into units (i.e., for a 300 dpi output device, it contains the value 1950); after incrementing, it contains the value 1951 (again, assuming a 300 dpi device). If you want to increment `LL` by 1 inch, append the proper scaling indicator. Likewise, when interpolating the value of a number register, specify that the value is in units. For example, the construct:

```
.nr IN 1i
.in \\n(IN
```

will produce unexpected results.  What you are really writing is:

```
.in 300m
```

(assuming a 300 dpi device) because the default scaling for an indent request is ems.
The proper usage is:

```
.in \\n(INu
```

## Number Registers as Global Variables

Number registers can be used in different ways.  First, and probably most important,
they can generalize a macro package.  For example, in ms, the default line length is
stored in a number register called LL.

Periodically, macros in the package may muck with the line length, and then reset
it to its default state.  Requests to reset the line length to its default value thus have the
form:

```
.ll \n(LLu   \" Single backslash within the body of text
```

or

```
.ll \\n(LLu   \" Double backslash within a macro definition
```

Because the line length is not "hard coded" in the document, users can change the line
length throughout simply by changing the default value stored in the number register.

You might wonder why this is necessary.  After all, you can simply set an initial
line length, and then increment it or decrement it as necessary.  And many macros take
this approach.  But there are other cases where the line length is a factor in another cal-
culation.

For example, the output text can be centered horizontally on the physical page
regardless of the line length if the page offset is set not absolutely, but in terms of the
line length:

```
.po (8.5i-\n(LLu)/2u
```

In general, it is good programming practice to place values that are used at many different places in a program into globally accessible variables.  To change the action of
the program, it is only necessary to change the value of the variable.  It is the same in
nroff and troff.  When we look at the overall design of a macro package in
Chapter 16, we'll return to this subject in more detail.

## Number Registers as Flags

In the chapters on the existing macro packages, you've also seen number registers used
as flags—signals to a macro to act in a certain way.  For example, in mm, paragraphs
are flush left by default, but if the user sets the Pt number register to 1, all paragraphs
will be indented.

Within the paragraph macro, there is a line that tests the `Pt` register, and acts accordingly:

```
.if \\n(Pt=1 .ti +\\n(Pin
```

This line actually uses number registers in both ways. If the number register `Pt` is set to 1, the macro indents by the value stored in another register, `Pi`.

One-character number register names can also be set from the command line, with `nroff` or `troff`'s `-r` option. This gives you the ability to construct macros that will act differently depending on command-line options. We'll show some examples of this in Chapter 16, when we discuss how to print a document on either an 8½-by-11 inch or a 6-by-9 inch page, simply by specifying a single command-line switch.

## Predefined Number Register Names

In addition to number registers set by the various macro packages, or set by macros you write, there are quite a few number registers whose usage is predefined by the formatter. You've already seen one of these—%, which always contains the current page number. Table 14-3 (and Table 14-4) list some of the most important preset registers, and Appendix B includes a complete listing. Not all of these registers will be meaningful at this point, but we'll tell you more about them as we go on.

### TABLE 14-3. Predefined Number Registers

| Register | Contents |
|----------|----------|
| %  | Current page number |
| dl | Width (maximum) of the last completed diversion |
| dn | Height (vertical size) of the last completed diversion |
| dw | Current day of the week (1 to 7) |
| dy | Current day of the month (1 to 31) |
| hp | Current horizontal place on the *input* line |
| ln | Output line number |
| mo | Current month (1 to 12) |
| nl | Vertical position of the last printed text baseline |
| yr | Last two digits of the current year |

The registers in Table 14-3 can be reset. For example, if you want to arbitrarily reset the page number to 1, you can type:

```
.nr % 1
```

The formatter will keep incrementing the register on each new page, but will count from the new baseline. (You might want to do this, for example, if you are following the convention used in many technical manuals, which number pages on a chapter-by-chapter basis, with a number made up of both the chapter number and the page number. In this case, the page number is reset to 1 at the start of each new chapter.)

Note that `%` is a true number register name, and don't let the special use of the `%` character in the `.tl` request confuse you. In `.tl`, `%` alone will interpolate the current page number; however, in any other place, you must specify the full number register interpolation `\n%`.

The set of registers in Table 14-4 cannot be modified. In reading their names, be sure to note that they are two-character names beginning with `.` (dot). If you are reading through one of the existing macro packages, it is easy either to confuse them with macros or requests, because they begin with a period, or to miss the period and read them as one-character names.

**TABLE 14-4. Read-Only Number Registers**

| Register | Contents |
| --- | --- |
| `.$` | Number of arguments available in the current macro |
| `.c` | Number of lines read from the current input file |
| `.d` | Current vertical place in current diversion; equal to `nl` if no diversion |
| `.f` | Current font position (1 to 4 in `otroff`) |
| `.H` | Available horizontal resolution in machine units |
| `.i` | Current indent |
| `.j` | Current adjustment mode (0 = `.ad l` or `.na`; 1 = `.ad b`; 3 = `.ad c`; 5 = `.ad r`) |
| `.L` | Line spacing set with `.ls` |
| `.l` | Current line length |
| `.n` | Length of text on previous line |
| `.o` | Current page offset |
| `.p` | Current page length |
| `.s` | Current point size |
| `.t` | Distance to the next trap (usually the page bottom) |
| `.u` | Equal to 1 in fill mode and 0 in no-fill mode |
| `.V` | Available vertical resolution in machine units |
| `.v` | Current vertical line spacing |
| `.w` | Width of previous character |
| `.z` | Name of current diversion |

The registers in Table 14-4 are particularly useful when you want to temporarily change some value (for example, the font) and then restore it, without having to know what was there before.

For example, if you print an italicized footer on each page, you might include the following requests in your page bottom macro:

```
.nr FT \\n(.f
.ft I

        .
        .
        .

.ft \\n(FT
```

This is safer than simply using the  .ft request without an argument to restore the previous font, which can create havoc if a user makes a font change within a definition of the footer string.

Be aware that registers with scaled values (e.g.,  .l for the line lengths or  .v for the current vertical spacing) contain those values as basic machine units (as do all number registers containing scaled values).  As described previously, this means you should append a  u whenever you want to use the contents of one of these registers as an argument to a request.

## Autoincrementing Registers

We've described how to increment the value stored in a register by prefixing the value you supply to the  .nr request with a plus sign (+), and how to decrement it by specifying a minus sign (-).

You can also *autoincrement* or *autodecrement* a register whenever you interpolate its value.  To make this work, you must supply two values to an initial  .nr request: the starting value and the increment value.  For example:

```
.nr TE 1 1
.nr ST 10 3
```

Then, when you interpolate the contents of the register, instead of using the standard \nx or  \n (xx, specify a plus or a minus after the  \n and before the register name. The value that is interpolated will be the original contents of the number register plus (or minus) the increment (or decrement) value.  At the same time, the value in the register will be updated by the increment value.  For example, assuming the initial definitions in the previous example:

```
\n+(TE \" Increment TE by 1, and interpolate the new value
\n-(ST \" Decrement ST by 3, and interpolate the new value
```

Number register interpolations of the normal sort can still be used and will, as always, simply give you the value currently stored in the register.

## Altering the Output Format

As we've seen, sometimes number registers are simply used to supply values to requests, or to pass information between macros.  But there are many cases in which the value of a number register is actually interpolated into the formatter output and printed. The page number register  % is a good example.  Although it might be used as the basis to test conditions in macros, it is usually printed as well.

The  .af (*alter format*) request allows you to specify the format in which to express the value of a number register.  This request takes two arguments, the name of the register to be affected and the format:

```
.af register format
```

The *format* codes are given in Table 14-5.

**TABLE 14-5. Format Codes**

| Format | Description | Numbering Sequence |
|--------|-------------|--------------------|
| 1 | Arabic | 0, 1, 2, 3, 4, 5, ... |
| i | Lowercase roman | 0, i, ii, iii, iv, v, ... |
| I | Uppercase roman | 0, I, II, III, IV, V, ... |
| a | Lowercase alphabetic | 0, a, b, c, ... z, aa, ab, ... zz, aaa, ... |
| A | Uppercase alphabetic | 0, A, B, C, ... Z, AA, AB, ... ZZ, AAA, ... |

In addition to the numbering sequences in Table 14-5, an arabic format having additional digits (e.g., 001) will result in a numbering sequence with at least that many digits (e.g., 001, 002, 003, ... ).

For example, to change to lowercase roman page numbering in the front matter of a book, you could write:

```
.af % i
```

(Note that, depending on exactly how a macro package implements page numbering, this may or may not work exactly as shown. Some macro packages interpolate % into another register and print the contents of that register. For example, `ms` stores the page number in the register `PN` and the request would be `.af PN i`.)

Alphabetic formats are generally used in macros for automatically numbered (or lettered) lists. We'll take a close look at some of these macros in Chapter 17.

## Removing Registers

With the very large number of possible register names (nearly 10,000 names are possible, given all one- and two-character combinations of the printing character set), it is unlikely that you will run out of number register names.

However, if your macros create a very large number of registers, the formatter can run out of internal storage space. For this reason, it may occasionally be necessary (or at least wise) to remove temporary registers that you no longer need, using the `.rr` request. For example:

```
.rr TE        \" Remove register TE
```

## ▪ Defining Strings ▪

In addition to macros and number registers, `nroff` and `troff` allow you to define character strings that will be stored and can be re-invoked at will. This is not intended as a general-purpose abbreviation function, although in certain cases it can be used that way. Rather, it is designed to allow you to store global string variables for use throughout a package, in much the same way that number registers provide numeric variables.

For example, in both ms and mm, you can define headers, footers, or both that will be printed on every page. To do this, the header or footer macro contains a reference to a predefined string. All the user has to do is give the string a value. The user doesn't have to modify the macro itself.

As we've already seen, to define a string, use the .ds (*define string*) request. For example:

```
.ds RH Tools for Building Macros  \" Define right header
```

String names, like macro and number register names, can have either one or two characters. However, unlike number registers, string names are drawn from the same pool as macro and request names, so you have to be careful not to conflict with existing names.

To interpolate the value of a string, use the escape sequence \**x* for a one-character name, or \* (*xx* for a two-character name. For example, our page top macro might include the lines:

```
.if o .tl '\\*(RH''%'    \" Print header string then page #
.if e .tl '%''\\*(RH'    \" Print page # then header string
```

Another good example of how to use this request (as well as how to use predefined number registers) is given by the technique used in ms and mm to build a date string.

The troff program reads in the date from the system clock into the predefined number registers mo (*month*), dy (*day*), and yr (*year*). To set a complete date string that users can easily reference, we might write the following requests in our macro package:

```
.if \n(mo=1 .ds MO January
.if \n(mo=2 .ds MO February
.if \n(mo=3 .ds MO March
.if \n(mo=4 .ds MO April
.if \n(mo=5 .ds MO May
.if \n(mo=6 .ds MO June
.if \n(mo=7 .ds MO July
.if \n(mo=8 .ds MO August
.if \n(mo=9 .ds MO September
.if \n(mo=10 .ds MO October
.if \n(mo=11 .ds MO November
.if \n(mo=12 .ds MO December
.ds DY \*(MO \n(dy, 19\n(yr
```

(Note that these requests do not need to be executed from within a macro. The register values can be interpolated when the macro package is first read in. For this reason, the string and number register interpolations shown here are not escaped with an additional backslash.)

Another request, .as (*append [to] string*), also allows you to add to the contents of an existing string. The last line of the previous sequence could also have been written:

```
.as MO \n(dy, 19\n(yr
```

to append the day and year to whatever value had been stored into MO. Here, this is a little contrived—it is better to maintain the month and the date as a whole in separate strings. However, the technique of appending to a string is used appropriately in the definition of a macro to produce numbered section headers, as we'll see in Chapter 17.

## ▪ Diversions ▪

So far, we have discussed macros that you define in advance as a sequence of stored requests. There is also another class of macros that are created by a process called *diversion*.

A diversion consists of temporary storage of text into a macro, which can be saved and output at a later time. In reading the chapters on ms or mm, you might have wondered how `troff` manages to move footnotes embedded anywhere in the text to the bottom of the page, or how it "floats" a figure, table, or block of text to the top of a succeeding page, after filling the current page with text that comes later in the input file.

The answer is simple: the formatter stores the text (or other output) in a macro created by diversion. (Such a macro is often called simply a diversion.) The size of the diversion is stored into number registers that you (your macros, that is) can test to see if the diversion will fit on the current page, and how much space you need to allocate for it. The macro package can then make decisions about how and where to place the contents of the diversion.

To create a diversion, use the `.di` (*divert*) request. This request takes as an argument the name of a macro. All subsequent text, requests, etc. will be processed normally, but instead of being output, they will be stored into the named macro. A `.di` request without an argument ends the diversion.

The output that has been stored in the diversion can now be output wherever you like, simply by invoking the macro named in the initial `.di` request. For many purposes, this invocation will be performed automatically by a page transition macro. We will look at this in more detail in succeeding chapters, but just to get the idea, let's look at a simple definition for a pair of keep macros.

(In general, diversions are handled by pairs of macros— one to start the diversion, the other to end it. However, there are other cases in which we will see that this is not necessary.)

Both ms and mm use diversions in their display macros. In ms, the display macros handle text positioning, and call lower-level macros called keep macros to make sure the text in the display stays on the same page.

The purpose of the keep macros, in case you are not familiar with this concept from earlier chapters, is to make sure that a block of text is not split across two pages. A typical example of a block that should not be split is a figure—whether it is reserved space for a figure, or an actual picture created with `pic` or some other graphics tool.

A simple macro to start a keep might look like this:

```
.de KS                  \" Keep Start
.br
.di KK
..
```

A simple macro to end a keep might look like this:

```
.de KE                  \" Keep End
.br
.di
.ne \\n(dnu
.nr fI \\n(.u
.nf
.KK
.if \\n(fI .fi
..
```

In both macros, the `.br` requests are extremely important; they flush any partial lines that have not yet been output. In the `.KS` macro, the break makes sure that the keep begins with the text following the macro; in `.KE`, it makes sure that the last partial line is included in the diversion.

It is also important to output the diversion in no-fill mode. If you don't, the text contained in the diversion will be filled and adjusted a second time, with unpredictable results. (Consider, for example, when the diversion includes an already formatted table. The table would be scrambled by a second pass.)

You can't just switch back to fill mode after you output the diversion, though. What if the body of the text was meant to be in no-fill mode? To get around this problem, you should save the value of `troff`'s read-only register `.u`, and test the saved value to see whether or not filling should be restored.

There are a few times when you might not want to follow this rule. For example, what should you do if there is a chance that the diversion will be output on a page where the line length is different? You still want to avoid processing the text twice. You can put the text into the diversion in no-fill mode, and can embed any formatting requests into the diversion by preceding them with a backslash (e.g., `\.in 5n`). Any requests treated in this way will be acted on when the diversion is output.

As always, it is important to specify the correct units. In the previous example, the value in `dn` is stored using basic device units (as is the case with all scaled values stored in a number register), so you *must* add a `u` on the end of the interpolation. For example, on a 300 dpi device, after a diversion 2 inches high, `dn` will contain the value 600. The request:

```
.ne \\n(dn
```

will always result in a page break because (in this example) what you are really writing is:

```
.ne 600
```

What you want to write is:

```
.ne \\n(dnu
```

Any text and requests that are issued between the initial .KS and the terminating .KE will be stored in the macro called .KK. The height of the last-completed diversion is always stored in the number register dn. We can simply say that we need (.ne) at least that much space. If the size of the diversion is greater than the distance to the bottom of the page, we simply start a new page. Otherwise, we output the text and continue as if the diversion had never happened.

The case of a floating keep, in which text that follows the keep in the source file floats ahead of it in the output, and fills up the current page, is more difficult to handle than the simple example just shown. However, this example should give you an idea of how to use diversions.

There is also a .da (*divert append*) request that adds output to an existing diversion. (A second .di given the same macro name as the first will overwrite the diversion's previous contents, but .da will add the new material to the end.)

The .da request has numerous applications. For example, consider footnotes. To calculate where to place the first footnote, you need to calculate the size of all the footnotes you want to put on the page. That's easy — just append them to the same diversion.

However, there are other far less obvious applications for appended diversions. For example, you can divert and append section headings or index entries to macros that will be processed at the end of the file to produce a table of contents or an index.

## ▪ **Environment Switching** ▪

The nroff and troff formatters allow you to issue many requests that globally affect the format of a document. The formatter is generally quite thorough in providing ways to change and restore the value of various parameters. This makes it relatively easy to change values such as the line length or fill/no-fill mode in order to treat certain blocks of text differently and then restore the original values.

Nonetheless, if you want to make major changes to a number of values, it can be awkward to save and restore them all individually. For this reason, nroff and troff provide a mechanism called *environment switching*. By default, text processing takes place in what is considered to be environment 0. The .ev request allows you to switch to either of two additional environments, referred to as environment 1 and environment 2.

For example, to change to environment 2, you would enter

```
.ev 2
```

To restore a previous environment, you simply issue an .ev request without an argument. Environments are stored in a "push down stack." So if you are using multiple environment switches, a sequence of .ev requests without arguments won't toggle you between two environments, but will actually backtrack the specified number of environment switches. That is:

```
.ev 1
do something
.ev 2
do something
.ev                      \" Go back to ev 1
.ev                      \" Go back to ev 0
```

If you use `.ev` with an argument, you will not pop the stack. For example, the requests:

```
.ev 2
.ev 0
```

will leave both environments on the stack. You might get away with this on one occasion, but if you do this in a macro that is used with any frequency, your stack will keep getting deeper until it overflows and the formatter fails with the message ''Cannot do ev.''

Within each environment, settings made with the following requests are remembered separately:

```
.c2 .cc .ce .cu .fi .ft .hc .hy .in .it .lc .ll .ls .lt
.mc .nf .nh .nm .nn .ps .sp .ss .ta .tc .ti .ul .vs
```

Number registers, macros, and strings are common to all environments. However, any partially collected lines are part of a given environment. If you switch environments without causing a break, these partial lines will be held till the environment that contains them is restored.

What this means is best shown by example:

```
.                \" Set parameters for environment 0
.ll 4.5i
.ad b
.ev 1            \" Switch to environment 1
.ll −10n         \" Set parameters for environment 1
.in +10n
.ad l
.ev              \" Restore previous environment (ev 0)
This text will be formatted using the parameters for
environment 0.  Notice that part of the last input
line appears to be lost when we switch environments.
It reappears when the environment is restored.
.ev 1
.sp              \" The break caused by this request is in ev 1
Now we've switched to environment 1.  Notice how the text
is now formatted using the parameters for environment 1.
Also notice that this time, we're going to issue an .sp
request after this sentence to cause a break and make sure
the last partial line is output before we leave this
environment.
.sp
```

```
.ev              \" Back once more to environment 0
This sentence will be preceded by the remainder of input
left over from the last time we were in this environment.
```

Here's the resulting output (from nroff):

```
This  text  will  be  formatted   using   the
parameters  for environment 0.  You'll notice
that part of the last input line  appears  to
be   lost   when   we   switch  environments.  It

        Now we've switched to environment 1.  Notice
        how the text is now formatted using the
        parameters for environment 1.  Also notice
        that this time, we're going to issue an .sp
        request after this sentence to cause a break
        and make sure the last partial line is output
        before we leave this environment.


reappears when the environment  is  restored.
This   sentence   will  be  preceded  by  the
remainder of the input  left  over  from  the
last time we were in this environment.
```

Environments are very powerful and versatile. The example given previously could have been handled more appropriately with a macro. However, as you will find, there are tasks that are best handled by an environment switch.

Printing footnotes is a primary example. Footnotes are usually collected in a diversion, which must be output at the bottom of the page without causing a break or other interference with the text.

Unfortunately, you must use environment switching with caution if you are working within one of the existing macro packages, because they may use different environments internally, and changing parameters in an environment may affect the operation of the package. For example, it was necessary to process the preceding example independently with nroff, and then read the resulting output into the source file, because the use of environments by the macro package that produced this book was incompatible with what we were trying to show.

### ▪ Redefining Control and Escape Characters ▪

There are special requests to reset the control characters that begin requests (. and ′ ) and the escape character:

```
.eo          \"Turn escape character off except for comments
.ec !        !" Set escape character to !
.ec \        \" Set escape character back to \
.cc #        \" Change control character from . to #
.c2 ^        \" Change no-break control character from ' to ^
```

As far as we can tell by experiment, turning the escape character off entirely with `.eo` does not affect the comment sequence `\"`; however, if you change the escape character with `.ec`, comments must be introduced by the new escape character.

We have not found a significant use for these requests in our own work, or in macros we've studied, although there are no doubt cases where they are precisely what is needed.

One application that immediately suggests itself is the representation of control and escape characters in the examples shown in this book. However, in practice there are many problems.

For example, if you use these requests in a pair of macros to frame examples, the closing macro must be invoked with the appropriate control character, creating inconsistencies for the user. Even more seriously, if control character translations are in effect during a page transition (something that is difficult to control) or other macro invoked by a trap, they will render that macro inoperable, unless it has been designed with the same control and escape characters.

Our preferred solution to this problem is to use the `.tr` request, which is discussed in the next chapter.

## · Debugging Your Macros ·

When using a markup language as complex as that provided by `nroff` and `troff`, it is easy to make mistakes, particularly when you are designing complex macros.

To limit the number of mistakes you make, you can take lessons from programmers in more general-purpose languages:

- Start by writing and testing small pieces of a complex macro. Then, after you know the pieces work, put them together. It is much easier to find a problem in a simple macro than in one that is already very complex.

- Be aware of interactions between the macro you are writing and other macros in the package. Initialize variables (number registers and strings) that might also be used by other macros.

- Include extensive comments, so you can reconstruct what you were trying to do when you go back to the macro later. (Errors often arise unexpectedly after the macro has been in use for a while, and you have a chance to exercise it fully. Be sure you can follow what you originally wrote.)

- Test each macro thoroughly before you put it into general use.

However, even with the best of intentions, you are likely to make mistakes. This short section is intended to give you a few pointers on how to track them down.

The term debugging is familiar even to nonprogrammers. In general, it refers to the process of finding errors in programs. I would like to suggest an alternate definition that may give you better insight into how to go about this process: *Debugging is the process of finding out what your macro really does, instead of what you thought it should do.*[*]

When you write a program or a macro, you have an idea in your mind of what you want to accomplish. When it doesn't do what you expect, you consider it an error.

But as we all know, computers are very literal. They generally do just what they are told. (The exception being when there is an error in some underlying layer of software that causes problems on a higher layer.) Therefore, the essence of debugging is to compare, on a step-by-step basis, exactly what the program or macro is actually doing with what you expect it to do.

There are several tools that you can use in debugging macros. First, and most obviously, you can look carefully at the output. Try to reconstruct the sequence of instructions and text that have been executed to produce the (presumably) undesirable result. Often, this will be all you need to do—think like a text formatter, and go through the requests that have been executed, in the order that they are executed.

You will often find that problems are due to an incorrect understanding of the action of one of the requests or escape sequences, so it may be advisable to consult the bible of macro programming, Joseph Osanna's extraordinarily dense but thorough *Nroff/Troff User's Guide*.

Secondly, you can use `nroff` or `troff` interactively. If you simply type:

```
$ nroff
```

or:

```
$ troff -a
```

the program will take standard input from the keyboard and send its results to standard output (the screen). The `troff -a` command creates an ASCII approximation of what the `troff` output would be, if you are using `ditroff`, you can also save the normal output in a file and look directly at the output. However, this output is in an obscure format and takes considerable time to learn.

With `troff -a`, special characters (such as underlines) are represented by their special character names. For example, underlining will show up as a sequence of `\(ul`s. Because proportional type is considerably more compact than the characters that appear on a terminal screen, lines will appear too long, and will wrap around on the screen. However, what you see does represent how `troff` will break the lines.

---

[*]I am indebted to Andrew Singer of Think Technologies for this definition. Andrew used similar words in describing to me the debugging philosophy of his company's innovative Pascal compiler for the Macintosh, Lightspeed Pascal.

Now, by typing in your macros (or reading them in from existing files with the
.so request), you can reproduce the environment of the formatter, and watch the
results as you type in text. As each line is completed in the input buffer, the formatted
result will be output. You can force output of a partially completed line with the .fl
(*flush*) request, which was designed for this purpose.

This method has definite limits, but has just as definite a place in pinning down
what the commands you type are doing.

Another debugging tool that you may find useful is the .ig (*ignore*) request. It
tells the formatter to ignore subsequent input, up to a specified terminator (.. by
default). The .ig request acts like .de, only the input is discarded. (The only
exception to this is that autoincremented registers whose values are interpolated within
the ignored block will still be incremented or decremented.)

This request is useful when you are trying to pin down exactly where in an input
file (or a long macro definition) a fatal error (one that causes the formatter to stop processing) occurs. By successively isolating parts of the file with .ig, you can locate
the problem more closely.

This request is also useful for "commenting out" extensive blocks of macro
definition or input text that you don't want in your output. It is much easier to bracket
a large block of input in this way than it is to insert comment characters at the beginning of each line.

Because you may want to "ignore" more than one macro definition, you may
want to get in the habit of specifying a special delimiter for the .ig request, so that
the "ignore" is not accidentally terminated by the end of the first macro definition.
This will also make it much easier to find the end of the ignored section. For example,
if you insert the line:

```
.ig ++
```

anywhere in your input, the formatter will ignore the input until it sees the request:

```
.++
```

The final tool provided for debugging is the .tm (*terminal message*) request, which
prints a message on standard error. This is particularly useful for tracking down errors
involving number registers. For example, if you have set a condition based on the
value of a number register, and the condition never seems to be satisfied, you might
want to insert .tm messages to print out the value of the number register at certain
points in your file. For example:

```
.tm Before calling B1, the value of BC is \n(BC
.B1
.tm After calling B1, the value of BC is \n(BC
```

(Note that there are no double backslashes before the number register interpolations,
because these requests are not made while you're inside a macro definition. From
inside a macro, be sure to double the backslashes, or you will get the value of the
number register at the time the macro was defined.)

A read-only number register that is useful in this regard is .c, which contains
the number of lines read from the current input file. This allows you to create messages

that will help you (or the user of your macros) find out where in the input file an error (or other event) occurs:

```
.tm  On input line \\n(.c, the value of BC was \\n(BC
```

(Here, there are double backslashes, because this example is intended to be inside a macro definition.) Sometimes it is helpful to follow just how far the formatter has gotten in a file. The most difficult errors to track are those that cause the formatter to quit without producing a block of output. A series of messages of the form:

```
.tm At top of page \\n%, I've processed \\n(.c input lines
```

inserted into the page top macro will help you determine how far the formatter has gotten, and can thus help locate an error. If the formatter is processing standard input rather than an individual file, the .c register will be empty.

Another register that you may find useful in printing error messages is .F, which contains the name of the current file. (Yes, the filename is a string, even though it's stored in a number register.)

The .R register is also useful. It contains the number of free number registers. You can print its value to see if you are running out of number registers or coming close to the limit. (tbl and eqn use many dynamic number registers, and it is possible to run out if you use a lot in your macros as well.)

Although we use the tools described here to debug our macros, we know that they don't always help you deal with the complexity of a macro package. The relationships among different macros are not always apparent. For instance, you can usually tell from looking at your output what macro is causing a problem; however, when you look at the macro definition, you might find that this macro is calling several other macros or testing registers that have been set elsewhere in the macro package. It soon leads to the wish for a debugging tool that traced the interpretation and execution of macro definitions.

At least one version of troff does support a *trace* facility. Users of SoftQuad's SQtroff can enable a trace mode to show the invocation of each request, diversion, trap, and macro call. For instance, suppose that a macro tests the value of a number register to determine whether a request should be executed. In trace mode, you can see at what point the .if request was invoked, whether it was evaluated as true or false, and determine the actual value of the number register at that point. SoftQuad has also taken another step to make debugging easier by improving troff's obscure error messages. In general, SoftQuad has enhanced standard troff in other ways that aid the process of macro writing and debugging, such as allowing longer names (up to 14 characters) for macros, requests, strings, registers, and fonts.

## ▪ Error Handling ▪

There are many different ways that users can get into trouble while coding documents, and your macros can help them identify and recover from problems. The three most common classes we have encountered are:

- A user fails to properly understand the action of the formatter itself. For example, he or she begins a text line with a single quote or period, or defines a special character (such as %) as an eqn delimiter. This problem becomes more pronounced as users try out more advanced capabilities without really understanding them.

- A user fails to properly understand the macro package. For example, he or she gives the wrong argument to a macro or specifies the wrong units.

- A user temporarily resets some condition, either directly or by failing to close a set of paired macros. This causes undesirable effects to propagate through the document.

The mm macros attempt to solve the first problem by creating so comprehensive a macro package that users never need use many low-level formatter requests. However, in doing so, its developers have created an environment that is in many ways more complex than the raw formatter environment itself. And in our opinion, no macro package is comprehensive enough to meet all user needs. Over time, users come up with formatting problems that they need to know how to solve on their own. There is no solution to this problem except better user education.

To some extent, you can compensate for the second problem by testing for arguments and printing error messages if a macro is misused. For example, if a macro requires an argument, consider printing a message if the user fails to supply it:

```
.if "\\$1"" .tm Line \\n(.c: .Se requires section \
number as first argument
```

Of course, by the time the user sees the error message, he or she has already formatted the document, and it is too late to do anything else but repair the damage and reprint. However, messages can sometimes make it easier for users to find errors and can give them warning to look more closely at their printout.

The .ab request takes things one step further—it lets you terminate processing if the formatter encounters a condition you don't like. For example, you could write a macro that aborts if it is called without a necessary argument:

```
.if !\\n(.$ .ab You forgot the argument!
```

The .ab request prints its argument as an error message, just like .tm. It just takes the further, definite step of quitting on the spot.

Probably more suitable, though, is a separate tool for checking macro syntax. Such a tool exists for mm in the mmcheck program. A program like this checks the syntax of macros and requests used in a document and reports possible errors.

This kind of approach is especially suitable for the third kind of error—the failure to close a set of paired macros.

## ▪ Macro Style ▪

As you develop more of your own macros, you might begin thinking about overall macro style. Developing macros that behave in a consistent, reliable way becomes all the more important as the number of new macros you have increases along with the number of people using them. Recognizing different styles of macro writing helps to suggest alternatives and improvements in the way a macro works.

If you have read the chapters on ms and mm in detail, or if you are already familiar with both of these packages, you have probably noticed that they embody somewhat different text-processing philosophies.

For example, ms generally attempts to recover and continue when it encounters a serious error, but mm aborts the formatting run. And although ms allows a certain amount of user customization (generally by providing a few number registers and strings that the user is expected to modify), it has nowhere near the complexity of mm in this regard. An mm user is expected to set up various number registers that affect the operation of many different macros.

In writing your own macros (especially ones that will be integrated with one of the existing packages), you should take some time to think about style, and how you want users to interact with your macros. This is most easily shown by comparing several different paragraph macros:

```
.de P               \" A very simple paragraph macro
.br
.ne 2v
.ti 2P
..


.de LP              \" An ms style flush left paragraph
.RT
.ne 1.1
.sp \\n(PDu
.ti \\n(.iu
..


.de PP              \" An ms style indented paragraph
.RT
.ne 1.1
.sp \\n(PDu
.ti +\\n(PIu
..


.deP                \" An mm style variable paragraph
.br                 \" Note that this is much
.sp (\\n(Ps*.5)u    \" simplified from true mm code
.ne 1.5v
```

```
.if\\n(.$>0&(0\\$1)  .ti+\\n(Pin
.if\\n(.$=0  .if\\n(Pt=1 .ti+\\n(Pin
..
```

The first example shows a very simple paragraph macro using a fixed indent value.

The second and third examples are adapted from ms. They show the use of an embedded reset macro (discussed in Chapter 16) and the specification of values such as indents and interparagraph spacing by means of number registers so that users can change them without rewriting the macro. The different types of paragraphs (flush left or indented) are handled by defining two different macros.

The fourth example is adapted from mm. It shows how a macro can be controlled in a number of different ways. First of all, the size of the paragraph indent can be controlled by the user, as in ms. Second, though, users can specify whether they want an indent for a particular paragraph by specifying an argument to the macro. Finally, they can specify whether all paragraphs are to be indented or flush left by setting the Pt (*paragraph type*) register.

Although you may not want to go as far as mm in giving different ways to affect the action of a macro, it is good to realize that all of these options are available and to draw on them as necessary.

However, it does make sense to be consistent in the mechanisms you use. For example, suppose you create macros to put captions on figures, tables, and examples. If you allow the user to control the amount of space before the caption with an optional argument, you ought to do so in all three analogous macros.

As much as possible, a user should be able to infer the action of a macro from its name, and should be able to guess at its arguments by analogy to other, similar macros in the same package. If you are capricious in your design, other users will have a much greater burden to shoulder when it comes time for them to learn your macros. Even if you are the only user of macros you develop, consistency will help you keep out of trouble as you gradually extend your package.

The issue of macro style really comes up as you begin to develop your own custom macro package, as you will see when we examine the elements of a macro package in Chapters 16 and 17.

# 15

# Figures and Special Effects

This chapter discusses a variety of formatter requests that you can use to draw figures and achieve special effects like overstriking and vertically stacked text. It also dissects some of the most complex macros we've seen so far, so it should advance your knowledge of how to write macros as well as your knowledge of its explicit subject matter.

## · Formatter Escape Sequences ·

Preprocessors like `tbl` and `pic` draw boxes, lines, and simple figures using an underlying library of formatter escape sequences that you can also use directly. The `eqn` preprocessor also uses many of these escape sequences, as well as others that are more appropriate for creating special effects with text characters.

The escape sequences are listed in Table 15-1. As you can see, there are quite a few! Fortunately, many of these need not be learned by the average user. The various preprocessors often allow a user to achieve the same effect more easily. Although `tbl` or `eqn` might seem difficult to learn, they are far simpler than the formatter commands they replace. For example, an `eqn` construct like `10% sup 5%` is easier to learn and type than an equivalent `troff` construct like:

```
10\s-3\v'-3p'5\v'3p'\s0
```

When it comes to drawing lines and figures, things get even more complex.

For this reason, many of the escape sequences we are about to discuss are not often used by the average person trying to achieve special effects. However, they are extremely useful to a developer of macros.

In this chapter, we'll cover the sequences for local vertical and horizontal motions and line drawing, because these requests are most commonly used in macros. In addition, we will show several large macros that do line drawing in order to demonstrate both the use of escape sequences and techniques for writing complex macros.

## TABLE 15-1. Formatter Escape Sequences

| Escape | Description |
|---|---|
| \v'*distance*' | Move *distance* vertically down the page. Precede *distance* with a minus sign to move back up the page. |
| \h'*distance*' | Move *distance* horizontally to the right. Precede *distance* with a minus sign to move back to the left. |
| \u | Move $^1/_2$ em up ($^1/_2$ line in nroff). |
| \d | Move $^1/_2$ em down ($^1/_2$ line in nroff). |
| \r | Move 1 em up (1 line in nroff). |
| \c | Join next line to current output line, even across a break. |
| \p | Cause a break, and adjust current partial output line. |
| \x'*distance*' | Add extra line space for oversize characters. |
| \(space) | Move right one space (distance determined by .ss). |
| \0 | Move right the width of a digit in the current font and size. |
| \| | Move right 1/6 em (ignored in nroff). |
| \^ | Move right 1/12 em (ignored in nroff). |
| \w'*string*' | Interpolate width of *string*. |
| \k*x* | Mark current horizontal place in register *x*. |
| \o'*xy*' | Overstrike characters *x* and *y*. |
| \z*c* | Output character *c* without spacing over it. |
| \b'string' | Pile up characters vertically (used to construct large brackets, hence its name). |
| \l'*Nc*' | Draw a horizontal line consisting of repeated character *c* for distance *N*. If *c* isn't specified, use _. |
| \L'*Nc*' | Draw a vertical line consisting of repeated character *c* for distance *N*. If *c* isn't specified, use \|. |
| \D'l *x,y*' | Draw a line from the current position to coordinates *x,y* (ditroff only). |
| \D'c *d*' | Draw a circle of diameter *d* with left edge at current position (ditroff only). |
| \D'e *d1 d2*' | Draw an ellipse with horizontal diameter *d1* and vertical diameter *d2*, with the left edge at the current position (ditroff only). |
| \D'a *x1 y1 x2 y2*' | Draw an arc counterclockwise from current position, with center at *x1,y1* and endpoint at *x1+x2,y1+y2* (ditroff only). |
| \D'~ *x1 y1 x2 y2...*' | Draw a spline from current position through the specified coordinates (ditroff only). |
| \H'*n*' | Set character height to *n* points, without changing the width (ditroff only). |
| \S'*n*' | Slant output *n* degrees to the right. Negative values slant to the left. A value of zero turns off slanting (ditroff only). |

Many of the escape sequences in Table 15-1 take arguments that must be delimited from any following text. The delimiter character is most often ′ or ^G (*CTRL-G*), but it can be any character. The first character following the escape sequence will be taken as the delimiter, and the argument list will be terminated when that same character is encountered a second time.

## ▪ Local Vertical Motions ▪

There are a number of escape sequences for *local* vertical motions. They are so called because they take place within a line, without causing a break or otherwise interrupting the filling and justification process.

However, this is not to say that the motions they cause are limited. For example, you can use \v, the vertical motion escape sequence, to move anywhere on the page, just as you can with the .sp request. However, the remainder of the line that has been collected in the formatter's internal buffers will be output in the new location just as if the motion had never taken place.

To make this point clearer, let's look at three examples of input text that use different types of vertical motion.

*What happens with* .sp:

*Input lines:*

```
Especially in troff, it is sometimes uncanny the way that
vertical motions can occur
.sp 12p
independently from the output of the text.
```

*Output lines:*

Especially in troff, it is sometimes uncanny the way that vertical motions can occur

independently from the output of the text.

*What happens with* ′sp:

*Input lines:*

```
Especially in troff, it is sometimes uncanny the way that
vertical motions can occur
'sp 12p
independently from the output of the text.
```

*Output lines:*

> Especially in `troff`, it is sometimes uncanny the way that vertical motions
>
> can occur independently from the output of the text.

*What happens with* `\v'12p'`:

*Input lines:*

```
Especially in troff, it is sometimes uncanny the way that
vertical motions can occur \v'12p'
independently from the output of the text.
```

*Output lines:*

> Especially in `troff`, it is sometimes uncanny the way that vertical motions
> can occur
>              independently from the output of the text.

As you can see, `.sp` causes a break as well as a downward movement on the page. The partially collected line is output before the movement takes place. With `'sp`, the line currently being collected is completely filled and output before the spacing takes place. With `\v`, the motion is completely independent of the process of filling and justification.

It is also independent of traps, as we discovered once when trying to put a pointing finger (☞) at the bottom of a page to indicate that the subject was continued on the overleaf. We used a macro invoked by the page bottom trap to print the finger. At first, we made the mistake of using `.sp -1` to move back up the page to place the finger. Unfortunately, this put `troff` into an endless loop around the trap position. The `\v` escape sequence, on the other hand, did the trick nicely. Since it does not change the current baseline spacing, it will not trigger a trap.

Long-winded examples aside, that is why `\v` is considered a local motion. In general, `\v` escape sequences are used in pairs to go away from, and then back to, the current vertical position.

A superscript is a good example of vertical motion using `\v`. For example, you could create a simple superscript macro like this:

```
.de SU
\\$1\s-2\v'-3p'\\$2\v'3p'\s0\\$3
..
```

This macro

- prints its first argument;
- reduces the point size;
- makes a 3-point reverse vertical motion;

- prints the second argument;

- makes a 3-point vertical motion to return to the original baseline;

- restores the original size;

- prints an optional third argument immediately following. (This allows punctuation to be introduced immediately following the superscript, rather than on
  the next line. If no third argument is supplied, this argument interpolation will
  be ignored.)

This macro could also be implemented using the \u (*up*) and \d (*down*) escape
sequences, which use a fixed ¹/₂-em distance. If you did this—or if you specified the
distance for the \v escape sequence in a relative unit like ems, instead of a fixed unit
like points—it would be essential to have both of the vertical motions either inside or
outside the font size change. For example, assuming that the current font size was 10
points:

```
.de SU
\\$1\u\s-2\\$2\d\s0\\$3
..
```

would produce an unbalanced effect, because the upward motion would be 5 points (¹/₂
em at 10 points), while the downward motion would be only 4 points (¹/₂ em at 8
points). This caution holds true whenever you mix font and size changes with local
motions.

### · Local Horizontal Motions ·

Much of what has been said about local vertical motions is true for local horizontal
motions. They take place independently of the process of filling and justification, and
so, if improperly used, can result in horrors like:

Look what happensyouwhenmake a mistake with \h!

which was produced by the line:

```
Look what happens when \h'-3m'you make a mistake with \h!
```

Horizontal motions are not as likely to take place in pairs as vertical motions. For
example, there are cases where you want to close up the space between two special
characters, or open up additional space on a line. For example, >>, produced by
>\h'-1p'>, looks better than >>.

In addition to \h, there are a number of escape sequences that affect horizontal
motion in specific ways.

For example, "\ " (it's quoted so you can see the blank space following the
backslash) will space over to the right by *exactly* one space. That sounds trivial, but it
isn't. When it justifies a line, troff feels free to expand the spaces between words.
(The default space size is normally 12/36 of an em, but can be reset with the .ss

request using units of 36ths of an em). The "\ " escape sequence makes sure that you get exactly one space. This is generally thought of as the unpaddable space character and is used when you want to keep two words together. However, it can also be used simply as a horizontal motion sequence.

Another useful sequence is \0. It provides exactly the width of a digit in the current font and size. (Unlike alphabetic characters, all digits are always the same width on the standard fonts, to allow them to line up properly in numeric displays.) The \0 sequence is most useful when you want to line up spaces and digits manually.

The two escape sequences \| and \^, which give, respectively, a 1/6 em and 1/12 em space, are useful when you want to create just a little bit of fixed space between two characters. (The normal space size created by an actual space character is 1/3 em, so these two characters give you, respectively, one-half and one-quarter of the normal interword spacing.) You may remember that we used \^ in Chapter 12 to create a little bit of space before and after the em dashes we were introducing into our files with sed.

## ▪ Absolute Motions ▪

As you've probably gathered from the preceding discussion, you can specify the distance for a horizontal or vertical motion using any of the units discussed in Chapter 4. The values can be given explicitly, or by interpolating the value of a number register. In addition, as discussed in Chapter 4, you can use a vertical bar (|) to indicate absolute motion relative to the top of the page or the left margin.

This is not as simple as it first appears. For vertical motions, you pretty much get what you expect. For example, .sp |2i, \v'|2i' will move you to a position 2 inches from the top of the page. Depending on where you are on the page before you issue the command, the generated motion will be either positive or negative.

For horizontal motions, things are a little more ambiguous. The absolute position indicator doesn't move you to an absolute position based on the output line, but on the *input* line. For example:

```
This is a test of absolute horizontal motion\h'|1i'_
```

produces:

    This is a test of abs<u>o</u>lute horizontal motion

But:

```
This is a test of
absolute horizontal motion\h'|1i'_
```

produces:

    This is a test of absolute horizontal <u>m</u>otion

What is really supplied as an argument to \h when you use the absolute position indicator is the *distance* from the current position on the input line to the specified position. Even though it looks the same, the argument will have a different value, depending on the length of the input line. And again, as with vertical motions, the actual movement may be positive (to the right) or negative (to the left), depending on the relationship between the current position and the absolute position specified.

It may appear odd to have these motions relative to the input line. However, as we will see (especially in line drawing), there is a method to the madness.

## ▪ **Line Drawing** ▪

Now we come to the fun part. Moving around on the page is of little use unless you plan to write something at the point you've moved to. Superscripts, subscripts, and overprinting provide some application of local motion, but local motions are most useful with the escape sequences for drawing lines and curves.

Applications range from underlining words in troff, to boxing single words (if you are writing computer manuals, this is very useful for showing the names of keys to be pressed), to drawing boxes around whole blocks of text, just like tbl does.

The \l sequence draws a horizontal line; \L draws a vertical line. Both escape sequences take two arguments, the second of which is optional. Both arguments should be enclosed together in a single pair of delimiters.

The first argument is the distance to draw the line. A positive value means to draw a horizontal line to the right, or a vertical line downward (depending on whether \l or \L is used). A negative value means to draw a line back to the left, or back up the page.

When you draw a line back to the left, either by explicitly specifying a negative value, or by specifying an absolute value (such as |0) that results in a negative movement, troff first moves back to the specified position, then draws the line from left to right. It is as if the line is drawn *from* the specified distance to the current position.

For example:

| | |
|---|---|
| \l'3i' | draws a line 3 inches to the right |
| \l'-3i' | draws a line from a position 3 inches to the left |
| \L'3i' | draws a line 3 inches down |
| \L'-3i' | draws a line 3 inches up |
| \L'|3i' | draws a line to a position 3 inches from the top of the page |

The optional second argument is the character with which to draw the line. By default, a horizontal line is drawn with the baseline rule—a horizontal line that is aligned with the bottom of the other characters on a line. However, if you want to underline text, be sure to use the underscore, which is printed in the space allotted for characters that descend below the line:

```
These_words_are_separated_by_baseline_rules.
These_words_are_separated_by_underscores.
```

The underscore is usually generated by the underscore character that appears above the hyphen on most keyboards. However, to be on the safe side, you should refer to it by

its special character name in troff—\(ul. (The baseline rule can be specified with
the sequence \(ru.)

Vertical lines are drawn by default with a character called the box rule (which can
be generated by the \(br escape sequence or the vertical bar character on most key-
boards). The box rule is a zero-width character—that is, when troff draws the box
rule, it does not space over as it does with other characters. This allows troff to
form exact corners with horizontal lines drawn with underrules. However, as you will
see, it may therefore require you to manually specify additional space to keep it from
crowding previous or succeeding characters.

Except in the case where you draw a line to the left, as described previously, the
current position at which text output will continue is changed to the endpoint of the
line. In drawing a box, you will naturally find yourself returning to the starting point.
However, if you are drawing a single line, you may need to use \v or \h to adjust
the position either before or after the line is drawn.

Let's look at a couple of examples. A simple macro to underline a word in
troff might look like this:

```
.de UL
\\$1\l'|0\(ul'\\$2
..
```

This example prints its argument, backs up a distance equal to the length of the argument *on the input line*, then draws a line from that point to the current position. The
optional second argument allows you to specify punctuation without separating it with
the space that is required if it were entered on the next input line. (This reverse motion
is implicit in the negative value generated by the absolute position request |0—that is,
the distance from the end of the word to the beginning of the line. Lines drawn with
\l and a negative distance generate a negative horizontal motion for the specified distance. The line is then drawn in a positive direction back to the current position.)

That is:

```
.UL Hello ,
```

produces:

Hello,

and:

```
.UL Hello
,
```

produces:

Hello ,

(In nroff, you can underline simply by using an italic font switch, or the .ul
request, because italics are represented in nroff by underlines.)

A macro to enclose a word (like the name of a key) in a box might look like this:

```
.de BX
\(br\|\\$1\|\(br\l'|0\(rn'\l'|0\(ul'\^\\$2
..
```

For example, the input text:

```
Press the
.BX RETURN
key.
```

will produce the line:

Press the ⎸RETURN⎹ key.

This macro prints a single box rule (\ (br), spaces over 1/6 em (\ |), prints the argument, spaces over another 1/6 cm space, and prints a concluding box rule. Then it draws two horizontal lines back to 0 (the beginning of the input line—that is, the width of the argument plus the two requested 1/6-em spaces).

The first horizontal line is drawn not with \ (ul but with another special character, the *root en* (\ (rn). This character is used when drawing equations to produce the top bar in a square root symbol, but it is just as useful when you want to draw a line over the top of some text without moving back up the page. The second horizontal line is drawn, as usual, with \ (ul.

Both lines can be drawn back to zero without compensating horizontal motions because, as we have already noted, horizontal lines drawn backwards actually generate a reverse horizontal motion followed by a line drawn back to the current position.

The macro concludes with an additional 1/12-em space (\^) and an optional second argument, designed to allow you to specify punctuation following the box.

A macro to box multiple lines of text (like this paragraph) is more complex. It requires the use of a diversion to capture the text to be boxed. The diversion can then be measured, and the lines drawn to fit. And when you are using diversions, you need two macros, one to start the diversion, and one to finish it, as in the following macros:

```
.de BS            \" Box Start
.br               \" Space down one line; cause break
.di bX            \" Start diverting input to macro bX
..
.de BE            \" Box End
.br               \" Ensure partial line is in bX
.nr bI 1n         \" Set "box indent"--space between
.                 \" box and text
.di               \" End diversion
.nr bW \\n(dlu    \" Set "box width" to diversion width
.nr bH \\n(dnu    \" Set "box height" to diversion height
.ne \\n(bHu+\\n(.Vu \" Make sure bH plus one line is
.                 \" left on page
```

```
.nr fI \\n(.u          \" Set fI to 1 if text is filled
.nf                    \" Specify no-fill before printing bX
.ti 0
.in +\\n(bIu           \" Add "box indent" to any other indent
.bX                    \" Output the text stored in macro bX
.in -\\n(bIu           \" Subtract bI to restore prev indent
.nr bW +2*\\n(b        \" Add 2x "box indent" to "box width"
.sp -1                 \" Compensate for baseline spacing
\l'\\n(bWu\(ul'\L'-\\n(bHu'\l'|0\(ul'\h'|0'\L'\\n(bHu'
.                      \" Draw box
.if \\n(fI .fi         \" Restore fill if prev text was filled
.sp                    \" Space down 1 line after box is drawn
..
```

There are a number of interesting things about these macros. First, they provide a good illustration of the use of diversions. Note that the macro causes a break (with either .br or .sp) before the diversion is started and before it is terminated. Note also how the predefined read-only registers dn and dl are used to measure the height and width of the diversion and therefore set the dimensions of the box. (The contents of these registers are not used directly when the lines are drawn because the registers are read-only, and the width needs to be adjusted to account for a small amount of spacing between the box rule and the text contained in the box.)

Second, because these macros are complex, they use quite a few number registers. We want to use register names that are mnemonic, but not use up names that might be useful for user-level macros. We get around this problem by using names that combine lowercase and uppercase letters. This is entirely a matter of convention, but one that we find preferable to mm's use of completely obscure internal register names like ;p.

Third, there is the actual line drawing—the point of this presentation. Let's look at this aspect of these macros in detail.

As we've discussed, bH and bW have been set to the height and width, respectively, of the diversion. Because the box rule is a zero-width character, however, the macro needs to allow a small amount of space between the sides of the box and the text it encloses. It does this by specifying a 1-en indent (which is added to any existing indent, in case the box occurs in a block of text that is already indented). When the diversion is output, it will thus be indented 1 en.

After the diversion is output, the indent is reset to its previous value. However, twice the value of the indent is added to the box width. The box will thus be drawn 2 ens wider than the text it encloses. The text will start in 1 en; the right side of the box will be drawn 1 en beyond the right margin.

The actual line to draw the box:

```
\l'\\n(BWu\(ul'\L'-\\n(BHu'\l'|0\(ul'\h'|0'\L'\\n(BHu'
```

draws a horizontal line using \(ul from the left margin to the distance specified by bW (*box width*), which, as we have seen, now includes a small extra margin. It then draws a line back up the page to the height specified by bH, and back across the page to the left margin again.

At this point, even though we have drawn the bottom, right, and top sides of the box, we are still at the top right corner of the box. The macro needs to move horizontally back to the left margin, because horizontal lines to the left are actually drawn *from* the left, and leave the current position the same as it was before the line was drawn. In this case we actually want to move to the left as well. Therefore, we must do so explicitly, by following the `\l' |0\ (ul'` request with a `\h' |0'`. Finally, the box is closed by drawing a vertical line back down the left side.

The current position is now at the start of the last line of the contents of the box, so the macro issues an `.sp` request to move down one line. Alternatively, you could write this macro in such a way that it leaves no additional space above and below the box, but lets the user leave space by issuing some kind of spacing or paragraph request.

By default, the box is drawn just long enough to surround the text it contains. (The number register `dl`, which is used to set the box width, contains the width of the text in the diversion.) For short lines in no-fill mode, the box will also be shorter:

```
Here are some short lines of text in no-fill mode.
Let's see how they come out.
```

This raises the idea that it might be nice to center a box that is shorter. A more complete set of box macros will do this, as well as let the user change the default box indent (the distance between the text and the edge of the box):

```
.de BS                      \" Box Start
.sp
.di bX
.nr bC 0                    \" Clear centering flag
.nr bI 0                    \" Clear box indent
.if "\\$1"C" .nr bC 1       \" Set flag if user wants centered
.if !"\\$2"" .nr bI \\$2n\" Set box indent if specified
..
.de BE                      \" Box End
.br
.if !\\n(bI .nr bI 1n       \" Set bI if not already set
.di
.nr bW \\n(dlu
.nr bH \\n(dnu
.ne \\n(bHu+\\n(.Vu
.nr fI \\n(.u
.nf
.ti 0
.nr iN \\n(.iu              \" Save current indent
.if \\n(bC .in +(\\n(.lu-\\n(bWu)/2u
.                           \" If centering, adjust indent
.in +\\n(bIu
.bX
.in -\\n(bIu
.nr bW +2*\\n(bIu
```

```
.sp -1
\l'\\n(bWu\(ul'\L'-\\n(bHu'\l'|0\(ul'\h'|0'\L'\\n(bHu'
.if \\n(fI .fi
.in \\n(iNu                  \" Restore original indent
.sp
..
```

Using the full macro, and specifying `.BS C 5n`, the box now looks like this:

> Here are some short lines of text in no-fill mode.
> Let's see how they come out with `.BS C 5n`.

These macros also provide insight into how to use number registers. For example, `B1` takes `C` as a possible argument to indicate that the box should be centered. Because the `B2` macro controls the output, there must be some way to communicate the user request for centering between `B1` and `B2`. The `B1` macro sets number register `BC` to 1 as a signal, or flag, to `B2` to do the centering. (Note that `BC` is first zeroed, to make sure that centering is not propagated into the current environment from a previous invocation of the box macros.)

Likewise, `BQ` is set as a flag to indicate whether justification is enabled. The box is drawn in no-fill mode, but the macro must reset filling if it was previously enabled. The read-only number register `.u` is nonzero if filling is in effect, so the lines:

```
.nr BQ \\n(.u
      .
      .
      .
.if \\n(BQ .fi
```

will execute the `.fi` request only if justification was previously in effect.

## Changing Line Weight

You may occasionally want to change the weight of a line you are drawing. The way to do this is simple: change the point size with either the `.ps` request or the `\s` escape sequence before drawing the line. For example:

```
\l'3i'
```

will produce:

———————————————————————

and:

```
\s20\l'3i'\s0
```

will produce:

———————————————————————

(This trick only works with \l and \L. It will not change the weight of lines drawn with any of the \D escape sequences.) You might also want to consider the text size when you are drawing boxes around text. For example, if you are using a macro like .BX (shown previously) to draw boxes around the names of keys, you might want to set the text 2 points smaller, either by specifying the font-switch codes as part of the argument:

```
.BX "\s-2RETURN\s0"
```

or by modifying the macro so that they are built right in:

```
.de BX
\(br\|\s-2\\$1\s0\|\(br\l'|0\(rn'\l'|0\(ul'\^\\$2
..
```

If either of these things were done, our earlier example would look like this, which is even better:

Press the ⃞RETURN⃞ key.

## Drawing Curves

The previous line drawing escape sequences work in nroff and otroff as well as ditroff. There are also additional drawing sequences that only work in ditroff. These escape sequences allow you to draw circles, arcs, ellipses, splines (curved lines between a series of coordinates), and straight lines.

Table 15-2 summarizes these sequences. The syntax of the escape sequences is familiar—an initial escape code is followed by a series of arguments enclosed in single quotation marks or some other user-supplied delimiter. In this case, though, all of the escape sequences begin with the same code—\D—with the type of item to be drawn (circle, arc, ellipse, spline, or straight line) given by the first argument.

TABLE 15-2. ditroff Escape Sequences for Drawing

| Escape | Description |
| --- | --- |
| \D'l $x,y$' | Draw a line from the current position to coordinates $x,y$. |
| \D'c $d$' | Draw a circle of diameter $d$ with left edge at the current position. |
| \D'e $d1\ d2$' | Draw an ellipse with horizontal diameter $d1$ and vertical diameter $d2$, with the left edge at the current position. |
| \D'a $x1\ y1\ x2\ y2$' | Draw an arc counterclockwise from the current position, with center at $x1,y1$ and endpoint at $x1+x2,y1+y2$. |
| \D'~ $x1\ y1\ x2\ y2\ldots$' | Draw a spline from the current position through the specified coordinates. |

Learning the geometry used by these escape sequences is best accomplished by example. Although we have shown the arguments to the line, arc, and spline sequences as if they were *x, y* coordinates, they are in fact `troff`'s usual vertical and horizontal distances. Read *x* as *horizontal* distance, and *y* as *vertical distance*. You can get very confused if you treat them as a true coordinate system.

Let's start simple, with individual fixed-size figures. The following input will produce the output shown in Figure 15-1:

```
.sp 1i
.in .5i
The circle starts here\D'c 1i'and ends here.
.sp 1i
The line starts here\D'l 1i -1i'and ends here.
.sp 1i
The ellipse starts here\D'e 2i 1i'and ends here.
.sp 1i
The arc starts here\D'a .5i 0 0 .5i'and ends here.
.sp 1i
The spline starts here
\D'~ .5i -.5i .5i .5i .5i .5i .5i -.5i'and ends here.
.sp .5i
.in 0
```

As you can see, arcs and splines are the most difficult figures to construct. Instinct cries out for the ability to draw an arc between two endpoints with the current position as the center of the arc. Instead, for consistency with the other figures, drawing begins at the current position, and the first set of values specify the center of the arc. This takes a little getting used to.

With splines, the problem is that distances are additive, and relative to the previous position, rather than to the initial position. Our familiarity with *x, y* coordinate systems leads us to think that the spline should be produced by a request like this:

```
\D'~ .5i -.5i 1i 0 1.5i .5i 2i 0'
```

(in which the *x* value increases relative to the origin rather than to the previous point) instead of by the request shown previously.

You may also have noticed something rather odd. Text continues right after the endpoint of the figure, yet the `.sp 1i` requests seem to give us 1 inch of space from the original baseline, regardless of the endpoint of the figure. This is most obvious with the line, which clearly moves back up the page. Yet the next figure is also spaced down 1 inch. This fact becomes even more obvious if we do this:

```
.sp 1i
The line starts here\D'l 1i -.5i'and ends here.
What happens to text that wraps and continues in fill mode?
```

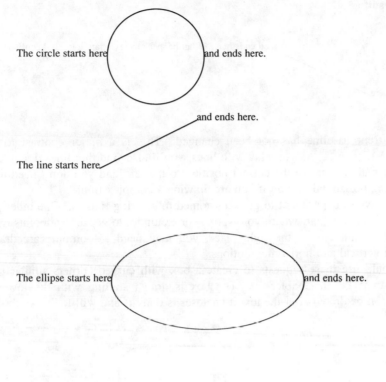

The circle starts here       and ends here.

and ends here.

The line starts here

The ellipse starts here       and ends here.

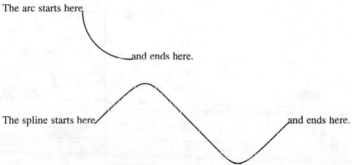

The arc starts here

and ends here.

The spline starts here       and ends here.

*Fig. 15-1.* Some Simple Figures

Here's the result:

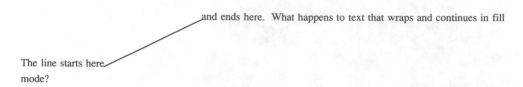

and ends here.  What happens to text that wraps and continues in fill

The line starts here
mode?

   The current baseline has not been changed.  This is a major contrast to lines drawn with  \L or  \l.  As you play with lines, you'll also find that lines drawn to the left with  \D really do move the current position to the left, and you don't need to add a compensating horizontal motion if you are drawing a complex figure.

   You'll have to experiment to get accustomed to drawing figures.  One other problem is to get figures to start where you want.  For example, to get the endpoints of arcs with various orientations in the right place, you may need to combine arc drawing requests with vertical and horizontal motions.

   You could use these requests to create a box with curved corners similar to the one done with  pic in Chapter 10.  The box is drawn starting with the lower left corner (so it can be drawn after the text it encloses is output) and will look like this:

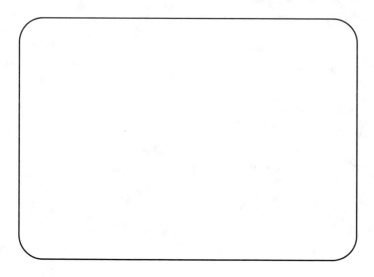

The box was drawn using the following drawing commands.  These commands are shown on separate lines for ease of reading.  To make them draw continuously, we need to add the  \c escape sequence to the end of each line.  This escape sequence joins succeeding lines as if the line feed were not there.  Warning: using fill mode will not achieve the same result, because the formatter will introduce spaces between each drawing command as if it were a separate word.

| | |
|---|---|
| `\v'-.25i'\c` | Go back up the page 1/4 inch |
| `\D'a .25i 0 0 .25i'\c` | Draw bottom left arc 1/4 inch down and to the right |
| `\D'l 3i 0'\c` | Draw horizontal line 3 inches to the right |
| `\D'a 0 -.25i .25i 0'\c` | Draw bottom right arc 1/4 inch up and to the right |
| `\D'l 0 -2i'\c` | Draw vertical line 2 inches back up the page |
| `\D'a -.25i 0 0 -.25i'\c` | Draw top right arc 1/4 inch up and to the left |
| `\D'l -3i 0'\c` | Draw horizontal line 3 inches to the left |
| `\D'a 0 .25i -.25i 0'\c` | Draw top left arc 1/4 inch down and to the left |
| `\D'l 0 2i'\c` | Draw vertical line 2 inches down the page |
| `\v'.25i'` | Restore original baseline position |

To build a complete macro to enclose examples in a simulated computer screen, we can adapt the `.B1` and `.B2` macros shown previously:

```
.de SS                     \" Start Screen with
.                          \" Curved Corners
.sp .5v
.ie !"\\$1"" .nr BW \\$1\" Get width from first arg
.el .nr BW 4i              \" or set default if not specified
.ie !"\\$2"" .nr BH \\$2\" Get height from second arg
.el .nr BH 2.5i            \" or set default if not specified
.br
.di BB
..
.de SE \" Screen End
.br
.nr BI 1n
.if \\n(.$>0 .nr BI \\$1n
.di
.ne \\n(BHu+\\n(.Vu
.nr BQ \\n(.j
.nf
.ti 0
.in +\\n(BIu
.in +(\\n(.lu-\\n(BWu)/2u
.sp .5
.BB
.sp +(\\n(BHu-\\n(dnu)
.in -\\n(BIu
.nr BH -.5i
.nr BW +2*\\n(BIu
.nr BW -.5i
\v'-.25i'\c
\D'a .25i 0 0 .25i'\c
\D'l \\n(BWu 0'\c
\D'a 0 -.25i .25i 0'\c
\D'l 0 -\\n(BHu'\c
```

```
\D'a −.25i 0 0 −.25i'\c
\D'l −\\n(BWu 0'\c
\D'a 0 .25i −.25i 0'\c
\D'l 0 \\n(BHu'\c
\v'.25i'
.sp −1.5
.if \\n(BQ .fi
.br
.sp .5v
..
```

Because a screen has a fixed aspect ratio, we don't want the box to be proportional to the text it encloses. Hence, we give the user of the macro the ability to set the box width and height. If no arguments are specified, we provide default values.

Because the box size is fixed, there are some additional steps necessary in the closing macro. First, we must decrement the specified box width and height by the distance used in drawing the curves, so that the user gets the expected size. Second, because the box is drawn from the lower left corner back up the page, we must make sure that the lower left corner is correctly positioned before we start drawing.

To do this, we again need to use a diversion. We measure the height of the diversion, then add enough additional space (.sp +(\\n(BHu−\\n(dnu)) to bring the starting point for drawing low enough so that the box is not drawn back over the text that precedes the invocation of .SS. (If you don't understand why this was done, delete this line from the macro, and watch the results.)

We've also centered the screen by default, and added a half-line of vertical spacing above and below the box. (As an exercise, modify the .BX macro to produce a key-cap with curved corners.)


## ▪ Talking Directly to the Printer ▪

Depending on the output device and postprocessor you are using, you may be able to send specialized control commands directly to your printer. For example, you may be able to embed raster graphics images (such as a file created on an Apple Macintosh with MacPaint) directly in your output. Or if you are using a PostScript-driven printer, you can integrate figures done with MacDraw, or issue PostScript commands to print grey screens over your text.

These capabilities are provided by the two requests \! and .cf, *copy filename [to standard output]* (ditroff only).

The \! request is the *transparent output* indicator. Any text following this escape sequence on a line is placed directly into the output stream, without any processing by troff. This makes it possible to insert control lines that will be interpreted by a postprocessor or an output device. (As mentioned in the last chapter, transparent output is also useful for embedding control lines in a diversion, to be executed when the text in the diversion is output.)

Likewise, the contents of the file specified as an argument to `.cf` are placed directly on standard output, without processing by `ditroff`.

Unfortunately, there is a catch! PostScript is a page-description language that resides in the printer. Before you can talk directly to the printer, you must get through the postprocessor that translates `ditroff` output into PostScript. If the postprocessor mucks with the data you send out, all bets are off.

As of this writing, TranScript, Adobe Systems' own `troff`-PostScript converter, does not allow you to use `\!`. However, with Pipeline Associates' `devps`, any lines beginning with `!` are ignored by the postprocessor, and go directly to the printer. This allows you to use transparent output by entering the sequence `\!!` followed by the appropriate PostScript commands. Or, if you are sending a PostScript file created on the Mac, use an editor to insert an exclamation point at the beginning of each line.

In any event, this is not a job for the novice, since you must learn PostScript as well as `troff`. Experiment with your printer and postprocessor, or ask around to see if other users have solutions you can adapt to your situation.

## ▪ Marking a Vertical Position ▪

There are many cases, both in macros and in the body of your text, where you may want to mark a spot and then return to it to lay down additional characters or draw lines.

The `.mk` request marks the current vertical position on the page; `.rt` returns to that position. This is useful for two-column processing. To give a simple example:

```
Two columns are useful when you have a linear list
of information that you want to put side-by-side, but don't
want to bother rearranging with the cut-and-paste programs.
.sp .5
.ll 2.5i
.nf
.mk
Item 1
Item 2
Item 3
.ll 5i
.in 2.75i
.rt
Item 4
Item 5
.in 0
.sp
```

This example produces the following output:

```
Two columns are useful when you have a linear list of
information that you want to put side-by-side, but
don't want to bother rearranging with the cut-and-paste
programs.

Item 1                                    Item 4
Item 2                                    Item 5
Item 3
```

Notice that it is entirely your responsibility to make sure that the second column doesn't overprint the first. In this example, we did this by manually adjusting the indent and the line length. In addition, because the second column is shorter than the first, a concluding `.sp` is necessary to return to the original position on the page. If this had not been done, subsequent text would overprint the last line of the first column.

Proper two-column processing for an entire document requires a much more complex setup, which must in part be handled by the page bottom macro. We'll look at that in detail in Chapter 16, but this example should be enough to give you the idea.

The `.mk` request can take as an argument the name of a number register in which to store the vertical position. This allows you to mark multiple positions on a page, and return to them by name. The `.rt` request always returns to the last position marked, but you can go to a position marked in a register using the `.sp` request:

```
.mk Q
.sp |\nQu
```

or (more to the point of the current discussion) with `\v`:

```
\v'|\nQu'
```

In addition, `.rt` can take as an argument a distance from the top of the page. That is:

```
.rt 3i
```

will return to a point 3 inches from the top of the page. The `.mk` request need not be used in this case.

## ▪ **Overstriking Words or Characters** ▪

There are a number of escape sequences that allow you to overstrike words or characters to create special effects. These include

- boldfacing an entire font by overstriking;
- marking and returning to a specific horizontal position;
- calculating the width of a word and backing up over it;
- centering two characters on top of each other;
- stacking characters vertically.

## Boldfacing a Font by Overstriking

The `.bd` request specifies that a font should be artificially boldfaced by overstriking. The request has two forms, one for ordinary fonts and one for the special font.

A request of the form:

`.bd` *font offset*

will overstrike all characters printed in *font* by overprinting them, with the second strike offset from the first by *offset*-1 basic units. The following:

`.bd` S *font offset*

will overstrike characters printed in the special font, while *font* is in effect. And:

`.bd` *font*
`.bd` S *font*

will restore the normal treatment of the font.

This request is particularly useful when you are boldfacing headings and want to account for special characters or italics in arguments supplied by the user. (This assumes that you don't have an explicit bold italic font.) Especially at sizes larger than 10 points, the stroke weights of bold and italic fonts can be quite different.

For example, assume that you had a macro that produced a boldface heading for a table:

```
.de Th   \" Table Heading
.ft B
.ce
Table \\$1: \\$2
.ft P
..
```

If the user supplied italics or special characters in the arguments to the macro, the contrast between the different character weights might not be as pleasing as it could be. For example:

```
.Th "3-1" "Special Uses for \(sr in \fItroff\fP"
```

would produce:

---

### Table 3-1: Special Uses for √ in *troff*

---

If the macro had `.bd` requests added like this:

```
.de Th   \" Table Heading
.ft B
.bd I 3
.bd S B 3
.ce
Table \\$1: \\$2
.ft R
```

```
.bd I
.bd S
..
```

the output would look like this:

---

**Table 3-1: Special Uses for √ in** *troff*

---

Another example is provided by the constant-width (CW) font used in this book. Because the font is optimized for the LaserWriter, where the ink bleeds slightly into the paper, the font is very light on the typesetter. Throughout this book, we have emboldened this font slightly, with the requests:

```
.bd CW 4
.bd S CW 4
```

This sentence shows how the `constant width` font looks without these requests.

## Marking and Returning to a Horizontal Position

Just as you can mark a vertical position, you can also mark and move to a specific horizontal position. This is chiefly useful for overstriking characters.

Just as you use a value stored into a register with the `.mk` request to indicate a fixed vertical location on the page, you mark a horizontal location with `\k`. Then, you can use the absolute position indicator `|` to specify the distance for `\h`.

To borrow an example from Kernighan's *Troff Tutorial*:

```
\kxword\h'|\nxu+2u'word
```

will artificially embolden *word* by backing up almost to its beginning, and then overprinting it. (At the start of *word*, `\k` stores the current horizontal position in register x. The `\h'|\nxu+2u'` sequence returns to that absolute position, plus 2 units—a very small offset. When *word* is printed a second time, an overstriking effect is created.)

This sequence might be useful if you were using a font that had no bold equivalent, and in circumstances where the `.bd` request could not be used because the special effect was not desired for all instances of that font on the same line. And, to be really useful, the sequence should probably be saved into a macro.

## The Width Function

The `\w` escape sequence returns the length of a string in units. For example:

```
\w'Hi there'
```

will tell you the length of the string *Hi there*.

This sequence returned by `\w` can be used as an argument with `\h` or with any horizontally oriented request (such as `.in`). This has many uses, which we'll introduce as we need them.

To give you an idea of how to use `\w`, though, we can rewrite the example used with `\k` as follows, to produce the same effect:

```
.de BD          \" Artificially embolden word
\\$1\h'-\w'\\$1'-2u'\\$1
..
```

This macro prints its first argument, then backs up the width of that argument, less two units. Then it prints the argument a second time— at a two-unit offset from the first. Hint: to avoid awkward constructions involving nested `\w` sequences, first read the width into a number register. For example, the previous macro could be rewritten like this:

```
.de BD          \" Artificially embolden word
.nr WI (\w'\\$1'-2u)
\\$1\h'-\\n(WIu'\\$1
..
```

In this case, the difference isn't so great; however, at other times the sequence can become too confusing to read easily.

## Overstriking Single Characters

Although `\k` provides a good method for overstriking an entire word, there are also more specialized functions for overstriking a single character.

The `\o` sequence takes up to nine characters and prints one on top of the other. This is most useful for producing accents, and so forth. For example, `\o'e^'` produces ê.

You can also produce other interesting character combinations, although you may need to tinker with the output to get it to look just right. For example, we once tried to simulate a checkmark in a box with the sequence: `\o'\(sq\(sr'`. (Note that the special character escape sequences are treated as single characters for the purpose of overstriking.) This example produced the following output:

☑

The square root symbol is too low in the box, so we tried to introduce some local motions to improve the effect, like this:

```
\o'\(sq\v'-4p'\(sr\v'4p''
```

Unfortunately, this didn't work. Although you can nest most escape sequences inside each other (as long as you use the correct number and order of delimiting quotation marks), local motions do not work with `\o`. However, there was a solution.

The `\z` sequence also allows overstriking, but in a different way. The `\o` sequence knows the width of each character, and centers them on top of each other. The `\z` sequence simply outputs the following character, *but does not space over it*. That means the current position after printing the character is the same as it was before the character was printed. A subsequent character will have its left edge at the same point as the character immediately following the escape sequence. Because \z does allow you to mix vertical motions with overstriking, it solved our problem.

Because all these escape sequences can be a bit much to type, we defined the checkmark in a box as a string:

```
.ds CK \z\(sq\\v'-4p'\(sr\\v'4p'
```

After we did that, simply typing \*(CK will produce ☑.

## Stacking up Characters

The \b sequence also does a kind of overstriking—it stacks the characters in the following string. It was designed for use with eqn. There are special bracket-building characters that are meant to stack up on top of each other. See Table 15-3.

**TABLE 15-3. Bracket-Building Characters**

| Character | Name | Description |
|-----------|------|-------------|
| ⌈ | \(lt | Left top of big curly bracket |
| ⌊ | \(lb | Left bottom |
| ⌉ | \(rt | Right top |
| ⌋ | \(rb | Right bottom |
| ⟨ | \(lk | Left center of big curly bracket |
| ⟩ | \(rk | Right center of big curly bracket |
| │ | \(bv | Bold vertical |
| ⌊ | \(lf | Left floor (left bottom of big square bracket) |
| ⌋ | \(rf | Right floor (right bottom) |
| ⌈ | \(lc | Left ceiling (left top) |
| ⌉ | \(rc | Right ceiling (right top) |

A typical invocation looks like this:

```
\b'\(lt\(lk\(lb'
```

which produces:

When you're creating a tall construct like this, you need to allow space so that it doesn't overprint preceding lines. You can create space above or below the line with .sp requests. However, this will cause breaks. Although 'sp might do the trick, it is sometimes hard to predict just where the break will fall.

The troff program has a special construct designed to solve just this problem of a tall construct in the middle of filled text. The \x request allows you to associate extra interline spacing with a word. A positive value specifies space above the line; a negative value specifies space below the line. So, when illustrating the previous bracket-building function, we could have shown the results inline, like this $\Big\{$, rather than in an example broken out by blank lines. Typing the sequence:

```
\b'\(lt\(lk\(lb'\x'9p'\x'-9p'
```

gives us the result we want.

The `\x` sequence is also useful when you want to allow extra space for an over-sized letter at the start of a paragraph. (You've probably seen this technique used in some books on the first paragraph of a new chapter. It was commonly used in illuminated manuscripts.)

An application of `\b` that you might find useful is to create vertically stacked labels. For example, consider the following macro, which will put such a label in the outside margin of a book:

```
.de SL
.mk          \" Mark current vertical position
.ft B        \" Change to bold font
.cs B 24     \" We'll explain this later
.po -.25i    \" Shorten the page offset by 1/4 inch
.lt +.5i     \" Extend the title length used by .tl
.            \"  This request will be explained later
.if e .tl '\b:\\$1:'''   \" Use .tl to put stacked label
.if o .tl '''\b:\\$1:'   \"   in the margins
.lt -.5i     \" Restore original title length
.po +.25i    \" Restore original page offset
.cs B        \" We'll explain this later
.ft          \" Restore original font
.rt          \" Return to original vertical position
..
```

So, for example:

```
.SL "Clever Trick!"
```

will produce the effect shown in the margin.

## ▪ Tabs, Leaders, and Fields ▪

We discussed tabs in Chapter 4. However, there are a couple of additional points that need to be covered. When you enter a tab on a typewriter, the typing position shifts over to a predefined *position*, or tab stop. In `nroff` and `troff`, what is actually generated is the *distance* from the current position *on the input line* to the next tab stop.

What this means is best illustrated by an example that will *not* work. Suppose you want to create a table of contents in which one entry (the page number) is all the way over to the right margin, and the other (the heading) is indented from the left, like this:

C<br>
l<br>
e<br>
v<br>
e<br>
r<br>
<br>
T<br>
r<br>
i<br>
c<br>
k<br>
!

You might be tempted to code the example as follows (where a tab is shown by the symbol |———| ):

```
.ta 6.5iR
Getting Started|———|1-1
.in .5i
Turning On the Power|———|1-2
Inserting Diskettes|———|1-3
```

This will not work.  Indents cannot be combined with tabs.  A tab character generates the distance from the current position on the input line to the tab stop.  Therefore, the page number will be indented an additional half-inch—extending out into the right margin—instead of staying where you put it.

The way to achieve this effect (in no-fill mode) is to use either spaces or tabs to manually indent the first text string.

When you use right or center-adjusted tabs, the text to be aligned on the tab is the entire string (including spaces) from one tab to the next, or from the tab to the end of the line.  Text is aligned on a right-adjusted tab stop by subtracting the length of the text from the distance to the next tab stop; text is aligned on a center-adjusted tab stop by subtracting half the length of the text from the distance.


## Using Leaders

A leader works like a tab; however, it produces a character string instead of horizontal motion.  A single character is repeated until a specific horizontal position is reached. There is actually a leader character, just as there is a tab character.  But there is no key for it on most keyboards, so it is not obvious how to generate it.  The magic character is ^A (*CTRL-A*), and you can insert it into a file with  vi  by typing ^V^A (*CTRL-V*, *CTRL-A*).

If you insert a ^A into your file where you would normally insert a tab (incidentally, the tab itself is equivalent to ^I, and will show up as such if you display a line with  ex's  :l command), you will generate a string of dots.  For example:

```
.nf
.ta 1i 2.5i 3.5i
|———|First^ASecond^AThird
.fi
```

will produce:

```
┌──────                                                                    ──────┐
│                                                                               │
│              First .....................................Second ..................Third                │
│                                                                               │
└──────                                                                    ──────┘
```

You can change the leader character from a period to any other single character with the
`.lc` request. For example, you could create a fill-in-the-blanks form like this:

```
.nf
.ta 1i 3iR
.lc _
Signature:|———|^A
Date:|———|^A
.fi
```

This example would produce the following output in `troff`:

```
  _____                                    _____
 |
 |     Signature:         _____
 |     Date:              _____
```

As you can see from the example, tabs and leaders can be combined effectively to line
up both ends of the underlines.

A second way to create leaders is to redefine the output of the tab character with
`.tc`. This request works just like `.lc`, only it redefines what will be output in
response to a tab character. For example, if you issue the request:

```
.tc .
```

a tab character (^I) generates a string of repeated dots, just like a leader (^A). However,
you will then lose the ability to intermix tabs and leaders on the same line, as in the
previous example.

Issuing a `.tc` request without an argument will restore the default value, which
generates motion only. (Incidentally, the same is true of `.lc`—that is, `.lc` without
an argument will cause leaders to generate motion only, just like tabs. To reset the
leader character to its default value, you need to request `.lc .`).

## Using Fields

In addition to tabs and leaders, `nroff` and `troff` support *fields*, which are blocks
of text centered between the current position on the input line and the next, or between
two tab stops.

The `.fc` request allows you to specify a delimiter that indicates the boundaries
of the field, and a second character (called the *pad* character) that divides the contents
of the field into subfields. A blank space is the default pad character. The `.fc`
request without any arguments turns off the field mechanism. This request is a little
difficult to explain, but easy to illustrate. The requests:

```
.nf
.ta 1i 3i
.fc #
|———|#Hi there#
|———|#Hi how are you#
.fc
.fi
```

will produce the following output:

```
                    Hi                           there
                    Hi         how        are    you
```

Within the field, the pad character (a space by default) is expanded so that the text evenly fills the field.  The first line contains only a single space, so the two words are adjusted at either end of the field.  The second line contains three spaces, so the words are evenly spaced across the field.

By specifying a pad character other than a space, you can achieve fine control over spacing within the field.  For example, if we modify the input like this:

```
.fc # ^
|———|#Hi^how are^you#
.fc
```

we'll get this result:

```
                    Hi            how are          you
```

What's this good for?  To return to our *fill-in-the-blanks* example, the construction:

```
.nf
.ta .5i 2i 2.5i 4i
.fc # ^
.lc _
|———|^A|———|^A
.sp .5
|———|#^Signature^#|———|#^Date^#
.fc
.lc .
.fi
```

would produce the following output:

```
              Signature                    Date
```

You should also know that  .fc, like many other advanced formatter requests, is used by the  tbl preprocessor to create complex tables.  It is wise to avoid using it inside a table.

## Using Tabs and Leaders in Macros

Within a macro definition, tabs and leader characters are not interpreted.  They will take effect when the macro is used, not when it is defined.  Within a macro definition, you can also specify tabs and leaders with the escape sequences  \t  and  \a.  These sequences are also not interpreted until the macro is used, and can be substituted for the actual tab or leader characters whenever interpretation is to be delayed.

## ▪ Constant Spacing ▪

One font that you may frequently encounter, especially in the `ditroff` environment, is called `CW` (*constant width*). It is the font used in this book for examples. It has become something of a convention in computer books to print all "computer voice" examples—input from the keyboard, the contents of a file, or output on the screen—in a constant-width font. (This convention is based on the fact that in many computer languages, precise indentation is syntactically or at least semantically significant, and the variable-width typesetting fonts cannot preserve the alignment of the original text.) When you use a constant-width font, you are essentially asking `troff` to act like `nroff`—to work in a realm where all characters, and all spaces, are of identical width.

To use the constant-width font in `ditroff`, request it like any other font, using either the request `.ft CW` or the escape sequence `\f(CW`. In `otroff`, depending on the output device, you could use constant width by using a preprocessor called `cw`, which got around the four font `troff` limit by handling the constant-width font in a separate pass. See the description of `cw` in your *UNIX Reference Manual* if you are interested in the details. (There are other ways to do this as well, depending on the output device and the postprocessor you are using to drive it. For example, we used `otroff` with TextWare International's `tplus` postprocessor and the HP LaserJet. To get around the font limit, we set a convention *in the postprocessor* that 11-point type was actually constant width, and then used the `.cs` and `.ss` requests to give `troff` the correct spacing.)

There is also a request that allows you to simulate the effect of a constant-width font even when you are using a variable-width font. The `.cs` request tells `troff`: "Use the spacing I give you, even if it doesn't match what you've got in your width tables." The request takes up to three arguments. The first two arguments are the most commonly used. They are the font to be so treated and the width to be used, in 36ths of an em. By default, the em is relative to the current type size. By using the optional third argument, you can use the em width of a different type size. So, for example:

```
.cs B 21
Space the bold font at 21/36 of an em.
.cs B 21 12
Space the bold font at 21/36 of a 12-point em.
```

Let's see what we get with these requests:

---

**Space the bold font at 21/36 of an em.**
**Space   the   bold   font   at   21/36   of   a   12-**
**point em.**

---

To return to normal spacing for the font, use `.cs` without a width argument. For example:

```
.cs  B
```

will return control of spacing for the bold font to `troff`'s width tables.

Although the results are not always aesthetically pleasing, it may be necessary to use this request if you have a real need to represent constant-width text. It is also useful for special effects. For example, you may have noticed that in the headings of each chapter of this book, the word *Chapter* is broadly and evenly spaced, and the boxes underneath align with the letters. This was done with the `.cs` request.

The `.cs` request is also useful when you are creating vertically stacked labels, as shown earlier in this chapter. Normally, characters are positioned with their left edge at the current position on the output line. When constant spacing with `.cs` is in effect, the left corner of the *character box* is placed at that position, and the character itself is centered in the box. You can see the difference between this graphically in the following example:

```
.sp  .7i
.ft  B
.in  1i
.mk
\b'Variable'
.in  3i
.rt
.cs  B  24
\b'Constant'
.br
.cs  B
.ft
.in  0
.sp  .7i
```

which produces:

```
        V               C
        a               o
        r               n
        i               s
        a               t
        b               a
        l               n
        e               t
```

The `.ss` request is a closely related request that sets the space size. The default size of an interword space in `troff` is 12/36 of an em; for true constant-width effects, you should set it to the same size as the font spacing you have set with `.cs`.

## ▪ **Pseudo-Fonts** ▪

Using the `.bd` request to create a bold italic is not the only way to simulate a nonstandard font, at least in `ditroff`. In `ditroff`, there are two new escape sequences, `\S` and `\H`. The `\S` sequence slants characters by a specified number of degrees. (Positive values slant characters to the right; negative values slant characters back to the left.) For example:

    `\S'15'`

will slant characters 15 degrees to the right. This can be used to create a pseudo-italic font. The `\S` sequence without an argument turns off slanting.

The `\H` sequence sets the character height to a specified point size without changing the width. For example, if type is currently being set at 10 point, the construct:

    `\H'12'`

will create characters that are 12 points high, but only 10 points wide (assuming you are at the default 10-point size). A height value of 0 turns off the function.

These escape sequences will only work on certain output devices. You'll have to experiment to find whether or not they'll work in the setup you're using.

## ▪ **Character Output Translations** ▪

"Garbage in, garbage out" is a truism of computer science. You get out of a computer what you put in. However, there are cases in `nroff` and `troff` in which what you put in is not the same as what you get out.

The first of these cases is only true for `troff`. It involves a special class of characters called *ligatures*. As we've previously discussed, typeset characters have different widths. Even so, when two narrow characters are printed together, such as a pair of *f*'s, or an *f* and an *i*, there is excess space between the characters.

To get around this problem, there are special characters called ligatures, which are really single characters designed so that they appear the same as a pair of narrow characters. (These are truly single characters, defined as such in `troff`'s character set.)

The ligature characters and the equivalent individual characters are:

| Input | Ligature | Equivalent Characters |
|-------|----------|----------------------|
| `\(fi` | fi | fi |
| `\(fl` | fl | fl |
| `\(ff` | ff | ff |
| `\(Fi` | ffi | ffi |
| `\(Fl` | ffl | ffl |

The `troff` formatter automatically converts any of these groups of characters to the equivalent ligature, although all ligatures are not supported by every output device.

(For example, *fi* and *fl* are the only ones in the standard PostScript fonts.)  You can turn this conversion off with the request:

```
.lg 0
```

and restore it with:

```
.lg
```

Normally, you won't need to do this, but there are special cases in which it may hang you up, and you'll need to know what to do.  We'll get to one of them in a moment.

The  `.tr` (*translate*) request provides a more general facility for controlling output character conversions.  It takes one or more pairs of characters as an argument.  After such a translation list has been defined,  `troff` will always substitute the second character in each pair for the first, whenever it appears in the input.

Let's look at some examples.  First, consider the case encountered throughout this book, in which we illustrate the syntax of various requests without actually executing them.  For example, we want to show a period at the start of a line or the backslash that starts an escape sequence, without actually having them executed.

We could simply insulate the special characters from execution.  For example, we can put the zero-width character  `\&` in front  of a period that begins a request, and we can double all backslashes (`\\` will appear as  `\` in the output) or use the  `\e` escape sequence, to print `\`.

However, this grows tedious and hard to read in the input file.  Another approach is to do a character translation:

```
.tr #.%\\          \" Translate # to ., % to \
```

(As usual, we have to double the backslash.)  Now, whenever  `#` appears in the input, `.` appears in the output, and whenever  `%` appears in the input,  `\` appears in the output. So, in our examples, we can actually type:

```
#sp 1i            %" Space down one inch
```

But what appears on the page of this book is:

```
.sp 1i            \" Space down one inch
```

The translations are built into the example start and end macros.  (The end macro resets the characters to their normal values.)

If you translate characters with  `.tr`, be sure to restore their original values correctly when you are done.  To reset the previous translation to the normal character values, the request is:

```
.tr ##%%          \" Translate # to #, % to %
```

In addition, the translation must be in effect at the time the line is output.  If you translate characters without first causing a break, any partially filled line will be affected by the translation.

It is also possible (and recommended in some of the  `troff` documentation) to use  `.tr` to substitute some other character (usually  `~`) for a space.  This creates an equivalent to the unpaddable space.

```
.tr ~
```

This will allow you to type single characters for unpaddable spaces; your input text will be more readable and will line up properly on the screen.

Yet another application of `.tr`, and one that you will find useful in designing macros for chapter headings and so on, is to translate lowercase input into uppercase, and then back again:

```
.de UC  \" Translate input to uppercase
.tr aAbBcCdDeEfFgGhHiIjJkKlLmMnNoOpPqQrRsStTuUvVwWxXyYzZ
\\$1
.br
.tr aabbccddeeffgghhiijjkkllmmnnooppqqrrssttuuvvwwxxyyzz
..
```

(The break is important. These character translations must be in effect at the time the line is output, not when it is read into the buffer.)

It is in this last case that you may have trouble with ligatures. If the `.UC` macro were defined as shown in the previous example, the line:

```
.UC troff
```

might produce the following output:

> TROﬀ

To have the macro work correctly, we would need to turn ligatures off (`.lg 0`) for the duration of the translation.


## ▪ Output Line Numbering ▪

Do you remember the treatment of the `proof` shell script in Chapter 12? It was such a long example that it required line numbers that could be referred to later in the text. The `nroff` and `troff` programs provide requests that allow you to automatically number output lines as was done in that example.

The `.nm` (*number*) request turns numbering on or off. The request:

```
.nm [±]N
```

will turn numbering on, with the next line numbered *N*. For example, the next paragraph is numbered with `.nm 1`.

1     A 3-digit arabic number followed by a space is placed at the start of each line.
2 (Blank lines and lines containing formatter requests do not count.) The line length is
3 not changed, so this results in a protruding right column, as in this paragraph. You may
4 need to decrease the line length (by `\w'000 '`u) if you are numbering filled text
5 rather than an example in no-fill mode. (Be sure to notice the space following the three
6 zeroes.) We'll do that from now on, so only the current paragraph will protrude.

There are several optional arguments as well: a step value, the separation
2 between the number and the beginning of the line, and an indent that will be added
to the line. By default, the step value is 1, the separation is 1, and the indent is 0.
4 For example, if you specified:

```
.nm 1 2
```

6 every second line would be numbered, as was done at the start of this paragraph.

The `.nn` (*not numbered*) request allows you to temporarily suspend numbering for a specified number of lines, as was done for this paragraph using the request
`.nn 4`. The specified number of lines is not counted. This could be useful if you
were interspersing numbered lines of code with a textual discussion.

To turn numbering off entirely, use `.nm` without any arguments. We'll do
8 that now.

The last line number used by `.nm` is saved in the register `ln`, and it is possible
to restart numbering relative to that number by preceding the initial line number you
give to `.nm` with a + or a −. For example, to restart numbering at exactly the point
it was turned off, you can use this request:

```
.nm +0
```

Let's do that now. As you can see, numbering resumes just where it left off, with
10 the same step value and indent, as if no intervening lines had been present. After
this line, we'll turn numbering off entirely.

When using `.nm` in fill mode, you have to watch for breaks. Because `.nm` itself
does not cause a break, it make take effect on the output line above where you expect it.
You may need to force an explicit break before `.nm` to make sure numbering starts on
the next line.

## · **Change Bars** ·

The `.mc` (*margin character*) request allows you to print "change bars" or other marks |
in the margin, as was done with this paragraph. This is especially useful if you are |
revising a document, and want to indicate to reviewers which sections have changed.

You can specify any single character as the margin character—so don't restrict
yourself to change bars when thinking up uses for this request. For example, you could
use an arrow, or the left-hand character (\ (lh) to draw attention to a particular point in
the text, like this. (These characters are oddly named. The right-hand character ☛
(\ (rh) is a left-hand that points to the right (☛); the left-hand character (\ (lh) is a
right hand that points to the left (☚). These characters are mapped onto arrows on
some output devices.)

You can control the distance the mark character appears from the margin with an
optional second argument. If no argument is given, the previous value is used; if there
is no previous value, the default distance is `0.2i` in `nroff` and `1m` in `troff`.

Incidentally, on many UNIX systems, there is a version of `diff`, called `diffmk`, that will compare two versions of a file, and produce a third file containing `.mc` requests to mark the differences. Additions and changes are marked with a bar in the margin, as shown previously. Deletions are marked with an asterisk.

In our business, we find this very useful for producing interim drafts of technical manuals. We archive the first draft of the manual, as it was turned in to our client. Then, after review changes have been incorporated, we use `diffmk` to produce an annotated version for second draft review:

```
$ diffmk draft1 draft2 marked_draft
$ ditroff ... marked_draft
```

This could also be done by manually inserting `.mc` requests as the edits were made. But, as stated in Chapter 12, why not let the computer do the dirty work?

## ▪ Form Letters ▪

No formatter would be complete without the ability to create form letters that merge existing text with externally supplied data. The `nroff` and `troff` programs are no exception in providing requests to handle this type of problem.

The `.rd` (*read*) request allows you to read from standard input. This request prints a prompt on standard error (the user's terminal) and reads input up to a pair of newlines. For example, you could have a form letter constructed like this:

```
.nf
.rd Enter_the_person's_name
.rd Enter_the_company
.rd Enter_the_street
.rd Enter_the_city,_state,_and_zip
.sp
.fi
Dear
.rd Enter_the_salutation
.sp
        .
        .
        .
```

Unfortunately, `.rd` terminates the prompt at the first space, and does not recognize quotation marks to delimit an entire string as the prompt. As a result, for a wordy prompt, you must tie the string together using an unobtrusive character like an underscore, as was done here.

Here's what would happen when this letter is formatted:

```
$ nroff letter | lp

Enter_the_person's_name:  Tim O'Reilly

Enter_the_company:   O'Reilly & Associates, Inc.
```

```
Enter_the_street:   981 Chestnut Street

Enter_the_city,_state,_and_zip:   Newton, MA 02164

Enter_the_salutation:   Tim:
```

Note that a colon is appended to the prompt, and that the *RETURN* key must be pressed twice after each response. If no prompt is specified, `.rd` will ring the terminal bell when it expects input.

In addition, the input need not come from the keyboard. It can come from a pipe or from a file. There are two other requests that come in handy to create a true form letter generation capability.

The `.nx` (*next*) request causes the formatter to switch to the specified file to continue processing. Unlike the `.so` request discussed in Chapter 4, it doesn't return to the current file. The `.ex` request tells the formatter to quit.

You can put these requests together with `.rd`. First, create a list of variable data (like names and addresses) either in a file or as the output of a database program. Then pipe this file to the formatter while it is processing a letter constructed like this:

```
.nf
.rd
.rd
.rd
.sp
.fi
Dear
.rd

        Body of letter here

Sincerely,


Jane Doe
.bp
.nx letter
```

The `.nx` request at the end of the form letter causes the file to reinvoke itself when formatting is complete. Assuming that the standard input contains a sequence of name, street, city (*et al*), and salutation lines, one line for each `.rd` request, and address block, in the data file, that are each separated by pairs of newlines, you can generate an endless sequence of letters.

However, be warned that formatting will continue in an endless loop, even when the standard input has run out of data, unless you terminate processing. This is where `.ex` comes in. By putting it at the end of the list of names coming from standard input, you tell the formatter to quit when all the data has been used.

The command line to produce this marvel (assuming a form letter in a file called `letter` and a list of names followed by an `.ex` request in a file called `names`) would be:

```
$ cat names | nroff letter | lp
```

or:

```
$ nroff < names | lp
```

It is possible to imagine a more extensive data entry facility, in which a variety of blank forms are constructed using `troff`, and filled in with the help of a data entry front end.* To generalize the facility, you could associate the various fields on the form with number register or string names, and then interpolate the number or string registers to actually fill in the form.

This approach would allow you to reuse repeated data items without having to query for them again. Even more to the point, it would allow you to construct the data entry facility with a program other than `troff` (which would allow features such as data entry validation and editing, as well as increased speed). The data entry front end would simply need to create as output a data file containing string and number register definitions.

## ▪ Reading in Other Files or Program Output ▪

In addition to `.nx`, don't forget the `.so` (*source*) request, which allows you to read in the contents of another file, and then return to the current file.

We've mentioned this request briefly in the context of reading in macro definitions. However, you can also use it to read in additional text. In our business, we've found it very useful in certain types of manuals to break the document into many separate files read in by `.so`. For example, we often need to write alphabetically-ordered reference sections in programming manuals. Unfortunately, the developers often haven't finalized their procedure names. If the section consists of a list of `.so` requests:

```
.so BEGIN_MODULE
.so BUFFER
.so CONFIGURE
    .
    .
    .
```

the job of reorganization is trivial—all you need to do is change the filenames and realphabetize the list.

---

*For this idea, I am indebted to a posting on Usenet, the UNIX bulletin board network, by Mark Wallen of the Institute for Cognitive Science at UC San Diego (Usenet Message-ID: <203@sdics.UUCP>, dated June 13, 1986).

The only caution, which was mentioned previously in Chapter 8, is that you can't include data that must be handled by a preprocessor, such as tables and equations. A quick look at the command line:

```
$ tbl file | nroff
```

will show you that the preprocessor is done with the file before the formatter ever has a chance to read in the files called for by the `.so` request. Some systems have a command called `soelim` that reads in the files called for by `.so`. If you use `soelim` to start the file into the pipeline, there is no problem.

One useful tip: if you are using `soelim`, but for some reason you *don't* want `soelim` to read in a file because you would rather it were read in by `troff`, use `'so` rather than `.so` to read in the file. The `soelim` command will ignore the `'so` request.

Another interesting request is `.sy`. This request executes a specified system command. If the command has output, it is not interpolated into the `troff` output stream, nor is it saved. However, you can redirect it into a file, and read that file into `troff` with `.cf` (or with `.so`, if you want it processed by `troff` instead of sent directly to the output stream).

# 16

# What's in a Macro Package?

In Chapters 4, 14, and 15, you've seen almost all of the individual formatting requests that `nroff` and `troff` provide, and many examples of groups of requests working together in macros. However, writing individual macros is still a far cry from putting together a complete package.

In Chapters 5 and 6, you've seen the features built into the ms and mm macro packages, so you can imagine the amount and complexity of macro definitions. Perhaps you have even looked at a macro package and determined that it was impossible to decipher. Nonetheless, it is possible even as a beginner to write your own macro package or to make extensions to one of the existing packages.

In this chapter, we'll look at the structure of a macro package—the essentials that allow you to handle basic page formatting. Then, in the next chapter, we'll look at a macro package with extensions for formatting large technical manuals or books. Even if you have no plans to write a new macro package, this chapter will help you understand and work with existing packages.

## · Just What Is a Macro Package, Revisited ·

When considering what a macro package is, you might think only of the visible features provided by macros in existing macro packages. But a macro package is more than a collection of user macros that implement various features. Failing to understand this fact might cause someone to import an mm macro into an ms-based macro package, and never understand why this macro fails to work.

Individual macros are dependent upon other elements of the macro package, which sometimes makes it hard to isolate a particular macro, even for purposes of understanding what it does. These interdependencies also make it difficult to understand what a macro package is doing. That is why we want to look at the underlying structure of a macro package, and not just the obvious features it provides. We want to look first at what a macro package *must* do before we look at what it *can* do.

A macro package is a structure for producing *paged* documents. The `nroff` and `troff` formatters do the actual collecting and formatting of lines of text, as steadily as a bricklayer placing bricks in a row. But they do not define the structure that is so obvious by the end result. Fundamentally, it is the macro package that defines the placement of lines on a page. At a minimum, a macro package must set traps and create macros to handle page transitions. It usually also defines the layout of the physical page.

A macro package may also provide a way to arrange the parts of a documents and affect their appearance. Remember the distinction we made earlier between *formatting* and *formats*. A format reflects the type of document being produced, just as a floor plan reflects the functions of rooms in a building. For instance, a technical manual might consist of chapters and sections that require headings. Other elements might be bulleted lists and numbered lists, a table of contents, and an index. These elements help readers to identify and to locate important parts of the document. But these features— so obviously important to users—are really not the essential elements in a macro package.

Page formatting is the foundation of a macro package, and this foundation must be solid before you can build a variety of custom document formats.

## New or Extended?

The first question to ask when you contemplate writing a whole new package is whether you need to do it all yourself or can simply build on an existing package.

There are benefits to either approach. The existing macro packages are quite complex (especially `mm`). It can be easier to start over, writing only the macros you need, than to learn the intricate internals of `ms` or `mm`. A custom macro package can be quite small, including only macros for page transition (which can be minimal, as we shall see) and whatever other macros you want. This is the best approach if you have something specific in mind.

As with all programming projects, though, you may find your package growing larger than intended, as your needs and understanding grow and you start to add features. A macro package begun haphazardly can also end that way, without any consistent structure.

If you do find yourself wanting to create an entire macro package, rather than just a few macros, you should think about modular programming techniques. Modular programming suggests that you break the tasks to be performed by a program into the smallest possible functional units, then build up larger tasks with each of these smaller units. This not only helps with debugging and testing of new macros, but also makes it much easier to write macros, because you end up with a library of low-level general-purpose macros that perform important functions. You don't have to reinvent the wheel for each new macro.

There are numerous advantages to building on the existing packages, especially if you want to have a general-purpose package:

- They already contain a wide range of useful macros that you not only can use directly, but can call on within new macros.

- They are tested and proven. Unless you are very experienced at text processing, it is difficult to foresee all of the kinds of problems that can arise. When you write your own package, you may be surprised by the kinds of errors that are filtered out by the design of ms or mm.

- If you are familiar with ms or mm, adding a few extended macros to your repertoire is easier than learning an entire new package.

- It can be easier than you expect to modify or add to them.

In our own work, we have chosen to extend the ms macro package rather than to build an entirely new package. In this chapter, though, we're going to take a hybrid approach. We'll build a minimal ms-like package that illustrates the essentials of a macro package and allows users who don't have access to the full ms package to make use of some of the extensions described in this and later chapters.

In this "mini-ms" package, we have sometimes pared down complex macros so it is easier to understand what they are doing. We try to uncover the basic mechanism of a macro (what it *must* do). As a caveat to this approach, we realize that simplifying a macro package can reduce its functionality. However, we see it as part of the learning process, to recognize that a macro in a certain situation fails to work and understand the additional code needed to make it work.

## Implementing a Macro Package

As discussed in Chapter 4, the actual option to nroff and troff to invoke a macro package is −m*x*, which tells the program to look in the directory /usr/lib/tmac for a file with a name of the form tmac.*x*. This means you can invoke your own macro package from the command line simply by storing the macro definitions in a file with the appropriate pathname. This file will be added to any other files in the formatting run.

If you don't have write privileges for /usr/lib/tmac, you can't create the tmac.*x* file (although your system administrator might be willing to do it for you). But you can still create a macro package. You will simply have to read it into the formatter some other way. You can either

- include it at the start of each file with the .so request:

    ```
    .so /usr/fred/newmacros
    ```

- or list it on the command line as the first file to be formatted:

    ```
    $ nroff /usr/fred/newmacros myfile
    ```

Nor do the macros need to be stored in a single file. Especially if you are using a package as you develop it, you may want to build it as a series of small files that are called in by a single master file. You may also want to have different versions of some macros for `nroff` and `troff`. So, for example, the mh (Hayden) macros used to format this book are contained in many different files, which are all read in by `.so` requests in `/usr/lib/tmac/tmac.h`:

```
.so /work/macros/hayden/startup
.so /work/macros/hayden/hidden
.so /work/macros/hayden/ch.heads.par
.so /work/macros/hayden/display
.so /work/macros/hayden/ex.figs
.so /work/macros/hayden/vimacs
.so /work/macros/hayden/lists
.so /work/macros/hayden/stuff
.so /work/macros/hayden/index
.so /work/macros/hayden/cols
```

Or, like mm, you might have two large files, one for `nroff` and one for `troff`. In `/usr/lib/tmac/tmac.m`, you find:

```
.if n .so /usr/lib/macros/mmn
.if t .so /usr/lib/macros/mmt
```

In extending an existing macro package, you are not restricted to creating a few local macro definitions that must be read into each file. You can make a complete copy of one of the existing packages, which you can then edit and add to. Or even better, you can read the existing package into your own package with `.so`, and then make additions, deletions, and changes. For example, you might create a superset of ms as follows:

```
.\" /usr/lib/tmac/tmac.S - superset of ms - invoke as -mS
.so /usr/lib/tmac/tmac.s      \" Read in existing package
.so /usr/macros/S.headings
.so /usr/macros/S.examples
.so /usr/macros/S.toc
        .
        .
        .
```

## · Building a Consistent Framework ·

One of the chief factors that distinguishes a macro package from a random collection of macros is that the package builds a consistent framework in which the user can work.
This consistent framework includes:

- Setting traps to define the top and bottom of each page. This is the one essential element of a macro package, because it is the one thing `nroff` and `troff` do not do.

- Setting default values for other aspects of page layout, such as the page offset (left margin) and line length. (The default page offset in `nroff` is 0, which is not likely to be a useful value, and `troff`'s default line length of 6.5 inches is really too long for a typeset line.)

- Setting default values for typographical elements in `troff` such as which fonts are mounted, the point size and vertical spacing of body copy and footnotes, adjustment type, and hyphenation.

- Giving the user a method to globally modify the default values set in the macro package, or temporarily modify them and then return to the defaults.

In a very simple macro package, we might set up default values for `troff` like this:

```
.po 1i      \" Set page offset to one inch
.ll 6i      \" Set line length to six inches
.ad l       \" Adjust left margin only
.hy 14      \" Hyphenate, using all hyphenation rules
.wh 0 NP    \" Set new page trap at the top of the page
.           \" (see below for details)
.wh -1i FO \" Set footer trap
```

(We are assuming here that `troff`'s default values for point size and vertical spacing are acceptable. In `otroff`, we also need to mount the default fonts with `.fp`, as described in Chapter 4; in `ditroff`, a default set of fonts is already mounted.)

Simply setting up explicit default values like this will do the trick, but for a more effective and flexible macro package, you should take the further step of storing default values into number registers. This has numerous advantages, as we'll see in a moment.

## Using Number Registers to Increase Flexibility

Writing `troff` macros is essentially a kind of programming. If you pay heed to the principles learned by programmers, you will find that your macros are more effective, if at first somewhat more complex to write and read.

One important lesson from programming is not to use explicit (so called "hardcoded") values. For example, if you supply the indent in a paragraph macro with an explicit value, such as:

```
.in 5n
```

you make it difficult for users to change this value at a later time. But if you write:

```
.in \\n(INu
```

the user can change the indent of all paragraphs simply by changing the value stored in number register `IN`. Of course, for this to work, you must give a default value to the `IN` register.

In programming, the process of setting variables to a predefined starting value is called *initialization*. To give you an idea of the kinds of variables you might want to initialize, Table 16-1 lists the values stored into number registers by the `ms` macros.

**TABLE 16-1. Number Registers Used in ms**

| Description | Name | Value | |
|---|---|---|---|
| | | `troff` | `nroff` |
| Top (header) margin | HM | `1i` | `1i` |
| Bottom (footer) margin | FM | `1i` | `1i` |
| Point size | PS | `10p` | `1P` |
| Vertical spacing | VS | `12p` | `1P` |
| Page offset | PO | `26/27i` | `0` |
| Line length | LL | `6i` | `6i` |
| Title length | LT | `6i` | `6i` |
| Footnote line length | FL | `\\n(LLu*11/12` | `\\n(LLu*11/12` |
| Paragraph indent | PI | `5n` | `5n` |
| Quoted paragraph indent | QI | `5n` | `5n` |
| Interparagraph spacing | PD | `0.3v` | `1v` |

The mm package uses *many* more number registers—in particular, it uses number registers as flags to globally control the operation of macros. For example, in addition to registers similar to those shown for ms in Table 16-1, there are registers for paragraph type, numbering style in headings, hyphenation, spacing between footnotes, as well as counters for automatic numbering of figures, examples, equations, tables, and section headings. (See Appendix B for a complete listing.) However, the registers used in ms should give you a sufficient idea of the kinds of values that can and should be stored in registers.

## An Initialization Sequence

In the ms macro package, a major part of the initialization sequence is performed by the .IZ macro.* This macro is executed at the start of a formatting run; then it is removed. Let's take a look at a *much* simplified version of the initialization sequence for an ms-like package:

```
.de IZ            \" Initialization macro
.                 \" Initialize Number Registers
.nr HM 1i         \" Heading Margin
.nr FM 1i         \" Footing Margin
.nr PS 10         \" Point Size
.nr VS 12         \" Vertical Spacing
.nr PO 1i         \" Page Offset
.nr LL 6i         \" Line Length
```

---

*There's no real reason why this sequence needs to be put in a macro at all, other than the consistency of putting two backslashes before number registers when they are read in.

```
.nr LT 6i                    \" Length of Titles for .tl
.nr FL \\n(LLu*11/12         \" Footnote Length
.nr PI 5n                    \" Paragraph Indent
.nr QI 5n                    \" Quoted Paragraph Indent
.nr PD 0.3v                  \" Interparagraph Spacing
.                    \" Set Page Dimensions through requests
.ps \\n(PS
.vs \\n(VS
.po \\n(POu
.ll \\n(LLu
.lt \\n(LTu
.hy 14       \" Specify hyphenation rules
.            \" Set Page Transition Traps
.wh 0 NP
.wh -\\n(FMu FO
.wh -\\n(FMu/2u BT
..
.IZ                  \" Execute IZ
.rm IZ               \" Remove IZ
```

As you can see, the initialization sequence stores default values into registers, then actually puts them into effect with individual formatting requests.

A number of the points shown in this initialization sequence will be a bit obscure, particularly those relating to trap positions for top and bottom margins. We'll return to the topic of page transitions shortly.

## A Reset Macro

After you have initialized number registers, the next question is how to make use of the default values in coding. Some registers, like a paragraph indent, will be used in a paragraph macro. But where, for example, might you use the LL register?

First of all, as suggested, putting default values into number registers allows users to change values without modifying the macro package itself. For instance, a user can globally change the interparagraph spacing just by putting a new value into the PD register.

However, the package itself can use these registers to periodically *reset* the default state of various formatting characteristics.

The ms package defines a macro called .RT (*reset*), which is invoked from within every paragraph macro. The .RT macro

- turns off centering—.ce 0;

- turns off underlining—.ul 0;

- restores the original line length—.ll \\n(LLu;

- restores the original point size and vertical spacing—.ps \\n(PS and .vs \\n(VS;

- restores the indent that was in effect before any .IP, .RS, or .RE macros were called (too complex to show here);

- changes back to the font in position 1—.ft 1;

- turns off emboldening for font 1—.bd 1;

- sets tab stops every 5n—.ta 5n 10n 15n 20n...;

- turns on fill mode—.fi.

This is part of the ms error recovery scheme. Rather than aborting when it encounters an error, ms frequently invokes the .RT macro to restore reasonable values for many common parameters.

If you have used ms for a while, and then switch to another package, you may find all kinds of errors cropping up, because you've come to rely on this mechanism to keep unwanted changes from propagating throughout a document. For example, suppose you create a macro that decrements the line length:

```
.ll -5n
```

but you forget to increment it again. You may never notice the fact, because ms will restore the line length at the next paragraph macro. Other packages are far less forgiving.

Unless you plan to explicitly test for and terminate on error conditions, it is wise to implement a reset facility like that used by ms.

A simple ms-like reset macro follows:

```
.de RT \" Reset
.ce 0          \" Turn off centering, if in effect
.ul 0          \" Turn off underlining, if in effect
.ll \\n(LLu    \" Restore default line length
.ps \\n(PS     \" Restore default point size
.vs \\n(VS     \" Restore default vertical spacing
.ft 1          \" Return to font in position 1
.ta 5n 10n 15n 20n 25n 30n 35n 40n 45n 50n 55n 60n 65n 70n
.fi            \" Restore fill mode
..
```

The ms version of .RT also ends any diversion invoked outside of the standard ms macros that create diversions. Thus, a reset may occur within a keep (.KS, .KE), footnotes (.FS, .FE), boxed material (.B1, .B2), and tables (.TS, .TE) without ending the diversion.

If you look at the actual ms reset macro, you will see that it calls another macro, named .BG, the very first time it is itself called. The .BG macro removes the macros associated with the unused Bell Labs technical memorandum formats (because the format has already been determined at that point). Like .IZ, the .BG macro is only called once during a formatting run. In our emulation, we don't make use of the

Technical Memorandum macros so we have not implemented the .BG macro. However, one could easily apply the idea behind the .BG macro: to execute a macro before we begin processing the body of a document. This can be useful if a format requires a number of preliminary or header macros that supply information about the document.

### ▪ Page Transitions ▪

A single page transition macro is the only macro that *must* be implemented for nroff and troff to produce paged output. An example of this simplest of all possible macro packages follows.*

```
.de NP    \" New Page
'bp
'sp 1i
'ns
..
.wh -1.25i NP
.br
.rs
.sp |1i
```

The page transition is triggered by a *trap* set 1.25 inches from the bottom of the page. When output text reaches the trap, the .NP macro is executed, which breaks the page (but not the line), spaces down 1 inch, and enters no-space mode. The three lines following the macro and trap definition take care of the special case of the first page, for which the .NP macro is not invoked.

The .wh request, which sets the location of the traps used for page transition, interprets the value 0 as the top of the page. Negative values are interpreted relative to the bottom of the page. So, for example, assuming that the page length is 11 inches, the requests:

```
.wh 10i BT \" Bottom Title Macro
```

and:

```
.wh -1i BT \" Bottom Title Macro
```

are equivalent. The second form is the most common.

This simple "package" provides only one macro for page transition. The bottom margin of the text portion of the page is determined by the trap location; the top margin by a spacing request in the macro executed at the trap. However, it is far more common to work with at least two page transition macros: one for the page top and one for the bottom.

---

*This "package" was contributed by Will Hopkins of VenturCom, Inc.

An example of a two-trap, two-macro macro package is given below:

```
.wh 0 NP
.wh -1i FO
.de NP                                    \"New Page
'sp 1i
.tl 'Top of Page \\n%'''   \".tl does not cause break
'sp |2i
'ns
..
.de FO                                    \"Page Footer
'sp .25i
.tl ''Page Bottom''
'bp
..
```

A trap is set at the top of the page (.wh 0) to execute the .NP macro. This macro provides a top margin and outputs a title in that space. The formatter begins processing lines of text until the bottom of the page trap is encountered. It invokes the .FO macro, which supplies a footer margin and outputs a centered title. The .FO macro then causes a page break, which in turn invokes .NP at the top of the new page. It is important that both of these macros avoid causing a break, so that text in fill mode will continue smoothly onto the next page.

By setting traps for both the top and bottom of a page you have more control over the size of the bottom and top margins, the placement of headers and footers, and advanced features like footnotes and multiple-column processing.

Take some time to experiment with this bare bones macro package. If you place it in a file, such as pagemacs, you can use it to format text files, as in the following example:

```
$ nroff pagemacs text
```

## No-Space Mode in Page Transitions

No-space mode is often used in a page transition macro to keep space from being output at the top of a page. It is standard page makeup for the top line of each page to begin at the same point. Without no-space mode, a spacing request (such as prespacing in a paragraph macro) that falls just before the page transition would result in space being output at the top of the page, causing uneven positioning of the top line of the page.

Any output text lines restore space mode, so you don't have to explicitly turn it back on. However, if you explicitly want to put space at the top of the page (to paste in a figure, for example), use .rs (*restore spacing*) before the spacing request. The following sequence can be used to start a new page and space down 2 inches below the top margin:

```
'bp
.rs
'sp 2i
```

This works in all cases, except on the first page.  You must force a break on the first page before you can restore spacing.  An `.fl` request will do the trick:

```
.fl
.rs
.sp 3i
.ce
A Title on a Title Page
.bp
```

The `.fl` request is useful when you want to flush the line buffer and cause a break.

## The First Page

As you might expect from the previous example, the first page is unlike others that follow it.  That is because there is no automatic transition to the first page.  To get around this, the formatter causes a "pseudo-page transition" when it first encounters a break or begins processing text outside a diversion.

For the top of page trap to be executed on the first page, you must set the trap and define the top of page macro before specifying any request that causes a break or initiates processing.  You can test this with the sample macros by putting an explicit `.br` request before the `.NP` macro definition.  After that test, try replacing `.br` with a `.tl` request.  Even though this request does not cause a break, it does initiate processing of text, and so the `.NP` macro is not executed.

## ▪ Page Transitions in ms ▪

Let's take a closer look now at the trap positions we set in the initialization sequence for our ms-like package, together with the definitions of the macros placed at those positions:

```
.de IZ
         .
       .   .
         .
.                      \" Set Page Transition Traps
.wh 0 NP
.wh -\\n(FMu FO
.wh -\\n(FMu/2u BT
.                      \" Define Page Transition Macros
..
.de NP                 \"     New Page Macro
'sp \\n(HMu/2u
.PT
```

```
'sp |\\n(HMu
'ns
..
.de FO              \"      Footer Macro
'bp
..
.de PT              \"      Page Top Title Macro
.tl '\\*(LH'\\*(CH'\\*(RH'
..
.de BT              \"      Bottom Title Macro
.tl '\\*(LF'\\*(CF'\\*(RF'
'sp .5i
..
```

You'll notice a couple of differences from our earlier example. Instead of specifying "hard-coded" values for trap locations, we have set up a top margin value in the register HM (*header margin*) and a bottom margin value in FM (*footer margin*).

Now we have three trap locations and four page transition macros. In the simplified form shown here, you may wonder why so many macros are used for this simple task. We'll look at that later, as we show some of the additional things that are done in these macros. But for the moment, let's focus on what these macros are. Their trap locations are shown in Figure 16-1.

- .NP (*new page*) is invoked by a trap at the top of each page (.wh 0 NP). It spaces down ½ the distance specified in the HM register, calls the PT macro, and then spaces down the full distance specified by the header margin.

- .PT (*page title*) prints out a three-part title consisting of user-definable strings LH, CH, and RH (*left header, center header,* and *right header*).

- .FO (*footer*) is invoked by a trap at the distance from the bottom of the page specified by the FM register (.wh -\\n(FMu FO). This macro causes a break to a new page. Note the use of 'bp rather than .bp so that any partially filled line is not output, but is held till the next page.

- .BT (*bottom title*) is invoked by a trap at ½ the distance from the bottom of the page specified by the FM register (.wh -\\n(FMu/2u BT).

Although this sequence is different than our earlier example, it is about as easy to understand. The main difference, however, is that there are two traps at the bottom of the page. The first (FO) causes a page break, and the second (BT) places the footer. Even though the first trap caused a page break, *the formatter keeps going till it reaches the true bottom of the page specified by the page length.* On its way, it passes the second trap that invokes .BT.

The use of the four page transition macros is slightly inconsistent in ms; .PT is invoked from .NP, but .BT, which could just as well be invoked by .FO, is instead invoked by a trap.

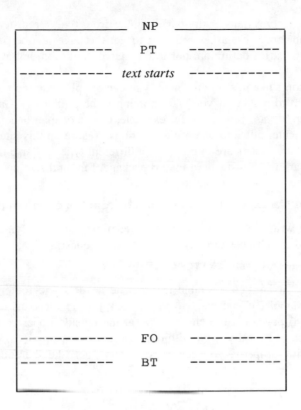

**Fig. 16-1.** Top and Bottom Margins

## Headers and Footers

Most books, and many shorter documents, include headers and footers. In books, headers often include the title of the book on the left-hand page, and the title of the chapter on the right. The footer typically includes the page number, either centered or in the lower outside corner, alternating from left to right. (Although all three elements are usually present, they can be in different positions depending on the book design.)

As previously mentioned, the .tl request was designed specifically for producing the three-part titles used in headers and footers. The ms package uses this request in both the PT and BT macros, filling the three fields with symmetrically named string invocations. If the string is undefined, the field is blank.

The macro package itself may define one or more of the fields. The .IZ macro from ms contains this piece of code:

```
.if "\\*(CH"" .ds CH "- \\\\n(PN -
.if n .ds CF "\\*(DY
```

The ms macros define the center header as the page number set off by hyphens. For nroff only, the center footer is set to the current date. (An nroff-formatted document is assumed to be a draft, but a troff-formatted document is assumed to be final camera-ready copy.)

The ms macros transfer the page number from the % register to one called PN. Note the number of backslashes required to get the page number output at the proper time—not in the string definition, nor in the macro definition, but at the time the title is output.

If you don't like this arrangement, you can simply redefine the strings (including redefining them to nothing if you want nothing to be printed). As a developer of macros built on top of ms, you could, for example, have a chapter heading macro automatically set the chapter title into one of these strings. (More on this later.)

Headers and footers are often set in a different type and size than the body of the book. If you are using a standard macro package, font and size changes can simply be embedded in the header or footer strings:

```
.ds LH "\fIAn Introduction to Text Processing\fP
```

Or, if you are writing your own macros or redefining an underlying package like ms, you can embed the changes directly into the .tl request:

```
.tl '\s-2\\*(LF'\\*(CF'\\*(RF\s0'
```

Another point: it is often desirable to alternate headers and footers on odd and even pages. For example, if you want to put a book title at the outside upper corner of a left-hand (even) page, and the chapter title at the outside upper corner of a right-hand (odd) page, you can't really work within the structure ms provides.

To do this properly, you could use a construct like the following within your .PT macro:

```
.if e .tl '\\*(TI'''
.if o .if \\n%-1 .tl '''\\*(CH'
```

where the string TI holds the title of the book, and CH holds the title of the chapter. If it's an odd page, we also test that it's not the first page. By invoking specific strings, you do lose the generality of the mechanism provided by ms.

## Page Numbers in Three-Part Titles

Inasmuch as the chief application of three-part titles is in producing header and footer lines from within page transition macros, there is a special syntax for including page numbers. A % character anywhere in a title will be replaced with the current page number. This saves the trouble of having to do a proper number register interpolation and makes it easier for unsophisticated users of ms or mm to include page numbers in header and footer strings.

Whenever nroff or troff makes use of a character in a special way, you can be sure there is a back door that allows you to change that character. The .pc (*page character*) request allows you to specify that some other character than % should perform this function:

```
.pc ^        \" Use ^ instead of % to print page # in .tl
```

This does not change the name of the % number register, which also contains the page number.

## Title Length

The other thing you can adjust is the length of the three-part title produced by `.tl`. Usually it is set to the same length as a text line, but this need not be so. Title length is specified independently of line length with the `.lt` (*length [of] title*) request. For example:

```
.lt 6.5i
```

The title length is *not* independent of the page offset, so if you want a title that is longer than the line length, yet centered on the page, you will need to muck with the page offset as well. (Note that this is most likely to occur within a page transition macro.)

```
.po 1i                              \" Page Layout Defaults
.ll 6.5i
     .
     .
     .
.lt 7i
.tl 'Alcuin User's Guide''%'  \" Title will extend 1/2 inch
     .                        \" past right margin
     .
     .
.po -.25i
.lt 7i
.tl 'Alcuin User's Guide''%'  \" Title will extend 1/4 inch
.po +.25i                     \" on either side
```

An `.lt` request without an argument will restore the previous title length.

## ▪ Some Extensions to the Basic Package ▪

Thus far, we've looked at what it will take to implement a small ms-like macro package. Now let's look at some extensions to the basic structure of the package that will make it more flexible. These extensions could be added to the minimal package shown earlier in this chapter, or they could be added to a full ms package, as we have done at our own site.

## Changing Page Size

As mentioned earlier, the initialization sequence usually sets up default values for line length, page offset, and the placement of the top and bottom traps. In the standard ms package, all of these values are set up to produce an $8^1/2$-by-11 inch page.

This is fine for nroff, but with troff, one might well want to produce a different page size. For example, many books are typeset for a $5^1/2$-by-$8^1/2$ inch page.

The most obvious move is to change the page length:

```
.pl 8.5i
```

and then reset the line length, title length, and page offset using the standard registers `ms` provides.

This may not work if your output device uses continuous-roll paper, such as a typesetter. However, in `nroff`, or when using `troff` with a sheet-fed laser printer, this may split your formatted output pages across physical sheets of paper. (Some devices translate a `.bp` into a page eject code or *formfeed*; others simply add blank lines to push text onto the next physical page. For this reason, it is perhaps preferable to think of `.pl` as the *paper length* rather than the *page length*.)

In addition, when you are printing a small page, it is nice to print cut marks to show the location of the page boundaries. If you change the page length, any cut marks you place will be off the page that `troff` knows about, and will not be printed.

For both of these reasons, we took a different approach. We modified the `ms` `.IZ` macro so that changing the header and footer margins would effectively change the page size, instead of just the margins. (In standard `ms`, you can change the size of the top and bottom margins, but this doesn't change the page size, because the placement of the footers is fixed after the initialization macro has been called. The trap position for `FO` is reset at the top of every page, thus taking into account changes in the value of the `FM` register. But the trap position for `BT` is never touched after `.IZ` has been executed.)

In our package, we decided to set up some standard page sizes as part of `.IZ`. In our business, writing and producing technical manuals, we often print books in both sizes. Early drafts are printed on the laser printer in 8½ by 11 format; later drafts and final camera-ready copy are produced in 5½ by 8½ format. We also produce quick-reference documents in a narrow 6-panel card or pamphlet. The user selects the size by specifying a command-line switch. This approach has the advantage of letting the user change all of the parameters associated with a given size with one easy command.

The `.IZ` macro in our mini-`ms` package now looks like this:

```
.de IZ                       \"  Initialization macro
.                            \"  Initialize Number Registers
.                            \"  Quick Reference Card size
.if \\nS=2 \{\
.        nr pW 3.5i          \"  Page Width
.        nr tH 1.25i         \"  Trim Height adjustment
.        nr LL 2.8i          \"  Line Length
.        nr LT 2.8i\}        \"  Title Length
.                            \"  5 1/2 by 8 1/2 size
.ie \\nS=1 \{\
.        nr pW 5.5i          \"  Page Width
.        nr tH 1.25i         \"  Trim Height adjustment
.        nr LL 4.25i         \"  Line Length
.        nr LT 4.25i\}       \"  Title Length
.                            \"  8 1/2 by 11 size
.el \{\
.        nr pW 0             \"  Page Width
```

```
.       nr tH 0                \" Trim Height adjustment
.       nr LL 6i               \" Line Length
.       nr LT 6i\}             \" Title Length
.                       \"Values independent of page size
.nr FM 1i                      \" Footer Margin
.nr HM 1i                      \" Header Margin
.nr PO 1i                      \" Page Offset
.nr PS 10                      \" Point Size
.nr VS 12                      \" Vertical Spacing
.nr FL \\n(LLu*11/12           \" Footnote Length
.nr PI 5n                      \" Paragraph Indent
.nr QI 5n                      \" Quoted Paragraph Indent
.nr PD 0.3v                    \" Interparagraph Spacing
.                  \" Set Page Dimensions through requests
.ps \\n(PS
.vs \\n(VS
.po \\n(POu
.ll \\n(LLu
.lt \\n(LTu
.ft 1
.hy 14                         \" Specify hyphenation rules
.                              \" Set Page Transition Traps
.wh 0 NP                       \" Top of page
.wh -(\\n(FMu+\\n(tHu) FO       \" Footer
.wh -((\\n(FMu/2u)+\\n(tHu) BT \" Bottom titles
.if \\nS .wh -\\n(tHu CM        \" Position of bottom mark
..
```

The `.NP` macro has been modified as follows:

```
.de NP                         \" New Page Macro
'sp \\n(tHu                    \" Space down by trim height
.ie \\nS \{\
.       CM                     \" If small format, print cut mark
'       sp \\n(HMu/2u-1v\}\"   Correct baseline spacing
.el 'sp \\n(HMu/2u             \" Space down by half HM
.PT
'sp |\\n(HMu+\\n(tHu           \" Space to HM plus adjustment
'ns
..
```

By simply setting the `S` (*size*) register from the command line, the user can choose from one of three different sizes. For example:

$ **ditroff -Tps -rS1** *textfile* **| devps | lp**

will choose the 5$\frac{1}{2}$-by-8$\frac{1}{2}$ page size.

What we've done here is to assume that the paper size is still $8\frac{1}{2}$ by 11. We've defined a fudge factor, which we've called the *trim height adjustment*, and stored it in a register called tH. If the user has set the size register from the command line, we use this adjustment factor to:

- shift the location of the footer trap:

```
.wh -(\\n(FMu+\\n(tHu) FO
```

- shift the location of the bottom title trap:

```
.wh -((\\n(FMu/2u)+\\n(tHu) BT
```

- place a new trap to print cut marks at the true bottom of the page:

```
.if \\nS .wh -\\n(tHu CM
```

- space down at the start of the .NP macro:

```
'sp \\n(tHu
.ie \\nS \{\
.        CM
'        sp \\n(HMu/2u-1v\}
.el 'sp \\n(HMu/2u
.PT
'sp |\\n(HMu+\\n(tHu
```

Note that in .NP we need to adjust for the extra line spacing that occurs as a result of printing the cut marks. Otherwise, the .PT macro would be invoked one line lower on a page with cut marks than on one without.

## Cut Marks

We've mentioned that if you are producing typeset or laser-printed copy on less than an $8\frac{1}{2}$ by 11 page, it is usually desirable to place marks showing the actual page boundary. The paper is then cut on these marks in preparation for pasteup on camera-ready boards.

As you've seen in the preceding discussion, we print the cut mark at the top of the page from the .NP macro, after spacing down by the desired trim height. The cut marks at the bottom of the page are printed by calling the cut mark macro with a trap placed at the trim height from the bottom of the page.

As you'll notice, the execution of the cut mark macro is conditioned on the presence of the S register, which indicates that the user has requested a small page.

Here's a simple version of the actual cut mark macro:

```
.de CM                      \" Cut Mark macro
'po -(\\n(pWu-\\n(LLu/2u)    \" Center cut mark around text
.lt \\n(pWu                  \" Set title length for cut mark
'tl '+''+'                   \" Print cut mark
```

```
.lt \\n(LTu              \" Reset title length
'po +(\\n(pWu-\\n(LLu/2u) \" Reset page offset
..
```

As with all activity that takes place during the page transition, it is very important that nothing in the cut mark macro causes a break. For this reason, all break causing requests are started with the no-break control character (`'`), and the cut marks themselves are printed with `.tl`, which doesn't cause a break. (The other way to avoid breaks is to do all of your page transition work in a different environment, but doing this uses up one of the environments, which might be better used for another purpose.)

We've specified the width of the page in the `pW` register. To center the cut marks around the text, we adjust the page offset by the difference between the page width and half the line length. Then we set the title length to the page width, and actually print the cut marks with `.tl`. Then, of course, we reset the original page offset and title length.

In the implementation shown, we use simple plus signs to create the cut marks. This creates a slight inaccuracy, because the page width will be from end to end of the plus signs, and the height from baseline to baseline, rather from the center of the plus as we'd like.

There are two ways that we could deal with this. One is to fudge the height and the width to account for the character widths. The other is to use a specially drawn mark that will put the actual cut lines at the edge rather than the center of the figure.

A very simple way to do this is to use the box rule, the root-en, and the underrule. Because the cut marks are no longer symmetrical, though, we'll need to give the cut mark macro an argument to specify whether we're at the top or the bottom of the page:

```
.de CM                   \" Cut Mark macro
'po -(\\n(pWu-\\n(LLu/2u) \" Center cut mark around text
'lt \\n(pWu               \" Set title length for cut mark
.ie "\\$1"T" 'tl '\(br\(rn''\(rn\(br'  \" Print cut mark
.el 'tl '\(br\(ul''\(ul\(br'
'lt \\n(LTu               \" Reset title length
'po +(\\n(pWu-\\n(LLu/2u) \" Reset page offset
..
```

When we invoke `.CM` from within `.NP`, we'll just have to add the argument `T` to specify we're at the top.

The cut marks will look like this:

## ▪ Other Exercises in Page Transition ▪

We've looked at the basic mechanism for page transition, and shown one way to extend that mechanism to allow the user to select different page sizes. We have not exhausted the topic of page transition, however. Before we begin to discuss the development of macros that prescribe document formats, rather than basic page formatting, we will briefly consider these topics:

- Footnotes
- Multicolumn processing
- Page top resets
- Handling widows and orphans

### Footnotes

Footnotes make page transition an even more complex exercise. Anyone who has typed footnotes on a typewriter knows the problem. Because the presence of a footnote shortens the space available on the page for regular text, you need to know the size of the footnote before you know if its reference will fit on the bottom of the current page, or will be pushed to the top of the next. There is always the possibility of a classic Catch-22: a footnote whose reference falls at the bottom of the page only if the footnote itself isn't printed there.

Let's look first at a very simple footnote mechanism—one that has a reasonable chance of failure in the face of heavy demand, but nonetheless illustrates the basic mechanism at work.

The first thing we need to know is the position of the page bottom trap for a normal page—one without any footnotes. For example, in ms, we know that its location is $-\backslash\backslash$n(FMu. (Now ms has a perfectly good footnote mechanism, but for purposes of argument, we're going to pretend we need to add one.)

All we really need to do, on the simplest level, is to save footnotes in a diversion, measure them, then move the footer trap back up the page by a distance equal to the size of the diversion.

In the new page macro, we initialize (reset to 0) a counter (fC) that will tell us if there are any footnotes on the page and how many. (We want to handle the first footnote differently than others on that page.) We also initialize a bottom position for printing footnotes (Fb) and initialize it with the value of the standard footer margin. (This will be the starting point that will be decremented as footnotes are encountered.) Last, we provide a reset that restores the page footer trap at the standard footer margin if it has been changed because of footnotes on a previous page.

```
.                         \" Add to .NP
.nr fC 0 1                \" Initialize footnote counter
.nr Fb 0-\\n(FMu          \" Initialize footnote position
.ch FO -\\n(FMu           \" Reset normal footer location
```

Now, a pair of footnote macros are required to open and close a diversion:

```
.de FS              \" Footnote Start
.nr fC 1            \" Set flag that there are footnotes
.ev 1               \" Use environment 1
.da FN              \" Divert text of footnote
.if \\n(fC=1 \{\    \" If first footnote
\l'1i'              \" Print 1 inch line before it
.br\}
..
.de FE              \" Footnote End
.br
.di                 \" End diversion
.ev                 \" Restore environment
.nr Fb -\\n(dn      \" Decrement footnote position by
.                   \" size of diversion;
.                   \" note that Fb is already negative.
.                   \" Reset footer trap
.ie (\\n(nl+1v)>(\\n(.p+\\n(Fb) .ch FO \\n(nlu+1vu
.el .ch FO -\\n(Fb
..
```

The footnotes are processed in a separate environment. This environment needs to be initialized, perhaps as part of the `.IZ` macro, or as part of the `.FS` macro the very first time it is called. The latter method makes it easier for users to change settings for this environment. It is recommended that you preserve a separate environment (either 1 or 2) for footnote processing. Here is a sample initialization sequence:

```
.ev 1       \" Initialize first environment for footnotes
.ps 8
.vs 10
.ll \\n(FLu \" FL was initialized to 11/12 of LL
.ev
```

The `.FS` macro opens a diversion (`.da FN`) into which we append the text of the footnote. Before the first footnote on a page, the `.FS` macro adds a one-inch reference line to mark the beginning of footnotes. After we have closed the diversion in the `.FE` macro, we obtain the size of it from the read-write register `.dn`. This amount is used to increase `Fb` (two negatives amounts are added together) and change the location of the footer trap further up the page.

Before changing that trap, the footnote end macro has to find out if the new footer trap will be placed above or below the current location. If the new trap location is below where we are, all is well; the page trap is moved up to that location. However, if the current footnote places the location above the current position, there's going to be trouble. In this case, we need to execute the footer macro immediately.

The `troff` formatter keeps the current page position in the `nl` register, and the page length in the register `.p`. As a result, we can set the trap position based on a conditional:

```
.ie (\\n(nl+1v)>(\\n(.p+\\n(Fb)  .ch FO \\n(nlu+1vu
.el .ch FO -\\n(Fb
```

If the footnote won't fit, this code puts the trap one line below the current position; otherwise, the footer trap location is moved up the page.

Now we'll have to redefine the footer macro to print the diverted footnotes, if there are any:

```
.de FO                  \" Redefine FO
.if \\n(fC\{\
.ev1                    \" Invoke first environment
.nf                     \" Good practice when outputting diversions
.FN                     \" Print diversion
.rm FN                  \" Remove printed diversion
.ev\}
'bp                     \" Now break page
..
```

Because the footnote macros are complicated, it might be a useful aside to look at the process of debugging these macros. We used several .tm requests to report (to standard error) on the sequence of events during a formatting run of a file that included footnotes. What we wanted to know was the location of the footer trap and when it was sprung. Inside the .FE macro, we inserted .tm requests to show which of the conditional .ch requests were executed.

```
.ie (\\n(nl+1v)>(\\n(.p+\\n(Fb) \{\
.tm !!!!!! FE: Change trap to current location (\\n(nl+1v)
.ch FO \\n(nlu+1vu \}
.el \{\
.tm !!!!!! FE: Move trap up the page (\\n(Fbu)
.ch FO -\\n(Fb \}
```

Then, inside the .FO macro, we inserted messages to locate two positions on the page: where the footer macro is invoked by the trap and where the footnotes have been output.

```
.de FO
.tm !!!! FO: position is \\n(nl (\\n(.p+\\n(Fb) BEFORE
.
.
.
.tm !!!! FO: position is \\n(nl AFTER footnotes
'bp
..
```

To see these terminal messages without the formatted text, we invoke nroff and redirect output to /dev/null. (tmacpack is a small macro package used for testing these macros.)

```
$ nroff tmacpack textfile > /dev/null
!!!!!! FE: Move trap up the page (-360u)
!!!!!! FE: Move trap up the page (-440u)
!!!!!! FE: Move trap up the page (-520u)
!!!!!! FE: Move trap up the page (-680u)
!!!! FO: position is 1980 (2640+-680) BEFORE
!!!! FO: position is 2420 AFTER footnotes
!!!!!! FE: Move trap up the page (-360u)
!!!!!! FE: Move trap up the page (-440u)
!!!!!! FE: Move trap up the page (-520u)
!!!!!! FE: Change trap to current location (2100+1v)
!!!! FO: position is 2140 (2640+-640) BEFORE
!!!! FO: position is 2580 AFTER footnotes
!!!!!! FE: Move trap up the page (-320u)
!!!! FO: position is 2320 (2640+-320) BEFORE
!!!! FO: position is 2400 AFTER footnotes
```

Part of the reason for making this aside is the difficulty of writing effective footnote macros. It requires a fair amount of testing to make sure they work in all cases. When we spring the footer trap for the second time, the messages alert us to a problem—the Catch-22 we mentioned earlier. The formatter encountered a footnote on the last input line. The only way to fit both the footnote reference and the footnote on the same page was to ignore the footer margin and let the footnote run into it.

Standard ms provides a better way of handling this overflow. In addition, the *Nroff/Troff User's Manual* describes a similar mechanism. Our simplified version, adequate only for demonstration of this mechanism, will borrow from both of these sources. (It might be said that a "working" version requires several empirically discovered fudge factors or, as Joseph Ossanna called them, "uncertainty corrections".)

The problem is how to split the footnote overflow if it extends beyond where we want the bottom of the page to be. The solution is to put *two* trap-invoked macros at the original (standard) page bottom location. The trap mechanism in troff allows only one macro to be executed by a trap at a given location. If you write:

```
.wh -\\n(FMu M1    \"Place first macro
.wh -\\n(FMu M2    \"Overwrite first macro at this location
```

all you will succeed in doing is wiping out the first placement with the second.

However, you can *move* a trap location to an occupied position. The second trap "hides" the first and renders it ineffective, but the first is still in place and is restored if the second subsequently moves off the spot.

So here's what we do in our trap initialization:

```
.wh 16i FO          \" Put regular footer out of the way
.                   \" (way off the page)
.wh -\\n(FMu FX     \" Place footnote overflow macro
.ch FO -\\n(FMu     \" Hide footnote overflow macro
```

The .FX (*footnote overflow*) macro will be invoked only if the FO trap is moved (as it will be whenever there are footnotes on the page). In .FX, all we do is start another diversion, so that excess footnote text that would overflow at the bottom of the page is saved for the next:

```
.de FX                 \" Footnote overflow
.if \\n(fC .di eF      \" Divert extra footnote
..
```

(We'll explain the reason for the test in a moment.)

Odd as it may seem, this diversion can be terminated from the footer macro `.FO`, even though that macro is invoked before the footnote overflow macro! Because the `.FN` diversion inside the `.FO` macros springs the footnote overflow trap and starts the overflow diversion, we can close that diversion by a request in `.FO` following the diversion.

The code in `.FO` now looks like this:

```
.nr dn 0               \" Reset diversion size register
.if \\n(fC \{\         \" If there are footnotes
.ev 1
.nf
.FN
.rm FN
.if'\\n(.z'eF'.di      \" End diversion opened by FX
.ev
.nr fC 0 \}            \" Done with footnotes
'bp
```

There are several things here that need further explanation. The number register `.z` always contains the name of the last completed diversion. (Don't ask us how they manage to put a string into a number register!) If our overflow diversion was this last completed diversion, we terminate it:

```
.if '\\n(.z'eF'.di
```

Then, we must take care of another eventuality. If we get this far *without* triggering the overflow trap—that is, if `.FN` did fit on the page—we want to disable the overflow macro, which we can do by zeroing our count register `fC`.

Now on the next page we have to handle any footnote overflow. We write a new macro that invokes `.FS` and `.FE` to output the overflow diversion (`.eF`) into the normal footnote diversion (`.FN`).

```
.de Fx         \" Process extra footnote
.FS
.nf            \" No-fill mode
.eF            \" Overflow diversion
.fi
.FE
.rm eF
..
```

In the new page macro, we add a test to check if the last diversion amounted to anything, and if it did, we invoke the `.Fx` macro.

```
      .                          \" added to .NP
    .if \\n(dn .Fx
      .
```

To test this new feature, we might add messages inside `.FX`, the macro invoked by a hidden trap to open a diversion that collects any footnote overflow, and inside `.Fx`, the macro that redirects the overflow back into the normal footnote diversion. You should be able to accomplish this part on your own, as well as to venture into areas that we did not cover (such as automatic numbering or marking of footnotes.) Before implementing a footnote mechanism, we urge you to study the mechanisms in one of the existing macro packages. However, following the chain of events from when a footnote is encountered to when it is output in the footer macro—on the current page or on the next—may seem like a `troff` exercise equivalent to what Alfred Hitchcock called a MacGuffin: a hopelessly complicated plot not meant to be figured out but that supplies a reason for many entertaining scenes.

### Multicolumn Processing

While we're still on the subject of page transition, we should look briefly at how multi-column processing works.

Multiple columns are generally produced by using the mark and return mechanism—`.mk` and `.rt`—and by manipulating the line length and page offset for each successive column. The basic trick is to have the page bottom macro check if multiple columns are in effect, and if so, whether or not the current column is the last one.

A simple macro to initiate two-column processing might look like this*:

```
.de 2C
.mk                              \" Mark top position
.nr CL 0 1                       \" Initialize column count flag
.ie \\$1 .nr CW \\$1             \" Test arg 1 for Column Width
.el   nr CW 2.75i                \" or set default CW
.ie \\$2 .nr GW \\$2             \" Test arg 2 for Gutter Width
.el .nr GW .5i                   \" or set default GW
.                                \" Save current one-column settings
.nr pO \\n(.o                    \" Save current page offset
.nr lL \\n(LLu                   \" Save original line length
.nr LL \\n(CWu                   \" Set line length to Column Width
.ll \\n(LLu                      \" Set line length to Column Width
..
```

---

*Despite similar macro and number register names, this is *not* the two-column macro used in `ms`. The `ms` package provides a more general multiple column macro, `.MC`, of which `.2C` is a specialized call.

(We must save the default line length in a new register and redefine LL, or else a paragraph macro, or any other macro that calls .RT, will interfere with two-column processing.)

The page footer needs to include the following requests:

```
.de FO                        \" New footer macro
.ie \\n+(CL<2\{\              \" If incremental column count < 2
'po+(\\n(CWu+\\n(GWu)         \" then increase page offset
'rt                           \" Return to mark
'ns \}                        \" Enter no-space mode
.el \{\                       \" Otherwise
'po \\n(pOu                   \" Restore original page offset
'bp \}                        \" Start a new page
..
```

Because two-column processing is likely to continue beyond a single page, we need to modify the page top macro to mark the top of the page and initialize (set to zero) the column count register. The two requests at the bottom of the definition have been added:

```
.de NP                        \"New Page Macro
'sp \\n(HMu/2u
.PT
'sp |\\n(HMu
'ns
'mk                           \"Mark top of page
.if \\n(CL .nr CL 0 1         \"Reset autoincrementing column count
..
```

After the CL register has been created by .2C, it can also be used as a flag that two-column processing is in effect. The page top resets it to 0 to start the first column on a new page.

The macro to return to single-column processing looks like this:

```
.de 1C
.rr CL           \" Remove column count register
.po \\n(POu      \" Reset original page offset
.nr LL \\n(lLu
.ll \\n(LLu      \" and line length
.bp              \" Start a new page
..
```

The column count register is removed, and the original page offset and line length are restored. Unfortunately, using this mechanism, you cannot return to single-column mode on the same page, without resorting to extensive use of diversions. If the first column has already gone to the bottom of the page, there is no way for a prematurely terminated second column to ''go back'' and fit the text into two even-sized columns on the same page.

## Page Top Resets

We've already discussed the use of a reset macro from within paragraphs to deal with common errors. Page transitions are also a convenient place to put some different kinds of resets. Like paragraphs, you can rely on their regular occurrence and can therefore trap certain conditions.

In particular, you can use them when you want an effect to take place for only one page and then stop. For example, in our business, we are often required to produce not just complete manuals, but replacement pages to be inserted into an existing manual. Sometimes the update page will be exactly the same size as the original, but often it is longer, and requires additional space.

To avoid changing the numbering on subsequent pages, additional full or partial pages are inserted with a special numbering scheme. For example, if a page is numbered 3-4 (section 3, page 4), and changes to that page run on to an additional page, the new page will be numbered 3-4a.

In this situation, we need to temporarily change the way page numbers are handled, then change back when the page is done. We've defined a macro called .UN, which looks like this:

```
.de UN                  \" Update page numbering macro
.nr Un 1                \" Set flag to test on page break
.nr % -1
.ie !"\\$1"" .as NN \\$1
.el .as NN a
..
```

Our extended ms macro package normally puts the section number (sE) and the page number (PN), separated by a hyphen, into the string NN. In this macro, we simply append a letter to that string. By default we add the letter *a*, but we give the user the option to specify another letter as an argument to the macro, so pages can be numbered 3-4, 3-4a, 3-4b, and so on. To use the macro, the user simply enters it anywhere on the update page. Voilá! The page number now has an *a* on the end.

Notice that the original page number register (%) was first decremented, so that this new page will have the same number as the previous one. More to the point of this discussion, notice that the macro sets the Un number register to 1 as a flag that update numbering is in effect.

This flag is tested in the page top macro for the next page, and if it is set, the original page numbering scheme is restored as follows:

```
.if \\n(Un=1 \{\
.       ds NN \\\\n(sE-\\\\n(PN
.       nr Un 0\}
```

(Note that four backslashes are required in the number register interpolations used in defining NN because the string definition will be interpreted twice, once when the macro is defined, and once when it is executed.)

Keep this trick in mind because there are many cases in which you can use the page bottom or page top macro to reset conditions that you don't want to carry across more than one page. We'll see another in just a moment.

## Handling Widows and Orphans

Widows and orphans are the bane of any markup language—the one real advantage of current *wysiwyg* systems. A widow is a single or partial line from the end of a paragraph left over at the start of the next page. An orphan is a single line from the start of a paragraph left alone at the bottom of a page. Both of these are considered poor page layout.

As we've discussed, a macro package can take care of orphans simply by including an .ne request in the paragraph macro. Widows are much harder to take care of, because you don't know where the end of the paragraph will fall until you reach it.

In nroff and troff, the only way you can handle this problem is to process each paragraph in a diversion, find out how long it was, then go back and break it up if necessary. This greatly increases processing time, and is probably not worth the effort.

You could limit the extra work by testing the position on the page and only diverting paragraphs that occur within range of the page bottom. However, even so, this is a difficult problem you may not want to attempt.

It may be satisfactory to give users an increased capability for dealing with widows when they do occur. Normally, the solution is to print out the document, find any offending widow lines, then go back and manually break the pages a line earlier. However, sometimes it is inconvenient to break the paragraph earlier—it would be better to add the line to the bottom of the current page.

In standard ms, the location of the footer trap is reset to $-\backslash n$ (FMu in the .NP macro at the top of every page. The user can get extra length on a page just by changing the value of FM on the preceding page.

We could also write a macro that would let the user make the change on the offending page. For example, in ms:

```
.de EL                      \" Extra Line macro
.nr eL 1                    \" Set flag
.ch FO -(\\n(FMu-1v)u       \" Put trap one line lower
..
```

All the user has to do is to introduce this macro anywhere on the page to be affected. It is your job as macro developer to reset the normal page length—and the most likely place is in the page top macro for the next page:

```
.if \\n(eL=1 \{\
.ch FO -\\n(FMu              \" Reset to normal location for ms
.nr eL 0\}                   \" Clear flag
```

# An Extended ms Macro Package

In the previous chapter, we've looked at some of the essential elements of a macro package—the innards that make it tick. However, few people will write a macro package just because they think they can do a better job at the basics than ms or mm. More often, users who need specific formatting effects will build a macro set to achieve those effects.

The macros used to produce this book are a good example of a custom macro package. They were developed to create a distinctive and consistent style for a series of books on UNIX by different authors. Although this macro package must of course do all of the basics we've talked about, many of its macros provide solutions to more specific problems. For example, there are macros for showing side-by-side before and after screens for vi and macros for inserting italicized commentary in examples.

To illustrate more concretely the issues that force you to create or significantly extend a macro package, this chapter will look at a set of extended ms macros for typesetting technical manuals. Extensions built into this package fall into two major categories:

- Extensions that make it easier to control the appearance of a document, particularly the page size (described in the last chapter) and the style of section headings, tables, and figures.

- Extensions that address needs of books, manuals, and other documents larger than the technical papers that ms and mm were originally designed for. These extensions include improved methods for handling tables of contents and indexes.

One of the chief weaknesses of the ms and mm packages is that they were designed for smaller documents. For example, ms does not provide table of contents generation, and the approach used by mm is suitable only for short documents. Neither package supports automatic index generation. In this chapter and the next, we will also look at ways to redress these problems.

## ▪ Creating a Custom Macro Package ▪

In this chapter, we will present an extended macro package designed for technical documentation. Based on the ms macro package, these extensions were originally developed by Steve Talbott of Masscomp; they have been extended and altered during several years of use in our technical writing and consulting business. Because we needed to produce technical manuals for a number of different clients, we needed a macro package that allowed us the flexibility to achieve a variety of document formats.

An important step in implementing this package was to establish the relation of new and redefined macros to the original ms package. We wanted to read in the standard tmac.s package, and then simply overwrite or remove unwanted macros. Then we organized our extensions into three groups: redefinitions of standard ms macros, common macros we added to provide specific features or capabilities for all documents, and format macros that were most often used to control the appearance or structure of a document.

The format macros can be modified for the specifications of a unique document format. Each format design has its own file, and the user only needs to specify which of these formats are to be read in during the formatting run.

Following is a summary of the steps we followed to implement our mS macro package. While describing this implementation, we don't pretend that it is unique or right for all uses; we do hope that it suggests ways to set up your own custom package.

1.  Create a new directory to store the macro files.

2.  Make a working copy of tmac.s and any subordinate files it reads in, moving them to a new directory.

3.  Create the tmac.Sredefs file to contain definitions of standard ms macros that we've redefined, such as .IZ.

4.  Create the tmac.Scommon file to contain utility and feature macros available in all formats. The list macros described in this chapter are kept here.

5.  Create separate files containing definitions for unique document formats.

6.  Set up tmac.S to control which files are read in and to handle certain parameters that might be set from the command line.

7.  Put tmac.S in /usr/lib/tmac, either by placing the file in that directory or by creating a tmac.S file that sources the tmac.S file in the macro directory.

The master file of this package is tmac.S, although it does not contain any macro definitions. It allows users to set some parameters from the command line, and then it reads in the standard ms macro package and the two files that contain redefinitions and common macros. Last, it checks the value of a number register (v) to determine which group of format macros are to be read in.

Here's what our `tmac.S` file looks like:

```
.\"  tmac.S - the main format macro package
.
.so /work/macros/tmac.s          \" Read in standard ms
.so /work/macros/tmac.Sredefs    \" Redefinitions of macros
.so /work/macros/tmac.Scommon    \" Common utility macros
.                    \" Check register v for version
.                    \"  and read in special format macros
.ie \nv \{\
.if \nv=9 .so /work/macros/tmac.Stest
.if \nv=8 .so /work/macros/tmac.Squickref
.if \nv=7 .so /work/macros/tmac.Slarge
.if \nv=6 .so /work/macros/overheads
.if \nv=5 .so /work/macros/tmac.Straining
.if \nv=4 .so /work/macros/tmac.Sprime
.if \nv=3 .so /work/macros/tmac.Scogx
.if \nv=2 .so /work/macros/tmac.Smanuals
.if \nv=1 .so /work/macros/tmac.Snutshell\}
.el .so /work/macros/tmac.Sstandard
```

The −r option to `nroff` and `troff` is used to select a particular version of the format macros. For instance, the first set of format macros is designed for producing our Nutshell Handbooks. To format a document using the macros defined in `tmac.Snutshell`, a user would enter:

**$ ditroff −Tps −mS −rv1 ch01 | devps | lp**

One of the files, `tmac.Stest`, is available for use during the development and testing of new versions of the macros. We'll look at some of the different formats later in this chapter.

A few other details about this implementation may help you customize a package. Both ms and mm include a number of Bell-specific macros that are not very useful for users outside of AT&T. For example, it is unlikely that you will require the various styles of technical memoranda used internally at Bell Labs. Unused macro definitions need not get in your way, but they do use up possible names and number registers that may conflict with what you want to do. The `.rn` macro allows you to rename a macro; `.rm` will remove the definition of a macro.

You may want to remove selected macros. For example, you might want to start the modifications to a macro package built on ms with the following request:

```
.rm TM IM MF MR EG OK RP TR S2 S3 SG IE [] ][ [. .] [o  \
    [c [5 [4 [3 [2 [1 [0 [< ]< [> ]> [- ]-
```

(Note the use of the backslash to make this apparent two-line request into a single long line.)

There is a slight performance loss in reading in a large macro package, and then removing a number of the macros. For efficiency, you'd be better off removing the undesirable macros from your copy of the ms source file.

Reading in `tmac.Sredefs` after `tmac.s` overwrites some of the standard `ms` macros with our own definitions. The standard versions are thus not available. If you want to retain a standard macro definition, you can make it available under a different name. Use the `.rn` request to rename the standard macro before overwriting its definition.

As discussed in the previous chapter, we redefined the `.IZ` macro to allow the setting of various page sizes. Because the standard `.IZ` macro is invoked from `tmac.s` at the start of the formatting run, we can't simply overwrite its definition. We must either delete the standard `.IZ` macro definition or comment out its invocation. Then the new `.IZ` macro in `tmac.Sredefs` will be executed.

As you develop your own set of extensions, you will undoubtedly consider additional modifications. Appendix F lists the set of extended macros that we use. You may not need many of the specialized macros provided in this package. But it wil! show you how to build on an existing package and how easy it is to modify the appearance of a document.

## ▪ Structured Technical Documents ▪

The `ms` and `mm` packages provide a number of macros to produce title pages, abstracts, and so on for technical memoranda. Subsections can be numbered or unnumbered.

Anyone who has used the *UNIX Programmers' Manual* is familiar with the output of these packages. The technical papers collected in that volume bear superficial resemblance to the chapters of a book. However, they lack continuity—section, figure, and table numbers, where present, are relative only to the current section, not to the entire volume.

A macro package designed for producing technical books or manuals may need at least some modification to produce section headings. Chapter and section headings should make the structure of a document visible. In a nontechnical book, chapters are often the only major structural element. They divide the book into major topics, and give readers stopping points to digest what they have read.

Chapters are usually distinguished from a formatting point of view by a page break and some kind of nonstandard typesetting. For example, a chapter number and title may be set in large type, and the text may begin lower on the page.

In technical books and manuals, which are often not read straight through as much as they are used for reference, frequent section headings within a chapter give the reader guideposts. There are often several levels of heading—more or less depending on whether the book is intended primarily for reading or for reference. This book uses three levels of headings within a chapter, one for major changes in topic, the others for less significant changes.

Section headings can be distinguished merely by type font and size changes, as in this book, or by section numbering as well. Properly used, section numbers can be very helpful in a technical manual. They allow detailed cross references to different parts of the book without using page numbers. Referencing by page numbers can result in errors because page numbers are not fixed until the book is done.

Detailed breakdown of a chapter into subsections can also help the writer of a technical manual. Because a manual (unlike an essay or other free-form work of non-fiction) has definite material that must be covered, it can be written successfully from an outline. It is often possible to write technical material by entering the outline in the form of section and subsection headings and then filling in the details.

In this approach, numbered sections also have a place because they make the outline structure of the document more visible. In reviewing technical manuals, we can often identify many weaknesses simply by looking at the table of contents. Sections in a technical manual should be hierarchical, and the table of contents should look effective *as an outline*. For example, a chapter in our hypothetical *Alcuin User's Guide* might look like this:

```
Chapter Two:  Getting Started with Alcuin

2.1      Objectives of this Session

2.2      Starting Up the System
2.2.1      Power-up Procedure
2.2.2      Software Initialization

2.3      Creating Simple Glyphs
2.3.1      Opening Font Files
2.3.2      Using the Bit Pad
2.3.2.1      The Cell Coordinate System
2.3.2.2      Pointing and Clicking
               .
               .
               .
```

How much easier it is to see the structure than in a case where the proper hierarchical arrangement of topics has not been observed. How often have you seen a ''flat'' table of contents like this:

```
Chapter Two:  Using Alcuin

2.0      Starting Up the System
2.1      Power-up Procedure
2.2      Software Initialization
2.3      Creating Simple Glyphs
2.4      Opening Font Files
2.5      Using the Bit Pad
2.6      The Cell Coordinate System
2.7      Pointing and Clicking
               .
               .
               .
```

Even when numbered section headings are not appropriate, they can be a useful tool for a writer during the draft stage, because they indicate where the organization has not been properly thought through. For example, we often see manuals that start with a general topic and then describe details, without a transitional overview.

A macro package should allow the writer to switch between numbered and unnumbered headings easily. Both mm and ms do provide this capability, and we want to include it in our macros. However, we also want to include more flexibility than either of these packages to define the format of headings.

Because headings are the signposts to the book's structure, changing their appearance can make a big difference in how the book is read. Different levels of headings need to stand out from the text to a greater or lesser degree, so that readers can easily scan the text and find the topic that they want.

The mechanisms for emphasis (in troff) are font and size changes, and the amount of space before and after a heading. Underlining and capitalization can also be used (especially in nroff but also in troff) for alternate or additional emphasis.

In our package, we include five levels of heading: a chapter-level heading and four levels of numbered or unnumbered subsection headings.

As described in the previous section, our custom macro package incorporates several different versions of the basic macros required to produce technical documents. In each version, the name of the heading macro is the same, but its definition is modified slightly to produce a different appearance. These different versions help us conform to the document styles used by our clients. Whenever we have a client who needs a new format, we customize the macro definitions, rather than add new macros.

The beauty of this approach is that the input macros the user needs to enter in a document are identical, or nearly so. Thus, we don't increase the number of new macros that our users must learn, and it eliminates the recoding of existing documents to achieve a new format.

This approach is also useful when you support different types of output devices. Originally, our designs were developed for the HP LaserJet printer, which supports a limited set of fonts and sizes. When we purchased an Apple LaserWriter and Linotronic L100 typesetter, our formatting options increased, making available multiple fonts and variable point sizes. In an environment supporting multiple types of printers, you might want to adapt formats for specific printers.

### The Chapter Heading

The chapter heading is in a class by itself, because it requires more emphasis than subsection headings, and because the macro that produces it may need to initialize or reset certain registers used within the chapter (such as section, figure, or table numbers).

In an arbitrary reversal of terminology, we call our chapter macro .Se (*section*). It could just as well be called .CH for chapter, but we use .Ch for a subsection heading (as we'll see in a moment) and want to avoid confusion. In addition, this macro can be used for appendices as well as chapters, so the more general name seems appropriate.

The chapter heading has three major parts:

- chapter-specific register initialization, including registers for section numbering, table and figure numbering, and page numbering

- appearance of the actual chapter break

- table of contents processing

Because this is a long macro definition, let's look at it in sections.

```
.de Se              \" section; $1 = number; $2 = name;
.                   \" $3 = type (Chapter, Appendix, etc)
.                   \"
.                   \" 1. Number Register Initialization
.                   \"
.ie !"\\$1"" \{.             \" Test for sect number
.      nr sE \\$1            \" Assign to register sE
.      if !\\n(sE \{.        \" Test if not a numeric
.         .af sE A           \"  Handle appendices
.         if "\\$1"A" .nr sE 1
.         if "\\$1"B" .nr sE 2
.         if "\\$1"C" .nr sE 3
.         if "\\$1"D" .nr sE 4
.         if "\\$1"E" .nr sE 5
.         if "\\$1"F" .nr sE 6
.         if "\\$1"G" .nr sE 7
.         if "\\$1"H" .nr sE 8
.         if "\\$1"I" .nr sE 9
.         if "\\$1"J" .nr sE 10\}\}
.                             \" Only go as far as J
.el \{\
.      nr sE 0
.      tm Preface or if Appendix past letter J:
.      tm     Set number register sE to position
.      tm     of that letter in the alphabet
.      tm     and alter register format:
.      tm      For Appendix K, enter:
.      tm        .Se K "Title"
.      tm        .nr sE 11
.      tm        .af sE A
.\}
.if \\n%>1 .bp          \" Check if consecutive sections
.                       \"  in same file and break page
.nr % 1                 \" Now reset page number
.nr PN 1
.af PN 1
.ie !"\\$1"" \{.        \" Test for sect number
.                       \"  to set page number type
```

```
.        ds NN \\\\n(sE-\\\\n(PN
.        ds H1 \\n(sE        \" Set for subsection numbering
.        \}
.el \{
.        ds NN \\\\n(PN
.        nr sE 0\}
.ds RF \\\\*(NN            \" Assign page number to footer
.nr fG 0                   \" Initialize figure counter
.nr tB 0                   \" Initialize table counter
```

The macro first initializes a number of registers. Chapters are usually numbered on the first page, along with the title. If subsections are to be numbered, the chapter number is the root number for all headings. We need to take this number as an argument, and store it into a register for later use.

Because appendices are usually lettered rather than numbered, we also need to consider the special case of appendices. (This could be done with a separate macro; however, this package uses a single multipurpose macro.) The code for this is quite cumbersome, but works nonetheless: if the first argument to the macro is non-numeric, it is tested to see if it is one of the first ten letters in the alphabet. If so, a number is stored into the register, but the output format is changed to alphabetic.

If the argument is not a letter between A and J, a message is printed. This message is more verbose than you would generally want to use, but it is included to make the point that you can include detailed messages.

The macro next sets up the special page numbering scheme used in many computer manuals—the chapter number is followed by a hyphen and the page number (e.g., 1-1). This numbering scheme makes it easier to make last minute changes without renumbering and reprinting the entire book.

Finally, the macro initializes counters for automatically numbering figures and tables. We'll see how these are used in a few pages.

The next portion of the macro is the part that is most variable—it controls the actual appearance of the chapter heading. This is the part of the macro that has led us to develop several different versions.

In designing chapter headings, let your imagination be your guide. Look at books whose design you like, and work from there. Three different designs we used on the HP LaserJet are shown in Figure 17-1. (These designs are a compromise between aesthetics and the capabilities of the output device.) This book is another model.

The macro for the first heading in Figure 17-1 is used as follows:

```
.Se 2 "Getting Started with Alcuin"
```

or:

```
.Se A "Summary of Alcuin Drawing Primitives" "Appendix"
```

The heading starts on a new page. If a third argument is not present, it is assumed that the section type is *Chapter*, and the section is labeled accordingly. An alternate section type can be specified in the optional third argument. This argument is usually *Appendix* but can be any string the user wants printed before the section number.

**CHAPTER 2**
**GETTING STARTED WITH ALCUIN**

---

2

Getting Started with Alcuin

Chapter 2
Getting Started with Alcuin

*Fig. 17-1.* Some Different Styles of Chapter Heading

The portion of the macro definition that creates the first heading in Figure 17-1 follows:

```
.\" Part 2 of Se Macro: Output chapter heading
.RT
.in 0
.lg 0                           \" Disable ligature before .tr
.                               \" Translate title to uppercase
.tr aAbBcCdDeEfFgGhHiIjJkKlLmMnNoOpPqQrRsStTuUvVwWxXyYzZ
.sp
.na
.                               \" Test for section type argument
.ie !"\\$3"" .ds cH \\$3
.el .ds cH Chapter              \" Default is chapter
.                               \" If section number supplied
.                               \" output section number and type
.                               \" in 14 pt. bold.
.if !"\\$1"" \{\
\s14\f3\\*(cH \\$1\f1\s0
\}
.                               \" If no section number but
.                               \" there is a type (i.e., Preface)
.                               \" then output section type
.if "\\$1"" .if !"\\$3"" \{\
\s14\f3\\*(cH\f1\s0
\}
.sp 5p
.                               \" Test for section title
.                               \" Print it in 14 pt. bold
.if !"\\$2"" \{\
\s14\f3\\$2\f1\s0
\}
.sp 6p
.ad b
.Hl                             \" Draw line
.                               \" Retranslate arguments
.tr aabbccddeeffgghhiijjkkllmmnnooppqqrrssttuuvvwwxxyyzz
.sp 3
.ns                             \" Enable no-space mode
```

There are a couple of points you may want to note about this code:

- The actual section title, as specified in the second argument, is forced to all uppercase using the .tr request.

- The horizontal line under the title is drawn using a utility macro called .Hl (*horizontal line*), which simply draws a line the width of the page, less any indent that is in effect:

```
.de Hl    \" Horizontal line.   $1 = underline char
.br
\l'\\n(.lu-\\n(.iu\&\\$1'
.br
..
```

- No-space mode is turned on at the end of the macro, to inhibit inconsistent spacing caused by users placing spacing requests or paragraph macros after the .Se macro. All of the heading macros use this technique because inconsistent spacing around headings will give the page an uneven look.

An alternate definition for this section of the macro follows. This code produces the second heading shown in Figure 17-1.

```
.\" Part 2 of Sc Macro (Alternate):
.ad r               \" Right justified
.fl
.rs
.sp .75i            \" Move down from top
.                   \" Section number in 24 pt. bold
.if !"\\$1"" \{\
\s24\f3\\$1\f1\s0\}
.sp 12p
.                   \" Section title in 20 pt. bold
.if !"\\$2"" \s20\f3\\$2\fP\s10
.sp 12p
.                   \" Optional 2nd line of title
.if !"\\$3"" \s20\f3\\$3\fP\s10
.sp 3
.ad b
.ns
```

This version is much simpler; it doesn't print the section type at all, just the number or letter. However, because it prints a right-justified title, we have given the user the option of splitting a long title into two parts.

The final part of the macro (in either version) adds the section title to the table of contents. As was the case with .Hl, this is done by an internal utility routine that is defined elsewhere. We'll discuss how this works later.

```
.                   \" Last Part of Se Macro
.                   \" Now do toc
.tC \\$1 \\$2 \\$3
..
```

### A Mechanism for Numbered Headings

Before we describe the lower-level headings used within a chapter, we need to explore how to generate automatically numbered sections. We have defined a version of the ms .NH macro that is called internally by our own heading macros. It has the same name and uses the same internal registers as the ms macro, but the font and spacing requests specified in the ms .NH macro are removed. All that this macro now does is generate the section number string.

```
.de NH                        \" redefine from -MS
.nr NS \\$1                    \" Set NS to arg 1
.if !\\n(.$ .nr NS 1          \" Set NS to 1 if no arg
.if !\\n(NS .nr NS 1          \"  or NS is null or negative
.nr H\\n(NS +1                \" Increment Heading level register
.                             \" Test which level is in effect
.if !\\n(NS-4 .nr H5 0        \" then reset lower levels to 0
.if !\\n(NS-3 .nr H4 0
.if !\\n(NS-2 .nr H3 0
.if !\\n(NS-1 .nr H2 0
.                                  \" Put together section number
.if !\\$1 .if \\n(.$ .nr H1 1      \" Set first level
.ds SN \\n(H1                      \" Begin building SN
.ie \\n(NS-1 .as SN .\\n(H2        \" == 1.1 2nd level
.el .as SN .                       \"   or == 1.
.if \\n(NS-2 .as SN .\\n(H3        \" == 1.1.1     3rd
.if \\n(NS-3 .as SN .\\n(H4        \" == 1.1.1.1   4th
.if \\n(NS-4 .as SN .\\n(H5        \" == 1.1.1.1.1 5th
'ti \\n(.iu
\\*(SN                             \" Output SN string
..
```

This macro repays study, because it shows several clever ways to use number registers. First, the argument to the macro is placed into a number register. This register is then used to select which of a series of further registers will be incremented:

```
.nr NS \\$1

        .

        .

        .

.nr H\\n(NS +1
```

If the macro is called as .NH 1, register H1 will be incremented; if the call is .NH 2, register H2 will be incremented, and so on. Then, depending on the value of that same NS register, the appropriate register value will be appended to the section number string SN.

## Subsection Headings

In our package, we allow four levels of subsection headings, created by macros called
.Ah (*A head*) through .Dh (*D head*). The macros for all four levels have the same
essential structure; they differ only in the appearance of the printed text. Again, we
have different styles for different clients.

The distinction between levels of headings in one of those styles is as follows:

- The A head prints the heading in 14-point bold type, all uppercase, with 26
  points of space above the heading and 18 points below.

- The B head prints the heading in 14-point bold type, mixed case, with 23
  points of space above the heading and 15.5 points below.

- The C head prints the heading in 12-point bold type, mixed case, with 18
  points of space above the heading and 12 points below.

- The D head prints the heading in 10-point bold type, mixed case, with 18
  points of space above the heading and none below. The heading actually runs
  into the text and is separated from it only by a period.

All levels of headings can be either numbered or unnumbered, depending on the state of
a number register called nH. If nH is 0, headings are unnumbered; if it is 1, they are
numbered.

Here is one version of the .Ah macro. From this example, you should be able to
build the lower-level headings as well.

```
.de Ah               \" A-heading ; $1 = title
.sp 26p
.RT
.ne 8                \" Need room on page
.ps 14               \" 14 pt. on 16 pt. heading
.vs 16
.lg 0
.tr aAbBcCdDeEfFgGhHiIjJkKlLmMnNoOpPqQrRsStTuUvVwWxXyYzZ
.bd I 4              \" Embolden italic font (optional)
\f3\c                \" Bold font, concatenate next input
.if \\n(nH \{.       \" if producing numbered heads
.        ie \\n(sE .NH 2    \" If chapter (Se macro) is
.                          \" numbered, then 2nd level
.        el .NH 1\}         \" If not, 1st level head
\&\\$1\f1            \" Output title
.LP 0                \" Paragraph reset; (0 = no space)
.                    \"  RT resets default point size
.bd I                \" Turn off emboldening
.tr aabbccddeeffgghhiijjkkllmmnnooppqqrrssttuuvvwwxxyyzz
.lg
.sp 18p
.ns
```

```
.tC \\*(SN \\$1 Ah      \" Output TOC info
..
```

Some pointers: First, whenever you force capitalization with `.tr`, be sure to turn off ligatures, because they do not capitalize. Second, when you boldface a user-supplied string, it is wise to artificially embolden italics as well, in case the user embeds an italic font switch in the heading. Third, don't forget to enter no-space mode to ensure consistent spacing following the heading.

As you can see, the `.NH` macro is called to generate a section heading only if the nH register has been set. In addition, the macro checks to make sure that a major section number has been specified by the `.Se` macro. As you may recall, `.Se` sets the first number in the numbered heading string (H1). If `.Se` has been called, the subsection headings start at level 2, otherwise they start from the top.

To make it very easy for even novice users to specify whether they want numbered or unnumbered headings, the package includes a macro called `.Nh` (*numbered headings*) that turns numbering on or off:

```
.de Nh     \" Numbered headings; $1 = turn on (1) or off (0)
.          \" $1 = 2 will cause only A heads to be numbered
.nr nH \\$1
..
```

This is a matter of macro package style, as mentioned earlier. Steve Talbott's style, when he initially developed this package, was to code everything as macros, even where the macro simply sets a number register or defines a string. This makes the package very easy to learn, because you can give a new user a concise, unambiguous list of macros to enter into a file.

Other examples of this style include the `.Ti` and `.St` (*title* and *subtitle*) macros, described in Appendix F, which simply define the ms RF and LF strings for running footers. Because of the mnemonically named macros, new users don't have to remember whether the title goes in the right footer or the left, and so on. They simply enter the title of the book and chapter as arguments to the respective macros. The disadvantage is that users are insulated from an understanding of what is really going on, which may be an obstacle to learning more advanced skills.

## An Alternate Definition

To give you an idea of how easy it is to change the look of a document by redefining a few macros, let's look at how we could redefine the heading for this section. One popular layout style in technical manuals uses a very wide left margin in which only the headings are printed, as follows.

An Alternate Definition

To give you an idea of how
easy it is to change the
look of a document...

Here's the modified macro to produce this heading:

```
.de Ah                  \" A-heading; alternate version
.                       \" Requires resetting default page
.                       \" (PO) to allow for extra offset.
.                       \" .nr PO 2.5i for 1.5 extra offset
.nr Po 1.5i             \" Set amount of extra offset
.nr Gw .2i              \" Set width of gutter
.mk                     \" Mark vertical position
.po -1.5i               \" Set new page offset
.ll \\n(Pou-\\nGwu
.ps 12                  \" Set 12 pt. on 14 pt.
.vs 14
\&\f3\\$1\f1            \" Output header in bold
.rt                     \" Return to vertical position
.po \\n(POu             \" Reset default page offset
.LP 0                   \" Reset point size and line length
.ns
.tC \\*(SN \\$1 Ah      \" Output TOC info
..
```

## ▪ Figure and Table Headings ▪

In technical manuals, it is common to number and title all figures and tables, both for easy reference from within the text, and for collection into lists of figures and tables that will appear in the table of contents.

These macros are easy to construct and, apart from whatever appearance you decide to give them, nearly identical in content. There is a "start" macro and an "end" macro:

```
.de Fs                  \" Start figure; $1= reserved space;
.                       \"               $2= F, floating figure
.RT
.if "\\$2"F" \{.        \" Figure can float
.       nr kF 1
.       KF\}
.if \\$1 \{.            \" Specify amount of space
.       ne \\$1         \"   required for paste-up
.       fl
.       rs
.       sp \\$1\}
..
.de Fe                  \" Figure end; $1 = title
.sp
.bd I 3
.nr fG +1               \" Increment Figure counter
```

```
.                           \" then determine format
.ie \\n(Se .ds fG \\*(H1-\\n(fG
.el .ds fG \\n(fG
.ce                         \" Output centered figure
\f3Figure \\*(fG.  \\$1\f1
.tC "\\*(fG" "\\$1" "Figure"
.bd I
.sp
.if \\n(kF=1 .KE    \" End keep if in effect
.tC "\\*(fG" "\\$1" "Figure"  \" Output TOC info
..
```

As you can see, the .Fs (*figure start*) macro allows the user to reserve space for a figure to be pasted in, and for it to float to a new page, using the ms "floating keep" mechanism.

Neither of these options are necessary. The macro can simply bracket a figure created with pic, for example, in which case all that the macro provides is a consistent amount of space before the figure starts.

The .Fe (*figure end*) macro does most of the work. If a keep is in effect, .Fe terminates it. In addition, it prints the figure caption below the figure and adds a consistent amount of space below the caption. The figure is automatically numbered with the section number, and a figure number that is incremented each time the macro is called. As you may remember, this figure number register, fG, was initialized to 0 in .Se.

To give the user some options with figure numbering, a second argument allows the user to turn it off entirely. In addition, if the section is unnumbered, the section number and hyphen will be omitted. To accomplish this involves a little juggling of strings and number registers (which is something you should plan to get used to when you write macros). Notice that we use the string H1 for the section number rather than the section number register itself (sE), because we went to some trouble in the .Se macro to handle lettered appendices as well as numbered chapters.

You could easily add optional appearance features to this macro. For example, in one implementation, we draw a horizontal line above and below the figure, and print the caption left justified and in italics below the bottom line.

The figure end macro also calls the table of contents macro, which will be described later.

The macros for labeling tables are very simple, because the standard .TS and .TE macros do everything necessary except providing consistent pre- and post-spacing and printing the caption. In this case, the caption is at the top:

```
.de Ts                              \" Table start; $1 = title
.nr tB +1                           \" Increment Table counter
.                                   \"   Determine format
.ie \\n(Se .ds tB \\*(H1-\\n(tB \" Section Table
.el .ds tB \\n(tB
.sp
.ce 2                               \" Output label and
```

```
\f3Table \\*(tB.              \" title on 2 lines
\&\\$1\f1
.tC "\\*(tB" "\\$1" "Table"   \" Output TOC info
.bd I
.LP                           \" Paragraph reset
..
.de Te    \" Table end -- no arguments
.RT                           \" Reset
.sp
..
```

## ▪ Lists, Lists, and More Lists ▪

One of the significant features lacking in the ms macros is the ability to generate automatically numbered or lettered lists. You can use the .IP macro and number or letter a list yourself—but what good is a computer if it can't handle a task like this?

One of the nicest features of Steve Talbott's extended ms package is its set of comprehensive, general-purpose list generation macros. There are three macros: .Ls (*list start*), .Li (*list item*), and .Le (*list end*). Unlike mm, in which different types of lists must be specified using different macros, here you request a different type of list by giving an argument to the .Ls macro. You can request any of the types of lists in Table 17-1.

### TABLE 17-1. List Types

| Argument | List Type |
|:---:|:---|
| A | Alphabetic with uppercase letters |
| a | Alphabetic with lowercase letters |
| B | Bulleted with • by default |
| N | Numbered with arabic numerals |
| R | Numbered with uppercase roman numerals |
| r | Numbered with lowercase roman numerals |

The bulleted list uses the bullet character (•) by default. However, as you will see, the macro allows you to specify an alternate bullet using an optional third argument. This "bullet" could be a dash, a box (\(sq), a checkmark (\(sr), or any other character.

Lists can be nested, and there is a default list type for each level of nesting, so the type argument does not really need to be specified.

Here's the list start macro:

```
.nr 10 0 1        \" Initialize nested list level counter
.de Ls
.\" list start; $1 = A(LPHA), a(alpha), B(ullet), N(umeric),
.\"                 R(oman), r(oman);  $2 = indent
.\"                 $3 = alternate bullet character
.br
.if !"\\$1"A" .if !"\\$1"B" .if !"\\$1"N" .if !"\\$1"R" \
.       if !"\\$1"r" .if !"\\$1"a" .if !"\\$1"" \
.       tm Ls: Need A a B N R r or null as list type
.nr 1\\n+(10 0 1
.ie "\\$1"" \{\                          \"Set defaults
.       if "\\n(10"1" .af 1\\n(10 1    \"Numeric at 1st level
.       if "\\n(10"2" .af 1\\n(10 a    \"lc alpha at 2nd level
.       if "\\n(10"3" .af 1\\n(10 i    \"lc roman at 3rd level
.       if "\\n(10"4" .ds 1\\n(10 \(bu\"Bullet at 4th level
.       if "\\n(10"5" .ds 1\\n(10 \f3\-\f1\"Dash at 5th level
.       if \\n(10-5 .ds 1\\n(10\(bu  \"Bullet above 5th level
.       if \\n(10-3 .nr 1\\n(10 0-1 \}
.el \{\
.       if "\\$1"A" .af 1\\n(10 A
.       if "\\$1"a" .af 1\\n(10 a
.       if "\\$1"B"\{\
.           if "\\$3"" .ds 1\\n(10 \(bu
.           if !"\\$3"" .ds 1\\n(10 \\$3
.           nr 1\\n(10 0-1\}
.       if "\\$1"R" .af 1\\n(10 I
.       if "\\$1"r" .af 1\\n(10 i \}
.ie !"\\$2"" .nr i\\n(10 \\$2    \" List indent
.el .nr i\\n(10 5                \" Default indent
.RS
..
```

When you first look at this macro, you may be a little overwhelmed by the complex number register names. In fact, there is not much to it.

One number register, 10, is used as a counter for nested lists. As you can see, this register is initialized to 0 outside of the list macro definition itself. Then, when the .Ls macro is called, this register is autoincremented at the same time as it is used to define the *name* of another number register:

```
.nr 1\\n+(10 0 1
```

It is this second number register interpolation—1\\n+(10—that is actually used to number the list. This is a technique we promised to show you back when we were first describing number registers. We create a series of related number register names by interpolating the value of another register as one character in the name.

Think this through for a moment. The first time .Ls is called, the request:

```
.nr l\\n+(10 0 1
```

defines a number register that is actually called `11` (the letter *l* followed by the value of number register `10`—which is 1). A second call to `.Ls` without closing the first list (which, as we shall see, bumps the counter back one) will define number register `12`, and so on.

In a similar way, another series of number registers (i\\n(10) allows a different indent to be specified for each nested level, if the user so desires.

With the exception of the bulleted list, all of the different list types are numbered using the same number register (`1n`, where *n* is the nesting depth). The different types of lists are created simply by changing the output format of this register using the `.af` request.

Here's the `.Li` macro:

```
.de Li  \" List item;  $1 = 0 no blank line before item
.br
.if "\\$1"0" .ns
.ie "\\n(l\\n(10"-1" .IP "\\*(1\\n(10" "\\n(i\\n(10"
.el \{\
.nr l\\n(10 +1
.IP "\\n(l\\n(10." "\\n(i\\n(10" \}
..
```

The actual list counter itself (as opposed to the nesting counter) is incremented, and the appropriate value printed.

The number and the associated text is positioned with the standard ms `.IP` macro. If you don't have access to the ms macros, you could simulate the action of the `.IP` macro as follows:

```
.de IP
.nr Ip 1
.sp \\n(PDu
.in \\$2u
.ti -\\$2u
.ta \\$2u
\\$1\t\c
..
```

However, there is one drawback to using an `.IP`-style macro as the basis of the list.

- The `.IP` macro puts its argument at the left margin, as was done with this sentence.

- Instead, we'd like something that puts the mark in the middle of the indent, as was done with this sentence.

Here's the macro that produced the second example:

```
.de IP
.nr Ip 1
.sp \\n(PDu
.in \\$2u
.nr i1 \\$2/2u+\w'\\$1'    \" Amount to move left
.nr i2 \\$2-\w'\\$1'       \" Amount to move back
.ta \\n(i2u
.ti -\\n(i1u
\\$1\t\c
..
```

This version of the macro places the mark not just at a position half the depth of the indent, but exactly in the middle of the indent by adjusting the indent by the width of the mark argument. Number registers are used for clarity, to avoid nesting the various constructs too deeply.

(Note that this simplified .IP macro lacks some of the functionality of the ms .IP macro, which saves the current indent and therefore allows you to nest indents by using the .RS and .RE macros.)

If you are using ms, and you want to create a macro that puts the mark in the center of the indent, be sure to name this macro something other than .IP, so that you don't conflict with the existing macro of that name.

Here's the list end:

```
.de Le  \" List end; $1=0 no blank line following last item
.br
.rr l\\n(l0
.rr i\\n(l0
.rm l\\n(l0
.nr l0 -1
.RE
.ie !\\n(l0 \{\
.        ie "\\$1"0" .LP 0
.        el .LP\}
.el .if !"\\$1"0" .sp \\n(PDu
..
```

This macro removes the list numbering registers and strings, decrements the nested list counter, and calls the ms .RE macro to "retreat" back to the left (if necessary because of a nested loop). Finally, it leaves a blank line following the end of the list. (As you might remember, PD is the ms register containing the *paragraph distance*—0.3v by default.)

## ▪ Source Code and Other Examples ▪

In a technical manual, there are often further issues brought out by the need to show program source code or other material that loses essential formatting if it is set with proportional rather than monospaced type.

As previously discussed, the basic trick in ditroff is to use the CW font. If you are using otroff, you will need to use the cw preprocessor (see your UNIX manual for details) or some other type of workaround. (When we were using otroff, our print driver allowed font substitutions based on size. We told the driver to use the printer's constant-width font whenever troff used a point size of 11. Then, we wrote a macro that changed the point size to 11, but used .cs to set the character spacing to the actual size for the printer's constant-width font. This was not a very elegant solution, but it worked—so if you are stuck with otroff, don't despair. Put your ingenuity to work and you should come up with something.)

Besides the change to the CW font, though, there are several other things we'd like to see in a macro to handle printouts of examples. We'd like examples to be consistently indented, set off by a consistent amount of pre- and post-line spacing, and set in no-fill mode.

Here's an example of a pair of macros to handle this situation:

```
.de Ps\" Printout start; $1 = indent (default is 5 spaces)
.br
.sp \\n(PDu
.ns
.nr pS \\n(.s  \" Save current point size
.nr vS \\n(.v  \" Save current vertical spacing
.nr pF \\n(.f  \" Save current font
.nr pI \\n(.i  \" Save current indent
.ps 8
.vs 10
.ft CW
.ie !"\\$1"" .in +\\$1n
.el .in +5n
.nf
..
.de Pe  \" Printout end; $1 non-null, no concluding
.br
.if "\\$1"" .sp \\n(PDu
.ps \\n(pSu
.vs \\n(vSu
.ft \\n(pF
.in \\n(pIu
.rr pS
.rr vS
.rr pF
.rr pI
.fi
..
```

The trick of saving the current environment in temporary registers is a useful one. The alternative is to use a separate environment for the printouts, but this assumes that the available environments are not already in use for some other purpose. You could also call a reset macro to restore the default state—but this may not actually be the state that was in effect at the time.

In addition, you shouldn't rely on `troff`'s ability to return to the previous setting by making a request like `.ll` without any argument. If you do so, an error might result if the user has himself made an `.ll` request in the interim.

In short, you should either save registers or use a different environment whenever you change formatting parameters in the opening macro of a macro pair. Then restore them in the closing macro of the pair.

## · Notes, Cautions, and Warnings ·

Another important macro for technical manuals is one that gives a consistent way of handling notes, cautions, and warnings. (Traditionally, a note gives users important information that they should not miss, but will not cause harm if they do. A caution is used for information that, if missed or disregarded, could lead to loss of data or damage to equipment. A warning is used for information that is critical to the user's life or limb.)

Obviously, this is a simple macro—all that is required is some way of making the note, caution, or warning stand out from the body of the text. You could redefine the macro shown here in any number of ways depending on the style of your publications.

```
.de Ns \" note/caution/warning; $1 = type "N", "C", "W"
.sp 2
.ne 5
.ce
.if !"\\$1"N" .if !"\\$1"C" .if !"\\$1"W" \{\
.  tm "Need N, C, or W as argument for Ns macro—using N"
\f3NOTE\f1\}
.if "\\$1"N" \f3NOTE\f1
.if "\\$1"C" \f3CAUTION\f1
.if "\\$1"W" \f3WARNING\f1
.sp
.ns
.nr nI \\n(.iu       \" Save current indent, if any
.nr nL \\n(.lu       \" Save current line length
.ie \\nS>0 .nr IN 5n\" Make indent less if in small format
.el .nr IN 10n       \" Larger indent for full-size page
.in +\\n(INu         \" Indent specified amount
.ll -\\n(INu         \" Decrement line length same amount
..
.de Ne \" "note end"; no args
.in \\n(nIu          \" Restore previous indent
.ll \\n(nLu          \" Restore previous line length
.rr nI               \" Remove temporary registers
.rr nL
.sp 2
..
```

A warning looks like this:

---

**WARNING**

You should be careful when reading books on `troff`, because they can be damaging to your health. Although escape sequences are allowed, they are not exactly high adventure.

---

A different version of a caution macro is shown below. It uses a graphic symbol to mark a caution statement.

---

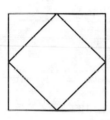

**CAUTION**

One client had a convention of marking a caution statement with a large diamond in a square. These diamonds will appear in a second color in the printed book.

---

To produce the escape sequences to draw the symbol, we used `pic`, processing the description and capturing it in a file. Then we read it into our macro definition. (We could also have produced the escape sequences to draw the symbol without `pic`'s help; this would result in much more compact code.) The drawing of the symbol does take up most of the `.Gc` macro definition. Before we actually output the symbol, the current vertical position is marked. After it is output, we mark its bottom position. Then we return to the top before placing the warning label and processing the text. After the caution statement is output, the closing macro, `.GE`, checks the current vertical position against the bottom position of the symbol.

```
.de Gc \"Graphic Caution Macro
.ne 10
.mk a                    \" Mark current top position
.br                      \" pic output belongs here
\v'720u'\D'l0u -720u'
.sp -1
\D'l720u 0u'
.sp -1
\h'720u'\D'l0u 720u'
.sp -1
\h'720u'\v'720u'\D'l-720u 0u'
.sp -1
\h'360u'\D'l360u 360u'
.sp -1
```

```
\h'720u'\v'360u'\D'l-360u 360u'
.sp -1
\h'360u'\v'720u'\D'l-360u -360u'
.sp -1
\v'360u'\D'l360u -360u'
.sp -1
.sp 1+720u            \" End of pic output
.sp
.mk q                 \" Mark bottom of symbol
.sp |\\nau            \" Move back to top (.mk a)
.in +1.5i             \" Indent to right of symbol
.ll -.5i              \" Reduce line length
.sp .5v
.ce
\f3CAUTION\f1         \" Output Caution label
.sp .3v
.
.de GE                \" Graphic Caution end
.br
.sp
.in                   \" Reset previous settings
.ll
.                     \" If bottom of symbol (.mk q)
.                     \" is below current vertical position
.                     \" then move to that position
.if \\nqu>\\n(nlu+\\n(.vu .sp |\\nqu
.sp .3v
..
```

## ▪ Table of Contents, Index, and Other End Lists ▪

Here's the part you've all been waiting for.  One of the nicest things a formatter can do
for a writer is automatically generate lists such as a table of contents and an index.
These are very time consuming to produce manually, and subject to error.  There are
basically two ways to do the trick, and both apply to an index as well as a table of contents, endnotes, and other collected lists.

The technique used by  mm, which generates an automatic table of contents at the
end of each formatting run, is to collect headings into a diversion using the  .da
request.  This diversion is then output from within a special macro called the "end
macro," which we have yet to discuss.

The second technique is to use the  .tm request to write the desired information
to standard error output.  Then that output is redirected to capture the messages in a file,
where they can be edited manually or automatically processed by other programs.

The advantage of the first approach is that it is clean and simple, and entirely internal to the formatter. However, it is really suitable only for short documents. A long document such as a book is not normally formatted in a single pass, but chapter by chapter. It is not desirable to format it all at once just to get the table of contents at the end. In addition, a large document generally will end up creating a large diversion—often one that is too large for troff to handle.

The second approach, on the other hand, opens up all kinds of possibilities for integration with other tools in the UNIX environment. The output can be saved, edited, and processed in a variety of ways. As you can imagine from our philosophy of letting the computer do the dirty work, this is the approach we prefer.

However, there is still a place for diversions, so we'll take a close look at both approaches in the sections that follow.

### Diverting to the End

Although we prefer to create our major end lists—the table of contents and index—by writing to stderr, we find it very useful to use diversions for another type of list.

We've added a couple of special macros that allow a writer to insert remarks intended specifically for the reviewers of a draft document or for personal use. Because technical reviewers frequently miss questions embedded in the text, we designed the .Rn macro to highlight notes. This macro makes these remarks stand out in the text and then collects them for output again at the end of the document.

```
.de Rn   \" Note to reviewers : $1 = Note
.        \" Print note in text and at end
.                        \" Output note first
.sp
\f3Note to reviewers:\fP \\$1
.sp
.ev 2
.da rN                   \" Then append into diversion
.sp 0.2v
.in 0
.ie "\\*(NN"" \(sq Page \\n(PN: \\$1
.el \(sq Page \\*(NN: \\$1
.br
.da
.nr RN 1                 \" Flag it for EM
.ev
..
```

Another macro, .Pn, is used to collect a list of personal notes or reminders and output them on a page at the end. These notes do not appear in the body of the text.

```
.de Pn     \" Personal Note; $1= note
.          \" Note listed at end, but not in text
.ev2
.if \\n(Pn<1 .nr Pn 0 1   \" Set up autoincrement counter
```

```
.da pN
.br
.IP "\\n+(Pn." 5n
\\$1
.ie "\\*(NN"" (Page \\n(PN)
.el (Page \\*(NN)
.br
.da
.nr pN 1                         \" Flag it for EM
.ev
..
```

Only the `.Rn` macro produces output in the body of the document, but both macros append the notes into a diversion that we can process at the end of the document. The *divert and append* (`.da`) macro creates a list of notes that can be output by invoking the macro created by the diversion.

For each macro, we format the lists slightly differently. In the `.Rn` macro, we print a box character (□) (to give the feeling of a checklist), then the page number on which the review note occurred. This allows the reviewer or the writer to easily go back and find the note in context. In the `.Pn` macro, we use an autoincrementing counter to number personal notes; this number is output through `.IP`. It is followed by the note and the page reference in parentheses.

The formatting of text inside a diversion can be tricky. The text could be formatted twice: when it is read into the diversion, and when the diversion is output. The one thing to keep in mind is that you don't want line filling to be in effect both times. If line filling is in effect when the text is read into the diversion, you should turn it off when the diversion is output. You can also use transparent output (\!) to hide macros or requests so that they will be executed only at the time the diversion is output. We have also taken the precaution of processing the diversion in a separate environment.

Now what about printing the list at the end? Well, as it turns out, `nroff` and `troff` include a special request called `.em` that allows you to supply the name of a macro that will be executed at the very end of the processing run, after everything else is finished.

The `.em` request allows you to define the name of a macro that will be executed when all other input has been processed. For example, the line:

```
.em EM
```

placed anywhere in a file or macro package, will request that the macro `.EM` be executed after everything else has been done. The definition of `.EM` is up to you.

The `ms` macros already have specified the name of this macro as `.EM`, the *end macro*. In its usual obscure way, `mm` calls its end macro `.)q`. If you are writing your own package, you can call it anything you like. You can either edit the existing end macro, or simply add to it using the `.am` (*append to macro*) request.

All that `ms` does with this macro is to process and output any diversions that have not been properly closed. (This might happen, for example, if you requested a floating keep, but its contents had not yet been printed out.)

The end macro is a good place to output our own special diversions that we've saved for the end. What we need to do now is to add some code for processing our list of review notes:

```
.de EM
.br
.if \\n(RN=1 \{\
\&\c
'bp
.
.
.ce
\f3NOTES TO REVIEWERS\f1
.sp 2
Reviewers, please address the following questions:
.sp
.ev 2
.nf
.rN
.ev
.\}
.if \\n(pN=1 \{\
.br
\&\c
'bp
.
.ce
\f3Notes To Myself:\f1
.sp 2
.ev 2
.nf
.pN
.ev
.\}
..
```

(Note: we have found that to print anything from the .EM macro in the standard ᴍs package, it is necessary to invoke .NP explicitly following a page break. However, when using our simplified version of this package as shown in the last chapter, our .EM does not need a .NP.) The list collected by the .Rn macro is printed on a new page, looking something like this:

**NOTES TO REVIEWERS**

Reviewers, please address the following questions:

□ Page 3-1:  Why can't I activate the bit pad before opening a font file?

□ Page 3-7:  Is there a size restriction on illuminated letters?

## A Diverted Table of Contents

Given the preceding discussion, it should be easy for you to design a diverted table of contents. The magic `.tC` macro we kept invoking from our headings might look something like this:

```
.de tC   \" table of contents; $1=sect number;
.                               $2=title; $3=type
.if "\\$3"\\*(cH"\{\
.da sL          \" Divert and append to section list
.sp 3
\\*(cH \\$1:    \\$2
.sp 1.5
.da
.\}
.if "\\$3"Ah"\{\
.da sL          \" Divert and append to section list
.br
\\$1        \\$2\\a\\t\\*(NN
.br
.da
.\}
.if "\\$3"Bh"\{\
.da sL          \" Divert and append to section list
.br
\\$1       \\$2\\a\\t\\*(NN
.br
.da
.\}
.if "\\$3"Figure" \{\
.da fL          \" Divert and append to figure list
\\$1  \\$2\\a\\t\\*(NN
.da
.\}
.if "\\$3"Table" \{\
.da tL          \" Divert and append to table list
\\$1  \\$2\\a\\t\\*(NN
```

```
.da
.\}
..
```

The diversion sL is set up to handle the main heading (chapter, appendix, unit, or section) and two levels of subheadings (A-heads or B-heads). The diversions fL and tL are set up to compile lists of figures and tables, respectively.

In the end macro, to print the table of contents, you have to cause a break to a new page, print: introductory captions, and so on, and then follow by outputting the collected diversion of each type. The following example shows the code to print:

```
.br                 \" Automatically invoke diverted toc
\&\c                \" by including these lines in EM macro
'bp                 \" Or place in own macro
.ta  \\n(LLu-5n \\n(LLuR
.cc
\f3Table of Contents\fR
.sp 2
.nf                 \" Process in no-fill mode
\\t\f3Page\fP
.sL
.rm sL              \" Clear diversion
.                   \" Add code here to output figure
.                   \" and table list diversions
```

We set two tab stops based on the default line length (\n(LLu). The second tab stop is used to set a right-adjusted page number in the right margin. The first tab stop is used to run a leader from the entry to the page number. The escape sequences that output the leader and tab (\a and \t) were specified in the .tC macros. (And to protect the escape sequence inside a diversion an extra backslash was required.)

Now we can obtain a table of contents each time we format the document. The format of the table of contents shows the hierarchical structure of the document:

---

**Table of Contents**

                                                          **Page**

Chapter Two: Getting Started with Alcuin

---

## When Diversions Get Too Big

One of the major problems with collecting a table of contents in a diversion is that, with a large document, the diversions quickly grow too large for the formatter to handle. It will abort with a message like "Out of temp file space."

The solution is to break up your diversions based on the number of entries they contain. One way to do this is to base the name of the diversion on a number register, and do some arithmetic to increment the name when the diversion has been added to a certain number of times.

For example, instead of just diverting to a macro called .sL, we could divert to one called x*n*, where *n* is a number register interpolation generated as follows:

```
.de tC
    .
    .
    .
.nr xX +1
.nr x0 \\n(xX/100+1
.da x\\n(x0
    .
    .
    .
```

Each time .tC is called, register xX is incremented by 1, and its value, divided by 100, is placed into another register, x0. Until the value of register xX exceeds 100—that is, until .tC has been called 99 times—x0 will be equal to 1. From 100 to 199, x0 will be equal to 2, and so on.

Accordingly, the actual macro into which output is diverted—represented as x\\n(x0—will first be x1, then x2, and so on.

When it comes time to output the collected entries, instead of calling a single diversion, we call the entire series:

```
.x1
.x2
.x3
.x4
```

Here, we are assuming that we will have no more than 400 entries. If there are fewer entries, one or more of these diverted macros may be empty, but there's no harm in that. If there are more than 400, the contents of .x5 (*et al*) would still have been collected, but we would have failed to print them out. We have the option of adding another in the series of calls in the end macro, or rebuking the user for having such a large table of contents!

## Writing to Standard Error

Although we've answered one of the objections to a diverted table of contents by the register arithmetic just shown, there is another, more compelling reason for not using this approach for large documents: there is no way to save or edit the table of contents.

It is produced on the fly as part of the processing run and must be recreated each time you print the document.

For a very large document, such as a book, this means you must format the entire book, just to get the table of contents. It would be far preferable to produce the table of contents in some form that could be saved, so the tables from each chapter could be assembled into a single large table of contents for the entire book.

(Incidentally, producing a table of contents for a large document introduces some other issues as well. For example, you may want to have an overall table of contents that shows only top-level headings, and individual chapter table of contents that give more detail. Working out the macros for this approach is left as an exercise for the reader.)

The best way to produce a table of contents for a large book is simply to write the entries to standard error using .tm, and rely on an external program to capture and process the entries.

In ditroff, you can instead use the .sy request to execute the echo command and redirect the entries to a file. An example of this method might be:

```
.sy echo \\$1 \\$2\a\t\\*(NN >> toc$$
```

However, this approach causes additional system overhead because it spawns echo subprocesses. Also, because it does not work with otroff, we have used the more general approach provided by .tm.

Our .tC macro might look like this:

```
.de tC   \" Standard error; table of contents;
.        \" $1=sect number; $2=title; $3=type
.if "\\$3"\\*(cH"\{\
.tm ><CONTENTS:.sp 3
.tm ><CONTENTS:\\*(cH \\$1\\$2
.tm ><CONTENTS:.sp 1.5
.\}
.if "\\$3"Ah" .tm ><CONTENTS:\\$1   \\$2\a\t\\*(NN
.if "\\$3"Bh" .tm ><CONTENTS:\\$1      \\$2\a\t\\*(NN
.if "\\$3"Figure" .tm ><FIGURE:\\$1   \\$2\a\t\\*(NN
.if "\\$3"Table" .tm ><Table:\\$1   \\$2\a\t\\*(NN
..
```

Instead of diverting the section lists to separate macros from the lists of figures and tables, we send all entries out to standard error.

To capture this output in a file, we simply need to redirect the error output:

```
$ ditroff -Tps ... 2> toc
```

To do this, we will use our format shell script, which was introduced in Chapter 12, and will be revisited in the next (and final) chapter.

Because actual error messages might be present in the output, we prefix a label indicating the type of entry, for example:

```
><CONTENTS:
><FIGURE:
><TABLE:
```

It will be up to some outside program to separate the different groups of entries and subject them to further processing. We'll use a sed script to separate the entries in the table of contents from the figure lists, table lists, and index entries. (In the next chapter, we'll look at the post-processing of these entries.) Now let's look at a macro to generate index entries that will also be written to standard error.

## Indexes

A simple index can be handled in much the same way as a table of contents. A macro for a simple index might look like this:

```
.de XX
.                       \" Section-page number set up
.                       \"  by Se macro in string NN
.tm INDEX:\\$1\t\\*(NN
..
```

You might also want to have a macro that doesn't print the page number, but is just used for a cross-reference:

```
.de XN  \" Cross-reference Index entry, no page number
.tm INDEX:\\$1
..
```

You might also want a macro pair that will index over several different pages:

```
.de IS                 \" Index macro
.                      \" Interpolate % for page number
.ie \\n(.$=1 .tm INDEX:\\$1, \\n%
.el \{\
.nr X\\$2 \\n%
.ds Y\\$2 \\$1 \}
.if \\n(.t<=1P .tm *\\$1* near end of page
.if \\n(nl<1.2i .tm *\\$1* near top of page
..
.de IE                 \" Index end macro
.ie !\\n(.$=1 .tm IE needs an argument!
.el .tm INDEX:\\*(Y\\$1, \\n(X\\$1-\\n%
.if \\n(.t<=1P .tm *\\*(Y\\$1* near end of page
.if \\n(nl<1.2i .tm *\\*(Y\\$1* near top of page
..
```

The .IS macro prints out an entry, just like .XX. However, in addition, it saves the argument into a string, and takes a letter or digit as an optional second argument. This second argument is used to define a number register and string that will be saved, and not printed until the index and macro is called with the same argument.  The index and macro print the starting number, followed by a hyphen and the current page number.

All of this discussion still avoids one major issue.  The real trick of indexing is what you do with the raw output after you have it, because a great deal of sorting, concatenation, and reorganization is required to rearrange the entries into a meaningful order.  Fortunately or unfortunately, this topic will have to wait until the next chapter.

# 18

# Putting It All Together

Before returning to the topic of table of contents and index processing, using shell tools that we will build, let's review what we've covered so far.

We started with a promise to show you how the UNIX environment could support and enhance the writing process. To do that, we've had to delve into many details and may have lost the big picture.

Let's return to that big picture here. First, UNIX provides what any computer with even rudimentary word-processing capabilities provides: the ability to save and edit text. Few of us write it perfectly the first time, so the ability to rewrite the parts of a document we don't like without retyping the parts we want to keep is a major step forward.

However, no one will argue that UNIX offers better tools at this simple level than those available in other environments. The vi editor is a good editor, but it is not the easiest to learn and lacks many standard word-processing capabilities.

Where UNIX's editing tools excel is in performing complex or repetitive edits. A beginner may have little use for pattern matching, but an advanced user cannot do without it. Few, if any, microcomputer-based or standalone word processors can boast the sophisticated capabilities for global changes that UNIX provides in even its most primitive editors.

When you go beyond vi, and begin to use programs such as ex, sed, and awk, you have unmatched text-editing capabilities—power, if you will, at the expense of user friendliness.

Second, UNIX's hierarchical file system, multiuser capabilities, and ample disk storage capacity make it easy to organize large and complex writing jobs—especially ones involving the efforts of more than one person. This can be a major advantage of UNIX over microcomputer-based or dedicated word processors.

Anyone who has tried to write a multiauthor work on a floppy-based system knows how easy it is to lose track of the latest version of a file, and to get lost among a multitude of disks. UNIX makes it easy to share files, and to set up a consistent framework for managing them.

In addition to storing multiple versions of documents on line, you can use the file system to set up specific environments for writing. For example, a separate `.exrc` file in each directory can define abbreviations and command maps specific to a book or section.

Third, UNIX provides a wide range of formatting tools. Using `troff`, `pic`, `tbl`, and `eqn`, you can easily typeset books. This is not as unique and powerful a capability as it was even two or three years ago. The advent of low-cost laser printers and *wysiwyg* "desktop publishing" tools like Microsoft WORD, MacWrite, and Aldus Pagemaker allow PC users to do typesetting as well.

However, despite the glamor of desktop publishing, and the easy-to-use appeal of products for the Macintosh, the UNIX typesetting facilities offer many advantages. Chief among these advantages is the very feature in which `troff` at first seems much weaker than its low-end competitors, namely, the use of embedded codes to control formatting.

*Wysiwyg* systems are easy for beginners to use, and they are very satisfying because you can immediately see what you are going to get on the printed page. But have you ever tried to make a global font change in MacWrite? Or had to make a change to a document after it was "pasted up" with Pagemaker? Or had to wait endlessly while Microsoft WORD reformats an entire document after you change the margins?

Because `troff` codes can be edited, just like any other text in a file, it is very easy to change your mind about formatting and make global changes. And after you have mastered the art of writing macros, it is even easier to change formats simply by changing macro definitions. And because the editing and formatting functions are separate, you don't have to wait for the computer while you are making those changes—that happens while you print.

This is not to say that `troff` is superior to the best possible *wysiwyg* system. High-end systems from companies like Interleaf, Xyvision, and Texet offer power, speed, and ease of use all at once. Unfortunately, the software is costly, and requires the use of high-cost bit mapped workstations. This can lead to a bottleneck in document production unless you have enough money to spend on hardware. Because `troff` requires only a standard alphanumeric terminal, it provides much more "bang for the buck."

There is no question that the publishing system of the future will be a *wysiwyg* system. But for now, a low-cost UNIX system with `vi` and `troff` is still one of the most cost-effective publishing systems around.

This brings us to the final strength of UNIX—its extensibility. More than an operating system or a collection of programs, UNIX is a philosophy of computing. Let's consider an analogy. The Volkswagen beetle was a unique automobile of the sixties and seventies. Its simple design was one of the reasons that made it popular; the "bug" was user-maintainable. VW owners ("users") could tinker with their cars, performing such tasks as changing spark plugs by hand. They scoffed at owners of other cars who depended upon mechanics. It is perhaps this same feeling of independence— let me do it myself—that the UNIX environment fosters in its users. There are many quite capable software environments that are packaged to keep users out. In some ways, the secret of UNIX is that its working parts are visible. The UNIX environment, like the VW beetle, is designed so that users can take it apart and put it back together. UNIX is a philosophy of computing. As we've stressed again and again, UNIX provides general-purpose tools, all of which are designed to work together.

No single program, however well thought out, will solve every problem. There is always a special case, a special need, a situation that runs counter to the expected. But UNIX is not a single program: it is a collection of hundreds. And with these basic tools, a clever or dedicated person can devise a way to meet just about any text-processing need.

Like the fruits of any advanced system, these capabilities don't fall unbidden into the hands of new users. But they are there for the reaching. And over time, even writers who want a word processor they don't have to think about will gradually reach out for these capabilities. Faced with a choice between an hour spent on a boring, repetitive task and an hour putting together a tool that will do the task in a flash, most of us will choose to tinker.

The index and table of contents mechanism in this chapter is a good example of putting together individual UNIX tools to do a job that no one of them can easily do alone. Its explanation is a fitting end to this book, which has tried throughout to put the UNIX text-processing tools in a wider context.

## ▪ Saving an External Table of Contents ▪

As discussed in the last chapter, `troff` does provide a mechanism (namely diversions) to collect and process a table of contents directly within the formatter. However, this approach is best suited to short documents, because it requires that the entire document be reformatted to produce the table of contents.

Likewise, you could even produce and sort an index entirely within `troff`, though the effort required would be large. (In fact, a recent article on Usenet, the on-line UNIX news network, described an implementation of a sort algorithm using `troff` macros. It is painfully slow—it was done just to prove that it could be done, rather than for practical application.)

The beauty of UNIX, though, is that you don't have to stretch the limits of `troff` to do everything necessary to produce a book. Just as editing is separated from formatting, you can separate processing the table of contents and the index from formatting the rest of the text.

The `troff` formatter provides the basic mechanisms for producing the raw material—the lists of headings or index terms, accompanied by the page numbers on which they occur. However, the actual saving and processing of the raw material is done with `make`, `sed`, `awk`, `sort`, and the shell.

In Chapter 12, we began to look at how a shell script (which we called `format`) could manage the formatting process. We used the programming power of the shell not only to save the user the trouble of remembering command-line options and complicated postprocessor names, but also to apply the power of `sed` to various ancillary formatting tasks.

The collection of a table of contents and index requires that we first return to this script. As we left Chapter 17, both the table of contents and the index macros simply write data to standard error.

A Bourne shell user can redirect this error output to a file using the following syntax:

$ **ditroff** *file* **2>** *tocfile*

The problem is that the table of contents, index entries, and potential formatter error messages are all captured in the same file. We need a mechanism for parsing this file into its separate elements. The user could do this manually, but it is far better to let a program do it.

The first step is to redirect all of the error output from the formatter to a temporary file. After formatting is done, we can use sed to search for the identifying strings that we introduced as part of the "error message" and output the matching lines into separate files. True error messages should be sent back to the screen, and the temporary file removed.

The trick here is naming the files into which the saved data is stored by sed. It is not appropriate simply to append table of contents data to one file, because we are likely to reformat a document many times while rewriting and revising it. Instead, we want to have a unique table of contents file and a unique index file for each source file that we format. The best way to do this without cluttering up the current directory is to create a subdirectory for each type of data we want to save—toc, index, and so on.

Let's look at how we did these things in the format script:

```
roff="ditroff -Tps"; files=""; options="-mS"
pre="| ditbl"; post="| devps "
sed="| sed -f /work/macros/new/cleanup.sed"
pages=""; toc="2>/tmp$$"; lp="| lp -s"
if [ ! -d index a ! -d toc ]; then
    echo "No index and toc. Use the buildmake command."
    toc="2>/dev/null"
fi
while [ "$#" != "0" ]; do
    case $1 in
      -?) echo "Format Options are:"
          echo "-m*    Specify other macro package ( mm)"
          echo "-s     Use small format (5-1/2 by 8-1/2)"
          echo "-o     Print selected pages"
          echo "-cg    Format for Compugraphic typesetter"
          echo "-E     Invoke EQN preprocessor"
          echo "-P     Invoke PIC preprocessor"
          echo "-G     Invoke GRAP & PIC preprocessors"
          echo "-x     Redirect output to /dev/null"
          echo "-y     Invoke nroff; pipe output to screen";
          echo "-a     Set interactive troff -a option"
          echo "-*     Any troff option"; exit;;
      -m*) options="$1";;
```

```
        -s) options="$options -rS1 -rv1";;
        -o) pages="$pages -o$1";toc="2>/dev/null";;
       -cg) roff="ditroff -Tcg86"; post="| ditplus -dtcg86";;
        -E) pre="$pre | dieqn";;
        -P) pre="| pic -T720 -D $pre";;
        -G) pre="| grap | pic -T720 -D $pre";;
        -x) options="$options -z"; post=""; lp="";;
        -y) roff="nroff"; post=""; lp="| col | pg";;
        -a) post=""; options="$options -a";;
        -*) options="$options $1";;
         *) if [ -f $1 ]; then
               files="$files $1"
               txfile="$1"
               if [ -d /print ]; then touch /print/$txfile
            else
               echo "USAGE: format (options) files"
               echo "To list options, type format -? "; exit
            fi;;
    esac
    shift
done
if [ -n "$files" -o ! -t 0 ]; then
# Use soelim to expand .so's in input files
#    otherwise use cat to send files down pipe.
 eval "cat $files $sed $pre |
        $roff $options - $toc $post $pages $toc $lp"
else echo "fmt:  no files specified"; exit
fi
if [ -f tmp$$ ]; then
    if [ -d toc ]; then
    sed -n -e "s/^><CONTENTS:\(.*\)/\1/p" tmp$$ > toc/$txfile
    fi
    if [ -d index ]; then
    sed -n -e "s/^><INDEX:\(.*\)/\1/p" tmp$$ > index/$txfile
    fi
    if [ -d figlist ]; then
    sed -n -e "s/^><FIGURE:\(.*\)/\1/p" tmp$$ > figlist/$txfile
    fi
    if [ -d tablist ]; then
    sed -n -e "s/^><TABLE:\(.*\)/\1/p" tmp$$ > tablist/$txfile
    fi
    sed -n "/^></!p"
    rm /tmp$$
fi
exit
```

Now, for example, when we format a file called `ch01`, a file of the same name will be written in each of the four subdirectories `toc`, `index`, `figlist`, and `tablist`. Each time we reformat the same file, the output will overwrite the previous contents of each accessory file, giving us the most up-to-date version. When we use the −o option for only partial formatting, writing out of these files is disabled by redirecting error output to `/dev/null`, so that we don't end up with a partial table of contents file.

There's also a −x option, to allow us to format a file to produce the table of contents and index without producing any regular output. This option uses `troff`'s −z option to suppress formatted output, and sets the `post` and `lp` shell variables to the null string.

(You may also notice the −cg option, which specifies a different device to both `troff` and the postprocessor—in this case, a Compugraphic typesetter instead of an Apple LaserWriter. This is included as an aside, to give you an idea of how this is done.)

The contents of the `toc`, `figlist`, and `tablist` directories can be assembled into a complete table of contents, or formatted on the spot for a chapter-level table of contents. We can use the following simple sequence of commands (which could be saved into a shell script):

```
echo .ta \n(LLu-5n \n(LLuR  > book.toc
echo .ce >> book.toc
echo \f3TABLE OF CONTENTS\fP >> book.toc
echo .sp 2 >> book.toc
echo "\t\f3Page\fP" >> book.toc
cat  /toc/ch?? /toc/app?  >> book.toc
echo .bp >> book.toc
cat  /figlist/ch?? /figlist/app? >> book.toc
echo .bp >> book.toc
cat  /tablist/ch?? /tablist/app? >> book.toc
```

The resulting `book.toc` source file looks like this:

```
.ta \n(LLu-5n \n(LLuR
.ce
\f3TABLE OF CONTENTS\fP
.sp 2
|———|\f3Page\fP
.sp 3
Chapter 1  Introduction to Alcuin
.sp 1.5
1.1    A Tradition of Calligraphic Excellence\a\t1-2
1.2    Illuminated Bit-Mapped Manuscripts\a\t1-4
.sp 3
Chapter 2  Getting Started with Alcuin
.sp 1.5
2.1    Objectives of this Session\a\t2-1
2.2    Starting Up the System\a\t2-2
```

```
2.2.1       Power-up Procedure\a\t2-2
  .
  .
  .
```

The index will require more serious postprocessing.

## ▪ Index Processing ▪

It is relatively simple to assemble the components of a table of contents into sequential order, but it is much more difficult to process the index entries, because they must be sorted and manipulated in a variety of ways.

This is one of the most complex tasks presented in this book. So let's start at the beginning, with the raw data that is output by troff, and directed to our index subdirectory by the format shell script. For illustration, we'll assume a sparse index for a short book containing only three chapters.

As you may recall, the user creates the index simply by entering macro calls of the form:

```
.XX "input devices"
```

or:

```
.XX "input devices, mouse"
```

or:

```
.XR "mouse (see input devices)"
```

throughout the text. Both macros write their arguments to standard output; the .XX macro adds the current page number, but the .XR (*cross reference*) macro does not. The user is responsible for using consistent terminology, capitalization, and spelling. A comma separates optional subordinate entries from the major term.

An index term should be entered on any page that the user wants indexed—at the start and end of a major topic, at least, and perhaps several in between if the discussion spans several pages.

In our example, entries are saved into the three files ch01, ch02, and ch03 in the order in which they appear in the respective input files. The indexing term entered by the user is printed, separated from the current page number by a tab. Certain cross reference entries do not have a page number. The content of the raw index files after chapters 1 through 3 have been formatted follows. (Here, and in the following discussion, a tab is represented by the symbol |————|.)

```
$ cat index/ch??
Alcuin, overview of|————|1-1
illuminated manuscripts|————|1-1
fonts, designing|————|1-2
Alcuin, supported input devices|————|1-2
input devices|————|1-2
input devices, mouse|————|1-2
input devices|————|1-2
mouse (see input devices)
```

```
input devices, bit pad|————|1-3
bit pad (see input devices)
input devices|————|1-3
startup, of system|————|2-1
power, location of main switch|————|2-1
power, for graphics display|————|2-1
startup, of system|————|2-2
input devices, mouse|————|2-2
input devices, bit pad|————|2-3
fonts, selecting|————|3-1
glyphs, designing|————|3-2
extra line space|————|3-3
symbolic names|————|3-3
@ operator|————|3-4
```

To create a presentable index from this raw data, we need to do the following:

- Sort the entries into dictionary order, and remove duplicates, if any. (Duplicate entries occur whenever the user enters .XX macros with the same argument over several input pages, and two or more of those entries fall on the same output page.)

- Combine multiple occurrences of the same term, appending a complete list of page numbers and properly subordinating secondary terms.

- Introduce formatting codes, so that the resulting file will have a pleasing, consistent appearance.

Just how complex a task this is may not be immediately apparent, but rest assured that it takes the combined operation of sort, uniq, and several different awk and sed scripts to do the job properly.

Fortunately, we can hide all of this complexity within a single shell program, so that all the user needs to type is:

```
$ cat index/files | indexprog > book.ndx
```

## Sorting the Raw Index

The first part of indexprog processes the index entries before they are passed to awk. The sort program prepares a list of alphabetical index entries; uniq removes duplicate entries.

```
sort -t\|————| -bf +0 -1 +1n | uniq
```

The options to the sort command specify primary and secondary sort operations, affecting the first and second fields separately. The -t option specifies that a tab character separates fields. The primary sort is alphabetic and performed on the indexing term; the secondary sort is numeric and performed on the page number. The primary sort is also controlled by the following options: the -b option (ignore leading blanks

in making comparisons) is a safety feature; the  −f (fold uppercase and lowercase
letters) is more important because the default sort order places all uppercase letters
before all lowercase ones; and  +0  −1 ensures that the alphabetic sort considers only
the first field.  The secondary sort that is performed on the second field (+1n) is
numeric and ensures that page numbers will appear in sequence.

Now let's look at the index entries after they have been sorted:

```
@ operator|————|3-4
Alcuin, overview of|————|1-1
Alcuin, supported input devices|————|1-2
bit pad (see input devices)
extra line space|————|3-3
fonts, designing 1-2
fonts, selecting|————|3-1
glyphs, designing|————|3-2
illuminated manuscripts|————|1-1
input devices|————|1-2
input devices|————|1-3
input devices, bit pad|————|1-3
input devices, bit pad|————|2-3
input devices, mouse|————|1-2
input devices, mouse|————|2-2
mouse (see input devices)
power, for graphics display|————|2-1
power, location of main switch|————|2-1
startup, of system|————|2-1
startup, of system|————|2-2
symbolic names|————|3-3
```

Multiple entries that differ only in their page number are now arranged one after the
other.

The  sort command is a simple way to obtain a sorted list of entries. However,
sorting can actually be a complicated process.  For instance, the simple  sort command that we showed above obviously works fine on our limited sample of entries.
And while it is designed to process entries with section-page numbering (*4-1, 4-2, 4-3*),
this command also works fine when sorting entries with continuous page numbering (*1,
2, 3*).

However, section page numbering does present a few additional problems that we
did not encounter here.  Two-digit section numbers and page numbers, as well as
appendices (*A-1, A-2, A-3*) will not be sorted correctly.  For instance, this might cause
the indexing program to produce the following entry:

```
Alcuin, software  A-2, 1-1, 1-10, 1-3, 11-5, 2-1
```

There are two ways to handle this problem.  One is to change the indexing macro in
troff so that it produces three fields.  Then the sorting command can sort on the section number independent of the page number.  (Because our  awk portion of the index-

ing program is set up to operate on entries with one or two fields, you'd have to change the program or use a sed script to reduce the number of fields.)

The second method uses sed to replace the hyphen with a tab, creating three fields. Actually, we run a sed script *before* the entries are sorted and another one *after* that operation to restore the entry. Then sort will treat section numbers and page numbers separately in secondary numeric sort operations, and get them in the right order.

The only remaining problem is how to handle appendices. What happens is that when a numeric sort is performed on section numbers, lettered appendices are sorted to the top of the list. This requires cloaking the letter in a numeric disguise. Presuming that we won't have section numbers greater than 99, our sed script prepends the number 100 to each letter; this number is also removed afterwards.

```
sed '
    s/|———|\([0-9][0-9]*\)-/|———|\1|———|/
    s/|———|\([A-Z]\)-/|———|100\1|———|/' |
sort -t\    -bf +0 -1 +1n +2n | uniq |
sed '
    s/|———|100\([A-Z]\)|———|/|———|\1-/
    s/\(|———|.*\)|———|/\1-/'
```

Now the sorting operation of our index program handles a wider range of entries.

## Building the Page Number List

The next step is more complex. We must now combine multiple occurrences of each term that differ only in the page number, and combine all of the page numbers into a single list. The awk program is the tool of choice. We can use a script for comparing and manipulating successive lines similar to the one described in Chapter 13. We begin by building the page number list for each entry.

```
awk '
BEGIN { ORS = ""; FS = "|———|" }
NF == 1 { if (NR == 1) printf ("%s", $0);
          else printf ("\n%s", $0) }
NF > 1 {
  if ($1 == curr)
    printf (",%s", $2)
  else {
    if (NR == 1) printf ("%s", $0)
    else printf ("\n%s", $0)
    curr = $1
    }
}'
```

First, the program sets the output record separator (ORS) to the null string, rather than the default newline. This means that output records will be appended to the same line, unless we specify an explicit newline.

Second, it sets the field separator (FS) to the tab character. This divides each index entry into two fields: one containing the text, the other containing the page number. (As you may recall, the page number is separated from the text of the entry by a tab when it is output from troff.)

Then, if the number of fields (NF) is 1 (that is, if there is no tab-separated page number, as is the case with cross reference entries generated with .XR), the program prints out the entire record ($0). If this is not the first line in the file (NR = 1), it precedes the record with an explicit newline (\n).

If the number of fields is greater than 1 (which is the case for each line containing a tab followed by a page number), the program compares the text of the entry in the first field ($1) with its previous value, as stored into the variable curr.

The next few lines might be easier to understand if the condition were written in reverse order:

```
if ($1 != curr)
{ if (NR == 1) printf ("%s", $0)
  else printf ("\n%s", $0)
  curr = $1
}
else printf (",%s", $2)
```

If the first field is not equal to curr, then this is a new entry, so the program prints out the entire record (again preceding it with an explicit newline if this is not the first line of the file). The value of curr is updated to form the basis of comparison for the next record.

Otherwise (if the first field in the current record is the same as the contents of the variable curr), the program appends a comma followed by the value of the second field ($2) to the current record.

The output after this stage of the program looks like this:

```
@ operator|——————|3-4
Alcuin, overview of|——————|1-1
Alcuin, supported input devices|——————|1-2
bit pad (see input devices)
extra line space|——————|3-3
fonts, designing 1-2
fonts, selecting|——————|3-1
glyphs, designing|——————|3-2
illuminated manuscripts|——————|1-1
input devices|——————|1-2,1-3
input devices, bit pad|——————|1-3,2-3
input devices, mouse|——————|1-2,2-2
mouse (see input devices)
power, for graphics display|——————|2-1
power, location of main switch|——————|2-1
startup, of system|——————|2-1,2-2
symbolic names|——————|3-3
```

## Subordinating Secondary Entries

The next trick is to subordinate secondary entries under the main entry, without reprinting the text of the main entry. In addition, we want to represent consecutive page numbers as a range separated by two dots (..) rather than as a list of individual pages. We'll show this script in two sections:

```
 1  awk '
 2  BEGIN  { FS = "|———|"; }
 3  {
 4  n = split ($1, curentry, ",")
 5  if (curentry[1] == lastentry[1])
 6    printf (" %s", curentry[2])
 7  else {
 8    if (n > 1) printf ("%s\n  %s", curentry[1], curentry[2])
 9    else printf ("%s", $1)
10    lastentry[1] = curentry[1]
11  }
12 }
```

This section of the script uses awk's split function to break the first field into two parts, using a comma as a separator.

There are several cases that the program has to consider:

- The text of the entry does not contain a comma, in which case we can just print the entire first field. See line 9: printf ("%s", $1).

- The entry does contain a comma, in which case we want to see if we have a new primary term (curentry[1]) or just a new secondary one (curentry[2]).

- If the primary term is the same as the last primary term encountered (and saved into the variable lastentry), we only need to print out the secondary term. See line 6: printf ("%s", curentry[2]).

- Otherwise, we want to print out both the primary and secondary terms: See line 8: printf ("%s\n %s", curentry[1], curentry[2]).

For example:

```
@ operator|———|3-4
Alcuin, overview of|———|1-1
Alcuin, supported input devices|———|1-2
```

When the first line is processed, the split will return a value of 0, so the entire line will be output.

When the second line is processed, lastentry contains the string @ operator, curentry[1] contains *Alcuin*, and curentry[2] contains *overview of*. Because lastentry is not the same as curentry[1], the program prints out both curentry[1] and curentry[2].

When the third line is processed, curentry[1] again contains the word *Alcuin*, but curentry[2] contains the words *supported input devices*. In this case, only curentry[2] is printed.

The next part of the script, which follows, looks considerably more complicated, but uses essentially the same mechanism. It splits the second field on the line (the page number list) on the hyphens that separate section number from page number. Then, it compares the various sections it has split to determine whether or not it is dealing with a range of consecutive pages. If so, it prints only the first and last members of the series, separating them with the range notation (..).

If you were able to follow the previous portion of the script, you should be able to piece this one together as well:

```
NF == 1{ printf ("\n") }
(NF > 1) && ($2 !~ /.*_.*/) {
  printf ("\t")
  n = split ($2, arr, ",")
  printf ("%s", arr[1])
  split (arr[1], last, "-")
  for (i = 2; i <= n; ++i) {
  split (arr[i], curr, "-")
  if ((curr[1] == last[1])&&(curr[2]/1 == last[2]/1+1)) {
    if (i != n) {
      split (arr[i+1], follow, "-")
      if ((curr[1] != follow[1])||(curr[2]/1+1 != follow[2]/1))
        printf ("..%s", arr[i])
    } else printf ("..%s", arr[i])
  } else printf (", %s", arr[i])
  last[1] = curr[1]; last[2] = curr[2]
}
printf ("\n")
}'
```

The output from this awk program (in sequence with the previous ones) now looks like this:

```
@ operator|———|3-4
Alcuin
    overview of|———|1-1
    supported input devices|———|1-2
bit pad (see input devices)
extra line space|———|3-3
fonts
    designing 1-2
    selecting|———|3-1
glyphs
    designing|———|3-2
illuminated manuscripts|———|1-1
input devices|———|1-2..1-3
    bit pad|———|1-3, 2-3
    mouse|———|1-2, 2-2
mouse (see input devices)
```

```
power
   for graphics display|————|2-1
   location of main switch|————|2-1
startup
   of system|————|2-1..2-2
symbolic names|————|3-3
```

That's starting to look like an index!

## Adding Formatting Codes

We could simply quit here, and let the user finish formatting the index. However, awk can continue the job and insert formatting codes.

We'd like awk to put in headings and divide the index into alphabetic sections. In addition, it would be nice to insert indentation requests, so that we can format the index source file in fill mode so that any long lines will wrap correctly.

Let's look at the coded output before we look at the script that produces it. Only the beginning of the output is shown:

```
.ti -4n
@ operator|————|3-4
.br

.ne 4
.ti -2n
\fBA\fR
.br
.ne 2
.ti -4n
Alcuin
.br
.ti -4n
   overview of|————|1-1
.br
.ti -4n
   supported input devices|————|1-2
.br

.ne 4
.ti -2n
\fBB\fR
.br
.ne 2
.ti -4n
bit pad (see input devices)
.br
```

```
.ne 4
.ti -2n
\fBE\fR
.br
.ne 2
.ti -4n
extra line space|————|3-3
.br
```

Here's a script that does this part of the job:

```
awk '
BEGIN  {OFS = ""
  lower = "abcdefghijklmnopqrstuvwxyz"
  upper = "ABCDEFGHIJKLMNOPQRSTUVWXYZ"
}
NF > 0 {
  if ($0 !~ /^ .*/) {
    n = 1
    while ((newchar = substr($1,n,1)) !~ /[A-Za-z]/) {
      n = n + 1
      if (n == 100) {# bad line
        newchar = oldchar
        break
      }
    }
    if (newchar ~ /[a-z]/) {
      for (i = 1; i <= 26; ++i) {
        if (newchar == substr (lower, i, 1)) {
          newchar = substr (upper, i, 1)
          break
        }
      }
    }
    if (substr($1,1,1) ~ /[0-9]/)
      newchar = ""
    if (newchar != oldchar) {
      printf ("\n\n%s\n", ".ne 4")
      printf ("%s\n", ".ti -2n")
      printf ("%s%s%s\n", "\\fB", newchar, "\\fR")
      printf ("%s\n", ".br")
      oldchar = newchar }
    printf ("%s\n", ".ne 2")
  }
  printf ("%s\n", ".ti -4n")
  printf ("%s\n", $0)
```

```
    printf ("%s\n", ".br")
}'
```

Every line in the input (NF > 1) will be subjected to the last three lines in the program. It will be surrounded by formatting codes and printed out.

```
        printf ("%s\n", ".ti -4n")
        printf ("%s\n", $0)
        printf ("%s\n", ".br")
```

The rest of the script checks when the initial character of a primary entry changes and prints a heading.

As you may have noticed, in the output of the previous script, secondary entries were indented by three leading spaces. They can be excluded from consideration at the outset by the condition:

```
    if ($0 !~ /^ .*/) {
```

All other lines are checked to determine their initial character. The awk program's substr function extracts the first letter of each line. Then, much as it did before, the program compares each entry with the previous until it detects a change.

The program is basically looking for alphabetic characters, but must test (especially in computer manuals) for strings that begin with nonalphabetic characters. (If it doesn't do this, it will loop endlessly when it comes to a string that doesn't begin with an alphabetic character.) If the program loops 100 times on a single line, it assumes that the character is nonalphabetic, breaks out of the loop, and goes on to the next line.

When the program finds a change in the initial alphabetic character, it prints a heading consisting of a single capital letter and associated formatting requests.

Primary terms beginning with nonalphabetic characters are output without causing a change of heading. (Because they are already sorted to the beginning of the file, they will all be listed at the head of the output, before the A's.)

## Final Formatting Touches

Having come this far, it hardly seems fair not to finish the job, and put in the final formatting codes that will allow us to format and print the index without ever looking at the source file (although we should save it to allow manual fine tuning if necessary)

A simple sed script can be used for these final touches:

```
sed "1i\\
.Se \"\" \"Index\"\\
.in +4n\\
.MC 3.15i 0.2i\\
.ds RF Index - \\\\\\\\n(PN\\
.ds CF\\
.ds LF\\
.na
s/|————|/   /"
```

Assuming that we're using our extended ms macros, these initial macros will create the section heading *Index*, print the index in two columns, and use a page number of the form Index − *n*. (Note how many backslashes are necessary before the number register invocation for PN. Backslashes must be protected from the shell, sed, and troff. This line will be processed quite a few times, by different programs, before it is output.)

Finally, the script converts the tab separating the index entry from the first page number into a pair of spaces.

## Special Cases

But our indexing script is not complete. There are a number of special cases still to consider. For example, what about font changes within index entries? In a computer manual, it may be desirable to carry through ''computer voice'' or italics into the index.

However, the troff font-switch codes will interfere with the proper sorting of the index. There is a way around this—awkward, but effective. As you may recall, we use a sed script named cleanup.sed called from within format. This script changes double quotation marks to pairs of matched single quotation marks for typesetting, and changes double hyphens to em dashes. We can also use it to solve our current problem.

First, we add the following lines to cleanup.sed:

```
/^\.X[XR]/{
        s/\\\(fP\)/%%~/g
        s/\\\(fS\)/%%~~/g
        s/\\\(fB\)/%%~~~/g
        s/\\\(fI\)/%%~~~~/g
        s/\\\(fR\)/%%~~~~~/g
        s/\\\(f(CW\)/%%~~~~~~/g
}
```

Within an .XX or .XR macro, the script will change the standard troff font-switch codes into an arbitrary string of nonalphabetic characters.

Then we add the −d option (*dictionary order*) to our initial sort command in the index program. This option causes sort to ignore nonalphabetic characters when making comparisons. (The exception will be lines like @ *operator*, which contain no alphabetic characters in the first field. Such lines will still be sorted to the front of the list.)

Finally, we use the concluding sed script in the indexing sequence to restore the proper font-switch codes in the final index source file:

```
s/%%~~~~~~/\\\\f(CW/g
s/%%~~~~~/\\\\fR/g
s/%%~~~~/\\\\fI/g
s/%%~~~/\\\\fB/g
s/%%~~/\\\\fS/g
s/%%~/\\\\fP/g
```

We might also want to consider the case in which a leading period (as might occur if we were indexing `troff` formatting requests) appears in an index entry. Inserting the following line one line from the end of the last `awk` script we created will do the trick. These lines insulate `troff` codes in index entries from the formatter when the index source file is processed by `troff` for final printing:

```
if ($0 ~ /^\..*/) printf ("\\&")
if ($0 ~ /^%%~~*\./) printf ("\\&")
```

Lines beginning with a `.` will be preceded with a `troff` zero-width character (`\&`).

## The Entire Index Program

We have broken the indexing process into stages to make it easier to understand. However, there is no need to keep individual `awk` and `sed` scripts; they can be combined into a single shell program simply by piping the output of one portion to another, within the shell program.

Here's the whole program, as finally assembled:

```
sed '
    s/|————|\([0-9][0-9]*\)-/|————|\1|————|/
    s/|————|\([A-Z]\)-/|————|100\1|————|/' |
sort -t\|————| -bdf +0 -1 +1n +2n | uniq |
sed '
    s/|————|100\([A-Z]\)|————|/|————|\1-/
    s/\(|————|.*\)|————|/\1-/' |
awk '
BEGIN { ORS = ""; FS = "|————|" }
NF == 1 { if (NR == 1) printf ("%s", $0);
          else printf ("\n%s", $0) }
NF > 1 {
  if ($1 == curr)
    printf (",%s", $2)
  else {
    if (NR == 1) printf ("%s", $0)
    else printf ("\n%s", $0)
    curr = $1
    }
}' | awk '
BEGIN { FS = "|————|"; }
{
n = split ($1, curentry, ",")
if (curentry[1] == lastentry[1])
  printf ("  %s", curentry[2])
else {
  if (n > 1) printf ("%s\n  %s", curentry[1], curentry[2])
```

```
        else printf ("%s", $1)
        lastentry[1] = curentry[1]
        }
}
NF == 1{ printf ("\n") }
(NF > 1) && ($2 !~ /.*_.*/) {
    printf ("\t")
    n = split ($2, arr, ",")
    printf ("%s", arr[1])
    split (arr[1], last, "-")
    for (i = 2; i <= n; ++i) {
    split (arr[i], curr, "-")
    if ((curr[1] == last[1]) && (curr[2]/1 == last[2]/1+1)) {
        if (i != n) {
            split (arr[i+1], follow, "-")
            if ((curr[1] != follow[1])||(curr[2]/1+1 != follow[2]/1))
                printf ("..%s", arr[i])
        } else printf ("..%s", arr[i])
    } else printf (", %s", arr[i])
    last[1] = curr[1]; last[2] = curr[2]
}
printf ("\n")
}' | awk '
BEGIN  {OFS = ""
    lower = "abcdefghijklmnopqrstuvwxyz"
    upper = "ABCDEFGHIJKLMNOPQRSTUVWXYZ"
}
NF > 0 {
    if ($0 !~ /^ .*/) {
        n = 1
        while ((newchar = substr($1,n,1)) !~ /[A-Za-z]/) {
            n = n + 1
            if (n == 100) {# bad line
                newchar = oldchar
                break
            }
        }
        if (newchar ~ /[a-z]/) {
            for (i = 1; i <= 26; ++i) {
                if (newchar == substr (lower, i, 1)) {
                    newchar = substr (upper, i, 1)
                    break
                }
            }
        }
```

```
      if (substr($1,1,1) ~ /[0-9]/)
        newchar = ""
      if (newchar != oldchar) {
        printf ("\n\n%s\n", ".ne 4")
        printf ("%s\n", ".ti -2n")
        printf ("%s%s%s\n", "\\fB", newchar, "\\fR")
        printf ("%s\n", ".br")
        oldchar = newchar
      }
      printf ("%s\n", ".ne 2")
    }
    printf ("%s\n", ".ti -4n")
    if ($0 ~ /^\..*/) printf ("\\&")
        if ($0 ~ /^%%~~*\./) printf ("\\&")
    printf ("%s\n", $0)
    printf ("%s\n", ".br")
}' | sed "11\\
.Se \"\" \"Index\"\\
.in +4n\\
.MC 3.4i 0.2i\\
.ds RF Index - \\\\\\\\\n(PN\\
.ds CF\\
.ds LF\\
.na
s/%%~~~~~~/\\\\\f(CW/g
s/%%~~~~~/\\\\\fR/g
s/%%~~~~/\\\\\fI/g
s/%%~~~/\\\\\fB/g
s/%%~~/\\\\\fS/g
s/%%~/\\\\\fP/g"
```

The result of all this processing is source text that can be piped directly to the formatter, saved in a file for later formatting (or perhaps minor editing), or both (using tee to "split" standard output into two streams, one of which is saved in a file).

Assuming that the various raw source files produced by troff are stored in a subdirectory called indexfiles, and that the index script is called indexprog, we can format and print the index as follows:

```
$ cat indexfiles/* | indexprog | ditroff -mS | ... | lp
```

The result will look something like this:

# INDEX

### ▪ Let make Remember the Details ▪

Even though we've hidden the really complex details of index processing inside a shell script, and the format shell script itself handles a lot of the dirty work, there is still a lot for the user to keep track of.  The make utility introduced in Chapter 11 can take us a long way towards making sure that everything that needs to happen for final production of the finished book comes together without a hitch.

Here are some of the things we want to make sure have been done:

- All of the relevant sections have been printed in their most up-to-date form. Odd as it may seem, it is possible to have last minute changes to a file that never make it into the printed book.

- The book has been proofed using whatever automatic tools we have provided, including the proof and double shell scripts (or wwb if you have it). All ''review notes'' embedded in the text must also be satisfied and removed.

- An updated table of contents and index have been printed.

You can probably think of others as well.

The make utility is the perfect tool for this job. We've already seen in Chapter 11 how it can be used to specify the files (and the formatting options) required for each section of the book. Unfortunately, this part of the job requires that you keep formatted output files, which are quite large. If disk space is a problem, this drawback might lead you to think that make isn't worth the bother.

However, with a little thought, you can get around this restriction. Instead of keeping the formatted output file, you can keep a zero-length file that you touch whenever you format the source file. You could add the following line to the end of the format script:

```
touch print/$file
```

Or, if you use make itself to print your document, you could put the touch command into the makefile. Your makefile might look like this:

```
book : print/ch01 print/ch02 print/ch03...

print/ch01 : ch01
    sh /usr/local/bin/format -mS -rv1 -rS2 ch01
    touch print/ch01

print/ch02 : ch02
    sh /usr/local/bin/format -mS -P -rv1 -rS2 ch02
    touch print/ch02
                    .
                    .
                    .
```

Notice that in order to execute the local formatting shell script, it is necessary to execute sh and specify the complete pathname. The options specified with the format shell script can be specific to each file that is formatted. However, generally you want to use the same options to format all the files that make up a particular document. Using variables, you can create a more generalized makefile that is easier to change.

```
FORMAT: sh /usr/local/bin/format
OPTIONS: -mS -P -rv1 -rS2

book : print/ch01 print/ch02 print/ch03...

print/ch01 : ch01
    $(FORMAT) $(OPTIONS) ch01
    touch print/ch01

print/ch02 : ch02
    $(FORMAT) $(OPTIONS) ch02
    touch print/ch02
                    .
                    .
                    .
```

The variables used by make are set like shell variables. But when they are referenced, the name of the variable must be enclosed in parentheses in addition to being prefixed with a dollar sign.

A user can now easily edit the OPTIONS variable to add or remove options. You could also place additional options on the command for a particular file. This is not necessary, though, just because some of the files have tables, equations, or pictures and others don't. Other than the small bit of extra processing it requires, there's no reason not to run the preprocessors on all files.

Our makefile can be further expanded. To make sure that our index and table of contents are up-to-date (and to automate the process of creating them out of the individual raw output files that the format script creates), we can add the following dependencies and creation instructions:

```
book: print/ch01 ... proof/ch01 ... book.index book.toc
                          .
                          .
                          .

print/ch01 : ch01
                          .
                          .
                          .

book.index : index/ch01 index/ch02 ...
    cat index/* | sh /usr/local/bin/indexprog > book.index

book.toc : toc/ch01...figlist/ch01...tablist/ch01...
        echo .ta \n(LLu-5n \n(LLuR  > book.toc
        echo .ce >> book.toc
        echo \f3TABLE OF CONTENTS\fP >> book.toc
        echo .sp 2 >> book.toc
        echo "\t\f3Page\fP" >> book.toc
    cat toc/ch01...toc/appz >> book.toc
    echo '.bp' >> book.toc
    cat figlist/ch01...figlist/appz >> book.toc
    echo '.bp' >> book.toc
    cat tablist/ch01...tablist/appz >> book.toc

toc/ch01 : ch01
  $(FORMAT) $(OPTIONS) -x ch01
toc/ch02 : ch02
  $(FORMAT) $(OPTIONS) -x ch02
                          .
                          .
                          .

index/ch01 : ch01
  $(FORMAT) $(OPTIONS) -x ch01
                          .
```

```
                              .
                              .
                              .
    figlist/ch01 : ch01
      $(FORMAT) $(OPTIONS) -x ch01
                              .
                              .
                              .

    tablist/ch01 : ch01
      $(FORMAT) $(OPTIONS) -x ch01
                              .
                              .
                              .
```

Because we have directories named `toc` and `index`, we give our source files names such as `book.toc` and `book.index`.

We can therefore enter:

**$ make book.toc**

and the table of contents will be compiled automatically. When you enter the above command, the `make` program recognizes `book.toc` as a *target.* It evaluates the following line that specifies several dependent components.

```
    book.toc: toc/ch01 toc/ch02 toc/ch03
```

In turn, each of these components are targets dependent on a source file.

```
    toc/ch02: ch02
      $(FORMAT) $(OPTIONS) -x ch02
```

What this basically means is that if changes have been made to to `ch02` since the file `book.toc` was compiled, the source file will be formatted again, producing new toc entries. The other files, assuming that they have not been changed, will not be re-formatted as their entries are up-to-date.

We can add other "targets", for instance, to check whether or not every chapter in the book has been proofed since it was last edited. Based on when the dependent components were last updated, you could invoke the `proof` program on the associated file, `grep` for Review Note macros, or just print a message to the user reminding him or her to proof the file.

To do this, we create a pseudo-target. If no file with the name `proof` exists, it can never be up-to-date, so typing:

**$ make proof**

will automatically force proofing of the document according to the rules you have specified in the makefile.

The `print` directory also serves as a pseudo-target, useful for printing individual chapters. Users don't have to remember the formatting options that must be specified for a particular file.

And if all these reasons don't convince you to learn `make` and begin constructing makefiles for large documents, perhaps this next benefit will. It gives you a simple two-word command to print an entire book and its apparatus.

```
$ make book
```

When you enter this command, each formatting command as it is being executed will be displayed on the screen. If you wish to suppress these messages while you do other work, invoke make with the −s option or place the line .SILENT: at the top of the makefile.

## Building the Makefile

You are limited only by your imagination and ingenuity in organizing your work with a makefile. However, the more complex the makefile, the longer it gets, and the more difficult for inexperienced users to create.

You can get around this problem too—just write a shell script to build the makefile, taking as arguments the files that make up the document. Here's such a script, called buildmake, that will produce a makefile similar to the one just described. (The make utility requires that the actions to be performed for each target begin with a tab. Such explicit tabs are shown in the following script by the symbol |————|.)

```
if [ $# -eq 0 ]; then
    echo "USAGE: buildmake files"
    echo "(You must specify the files that make up the book)"
    exit
fi
if [ ! -d print ]; then
    mkdir print
    mkdir proof
fi
if [ ! -d index ]; then
    mkdir index
fi
if [ ! -d toc ]; then
    mkdir toc
    mkdir figlist
    mkdir tablist
fi
for x
do
    prifiles="$prifiles print/$x"
    profiles="$profiles proof/$x"
    tcfiles="$tcfiles toc/$x"
    xfiles="$xfiles index/$x"
    fgfiles="$fgfiles figlist/$x"
    tbfiles="$tbfiles toc/$x"
done
echo ".SILENT:" > makefile
```

```
echo "FORMAT = sh /usr/local/bin/format" >> makefile
echo "OPTIONS = -mS" >> makefile
echo "INDEXPROG = sh /usr/local/bin/indexprog">>makefile
echo "book : $prifiles $profiles book.toc book.index">>makefile
echo "book.index : $xfiles/" >> makefile
echo "|————|cat $xfiles | $(INDEXPROG) > book.index">>makefile
echo "|————|$(FORMAT) $(OPTIONS) book.index" >> makefile
echo "book.toc : $tcfiles" >> makefile
echo "|————|echo .ta \n(LLu-5n \n(LLuR  > book.toc">>makefile
echo "|————|echo .ce >> book.toc" >> makefile
echo "|————|echo \f3TABLE OF CONTENTS\fP >> book.toc">>makefile
echo "|————|echo .sp 2 >> book.toc" >> makefile
echo "|————|echo "\t\f3Page\fP" >> book.toc" >> makefile
echo "|————|cat /work/lib/toc_top > book.toc" >> makefile
echo "|————|cat $tcfiles >> book.toc" >> makefile
echo "|————|echo .bp >> book.toc" >> makefile
echo "|————|cat $fgfiles >> book.toc" >> makefile
echo "|————|echo .bp >> book.toc" >> makefile
echo "|————|cat $tbfiles >> book.toc" >> makefile
echo "|————|$(FORMAT) $(OPTIONS) book.toc" >> makefile
for x
do
    echo "print/$x : $x" >> makefile
    echo "|————|$(FORMAT) $(OPTIONS) $x" >> makefile
    echo "proof/$x : $x" >> makefile
    echo "|————|echo $x has not been proofed" >> makefile
    echo "toc/$x : $x" >> makefile
    echo "|————|$(FORMAT) $(OPTIONS) -x $x" >> makefile
    echo "index/$x : $x" >> makefile
    echo "|————|$(FORMAT) $(OPTIONS) -x $x" >> makefile
done
```

To create a complex makefile, all the user needs to do is type:

$ **buildmake** *files*

In addition, the user may want to manually edit the first line of the makefile, which specifies formatter options.

## · Where to Go from Here ·

Large as this book is, it is far from comprehensive. We have covered the basic editing and formatting tools in some detail, but even there, topics have been glossed over. And when it comes to the more advanced tools, programs not explicitly designed for text processing, much has been left out.

The sheer size and complexity of UNIX is one of its fascinations. To a beginner, it can be daunting, but to an advanced user, the unknown has an appeal all its own. Particularly to a technical writer, for whom the computer is a subject as well as a tool, the challenge of taking more control over the process of book production can be endlessly fascinating. The subject and the method of inquiry become ever more intertwined, until, in Yeats's immortal phrase:

How can you know the dancer from the dance?

# Editor Command Summary

This section is divided into five major parts, describing the commands in the text editors vi, ex, sed, and awk, and the pattern-matching syntax common to all of them.

### · Pattern-Matching Syntax ·

A number of UNIX text-processing programs, including ed, ex, vi, sed, and grep, allow you to perform searches, and in some cases make changes, by searching for text patterns rather than fixed strings. These text patterns (also called regular expressions) are formed by combining normal characters with a number of special characters. The special characters and their use are as follows:

.
Matches any single character except newline.

*
Matches any number (including zero) of the single character (including a character specified by a regular expression) that immediately precedes it. For example, because . means "any character," .* means "match any number of any characters."

[...]
Matches any one of the characters enclosed between the brackets. For example, [AB] matches either A or B. A range of consecutive characters can be specified by separating the first and last characters in the range with a hyphen. For example, [A-Z] matches any uppercase letter from A to Z, and [0-9] matches any digit from 0 to 9. If a caret (^) is the first character in the brackets, the comparison is inverted: the pattern will match any characters *except* those enclosed in the brackets.

\\{*n,m*\\}  Matches a range of occurrences of the single character (including a character specified by a regular expression) that immediately precedes it. *n* and *m* are integers between 0 and 256 that specify how many occurrences to match. \\{*n*\\} matches exactly *n* occurrences, \\{*n*,\\} matches at least *n* occurrences, and \\{*n,m*\\} matches any number of occurrences between *n* and *m*. For example, A\\{2,3\\} matches either AA (as in AARDVARK) or AAA (as in AAA Travel Agency) but will not match the single letter A. This feature is not supported in all versions of vi.

^  Requires that the following regular expression be found at the beginning of the line.

$  Requires that the preceding regular expression be found at the end of the line.

\\  Treats the following special character as an ordinary character. For example, \\. stands for a period and \\* for an asterisk.

\\( \\)  Saves the pattern enclosed between \\( and \\) in a special holding space. Up to nine patterns can be saved in this way on a single line. They can be ''replayed'' in substitutions by the escape sequences \\1 to \\9. This feature is not used in grep and egrep.

\\*n*  Matches the *n*th pattern previously saved by \\( and \\), where *n* is a number from 0 to 9 and previously saved patterns are counted from the left on the line. This feature is not used in grep and egrep.

The egrep and awk programs use an extended set of metacharacters:

*regexp*+  Matches one or more occurrences of the regular expression (*regexp*).

*regexp*?  Matches zero or one occurrences of the regular expression.

*regexp* | *regexp*  Matches lines containing either *regexp*.

(*regexp*)  Used for grouping in complex regular expressions (e.g., with | above).

Regular expressions in ex (: commands from vi) offer some different extensions:

\\<  Constrains the following pattern to be matched only at the beginning of a word.

\\>  Constrains the following pattern to be matched only at the end of a word.

\\u  Appended to the *replacement* string of a substitute command, converts first character of replacement string to uppercase.

\U       Appended to the *replacement* string of a substitute command, converts entire replacement string to uppercase.

\l       Appended to the *replacement* string of a substitute command, converts first character of replacement string to lowercase.

\L       Appended to the *replacement* string of a substitute command, converts entire replacement string to uppercase.

## ▪ The vi Editor ▪

### Command-Line Syntax

There are two commands to invoke the vi editor:

    vi [*options*] [*file(s)*]

or:

    view [*file(s)*]

If a file is not named, vi will open a file that can be given a name with the .f command or when it is saved using the :w command. If more than one file is named, the first file is opened for editing and :n is used to open the next file. The view command opens the first *file* for read-only use; changes cannot be saved.

*Options:*

| | |
|---|---|
| −l | Open file for editing LISP programs |
| −r | Recover file |
| −R | Open file in read-only mode; same as using view |
| −t.*tag* | Start at *tag* |
| −x | Open encrypted file |
| + | Open file at last line |
| + *n* | Open file at line *n* |
| +/*pattern* | Open file at first occurrence of *pattern* |
| −w*n* | Set window to *n* lines |

### Operating Modes

After the file is opened, you are in command mode. From command mode, you can invoke insert mode, issue editing commands, move the cursor to a different position in the file, invoke `ex` commands or a UNIX shell, and save or exit the current version of the file.

The following commands invoke insert mode:

```
a A i I o O R s S
```

While in insert mode, you can enter new text in the file. Press the *ESCAPE* key to exit insert mode and return to command mode.


## Command Syntax

The syntax for editing commands is:

[*n*] *operator* [*n*] *object*

The commands that position the cursor in the file represent objects that the basic editing operators can take as arguments. Objects represent all characters up to (or back to) the designated object. The cursor movement keys and pattern-matching commands can be used as objects. Some basic editing operators are:

c     Change
d     Delete
y     Yank or copy

If the current line is the object of the operation, then the operator is the same as the object: `cc`, `dd`, `yy`. *n* is the number of times the operation is performed or the number of objects the operation is performed on. If both *n*'s are specified, the effect is *n* times *n*.

The following text objects are represented:

*word*        Includes characters up to a space or punctuation mark. Capitalized object is variant form that recognizes only blank spaces.

*sentence*    Up to . ! ? followed by two spaces.

*paragraph*   Up to next blank line or paragraph macro defined by `para=` option.

*section*     Up to next section heading defined by `sect=` option.

Examples:

2cw       Change the next two words
d}        Delete up to the next paragraph
d^        Delete back to the beginning of the line

| | |
|---|---|
| 5yy | Copy the next five lines |
| 3dl | Delete three characters to the right of the cursor |

## Status Line Commands

Most commands are not echoed on the screen as you input them. However, the status line at the bottom of the screen is used to echo input for the following commands:

| | |
|---|---|
| / ? | Start pattern-matching search forward (/) or backwards (?) |
| : | Invoke an ex command |
| ! | Invoke a UNIX command that takes as its input an object in the buffer and replaces it with output from the command |

Commands that are input on the status line must be entered by pressing the *RETURN* key. In addition, error messages and output from the ^G command are displayed on the status line.

## Summary of vi Commands

| | |
|---|---|
| . | Repeat last command (insert, change, or delete). |
| ^@ | Repeat last command. |
| @*buffer* | Execute command stored in *buffer*. |
| a | Append text after cursor. |
| A | Append text at end of line. |
| ^A | Unused. |
| b | Back up to beginning of word in current line. |
| B | Back up to word, ignoring punctuation. |
| ^B | Scroll backward one window. |
| c | Change operator. |
| C | Change to end of current line. |
| ^C | Unused. |
| d | Delete operator. |
| D | Delete to end of current line. |
| ^D | Scroll down half-window. |
| e | Move to end of word. |
| E | Move to end of word, ignoring punctuation. |
| ^E | Show one more line at bottom of window. |
| f | Find next character typed forward on current line. |
| F | Find next character typed back on current line. |

| | |
|---|---|
| ^F | Scroll forward one window. |
| g | Unused. |
| G | Go to specified line or end of file. |
| ^G | Print information about file on status line. |
| h | Left arrow cursor key. |
| H | Move cursor to home position. |
| ^H | Left arrow cursor key; *BACKSPACE* key in insert mode. |
| i | Insert text before cursor. |
| I | Insert text at beginning of line. |
| ^I | Unused in command mode; in insert mode, same as *TAB* key. |
| j | Down arrow cursor key. |
| J | Join two lines. |
| ^J | Down arrow cursor key. |
| k | Up arrow cursor key. |
| K | Unused. |
| ^K | Unused. |
| l | Right arrow cursor key. |
| L | Move cursor to last position in window. |
| ^L | Redraw screen. |
| m | Mark the current cursor position in register (a-z). |
| M | Move cursor to middle position in window. |
| ^M | Carriage return. |
| n | Repeat the last search command. |
| N | Repeat the last search command in reverse direction. |
| ^N | Down arrow cursor key. |
| o | Open line below current line. |
| O | Open line above current line. |
| ^O | Unused. |
| p | Put yanked or deleted text after or below cursor. |
| P | Put yanked or deleted text before or above cursor. |
| ^P | Up arrow cursor key. |
| q | Unused. |
| Q | Quit `vi` and invoke `ex` |
| ^Q | Unused in command mode; in input mode, quote next character. |
| r | Replace character at cursor with the next character you type. |
| R | Replace characters. |
| ^R | Redraw the screen. |
| s | Change the character under the cursor to typed characters. |
| S | Change entire line. |
| ^S | Unused. |
| t | Move cursor forward to character before next character typed. |
| T | Move cursor back to character after next character typed. |
| ^T | Unused in command mode; in insert mode, used with *autoindent* option set. |

| | |
|---|---|
| u | Undo the last change made. |
| U | Restore current line, discarding changes. |
| ^U | Scroll the screen upward half-window. |
| v | Unused. |
| V | Unused. |
| ^V | Unused in command mode; in insert mode, quote next character. |
| w | Move to beginning of next word. |
| W | Move to beginning of next word, ignoring punctuation. |
| ^W | Unused in command mode; in insert mode, back up to beginning of word. |
| x | Delete character under the cursor. |
| X | Delete character before cursor. |
| ^X | Unused. |
| y | Yank or copy operator. |
| Y | Make copy of current line. |
| ^Y | Show one more line at top of window. |
| z | Redraw the screen, repositioning cursor when followed by CR at the top, . at the middle, and − at the bottom of screen. |
| ZZ | Exit the editor, saving changes. |
| ^Z | Unused. |

## Characters Not Used in Command Mode

The following characters are unused in command mode and can be mapped as user-defined commands.

| | | | |
|---|---|---|---|
| ^A | g | K | ^K |
| ^O | q | ^T | v |
| V | ^W | ^X | ^Z |
| * | \ | _ (underscore) | |

## vi set Options

The following options can be specified with the : set command.

| Option (Abbreviation) | Default | Description |
|---|---|---|
| autoindent (ai) | noai | Indents each line to the same level as the line above. Use with shiftwidth option. |

| autoprint (ap) | ap | Changes are displayed after each editor command. (For global replacement, last replacement displayed.) |
|---|---|---|
| autowrite (aw) | noaw | Automatically writes (saves) file if changed before opening another file with :n or before giving UNIX command with :!. |
| beautify (bf) | nobf | Ignores all control characters during input (except tab, newline, or formfeed). |
| directory (dir) | =tmp | Names directory in which ex stores buffer files. (Directory must be writable.) |
| edcompatible | noed-compatible | Uses ed-like features on substitute commands. |
| errorbells (eb) | errorbells | Error messages ring bell. |
| hardtabs (ht) | =8 | Defines boundaries for terminal hardware tabs. |
| ignorecase (ic) | noic | Disregards case during a search. |
| lisp | nolisp | Indents are inserted in appropriate LISP format. () {} [[ and ]] are modified to have meaning for *lisp*. |
| list | nolist | Tabs print as ^I; ends of lines are marked with $. (Used to tell if end character is a tab or a space.) |
| magic | magic | Wildcard characters . * [ are special in *patterns*. |
| mesg | mesg | Permits messages to display on terminal while editing in vi. |
| number (nu) | nonu | Displays line numbers on left of screen during editing session. |
| open | open | Allows entry to *open* or *visual* mode from ex. |

| | | |
|---|---|---|
| optimize<br>(opt) | noopt | Deletes carriage returns at the end of lines when printing multiple lines; speeds output on dumb terminals when printing lines with leading white space (blanks or tabs). |
| paragraphs<br>(para) | =IPLPPPQP<br>LIpplpipbp | Defines paragraph delimiters for movement by { or }. The pairs of characters in the value are the names of nroff/troff macros that begin paragraphs. |
| prompt | prompt | Sets ex prompt (:). |
| readonly<br>(ro) | noro | Any writes (saves) of a file will fail unless you use ! after the write (works with w, ZZ, or autowrite). |
| redraw<br>(re) | noredraw | Terminal will redraw the screen whenever edits are made (insert mode pushes over existing characters; deleted lines immediately close up). Default depends on line speed and terminal type. noredraw is useful at slow speeds on a dumb terminal; deleted lines show up as @, and inserted text appears to overwrite existing text until you press *ESC*. |
| remap | remap | Allows nested map sequences. |
| report | =5 | Size of a large edit (i.e., number of lines affected by a single edit) that will trigger a warning message on bottom line of screen. |
| scroll | =[½ window] | Amount of screen to scroll. |
| sections | =SHNHH HU | Defines section delimiters for { } movement. The pairs of characters in the value are the names of nroff/troff macros that begin sections. |
| shell<br>(sh) | =/bin/sh | Pathname of shell used for shell escape (:!) and shell command (:sh). Value is derived from shell environment. |

| `shiftwidth`<br>`(sw)` | `sw=8` | Defines number of spaces to indent when using the `>>` or `<<` commands in the `autoindent` option. |
|---|---|---|
| `showmatch`<br>`(sm)` | `nosm` | In `vi`, when ) or } is entered, cursor moves briefly to matching ( or {. (If match is not on the screen, rings the error message bell.) Very useful for programming. |
| `showmode`<br>`(smd)` | `nosmd` | (System V, Release 2 `vi` only). The string *Input Mode* is printed on the command line whenever input mode is entered. |
| `slowopen`<br>`(slow)` | | Holds off display during insert. Default depends on line speed and terminal type. |
| `tabstop`<br>`(ts)` | `=8` | Sets number of spaces that a *TAB* indents during editing session. (Printer still uses system tab of 8.) |
| `taglength`<br>`(H)` | `=0` | Defines the number of characters that are significant for tags. Default (zero) means that all characters are significant. |
| `tags` | `=tags`<br>`/usr/lib/tags` | Pathname of files containing tags. (See the `tag(1)` command.) By default, system searches `/usr/lib/tags` and the file `tags` in the current directory. |
| `term` | | Terminal type. |
| `terse` | `noterse` | Displays briefer error messages. |
| `timeout` | `timeout` | Macros "time out" after 1 second. |
| `ttytype` | | Terminal type. |
| `warn` | `warn` | Displays *No write since last change* as warning. |
| `window`<br>`(w)` | | Shows a certain number of lines of the file on the screen. Default depends on line speed and terminal type. |
| `wrapscan`<br>`(ws)` | `ws` | Searches wraparound end of file. |

| wrapmargin<br>(wm) | =0 | Defines right margin. If greater than zero, automatically inserts carriage returns to break lines. |
| writeany<br>(wa) | nowa | Allows saving to any file. |

## ▪ The ex Editor ▪

The ex editor is a line editor that serves as the foundation for the screen editor, vi. All ex commands work on the current line or a range of lines in a file. In vi, ex commands are preceded by a colon and entered by pressing *RETURN*. In ex itself, the colon is supplied as the prompt at which you enter commands.

The ex editor can also be used on its own. To enter ex from the UNIX prompt:

> ex *filename*

Any of the options described for invoking vi may also be used with ex. In addition, the vi command Q can be used to quit the vi editor and enter ex.

To exit ex:

| x | Exit, saving changes |
| q! | Quit, without saving changes |
| vi | Enter vi from ex |

To enter an ex command from vi:

> :*address command options*

The colon (:) indicates an ex command. The *address* is a line number or range of lines that are the object of the *command*.

The following options can be used with commands:

| ! | Indicates a variant form of the command. |
| *parameters* | Indicates that additional information can be supplied. A parameter can be the name of a file. |
| *count* | Is the number of times the command is to be repeated. |
| *flag* | #, p, and l indicate print format. |

Unlike vi commands, the *count* cannot precede the command as it will be taken for the *address*. d3 deletes three lines beginning with the current line; 3d deletes line 3.

As you type the address and command, it is echoed on the status line. Enter the command by pressing the *RETURN* key.

## Addresses

If no address is given, the current line is the object of the command. If the address specifies a range of lines, the format is:

   *x*, *y*

where *x* and *y* are the first and last addressed lines. *x* must precede *y* in the buffer. *x* and *y* may be line numbers or primitives. Using ; instead of , sets the current line to *x* before interpreting *y* (that is, the current position will be at *x* at the completion of the command). 1, $ addresses all lines in the file.

The following address symbols can be used:

| | |
|---|---|
| . | Current line |
| *n* | Absolute line *number* |
| $ | Last line |
| % | All lines, same as 1, $ |
| *x*− \| +*n* | *n* line before or after *x* |
| -[*n*] | One or *n* lines previous |
| + [*n*] | One or *n* lines ahead |
| '*x* | Line marked with *x* |
| ' ' | Previous context |
| /*pat*/ or ?*pat*? | Ahead or back to line matching *pat* |

## ex Commands

| | |
|---|---|
| abbrev | ab [*string text*]<br>Define *string* when typed to be translated into *text*. If *string* and *text* are not specified, list all current abbreviations. |
| append | [*address*]a[!]<br>*text*<br><br>.<br>Append *text* at specified *address*, or at present address if none is specified. With the ! flag, toggle the autoindent setting during the input of *text*. |

args
ar
Print the members of the argument list, with the current argument printed within brackets ([ ]).

change
[*address*]c[!]
*text*
.
Replace the specified lines with *text*. With the ! flag, toggle the autoindent setting during the input of *text*.

copy
[*address*]co*destination*
Copy the lines included in *address* to the specified *destination* address. The command t is a synonym for copy.

delete
[*address*]d[*buffer*]
Delete the lines included in *address*. If *buffer* is specified, save or append the text to the named buffer.

edit
e[!] [+*n*] *file*
Begin editing on *file*. If the ! flag is used, do not warn if the present file has not been saved since the last change. If the +*n* argument is used, begin editing on line *n*.

file
f [*filename*]
Change the name of the current file to *filename*, which is considered "not edited." If no *filename* is specified, print the current status of the file.

global
[*address*]g[!]/*pattern*/[*commands*]
Execute *commands* on all lines that contain *pattern*. If *commands* are not specified, print all such lines. If the ! flag is used, execute *commands* on all lines not containing *pattern*.

insert
[*address*]i[!]
*text*
.
Insert *text* at line before the specified *address*, or at present address if none is specified. With the ! flag, toggle the autoindent setting during the input of *text*.

join
[*address*]j[*count*]
Place the text in the specified range on one line, with white space adjusted to provide two blank characters after a (.), no blank characters if a ) follows, and one blank character otherwise.

k
[*address*]k*char*
Mark the given *address* with *char*.

list

[*address*]l[*count*]
Print the specified lines in an unambiguous manner.

map

map *char commands*
Define a macro named *char* in visual mode with the specified sequence of *commands*. *char* may be a single character, or the sequence #*n*, representing a function key on the keyboard.

mark

[*address*]ma*char*
Mark the specified line with *char*, a single lowercase letter. Return later to the line with ' x.

move

[*address*]m*destination*
Move the lines specified by *address* to the *destination* address.

next

n[!][[+*command*] *filelist*]
Edit the next file in the command-line argument list. Use args for a listing of arguments. If *filelist* is provided, replace the current argument list with *filelist* and begin editing on the first file; if *command* is given (containing no spaces), execute *command* after editing the first such file.

number

[*address*]nu[*count*]
Print each line specified by *address* preceded by its buffer line number. # may be used as an abbreviation for number as well as nu.

open

[*address*]o[/*pattern*/]
Enter open mode at the lines specified by *address*, or lines matching *pattern*. Exit open mode with Q.

preserve

pre
Save the current editor buffer as though the system had crashed.

print

[*address*]p[*count*]
Print the lines specified by *address* with nonprinting characters printed. P may also be used as an abbreviation.

put

[*address*]pu[*char*]
Restore previously deleted or yanked lines from named buffer specified by *char* to the line specified by *address*; if *char* is not specified, the last deleted or yanked text is restored.

quit

q[!]
Terminate current editing session. If the file was not saved since the last change, or if there are files in the argument list that have not yet be accessed, you will not be able to quit without the ! flag.

read            [*address*]r[!] [*file*]
                Copy the text of *file* at the specified *address*. If *file* is not specified,
                the current filename is used.

read            [*address*]r !*command*
                Read in the output of *command* into the text after the line specified
                by *address*.

recover         rec [*file*]
                Recover *file* from system save area.

rewind          rew[!]
                Rewind argument list and begin editing the first file in the list. The
                ! flag rewinds without warning if the file has not been saved since
                the last change.

set             se *parameter parameter2* ...
                Set a value to an option with each *parameter*, or if no *parameter* is
                supplied, print all options that have been changed from their
                defaults. For Boolean-valued options, each *parameter* can be
                phrased as *option* or *nooption*; other options can be assigned with
                the syntax, *option=value*.

shell           sh
                Create a new shell. Resume editing when the shell is terminated.

source          so *file*
                Read and execute commands from *file*.

substitute      [*address*]s[[/*pattern*/*repl*/]*options*][*count*]
                Replace each instance of *pattern* on the specified lines with *repl*. If
                *pattern* and *repl* are omitted, repeat last substitution. The following
                options are supported:
                        g       Substitute all instances of *pattern*
                        c       Prompt for confirmation before each change

t               [*address*]t *destination*
                Copy the lines included in *address* to the specified *destination*
                address.

ta              [*address*]ta *tag*
                Switch the focus of editing to *tag*.

unabbreviate una *word*
                Remove *word* from the list of abbreviations.

undo            u
                Reverse the changes made by the last editing command.

| | |
|---|---|
| unmap | unm *char*<br>Remove *char* from the list of macros. |
| v | [*address*]v / *pattern* / [*commands*]<br>Execute *commands* on all lines not containing *pattern*. If *commands* are not specified, print all such lines. |
| version | ve<br>Print the current version number of the editor and the date the editor was last changed. |
| visual | [*address*]vi [*type*] [*count*]<br>Enter visual mode at the line specified by *address*. Exit with Q. *type* is either −, ^, or . (see the z command). *count* specifies an initial window size. |
| write | [*address*]w[!] [[>>] *file*]<br>Write lines specified by *address* to *file*, or full contents of buffer if *address* is not specified. If *file* is also omitted, save the contents of the buffer to the current filename. If >> *file* is used, write contents to the end of the specified *file*. The ! flag forces the editor to write over any current contents of *file*. |
| write | [*address*]w ! *command*<br>Write lines specified by *address* to *command* through a pipe. |
| wq | wq[!]<br>Write and quit the file in one movement. |
| xit | x<br>Write file if changes have been made to the buffer since last write, then quit. |
| yank | [*address*]ya[*char*][*count*]<br>Place lines specified by *address* in named buffer indicated by *char*. If no *char* is specified, place in general buffer. |
| z | [*address*]z[*type*][*count*]<br>Print a window of text with line specified by *address* at the top. *type* is as follows: |

    +    Place specified line at the top of the window (default)
    -    Place specified line at bottom of the window
    ^    Print the window before the window associated with type −
    =    Place specified line in the center of the window and leave the current line at this line

*count* specifies the number of lines to be displayed.

!              *[address]! command*

Execute *command* in a shell. If *address* is specified, apply the lines contained in *address* as standard input to *command*, and replace the lines with the output.

=            *[address]=*

Print the line number of the line indicated by *address*.

< >       *[address]<[count]*

or *[address]  >  [count]*

Shift lines specified by *address* in specified direction. Only blanks and tabs are shifted in a left shift (<).

*address*     *address*

Print the lines specified in *address*.

*RETURN*     *RETURN*

Print the next line in the file.

&            *[address]&[options][count]*

Repeat the previous substitute command.

~            *[address]~[count]*

Replace the previous regular expression with the previous replacement pattern from a `substitute` command.

## ▪ **The `sed` Editor** ▪

`sed` *[options] file(s)*

The following options are recognized:

      −n          Only print lines specified with the p command, or the p flag of the s command

      −e *cmd*    Next argument is an editing command

      −f *file*     Next argument is a file containing editing commands

All `sed` commands have the general form:

      *[address][, address][!]command [arguments]*

The `sed` editor copies each line of input into a pattern space. `sed` instructions consist of addresses and editing commands. If the address of the command matches the line in the pattern space, then the command is applied to that line. If a command has no address, then it is applied to each input line. It is important to note that a command affects the contents of the space; subsequent command addresses attempt to match the line in the pattern space, not the original input line.

## Pattern Addressing

In a `sed` command, an *address* can either be a line number or a *pattern*, enclosed in slashes (*/pattern/*). Address types cannot be mixed when specifying two addresses. Patterns can make use of regular expressions, as described at the beginning of this appendix. Additionally, `\n` can be used to match any newline in the pattern space (resulting from the N command), but not the newline at the end of the pattern space. If no pattern is specified, *command* will be applied to all lines. If only one address is specified, the command will be applied to all lines between the first and second addresses, inclusively. Some commands can only accept one address.

The `!` operator following a pattern causes `sed` to apply the command to all lines that do not contain the pattern.

A series of commands can be grouped after one pattern by enclosing the command list in curly braces:

[*/pattern/*][, */pattern/*]{
*command1*
*command2*
}

## Alphabetical List of Commands

:
: *: label*
Specify a label to be branched to by `b` or `t`. *label* may contain up to eight characters.

=
: [*/pattern/*]=
Write to standard output the line number of each line addressed by *pattern*.

a
: [*address*]a\
*text*
Append *text* following each line matched by *address*. If *text* goes over more than one line, newlines must be "hidden" by preceding them with a backslash. The insertion will be terminated by the first newline that is not hidden in this way. The results of this command are read into the pattern space (creating a multiline pattern space) and sent to standard output when the list of editing is finished or a command explicitly prints the pattern space.

b
: [*address1*][, *address2*]b[*label*]
Branch to *label* placed with `:` command. If no *label*, branch to the end of the script. That is, skip all subsequent editing commands (up to *label*) for each addressed line.

c
    *[address1][, address2]*c\
    *text*
    Replace pattern space with *text*. (See a for details on *text*.)

d
    *[address1][, address2]*d
    Delete line in pattern space. Thus, line is not passed to standard output and a new line of input is read; editing resumes with first command in list.

D
    *[address1][address2]*D
    Delete first part (up to embedded newline) of multiline pattern created by N command and begin editing. Same as d if N has not been applied to a line.

g
    *[address1][, address2]*g
    Copy contents of hold space (see h or H command) into pattern space, wiping out previous contents.

G
    *[address1][, address2]*G
    Append contents of hold space (see h or H command) to contents of the pattern space.

h
    *[address1][, address2]*h
    Copy pattern space into hold space, a special buffer. Previous contents of hold space are obliterated.

H
    *[address1][, address2]*H
    Append pattern space to contents of the hold space. Previous and new contents are separated by a newline.

i
    *[address1]*i\
    *text*
    Insert *text* before each line matched by *address*. (See a for details on *text*.)

n
    *[address1][, address2]*n
    Read next line of input into pattern space. Current line is output but control passes to next editing command instead of beginning at the top of the list.

N
    *[address1][, address2]*N
    Append next input line to contents of pattern space; the two lines are separated by an embedded newline. (This command is designed to allow pattern matches across two lines.)

p
    *[address1][, address2]*p
    Print the addressed line(s). Unless the −n command-line option is used, this command will cause duplication of the line in the output. Also used when commands change flow control (d, N, b).

P         [*address1*][, *address2*]P
Print first part (up to embedded newline) of multiline pattern created by N command. Same as p if N has not been applied to a line.

q         [*address*]q
Quit when *address* is encountered. The addressed line is first written to output, along with any text appended to it by previous a or r commands.

r         [*address*]r *file*
Read contents of *file* and append after the contents of the pattern space. Exactly one space must separate the r and the filename.

s         [*address1*][, *address2*]s/*pattern*/*replacement*/[*flags*]
Substitute *replacement* for *pattern* on each addressed line. If pattern addresses are used, the pattern // represents the last pattern address specified. The following flags can be specified:
> g     Replace all instances of /*pattern*/ on each addressed line, not just the first instance.
>
> p     Print the line if a successful substitution is done. If several successful substitutions are done, multiple copies of the line will be printed.
>
> w *file* Write the line to a *file* if a replacement was done. A maximum of ten different *files* can be opened.

t         [*address1*][, *address2*]t [*label*]
Test if successful substitutions have been made on addressed lines, and if so, branch to *label*. (See b and :.) If label is not specified, drop to bottom of list of editing commands.

w         [*address1*][, *address2*]w *file*
Write contents of pattern space to *file*. This action occurs when the command is encountered rather than when the pattern space is output. Exactly one space must separate the w and the filename. A maximum of ten different files can be opened.

x         [*address1*][, *address2*]x
Exchange contents of the pattern space with the contents of the hold space.

## ▪ awk ▪

An awk program consists of patterns and procedures:

> *pattern* {*procedure*}

Both are optional. If *pattern* is missing, {*procedure*} will be applied to all lines. If {*procedure*} is missing, the line will be passed unaffected to standard output (i.e., it will be printed as is).

Each input line, or record, is divided into fields by white space (blanks or tabs) or by some other user-definable record separator. Fields are referred to by the variables $1, $2,..., $n. $0 refers to the entire record.

## Patterns

Patterns can be specified using regular expressions as described at the beginning of this appendix.

> *pattern* {*procedure*}
> The following additional pattern rules can be used in awk:

- The special pattern BEGIN allows you to specify procedures that will take place before the first input line is processed. (Generally, you set global variables here.)

- Interrupt place after the last input line is processed.

- ^ and $ can be used to refer to the beginning and end of a field, respectively, rather than the beginning and end of a line.

- A pattern can be a relational expression using any of the operators <, <=, ==, !=, >=, and >. For example, $2 > $1 selects lines for which the second field is greater than the first. Comparisons can be either string or numeric.

- Patterns can be combined with the Boolean operators || (or), && (and), and ! (not).

- Patterns can include any of the following predefined variables. For example, NF > 1 selects records with more than one field.

## Special Variables

| | |
|---|---|
| FS | Field separator (blank and tab by default) |
| RS | Record separator (newline by default) |
| OFS | Output field separator (blank by default) |
| ORS | Output record separator (newline by default) |
| NR | Number of current record |
| NF | Number of fields in current record |
| $0 | Entire input record |

$1, $2, ..., $n    First, second, ... *n*th field in current record, where
fields are separated by FS

## Procedures

Procedures consist of one or more commands, functions, or variable assignments,
separated by newlines or semicolons, and contained within curly braces. Commands
fall into four groups:

- variable or array assignments

- printing commands

- built-in functions

- control flow commands

## Variables and Array Assignments

Variables can be assigned a value with an = sign. For example:

    FS = ``,''

Expressions using the operators +, −, /, and % (modulo) can be assigned to variables.

Arrays can be created with the split function (see following awk commands)
or can be simply named in an assignment statement. ++, +=, and −= are used to
increment or decrement an array, as in the C language. Array elements can be subscripted with numbers (*array*[1],...,*array*[*n*]) or with names. (For example, to count
the number of occurrences of a pattern, you could use the following program:

    /pattern/ {n["/pattern/"]++}
    END {print n["/pattern/"] }

## awk Commands

for

    for (i=lower;i<=upper;i++)
        command
    While the value of variable *i* is in the range between *lower* and
    *upper*, do *command*. A series of commands must be put within
    braces. <= or any relational operator can be used; ++ or −− can
    be used to decrement variable.

| | |
|---|---|
| `for` | `for` *i* `in` *array*<br>   *command*<br>For each occurrence of variable *i* in *array*, do *command*. A series of commands must be put inside braces. |
| `if` | `if` (*condition*)<br>   *command*<br>`[else]`<br>   [*command*]<br>If *condition* is true, do *command(s)*, otherwise do *command* in `else` clause. *condition* can be an expression using any of the relational operators `<`, `<=`, `==`, `!=`, `>=`, or `>`, as well as the pattern-matching operator `~` (e.g., `if $1 ~ /[Aa].*/`). A series of commands must be put within braces. |
| `length` | *x* = `length` (*arg*)<br>Return the length of *arg*. If *arg* is not supplied, `$0` is assumed. |
| `log` | *x*–`log` (*arg*)<br>Return logarithm of *arg*. |
| `print` | `print` [*args*]<br>Print *args* on output. *args* is usually one or more fields, but may also be one or more of the predefined variables. Literal strings must be surrounded by quotation marks. Fields are printed in the order they are listed. If separated by commas in the argument list, they are separated in the output by the character specified by `OFS`. If separated by spaces, they are concatenated in the output. |
| `printf` | `printf` "*format*, "*expression(s)*<br>Formatted print statement. Fields or variables can be formatted according to instructions in the *format* argument. The number of arguments must correspond to the number specified in the format sections.<br><br>*Format* follows the conventions of the C language's `printf` statement. Here are a few of the most common formats: |

          `%`*n*.*m*d    a floating point number;
                        *n* = total number of digits.
                        *m* = number of digits after decimal point.
          `%`[`–`]*nc*   *n* specifies minimum field length for
                        format type *c*. `–` justifies value in
                        field; otherwise value is right justified.

       *Format* can also contain embedded escape sequences: `\n` (newline) or `\t` (tab) are the most common.

       Spaces and literal text can be placed in the *format* argument by surrounding the entire argument with quotation marks. If there are multiple expressions to be printed, you should specify multiple formats.  An example is worth a thousand words.  For an input file containing only the line:

    5  5

The program:

    {printf (''The sum on line %s is %d \n'', NR, $1+$2)}

will produce:

    The sum on line 1 is 10.

followed by a newline.

split           $x$ = split (*string*, *array* [, *sep*])
                Split       *string*       into       elements       of       array
                array[1], . . . , array[*n*].  *string* is split at each occurrence
                of separator *sep*.  If *sep* is not specified, FS is used.  The number
                of array elements created is returned.

sprintf         $x$ = sprintf ("*format*", *expression*)
                Return the value of *expression*(s), using the specified *format* (see
                printf).

sqrt            $x$ = sqrt(*arg*)
                Return square root of *arg*.

substr          $x$ = substr (*string*, *m*, [*n*])
                Return substring of *string* beginning at character position *m* and con-
                sisting of the next *n* characters.  If *n* is omitted, include all charac-
                ters to the end of *string*.

while           while (*condition*)
                    *command*
                Do *command* while *condition* is true (see if for a description of
                allowable conditions).  A series of commands must be put within
                braces.

# B

# Formatter Command Summary

This appendix is divided into ten subsections, each covering a different facet of the nroff/troff formatting system. These sections are:

- nroff/troff command-line syntax

- nroff/troff requests

- escape sequences

- predefined number registers

- special characters

- the ms macro package

- the mm macro package

- the tbl preprocessor

- the eqn preprocessor

- the pic preprocessor

In the following sections, italics are used for values that you supply. Optional arguments to requests or macros are enclosed in brackets.

## ▪ **nroff/troff** Command-Line Syntax ▪

nroff [*options*] [*files*]

| | |
|---|---|
| −c*name* | Prepend /usr/lib/macros/cmp.n.[dt].*name* to *files* (old versions of nroff only). |
| −e | Space words equally on the line instead of in full multiples of the space character. |
| −h | Use tabs in large spaces. |
| −i | Read standard input after *files* are processed. |
| −k*name* | Compact macros and output to [dt].*name* (old versions of nroff only). |
| −m*name* | Prepend /usr/lib/tmac/tmac.*name* to *files*. |
| −n*n* | Number first page *n*. |
| −o*list* | Print only pages contained in *list*. Individual pages in *list* should be separated by commas; a page range is specified by *n−m*; *n−* indicates from page *n* to the end. |
| −q | Invoke simultaneous input/output of .rd requests. |
| −r*an* | Set register *a* to *n*. |
| −s*n* | Stop every *n* pages. |
| −T*name* | Output is for device type *name*. Values are shown in Table B-1. (Check your manual for other devices, especially those supported by the mm command.) |
| −u*n* | Embolden characters by overstriking *n* times. |
| −z | Throw away output except messages from .tm request. |

**TABLE B-1. Device Names for nroff**

| Abbreviation | Used for |
|---|---|
| 37 | TELETYPE Model 37 terminal (default for nroff) |
| 450 | DASI 450 terminal (default for mm) |
| tn300 | GE TermiNet 300 printer |
| 300 | DASI 300 terminal |
| 832 | Anderson Jacobson 832 printer |
| 2631 | Hewlett-Packard 2631 |
| 4000a | Trendata 4000a |
| 8510 | C. Itoh printer |
| lp | ASCII line printer |
| X | EBCDIC line printer |

## troff Options

troff [*options*] [*files*]

| | |
|---|---|
| −a | Send printable ASCII approximation to standard output. otroff sends its output directly to a connected typesetter unless the −t or −a option is specified, in which case it is sent to standard output. ditroff always writes to standard output. |
| −b | Report phototypesetter status (otroff only). |
| −c*name* | Prepend /usr/lib/macros/cmp.t.[dt].*name* to *files* (otroff only). |
| −f | Do not stop the phototypesetter when the formatting run is done (otroff only). |
| −F*dir* | Format output for device name using the font tables in directory *dir* instead of /usr/lib/font (ditroff only). |
| −i | Read standard input after files. |
| −k*name* | Compact macros and output to [dt].*name* (otroff only). |
| −m*name* | Prepend /usr/lib/tmac/tmac.*name* to *files*. |
| −n*n* | Number first page *n*. |
| −o*list* | Print only pages contained in *list*. Individual pages in *list* should be separated by commas. A page range is specified by *n−m*; *n−* indicates from page *n* to the end. |
| −p*n* | Print all characters in point size *n*, but retain motions for sizes specified in document (otroff only). |
| −q | Do not echo .rd requests. |
| −r*an* | Assign value *n* to register *a*. |
| −s*n* | Stop every *n* pages. |
| −t | Send output to standard output instead of directly to the phototypesetter (otroff only). |
| −T*name* | Format output for device *name* using the device description and font width tables in /usr/lib/font/dev*name* (ditroff only). |
| −w | If the phototypesetter is busy, wait until it is free (otroff only). |

## ▪ nroff/troff Requests ▪

| | |
|---|---|
| .ab [*text*] | Abort and print *text* as message. If *text* is not specified, the message *User Abort* is printed. |
| .ad [*c*] | Adjust one or both margins if filling is in effect (see .fi). *c* can be: |

            b or n     Adjust both margins

            c         Center all lines

|  | l | Adjust left margin only |
|---|---|---|
|  | r | Adjust right margin only |

.af *r c*  Assign format *c* to register *r*. *c* can be:

|  | 1 | 0, 1, 2, etc. |
|---|---|---|
|  | 001 | 000, 001, 002, etc. |
|  | i | Lowercase roman |
|  | I | Uppercase roman |
|  | a | Lowercase alphabetic |
|  | A | Uppercase alphabetic |

.am *xx yy*  Append to macro *xx*; end append at call of *yy* (default *yy* = ..).

.as *xx string*  Append to *string xx*.

.bd *f n*  Overstrike characters in font *f*, *n* times.

.bd *f s n*  Overstrike special font *s*, *n* times when font *f* is in effect.

.bp [*n*]  Begin new page.  Number next page *n*.

.br  Break to a new line (output partial lines).

.c2 *c*  Set no-break control character to *c* (default ′).

.cc *c*  Set control character to *c* (default .).

.cf *file*  Copy contents of *file* into output, uninterpreted (ditroff only).

.ce [*n*]  Center next *n* lines; if *n* is 0, stop centering (default *n* = 1).

.ch *xx* [*n*]  Change trap position for macro *xx* to *n*.  If *n* is absent, remove the trap.

.cs *f n m*  Use constant character spacing for font *f* of *n*/36 ems.  If *m* is given, the em is taken to be *m* points.

.cu [*n*]  Continuous underline (including interword spaces) on next *n* lines.  If *n* is 0, stop underlining.  Italicize in troff. (See .ul.)

.da [*xx*]  Divert following text, appending it to macro *xx*.  If no argument, end diversion.

.de *xx* [*yy*]  Define macro *xx*.  End definition at .*yy* (default .yy = ..).

.di [*xx*]  Divert following text to newly defined macro *xx*.  If no argument, end diversion.

.ds *xx string*  Define *xx* to contain *string*.

.dt *n xx*  Install diversion trap to invoke macro *xx* at position *n*.

.ec [*c*]  Set escape character to *c* (default \).

.el *anything*  Else portion of if-else.  See .ie.

.em *xx*  Set end macro to *xx*.

.eo  Turn escape character mechanism off.  See .ec.

.ev [*n*]  Change environment to *n*.  If no argument, restore previous environment ($0 \leq n \leq 2$ = initial value 0).

.ex  Exit from formatter.

.fc *a b*  Set field delimiter to *a* and pad character to *b*.

| | |
|---|---|
| `.fi` | Turn on fill mode (default: fill is on). |
| `.fl` | Flush output buffer. |
| `.fp` *n f* | Assign font *f* to position *n*. |
| `.ft` *f* | Change font to *f*. |
| `.hc[c]` | Change hyphenation-indication character used with `.hw` to *c* (default −). |
| `.hw` *words* | Specify hyphenation points for *words* (e.g., `.hw spe-ci-fy`). |
| `.hy` *n* | Turn hyphenation on ($n{\geq}1$) or off ($n{=}0$). |

|  | |
|---|---|
| $n{=}1$ | Hyphenate whenever necessary |
| $n{=}2$ | Don't hyphenate last word in page or diversion |
| $n{=}4$ | Don't split off first two characters of word |
| $n{=}8$ | Don't split off last two characters of word |
| $n{=}14$ | Use all three restrictions |

| | |
|---|---|
| `.ie` *c anything* | If portion of `if-else`. See `.el`. |
| `.if !`*c anything* | If condition *c* is false, do *anything*. |
| `.if` *n anything* | If expression *n* >0, do *anything*. |
| `.if !`*n anything* | If expression $n \leq 0$, do *anything*. |
| `.if` *' string1' string2' anything* | |
| | If *string1* and *string2* are identical, do *anything*. |
| `.if !`*' string1' string2' anything* | |
| | If *string1* and *string2* are not identical, do *anything*. |
| `.ig` *yy* | Ignore following text, up to line beginning with `.yy`. |
| `.in [±][n]` | Set indent to *n* or increment indent by ±*n*. If no argument, restore previous indent. |
| `.it` *n xx* | Set input line count trap to invoke macro *xx* after *n* lines of input text have been read. |
| `.lc` *c* | Set leader repetition character to *c*. (See `.tc`.) Leaders are invoked by `\a`. |
| `.lg` *n* | Turn ligature mode on if *n* is absent or nonzero. |
| `.ll [+][n]` | Set line length to *n* or increment line length by ±*n*. If no argument, restore previous line length (default 6.5 inches). |
| `.ls` *n* | Set line spacing to *n*. If no argument, restore previous line spacing (initial value 1). |
| `.lt` *n* | Set title length to *n*. If no argument, restore previous value. |
| `.mc [c] [n]` | Set margin character to *c*, and place it *n* spaces to the right of margin. If *c* is missing, turn margin character off. Default for *n* is 0.2 inches in `nroff` and 1 em in `troff`. |
| `.mk [r]` | Mark current vertical place in register *r*. Return to mark with `.rt`, or `.sp|\n`*r*. |
| `.na` | Do not adjust margins. (See `.ad`.) |
| `.ne` *n* | If *n* lines do not remain on this page, start new page. |
| `.nf` | No filling or adjusting of output lines. (See `.ad` and `.fi`.) |

| | |
|---|---|
| .nh | Turn hyphenation off. (See .hy.) |
| .nm [n m s i] | Number output lines ($n \geq 0$) or turn numbering off ($n=0$). $\pm n$ sets initial line number; m sets numbering interval; s sets separation of numbers and text; i sets indent of text. |
| .nn n | Do not number next n lines, but keep track of numbering sequence, which can be resumed with .nm+0. |
| .nr r n [m] | Assign the value n to number register r and optionally set autoincrement to m. |
| .ns | Turn no-space mode on. (See .rs.) |
| .nx file | Switch to file and do not return to current file. (See .so.) |
| .os | Output saved space specified in previous .sv request. |
| .pc c | Set page number character to c. |
| .pi cmd | Pipe output of troff to cmd instead of to standard output. |
| .pl [±][n] | Set page length to n or increment page length by $\pm n$. If no argument, restore default (default 11 inches). |
| .pm | Print names and sizes of all defined macros. |
| .pn [±][n] | Set next page number to n, or increment page number by $\pm n$. |
| .po [±][n] | Offset text a distance of n from left edge of page, or increment the current offset by $\pm n$. If no argument, restore previous offset. |
| .ps n | Set point size to n (troff only). (Default 10 points.) |
| .rd [prompt] | Read input from terminal, after printing optional prompt. |
| .rm xx | Remove macro or string xx. |
| .rn xx yy | Rename request, macro, or string xx to yy. |
| .rr r | Remove register r. |
| .rs xx yy | Restore spacing. (Turn no-space mode off; see .ns.) |
| .rt [±n] | Return (upward only) to marked vertical place, or to $\pm n$ from top of page or diversion. (See .mk.) |
| .so file | Switch out to file, then return to current file. (See .nx.) |
| .sp n | Leave n blank lines (default 1). |
| .ss n | Space character size set to n/36 em (no effect in nroff). |
| .sv n | Save n lines of space; output such space with .os. |
| .sy cmd [args] | Execute UNIX command cmd with optional arguments (ditroff only). |
| .ta n[t] m[t] | Set tab stop at positions n, m, etc. If t is not given, tab is left adjusting; if t is:<br>R  Right adjust<br>C  Center |
| .tc c | Define tab character as c (e.g., .tc . will draw a string of dots to tab position). |
| .ti [±][n] | Indent next output line n spaces, or increment the current indent by $\pm n$ for the next output line. |

| | |
|---|---|
| `.tl 'l'c'r'` | Specify left (*l*), centered (*c*), right (*r*) title. |
| `.tm` *text* | Terminal message. (Print *text* on standard error.) |
| `.tr` *ab* | Translate character *a* to *b*. |
| `.uf` *f* | Underline font set to *f* (to be switched to by `.ul`). |
| `.ul` [*n*] | Underline (italicize in `troff`) next *n* input lines. Do not underline interword spaces. |
| `.vs` [*n*] | Set vertical line spacing to *n*. If no argument, restore previous spacing (default 1/6 inch in `nroff`, 12 points in `troff`). |
| `.wh` *n xx* | When position *n* is reached, execute macro *xx*; negative values of *n* are with respect to page bottom. |

## ▪ Escape Sequences ▪

| | |
|---|---|
| `\` | To prevent or delay the interpretation of `\`. |
| `\e` | Printable version of the *current* escape character. |
| `\´` | ´ (acute accent); equivalent to `\(aa`. |
| `\`` | ` (grave accent); equivalent to `\(ga`. |
| `\-` | – Minus sign in the *current* font. |
| `\.` | Period (dot). (See `de`.) |
| `\` (space) | Unpaddable space-size space character. |
| `\0` | Digit width space. |
| `\|` | 1/6-em narrow space character (zero width in `nroff`). |
| `\^` | 1/12-em half-narrow space character (zero width in `nroff`). |
| `\&` | Nonprinting, zero-width character. |
| `\!` | Transparent line indicator. |
| `\"` | Beginning of comment. |
| `\\$N` | Interpolate argument $1 \leq N \leq 9$. |
| `\%` | Default optional hyphenation character. |
| `\(xx` | Character named *xx*. |
| `\*x`, `\*(xx` | Interpolate string *x* or *xx*. |
| `\a` | Noninterpreted leader character for use in macros. |
| `\b´abc...´` | Bracket building function—stack *abc*... vertically. |
| `\c` | Interrupt text processing. |
| `\d` | Downward 1/2-em vertical motion (1/2 line in `nroff`). |
| `\D´l x,y´` | Draw a line from current position to coordinates *x,y* (`ditroff` only). |
| `\D´c d´` | Draw circle of diameter *d* with left edge at current position (`ditroff` only). |

| | |
|---|---|
| \D´e *d1 d2*´ | Draw ellipse with horizontal diameter *d1* and vertical diameter *d2*, with left edge at current position (`ditroff` only). |
| \D´a *x1 y1 x2 y2*´ | Draw arc counterclockwise from current position, with center at *x1,y1* and endpoint at *x1+x2,y1+y2* (`ditroff` only). |
| \D´~ *x1 y1 x2 yx . . .*´ | Draw spline from current position through the specified coordinates (`ditroff` only). |
| \f*x*,\f (*xx*,\f*N* | Change to font named *x* or *xx* or to position *N*. |
| \h´*N*´ | Local horizontal motion; move right *N* (negative left). |
| \H´*n*´ | Set character height to *n* points, without changing width (`ditroff` only). |
| \j*x* | Mark horizontal place on output line in register *x*. |
| \k*x* | Mark horizontal place on input line in register *x*. |
| \l´*Nc*´ | Horizontal line drawing function (optionally with *c*, default _ ). |
| \L´*Nc*´ | Vertical line drawing function (optionally with *c*, default ǀ). |
| \n*x*,\n (*xx* | Interpolate number register *x* or *xx*. |
| \o´*abc...*´ | Overstrike characters *a*, *b*, *c*... |
| \p | Break and spread output line. |
| \r | Reverse 1-em vertical motion (reverse line in `nroff`). |
| \s*N*,\s±*N* | Point-size change function. |
| \S´*n*´ | Slant output *n* degrees to the right (`ditroff` only). Negative values slant to the left. A value of zero turns off slanting. |
| \t | Noninterpreted horizontal tab. |
| \u | Reverse (up) 1/2-em vertical motion (1/2 line in `nroff`). |
| \v´*N*´ | Local vertical motion; move down *N* (negative up). |
| \w´*string*´ | Interpolate width of *string*. |
| \x´*N*´ | Extra line-space function (negative before, positive after). |
| \z*c* | Print *c* with zero width (without spacing). |
| \{ | Begin conditional input. |
| \} | End conditional input. |
| \(newline) | Concealed (ignored) newline. |
| \*X* | *X*, any character *not* listed above. |

# ▪ **Predefined Number Registers** ▪

## Read-Only Registers

| | |
|---|---|
| .$ | Number of arguments available at the current macro level. |
| .$$ | Process ID of troff process (ditroff only). |
| .A | Set to 1 in troff, if −a option used; always 1 in nroff. |
| .H | Available horizontal resolution in basic units. |
| .T | In nroff, set to 1 if −T option used; in troff, always 0; in ditroff, you can print the value of −T with the string \*(.T. |
| .V | Available vertical resolution in basic units. |
| .a | Extra line space most recently utilized using \x´N´. |
| .c | Number of *lines* read from current input file. |
| .d | Current vertical place in current diversion; equal to nl if no diversion. |
| .f | Current font as physical quadrant (1 to 4 in otroff; no limit in ditroff). |
| .h | Text baseline high-water mark on current page or diversion. |
| .i | Current indent. |
| .j | Current adjustment type (0=.adl or .na; 1=.adb; 3=.adc; 5=.adr). |
| .l | Current line length. |
| .n | Length of text portion on previous output line. |
| .o | Current page offset. |
| .p | Current page length. |
| .s | Current point size. |
| .t | Distance to the next trap. |
| .u | Equal to 1 in fill mode and 0 in no-fill mode. |
| .v | Current vertical line spacing. |
| .w | Width of previous character. |
| .x | Reserved version-dependent register. |
| .y | Reserved version-dependent register. |
| .z | Name of current diversion. |

## Read/Write Registers

| | |
|---|---|
| % | Current page number. |
| ct | Character type (set by width function). |
| dl | Width (maximum) of last completed diversion. |
| dn | Height (vertical size) of last completed diversion. |
| dw | Current day of the week (1 to 7). |

| | |
|---|---|
| `dy` | Current day of the month (1 to 31). |
| `hp` | Current horizontal place on input line. |
| `ln` | Output line number. |
| `mo` | Current month (1 to 12). |
| `nl` | Vertical position of last printed text baseline. |
| `sb` | Depth of string below baseline (generated by `width` function). |
| `st` | Height of string above baseline (generated by `width` function). |
| `yr` | Last two digits of current year. |

## ▪ Special Characters ▪

### On the Standard Fonts

The following special characters are usually found on the standard fonts:

| | | | | | |
|---|---|---|---|---|---|
| ' | ´ | close quote | fi | `\(fi` | fi ligature |
| ' | ` | open quote | fl | `\(fl` | fl ligature |
| — | `\(em` | 3/4 em dash | ff | `\(ff` | ff ligature |
| - | – | hyphen | ffi | `\(Fi` | ffi ligature |
| - | `\(hy` | hyphen | ffl | `\(Fl` | ffl ligature |
| – | `\-` | current font minus sign | ° | `\(de` | degree |
| • | `\(bu` | bullet | † | `\(dg` | dagger |
| □ | `\(sq` | square | ′ | `\(fm` | foot mark |
| _ | `\(ru` | rule | ¢ | `\(ct` | cent sign |
| ¹/₄ | `\(14` | 1/4 | ® | `\(rg` | registered trademark |
| ¹/₂ | `\(12` | 1/2 | © | `\(co` | copyright |
| ³/₄ | `\(34` | 3/4 | | | |

### On the Special Font

The following characters are usually found on the special font except for the uppercase Greek letter names followed by † which are mapped into uppercase English letters in whatever font is mounted on font position one (default is Times Roman).

## Miscellaneous Characters

| | | | | | | |
|---|---|---|---|---|---|---|
| § | \(sc | section | ↓ | \(da | down arrow |
| ´ | \(aa | acute accent | \| | \(br | box rule |
| ` | \(ga | grave accent | ‡ | \(dd | double dagger |
| _ | \(ul | underrule | ☞ | \(rh | right hand |
| → | \(-> | right arrow | ☜ | \(lh | left hand |
| ← | \(<- | left arrow | ○ | \(ci | circle |
| ↑ | \(ua | up arrow | | | |

## Mathematic Symbols

| | | | | | | |
|---|---|---|---|---|---|---|
| + | \(pl | math plus | ∪ | \(cu | cup (union) |
| − | \(mi | math minus | ∩ | \(ca | cap (intersection) |
| = | \(eq | math equals | ⊂ | \(sb | subset of |
| * | \(** | math star | ⊃ | \(sp | superset of |
| / | \(sl | slash (matching backslash) | ⊆ | \(ib | improper subset |
| √ | \(sr | square root | ⊇ | \(ip | improper superset |
| | \(rn | root en extender | ∞ | \(if | infinity |
| ≥ | \(>= | greater than or equal to | ∂ | \(pd | partial derivative |
| ≤ | \(<= | less than or equal to | ∇ | \(gr | gradient |
| ≡ | \(== | identically equal | ¬ | \(no | not |
| ≠ | \(~= | approx equal | ∫ | \(is | integral sign |
| ~ | \(ap | approximates | ∝ | \(pt | proportional to |
| ≠ | \(!= | not equal | ∅ | \(es | empty set |
| × | \(mu | multiply | ∈ | \(mo | member of |
| ÷ | \(di | divide | \| | \(or | or |
| ± | \(+- | plus-minus | | | |

## Bracket Building Symbols

| | | |
|---|---|---|
| ⌠ | \(lt | left top of large curly bracket |
| { | \(lk | left center of large curly bracket |
| ⌡ | \(lb | left bottom of large curly bracket |
| ⌠ | \(rt | right top of large curly bracket |
| } | \(rk | right center of large curly bracket |
| ⌡ | \(rb | right bottom of large curly bracket |
| ⌈ | \(lc | left ceiling (top) of large square bracket |
| \| | \(bv | bold vertical |
| ⌊ | \(lf | left floor (bottom) of large square bracket |
| ⌉ | \(rc | right ceiling (top) of large square bracket |
| ⌋ | \(rf | right floor (bottom) of large square bracket |

## Greek Characters

| | | | | | | |
|---|---|---|---|---|---|---|
| α | \(*a | alpha | | A | \(*A | Alpha† |
| β | \(*b | beta | | B | \(*B | Beta† |
| γ | \(*g | gamma | | Γ | \(*G | Gamma |
| δ | \(*d | delta | | Δ | \(*D | Delta |
| ε | \(*e | epsilon | | E | \(*E | Epsilon† |
| ζ | \(*z | zeta | | Z | \(*Z | Zeta† |
| η | \(*y | eta | | H | \(*Y | Eta† |
| θ | \(*h | theta | | Θ | \(*H | Theta |
| ι | \(*i | iota | | I | \(*I | Iota† |
| κ | \(*k | kappa | | K | \(*K | Kappa† |
| λ | \(*l | lambda | | Λ | \(*L | Lambda |
| μ | \(*m | mu | | M | \(*M | Mu† |
| ν | \(*n | nu | | N | \(*N | Nu† |
| ξ | \(*c | xi | | Ξ | \(*C | Xi |
| o | \(*o | omicron | | O | \(*O | Omicron† |
| π | \(*p | pi | | Π | \(*P | Pi |
| ρ | \(*r | rho | | P | \(*R | Rho† |
| σ | \(*s | sigma | | Σ | \(*S | Sigma |
| ς | \(ts | terminal sigma | | | | |
| τ | \(*t | tau | | T | \(*T | Tau† |
| υ | \(*u | upsilon | | Y | \(*U | Upsilon |
| φ | \(*f | phi | | Φ | \(*F | Phi |
| χ | \(*x | chi | | X | \(*X | Chi† |
| ψ | \(*q | psi | | Ψ | \(*Q | Psi |
| ω | \(*w | omega | | Ω | \(*W | Omega |

# ▪ The ms Macros ▪

## Summary of ms Macros

| | |
|---|---|
| .1C | Return to single-column format. |
| .2C | Start two-column format. |
| .AB | Begin abstract. |
| .AE | End abstract. |
| .AI *name* | Name of author's institution (used in cover sheet). |
| .AU *name* | Author's name (used in cover sheet). |
| .B [*text*] | Print *text* in boldface. If *text* is missing, equivalent to .ft 3. |

| | |
|---|---|
| .B1 | Enclose following text in a box. |
| .B2 | End boxed text. |
| .BX *word* | Surround *word* in a box. |
| .DA | Print date on each page. |
| .DS | Start displayed text. |
| .DSB | Start left-justified block, centered. |
| .DSC | Start centered display. |
| .DSL | Start left-centered display. |
| .DE | End displayed text. |
| .EQ | Begin equation. |
| .EN | End equation. |
| .FS | Start footnote. |
| .FE | End footnote. |
| .I [*text*] | Print *text* in italics. If *text* is missing, equivalent to .ft 2. |
| .IP *label n* | Indent paragraph *n* spaces with hanging *label*. |
| .KS | Start keep. |
| .KE | End of keep or floating keep. |
| .KF | Begin floating keep. |
| .LG | Increase type size by two points (troff only). |
| .LP | Start block paragraph. |
| .ND | Change or omit date. |
| .NH *n* | Numbered section heading, level *n*. |
| .NL | Restore default type size (troff only). |
| .PP | Start indented paragraph. |
| .R [*text*] | Print *text* in roman. If *text* is missing, equivalent to .ft 1. |
| .RP | Initiate title page for a ''released paper.'' |
| .RS | Increase relative indent one level. Use with .IP. |
| .RE | End one level of relative indent. |
| .SG | Signature line. |
| .SH | Unnumbered section heading. |
| .SM | Decrease type size by two points (troff only). |
| .TL | Title line. |
| .TS [H] | Start table. H will put table header on all pages. Use this option with following TH |
| .TH | Table header ends. Must be used with .TS H. |
| .TE | End table. |
| .UL | Underline following text, even in troff. |

## Internal Macros Worth Knowing About

.IZ      Basic initialization; executed automatically before any text is processed. It is then removed, and cannot be invoked again.

.RT      Reset. Invoked by all paragraph macros, plus .RS, .RE, .TS, .TE, .SH, and .NH. Resets various values to defaults stored in number registers listed below.

.BG      Prints cover sheet, if any. Also performs some special first page initialization. Invoked once by the very first .RT in a document.

.NP      New page. Invoked at the top of each page. Performs various page top resets, and calls .PT.

.PT      Page titles. Contains running headers. Can be redefined. Invoked by .NP at \n(HMu from the top of the page.

.BT      Bottom titles. Continuous running footers. Invoked by trap at \n(FMu/2u from the bottom of the page.

.FO      Footer. The bottom of the text on the page. Invoked by trap at \n(FMu.

## Number Registers Containing Page Layout Defaults

CW      Column width (default 7/15 of line length).

FL      Footnote length (default 11/12 of line length).

FM      Bottom margin (default 1 inch).

GW      Intercolumn gap width for multiple columns (default 1/15 of line length).

HM      Top margin (default 1 inch).

LL      Line length (default 6 inches).

LT      Title length (default 6 inches).

PD      Paragraph spacing (default 0.3 of vertical spacing).

PI      Paragraph indent (default 5 ens).

PO      Page offset (default 26/27 inches).

PS      Point size (default 10 points).

VS      Vertical line spacing (default 12 points).

## Predefined and User-Definable Strings

| | |
|---|---|
| DY | The current date. |
| LH | Left header, printed by `.tl '\\*(LH'\\*CH'\\*(RH'` in PT macro. Null unless user-defined. |
| CH | Center header, printed by `.tl '\\*(LH'\\*CH'\\*(RH'` in PT macro. Null unless user-defined. |
| RH | Right header, printed by `.tl '\\*(LH'\\*CH'\\*(RH'` in PT macro. Null unless user-defined. |
| LF | Left footer, printed by `.tl '\\*(LH'\\*CH'\\(RH'` in BT macro. Null unless user-defined. |
| CF | Center footer, printed by `.tl '\\*(LH'\\*CH'\\RH'` in BT macro. Contains PN by default. |
| RF | Right footer, printed by `.tl '\\*(LH'\\*CH'\\RH'` in BT macro. Contains PN by default. |

## Reserved Macro and String Names

The following macro and string names are used by the ms package. Avoid using these names for compatibility with the existing macros. An italicized *n* means that the name contains a numeral (generally the interpolated value of a number register).

| | | | | | | | |
|---|---|---|---|---|---|---|---|
| ' | AX | DA | FL | KJ | OD | RT | TR |
| .] | B | DW | FN | KS | OK | S0 | TS |
| : | B1 | DY | FO | LB | PP | S2 | TT |
| [. | B2 | EE | FS | LG | PT | S3 | TX |
| [c | BB | EG | FV | LP | PY | SG | UL |
| [o | DG | EL | FX | LT | QE | SH | US |
| ^ | BT | EM | FY | MC | QF | SM | UX |
| ` | BX | EN | HO | ME | QP | SN | WB |
| ~ | C | E*n* | I | MF | QS | SY | WH |
| 1C | C1 | EQ | IE | MH | R | TA | WT |
| 2C | C2 | EZ | IH | MN | R3 | TC | XF |
| AB | CA | FA | IM | MO | RA | TD | XK |
| AE | CC | FE | I*n* | MR | RC | TE | XP |
| AI | CF | FF | IP | ND | RE | TH | |
| A*n* | CH | FG | IZ | NH | R*n* | TL | |
| AT | CM | FJ | KD | NL | RP | TM | |
| AU | CT | FK | KF | NP | RS | TQ | |

The following number register names are used by the ms package. An italicized *n* means that the name contains a numeral (generally the interpolated value of another number register).

| #T | EF | H5 | IX | MF | OJ | QP | TV |
|----|----|----|----|----|----|----|----|
| AJ | FC | HM | I# | MG | PD | RO | TY |
| AV | FL | HT | J# | ML | PE | SJ | TZ |
| BC | FM | IO | KG | MM | PF | ST | VS |
| BD | FP | IF | KI | MN | PI | T. | WF |
| BE | GA | IK | KM | NA | PN | TB | XX |
| BH | GW | IM | L1 | NC | PO | TC | YE |
| BI | H1 | IP | LE | ND | PQ | TD | YY |
| BQ | H2 | IR | LL | NQ | PS | TK | ZN |
| BW | H3 | IS | LT | NS | PX | TN |    |
| CW | H4 | IT | MC | NX | QI | TQ |    |

Note that with the exception of [c and [o, none of the number register, macro, or string names contain lowercase letters, so lowercase or mixed case names are a safe bet when you're writing your own macros.

<br>

## · The mm Macros ·

### Summary of mm Macros

.1C   Return to single-column format.

.2C   Start two-column format.

.AS [*x*][*n*]   Start abstract type *x*, indent *n* spaces. (Used with .TM and .RP only.) (Types: 1=abstract on cover sheet and first page; 2=abstract only on cover sheet; 3=abstract only on Memorandum for File cover sheet.) End with .AE.

.AE   End abstract. Begin with .AS.

.AF [*company name*]

   Alternate format for first page. Change first page "Subject/Date/From" format. If argument is given, other headings are not affected. No argument suppresses company name and headings.

.AL [*x*][*n*]   Start list type *x* (1, A, a, I, or i), indent *n* spaces. If third argument is 1, don't put a blank line between items. Default is numbered listing, indented 5 spaces.

.AT *title*   Author's *title* follows.

.AU *name*   Author's *name* and other information follows.

.AV *name*   Approval signature line for *name*.

.B [*w*] [*x*]...   Set *w* in bold (underline in nroff) and *x* in previous font; up to six arguments.

.BS   Begin block of text to be printed at bottom of page, after footnotes (if any), but before footer.

| | |
|---|---|
| `.BE` | End bottom block and print after footnotes (if any), but before footer. |
| `.BI` [*w*] [*x*] | Set *w* in bold (underline in `nroff`) and *x* in italics; up to 6 arguments. |
| `.BL` [*n*] [*l*] | Start bullet list and indent text *n* spaces. If second argument is 1, don't put a blank line between items. |
| `.BR` [*w*] [*x*] | Set *w* in bold (underline in `nroff`) and *x* in roman; up to six arguments. |
| `.CS` [*pgs*] [*other*] [*tot*] [*figs*] [*tbls*] [*ref*] | Cover sheet numbering information. |
| `.DF` [*x*] [*y*] | Start floating display of type *x* and mode *y*, with indent *n*. (Default is no indent, no-fill mode.) End with `.DE`. *x* is: `L` (no indent), `I` (indent standard amount), `C` (center each line individually), or `CB` (center as a block). *y* is: `N` (no-fill mode) or `F` (fill mode). |
| `.DS` | Start floating or static display of type *x* and mode *y*, with indent *n*. Type and mode are as in `.DF`. End with `.DE`. |
| `.DE` | End floating or static display started with `.DS` or `.DF`. |
| `.DL` [*n*] [*l*] | Start dashed list and indent text *n* spaces. If second argument is 1, no space between items. |
| `.EC` [*caption*] [*n*] [*f*] | Equation *caption*. Arguments optionally override default numbering, where flag *f* determines use of number *n*. If *f*=0 (default), *n* is a prefix to number, if *f*–1, *n* is a suffix, if *f*–2, *n* replaces number. |
| `.EF` [*text*] | Print *text* as the footer on all even pages. *text* has the format: 'left' center 'right'. |
| `.EH` [*text*] | Print *text* as the heading on all even pages. *text* has the format: 'left' center 'right'. |
| `.EQ` [*text*] | Start equation display using *text* as label. |
| `.EN` | End equation display. |
| `.EX` [*caption*] [*n*] [*f*] | Exhibit *caption*. Arguments optionally override default numbering, where flag *f* determines use of number *n*. If *f*=0 (default), *n* is a prefix to number; if *f*=1, *n* is a suffix; if *f*=2, *n* replaces number. |
| `.FC` [*text*] | Use *text* for formal closing. |
| `.FD` [*0-11*] | Setup default footnote format. |
| `.FS` [*c*] | Start footnote using *c* for indicator. Default is numbered footnote. |
| `.FE` | End footnote. |
| `.FG` [*title*] | Figure *title* follows. |
| `.H`*n* [*heading*] | Numbered *heading* level *n* follows. |
| `.HC` [*c*] | Use *c* as hyphenation indicator. |

.HM [*mark*]     Heading *mark* style follows arabic (1 or 001), roman (i or I), or alphabetic (a or A).

.HU *heading*    Unnumbered *heading* follows.

.HX     User-supplied exit macro before printing heading.

.HY     User-supplied exit macro in middle of printing heading.

.HZ     User-supplied macro after heading.

.I [*w*] [*x*]   Set *w* in italics (underline in nroff) and *x* in previous font. Up to six arguments.

.IB [*w*] [*x*]  Set *w* in italics (underline in nroff) and *x* in bold. Up to six arguments.

.IR [*w*] [*x*]  Set *w* in italics (underline in nroff) and *x* in roman.

.LB *n m pad type* [*mark*] [LI-*space*] [LB-*space*]

List beginning. Allows complete control over list format. It takes the following arguments:

*n* — Text indent.

*m* — Mark indent.

*pad* — Padding associated with mark.

*type* — If 0, use the specified *mark*. If nonzero, and *mark* is 1, A, a, I, i, list will be automatically numbered or alphabetically numbered or alphabetically sequenced. In this case, *type* controls how the *mark* will be displayed. For example, if *mark* is 1, *type* will have the following results:

| Type | Format |
|------|--------|
| 1 | 1. |
| 2 | 1) |
| 3 | (1) |
| 4 | [1] |
| 5 | <1> |
| 6 | {1} |

*mark* — The symbol or text that will be used to start each list entry. *mark* can be null (creates hanging indent), a text string, or 1, A, a, I, or i to create an automatically numbered or lettered list. Format of the *mark* will be affected by *type*.

LI-*space* — The number of blank lines to be output between each following .LI macro (default 1).

LB-*space* — The number of blank lines to be output by the LB macro itself (default 0).

.LC [*n*]   Clear list level *n*.

.LE     End list.

.LI [*mark*]    Item in list and specify *mark*.

.ML *mark* [*n*] [*1*]

Start marked list, indent *n* spaces. If third argument is 1, no space between items in list.

.MT [*type*] [*title*]
    Specify memorandum *type* and *title*. *type* is:
        " " = No type
        0 = No type
        1 = Memorandum for file (default)
        2 = Programmer's notes
        3 = Engineer's notes
        4 = Released paper
        5 = External letter
        *string* = *string* is printed.
    *title* is user-supplied text prefixed to page number.

.ND *date*
    New date. Change date to *date*.

.nP
    Double-line indent on paragraph start.

.NS [*type*]
    Notation start. Specify notation *type*. *type* is:
        " " = Copy to
        0 = Copy to
        1 = Copy (with att.) to
        2 = Copy (no att.) to
        3 = Att.
        4 = Atts.
        5 = Enc.
        6 = Encs.
        7 = Under Separate Cover
        8 = Letter to
        9 = Memorandum to
        10 = Copy (with atts.) to
        11 = Copy (without atts.) to
        12 = Abstract Only to
        13 = Complete Memorandum to
        *string* = Copy *string* to

.NE
    Notation end.

.OF [*text*]
    Print *text* as the footer on all odd pages. *text* has the format: 'left' center 'right'.

.OH [*text*]
    Print *text* as the heading on all odd pages. *text* has the format: 'left' center 'right'.

.OK [*topic*]
    Other keywords. Specify *topic* for TM cover sheet.

.OP
    Force an odd page.

.P [*type*]
    Start paragraph type. *type* is: 0 = left justified (default), 1 = indented, 2 = indented except after .H, .LC, .DE.

.PF [*text*]
    Print *text* as the page footer on all pages. *text* has the format: 'left' center 'right'.

.PH [*text*]
    Print *text* as the page heading on all pages. *text* has the format: 'left' center 'right'.

.PM [*type*]
    Proprietary marking on each page (*type*: P=PRIVATE; N=NOTICE).

| | |
|---|---|
| `.PX` | Page-heading user exit. |
| `.R` | Return to roman font (end underlining in `nroff`). |
| `.RB [w] [x]` | Set *w* in roman and *x* in bold. |
| `.RD [input]` | Read *input* from terminal. |
| `.RI [w] [x]` | Set *w* in roman and *x* in italics. |
| `.RS [arg]` | Start automatically numbered reference. *arg* manually specified reference number. |
| `.RF` | End of reference text. |
| `.RL [n] [1]` | Start reference listing, indent text *n* spaces. If second argument is 1, no space between list items. |
| `.RP` | Produce reference page. |
| `.S [n] [m]` | Set point size to *n* and vertical spacing to *m* (`troff` only) (defaults: 10 or 12). Alternatively, either argument can be specified as ±*n*/*m* to increment/decrement current value, `D` to use default, `C` to use current value, `P` to use previous value. |
| `.SA [n]` | Set right margin justification to *n*. *n* is:  0 = no justification or 1 = justification. (Defaults: no justification for `nroff`, justification for `troff`.) |
| `.SG [name]` | Use *name* for signature line. |
| `.SK n` | Skip *n* pages. |
| `.SM x[y][z]` | Reduce string *x* by one point. If strings *x, y,* and *z* are specified, *y* is reduced by one point. |
| `.SP [n]` | Leave *n* blank vertical spaces. |
| `.TB [title][n][f]` | Supply table *title*. Arguments optionally override default numbering, where flag *f* determines use of number *n*. If *f*=0 (default), *n* is a prefix to number; if *f*=1, *n* is a suffix; if *f*=2, *n* replaces number. |
| `.TS [H]` | Start table. `H` will put table header on all pages. Use this option with following `.TH`. |
| `.TH N` | Table header ends. Must be used with `.TS H`. `N` = only print table headers on new page. |
| `.TE` | End table. |
| `.TC [level] [level] [tab] [head1]...` | |
| | Generate table of contents. |
| `.TL` | Title of memorandum follows on next line. |
| `.TM [n]` | Number a technical memorandum *n*. (Up to nine may be specified.) |
| `.TP` | Top-of-page macro. |
| `.TX` | User-supplied exit for table-of-contents titles. |
| `.TY` | User-supplied exit for table-of-contents header. |
| `.VL n [m] [1]` | Start variable item list. Indent text *n* spaces and mark *m* spaces. If third argument is 1, no space between list items. |
| `.VM [n] [m]` | Add *n* lines to top margin and *m* lines to bottom. |

| `.WC [x]` | Change column or footnote width to *x*. *x* is: | |
|---|---|---|
| | `FF` | All footnotes same as first |
| | `-FF` | Turn off `FF` mode |
| | `N` | Normal default mode |
| | `WD` | Wide displays |
| | `-WD` | Use default column mode |
| | `WF` | Wide footnotes |
| | `-WF` | Turn off `WF` mode |

## Predefined String Names

| `BU` | Bullet; same as `\(bu`. |
|---|---|
| `Ci` | List of indents for table of contents levels. |
| `DT` | Current date, unless overridden. Month, day, year (e.g., July 28, 1986). |
| `EM` | Em dash string (em dash in `troff` and a double hyphen in `nroff`). |
| `F` | Footnote number generator. |
| `HF` | Fonts used for each level of heading (1=roman, 2=italic, 3=bold). |
| `HP` | Point size used for each level of heading. |
| `Le` | Title set for *List Of Equations*. |
| `Lf` | Title set for *List Of Figures*. |
| `Lt` | Title set for *List Of Tables*. |
| `Lx` | Title set for *List Of Exhibits*. |
| `RE` | SCCS Release and Level of mm. |
| `Rf` | Reference number generator. |
| `Rp` | Title for references. |
| `TM` | Trademark string. Places the letters *TM* one-half line above the text that it follows. |

## Number Registers Used in mm

A dagger (†) next to a register name indicates that the register can *only* be set from the command line or before the mm macro definitions are read by the formatter. Any register that has a single-character name can be set from the command line.

| | |
|---|---|
| A† | If set to 1, omits technical memorandum headings and provides spaces appropriate for letterhead. See `.AF` macro. |
| Au | Inhibits author information on first page. See `.AU` macro. |
| C† | Flag indicating type of copy (original, draft, etc.). |
| Cl | Level of headings saved for table of contents (default 2). See `.TC` macro. |
| Cp | If set to 1, list of figures and tables appear on same page as table of contents. Otherwise, they start on a new page. (Default is 1.) |
| D† | If set to 1, sets debug mode (default 0). If set, mm will continue even when it encounters normally fatal errors. |
| De | If set to 1, ejects page after each floating display. (Default is 0.) |
| Df | Format of floating displays. See `.DF` macro. |
| Ds | Sets the pre- and post-space used for static displays. |
| E† | Font for the Subject/Date/From: 0=bold; 1=roman. (Default is 0.) |
| Ec | Equation counter, incremented for each `.EC` macro. |
| Ej | Heading level for page eject before headings. (Default is 0, no eject.) |
| Eq | If set to 1, places equation label at left margin. (Default is 0.) |
| Ex | Exhibit counter, incremented for each `.EX` macro. |
| Fg | Figure counter, incremented for each `.FG` macro. |
| Fs | Vertical spacing between footnotes. |
| H1-H7 | Heading counters for levels 1-7, incremented by the `.H` macro of corresponding level or the `.HU` macro if at level given by the Hu register. The H2-H7 registers are reset to 0 by any `.H` (or `.HU`) macro at a lower-numbered level. |
| Hb | Level of heading for which break occurs before output of body text (default 2 lines). |
| Hc | Level of heading for which centering occurs (default 0). |
| Hi | Indent type after heading. (Default 1=paragraph indent.) Legal values are: 0 left justified, 1 indented, 2 indented except after `.H`, `.LC`, `.DE`. (Default is 0.) |
| Hs | Level of heading for which space after heading occurs. (Default = 2; `.H2`.) |
| Ht | Numbering type of heading: single (1) or concatenated (0). (Default is 0.) |
| Hu | Sets level of numbered heading that unnumbered heading resembles. (Default = 2; `.H2`.) |
| Hy | Sets hyphenation. If set to 1, Hy enables hyphenation. (Default is 0.) |
| L† | Sets length of page. (Default is 66v.) |
| Le | Flag for list of equations following table of contents. 0 = do not print; 1 = print. (Default is 0.) |

| | |
|---|---|
| Lf | Flag for list of figures following table of contents. 0 = do not print; 1 = print. (Default is 0.) |
| Li | Default indent of lists. (Default is 5.) |
| Ls | List spacing between items by level. (Default = 6, spacing between all levels of list.) |
| Lt | Flag for list of tables following table of contents. 0 = do not print; 1 = print (Default is 0.) |
| Lx | Flag for list of exhibits following table of contents. 0 = do not print; 1 = print (Default is 0.) |
| N† | Page numbering style. 0=header on all pages; 1=header printed as footer on page 1; 2=no header on page 1; 3=section page as footer; 4=no header unless .PH defined; 5=section page and section figure as footer. (Default is 0.) |
| Np | Numbering style for paragraphs. 0 = unnumbered; 1 = numbered. |
| O | Offset of page. For nroff, this value is an unscaled number representing character positions. Default is 9 (7.5i). For troff, this value is scaled. Default is .5i. |
| Oc | Table of contents page numbering style. 0=lowercase roman; 1=arabic. (Default is 0.) |
| Of | Figure caption style. 0=period separator; 1=hyphen separator. (Default is 0.) |
| P | Current page number. |
| Pi | Amount of indent for paragraph. (Default is 5 for nroff, 3 for troff.) |
| Ps | Amount of spacing between paragraphs. (Default is 3v.) |
| Pt | Paragraph type. Legal values are: 0 left justified, 1 indented, 2 indented except after .H, .LC, .DE. (Default is 0.) |
| Pv | Inhibits "PRIVATE" header. See .PV macro for values. |
| Rf | Reference counter, incremented for each .RS. |
| S† | Default point size for troff. Default is 10. (Vertical spacing is \n5+2.) |
| Si | Standard indent for displays. (Default is 5 for nroff, 3 for troff.) |
| T† | Type of nroff output device. Causes register settings for specific devices. |
| Tb | Table counter, incremented for each .TB. |
| U* | Underlying style (nroff) for .H and .HU. If not set, use continuous underline; otherwise, don't underline punctuation and white space. (Default is 0.) |
| W† | Width of page (line and title length). (Default is 6i.) |

## Other Reserved Macro and String Names

In mm, the only macro and string names you can safely use are names consisting of a single lowercase letter, or two character names whose first character is a lowercase letter and whose second character is *anything but* a lowercase letter. Of these, c2 and nP are already used.

## · `tbl` Command Characters and Words ·

| | |
|---|---|
| `.TS` | Start table. |
| `.TE` | End table. |
| `.TS H` | Used when the table will continue onto more than one page. Used with `.TH` to define a header that will print on every page. |
| `.TH` | With `.TS H`, ends the header portion of the table. |
| `.T&` | Continue table after changing format line. |

## Options

Options affect the entire table. The options should be separated by commas, and the option line must be terminated by a semicolon.

| | |
|---|---|
| `center` | Center with current margins. |
| `expand` | Flush with current right and left margins. |
| (*blank*) | Flush with current left margin (default). |
| `box` | Enclose table in a box. |
| `doublebox` | Enclose table in two boxes. |
| `allbox` | Enclose each table entry in a box. |
| `tab` (*x*) | Define the tab symbol as *x*. |
| `linesize` (*n*) | Set lines or rules (e.g., from box) to *n* point type. |
| `delim` (*xy*) | Recognize *x* and *y* as the `eqn` delimiters. |

## Format

The format line affects the layout of individual columns and rows of the table. Each line contains a key letter for each column of the table. The column entries should be separated by spaces, and the format section must be terminated by a period. Each line of format corresponds to one line of the table, except for the last, which corresponds to all following lines up to the next `.T&`, if any.

### Key letters

| | |
|---|---|
| c | Center. |
| l | Left justify. |
| r | Right justify. |
| n | Align numerical entries. |
| a | Align alphabetic subcolumns. |
| s | Horizontally span previous column entry across this column. |
| ^ | Vertically continue entry from previous row down through this row. |

### Other choices (must follow a key letter)

| | |
|---|---|
| b | Boldface. Must be followed by a space. |
| i | Italics. Must be followed by a space. |
| p$n$ | Point size $n$. |
| t | Begin any corresponding vertically spanned table entry at the top line of its range. |
| o | Equal width columns. |
| w ($n$) | Minimum column width. Also used with text blocks. $n$ can be given in any acceptable `troff` units. |
| v$n$ | Vertical line spacing. Used only with text blocks. |
| n | Amount of separation between columns (default is 3n). |
| \| | Single vertical line. Typed between key letters. |
| \| \| | Double vertical line. Typed between key letters. |
| _ | Single horizontal line. Used in place of a key letter. |
| = | Double horizontal line. Used in place of a key letter. |

## Data

The data portion includes both the heading and text of the table. Each table entry must be separated by a tab symbol.

| | |
|---|---|
| `.xx` | `troff` commands may be used (such as `.sp #` and `.ce #`). Do not use macros, unless you know what you're doing. |
| `\` | As last character in a line, combine following line with current line (`\` is hidden). |
| `\^` | Vertically spanned table entry. Span table entry immediately above over this row. |
| `_` or `=` | As the only character in a line, extend a single or double horizontal line the full width of the table. |
| `\$_` or `\$=` | Extend a single or double horizontal line the full width of the column. |
| `\_` | Extend a single horizontal line the width of the contents of the column. |
| `\R`$x$ | Print $x$'s as wide as the contents of the column. |
| `...T{` | Start text block as a table entry. Must be used with `w`$n$, column width option. |
| `...T}` | End text block. |

## ▪ eqn Command Characters ▪

| | |
|---|---|
| `.EQ` | Start typesetting mathematics |
| `.EN` | End typesetting mathematics |

## Character Translations

The following character sequences are recognized and translated as shown.

| | | | |
|---|---|---|---|
| `>=` | ≥ | `approx` | ≈ |
| `<=` | ≤ | `nothing` | |
| `==` | ≡ | `cdot` | · |
| `!=` | ≠ | `times` | × |
| `+-` | ± | `del` | ∇ |
| `->` | → | `grad` | ∇ |
| `<-` | ← | `. . .` | . . . |
| `<<` | ≪ | `, . . . ,` | , . . . , |
| `>>` | ≫ | `sum` | Σ |
| `inf` | ∞ | `int` | ∫ |
| `partial` | ∂ | `prod` | Π |
| `half` | ½ | `union` | ∪ |
| `prime` | ′ | `inter` | ∩ |

Digits, parentheses, brackets, punctuation marks, and the following words are converted to roman font when encountered:

```
sin cos tan sinh cosh tanh arc
max min lin log ln exp
Re Im and if for det
```

Greek letters can be printed in uppercase or lowercase. To obtain Greek letters, simply spell them out in the case you want:

| | | | |
|---|---|---|---|
| `alpha` | α | `sigma` | σ |
| `beta` | β | `tau` | τ |
| `gamma` | γ | `upsilon` | υ |
| `delta` | δ | `phi` | φ |
| `epsilon` | ε | `chi` | χ |
| `zeta` | ζ | `psi` | ψ |
| `eta` | η | `omega` | ω |
| `theta` | θ | `GAMMA` | Γ |
| `iota` | ι | `DELTA` | Δ |
| `kappa` | κ | `THETA` | Θ |
| `lambda` | λ | `LAMBDA` | Λ |
| `mu` | μ | `XI` | Ξ |
| `nu` | ν | `PI` | Π |
| `xi` | ξ | `SIGMA` | Σ |
| `omicron` | ο | `UPSILON` | Υ |
| `pi` | π | `PHI` | Φ |
| `rho` | ρ | `PSI` | Ψ |
| | | `OMEGA` | Ω |

The following words translate to marks on the tops of characters.

| | | | |
|---|---|---|---|
| x dot | $\dot{x}$ | x vec | $\vec{x}$ |
| x dotdot | $\ddot{x}$ | x dyad | $\overset{\leftrightarrow}{x}$ |
| x hat | $\hat{x}$ | x bar | $\bar{x}$ |
| x tilde | $\tilde{x}$ | x under | $\underline{x}$ |

## Words Recognized By  eqn

| | |
|---|---|
| above | Separate the pieces of a pile or matrix column. |
| back $n$ | Move backwards horizontally $n$ 1/100's of an em. |
| bold | Change to bold font. |
| ccol | Center a column of a matrix. |
| col??? | Used with a preceding  l  or  r  to left or right adjust the columns of the matrix. |
| cpile | Make a centered pile (same as pile). |
| define | Create a name for a frequently used string. |
| delim | Define two characters to mark the left and right ends of an  eqn  equation to be printed in line. |
| down $n$ | Move down $n$ 1/100's of an em. |
| fat | Widen the current font by overstriking it. |
| font $x$ | Change to font $x$, where $x$ is the one-character name or the number of a font. |
| from | Used in summations, integrals, and similar constructions to signify the lower limit. |
| fwd $n$ | Move forward horizontally $n$ 1/100's of an em. |
| gfont $x$ | Set a global font $x$ for all equations. |
| gsize $n$ | Set a global size for all equations. |
| up $n$ | Move up $n$ 1/100's of an em. |
| italic | Change to italic font. |
| lcol | Left justify a column of a matrix. |
| left | Create large brackets, braces, bars, etc. |
| lineup | Line up marks in equations on different lines. |
| lpile | Left justify the elements of a pile. |
| mark | Remember the horizontal position in an equation.  Used with  lineup. |
| matrix | Create a matrix. |
| ndefine | Create a definition which only takes effect when  neqn  is running. |
| over | Make a fraction. |
| pile | Make a vertical pile with elements centered above one another. |
| rcol | Right adjust a column of a matrix. |
| right | Create large brackets, braces, bars, etc. |
| roman | Change to roman font. |

| | |
|---|---|
| `rpile` | Right justify the elements of a pile. |
| `size` *n* | Change the size of the font to *n*. |
| `sqrt` | Draw a square root sign. |
| `sub` | Start a subscript. |
| `sup` | Start a superscript. |
| `tdefine` | Make a definition that will apply only for `eqn`. |
| `to` | Used in summations, integrals, and similar constructions to signify the upper limit. |
| `~` | Force extra space into the output. |
| `^` | Force a space one half the size of the space forced by `~` . |
| `{ }` | Force `eqn` to treat an element as a unit. |
| `' . . . '` | A string within quotation marks is not subject to alterations by `eqn`. |

## Precedence

If you don't use braces, `eqn` will do operations in the order shown in the following list.

```
dyad  vec  under  bar  tilde  hat  dot  dotdot
fwd   back   down   up
fat   roman  italic   bold   size
sub   sup   sqrt   over
from   to
```

These operations group to the left:

```
over   sqrt   left   right
```

All others group to the right.

---

## ▪ The `pic` Preprocessor ▪

In `pic` there are often dozens of ways to draw a picture, not only because of the many permissible abbreviations, but because `pic` combines the language of geometry with English. You can specify a line, for example, with direction, magnitude, and starting point, yet often achieve the same effect by simply stating, "from *there* to *there*."

Full descriptions of primitive objects in `pic` can be ended by starting another line, or by the semicolon character (;). A single primitive description can be continued on the next line, however, by ending the first with a backslash character (\). Comments may be placed on lines beginning with #.

## pic Macros

The following macros are used to delimit `pic` input from the body of the source file. Only text within these macros will be processed by `pic`.

.PS [*h* [*w*]]    Start `pic` description. *h* and *w*, if specified, are the desired height and width of the picture; the full picture will expand or contract to fill this space.

.PS <*file*    Read contents of *file* in place of current line.

.PE    End `pic` description.

.PF    End `pic` description and return to vertical position before matching PS.

## Declarations

At the beginning of a `pic` description, you may declare a new scale, and declare any number of variables.

    `pic` assumes you want a 1-to-1 scale, with 1 = one inch. You can declare a different scale, say 1 = one-*n*th of an inch, by declaring, `scale` = *n*.

    `pic` takes variable substitutions for numbers used in the description. Instead of specifying, `line right` *n*, you may use a lowercase character as a variable, for example, `a`, by declaring at the top of the description:

    `a` = *n*

You may then write `line right a`.

## Primitives

Primitives may be followed by relevant options. Options are discussed later in this section.

`arc` [`cw`] [*options*] [`` ` ` ``*text*`' '`]
    A fraction of a circle. (Default = 1/4 of a circle.) The `cw` option specifies a clockwise arc; default is counterclockwise.

`arrow` [*options*] [`` ` ` ``*text*`' '`] [`then . . .`]
    Draw an arrow. Essentially the same as `line` ->.

`box` [*options*] [`` ` ` ``*text*`' '`]
    Draw a box.

`circle` [*options*] [`` ` ` ``*text*`' '`]
    Draw a circle.

`ellipse` [*options*] [`` ``*text*`` ``]
> Draw an ellipse.

`line` [*options*] [`` ``*text*`` ``] [then . . .]
> Draw a line.

`move` [*options*] [`` ``*text*`` ``]
> A move of position in the drawing. (Essentially, an invisible line.)

`spline` [*options*] [`` ``*text*`` ``] [then . . .]
> A line, with the feature that a "then" results in a gradual (sloped) change in direction.

`` ``*text*`` ``
> Text centered at current point.


## Options

| | |
|---|---|
| `right` [*n*]<br>`left` [*n*]<br>`up` [*n*]<br>`down` [*n*] | Specifies direction of primitive; default is direction in which the previous description had been heading. Diagonals result by using two directions on the option line. Each direction can be followed by a specified length *n*. |
| `rad` *n*<br>`diam` *n* | Specifies a primitive to have radius *n* (or diameter *n*). |
| `ht` *n*<br>`wid` *n* | Specifies the height or width of the primitive to be *n*. For an arrow, line, or spline, refers to size of arrowhead. |
| `same` | Specifies a primitive of the same dimensions of the most recent matching primitive. |
| `at` *point* | Specifies primitive to be centered at *point*. |
| `with` .*position* `at` *point* | Specifies the designated *position* of the primitive to be at *point*. |
| `from` *point1* `to` *point2* | Specifies the primitive to be drawn from *point1* to *point2*. Points may be expressed as Cartesian coordinates or in respect to previous objects. |
| `->` | Specify the arrowhead to be directed forwards. |
| `<-` | Specify the arrowhead to be directed backwards. |
| `<->` | Specify the arrowhead to be directed both ways. |
| `chop` *n m* | Chop off *n* from beginning of primitive, and *m* from end. With only one argument, the same value will be chopped from both ends. |

|  |  |
|---|---|
| `dotted`<br>`dashed`<br>`invis` | Specifies the primitive to be drawn dotted, dashed, or to be invisible. Default is solid line. |
| `then...` | Continue primitive in a new direction. Relevant only to lines, splines, moves, and arrows. |

## Text

Place text within quotation marks. To break the line, break into two (or more) sets of quotation marks. Text always appears centered within the object, unless given one of the following arguments:

|  |  |
|---|---|
| `ljust` | Text appears left justified to the center. |
| `rjust` | Text appears right justified to the center. |
| `above` | Text appears above the center. |
| `below` | Text appears below the center. |

## Object Blocks

A complex object that is the combination of several primitives (for example, an octagon) can be treated as a single object by declaring it as a block:

```
Object:[
  description

     .
     .
     .

  ]
```

Brackets are used as delimiters. Note that the object is declared as a proper noun, hence it should begin with a capital letter.

## Macros

The same sequence of commands can be repeated by using macros. The syntax is:

```
define sequence %
  description

     .
     .
     .

  %
```

In this example, we have used the percent sign (%) as the delimiter, but any character that is not in the description may be used.

Macros can take variables, expressed in the definition as ''$1'' through ''$9''. Invoke the macro with the syntax: *sequence(value1,value2,...)*

## Positioning

In a `pic` description, the first action will begin at (0,0), unless otherwise specified with coordinates. Thus, the point (0,0) will move down and right on the drawing, as objects are placed above and to the left of the first object.

All points are ultimately translated by the formatter into x- and y-coordinates. You may therefore refer to a specific point in the picture by incrementing or decrementing by coordinates, i.e., `2nd ellipse - (3,1)`.

You may refer to the x- and y-coordinates of an object by placing `.x` or `.y` at the end. For example, `last box.x` will refer to the x-coordinate of the most recent box drawn. Some of the physical attributes of the object may also be referred to similarly, as follows:

| | |
|---|---|
| `.x` | X-coordinate of object's center. |
| `.y` | Y-coordinate of object's center. |
| `.ht` | Height of object. |
| `.wid` | Width of object. |
| `.rad` | Radius of object. |

Unless otherwise positioned, each object will begin at the point where the last object left off. If a command (or sequence of commands) is set off by braces ({ }), however, `pic` will then return to the point before the first brace.

### Positioning between Objects

When referring to a previous object, you must use proper names. This can be done two ways:

- By referring to it by order, e.g., `1st box`, `3rd box`, `last box`, `2nd last box`, etc.

- By declaring it with a name, in initial caps, on its declaration line, e.g., `Line1: line 1.5 right from last box.sw`

To refer to a point between two objects, or between two points on the same object, you may write: *fraction* `of the way between` *first.position* `and` *second.position* or (abbreviated) *fraction<first.position , second.position>*

## Corners

When you refer to a previous object, `pic` will assume that you mean the *center* of the object, unless you use a *corner* to specify a particular point on the object. The syntax is:

> *.corner* `of` *object*

for example, `.sw of last box`. You can also use an abbreviated syntax:

> *object.corner*

for example, `last box.sw`.

These *corners* may be:

| | |
|---|---|
| `n` | North (same as `t`) |
| `s` | South (same as `b`) |
| `e` | East (same as `r`) |
| `w` | West (same as `l`) |
| `ne` | Northeast |
| `nw` | Northwest |
| `se` | Southeast |
| `sw` | Southwest |
| `t` | Top (same as `n`) |
| `b` | Bottom (same as `s`) |
| `r` | Right (same as `e`) |
| `l` | Left (same as `w`) |
| `start` | Point where drawing of object began |
| `end` | Point where drawing of object ended |

You may also refer to the `upper right`, `upper left`, `lower right`, and `lower left` of an object.

## Numerical Operators

Several operators are functional in `pic`. These are:

| | |
|---|---|
| + | Addition |
| − | Subtraction |
| * | Multiplication |
| / | Division |
| % | Modulo |

## Default Values

| | | | |
|---|---|---|---|
| arcrad | 0.25 | ellipsewid | 0.75 |
| arrowwid | 0.05 | linewid | 0.5 |
| arrowht | 0.1 | lineht | 0.5 |
| boxwid | 0.75 | movewid | 0.5 |
| boxht | 0.5 | moveht | 0.5 |
| circlerad | 0.25 | scale | 1 |
| dashwid | 0.05 | textht | 0 |
| ellipseht | 0.5 | textwid | 0 |

# Shell Command Summary

This section describes the syntax of the Bourne Shell. It lists special characters, variables, and built-in programming commands used by the shell.

## Special Files

$HOME/.profile     Executed at shell startup.

## Special Characters for Filename Generation

| | |
|---|---|
| `*` | Match any string of characters. |
| `?` | Match any single character. |
| `[ . . . ]` | Match any of the enclosed characters. A pair of characters separated by a minus will match any character lexically between the pair. |

## Special Characters for Control Flow

| | |
|---|---|
| `|` | Perform pipeline (use output of preceding command as input of following command, e.g., `cat file | lpr`). |
| `;` | Separate sequential commands on the same line. |
| `&` | Run command in background (e.g., `lpr` *file*`&`). |
| `&&` | Execute command if previous command was successful (e.g., `grep` *string file* `&&` `lpr` *file*). |

| | |
|---|---|
| &#124;&#124; | Execute command if previous command was unsuccessful (e.g., grep *string1 file* &#124;&#124; grep *string2 file*). |
| ( ) | Execute commands enclosed in ( ) in a subshell; output from the entire set can then be redirected as a unit or placed in the background. |
| ′...′ | Take all characters between single quotation marks literally. (Don't allow special character meaning.) |
| \ | Take following character literally. |
| ″...″ | Take enclosed characters literally but allow variable and command substitution. |
| ′cmd′ | Use output of *cmd* as argument to another command. |
| # | Begin a comment in a shell file. |
| <*file* | Take input from *file*. |
| <<*string* | Read standard input up to a line identical to *string*. |
| >*file* | Redirect output to *file* (overwrite). |
| >>*file* | Redirect output to end of *file* (append). |
| >&*digit* | Duplicate standard input from *digit* e.g., 2>&1. |
| <&− | Close standard input. |
| >&− | Close standard output. |

## Variable Substitution

| | |
|---|---|
| *variable=value* | Set *variable* to *value*. |
| $*variable* | Use value of *variable*. |
| $*variable-value* | Use *variable* if set; otherwise set to *value*. For example: |
| $*variable*[:]-*value* | TERM=${1:-$TERM} will set the TERM variable to the value of the first argument to a shell script, if given, or else to the existing (default) value of TERM. |
| $*variable−value* | Use *variable* if not set; otherwise set to *value*. |
| $*variable*[:]=*value* | |
| $*variable?value* | Use *variable* if set; otherwise print *value* then exit. |
| $*variable*[:]?*value* | |
| $*variable+value* | Use *value* if *variable* is set; otherwise nothing. |
| $*variable*[:]+*value* | |

If the colon (:) is included in these expressions, a test is performed to see if the variable is non-null as well as set.

## Shell Parameters Set by the Shell under Execution

| | |
|---|---|
| $# | Number of command-line arguments. |
| $− | Options supplied in invocation or by the `set` command. |
| $? | Return value of last executed command. |
| $$ | Return process number of current process. |
| $! | Return process number of last background command. |

## Shell Variables Initially Set By `profile`

| | |
|---|---|
| $HOME | Default (home directory) value for the `cd` command. |
| $IFS | Internal field separators. |
| $MAIL | Default mail file. |
| $PATH | Default search path for commands. |
| $PS1 | Primary prompt string; default is `$`. |
| $PS2 | Secondary prompt string; default is `>`. |
| $TERM | Specifies the type of terminal. |

## Shell Functions

*name* ( ) {*command1*; ...; *commandn*}
> Create a function called *name* that consists of the commands enclosed in braces. The function can be invoked by name within the current script.

## Built-in Commands

*file*
> *file*
> Execute contents of *file*.

break
> break [*n*]
> Exit from a `for`, `while`, or `until` loop in *n* levels.

| | |
|---|---|
| case | case *value* in<br>  *pattern1* ) *commands* ; ;<br>    .<br>    .<br>    .<br>  *patternn* ) *commands* ; ;<br>esac<br>For each item in *list* that matches *pattern*, execute *command*. |
| cd | cd [*dir*]<br>Change current directory to *dir*. |
| continue | continue [*n*]<br>Resume *n*th iteration of a for, while, or until loop. |
| echo | echo *args*<br>Print *args* on standard output. |
| eval | eval [*arg* ...]<br>Evaluate arguments, then execute results. |
| exec | exec [*cmd*]<br>Execute *cmd* in place of current shell. |
| exit | exit [*n*]<br>Exit the shell with exit status *n*, e.g., exit 1. |
| export | export [*var* ...]<br>Export variable *var* to environment. |
| for | for *variable* [in *list* ...]<br>do<br>  *commands*<br>done<br>For variable *x* (in optional *list*) do *commands*. |
| if | if *condition*<br>  then *commands*<br>  [elif *condition2*<br>  then *commands2*] ...<br>  [else *commands3*]<br>fi<br>If *condition* is met, do list of *commands*, or else if *condition2* is met, do *commands2*, otherwise do *commands3*. (See test for a list of conditions.) |
| hash | hash *cmds*<br>Temporarily add *cmds* to search path. |

login            login [*user* ...]
                 Log in as another user.

newgrp           newgrp [*group* ...]
                 Change your group ID to *group*; if no argument, change back to your
                 default group.

pwd              pwd
                 Print current working directory.

read             read [*var* ...]
                 Read value of *var* from standard input.

readonly         readonly [*var* ...]
                 Mark variable *var* as read only.

return           return
                 Stop execution of current shell function and return to calling level.

set              set [*t*] [options]  [*arg* ...]
                 With no arguments, set prints the values of all variables known to
                 the current shell. The following options can be enabled (-option) or
                 disabled (+option).

                 --    Don't treat subsequent arguments beginning with − as
                       options.
                 −a    Automatically export all subsequently defined variables.
                 −e    Exit shell if any command has a nonzero exit status.
                 −k    Put keywords in an environment for a command.
                 −n    Read but do not execute commands.
                 −t    Exit after one command is executed.
                 −u    Treat unset variables as an error.
                 −v    Print commands as they are executed.
                 −x    Turn on trace mode in current shell (echo com-
                       mands in scripts as they are executed).
                 *arg* ... Assigned in order to $1, $2, ... $9.

shift            shift
                 Perform a shift for arguments, e.g., $2 becomes $1.

test             test *exp* | [*exp*]
                 Evaluate the expression *exp*. An alternate form of the command uses
                 [ ] rather than the word *test*. The following primitives are used to
                 construct *expression*.

                 −b *file*   True if *file* exists and is a block special file.
                 −c *file*   True if *file* exists and is a character special file.

| | |
|---|---|
| −d *file* | True if *file* exists and is a directory. |
| −f *file* | True if *file* exists and is a regular file. |
| −g *file* | True if *file* exists and its set-group-id bit is set. |
| −k *file* | True if *file* exists and its sticky bit is set. |
| −n *s1* | True if the length of string *s1* is nonzero. |
| −r *file* | True if *file* exists and is readable. |
| −s *file* | True if *file* exists and has a size greater than zero. |
| −t [*n*] | True if the open file whose file descriptor number is *n* (default is 1) is associated with a terminal device. |
| −u *file* | True if *file* exists and its set-user-id bit is set. |
| −w *file* | True if *file* exists and is writable. |
| −x *file* | True if *file* exists and is executable. |
| −z *s1* | True if the length of string *s1* is zero. |
| *s1* = *s2* | True if strings *s1* and *s2* are identical. |
| *s1* != *s2* | True if strings *s1* and *s2* are not identical. |
| *s1* | True if string *s1* is not the null string. |
| *n1* -eq *n2* | True if the integers *n1* and *n2* are algebraically equal. Any of the comparisons −ne, −gt, −ge, −lt, and −le may be used in place of −eq. |

times      times
Print accumulated process times.

trap      trap [*cmd*] [*n*]
Execute *cmd* if signal *n* is received. Useful signals include:

| | |
|---|---|
| 0 | Successful exit of command. |
| 1 | Hangup of terminal line. |
| 2 | Interrupt. |
| 15 | Process is killed. |

type      type *commands*
Print information about *commands*.

until      until *condition*
         [do *commands*]
done
Until *condition* is met, do *commands* (see test for conditions).

ulimit      ulimit [*size*]
Set maximum size of file that can be created to *size*; if no arguments, print current limit.

umask      umask [*nnn*]
Set file creation mask to octal value *nnn*.

unset   unset *vars* ...
      Remove definitions for variable *var*.

wait    wait [*n*]
      Wait for specified process with identification number (*n*) to terminate
      and report its status.

while   while *condition*
       [do *commands*]
      done
      While *condition* is met, do *commands* (see test for conditions).

*filename*   *filename*
      Read and execute commands from executable file *filename*.

# D

# Format of `troff` Width Tables

As discussed in Chapter 4, `troff` uses width tables stored in the directory `/usr/lib/font` to determine how to place text on the page. To do this, it needs to know how wide each character is.

For each type of `troff` output device supported by your system, there should be a directory called `/usr/lib/font/dev`xx, where *xx* is the name of the device. For example, on our system:

```
$ ls -F /usr/lib/font
devlj/
devps/
```

Within each of these directories resides an overall device description file, called DESC, and individual font files for the fonts on your system. These files exist both in ASCII and binary form. The binary files are created from the ASCII versions using a utility called `makedev`, and have the suffix `.out`.

On our system, here's what the font directory for the HP Laserjet contains:

```
$ ls /usr/lib/font/devl
B          DESC       I         S
B.out      DESC.outI.out        S.out
CW         HB         R         TY
CW.out     HB.out     R.out     TY.out
```

## • The DESC File •

The DESC file contains an overall description of the output device, including its resolution in dots per inch, the paper size, the fonts that will be mounted by default, the available point sizes, and a complete list of all the `troff` special character names supported on that device.

A DESC file might look something like the following example:

```
# HP LaserJet
fonts 6 R I B HB CW S
sizes 7 8 10 12 14 17 22 27 0
res 300
hor 1
vert 1
unitwidth 12
paperwidth 2400
paperlength 3300

charset
\|  \^  \-
fi fl ff Fi Fl
br vr ul ru
bu sq em hy 14 12 34 aa ga
        .
        .
        .
sc gr no is pt es mo
dd rh lh bs or ci
lt lb rt rb lk rk bv lf rf lc rc
```

The following keywords are used in the DESC file:

| | |
|---|---|
| fonts | The number of fonts to be mounted for the device, followed by a list of the font names (maximum is ten). The user can request other fonts from within a document. However, the fonts listed here will be "mounted" (by analogy with the CAT typesetter), and can by referenced by position (\f1, \f2 ...) as well as by name. |
| sizes | The sizes in which the various fonts are available. |
| res | The resolution of the output device, in dots per inch. |
| hor | The minimum number of units of resolution that the device can move in a horizontal direction. |
| vert | The minimum number of units of resolution that the device can move in a vertical direction. |
| unitwidth | The point size at which character widths are specified in the other files. |
| paperwidth | The width of the page in units of resolution (e.g., 8 inches x 300 = 2400, the width for the LaserJet, because it forces a 1/2-inch margin). |

paperlength      The length of the page in units of resolution (e.g., 11 inches x 300 = 3300, the length for the LaserJet).

biggestfont      The maximum number of characters in a font.

charset      The list of character names that are supported on this output device. The keyword should be on a line by itself; the list of characters starts on the next line.

\#      Begins a comment.

## · Font Description Files ·

For each font listed on the fonts line of the DESC file, there should be a font file with the same name. The font file contains a list of all the characters in the font, along with the width and other associated information.

A font file looks like this:

```
name R
internalname Roman

charset
        4       0       0
        8       0       0
vr      0       3       13
ru      25      0       17
        .
        .
        .
A       42      2       65
B       35      2       66
C       37      2       67
        .
        .
        .
w       40      0       119
x       28      0       120
y       28      1       121
z       25      0       122
        .
        .
        .
```

Four columns, separated by tabs, are listed for each character.

The first column lists the character name—either the letter, digit, or symbol, or a two-character `troff` special character name defined in the `charset` section of `DESC`.

The second column contains the width of the character in output device units. The width is the width of the character at the point size specified by the `unitwidth` keyword in `DESC`. For example, if `unitwidth` is 12, then from the portion of the table just shown, we know that a 12-point A in the roman font is 42 units wide. The `troff` formatter determines the width at other point sizes by scaling the `unitwidth` size.

The third column describes the character type—that is, whether it is an descender (1), ascender (2), both (3), or neither (0).

The fourth column contains the typeset code for the character. This code is the value that the output device will recognize to generate the character. This information is obtained from the typesetter or laser printer vendor. The code can be in decimal or octal form. (Octal is specified by a leading zero.)

In general, whomever supplied the driver for the output device will provide you with appropriate width tables for the supported fonts. However, you may have access to other public domain fonts for output devices that support downloadable raster fonts. In this case, you may need to build your own tables.

In addition, you may want to "tune" tables by adjusting the widths slightly if you find that the character spacing is poor. Creating a font table from scratch requires a magnifying glass, a micrometer, a good eye, and a lot of patience.

## ▪ Compiling Font Files ▪

After you are satisfied with your width tables, they need to be compiled using the `makedev` utility:

    $ **makedev DESC**          Compile all fonts in DESC

Running `makedev` on `DESC` will compile all of the fonts listed on the `fonts` line in that file. You can compile a font that is not included in `DESC` by specifying its name on the command line:

    $ **makedev B**          Compile the bold font

## ▪ Font Usage Limitations ▪

The user is not restricted to using the "mounted" fonts that have been listed in `DESC`. Any font supported by the output device, and for which a compiled width table exists, can be referred to from within a document. For example, if you had a Palatino font family named `PA`, `PB`, and `PI`, there should be files called:

```
    PA.out      PB.out      PI.out
```

One problem that is sometimes encountered is that troff has problems if a font that is used in this way is larger (in absolute file size) than the largest of the mounted fonts specified in DESC. The troff formatter only allocates enough memory for the largest font in DESC. If you encounter this problem, you can either strip unneeded characters out of the font, pad a font in DESC, or add the large font that is giving you trouble to DESC.

# E

# Comparing mm and ms

If you have both ms and mm on your system, you may be interested in looking at both packages, perhaps evaluating features. In general, ms has many of the same capabilities as mm. However, it lacks some essential features, such as automatically numbered lists and table of contents generation. On the other hand, it is much easier to learn the internals of ms, and therefore easier to extend it with your own macros.

## ▪ Paragraphs ▪

The basic paragraph types are block and indented.

| ms | mm | Description |
|------|------|-------------|
| .P | .LP | Begin a block paragraph. |
| .P 1 | .PP | Begin a paragraph with indented first line. |

In mm, the default paragraph type can be changed from block to indented by setting the number register Pt to 1 or 2. The ms macros lack this generalizing mechanism.

## ▪ Justification ▪

When using the nroff formatter, mm does not justify the right margin. .SA 1 turns on justification for both formatters. .SA 0 turns it off.

The ms macros do not provide a macro for inhibiting the normal justification of paragraphs. However, the .na request can be used to do this.

# ▪ Displays ▪

Displays are produced in a very similar way in both macro packages, using the DS/DE pair of macros. In mm, display are left justified; in ms, displays are indented. The options that allow you to change the placement of the display are basically the same.

The mm macros provide for static and floating displays (.DF). In ms, this is done with a separate pair of keep macros (KS/KF and KE).

In mm, you can turn on fill mode within the display and specify an indent from the right margin. This is used for quoted material and has its equivalent in ms with the QP or the QS/QE pair.

In addition, the same set of delimiter pairs for tbl, eqn, and pic are available in both packages.

# ▪ Formatting Lists ▪

The mm macros have sophisticated list formatting macros that are lacking in ms. The .IP macro in ms produces the equivalent of a variable item list in mm. In other words, you can get a numbered list by specifying the number as a label to an indented paragraph, but you cannot get an automatically numbered list.

# ▪ Change Font ▪

The .B (change to bold), .I (change to italic), and .R (change to roman) macros used for changing fonts are the same. The mm macros allow up to seven arguments for alternating with the previous font, but ms is limited to two.

# ▪ Change Point Size ▪

Both packages allow you to change point size. In mm, .S specifies a new point size and .SM reduces point size relative to the current size.

When you change the point size using ms macros, it is always done relative to the current point size. The .LG and .SM macros increase and decrease the current point size by 2 points. The .NL macro restores the default point size.

## ▪ Headers and Footers ▪

The mm macros provide macros for specifying a delimited string that will appear left justified, centered, and right justified in a page header or footer. The `.PH` macro defines a page header and `.PF` defines a page footer. In addition, mm provides variations of these macros for specifying headers and footers for odd and even pages.

The ms macros handle this through setting individual strings. To define a string that appears left justified in a header, use:

    .ds LH *string*

The other strings for the header are CH and RH; other strings for the footer are LF, CF, and RF.

## ▪ Section Headings ▪

Numbered and unnumbered section headings are available in both packages. The `.SH` and `.NH` macros are used in ms. The `.H` and `.HU` macros are used in mm. The main difference is where you specify the heading string. In mm, it is the first argument on the line with the macro. In ms, it follows on the line after the macro and continues up to the first paragraph macro.

## ▪ Footnotes ▪

The pair of macros used for footnotes is the same (`.FS` and `.FE`), although automatic numbering of footnotes is provided in mm. One difference is that in mm the footnote at the bottom of the page is printed in 8 points. The mm macros also provide a pair of macros (`.RF` and `.RE`) for collecting a page of references.

# F

# The format Macros

Throughout this book, we've made extensive references to portions of the extended ms macro package that we use in our technical writing business. These macros are used in conjunction with the format shell script to provide a complete document formatting environment.

This package was originally developed by Steve Talbott of Massachusetts Computer Corp. (MASSCOMP). We have extended and generalized it to meet the document design needs of many different clients.

The purpose of this appendix is to summarize, in one place, the function of the macros that the package contains. We have found that this set of macros covers the basic needs of people involved in the development of technical books and manuals.

The package relies on the existence of the underlying ms macros. In this sense, it is not a complete package. However, it is possible to define a simple subset of the ms macros to cover the basics if the full implementation of ms is not available.

For more information on the full implementation of these macros, please feel free to contact us in care of the publisher.

## · Summary of the Macros ·

The following list summarizes the user-callable macros in the format macro package.

| | |
|---|---|
| .[ABCD]h | A-level head, B-level head, and so on. |
| .Dr | Specify whether the current version is a draft. (Drafts are dated.) |
| .Fs | Start a figure. |

| | |
|---|---|
| .Fe *title* | Figure end. Figures are automatically numbered, and given the specified *title*. |
| .Hl [*c*] | Print a horizontal line the width of the page, using character *c*. (Default is underscore.) |
| .IOC [*strings*] | Start an interoffice memo. |
| .TO | List of names following .TO "" will be placed in separate distribution list. |
| .TO *name* | *name* is addressee. Maximum of five such .TO lines. |
| .DA *date* | *date* is date of the memo; will be included in page footer. |
| .ND *date* | *date* is date of the memo; will be omitted from page footer. |
| .FR *name* | *name* is sender. Maximum of five such .FR lines. |
| .CC *name* | *name* is person to receive copy of memo. Maximum of five .CC lines. |
| .SU *subject* | *subject* is subject of the memo. |
| .IP *label indent* [0] | Begin paragraph with ''hanging indent.'' Following text is indented, while *label* remains at the margin. |
| .LP [0] | Start a (left-justified) paragraph. 0 suppresses blank line. |
| .Ls [*type*] [*indent*] [*bullet*] | Start a (possibly nested) list. *type* is N (number), A (alphabetical uppercase), a (alphabetical lowercase), I (Roman numeral uppercase), i (Roman numeral lowercase), B (bullet). Default indent is 5. *bullet* is alternative bullet string (null string is acceptable). |
| .Li [0] | List item. 0 suppresses preceding blank line. |
| .Le [0] | End of innermost list. 0 suppresses preceding blank line. |
| .Lt [1 \| 2] | Enter address blocks and date (1), and salutation (2) of a letter. |
| .Nd *n* | Need *n* lines. If *n* lines do not remain on the page, eject new page. Unlike .ne, .Nd causes a break. |
| .Nh [1 \| 0] | Enable/disable numbered headings (enabled by default). |
| .Ns *type* | Start a NOTE of type N (Note), C (Caution), W (Warning), R (Review Note), or P (Private Note). Review notes are printed in the text and summarized in a list at the end. Private notes appear only in the end list. |

.Ne            End a note.

.OB *string*       Print an overbar (over a string).

.Ps [*indent*]     Start a "printout" (display). Text is printed in the  CW font and preserved as is—there is no filling.

.Pe            End a printout. See .Ps.

.Rh [0 | 1] [*desc*] *head* . . .
           Create reference page header.

.Se [*number*] [*title*]     Start a section (chapter). This sets up many defaults, and is desirable to use for most documents.

.SE            Screen end. End a computer screen illustration begun with .SS.

.SS [*width*] [*height*]     Start a screen illustration (box with curved corners). If width and height are not specified, scale to size of contents.

.Tc *level*        Specify what level of heading will be saved in the table of contents (Ah to Dh)

.Ti *text*         Title—goes in left page footer.

.St *text*         Subtitle—goes in right page footer.

.Ts *title*        Start a table with given caption. Tables are automatically numbered.

.Te            End a table. (Output a blank line.)

.XX *text*        Make an index entry out of *text*, with automatic addition of a page number.

.XN *text*        Make an index cross-reference out of *text* (no page number).

# A P P E N D I X
## G

# Selected Readings

The following books may be helpful either when you're starting out, or when you're ready to go on to more advanced topics.

## ▪ Introductory UNIX Texts ▪

Kochan, Steven G. and Patrick H. Wood. *Exploring the UNIX System*, Hasbrouck Heights, NJ: Hayden Book Co., 1984. A comprehensive introduction to the UNIX system. (371 pp.)

Todino, Grace. *Learning the UNIX Operating System*, Newton, MA: O'Reilly and Associates, Inc., Nutshell Handbooks, 1985. A brief introduction to essential UNIX skills, designed to be read and mastered in one or two sessions. (73 pp.)

## ▪ Advanced Topics ▪

Kernighan, Brian and Rob Pike. *The UNIX Programming Environment*, Englewood Cliffs, NJ: Prentice-Hall, 1984. The best introduction to the practical philosophy of UNIX programming. (240 pp.)

Kochan Steven G. and Patrick H. Wood. *UNIX Shell Programming*, Hasbrouck Heights, NJ: Hayden Book Co., 1985. A comprehensive and readable discussion of shell programming. (422 pp.)

Talbott, Steve. *Managing Projects with Make*, Newton, MA: O'Reilly and Associates Inc., Nutshell Handbooks, 1985. A concise but thorough description of the UNIX make utility. (63 pp.)

# I N D E X

# BRADY VS MANNING

Also by Gary Myers

Coaching Confidential
The Catch

# BRADY vs MANNING

## THE UNTOLD STORY OF THE RIVALRY THAT TRANSFORMED THE NFL

# GARY MYERS

THREE RIVERS PRESS
NEW YORK

To Allison, Michelle, Emily, and Andrew

# CONTENTS

# BRADY VS MANNING

# INTRODUCTION

Tom Brady was warming up at the old Foxboro Stadium prior to the first start of his career. It was the third game of the 2001 season, and the New England Patriots were already desperate. They had lost their first two games to the Cincinnati Bengals and New York Jets, they had just lost starting quarterback Drew Bledsoe with a sheared blood vessel in his chest that nearly killed him, and head coach Bill Belichick feared owner Robert Kraft was going to fire him even though it was only his second year in New England.

The Patriots were playing the Indianapolis Colts and their young superstar Peyton Manning, who was in his fourth season and already established as one of the best quarterbacks in the NFL.

Brady was a forgotten sixth-round pick in 2000. He'd thrown just three passes as a rookie but had played the final series after Bledsoe was hurt against the Jets and threw ten passes in the loss. Now all the pressure of the season was on him. If it had been put to a vote right then whether, thirteen years later, either Manning or Brady would have won four Super Bowls and three Super Bowl MVPs, Manning would have been a landslide winner, carrying all six New England states, especially the great state of Massachusetts.

Brady had fought for every snap he received at the University of Michigan and had overcome the indignity of having 198 players, including 6 quarterbacks, taken ahead of him before the Patriots wrote his name on the draft card that is displayed in the

Pro Football Hall of Fame in Canton, Ohio. Now, however, with Bledsoe out indefinitely, the Patriots starting job belonged to him.

The greatest rivalry in National Football League history began with a pregame introduction that was hardly necessary.

"Hey, Tom," a player wearing the Colts white jersey number 18 said, extending his hand.

Brady looked up. The player introduced himself.

"Peyton," he said to Brady.

Of course, Brady knew who he was. Everybody knew Peyton Manning. He was the number-one overall pick in the 1998 draft. He was the new fresh face of the league, with Dan Marino and John Elway nearing the end of their careers. Brady was impressed that Manning knew his name.

Brady smiled, but resisted saying what was going through his mind: *No shit. I know who you are.*

"That's funny," Manning said when the story was relayed to him years later.

"It was a very polite thing for him to do, especially being on our field," Brady said. "That really speaks to his character. He always does the right thing, says the right thing, acts the right way."

Manning learned from his father, Archie, to introduce himself even when he thinks the person knows who he is. "It's a Southern thing," Archie said. That's how he does it. That's what he taught his three sons.

"I like when people introduce themselves to me, because I meet a lot of people. So it helps," Peyton Manning said. "I don't assume anybody knows who I am automatically."

That was the start of an intense rivalry and a terrific friendship. Brady vs. Manning. Manning vs. Brady. Regardless of who comes first, they have been magic—like Magic vs. Bird.

Brady won that first meeting by 31 points over a Colts team that Manning, who had two interceptions returned for touchdowns in the game, said was "pretty terrible." Since then, Brady vs. Manning has been the most compelling matchup in the NFL. They faced each other seventeen times. Overall it was 11–6 for Brady, including 3–2 for Manning in the playoffs. Brady won the first two postseason matchups: the 2003 AFC Championship Game and again the next year in the divisional round, when Manning played for the Colts. Manning won the last three playoff games against Brady, all in AFC Championship Games: following the 2006 season with the Colts, seven years later in his second season in Denver, and then in the final meeting of this great rivalry in the 2015 AFC Championship Game.

**The argument has** been going on for more than a decade in stadiums, living rooms, luxury boxes, sports bars, fantasy leagues, and wherever they have high-definition televisions: Who is better, Brady or Manning?

The red, white, and blue confetti, the Patriots colors, coming down on Brady for the fourth time in his illustrious career after the Patriots beat the Seahawks in Super Bowl XLIX in Phoenix provides one answer. Brady leads Manning in Super Bowl victories 4–2. He leads him in Super Bowl appearances, 6–4. But he's also had the benefit of playing his entire career for Belichick, arguably the greatest coach since Vince Lombardi. Manning played for Jim Mora, Tony Dungy, and Jim Caldwell in Indianapolis, then three years for John Fox in Denver, and then for Gary Kubiak, who took over the Broncos in 2015. None of Manning's coaches approach Belichick in stature.

Who has been the better quarterback? Manning is the greatest regular-season player, not just quarterback, in the history of the NFL. You want Manning in the regular season. You don't lose much by taking Brady, but you definitely want Brady in January and on the first Sunday in February. By the time Brady picked up his fourth ring, he was 21–8 in the playoffs with the best post-season winning percentage in league history. Manning finished just 14–13.

When Brady won his first Super Bowl, he was the youngest quarterback to hold the trophy. When he won his fourth Super Bowl, he was the fourth-oldest quarterback to win it all. He has stood the test of time. The thirteen-year period between his first and latest Super Bowl victories is the longest sustained run of excellence of any quarterback in NFL history. The ten-year gap between his third and fourth titles is also the longest for any quarterback. Brady won the first nine playoff games of his career, resulting in three Super Bowl titles.

Manning holds the NFL record for touchdown passes in a season and career as well as most passing yards in a season and career, and finished tied with Brett Favre for most regular-season victories, with 186. He did it in 33 fewer games. Including the playoffs, Manning has a record 200 career victories, one more than Favre. Manning's passing numbers are far superior to Brady's, but Brady went into the 2016 season trailing Manning and Favre by only 14 regular-season victories but had 8 more playoff victories than Manning and 9 more than Favre. Manning is the oldest quarterback to win the Super Bowl and the only player to win five Most Valuable Player awards. Jim Brown, Johnny Unitas, and Favre are next with three. Brady has two. But . . . Brady has all those rings.

Sports is all about great rivalries. The gold standards: Manning vs. Brady. Ali vs. Frazier. Magic vs. Bird. Palmer vs. Nicklaus. Wilt vs. Russell.

The Manning-Brady rivalry doesn't have the sociological implications of Magic and Bird, of course, and they are never on the field at the same time, but their greatness and popularity transcend the ultimate team sport. Brady was number one in jersey sales for the nine-month period that ended January 31, 2016, according to nflshop.com. Manning was number three. That's impressive considering they've been around so long that you would think most people who wanted their jersey would have already purchased it. They played five elimination games against each other. Their rivalry defines an entire era of the NFL. Brady's most recent title tied him with Terry Bradshaw and Joe Montana for the most Super Bowl victories by a quarterback, and jumped him over Montana as the greatest quarterback in NFL history. Manning has had more heartache than happiness in the postseason. The Broncos' loss in the divisional round of the playoffs to the Colts following the 2014 season was the ninth time his team was eliminated in its first playoff game, the most one-and-dones ever for a quarterback, and the sixth time he had lost a home playoff game. Brady has been one-and done twice in his career and lost three home playoff games.

Their battles have been epic. The television ratings are astronomical. BradyManning has morphed into one word.

"I don't think there would be Tom who he is now if there wasn't Peyton and the Colts," said Tedy Bruschi, the former Patriots linebacker. "It just goes hand in hand. Manning-Brady. What if they were in different eras and didn't have each other to push each other against their respective teams? That's the finals. That's Bird-Magic. That's what everybody wants to see. That's classic football, a matchup you remember where you were when you saw certain playoff games or when it started snowing or the three interceptions by Ty Law or Peyton Manning finally winning his. I remember all that stuff. A lot of the best memories I have playing for the Patriots involved the Colts, involve Manning."

Dan Marino and John Elway were two of the best quarterbacks to ever play at the same time. They came into the NFL together in 1983 and their careers are often compared. But Brady was shocked when told that Elway and Marino played against each other just three times before Elway retired following the 1998 season. Two of the games were played in Elway's final year, including the only time they met in the playoffs. "How is that possible?" Brady asked.

That's what has made the Brady vs. Manning rivalry so special. They faced each other at least once every season except when Brady was hurt in 2008 and Manning was hurt in 2011. They competed twice in the same season six times.

**Brady is driving** from Foxboro to downtown Boston on a frigid November day in his black Lexus. I am in the passenger seat. He has just finished practice and a meeting prior to a Monday night game in Carolina in 2013, which the Patriots would lose and in which Brady would trail an official coming off the field, unloading a few F-bombs about a bad noncall in the end zone that cost the Patriots the game. Brady may have the look of a choirboy, but he's a cold-blooded killer on the field. Toward the end of a 2014 loss in Green Bay, when a pass by Aaron Rodgers picked up a key first down allowing the Packers to run out the clock and deprive Brady of one last chance to win the game, America became aware of the fire and passion that drive him.

"Fuck! Fuck! Fuck!" Brady could be seen yelling as he paced the sidelines.

That was not out of character for Brady, the league's best undercover trash-talker. "I couldn't watch all of the game. I was offended by the language I saw," joked then Jets coach Rex Ryan, who himself set a modern-day television record for F-bombs when the Jets appeared on *Hard Knocks* in 2010.

I am explaining the concept of *this book* to Brady on the way into Boston as he makes the nearly hour-long drive to the apartment he's living in with his Brazilian supermodel wife Gisele

Bundchen and their two children while his mansion in Brookline is under construction. I'm asking the questions, and he's answering them with a lot of thought and depth, taking his eyes off the road only at a red light or when traffic comes to a stop.

He likes the idea. He likes Manning. They are very good friends. Tom's father, Tom Brady Sr., and Archie text on Mondays during the season to ask each other about their sons and, as Tom Sr. says, "to let each other know the kids are all right." Surprisingly, after all these years, they have never met in person but feel connected through their quarterback sons.

Brady and Manning are only a year apart, the two oldest starting quarterbacks in a league that caters to the young. They have gone through many of the same experiences in the NFL. They can relate to each other. "It's been pretty cool," Brady said. "It's a pretty special rivalry."

Peyton has his younger brother Eli to share notes with, but Brady is the only other quarterback in his inner circle. At times, Brady has looked at Peyton as the older brother he never had, growing up in a house with three older sisters.

When Brady missed almost the entire 2008 season after tearing the anterior cruciate ligament (ACL) in his left knee in the first quarter of the season opener when Chiefs safety Bernard Pollard rolled into him, Manning supported him with encouraging text messages and phone calls. "I think you find out during those times who's with you," Manning said. "Everybody wants to talk to you when you're playing well, throwing touchdowns. Going through a tough time, being injured, people kind of look at you funny. You kind of reach out to Tom, tell him good luck, check in on him. When I got injured, it was the same deal. He had the same chance to do that for me. It does mean something."

When Manning missed the entire 2011 season following his fourth neck surgery, Brady was in frequent communication. "It's

nice to have a peer you can really rely on and you know is completely trustworthy," Brady said. "That's the kind of relationship
we have. It's nice to have people like that. I think it's been a natural
thing for us."

Their absence added another layer to the argument about who
was better. The Patriots still had an excellent season in 2008, an
11–5 record with backup Matt Cassel, but lost the division to the
Dolphins on a tiebreaker and a wild-card spot to the Ravens on a
tiebreaker. Yet when Manning was sidelined three years later, the
Colts bottomed out at 2–14.

Did that prove that Manning was better or more valuable? It
proved that Belichick had a better backup in Cassel and a better
team around him than Caldwell had with backups Kerry Collins,
Curtis Painter, and Dan Orlovsky and the team that future Hall
of Famer Bill Polian had constructed around them.

Would Brady have been Brady and Manning been Manning if
they hadn't had each other?

"One isn't bigger without the other. Tom completes Peyton
and Peyton completes Tom," said Dallas Clark, who played tight
end for the Colts from 2003 to 2011. "It makes their legacy in the
NFL that much greater by having one another and having the battles they had as individuals and with their teams. It's taken their
level of recognition, taken their impact on this game, to a whole
other level. What better sell is there than Manning vs. Brady? You
just say that and television ratings are shooting through the roof.
It was a battle. It was a grind."

Rodney Harrison, one of the hardest-hitting safeties to play in
the NFL, began his career with the Chargers in 1994 and played
nine years in San Diego. He joined the Patriots in 2003 and spent
the final six years of his career in New England playing with Brady
and against Manning.

"Let me tell you something: I'm so thankful to have played

in this era," Harrison said. "Sometimes people can look and say I played at the wrong time because of the contracts and the type of money. But to be able to witness two of the greatest quarterbacks ever to play the game, to have the professionalism, the mutual respect that they have for one another, it's tremendous. I'll be able to tell my kids exactly what I witnessed. I played against Tom. I played against Peyton. I just shake my head because people don't understand the greatness and consistency over so many years and what they've been able to accomplish." Brady has often been compared to Derek Jeter, the former New York Yankees shortstop, for both his demeanor and his accomplishments. I mentioned to Brady in the midst of his ten-year drought between Super Bowl titles that Jeter won his fourth World Series in 2000 and his fifth and final in 2009, with two World Series losses in between. Brady also lost two Super Bowls between his third and fourth titles.

"It's not like you are going to win six or seven Super Bowls," he said. "Why didn't Michael Jordan win twelve championships? He won six. That's still a ton. With how good the other players are, the level playing field, especially in the NFL in the salary-cap era, it's hard to win."

I suggest to Brady that he and Peyton are the Bird and Magic of the NFL. He doesn't ask which is which. If he did, I would say Manning is Bird—he can slice up a defense with his brains, precision passes, anticipation, and instincts. Brady is Magic, just as much a student of the game as Manning and Bird and Magic, but like Magic, he is more explosive, exciting, creative, spectacular, more volatile. Bird is from Indiana. Manning played most of his career in Indianapolis. Brady is from California. Johnson played his entire career in Los Angeles.

Magic vs. Bird. Brady vs. Manning.

"I definitely think that's a flattering thing," Brady said. "I think so highly of them. So when people say you guys are comparable,

that's very flattering. It's not why we play the game. It's not what
motivates me. It's not about my legacy. I couldn't care less about
that. I just want to win. That's what makes me feel the best. My
days are committed to that."

I am meeting with Manning at the Broncos practice facility
in Dove Valley outside downtown Denver after a June organized
team-activity day. He is friendly and accommodating as usual, and
as every reporter who has dealt with him over the years knows, he
never forgets your name. I met him for the first time the day before
he was drafted in 1998, when the NFL used to bring six players
to New York and invite the media to join them on a cruise ship
for a ride around the island of Manhattan with the opportunity to
interview the players. The ride would last two hours, but the work
was done in forty-five minutes. At that point, the players, media,
agents, and league officials along for the ride wanted to get off the
boat and go about their business, but there's not much to be done
when you are in the middle of the Hudson River with the captain
enthusiastically pointing out the Statue of Liberty.

Manning had been told in confidence by the Colts one day
earlier they would take him over Ryan Leaf, but with the draft
beginning in less than twenty-four hours, that preference was still
supposed to be a secret. Even Leaf didn't know. Although San
Diego, which was picking second, would be considered by most to
be a more desirable city than Indianapolis, Manning was focused
on the Colts.

He wanted to be the first pick in the draft. His father, Archie,
had been the number-two overall pick in 1971 by the Saints, one
spot after New England selected Jim Plunkett. Besides, Polian had
recently been hired to run the Colts; he had helped build four
Super Bowl teams in Buffalo and had put together the expansion
Carolina Panthers, who made it to the NFC championship game
in just their second season. San Diego's GM was Bobby Beathard,

who'd done his best work when he'd had Joe Gibbs as his coach in Washington. Neither the Colts nor the Chargers were any good, but Manning would have been insulted to be selected behind Leaf. He even promised Polian, if he drafted him, "We will win a championship. And if you don't, I promise I will come back and kick your ass." Brady still had one year left to play at Michigan on the day the Colts turned their franchise around by selecting Manning.

Peyton likes Brady very much. They've played golf together. They've had dinner together. Their wives have spent time together. Manning's brother Eli has defeated Brady twice in the Super Bowl. The Manning brothers have defeated Brady five times in the playoffs.

I also outline the book project, *Brady vs Manning*, to Peyton. He's into it.

What does he think about the Magic vs. Bird comparison?

"It's hard to compare football to basketball. In basketball, you're guarding each other, playing offense and defense at the same time," he said. "I have great respect for Tom and I knew I was going to have to try to play well in order to beat the Patriots because they were going to be extremely tough to play; they were extremely well coached, and Brady was their quarterback. You always knew that was a challenge."

The NFL has been an ATM without limits for a long time now, but the emergence of the Manning-Brady rivalry coincided with a tremendous growth spurt in the league. Robert Kraft bought the Patriots for $172 million in 1994, saving the ragtag franchise from moving to Saint Louis. Twenty-one years later, they were valued by *Forbes* at $3.2 billion, second behind the Dallas Cowboys at $4 billion, and Kraft's net worth was listed at $4.8 billion by *Forbes* in 2015.

Manning vs. Brady raised the visibility and marketability of the entire NFL brand and made owners throughout the league even richer, helping revenues expand to $10 billion annually by 2014. They have been the two faces of the league during the period when its popularity exploded worldwide. "The rivalry has been great for the fans and for the game of football," NFL commissioner Roger Goodell said. "Not only are they great performers, but it's almost what they do off the field that distinguishes them as even more special. They are leaders, they're maybe the hardest-working individual players, nobody outworks them, they prepare like nobody else. They are humble in the sense that they recognize the value of the team. They want their teams to take the same approach to the game of football. They are great ambassadors of the game because they love the game. You can't ask for two better guys."

Manning is wildly popular, not only in Indianapolis and Denver but around the country. Madison Avenue has capitalized on his appeal with all his commercials, ranging from pizza to automobiles to credit cards. Brady is beloved in Boston and is a civic treasure along with Bill Russell, Larry Bird, Bobby Orr, Carl Yastrzemski, and Big Papi. Outside their home areas, Brady stirs up more negative feelings than Manning. Why? He is resented for his tremendous success, his good looks, and his supermodel wife—and his connection to Bill Belichick.

Brady steered away from any negative headlines on or off the field for nearly all of the first fifteen years of his career—until the Indianapolis Colts alerted the NFL prior to the AFC championship game on January 18, 2015, that they suspected the Patriots were deflating footballs, which would make them easier for Brady to grip, especially on days when it is cold or rainy. That gave birth to Deflategate, one of the most bizarre controversies in the league's ninety-five-year history, leading Goodell to authorize severe penalties handed down by Troy Vincent, the league's vice president of football operations: the Patriots were fined $1 million and stripped of a first-round draft pick in 2016 and a fourth-round pick in 2017, and Brady was suspended for the first four games of the 2015 season, a sanction he successfully appealed and had overturned one week before the Patriots opened the defense of their Super Bowl championship against the Steelers. Judge Richard Berman of the U.S. District Court in New York ruled that Goodell had not treated Brady fairly during the process regarding, among other things, the sharing of evidence and being denied the ability to question NFL vice president Jeff Pash during Brady's appeal at the NFL office. Of course, the NFL immediately appealed Berman's ruling, and there was a hearing before three judges of the Second Circuit Court of Appeals in New York on March 3, 2016, forcing Brady to have his fate once again determined in court. In a surprisingly quick decision rendered on April 25, two of the three judges sided with the NFL, offering the opinion that Goodell had exercised his commissioner powers properly as outlined in the collective bargaining agreement. Brady's suspension was reinstated, and, pending any further appeals by him, he would have to sit out the first four games of the 2016 season.

Was this much ado about nothing? Did the footballs lose air pressure on their own due to atmospheric conditions, or did Brady and the Patriots cheat?

Each team prepares the footballs that its offense will use during the game. Until 2006, the home team was in charge of all the footballs, including those for the visitors, but Manning and Brady were behind a petition by quarterbacks to amend the rule and allow them to bring their own footballs on the road.

At halftime of the championship game in Foxboro, eleven of the Patriots footballs were retested. They were all under the 12.5-pounds-per-square-inch minimum, and that prompted Goodell to initiate a full-scale independent investigation by Ted Wells, a New York attorney. The Patriots tried to explain the discrepancy by citing the ideal gas law. The Wells Report, a 243-page account, was conducted over more than one hundred days and cost the NFL millions. It came to the conclusion, through mostly circumstantial evidence, that Brady was involved in a plot to have air taken out of the footballs prior to the championship game with the Colts after they were tested by referee Walt Anderson.

Wells used a connect-the-dots approach to decide that assistant equipment manager John Jastremski and clubhouse attendant Jim McNally were acting on Brady's desire to have the balls deflated. The report never accused Brady of telling Jastremski and McNally to deflate the footballs under the minimum, only that he liked them on the lower end of the 12.5-13.5 psi range. Wells cited a series of text messages between Jastremski and McNally (who referred to himself as The Deflator, which the Patriots later attributed to his desire to lose weight), and surveillance cameras catching McNally duck into a bathroom for a hundred seconds after Anderson had signed off on the twelve footballs the Patriots presented for the game. Wells wrote "that it is more probable than not that Brady was at least generally aware of the inappropriate activities of McNally and Jastremski involving the release of air from Patriots game balls."

Brady answered sixty-one questions during a thirty-minute press conference on January 22, four days after the title game and nearly four months before the release of the Wells Report. "I didn't alter the ball in any way," he said. "I feel like I have always played within the rules. I would never break any rules."

The footballs come out of the box a little slippery, and quarterbacks and equipment managers work them over until they have a comfortable feel. Then the quarterbacks choose the twelve they want in the game along with twelve backups. "When I pick those footballs out, at that point, to me, they're perfect," Brady said. "I don't want anyone touching the balls after that. I don't want anyone rubbing them, putting any air in them, taking any air out. To me, those balls are perfect, and that's what I expect when I show up on the field."

Deflategate overshadowed the Super Bowl for nearly two weeks, right up until kickoff. Brady, who never seems anxious, initially was nervous in that press conference as he was grilled with questions about air pressure, and for the first time in his career his integrity was questioned. Wells revealed in his report that Brady refused to turn over his cell phone or even allow his own attorney to pick out relevant e-mails and text messages when they interviewed him. The NFL considered that a lack of cooperation, which contributed to Brady's punishment.

The anti-Patriots faction will claim this taints Brady's legacy, even if the evidence would never get him convicted in a court of law. Patriots Nation will argue that Wells hardly proved the Patriots deflated the footballs and certainly didn't do enough to link Brady to any wrongdoing, although the consensus among quarterbacks is no equipment or clubhouse worker would make changes to the football unless directed by the quarterback. The impact on the game itself is arguable—Brady played much better in the second half of the 45–7 victory over the Colts when the footballs were fully inflated—but the issue is whether rules were broken.

Kraft accepted his penalties from the league after he initially considered fighting the fine and loss of draft picks. He is a league man, and although he has never acknowledged the Patriots did anything wrong, he felt compelled to back down. He has never doubted that Brady was innocent of any wrongdoing. "Tom Brady has our unconditional support," Kraft said. "Our belief in him has not wavered."

If Brady was breaking the rules, then it adds another talking point to the pro-Manning backers in the Brady vs. Manning argument. Could that explain why Brady outplayed Manning in so many cold-weather games in New England? Manning stayed clear of any Deflategate talk and any talk about Brady. "I'll speak it as clearly and slowly as I can," he said. "He's my friend; he'll always be my friend. I don't know what happened. I don't have much more than that for you."

*Brady vs Manning* will take you behind the scenes of the NFL's greatest rivalry between two of the all-time best quarterbacks. "I've been playing against Tom for a long time," Manning said. "You do form a friendship as well, besides just a football handshaking a guy after a game. I have enjoyed that. There's that fine line between asking questions that can benefit you as far as how does he train in the off-season, but at the same time, you do try to protect some secrets. I think he and I have a healthy respect, never crossing the line, asking something that is a little too football private for his team and for my team. At the same time, you are always trying to find ways to improve, to keep playing, to get better. There is really nobody better to talk to than somebody else trying to do the same thing."

One thing they don't talk about: Super Bowl rings. Brady has never brought up the medal count.

"I could never do that," he said. "He's had as great a career as anyone who has ever played the position. I feel I've had as great a career as I could have ever imagined or dreamed of. I've been lucky to have been on some great teams. That's what I think about. I want to be part of the reason why we continue to do well. If I'm not doing well, then someone else has to do it. That's how the NFL works."

Brady and Manning are icons of the game who have permanently carved a niche for themselves in its history, both individually and as part of something really special. Brady vs. Manning was the best long-running show in NFL history, and nobody wanted a series finale.

# 1

# FOR THE RECORD

Peyton Manning and his brother Eli talk often during the season, particularly during the week when one of them is facing a team the other has already played.

They are five years apart, and Peyton picked on Eli unmercifully as a kid—he used to pin him down and bang his knuckles against his chest until he was able to name all the schools in the Southeastern Conference (SEC), and when he mastered that, Peyton tested him on the names of all the NFL teams. But as adults, they count on each other as a trusted set of eyes and ears when studying an upcoming opponent.

In the final game of the 2007 season, Eli and the New York Giants were playing Tom Brady and the Patriots. The Patriots already had the number-one seed in the AFC wrapped up, and the Giants had secured a wild-card spot in the NFC. In other years, this game would have had all the ingredients for a meaningless three hours with the goal to rest the starters and make sure nobody picked up any new injuries going into the playoffs.

In the days before the game, Eli's cell phone rang. It was Peyton calling from Indianapolis. He wasn't offering advice on how to take advantage of the Patriots defense, although he finally seemed to have figured out how to beat Bill Belichick's complex schemes. The Colts had lost to New England by four points in the middle of the season when both teams were undefeated but Manning had won the previous three games.

Peyton needed a favor from Eli. More specifically, he needed Eli to ask the Giants defense for a favor.

Brady was having a magical season. He had thrown forty-eight touchdown passes in the first fifteen games, and the Patriots had won them all. Two more touchdowns and Brady would break the all-time single-season record, which happened to be held by Peyton Manning. He'd had forty-nine in 2004. One more victory and the Patriots would become the first team to put together a perfect 16–0 regular season.

Manning probably would have put the record out of Brady's reach had he played more than one series and thrown more than two passes in the final game of the '04 season against Denver. The Colts had already clinched their playoff seeding, and Tony Dungy only played Manning to keep his starting streak alive. The next week, when the game mattered in the wild-card round, the Colts played the Broncos again and Manning threw four touchdowns against the Denver defense.

Brady and Manning, even when they were not playing against each other, were linked once again.

Becoming the first team to go undefeated since the league went to a sixteen-game season in 1978 was motivation, but Brady and the Patriots had played with a chip on their shoulder all year after Belichick was turned in to the NFL by the Jets in the first game of the year for taping their defensive signals. Spygate, as the scandal became known, exposed a practice that had been going on for many years and that called into question the three Super Bowls that Brady and Belichick had already won together.

Belichick was out to prove that the taping was incidental to the Patriots' success, and he was on a mission for the rest of the 2007 season not only to win games, but to embarrass teams. After the opener, the Patriots won their next seven games by a combined 293–113, including a beatdown of the Redskins 52–7. Belichick humiliated Hall of Fame coach Joe Gibbs by running up the score, leaving Brady in the game until he had thrown his third touchdown pass to make it 45–0 on the first series of the fourth quarter. Belichick was taking out his anger on the Patriots' opponents even though he was the one caught cheating. And now, to complete the Patriots' undefeated season against the Giants in the Meadowlands, where Belichick had made a name for himself by winning his first two Super Bowl rings as defensive coordinator for Bill Parcells, would be perfect. He loved his twelve years with the Giants organization and had too much respect for coach Tom Coughlin—they worked together for three years with the Giants—to consider running up the score. He just wanted to win the game.

Coughlin decided he was going to go all-out to beat the Patriots to try to create momentum going into the playoffs after an up-and-down season. It was a questionable maneuver. New York was already locked in to the number-five playoff seed and couldn't afford any more injuries. The risk, Coughlin decided, was worth the reward. That was good news for the Manning precinct in Indianapolis. The outcome of this game meant little to the Colts, but Brady's stats meant everything to Peyton Manning.

He called his younger brother and asked him to relay a message to the defensive leaders: If the Patriots were going to get into the end zone, he sure would appreciate if it happened on the ground. No touchdown passes, please.

"He said it jokingly, but maybe a little serious in the mix," Eli Manning said. "I thought I would pass it on to Antonio Pierce."

It was no joke.

Anytime players say statistics are just numbers and they don't pay attention, they're not telling the truth. Manning might have been funny as guest host on *Saturday Night Live* and a tremendous pitchman in all those television commercials, but he has an ego, a big ego. Manning wanted that touchdown record to be enduring, just as Dan Marino did when he threw forty-eight back in 1984, shattering the old record of thirty-six set by Y. A. Tittle, which had stood since 1963. At least Marino's record lasted twenty years. Manning's was on the verge of being wiped out after just three.

Pierce, the Giants middle linebacker, had created headlines that week by saying that Brady walks around "like he's Prince Charles, like he's the golden boy," and complaining that Brady seemed indignant anytime a defensive player managed to lay hands on him. The Giants did not like Brady. They wanted to knock him around. They were happy to give it their best shot to do Eli's big brother a favor.

Eli walked over to Pierce in the locker room to relay the message from Peyton: "Hey, you know, if you guys can do whatever you can to not let him break the record, that would be great," Eli said. "It would be nice if the defense can go out there and not give up any touchdown passes."

Brady had thrown forty-eight touchdowns, but that was against the rest of the league. Pierce did not want him breaking the record against the Giants. Eli Manning is hard to read sometimes, even for his teammates. "You think the guy is joking, but then you look at his face," Pierce said. "He was serious about that."

Then Pierce laughed. "There might have been a little bit of an incentive for us to try and stop Tom Brady from getting that record," he said.

The Giants defensive players went out to dinner every Monday and Friday night. Pierce told Eli to inform Peyton that if the

Giants prevented Brady from breaking the record, they expected a "parting gift." He had it all planned out. He would round up the crew for a night in Manhattan with dinner at Del Frisco's, one of the best steak houses in New York. Pierce got the word to Peyton that if the Giants came through, he would be expected to pick up the check.

The night before the game, at the Hilton Hasbrouck Heights, the Patriots team hotel in New Jersey five miles north of Giants Stadium, backup quarterback Matt Cassel was being prepared by the New England offensive coaches to come into the game in relief of Brady, but he knew he wouldn't get in until the Patriots were comfortably ahead to secure the undefeated season and Brady had set the touchdown record. Based on how the season had gone, that figured to be sometime in the third quarter. "They were talking to me like, 'What are your favorite passes on the call sheet?'" Cassel said. "I'm like, 'Okay, I'm going to get in there and rock-and-roll.' Then it became a tight game and there wasn't even a question on the sideline. Those guys weren't coming out of the game. Brady definitely wasn't getting taken out of the game. The next thing I know, the fourth quarter rolls around and Brady is taking a knee, and we just went 16–0. I was like, 'Okay, well, maybe next year.'" He wasn't trying to jinx his friend, but Cassel did get his chance in 2008 when Brady tore his ACL in the first game.

The Giants held Brady without a touchdown pass in the first quarter. But on the first play of the second period, he completed a four-yard score to Randy Moss, tying Brady with Manning at forty-nine TD passes. It was also Moss's twenty-second TD catch of the season, tying him with Jerry Rice for the single-season record. Brady didn't throw a touchdown in the second or third quarter, giving Manning hope that he would at least end the season with a share of the record. It was a lot to ask. Brady came into the game averaging more than three touchdown passes per game. By the fourth quarter, it became clear that the Giants defense could no longer contain him; he was operating the highest-scoring offense in NFL history (a record Manning took ownership of in Denver in 2013). The Giants were playing inspired ball and giving the Patriots a huge scare, as they held a 28–16 lead early in the third quarter, still 28–23 going into the fourth.

Brady went deep to Moss down the right sideline on second down early in the fourth quarter, but he was unable to hold on. The Patriots came back with the exact same play on third down, knowing that the Giants secondary couldn't keep up with Moss. This time, Brady and Moss connected on a 65-yard touchdown with 11:06 remaining, which broke the records of Manning and Rice, putting Brady and Moss on top. It gave New England the lead for good. The Patriots eventually won 38–35 but lost to the Giants five weeks later in the Super Bowl when Brady was held to just one TD pass. Brady got the regular-season record. The Giants got the Super Bowl ring. On a smaller scale, they also would have liked to stop Brady from making history against them.

"We tried," Pierce said. "We didn't just try for Peyton. We obviously tried for ourselves. But that just tells you how competitive those guys are."

Brady was later told that Manning had implored the Giants defense through Eli to prevent him from breaking the record. He grinned, noting that the Giants didn't make it easy. "We worked for them that night," he said.

Brady understood that Manning was trying to protect his turf. Six years later, Manning had forty-seven touchdowns going into the Broncos' final two games of season. He needed three to tie Brady and four to take back the record. He tossed four in the next-to-last game against the Texans to get to 51. He was back on top. In the final game, needing a victory to secure the AFC's number-one seed over the Patriots, Manning threw another four in the first half against the Raiders. That gave him fifty-five. With the Broncos comfortably ahead 31–0 at the half, Manning took a seat on the bench.

"He wanted the record back," Pierce said. "Then he wanted to crush that record a little bit. He went up plus five. As much as Brady and Manning are gentlemen on the field and shake hands and head-nod, don't ever get it twisted one way or the other that these guys don't want to outdo the other."

Even when he broke the record, Manning had Brady on his mind. He predicted that Brady would break the record in 2014. "I have zero chance," Brady said with a laugh. "But it's a very nice thing for him to say."

Brady was right. He didn't break the record, and he didn't come close. He threw thirty-three touchdowns in 2014. He says he doesn't care about records. He cares about rings, and it became clear as the years ticked by in their careers that Manning would never catch him. One year apart, they each played the Seahawks in the Super Bowl. Manning and the Broncos lost 43–8. He threw just one touchdown pass, had the first snap fly over his head for a safety, and also threw two interceptions, one setting up a touchdown and the other returned for a touchdown. Brady and the Patriots won 28–24. Brady threw four touchdown passes and passed Joe Montana for the most TD passes in Super Bowl history. He overcame two bad interceptions, the first one costing the Patriots at least a field goal and the second setting up a Seahawks touchdown, but he threw a pair of fourth-quarter touchdown passes, including the game-winner with just 2:02 remaining. He completed 13 of 15 passes in the fourth quarter, including a perfect 8-for-8 on the final drive. He also broke Manning's Super Bowl record for completions, set just twelve months earlier. That postseason gap makes owning all the regular-season passing records even more important for Manning's legacy.

. . .

**It goes beyond** the pregame chat and postgame handshake for Peyton Manning and Tom Brady. That's all the public sees. They are supercompetitive athletes, especially when they play each other, but they have a relationship that goes beyond mutual respect. They relate to each other. They are the only two players in the last fifteen years who are bigger than the game. "They are much better friends than anybody knows," Archie Manning said.

Brady and Manning play golf together in California. They've had dinner together in Boston. They speak on the phone and often text each other good luck before games. "I wouldn't say I really root for them to win because of the impact it has on our team and our season," Brady said. "But I always want him to do well."

During the off-season in 2013, Brady was at his home in Brentwood, California, outside Los Angeles. He and Bundchen purchased the four-acre property for $11.75 million in 2008, spent four years having the 18,298-square-foot French-style house built, then wound up selling to Dr. Dre of Beats headphone fame for $40 million in the summer of 2014. The Brady bunch—they have a son, Benjamin, and a daughter, Vivian, and Tom has a son, Jack, who lives with his former girlfriend Bridget Moynahan—moved into a custom-built mansion in Brookline, Massachusetts, in the fall of 2014, about two hundred yards from the front door of Patriots owner Robert Kraft. They downsized to 18,000 square feet.

Manning and Brady played golf a "bunch of times," Brady said, during the off-season in 2013. They had a lot to talk about. Manning had just completed his first season with the Broncos and had lost in devastating fashion to the Ravens in double overtime at home in the divisional round of the playoffs. The following week, the Ravens went into Foxboro for the AFC championship game and defeated the Patriots. Joe Flacco had won the daily double, beating Manning and Brady back-to-back on the road in the playoffs, something Mark Sanchez was first to do, with the Jets in 2010.

Before training camp opened in the summer of 2013, Manning was on the West Coast with his wife, Ashley. "I'm in LA," Manning texted Brady. "If you're around, let me know."

The previous summer, Manning tried to get together with Brady in California, but the Bradys were out of town. This time, they were home. Brady invited Peyton and Ashley to their house for dinner. The Mannings were traveling without their son, Marshall, and daughter, Mosley, twins born in 2011, but the Bradys' two children were at home. The couples sat for three or four hours, two of the greatest players in football history in the privacy of the Brady home. No cameras, no tape recorders, no media, no TMZ. They didn't go into the backyard and throw footballs through a tire, and they didn't play *Madden NFL 13* with Manning picking Brady and Brady picking Manning.

The four of them sat and talked. Tom and Peyton, of course, did chat some football, most of it before joining the ladies at the dinner table. "We've always had a pretty good bond and spoken the same language," Brady said.

Chefs cooked the meal. Ashley and Gisele talked about their kids and their homes, and their conversation centered on "what wives talk about," Brady said. "Sometimes they will listen a little bit to what we are talking about. I think it's fascinating for both of them. It nice for them to be able to relate to each other in a sense, also, because they know what their husbands are like and how we think and what keeps us up at night. My wife will get in the car driving home with me after a game, and she just wants to talk about the game—what happened, why did you do this? I need to relax. I'm sure Peyton is very similar, because his wife is similar to my wife. They're just passionate about rooting for their husbands to do well."

It was the first time Ashley had spent time with Gisele. Peyton had met Gisele and spoken to her and Brady in the hallway outside the locker room when the Colts played New England in 2011, the year Manning was injured. He still made the trip and helped out the quarterbacks on the sideline.

Bundchen made headlines in February one year earlier following the Patriots' loss to the Giants in Super Bowl XLVI when she was critical of the Patriots receivers for dropped passes. Though she didn't name any names, Wes Welker, who was Brady's close friend, dropped a key pass in the fourth quarter on a Brady pass that twisted him around.

On her way to an elevator after the game, Bundchen was heckled by Giants fans, who shouted, "Eli rules" and "Eli owns your husband." She didn't immediately respond, but was caught on video speaking to those around her. "You have to catch the ball when you're supposed to catch the ball," she said. "My husband cannot throw the ball and catch the ball at the same time. I can't believe they dropped the ball so many times."

How could Welker not take what she said personally? The wife of his buddy was calling him out. Welker beat himself up after the game for not catching Brady's pass. He blamed himself. "Trust me, I wasn't happy about it, either," he said. "I don't think anybody was. I understand the frustration. Somebody caught it on camera. It's not that big a deal. They are good friends of mine and my wife. She is as sweet as she can be."

Bundchen is one of the most visible women in the world. Ashley Manning keeps a low profile and is rarely shown at games or in public with Manning. She is never quoted about her husband. But the women hit it off at the Brady house. "We had fun," Manning said. "Ashley has known Tom for quite some time. That was the first time getting to know his wife. It was great. Just the four of us. It was the off-season, not a ton of football talk, just two couples spending time together. We tried not to talk about football. Naturally, when Tom and I are alone playing golf or before dinner that night, obviously it's pretty natural that football is going to come up."

Manning and Brady are selective about what they allow their fans to know about their lives away from the field, but they hardly lead private lives. Brady has tried to control the message on his Facebook page. Two months after winning his fourth Super Bowl, he posted video showing him diving off a forty-foot cliff in Costa Rica into a pool of water, set to the music from *Superman*, which must have caused Robert Kraft's heart to skip a beat. Brady's comment on his page was "Never doing that again! #AirBrady." The next day, a video surfaced on the Internet of Brady teaming up with Michael Jordan in a three-on-three basketball game in the Bahamas. He then Photoshopped a picture of himself in a full body cast lying in a hospital bed with the caption "Jordan's crossover is no joke!" The cast on his left leg is signed by Jordan, and of course Brady is wearing his trademark eyeblack.

Manning is in half of all television commercials, or so it seems, and Bundchen is one of the highest-paid supermodels in the world; *Forbes* in 2014 placed her earnings for the previous twelve months at $47 million. Brady does just a fraction of the commercials that Manning does, and Ashley Manning is rarely seen.

Ashley Manning is one of the twenty-three limited partners of the Memphis Grizzlies of the NBA. She is from Memphis and became part of the group, which also includes singer and actor Justin Timberlake, to make sure the team didn't relocate. She reportedly made a $5 million investment to purchase 2.84 percent of the team. She and Peyton met through mutual friends before he enrolled at Tennessee in 1994. She went to Virginia. They were married in 2001.

"Ashley doesn't really like to be in the public," Brady said. "She has told that to me. She loves to be really low-key. It's really a great quality about her. I married a woman who happens to do what she does and is very good at it. There is a lot of popularity associated with that. I think, all in all, we're all kind of very homey, family-oriented people. We have public jobs. There's nothing I love to do other than play football. I know my wife loves to work and the career she has. That brings on a lot of other things. I know Ashley says she just likes to go sit in the box and, 'No one knows it, no one hears me, no one knows I'm there. I don't need to go out and show my face. I'll see Peyton after the game.' She kind of feels Peyton does his work, comes home, and she is there to take care of the family."

Brady and Peyton have a strong connection, but it can go only so far when it comes to sharing information. It's easier for Peyton with Eli than it is with Brady. After all, they are brothers and play in different conferences. There is never a time when they want the other to lose, except when they are playing each other, and even then, they root for each other to have big games. Peyton leads Eli 3–0 in Manning Bowl games.

The Patriots have always been battling Manning for playoff seeding, whether he has been with the Colts or the Broncos, so Tom and Peyton never root for each other to win, even though they want each other to do well and stay healthy. They share information about how to beat different teams but never discuss their own teams. "Kind of like pitchers sharing how to get hitters out," says Tony Dungy, who coached Peyton in Indianapolis for seven years.

Cassel is Brady's best friend in all the years he's played for the Patriots. He was Brady's backup from 2005 to 2008. When Brady suffered a torn ACL in the 2008 season, Cassel nearly led New England to the playoffs. Brady helped guide him through the season. Brady texted him the night before each game and the morning after. His play in Brady's absence made him a lot of money when he was traded to Kansas City following the season and signed a big contract that included $28 million in guaranteed money. During the years Cassel played in New England, Brady made sure to include him when Manning would come to Boston in the off-season and they would get together.

"When Tommy gets his knee blown out against the Chiefs, one of the first people to call him was Peyton," said Scott Pioli, the former Patriots vice president of personnel. "And he called him more than once, checking in on him. It revealed something to Tommy. It slowed Tommy down in terms of his thoughts toward Peyton. Not that he had any negative thoughts about him, but when you are that competitive with someone, you've got to find ways to hate them, because if you cross that line competing against someone that you genuinely and authentically care about, you might lose your edge."

Three years later, Manning missed the season following neck surgery. His career was in jeopardy. "Tommy told me it just wasn't the same playing the Colts without Peyton there," Pioli said. "He said he felt he lost somebody. That's why he gets so fired up to play Denver. He has never taken time to look at things in a historical context. He said, 'I'm finally realizing it. Facing Peyton has been one of the great elements of my career.'"

Manning won the Super Bowl following the 2006 season, beating Brady in the playoffs for the first time, erasing a 21–3 second-quarter deficit and then holding on to win 38–34 in the AFC championship game. Manning had business in Boston a few months later and was in touch with Brady to have dinner. Brady invited Cassel, Larry Izzo, Dan Koppen, and Will McDonough, a friend of Brady's who has managed both his career and Bundchen's. Heads turned when Brady and Manning and the group walked into a sushi restaurant and headed into a back room.

"They've got a great relationship and they have admiration for each other, too," Cassel said. "Anybody who plays this position knows how difficult it is to play at a high level, let alone be as consistent as the two of them have been over the years. I can only imagine the respect they have for one another, but the competitive fire burns in both of them."

As their lives have changed, their relationship has grown. "We have a lot in common," Brady said. "We both love doing what we do. We have families now, so it's different than the first time we kind of hung out."

Brady puts together a trip each year to travel to Louisville with several of his Patriots friends to attend the Kentucky Derby. Bruschi, Cassel, Welker, Rob Gronkowski, and Lonie Paxton have been on the excursion. One year, Archie Manning arranged a trip to the derby with sons Cooper, Peyton, and Eli and their wives and his wife, Olivia. Archie doesn't know much about horse racing, but he has a buddy in New Orleans who is pretty knowledgeable about the ponies. His friend advised him which horse to pick in each race. The night before the derby, the eight members of the Manning party met with Brady's group at a Kentucky Derby gala. As part of the deal, they had excellent seats together in the same area for the next day's races. Archie shared his friend's picks with Brady and his friends. Archie won three of the first four races, and the Patriots who bet on his tips cashed in too.

Peyton Manning has always been competitive whether playing Amazing Catches in the yard as a kid with his father and brothers or trying to beat Brady to get to the Super Bowl. After winning the three races and realizing his father was on a hot streak, he objected to his spreading the wealth. "Quit sharing those picks," Peyton said. "It's going to affect the odds."

There were more multimillionaires among the Mannings and the Patriots group than just about anywhere else in Churchill Downs, but Peyton was concerned that if too much money was placed on his father's picks, the payoff would be less. Archie wound up picking eight winners, including the derby winner. He went back the next year and didn't pick a single winner. They all thought it was funny, including Brady's group.

In the early part of the off-season of 2015, before things got busy with the workouts and minicamps, Brady and his father were invited to play at Augusta National Golf Club, site of the Masters Tournament. The father-son competition was set up by a friend who was also friends with Rory McIlroy, the number-one player in the world. McIlroy and his father, Brady and his father, and four others were on the course together. They had dinner at the golf club the night before playing three rounds in two days, and just coincidentally, Peyton Manning was there with his brothers Eli and Cooper, Broncos tight end Jacob Tamme, and Peyton's good friend John Lynch, who played for the Bucs and then for the Broncos prior to Peyton's arrival in Denver in 2012. Brady and Manning spoke briefly but didn't have a chance to play the famed course together. Brady went off the first tee with McIlroy. A couple of weeks later, he was playing basketball with Michael Jordan and McIlroy was playing in the Masters.

The two football superstars have relied on each other's friendship for many years, even though one of them was always in the way of the other on the road to the Super Bowl. "He's a great person and a good friend," Brady said. "When you are competing, it's a whole different story. But it's not like we're boxers and we're throwing punches at one another. We've never been on the same field at the same time. I have a lot of respect for him and what he is able to do. I think it's more of an appreciation, especially for a year like he had in 2013, the best year in the history of all NFL quarterbacks."

# 2

# THE FAMILY BUSINESS

Archie Manning was the second overall pick in the 1971 draft by the Saints. He has three sons who played football. Cooper was an accomplished receiver at Isidore Newman High School in New Orleans, even catching passes his senior year from younger brother Peyton, the starting quarterback. Suddenly, all the fighting that had gone on between them—brotherly love—came to a stop. "That's when I had to start kissing his butt or he wasn't going to throw it to me," Cooper said. "We had a big year. He threw it to me a ton. We got beat in the semifinals of the state tournament. That was a great year not only for us to grow closer and have to put up with each other and get along, but my parents also had a blast that year watching us play together. I caught seventy-five balls."

He earned a scholarship to play at Ole Miss, where his father had gone to school. But before he could even play in his first game, he was having numbness in his hands during preseason practices. He went to the Mayo Clinic in Minnesota and was diagnosed with spinal stenosis, a narrowing of the spinal column. He underwent surgery, ending his football career.

Peyton took the news hard that Cooper couldn't play anymore. According to published reports, Cooper wrote him an emotional letter: "I would like to live my dream of playing football through you. Although I cannot play anymore, I know I can still get the same feeling out of watching my little brother do what he does best. I know now that we are good for each other, because I need you to be serious and look at things from a different perspective. I am good for you, as well, to take things light. I love you, Peyt, and only great things lie ahead for you. Thanks for everything on and off the field."

When Peyton elected to enroll at Tennessee, the state of Mississippi all but broke down the front door of the Mannings' home in the historic Garden District of New Orleans. Archie was an Ole Miss icon, the greatest quarterback in the school's history. Peyton was born to play at Mississippi—it all but said that on his birth certificate—but he decided to create his own identity at Tennessee.

"When Peyton was being recruited, he had a hundred schools after him," Archie Manning said. "It really got turned up his junior year. You know him—Peyton kind of attacked recruiting. He did his due diligence. He wasn't going to let recruiting overwhelm him. He was going to overwhelm recruiting. It didn't bother him. In October of his senior year, he was still talking to forty schools. He was playing his season, doing his schoolwork. He handled it. He did recognize at some point, maybe at my suggestion, 'Peyton, you got to start eliminating some schools.'"

Archie explained to him that it wasn't fair to the schools to keep them hanging and prevent them from finalizing scholarships with other quarterbacks. Just about every school in the country wanted Peyton, including Michigan, which made it deep into the process. Of course, if Manning had showed up in Ann Arbor in 1994, either it would have ended any interest Michigan had in Brady or scared Brady away from enrolling one year later, or it would have been Brady vs. Manning dueling it out to see who played in "The Big House," Michigan Stadium, the world's second-largest stadium, seating over 110,000.

Taking his father's suggestion, Manning began to cut his list. He'd return home from football practice, do his schoolwork, and then take recruiting calls every night between eight thirty and ten o'clock. "He would come sit at the foot of our bed and say, 'Well, I cut Arizona State today. Good coach.' One night he came in and said, 'I just cut two schools and nobody thinks they're any good, but they have new coaches who are going to win. Coach Snyder at Kansas State and Coach Barnett at Northwestern.' A few years ago, I reminded him of that. I said, 'You were a prophet.' He had forgotten about that. I'm not saying he was right about everybody, but those two he was right about. He had a feel for it."

Manning took a visit to Michigan and liked the idea that if he wasn't going to pick Ole Miss, then he wouldn't have to play against them either if he got out of the South. "Michigan was a bailout," Archie said.

Michigan, Ole Miss, Tennessee, and Florida were Manning's final four. "I wanted to go to Ole Miss, I wanted to go to Florida, I wanted to go to Michigan," he said. "You have to pick one."

He loved Ole Miss and wasn't afraid of following in his father's footsteps. Even so, there were rumors that Mississippi was headed for probation, and the Mannings couldn't get a clear answer about what punishment awaited the program. That eliminated the Rebels. "They did go on probation," Archie Manning said. "If Peyton had gone there, he would have been able to play in only one bowl game and been on television only one year."

Peyton loved Michigan and offensive coordinator Cam Cameron, but ultimately decided he wanted to play in the SEC. Cameron wound up taking a job with the Redskins and later told the

Mannings that if it had looked as though Peyton was going to come to Michigan, he would have told him he was leaving before he committed to playing in Ann Arbor. Manning has never played well in cold weather in the NFL. Brady has thrived when it's freezing. Perhaps if Manning had chosen Michigan, he would have been better prepared to play in Foxboro in January.

That left Florida and Tennessee, in the other division of the SEC from Ole Miss. Manning looked at the quarterback depth chart and felt he would have a clearer path reaching his goal of starting by his sophomore year if he went to Knoxville. Archie was such a legend at Ole Miss that the speed limit on the Oxford campus was later set at 18 mph, a tribute to his uniform number. Peyton left it up to little brother Eli to rewrite the Mississippi record books. Eli was up to the challenge, and the speed limit around the football stadium on campus was subsequently set at 10 mph, the number Eli wore for the Rebels. Peyton may have pissed off the entire state of Mississippi, but Tennessee was more than happy to provide a comfortable landing spot.

Archie endured a good deal of the criticism for the Tennessee decision. He received nasty letters. He heard of friends talking behind his back. On his way to Jackson once, he stopped at a gas station and said a "good ole boy" gave him a hard time for letting Peyton go to Tennessee. "I let him make his own choice," Archie told the man.

Just like his brother, Eli was the number-one overall pick in the draft, in 2004 by the Chargers. He had declared he would go back to school before playing for San Diego, which was considered a dysfunctional organization. He wanted to play for the Giants, who were picking fourth. The Chargers and Giants couldn't agree on a predraft deal, but after San Diego took Manning and the Giants were on the clock with the fourth pick, they worked out a trade. New York agreed to select North Carolina State quarterback Philip Rivers for the Chargers and also to trade picks in the third and fifth rounds in 2004 and the first round in 2005 in exchange for Manning.

The Manning brothers are close friends. Cooper has lived vicariously through the accomplishments of his brothers and is a successful businessman in an energy investment banking firm in New Orleans. Archie used to stand on the front porch step of their New Orleans home and toss the football as Cooper, Peyton, and Eli would run out for passes. "They preferred when it was raining or wet because it was more fun to slide," Archie said.

The boys made some Amazing Catches. "They would start at one end of the yard and take off," Archie said. "We had a sidewalk that was about a third of the way, so I had to make sure they cleared it. They would cross the sidewalk, I would lay it out in front of them, and they would try to make diving catches. It was up to me to make it an amazing catch instead of a routine catch."

It was an entertaining game, and Peyton has turned out to be quite entertaining on and off the field. Eli is laid-back; nothing bothers him. Cooper has always been the one with the twinkle in his eye and, as a kid, mischief on his mind. When Archie was playing for the Saints, the team was very bad. They were called the 'Aints. Fans wore bags over their heads at the Superdome. Archie's wife, Olivia, would take Cooper and Peyton to the games to watch their father play. Eli was not born yet.

"We were six and four years old," Cooper said. "Some guys were there and left the bags in their seats. My Mom turned around and there we were; we had them on our heads, too. We didn't know what we were doing, of course. We thought Mom would get a laugh out of it. It helped her laugh because we were probably getting beat that afternoon."

Did he force Peyton to wear the bag?

"Monkey see, monkey do," he said. "That was probably the last time I had control over Peyton when he would do what I said. My grip has been slipping slowly."

Archie said when he heard about the boys wearing the bags, he laughed. Now if newspapers had caught the sons of the Saints starting quarterback wearing bags over their heads as the home team was stinking up the field once again, there might have been hell to pay in the Manning household. "Olivia was pregnant with Eli. We were 0–11, 0–12. We were in the dome and they were booing my ass," Archie said. "Cooper asks Olivia if they could boo, too. You almost got to laugh at something like that. Olivia was pretty pregnant and kind of looking for a reason to quit going to the games. And that was it. She was, 'Let's go. You can't boo and you can't come to any more games. So let's go.'"

Cooper still makes people laugh. Peyton was the son who kept his siblings in line.

"Peyton was pretty easy. He tried to please," Archie said. "I guess you could say Peyton was coachable. If you said, 'Don't cross the street,' he wasn't going to cross the street, and he was going to tell Cooper and Eli, 'Don't go across the street.'"

Eli is seven years younger than Cooper, so their relationship was different from that between Cooper and Peyton. Cooper was more of a big brother to Eli. "Peyton and I are two years apart," Cooper said. "We played a lot of sports together. We fought a lot. A lot of hoops games in the backyard that never finished because the game gets close and here come the elbows and here come the fists. I have very distinct memories of my dad begging and pleading with us, saying if we could ever get along, how lucky we were to have each other. Just compete and finish a game as opposed to fighting and fighting."

Archie was a tremendous athlete, the best in the family. He was fast and had a big arm; he just played on some of the worst teams in the NFL year after year and is the best quarterback in league history never to make the playoffs.

"Peyton is a good athlete, but that's not what made him the player he is today," Archie said. "He never ran fast and that always kind of bothered him. He's the only one of my three children that cared and was interested in what I did and dug up film and read stories. I was classified as a runner. I was pretty fast. It bothered Peyton."

"Dad, why am I not fast?" he asked.

"I don't know, Peyton. I don't know," Archie said.

They were years away from knowing each other, but Manning and Brady already had one thing in common: they were slow. In fact, Brady's forty-yard-dash time at the scouting combine in 2000 is legendary for being so painfully slow. He could've been clocked with an hourglass. Brady ran the forty in 5.28 seconds. Manning didn't run at the combine but was timed in his rookie year at 4.8.

"Peyton and Tom, golly, you wouldn't want to see that race," Archie said. "The fact Peyton wasn't fast made him say, 'Well, I want to be a quarterback.'"

**Brady grew up** with three older sisters. Maureen and Nancy were accomplished softball players. Julie played soccer. Julie married former Red Sox third baseman Kevin Youkilis in 2012. All the girls played in college. They all picked on their little Tommy. "Oh, yeah, it goes with the territory," Tom Brady Sr. said.

Tom Sr. has an estate-planning business with offices in the Bay Area, New York, and, quite conveniently, Boston. He and his wife, Galynn, attended 90 percent of Tom's games at Michigan, traveling to home and away games even when he was second or third on the depth chart. They went to all his Patriots games for the first four years he was starting, but now limit it to home games and a few road games each year. Archie tries to attend as many of Peyton's and Eli's home games as he can, but it became too much of a physical strain to get to road games.

Tom Sr. also let his son make his own decision about where to attend college, but he was distraught when he selected Michigan over Cal–Berkeley, which is just thirty-five miles across the San Francisco Bay from the Brady home in San Mateo. Tommy was his best friend, and he was moving across the country. Brady Sr. turned to a psychologist for help dealing with the separation from his son. He went through eight weeks of counseling. "Tommy and I, he's my best buddy. We spent so much time together," he said. "We'd play golf, go to ball games; I coached his games. When he decided to go to Michigan, it literally broke my heart." The sessions with the psychologist helped. "Oh yeah," he said. "I don't have any qualms about saying it."

Archie Manning and Tom Brady Sr. developed a friendship because of the rivalry of their sons. Just as Brady never brings up to Peyton that he has quite a big lead in Super Bowl championships, the Manning family doesn't brag that Eli beat Brady in Super Bowls XLII and XLVI.

"I'm trying to win a championship for the Giants and myself," Eli said. "It's not Manning vs. Brady. It's the Giants vs. New England. It's bigger than the two people or a last name."

Archie Manning says Peyton never really discusses the games against Brady with him. "He's been on the short end, but I don't think he's scarred by that," he said. "He's proud of the fact that they are recognized as certainly two of the top quarterbacks of an era. I'm glad he likes Tom. I'm glad Tom likes him. I'm glad they have a friendship. It wouldn't be good if they didn't like each other. Then, all of a sudden, there would be this built-in jealousy or hate. There's been a lot written about Peyton and Tom, and everybody wants to proclaim the greatest ever. I don't think you can do that with quarterbacks. Even Tom and Peyton and Drew Brees and Aaron Rodgers vs. Joe Montana or Roger Staubach or Terry Bradshaw, or how in the world can you go back and talk about people vs. Otto Graham, Sammy Baugh, and Johnny Unitas? To have a son who is kind of mentioned in that argument, I'm proud of that and I'm sure Tom Brady Sr. is, too."

Peyton Manning is a serious student of the history of the game. He was a Dan Marino fan growing up. The first start of his pro career, in the opening game of his rookie year in 1998, was against Marino and the Dolphins. Brady lived in Northern California; his first idol was Joe Montana and then Steve Young. Montana retired six years before Brady was drafted by the Patriots. Young retired the year before Brady came into the NFL. In the summer of 2003, Montana had Brady over to his house for lunch in the Bay Area. Brady said it was a dream come true.

Tom Brady Sr. admires Archie Manning for the class with which he's dealt with two sons achieving fame and greatness in the family business as the First Family of the NFL. "My internist would have had to do ulcer surgery four or five times by now," Brady Sr. said. "Archie is obviously a quality, quality guy."

Tom Sr. felt for Archie after the Broncos were crushed in the Super Bowl by Seattle. He texted his regrets. "It wouldn't have made a difference who was playing quarterback," Brady Sr. said. "Obviously, the fans of one guy tar and feather the other guys when the team loses. We are parents, I don't care what you say, you feel that. I just was commenting to him, as a dad to a dad, 'Hey, I feel your pain. I'm proud of your son. I'm proud of you guys.' This is a game. This isn't going to Iraq. Unfortunately, we lose focus. Our life is supposed to be determined by the outcome of a game? We have our priorities certainly misplaced when you are putting that much value on the final score."

Archie Manning still finds it hard to believe he has two sons who have been in five Super Bowls and won three. "Olivia and I try not to take it for granted," he said. "Along the way, we've tried to be sensible and good, supporting parents. Sometimes we look at each other and say, 'Can you believe this?' We're so proud. We just kind of pinch ourselves. Both of them are fortunate to be healthy.

As parents, we've been blessed. They had successful college careers and are getting to play for successful NFL franchises and winning Super Bowls."

Archie never pushed his sons to be quarterbacks. It's more than just having the quarterback genes. How many NFL quarterbacks have sons who turn out better than them? Certainly not Montana, whose two sons bounced around college football. Or Phil Simms, who had two sons make it to the NFL; his older son, Chris, started a playoff game for the Bucs, the first of four stops in a seven-year journeyman career interrupted by a frightening ruptured spleen suffered early in his career against Carolina. His younger son, Matt, was a Jets backup for several years before he was claimed on waivers in 2015 by Buffalo. All those young men had the burden of carrying the family name and trying to live up to the accomplishments of their fathers.

Brady came from a family of athletes, but not even Tom Sr. thought his only boy had a future in professional football. In fact, he was a good enough lefty-hitting catcher with a strong arm at Serra High School in San Mateo, the same school that produced Barry Bonds, to be drafted in the eighteenth round by the Montreal Expos in 1995. His father thinks that if he hadn't already accepted a scholarship to play football at Michigan, he might have been selected in the second or third round. The Manning brothers were destined to be quarterbacks. Not so with Brady. He didn't start playing football until he was a freshman in high school and didn't get on the field as a quarterback his first year even though his team finished 0–8 and didn't score a touchdown. He became the starter by default in his sophomore year when the previous year's number one quarterback decided not to play. Tom's mother played competitive soccer into her forties, and he inherited his athletic ability from her.

"To have all this stuff happen, I'm not sure if the word is *surreal* or whether it's *bizarre*," said Brady Sr. "When Tommy was growing up, he was a normal kid. He's still a normal son to us. He's so blessed with a wonderful wife. She's just awesome. They get along like ham and eggs. I've got three other kids, three daughters; they're just awesome. Tommy happens to have captured some celebrity, for whatever that's worth, and untoward wealth. The reality is, he's exactly the same guy; he's more sophisticated, but he's still the gentle, kind, loving son that we hoped he would be. All this other stuff is peripheral. He really digs his family, his sisters, his parents, and his own family. He's a great dad."

Manning could have made a fortune if he'd been able to cash in the value of the postage from all the recruiting letters he received. Brady was a recruiting afterthought. He didn't need to set aside ninety minutes every night after doing his homework to field calls from college head coaches. He put together a recruiting tape that he sent to schools, trying to sell himself.

Archie Manning sat back and let Peyton manage the recruiting process. Tom Brady Sr. did the same with Tom. He didn't accompany him on recruiting trips. He felt he needed to experience that on his own. He was privately rooting for him to stay home and play at Cal, but "I never expressed that to him," he said. Tom Sr. was not going to influence his son as to where to go to college.

They compiled a list of fifteen questions to ask reps from each school that was interested. "Tommy had to own the decision, because when things got really tough, I didn't want to be responsible for him turning around to me and saying, 'Jeez, you really wanted me to come here, but in my heart I didn't want to,'" Brady Sr. said.

Brady narrowed it down to three schools: Michigan, Cal, and Illinois.

He fell in love with Michigan and Ann Arbor. "I loved the social aspect. I loved the team. It was a great school," he said. "It was more of a feeling. Once I experienced that, I really didn't want to go anywhere else."

He visited Ann Arbor in the winter. Billy Harris, the defensive backs coach on Michigan head coach Gary Moeller's staff, was in charge of West Coast recruiting. He was concerned about a California kid being turned off by the arctic Midwestern winters. "We gave that old pitch: when you go pro, it might be somewhere where it snows," Harris said. "Thank goodness he went to Michigan, because it snows in New England. Now he can credit Michigan for helping him deal with bad-weather games."

NFL teams have been second-guessed forever because Brady lasted until the sixth round, the 199th pick of the 2000 draft. Still, it wasn't as if the Bradys packed up young Tommy and sent him to Ann Arbor expecting him to return as a first-round draft pick or become the greatest quarterback in NFL history. "Before he had gone off to Michigan, we had homed in on the fact that 'football probably isn't going to be your life,'" Brady Sr. said. "Those athletes go to school and there is not—even though people had hoped and expected it—a future in athletics."

So the father told the son as he was considering his final decision: "There is a very good probability that you will not have the success that you hoped to have. Whatever school you choose, you better decide, in conjunction with the athletics, that you want a degree from that school that means something that is going to get you on to the next level of your life. What school would be the school . . . that you would be proud to have that degree on the wall and it would launch you into your career, if football doesn't work out?"

As a result, "Before he decided on Michigan, that was one of the major, major criteria. It wasn't just football criteria," Brady Sr. said.

Brady wanted to be a Michigan man. He wanted to lead the Wolverines onto the field at The Big House in front of 110,000 screaming fans dressed in maize and blue. He wanted to walk down State Street after the game as the Michigan quarterback, the big man on campus. Football wasn't a significant enough presence back home at Berkeley, although the path to the field might have been quicker, especially after he had been the star of a summer camp at Cal and was promised he would start as a sophomore. Michigan people told him, "You would have to prove yourself to be the best if you are going to lead the best," and Brady wasn't going to run away from the challenge of working himself up the depth chart.

Before allowing him to sign the letter of intent, however, Brady Sr. called Harris. "Billy, the only thing that I know has to happen is we have to have somebody at Michigan who really wants Tommy. He wants to go where he's wanted. Does Gary Moeller want him?"

"Absolutely, he wants him," Harris said.

"I want that in blood. I want you to tell me truthfully that's the case," Brady Sr. said.

"I'll get back to you," Harris said.

Two days later, Moeller and Harris were in San Mateo having breakfast with the Brady men.

"Tommy, we got to change from what we've done," Moeller said. "We can't keep running with the same kind of system. You are our prototypical quarterback."

That sold Brady. He was going to Ann Arbor. He signed his letter of intent.

Brady didn't even have time to buy a couple of Michigan sweatshirts before Harris called. "I got good news and bad news," Harris said. "The good news is, we're going to play golf before next summer, and I'm going to see your family more often. The bad news is, I'm no longer at Michigan."

# 3

# GO BLUE OR BE BLUE

Lloyd Carr walks virtually unnoticed into Zingerman's Deli on the corner of Detroit and Kingsley on the North Side of Ann Arbor, one mile from the center of the beautiful University of Michigan campus. Zingerman's is a bucket-list stop in one of the great college towns in America, the place former Wolverines quarterback and now head coach Jim Harbaugh recommends when he's asked where to eat in town, and the lines often extend out the door and around the corner at lunchtime.

This was a quiet spring morning just past breakfast. The sun was making its first appearance since October. In two hours, the place would be packed, but at the time there were a few people on line downstairs, a group sitting at nearby tables, and in an upstairs dining room, a woman on her iPad on one side and a few students having breakfast on the other. That was about it.

Carr, a dignified man, a proud grandfather enjoying his retirement years, arrives to address one of the great unsolved mysteries of this generation in college football: the Michigan years of Tom Brady. How and why did Carr make him beg for every snap he received in his five years on campus?

Carr still lives in Ann Arbor. He retired following the 2007 season after putting together a 122–40 record in thirteen years. His legacy is set in stone: he won the national championship in 1997, giving him one more than the legendary Bo Schembechler. Michigan football has since fallen on hard times, Rich Rodriguez and Brady Hoke having been unable to get the Wolverines back into national championship contention. Tom Brady was very close to Hoke, who was a defensive assistant under Carr during Brady's years at Michigan. Brady was disappointed that Hoke was fired after the 2014 season, but he was excited that Harbaugh, after a falling-out with the 49ers, was coming back home to resurrect the proud program. Carr, still a visible face around campus, endorsed the Harbaugh hiring and was at his introductory press conference.

A handful of customers at Zingerman's approach and say, "Coach, good to see you. How you been?" as Carr carries a cup of coffee to the upstairs dining room. Nobody ever walks up to him on campus and asks, "What were you thinking when you had Tom Brady?" They could be thinking it, however. Just about everybody outside Ann Arbor is. How did the greatest quarterback in NFL history, a four-time Super Bowl champion and three-time Super Bowl MVP, get so overlooked that his father still holds a grudge against Carr for mistreating his son?

Brady's agony started the day Harris made the phone call to say he was leaving. Harris was Brady's main contact during the re-cruiting process, but he had taken a job as the defensive coordina-tor at Stanford, right in Brady's backyard. It was a nice promotion up the coaching ladder. Harris remained friends with the Brady family and even showed up at Brady's send-off party before he left for Michigan. He brought him a University of Michigan flag as a going-away present. Harris departed Ann Arbor for career advancement, but Michigan was in his heart. His two black Labs were named Maize and Blue. Harris was fired by Stanford after four seasons and took a job at Eastern Michigan. He and his wife sold their house in California, but his wife's job at Stanford didn't end for another four months. She lived with the Bradys at their home in San Mateo during the transition.

Harris's decision to leave Michigan before Brady even arrived left him without the one ally on the coaching staff he knew would always be in his corner. Moeller had pledged to Brady in the breakfast meeting that he wanted him to play for him. But in May 1995, a few months before Brady was to arrive on campus, Moeller was arrested following a drunken incident at a restaurant in Southfield, Michigan. He eventually pleaded no contest to disorderly conduct and assault charges and was fined $200. According to reports, he was intoxicated and punched a police officer in the chest.

One week later, Moeller was pushed out. He'd had a record of 44–13–1 in five seasons, with two Big Ten titles and a share of a third. This was more bad news for Brady. First the man who recruited him had taken a new job. Then the head coach who swore he wanted him was fired and replaced by Carr, the defensive coordinator, whom Brady didn't know. Carr was first promoted to head coach on an interim basis, but before the end of the 1995 season, the interim tag was removed. Carr had been a Michigan assistant for fifteen seasons, including the final ten of Schembechler. Brady had been abandoned. "Lo and behold, Tommy has nobody in the coaches' room rooting for him," Brady Sr. said.

The next year, quarterbacks coach Kit Cartwright left for Indiana.

"All the people that helped recruit Tommy to Michigan had left," Harris said. "That's what makes you feel bad. Now if there are any struggles, the people that are usually closest to you are the folks that recruited you."

There was no uncertainty for Manning at Tennessee. Phillip Fulmer was the head coach who recruited him to Knoxville, and he was there long after Manning graduated. David Cutcliffe was his offensive coordinator and quarterbacks coach when he arrived. Cutcliffe left to be the head coach at Ole Miss in 1998, following Manning's senior year. He then recruited Eli Manning to play for him at Mississippi. Cutcliffe later became the head coach at Duke and supervised Peyton Manning's throwing rehabilitation in Durham, North Carolina, following the neck surgery in 2011 that nearly ended his career.

Manning always trusted that the coaches had his back in Knoxville. He was prepared to sit during his freshman year and would have been fine with it, knowing he would rise to the top of the depth chart in his sophomore year. He didn't even have to wait that long.

But for Brady, it wasn't until he walked off the field following the Orange Bowl on January 1, 2000, after throwing for 369 yards and four touchdowns to beat Alabama in overtime, that he was finally appreciated as a Michigan man.

Brady has played with a chip on his shoulder during his entire career with the Patriots. He knew how hard it was for him to get on the field in Ann Arbor, knew he'd almost gone undrafted, and knew it took a freak injury to Drew Bledsoe to get him his first start in the NFL. He still goes out to every practice with the mind-set that he must excel to keep his job. It's what drives him. The Michigan experience made Brady who he is today—but not before it nearly broke him.

Brady was so discouraged at not being given a chance to play that he nearly transferred to Cal the season after redshirting as a freshman. He attempted only twenty passes in his first two years on the varsity team and didn't become the starter until his fourth year in the program. It wasn't until midway through his fifth and final season that Carr gave Brady his full endorsement. Only then did he have the job security not to have to look over his shoulder at phenom and local favorite Drew Henson, who was from nine-teen miles up the road on US 23 in Brighton. But then, almost as a warning that nothing worth having ever comes easy, Carr still benched him for one series in the final game of his career in the Orange Bowl.

It's not uncommon for teams in the NFL draft to overlook players who later become stars. Trying to figure out why Brady was never shown the love at Michigan until he was ready to leave is much harder. "It was a great learning experience for me," he said. "Everyone has their own journey, and my journey was a very competitive one. I was forced to compete on a daily basis. It wasn't, 'Okay, if you commit to Michigan, you're going to be the quarter-back your second year.' And that's probably how a lot of kids want it, you know? They didn't promise me anything."

That was part of the message Brady delivered when Wolver-ines coach Brady Hoke asked him to speak to his team on the eve of Michigan's 2013 season, a few hours before Brady was to play against the Detroit Lions at Ford Field in a preseason game. He was standing in front of ninety players at Schembechler Hall. All eyes were on him. This was Tom Brady, Super Bowl champion, but he spoke to them as Tom Brady, who was in one of their seats nearly twenty years earlier, unsure of where his football career and his life would take him. Hoke was sitting to Brady's left as he gave an impassioned speech without any notes.

Every man in this room is counting on you. And every player that's ever worn this helmet is counting on you. Because you guys are the ones that are lucky enough to play for Michigan. And not a lot of other kids around the country can do that. There's probably a lot of other kids that are sitting in meeting rooms across the country playing for some other teams. Not every kid is playing for Michigan. And this place is special to me. It's special to the guys that I played with. It's special to the guys that played before me. Because we love Michigan.

Now, I didn't have an easy experience. I didn't come in as a top-rated recruit. I didn't come in with the opportunity to play right away. I had to earn it. And you know what the greatest honor I've ever received as a player is? In my fourth year and in my fifth year, I was named team captain. That, to this day, is the single greatest achievement I've ever had as a football player, because the men in this room chose me to lead their team. And these were my best friends. These were the guys that knew that I liked to work, that knew that I loved football, that knew that I loved to play, that knew that I wanted to be the quarterback for Michigan. And all the lessons that I've learned here on State Street and in The Big House, that's still what I bring to practice today. And after fourteen years, I love the game more than I've ever loved it.

Where did I learn the love for the game? Where did I learn to practice? Where did I learn to compete? It was sitting in the same chairs that you guys are sitting in today.

On a wall behind where Brady was speaking was a sign: THE TEAM, THE TEAM, THE TEAM. In his career with the Patriots, Brady has never talked about individual achievement. It's always about the team.

Brady's success in the NFL raises the question of why Carr played Scott Dreisbach and Brian Griese over him for two years and then Griese over him in Brady's third year. Carr avoided any second-guessing at the time, because Griese, who went on to be an NFL journeyman playing for five teams, was the quarterback in the national championship season. Since Brady had not been given a chance to prove he belonged on the field, Wolverines fans had no idea of the talent that was sitting on the bench. Nobody was in The

Big House chanting "We Want Brady," except maybe Tom Sr., his wife, and his three daughters.

Patriots fans chanted, "Brady's better! Brady's better!" when he outplayed Peyton Manning in a 43–21 victory over the Broncos in Foxboro in 2014. It's easy to say now that hearing that made up for the disrespect he received from the Michigan fans and coaching staff, but those were five difficult years in the young man's life; he can never get them back.

Most of the criticism directed at Carr is based in hindsight on what Brady has become in the NFL. "I didn't expect anybody to defend me, and I've never defended myself," Carr said. "My deal was, 'Hey, I'm trying to win. I might be right, I might be wrong, but I'm going to do what I think gives us the best chance.' It is a big issue. It's a big part of who Tom Brady is. Nobody that I know could have handled it better."

Manning began his college career at Tennessee in 1994 third on the depth chart. Brady was buried at number seven when he arrived at Michigan in 1995, behind even senior Jason Carr, the head coach's son, who had thrown just fourteen passes in his first three years and would throw another ten in Brady's freshman year, when he was redshirted.

From the day Manning stepped onto the campus in Tennessee, there was no need for coach Phillip Fulmer to manage the expectations of Volunteers fans. They all knew it would not take long for him to take over. Senior Jerry Colquitt opened the 1994 season as Tennessee's starter, but after tearing his ACL on the seventh play of the first game at UCLA, he was replaced by Todd Helton, who went on to have an excellent baseball career as the Colorado Rockies first baseman. Helton suffered a knee injury in the fifth game, and when he came off the field, Manning, who had played some in the UCLA game and one other before Helton was injured, ran onto the field and never left. The next football game Manning didn't start was the season opener in 2011, the fourteenth year of his NFL career, when he was recovering from neck surgery.

Manning was not an instant hit in the huddle with his teammates, a fact he elaborated on as the keynote speaker at the 2014 valedictory exercises at the University of Virginia. Manning's wife, Ashley, was a 1997 Virginia graduate, and Manning visited her often when he was at Tennessee. The Virginia students selected Manning to give the address, and he was flattered. He took the honor very seriously, not that you would expect anything less from him. Manning doesn't do anything in his life without preparing. Manning told the students:

> It was the first time I ran into the huddle as a quarterback at Tennessee. We were playing at UCLA in the Rose Bowl, ninety-five thousand people in the stands, ABC broadcasting the game on national television, Keith Jackson and Bob Griese. Tennessee was ranked ninth in the country. UCLA was unranked. It was expected to be a blowout. I was third team on the depth chart, not expecting to play the entire game, much less the entire season. On the seventh play of the game, our starting quarterback tears his knee, and he is out for the year. Our backup quarterback was a guy named Todd Helton, who went on to have an eighteen-year Major League Baseball career. Let's just say, Todd was kind of thinking about that baseball signing bonus he was about to get. He wasn't real crazy about going into the game. So we're getting beat 21–0, and my coach turns to me, and he says, "Peyton, you're going in." And, boy, I didn't think I was nervous. I looked down and all the hair on my arms is just sticking up.
>
> So I'm jogging into the huddle, and I remembered something my dad had told me. He said, "Son, if you ever get into the huddle with the starters at any point in the season—it may be in the fourth quarter of a blowout, it may be just in prac-

tice, it doesn't matter—you be the leader, and you take control of that huddle. That's your job as the quarterback. You're just eighteen years old. Most of these seniors are twenty-one, twenty-two. It doesn't matter. Be the leader and take control of that huddle."

So I remember old Dad's advice, and I got into the huddle, and I said, "All right, guys, I know I'm just a freshman, but I can take us down the field right now, get us a touchdown, and get us back in this game. Let's go." Big left tackle, a guy named Jason Layman, about six five, 330 pounds, grabs me by the shoulder and says, "Hey, freshman, shut the blank up and call the blanking play." And I said, "Yes, sir." That was really great advice from my dad. I really appreciated that.

Archie watched the speech on the Internet. He laughed as Peyton told the story. "He went in there and gave his little leader talk, and the tackle told him to shut the eff up and call the effing play," Archie said. "It was kind of humbling."

It was a beautiful day in Charlottesville, Virginia, with the senior class sitting in front of Manning on the Lawn. He was insightful and witty. At one point he picked three students out of the crowd to catch passes from him. He eased their minds by sarcastically assuring them that if they dropped the ball, there was no way it would wind up on YouTube. All three caught easy ones. Manning joked that after he fired Nerf balls at child actors in a skit on *Saturday Night Live*, he received letters from mothers and grandmothers who watched the show with their nine-year-olds and were disappointed in him for throwing the ball so hard at the kids. He said he wrote back asking why their nine-year-olds were up late watching *SNL*.

By October of his senior year in high school, Manning was still talking to forty schools. Brady was down to three. If he chose Cal, his father could watch him play on Saturdays, and they could play golf on Sundays. Michigan and Illinois were far from home, and the winters would be brutal—tough for a kid from Northern California—but getting exposed to swirling snow, wind whipping his face, and temperatures around zero late in the season would be good prep work for the big leagues.

Tom Sr. made it clear that the decision would be his, and he would have to own it. If things didn't work out, he didn't want to be responsible for giving his son bad advice. He was there to support him and advise him but not influence him. As the process began to develop, as the skinny kid from San Mateo sent out videos and schools showed interest, Michigan became his choice.

**Brady arrived at** Michigan for the summer preseason practice and quickly knew there wasn't much chance he'd be seeing action as a freshman. Carr redshirted him. Dreisbach, a redshirt freshman, won the starting job in 1995 but was injured in the fifth game of the year, and Griese started the last nine games as Michigan went 9–4, including a loss to Texas A&M in the Alamo Bowl. Dreisbach returned in 1996 and beat out Griese, a fourth-year junior. Brady at least made it into two games.

The day he addressed the Michigan players in 2013, he didn't tell them about the turning point in his career when he nearly left in 1996. It was only his second year, but he wasn't able to jump over Dreisbach or Griese. Brady loved the school, but he was a football player and he wanted to play. He saw no opening to get on the field in the years ahead. He felt lost.

He set up a meeting with Carr early in the season. The worst fears of Brady Sr. were being realized. His son didn't have an advocate in the coaches' room. Carr was not impressed enough by what he was seeing on the practice field to consider starting him. Brady walked into Schembechler Hall and went up one flight of steps to Carr's second-floor office. There was a lot of history in that building and in the Michigan program, but Brady was ready to walk away.

The coach is from Hawkins County, Tennessee, and the pace of his speech is deliberate. He is not an intimidating man. Brady had just turned nineteen and was 2,372 miles from home, feeling as though a degree from one of the best schools in the country just might not be enough to make him stay.

Carr sat behind his desk. Brady sat in front of him.

Brady said, "Coach, I think I'm going to transfer."

"Why is that?"

"I don't think I'm ever going to play here, and I don't think I'm getting a fair chance."

"If you want to transfer, I'll give you your release, but I think it will be the biggest mistake you ever make. Look, you're in a very competitive situation here. All you guys have talent. The best advice I can give anybody in a competitive situation is that they come in here every single day prepared mentally and physically to compete at their very best. Don't be watching the other guy, hoping he has a bad day or doesn't do well. Just worry about getting better every day."

There was a pause.

Carr continued. "Look, you want to be the best, you've got to stick it out and try to beat out the best. Tom, have you talked to your dad?"

"Yeah."

"What does he say?"

"He will support whatever decision I make."

"Well, why don't you give it some thought tonight and come back tomorrow, and we'll talk again."

There was no doubt in Carr's mind about what Brady was going to do. Carr called his coaches together and told them, "Well, I think Tom's going to leave."

During recruitment, Brady Sr. also told his son, "So many kids

I see transfer from school to school to school to school, and that does a disservice to the kid's adolescence and to the kid's future, because he's running away from problems, and he's not confronting them head-on."

Brady went back to his apartment. If he left Michigan, he would sit out the rest of the 1996 season and the NCAA would have to rule whether he had to sit out 1997 as well. Carr was prepared to give him his release. He didn't want an unhappy player. Brady slept on his decision. He agonized over it.

"I really wasn't sure where my career was going to go," Brady said. "I just wasn't sure if I would ever get an opportunity to play."

Brady had just one school on his list if was going to leave Michigan. He would transfer back home to Cal–Berkeley. The coach, Keith Gilbertson, who had recruited Brady out of high school, had been replaced in 1996 by Green Bay Packers assistant Steve Mariucci, who had a reputation as an excellent quarterbacks coach. As it turned out, Mariucci was hired as the 49ers head coach after one season, which would have added him to the list of coaches who left campus before Brady even arrived, but Brady's decision was more about getting to play than about the coach. Brady debated in his mind about Cal.

"I was just really thinking if that was going to be a great opportunity for me," he said.

As he promised, Brady went back to see Carr at Schembechler Hall the next day. Carr was sitting behind his desk again. Brady was in front of him again. This time, Brady leaned over Carr's desk to get his point across. "Coach," he said with more confidence than he had the day before, "I've decided I'm going to stay at Michigan, and I'm going to prove to you I'm a great quarterback."

That's what Carr wanted to hear. He wasn't looking to run Brady off and get back his scholarship. He liked him. But he also made no promises about playing time. "He was always competitive from the first day, but I think what happened from that point on is, I would say he began to enjoy the struggle," Carr said. "He went out with the intention of showing his teammates what kind of quarterback he is."

Schembechler came up with the Michigan motto: Those Who Stay Will Be Champions.

The Michigan players touch that sign on the way out of the locker room on Saturdays. In his speech to Team 134, the Michigan team of 2013, Brady closed by speaking of the Schembechler saying that shaped his future: "You stick around, you fight, you work, you do everything you can every day for each other, and you'll be champions."

Griese took over as the starting quarterback as a third-year sophomore in 1995 after Dreisbach tore ligaments in the thumb on his throwing hand in practice. Michigan was 4–0 at the time. Dreisbach had surgery at the University of Michigan Hospital and didn't play again that season. Jason Carr, a fifth-year senior, was Griese's backup.

Dreisbach returned as the starter in 1996. Griese was the backup and didn't get a chance to win the job back until Dreisbach injured his elbow and suffered a concussion in the first half of the annual Thanksgiving weekend game against Ohio State, which was undefeated and ranked number two in the country. Michigan trailed 9–0 at the half, but Griese rallied the Wolverines to a 14–9 upset victory in Columbus, throwing for 120 yards, including a 69-yard touchdown to Tai Streets on the second play of the third quarter. The job was his for the rest of the year.

"It was a stellar performance," Carr said back then. "He came into a pressure situation and made no mistakes. It was really something to see."

Griese then started in the loss to Alabama in the Outback Bowl following the 1996 season. Brady may have decided to stay at Michigan, but his talk with Carr didn't produce an immediate change in his status. His résumé for the season: two games, five passes, three completions.

Brady was still a long way from playing, but his attitude had changed. He was out to win practice every day. He had committed to staying at Michigan. He wanted to prove to Carr that he was the best option at quarterback. He watched film until midnight. His teammates in his apartment building could hear him leaving at six a.m. to work out. Brady began scheduling visits with Greg Harden, Michigan's director of athletic counseling, who became his mentor. Harden couldn't do anything to get him on the playing field, but he became a big influence in Brady's life, helping him deal with his frustration, just as Brady Sr. had undergone counseling to help him deal with Tom's going to college so far away from home.

"Tommy was smart to grab help being offered," Brady Sr. said. "Greg was a major help in his life. Tommy was not getting a chance to play, and Greg helped him process the experience."

Griese had been traveling an even bumpier road than Brady. He was a lightly regarded high school player and came to Michigan as a walk-on. He didn't earn a scholarship until right before his freshman season when another player left the program. Then Griese was redshirted. His father, Bob, had been an excellent quarterback, winning the Rose Bowl for Purdue and then two Super Bowls for the Dolphins, including the victory that capped the Dolphins' magical undefeated 1972 season. He missed most of that season, however, after suffering a broken leg and dislocated ankle, but when his replacement, Earl Morrall, struggled in the AFC championship game, Don Shula went back to Griese. He helped beat the Steelers and then the Redskins in Super Bowl VII. Bob Griese was elected to the College Football Hall of Fame and the Pro Football Hall of Fame.

Brian Griese was to receive his degree in the spring of 1997, and even though he had one year of eligibility remaining as a fifth-year senior, he seriously considered giving up football and going to graduate school. He had not shown enough to be a midround draft pick or even to be drafted at all, and there was no guarantee he would beat out Dreisbach. He had a talk with his older brother, who convinced him to take one more shot at winning the job and getting to the Rose Bowl, just like their dad.

This was not good news for Brady. He was antsy to play, and the more experienced Griese presented another obstacle. Dreisbach also was back again. Carr had to make the right decision. The pressure was on him to win. When Moeller was forced out, Carr initially was named to replace him on an interim basis for the 1995 season by athletic director Joe Roberson. He was not considered a candidate for the job. Tony Dungy, then the defensive coordinator of the Minnesota Vikings, who was a Michigan native and later Manning's coach with the Colts, was on Roberson's list. Near the end of the season, Carr had done well enough to have the interim tag removed. He was 9–4 in his first season and 8–4 in his second—not acceptable by Michigan's lofty standards—and the 1996 group of seniors was the first in school history not to play in the Rose Bowl.

"It was a big year because we had lost four games in each of those previous four seasons and there was pressure," Carr said. "By that time, going into Tom's third year, we all knew that if he got a chance, if we needed him, he was ready."

Carr waited until just a few days before Michigan opened the season against Colorado in 1997 to announce that Griese would be the starting quarterback over Dreisbach, who was getting a cast removed from a sprained right wrist days before the game. "I think his decision making has improved, and I think he has shown great leadership skills," Carr said of Griese.

There was immediate discontent in the Brady household. Carr's decision was between Griese and Dreisbach. Brady was barely mentioned in any of the accounts of the quarterback competition that summer and didn't appear to be in Carr's thought process. "Tommy went in and said, 'I beat him out. You know I beat him out,'" Brady Sr. said. "Carr said no."

Brady's position on the depth chart was not the hot topic of conversation at the Michigan football training table. "Look, we're college kids. What do you know? It's an intense competitive environment where everybody essentially is trying to be the next man up or step into a role in the national spotlight," said Dhani Jones, a Michigan linebacker from 1996 to 1999. "I think Michigan was stacked with so many great quarterbacks. Everybody wants to come in and be The Man. I don't think Brady got the short end of any stick. I think that he actually came in at the appropriate time. Everybody is like, 'He should have started the entire time he was there.' Maybe if he started the entire time, he wouldn't be where he is now on the Patriots."

Jay Feely, the Wolverines kicker, was extremely close to Brady. Feely met his wife, Rebecca, when they were students at Michigan. Brady was in their wedding party. Feely knew how much not playing was getting to Brady. "I think he was probably very frustrated," he said, "the same as any guy who wasn't getting the opportunity to succeed or fail. I think that's what every guy wants, whether it's in college or the NFL. You want to be on the field. When you don't get on the field, you don't know whether you're good enough."

Feely said there wasn't any talk on the team that Brady deserved to be playing. "Nobody knew how good he could be. I don't know if *he* knew how good he could be. Everybody knew all along he was a great leader. That was one of his greatest qualities, his ability to bring guys together. He was always the central figure, even when he was the third-string quarterback. People are naturally drawn to him and his personality. But I don't think anybody in any way could honestly tell you that they saw the potential that was there to become one of the greatest ever."

Griese made Carr look smart in 1997. The Wolverines went 12–0, and their 21–16 victory over Washington State in the Rose Bowl allowed Carr to announce to the team in the locker room after the game that they were national champions. They were number one in the Associated Press writers' poll. Nebraska finished number one in the coaches' poll after beating Tennessee and Peyton Manning 42–17 in the Orange Bowl. Michigan beat Ryan Leaf, who in the coming months would be competing with Manning to be the first pick in the 1998 NFL draft. Griese was the MVP of the Rose Bowl, passing for 251 yards and three touchdowns. Bob Griese, his father, broadcast the game for ABC.

"I think it worked out pretty well," Carr said at Zingerman's. "Here's the thing. Griese had to compete just like Tom did to become the starter. There were people who questioned why Griese was the starter in 1997. Well, I think he did okay. We won the national championship."

As spring practice opened in 1998, Brady had a clear path to the starting job. Griese, a fourth-round pick of the Broncos, was gone from Ann Arbor. Dreisbach was back but had enjoyed limited success when he'd previously had the chance to play, and he was not durable. But there was trouble ahead for Brady.

"Drew Henson is growing up in the town next door. He's the local hero," Brady Sr. said. "He's the guy who has the six-page *Sports Illustrated* spread about him as the next Jim Thorpe or something. I have no doubt that Lloyd Carr had tremendous pressure on him to make the hometown boy the quarterback of the Michigan Wolverines. I also don't have any doubt, although I have no proof, that Lloyd Carr made a deal with the devil that Drew Henson would be his quarterback. So when Tommy comes through the ranks and goes from the bottom of the depth chart to competing for the starting job, Drew Henson, before he even steps on campus, is taking snaps with the first team."

When it was suggested to Carr that Brady was handicapped in his years at Michigan because he didn't recruit him and he wasn't his guy, Carr snapped, "What kind of question is that? The coach's job, the coach here, your job is to win."

Henson was a football, baseball, and basketball star at Brighton High School—he hit seventy home runs and threw fifty-two touchdown passes—and once Carr received a commitment from him to play for Michigan, making sure he received playing time was the only way to keep him from playing baseball full-time. Two months before Henson showed up for his first summer practice, the Yankees drafted him in the third round and gave him a $2 million signing bonus, planning that he would eventually become their third baseman. It didn't help Michigan that Yankees owner George Steinbrenner was a big Ohio State supporter and that by enticing Henson with a baseball career, he could also hurt the Buckeyes' arch rival.

Carr waited until August 27, just ten days before the 1998 season opener at Notre Dame, to name Brady as the Wolverines' starting quarterback. "Now at the same time, I had a freshman named Drew Henson," Carr said. "My stance has always been, 'Let's compete.' You're always trying to get better and you're always competing."

He made the announcement at Schembechler Hall that Brady would start, but just by the tone of his comments, it was clear he would be looking for the first opening to get Henson on the field. He had been practicing with the team for just two weeks after spending most of the summer in the Yankees minor-league system.

"I've been accused that I promised him playing time. All that stuff," Carr said. "I promised him the same thing I promised all the great athletes I recruited: an opportunity to compete. I have no problem with people questioning me for that. I was looking to the future. Henson, make no mistake, was talented. Tom, when he came here, was a great quarterback."

On the day he picked Brady to start, Carr said, "Tom Brady has paid his dues. He has worked extremely hard. He's a bright guy, he has a good arm, and he has the respect of his teammates. I'm anxious to see Tom play. He's got all the right stuff."

Brady won the job over Henson and Dreisbach, who was now a fifth-year senior, and Jason Kapsner, a third-year sophomore. When he was asked about Henson, Carr said he was "rapidly improving" and predicted he would see action in his freshman year.

"Drew has made excellent progress," said Carr, adding that Henson "has gotten better almost daily. He's picked up the offense well. He is without question the most talented quarterback I've been around. It's just a matter of continuing to compete and continuing to prepare. He's going to play some this year because he's not just 'another guy.' He's got everything you want. He is a guy who really adds a lot of mobility to that position."

Why Brady over Henson? "I think it goes back to the fact that Drew Henson has been here two weeks and Tom Brady's been here three years," Carr said. "Tom Brady knows the offense; he's a talented guy. Tom Brady is a fighter, he's a competitor, so I don't sell him short at all."

Brady sat for three years, but he finally had his chance. It didn't get any bigger than opening at Notre Dame. Touchdown Jesus and all. Michigan was the defending national champion, but two lost fumbles by the Wolverines in the third quarter led to two Notre Dame touchdowns that broke the game open after Brady had built a halftime lead. The Irish won 36–20. Carr was determined to get Henson experience by playing him one series per game.

"I'm getting a little bit old, but I have a pretty decent recollection of things that occurred," Brady Sr. said. "Our first game was at Notre Dame, and Drew Henson came in when we were down on the 2-yard line ready to score, to do a quarterback sneak. I think his first snap as a Michigan Wolverine was on Notre Dame's 2, and he fumbled the ball."

Michigan recovered and kicked a field goal. The irony is Brady has become one of the best quarterbacks in NFL history on short-yardage sneaks for first downs or touchdowns. Carr benched Brady late in the game with the outcome decided and Henson came in and threw a touchdown pass.

The next week, Michigan had its home opener against Syracuse and senior quarterback Donovan McNabb. Michigan Stadium was packed with 111,012 fans. Syracuse took a 17–0 lead in the second quarter, and Brady was temporarily knocked out of the game and replaced by Henson. When Michigan trailed 38–7 in the fourth quarter, Brady was benched and Henson came back in. The fans went wild at the mere sight of Henson. Two starts and Brady had been benched twice. He was outplayed by McNabb but would get a degree of retribution when he was better than McNabb in the Patriots' victory over the Philadelphia Eagles in Super Bowl XXXIX following the 2004 season.

The reaction that day at The Big House—the fans booing Brady and cheering Henson—helped create a quarterback controversy. "I put Henson in, some of the crowd—he's a local kid and had an unbelievable high school career—they are happy to see him play. We go down and score a touchdown and that ignites all of this," Carr said. "In the local paper, we had two writers following the team. One of them sides with Brady and the other takes Henson. I remember telling Tom, 'Look, this is what it's like being the Michigan quarterback.'"

Brady faced adversity when not playing. Now he was facing adversity while playing. What did the Michigan fans know about him? He was a California kid who nearly transferred, had to wait until his fourth year before he had a chance to start, and now was 0–2 taking over a team that had just won the national championship and was ranked fifth in the country in the Associated Press preseason poll. Henson was a local hero so good he was able to dictate to any college program interested that they couldn't bring in a quarterback in the class before him.

Carr didn't waver. He stayed with Brady, who then rewarded his coach's faith by ripping off eight straight victories. The winning streak ended at Ohio State in a 31–16 loss when Brady completed 31 of 56 passes for 375 yards and got the crap kicked out of him with seven sacks and many other big hits. "No man ever took the beating he took that day," Carr said. "He was bloodied but unbowed."

Michigan finished 10–3 with a share of the Big Ten championship, ending the season on New Year's Day with a 45–31 victory over Arkansas in the Citrus Bowl, the same bowl Manning had won after his sophomore and junior years. The Wolverines finished twelfth in the rankings. That should have been good enough to make Brady the unquestioned starter going into the 1999 season as a fifth-year senior. Henson skipped spring practice to play baseball and wasn't back with the team until summer camp. However, Carr was still going to make Brady fight for every snap right until his final game. He didn't let anybody outside of the team know that Brady would start until his team took the field for the season opener at home against Notre Dame. The Wolverines were ranked seventh in the preseason polls.

When he was asked a few days before the game who was starting, Carr said, "What time's the game?" When he was told it was three thirty, he said, "Three thirty? You'll see then."

It was Brady, but this time with a big, fat asterisk. Instead of working Henson into each game for one series, Carr came up with a bizarre plan: Brady would start and play the first quarter. Henson would play the second quarter. At halftime, he would decide who played the second half.

"I had two extremely talented guys, and I told them from the beginning that I was going to give them an opportunity to compete," Carr said. "Tom handled it. I can assure you he didn't like it. Neither did Henson. But Tom handled it like a champion. And I think it's because of the way he handled it, there's no one who didn't have great respect for him as a leader, as a teammate, and that includes me."

Brady had been voted captain by his teammates for the second year in a row. He had to set an example with his attitude and hard work. He knew he couldn't complain about Carr's rotation because it could divide the team. He just had to suck it up and hope that Carr would eventually just let him be his quarterback.

"I honestly could say I think I was completely oblivious to it. I can say that I probably didn't even think about it," Dhani Jones said. "I will say this: if I was Tom, I'd be frustrated. As a quarterback, you either want to know that you are in control or you're not in control. Who wants to come on and off the field? If I'm looking at it from Brady's perspective and seeing Henson out there and me out there and Henson out there and me out there, I'm pissed."

It might have been the strangest quarterback controversy in college football, but it didn't top what Tom Landry did in a Cowboys game at Chicago in 1971. He was unable to choose between Craig Morton and Roger Staubach. These were the days when most quarterbacks called their own plays. It was way before coaches would use hand signals to send in plays, and the coach-to-quarterback radio helmet was a concept as foreign as cell phones. Landry was one of the few coaches calling every play on the sideline. He would get the play to the quarterbacks by shuttling guards as his messengers. For the game in Chicago, instead of alternating the guards, he alternated Staubach and Morton every down, giving them the play on the sidelines. Obviously, that was a bad idea. After losing to the Bears, Landry settled on Staubach and the Cowboys went on to win their first Super Bowl.

Carr's plan worked early in the season, as Michigan opened with victories over Notre Dame, Rice, Syracuse, and Wisconsin. Brady earned the right to play the second half three times. Carr picked Henson in the game at Syracuse. "It was a turf field and Henson could run," Carr said. "He had good mobility."

Henson helped win the game as Brady stood on the sidelines at the Carrier Dome. In the locker room after the game, the team circled around the captains as they said a few words.

"It's a great win," Brady told his teammates to open his speech. He was hurting inside, but he was a team player. The team had won. That was the important thing.

"That was one of the most remarkable memories I have of him," Carr said. "I would say in athletics I've never seen a better example of leadership."

Brady started the next week against Purdue and won the right to play in the second half. In the sixth game, against Michigan State, Carr again picked Henson to open the second half. This time he played poorly, and Carr switched back to Brady, who nearly brought the Wolverines from behind. Carr then decided to end the platoon system and just put it all on Brady. The next week against Illinois at home, the Wolverines held a 27–7 lead but wound up losing 35–29 to a 24-point underdog. It was not Brady's fault. The defense fell apart. He threw for 307 yards.

That was the last time Brady lost in college. He did throw three interceptions against Penn State at Beaver Stadium, but he brought Michigan back from a 27–17 deficit in the fourth quarter to win 31–27. He won his last five college games, saving the best for last in a 35–34 overtime victory over Alabama in the Orange Bowl. Michigan finished fifth in the polls.

Somehow it seems fitting that when Michigan trailed 14–0 in the second quarter, Carr benched Brady for one series and put in Henson one last time. The Wolverines went three-and-out, and

Brady played the rest of the game. He rallied his team from 14–0 and 28–14 deficits. Alabama blocked a 36-yard field goal on the final play of the fourth quarter to send the game into overtime. On the first play of overtime, Brady rolled right and threw a 25-yard touchdown pass to Shawn Thompson. Alabama came right back and scored but the game ended when the Crimson Tide's Ryan Pflugner's extra point was wide right. Brady had played the game of his life, but consistent with the lack of appreciation he felt at Michigan, the Most Outstanding Player award went to sophomore wide receiver David Terrell, who caught ten passes for 150 yards and three touchdowns. Terrell would go on to become the first pick of the Chicago Bears, the eighth player selected in the 2001 draft, the same year Brady won his first Super Bowl. He was cut by the Bears after four seasons, and at Brady's urging, the Patriots signed his former Michigan receiver in the spring of 2005. Terrell didn't make it to the regular season as he was among the final cuts.

Brady Sr. was outside the gate at Pro Player Stadium following the Orange Bowl waiting for his son after the last game of his college career. It would usually take twenty-five or thirty minutes. After forty minutes, there was no sign of the Michigan quarterback. Brady Sr. decided to walk up the tunnel to look for his son. After a few steps, he saw Tom and Michigan quarterbacks coach Stan Parrish making their way toward him. Parrish was carrying Brady's duffel bag.

"Parrish said to me, 'Mr. Brady, I've been coaching twenty-five years, and I have never seen an athlete go through what your son has gone through and perform the way he performed and carry himself in such an outstanding manner.' He said, 'In twenty-five years of coaching, this kid has overcome more than any kid that I have ever seen.'"

Brady Sr. took a deep breath when relaying the story. "I talk about it, I get emotional about it," he said. "I will tell you this: Tommy never once complained to us about it. Not once."

Carr gets defensive when talking about how he handled Brady in his five years at Michigan and lists his accomplishments: he was 20–5 as a starter, beat Ohio State, beat Michigan State twice, won the Big Ten, and won two bowl games, including the Orange Bowl against the SEC champion, Alabama, in the final game of his college career.

"If you watched the last four or five games, you would see a guy that was unbelievable under pressure," Carr said. "The game at Penn State, go back and look at the last five minutes of that game. He brought us from behind against Ohio State to win and there's never been a better performance ever at Michigan than Brady's performance at the Orange Bowl.

"So here's the thing: people say he was not the starter. Well, you're watching a guy two years. Maybe the fact that I played Henson some in there may have influenced people. But it's all there on tape. Those last five games, he was sensational. What came to the surface there, going back to the Ohio State game, was his toughness, his leadership, his passion to win. All those things are part of who he is. I love Tom Brady, and no one respects him more than I do."

Henson had the starting job to himself in his junior year and led Michigan to a 9–3 record and a share of the Big Ten title. He then left to concentrate full time on his baseball career with the Yankees. If he had returned for his senior year to play football and if he played as well as he had in his junior year, the expansion Houston Texans were expected to take him with the first overall pick in the 2002 draft. They selected David Carr instead. Henson couldn't make it in baseball and tried to make a comeback in football. He signed with the Cowboys in 2004, and Bill Parcells started him in a Thanksgiving game against the Bears. Henson had an interception returned for a touchdown in the first half, so Parcells benched him at halftime and put in veteran Vinny Testaverde. Henson played with the Vikings and then his hometown Lions, but he had spent too much time away from football. His dream was to be a major-league baseball player. He had more talent as a quarterback but didn't give himself a chance. It was 2008; he was only twenty-eight, but his football and baseball careers were over.

Brady does not have bitter feelings for Carr, but Brady Sr. does. "I absolutely do. I don't harbor it against Michigan. I have Irish Alzheimer's. I forget everything but my grudges," he said. "I harbor it against Lloyd Carr. The way I feel about it really has no bearing. What's important is how Tommy feels about it. As a parent, I feel Tommy got screwed and many of my friends who were at Michigan, who were strong Michigan advocates and graduates— they felt he got screwed too. That's just the way it is. This wasn't a Michigan decision. This was a Lloyd Carr decision."

Brady learned from his years at Michigan never to take anything for granted. Even as a four-time Super Bowl champion, he goes out to practice every day with the goal to impress Bill Belichick enough to allow him to start the next game. He hates giving up first-team reps. Michigan taught him to fight for everything he wanted.

When Carr retired after the 2007 season, he received a very nice note from Tom Brady. "It was wonderful," Carr said. "We exchange mostly text messages. The one when I retired was special because look at what he has become. He's a Hall of Famer."

Carr has traveled in person several times to see Brady play in the NFL. He went to Miami. He went to Cleveland. "I had a lot of respect for him," Brady said. "I really enjoyed playing for him. He taught me a lot. It certainly wasn't easy, but I think that was the best thing for me. I really needed to be toughened up. I don't think it would have worked out in the long run had I not learned the will to compete and win. The whole competition at Michigan really helped establish that part of my character."

The national championship is Carr's legacy at Michigan, but so are the frustrating years of Tom Brady's college career.

"Did I think he was going to have a good career in the NFL? Absolutely. Did I think he was going to be a Hall of Famer after six or seven years in the league? I don't claim that," Carr said. "I'll say this: since I've retired, I've had a lot of time to think about a lot of things. In my opinion, if you took the greatest quarterbacks in the history of Michigan football, nobody played better than Tom Brady at Michigan."

# 4

# THE FRANCHISE QUARTERBACK

Bill Polian had been hired by Jimmy Irsay to run the Colts, and it was the perfect match—an owner passionate about his franchise and willing to open up his checkbook working with a team president who knew how to build championship contenders and spend money wisely.

Polian constructed the Buffalo Bills teams that went to four straight Super Bowls in the first four years of the 1990s. The Bills lost to the Giants, Redskins, and then the Cowboys twice and became the butt of jokes. As time passed, however, the Bills have been celebrated for getting to four straight Super Bowls rather than being ridiculed for losing all of them.

By the time they had lost the first three, Polian's time in Buffalo was up. He worked in the NFL office in New York for a brief period before Jerry Richardson hired him to put together the expansion Carolina Panthers, who were starting play in 1995. Polian knew his first priority was getting a quarterback. By the time he arrived in Buffalo in 1984, the Bills had already selected Jim Kelly as part of the great quarterback draft of 1983, which included future Hall of Famers John Elway and Dan Marino, but Kelly decided to sign with the Houston Gamblers of the USFL. He was from western Pennsylvania and had dreamed of playing at Penn State until Joe Paterno told him he wanted to make him a linebacker. Kelly had a linebacker's mentality, but he had a quarterback's arm. He went to the University of Miami instead, enjoyed the warm weather, and chose the hot Houston summers over the frigid Buffalo winters. He played in the USFL for three years until the league folded in the summer of 1986, and then Polian brought him to Buffalo. Kelly fell in love with the city and remained after his Hall of Fame career was over.

Polian knew he had to find a franchise quarterback to be the foundation of the expansion team. North Carolina was a college football haven but had been starved for an NFL team. The Panthers were awarded the first pick in their inaugural 1995 draft, and Polian traded down to the fifth spot and picked Penn State quarterback Kerry Collins. By their second season, the Panthers and the Jacksonville Jaguars, their expansion brothers, were in the conference championship game. They both lost, however.

Next stop: Indianapolis.

At the end of the 1997 season, Polian left the Panthers and was hired as the Colts president. He had one year remaining on his contract, and the Colts agreed to give up a third-round draft choice as compensation for Carolina to release him.

Polian walked into a gold mine. The Colts had just finished off a 3–13 disaster to earn the first pick in the draft. The day after the season ended, Irsay fired Bill Tobin, the director of football operations, and coach Lindy Infante, who made the playoffs with a 9–7 record in his first season, but got blown out by the Steelers in the playoffs, and then opened the '97 season with a ten-game losing streak.

By now, Polian had developed a reputation as a master builder, although one with a nasty temper. He sealed his 2015 election to the Pro Football Hall of Fame in the newly created contributors category by rescuing the Colts from obscurity. Jim Harbaugh had been the Colts quarterback the previous four years and had come close—a jump ball nearly caught in the end zone by Aaron Bailey in the 1995 AFC title game in Pittsburgh—to taking Indianapolis to the Super Bowl. Harbaugh was a beloved figure in Indianapolis—he once changed a driver's tire on the way home from a game—and has since developed into one of the best head coaches among all former NFL quarterbacks. Polian knew he was taking a quarterback with the first pick and Captain Comeback was not in the plans. Polian traded Harbaugh to the Ravens for a third-round pick six weeks after the season ended.

"Look, you've been great, but the new guy is going to play," Polian told Harbaugh.

Harbaugh was so competitive and so popular in the locker room that it would have been tough for any rookie if he had remained. Polian didn't want controversy as he began the rebuild. This was a new regime, and Polian was sitting with the first pick and two quarterbacks from which to choose: Peyton Manning and Ryan Leaf. He wanted a smooth transition.

Manning was the sure thing, the best quarterback prospect since John Elway. Leaf was the wild card—amazingly high upside but potential to be a big-time bust. Of course, it now seems like a no-brainer. Manning has gone on to a record-setting career and a Super Bowl win; he's one of only three quarterbacks to take two different teams to the Super Bowl. Leaf was the biggest draft dud of all time and had played himself out of the NFL by the time he should have just been getting warmed up. He lasted three years in San Diego—he missed his entire second season after a training-camp shoulder injury, which required surgery—and one in Dallas. He went about the next decade making headlines for all the wrong reasons and spending more than two years in jail for breaking into a house in Great Falls, Montana, and stealing prescription pills.

Polian walked into a conference room at the Colts headquarters on West Fifty-Sixth Street in Indianapolis for his first meeting with the scouts he inherited. He had his own ideas about Manning and Leaf but wanted to hear from the men in the field who had spent countless nights away from home scouting talent to bring to the Colts.

"I basically said two things: 'I'll learn to speak your language; you don't have to worry about speaking mine. Just go right ahead and do the things you had been doing under Bill Tobin,'" Polian said. "'And give me a preliminary opinion on Manning-Leaf. You don't have to go into the reasons; we'll get into that later on.'"

Polian had seen Manning play three times in person when he was working for the Panthers. He had seen Leaf play once. Eight scouts were in the room. Four voted for Manning. Four voted for Leaf. In the next meeting, he asked for one sentence about why they had made their choices. "What was interesting was that the Peyton people were not anti-Leaf," Polian said. "The Leaf people were pretty vehemently anti-Peyton."

He had four months to make a decision. He started to "zero-base it," as he put it, to go back through the whole process with his scouts and involve Jim Mora, whom he had hired as the Colts head coach, along with key offensive assistants Bruce Arians and Tom Moore. He went to the Colts video department and asked for a montage tape of every pass Manning and Leaf had thrown in their careers. "They kind of looked at me like, *What?*" Polian said.

Manning had thrown 1,381 passes at Tennessee. Leaf had thrown 880 passes at Washington State. That was a lot of tape to put together. This was before plays were easily accessible by computer. The scouting staff did as Polian asked, and right before the combine, he circulated the tape to his staff.

Six weeks before the draft, Chargers general manager Bobby Beathard, always known for taking chances and making big trades, held the third pick overall. He wanted Manning, and to a much lesser extent Leaf, but knew he had to come out of the draft with either one to fix San Diego's quarterback issues. The Chargers had finished 4–12 with Stan Humphries and Craig Whelihan at quarterback. Beathard had to move up one spot to guarantee that he'd get Manning or Leaf. He paid a fortune by trading his first- and second-round picks in the 1998 draft, his first-round pick in 1999, kick returner Eric Metcalf, and linebacker Patrick Sapp to the Cardinals to jump up just one spot.

"I think the consensus opinion is that two like that don't come along very often," Beathard said. "If we're going to be successful in getting that type of quarterback, we're going to have to give up something, and we really did."

Beathard insisted he would be happy with whichever quarterback the Colts didn't take. If that was his way of talking up Leaf and trying to trick Polian into taking him, Polian was too savvy to fall for that. Beathard liked Manning better.

Manning separated himself from Leaf at the combine in Indianapolis. On one of the first nights, Leaf had a 7:00 p.m. appointment with the Colts in their hotel suite at the Holiday Inn not far from the RCA Dome. Polian, Mora, Arians, and Moore were there for their allotted fifteen minutes. Interviews took place during a three-hour window until 10:00 p.m. Leaf didn't show up. "The scout who was in charge of trying to run him down was just flying around trying to reach somebody on the phone," Polian said. "Where is he? What is he doing?"

Sixteen years later, agent Leigh Steinberg said Leaf intentionally skipped the meeting to dissuade the Colts from taking him because Leaf wanted to play for the Chargers. The Leaf camp said at the time that there was confusion over the time of the meeting, but that apparently wasn't true. He just blew it off. The Colts were livid that Leaf skipped the meeting, but Polian denied that he had been manipulated into taking Manning. If Polian had liked Leaf better than Manning, he would have taken him. But that would have been hard. Leaf was a jerk and a knucklehead. Manning was a coach's dream.

The following night, Manning had his appointment with the Colts. Mora, the former New Orleans coach, had gotten to know him over the years through Archie Manning, who was doing the Saints games on the radio. Polian had never met Peyton. He told him he had seen him play a few times in college. "So we sat down and took out our binders, and he took out his binder, and he began to ask us questions," Polian said.

The horn blew after fifteen minutes. Manning had to move on to the next team. The Colts had interviews scheduled with other players. They never got to ask Manning a single question. He asked them all of his. "He got up and left and said, 'Nice to see you. See you down the road,'" Polian said. "I think it was Tom Moore who turned around and said, 'Well, he just interviewed us,' which, of course, as we got to know him, was his modus operandi."

Manning asked about the Colts offensive philosophy, their practice philosophy. "Nitty-gritty football," Polian said. "He had them all written out. Of course, he hasn't changed one iota."

Polian and his contingent planned to be at Leaf's campus workout, so they didn't attempt to reschedule an appointment with him at the combine. Manning had definitely taken the lead, but it was not yet a done deal. Polian approached Mora in mid-March with the idea of sending the tape that the video department had produced to Bill Walsh, the three-time Super Bowl champion coach of the 49ers who was one year away from returning to the 49ers as vice president and general manager. He was unattached in the spring of '98 and agreed to consult with the Colts on the two quarterbacks. Polian shipped the tape to Walsh, who was living in the Bay Area.

By late March, Polian was still waiting to hear from Walsh. He had already watched the tape three times himself and had charted each of the 2,261 throws. "You get paralysis by analysis," he said. "You begin to see ghosts."

On a quiet Sunday afternoon in April, he called Arians and Moore into his office. "It looks to me like Peyton's got a ceiling on his arm at about sixty yards. Beyond sixty yards, he's not all that accurate," Polian said.

"That might be true," Moore said. "But we won't throw any passes over sixty yards."

"You think I'm seeing ghosts?" Polian asked.

"Yeah, you are," Moore said. "Go look at somebody else."

Polian and his entourage took off for Knoxville to run Manning through a private workout. The perception was that Manning had just an average arm, definitely weaker than Leaf's. The Colts played in a dome, so except for outdoor games late in the season and in the playoffs, he didn't need to have a rocket arm like Elway's to cut through the nasty weather. Polian discovered at the workout that Manning's arm was a lot stronger than he had seen on tape.

Moore ran Manning through one of his favorite drills to test arm strength. The receiver stands five yards away. The quarterback has to throw the ball without a drop. The receiver moves back five yards at a time. They keep moving apart five yards at a time. "It's the perfect measure of arm strength and revolutions on the ball," Polian said. "Peyton's arm was plenty strong. Interestingly, he threw a heavy ball, the opposite of what people thought or said. That issue disappeared. He looked terrific in the workout. His footwork was perfect. It was a very, very impressive workout. Of course, it was a very impressive interview. We spent a lot more time with him." This time around, Manning even let the Colts ask some questions.

Tennessee coach Phillip Fulmer then gave the Colts a detailed analysis of Manning as a player. There were no doubts about his character. When the Colts group boarded their plane out of Knoxville, Polian turned to Moore and said, "So much for the stuff about arm strength."

They were off to Pullman to check out Leaf. They didn't run the workout; it was scripted. Multiple teams were present, and Leaf did it in shifts. As Beathard was walking out, Polian, Arians, and Moore were walking in. Polian watched Leaf throw and turned to Moore. "Wow, his arm isn't as strong as Peyton's."

Polian noticed that Leaf's "body definition" wasn't very good. "It was pretty obvious that he hadn't spent a lot of time in the weight room," he said.

He interviewed Leaf at great length. Washington State coach Mike Price was in the room at Leaf's request, even though Fulmer had not been present when the Colts had interviewed Manning in Knoxville. The interview with Leaf went horribly. Polian felt he wasn't professional, wasn't mature, not a football junkie like Manning. At the combine, Manning had asked the Colts whether, if they drafted him, he could come to Indianapolis the next day to start working out and learn the playbook. It was explained to him that college rules prohibited them from doing that right away. Classes had to be over even though he had already graduated.

"What are you going to do to get me up to speed?" Manning asked. "Can I go to a high school in Indianapolis? Can I cross the line into Kentucky? I'm going to be there. We are going to find a way around this rule, right?"

"We will find a way to get you the data," Polian said.

Leaf never asked those questions. He wouldn't even commit to coming to Indianapolis the day after the draft for a get-acquainted session if the Colts picked him. "I hadn't planned on it," he said.

He also hadn't planned to show up on the day rookies were allowed to report in early May. He had a trip planned to Las Vegas with friends. Polian's mind was made up. Then Walsh checked back in.

"He was strongly Peyton for a lot of principally technical reasons," Polian said. "We had a long discussion about technical things. He was sold on Peyton's balance, his ability to stay alive in the pocket, and his accuracy."

Walsh was doing this as a favor to Polian and didn't send him a bill. But Polian felt that wasn't right and sent him a "gratuity," he said, in the form of a check. The draft was still weeks away, but Polian reconvened his brain trust and conducted another Manning vs. Leaf vote. "Clearly, it was trending Peyton," he said. "The early returns were showing Peyton."

They brought him to Indianapolis when they wanted to double-check a minor physical issue. There was no problem. That's when Manning promised to win a championship for Polian if he took him but said that if he passed on him, he would regret it, because he'd come back and kick his ass.

What kept coming back to Polian was Leaf's immaturity, while Manning seemed equipped to handle the demands placed on an NFL quarterback. Polian received a call from Beathard. It was clear he wanted Manning, but he never made an offer to Polian to trade up one more spot. The Colts would have considered a deal only if they had Manning and Leaf dead even and could gain valuable extra draft picks. That might have been the case in January, but now the draft was ten days away.

"Give me a call and let me know who you're going to pick," Beathard said.

Polian called Mora into his office.

"What do you think?" Polian said.

"I think Peyton," Mora said.

"I think you're right. This is what we believe in. If we don't take this kid, we're turning our backs on everything we think we stand for," Polian said.

Arians and Moore were 100 percent for Manning. The scouts were still split. That didn't surprise Polian. "They had done all the work. They were married to the guy they were married to," he said.

Irsay, then just thirty-eight years old and in his second year as the Colts owner after his father, Robert Irsay, had died, was going to be investing an awful lot of money in Polian's decision. He sent a private plane to Knoxville to pick up Manning and bring him to Miami, where they dined at the Surf Club in early April, a few weeks before the draft.

"I'll win for you," Manning told him. Irsay said Manning's words sent chills down his spine. Manning looked straight at Irsay with piercing eyes and shook his hand as firmly as it could be shaken.

"Peyton was impressive," Irsay said. "He would've been great as an astronaut, too. NASA if not the NFL."

Now Irsay wanted to know whom Polian was going to select with the first pick. Manning, he said.

Irsay wanted to know why. "Shows you what a great scout I am," Polian said. "I said if we bust out Ryan, it's a total bust. We don't recoup anything. It's hit-or-miss. If we bust Peyton, if we're wrong on Peyton, which you can always be, the worst we get is Bernie Kosar. Not bad, but not an apt comparison, given what we know today. Jim and I both laughed, and that was essentially it."

The first day of the draft was on a Saturday. Archie Manning called Polian on Tuesday to ask when he would have a decision. Polian knew he was taking Manning, but if nobody was forcing him to make a decision with the draft four days away, he wasn't about to do it. The Colts had the right to sign Manning before the draft, and Polian could have had negotiating leverage with Tom Condon, Manning's agent, because the first pick was going to sign a bigger contract than the second pick. He chose not to use it. He didn't tell Archie. He finally told Peyton on Thursday, but made him promise not to say anything publicly. Irsay was going to be at the Theatre at Madison Square Garden to present a Colts jersey to Manning onstage, and Polian didn't want to take the spotlight away from his owner.

At the NFL's Friday draft event, on a boat that circled Manhattan for two hours, Manning had a secret. He knew the Colts were taking him, but he played dumb. Leaf said he didn't know, but based on Steinberg's account, he was hoping Indianapolis took Manning. Finally, on Friday night, about twelve hours before Commissioner Paul Tagliabue would announce the pick, word leaked that the Colts were indeed taking Manning. "I was taught to be a person of process," Polian said. "We went through the process. The process led us to the right answer."

The Colts and Chargers met in the third preseason game that summer in Indianapolis. The Chargers won 33–3, and Leaf outplayed Manning. He was 15 of 24 for 172 yards with an interception and a fumble and was sacked three times. Manning was 11 of 21 for 123 yards with two interceptions and no sacks.

"The whole Ryan-Peyton thing—we don't get into that," Manning said after the game. "That just slows me down from what I'm trying to do. All it does is take time away from that. I hope he does well. There's no controversy between him and me. All I want to do is play well for my team."

Leaf threw some bouquets Manning's way. "Peyton's the real deal. Everybody knows that," he said. The question after the game, Polian said, was whether Manning was a bust and whether he would ever make it.

The Colts and Chargers met again in the fifth game of the season in Indianapolis. This time, the Colts won 17–12. Manning and Leaf were each an abysmal 12 of 23. Manning threw for 137 yards with one touchdown and one interception. Leaf threw for 137 yards with no touchdowns and one interception. Manning was not sacked. Leaf was sacked four times. It was the first victory of Manning's pro career.

That was the last time they ever stepped on the same field. When Manning was starting to consistently put up big numbers, Leaf's career was just about over.

**Manning could have** owned New York in a much bigger way than his brother Eli did after winning two Super Bowls with the Giants. Peyton has a much more engaging personality, which is appealing to advertisers.

For the first month after the 1996 season, it looked as though Peyton could be the Jets best quarterback since Joe Namath. Bill Parcells had just worked his way out of his deal in New England and taken over as the Jets coach and general manager. New York had been a dreadful 1–15 under Rich Kotite and had the first pick in the '97 draft. The Jets quarterback was Neil O'Donnell, whom Parcells inherited and quickly learned to dislike. Kotite had signed O'Donnell to a five-year, $25 million contract in 1996, shortly after his two interceptions helped cost the Steelers a chance to beat Dallas in Super Bowl XXX.

Parcells-Manning was a match made in football heaven: Manning was obsessed with football, and Parcells was obsessed with players who were obsessed with football.

Just two events needed to happen and Manning could be the new Namath, minus the pantyhose, fur coats, and Super Bowl guarantees. Parcells had to assure Manning he would take him with the first pick in the draft. Manning had to declare for the draft and give up his senior season at Tennessee. He was going to be graduating in three years, so he could leave after his junior year and still have his degree, which was important to him and his family.

Manning was facing an April 4 deadline to declare for the April 19 draft. Parcells officially became the Jets coach after Tagliabue brokered a compensation settlement between the Jets and Patriots on February 10. He had already been hired and was working as the Jets GM after he left the Patriots shortly after coaching them in their loss to the Packers in the Super Bowl. Tagliabue's ruling made him the coach as well.

Parcells sat in his office at Weeb Ewbank Hall on the campus of Hofstra University in Hempstead, New York, studying tape of Manning. He was outstanding in his final game of the season, throwing for four TDs and 408 yards in Tennessee's 48–28 victory over Northwestern in the Citrus Bowl. The Jets were a team lacking in talent and poorly coached by Kotite, just off the worst season in team history. The Jets had some offensive playmakers in wide receivers Keyshawn Johnson and Wayne Chrebet, but Parcells knew he needed a lot of impact players on defense to get the program turned around.

He studied every throw Manning made as a junior. He liked what he saw. "I think the player is a very good player, and I'll just leave it at that," he said.

The NFL wants players to stay in school and discourages teams from speaking publicly about underclassmen. Parcells used that as a cover for one of the most dreadful mistakes he made in his Hall of Fame career. When Archie Manning called him twice before Peyton announced on March 5 that he would be returning to Tennessee for his senior year, he was all but begging Parcells to tell him whether or not he would take his son with the first pick in the draft. Peyton wanted to make an informed decision and needed answers from Parcells. He didn't want to enter the draft with the intention of playing for Parcells in New York and then have no control if Parcells traded the pick. He wanted clarity about what Parcells was thinking.

"Peyton wanted me to call him," Archie said.

He told Parcells he thought there was a good chance Peyton was going to return to school. That represented a change in thinking, because Peyton later said that during the 1996 season, he was "pretty intent on leaving." If Parcells guaranteed that Manning would be his pick, the feeling around the league at the time was that Manning would turn pro.

"I'm telling you, he's pretty torn," Manning told Parcells. "He'd like to be the first pick in the draft; he's got no problem with New York or the Jets. At the same time, he wants to play his senior year."

Parcells knew that if Manning came out and he selected him, he would be the Jets quarterback for the next fifteen years. He also knew that if he traded the pick, he could fill many of the Jets' holes. One close friend of Parcells suggested that he didn't believe in Manning as much as others did, and at that time in the NFL, before it became a league dominated by the passing game, Parcells wasn't convinced he needed a superstar quarterback to win, especially one coming to New York with as much hype as Manning. "I wasn't in any place to talk," Parcells said. "The league was very adamant about not making any commentary about what players should do. They were on your ass about it. They were watching the Jets. They were watching us like hawks."

Parcells said all he told Archie was to let him know if Peyton was coming out. "All this conjecture about if we just told him he would have come out—that's bullshit. He was committed to staying in school. That's what he wanted to do. He enjoyed college," Parcells said. "Nothing I can do about it."

Parcells never gave the Jets a chance. Backroom conversations happen all the time in the NFL. It would be foolish to suggest otherwise. If Parcells was unsure about Manning and didn't want to commit to taking him in early March, he had that right, although it was the wrong decision. But to say he was concerned about NFL rules makes little sense. If he wanted Peyton, all he had to do was tell Archie.

Was it all a moot point? Archie thinks Peyton would have stayed at Tennessee anyway, but he admits, "If Bill had come out and said, 'Peyton, you're my guy, I'm going to pick you,' it may have made it a little bit harder. But I swear he wanted to be a senior."

Manning finalized his decision to stay at Tennessee on a Sunday. Three days later, he walked into a packed press conference at Thompson-Boling Arena on the Tennessee campus to make his announcement. The anticipation was similar to that of three years earlier, when he revealed he was going to Tennessee instead of Ole Miss, Florida, or Michigan. The arena was filled with teammates, alumni, and students. Coach Phillip Fulmer and offensive coordinator David Cutcliffe were present. Not one person there wanted Manning to leave, and a huge roar went up when he said he was staying.

After the press conference, Archie and Peyton drove to a friend's house in Knoxville. Peyton was amazed that there had been so much suspense in the arena. "Do these people really think if I was going to leave, I would have had a press conference? Would I have gotten up there with Phil Fulmer, David Cutcliffe, my teammates, students, and alumni and say I'm going to go?" he said to his father in the car. "They didn't figure that out. I would have called that one in."

Manning had already begun working out with his teammates and hanging out with friends, and because he had taken between eighteen and twenty-two hours of classes in several semesters, he was a year ahead of schedule to get his degree in speech communications. He graduated with a 3.61 GPA. "I was in such a rush my first three years, I didn't have much chance to breathe," he said.

He evaluated all he had at Tennessee and decided to be a kid for one more year. He would lighten his course load in the fall and relax. He would take graduate classes. "I thought, *I'm not sure I'm really ready to leave this*," he said. "It was one of the best decisions I ever made. I got to be a senior in college. It's not a year you can ever get back. There was no guarantee the Jets were even going to draft me."

Would Parcells have taken Manning if he'd declared for the 1997 draft? "Yeah, we probably would have," he said. "That's a retrospective view, too. You know what I mean?" Parcells wound up trading the pick to the Rams, who selected offensive tackle Orlando Pace. Parcells now had the sixth overall pick. He traded down a second time and took linebacker James Farrior at number eight. Farrior became a much better player after he signed as a free agent with the Steelers in 2002 than he ever was with the Jets. Parcells passed on Pace when he traded out of the top spot and then traded away the chance to pick offensive tackle Walter Jones at the number-six spot. Pace and Jones are in the Pro Football Hall of Fame.

Manning wanted to return for his senior year to beat Florida, but he lost to the Gators for the third straight time as a starter. He'd also played as a backup in a shutout loss to Florida as a freshman. He wanted to win the national championship. Tennessee was 11–2 and finished seventh in the polls after losing 42–17 to Nebraska in the Orange Bowl. Michigan, with Tom Brady as a backup quarterback, won the writers' poll, and Nebraska won the coaches' poll to share the national championship. Manning wanted to win the Heisman but finished second to cornerback Charles Woodson, Brady's teammate at Michigan.

"Peyton Manning came back to win the Citrus Bowl again," quipped Florida coach Steve Spurrier. "You can't spell Citrus without the UT." Manning had won the Citrus Bowl after his sophomore and junior seasons.

When Spurrier was hired to coach the Redskins in 2002, his comments from five years earlier were mentioned to Manning. "The Tennessee-Florida rivalry is extremely intense. It was always 'Spurrier beat Peyton,'" he said. "I thought their defense was pretty good, too. Since I've been in pro ball, I've played in a few golf tournaments and been to a few banquets with Steve. We told stories and had a few beers together."

Spurrier couldn't wait to return to college ball after compiling a 12–20 record in two seasons in Washington. One of those victories came against Manning and the Colts.

Had Manning come out in 1997 and skipped his senior year, he and Parcells would have been quite a combination. They are pretty much the same person when it comes to football. Attention to detail. No shortcuts to winning. Holding everybody accountable. The two strong-willed personalities might have clashed every now and then, but if Parcells had had Manning, he surely would have coached the Jets for more than just three years. They could have won multiple championships together.

And Parcells would have enjoyed coaching Manning. "I would have liked it very much," he said. "I can tell pretty much what kind of guy he is. I would have liked it."

Parcells and Manning didn't know each other back then but went on to become good friends. Years ago, Manning was the guest of a lawyer friend of Parcells's for a round of golf at McArthur Golf Club in Hobe Sound, Florida, to which Parcells belongs. It's the course designed by pro golfer Nick Price. After the round, everybody was socializing, but there were Parcells and Manning off to the side engaged in a deep talk about football. When Parcells was running the Dolphins and the Colts were practicing at the Dolphins facility before Super Bowl XLIV, Parcells went down to the weight room to hang out with Manning, Jeff Saturday, and Dallas Clark.

Manning had a very tight inner circle, and when his career was in jeopardy following his fourth neck surgery and he was working out and trying to decide in 2012 whether to give it another shot, Parcells and former Giants quarterback Phil Simms were on his short list of consultants. "I was able to converse with him in a language that he understood," Parcells said. "How much do you got on your comeback route? How much on your long ball? Where are you on this or that? He was very candid."

Manning wanted Parcells to watch him throw, but they never did hook up, just as they didn't connect in 1997. Cutcliffe, who'd known Manning as an eighteen-year-old, guided him through the football part of his rehabilitation at Duke. Parcells was available for moral support. "I like the son of a bitch a lot. I really do. He's trying to win. And you can tease him," Parcells said.

Manning did a commercial for Buick. The car is giving him instructions as he drives. "So I leave him a little message," Parcells said. "If that Buick can tell you who is open on Sunday, why don't you just bring that Buick down to the sideline with you?"

Parcells rejected criticism of Manning's history of not being able to win big games in college or the NFL. "They like to kill heroes now," he said. "They do like to kill them."

# 5

# BRADY'S DRAFT DAZE

Just a few days before Tom Brady won his second Super Bowl, defeating the Panthers in Houston following the 2003 season, he was intercepted in practice by safety Rodney Harrison, who proceeded to show Brady up by high-stepping around the field at the Texans' indoor facility. Bill Belichick was running the two-minute session to finish things up, and the competition between the offense and the defense was typically intense. The Patriots were transitioning into their Super Bowl game mind-set. Brady is always in a game mind-set. The trash-talking and yelling between Brady and Harrison carried over into the locker room. "Some bad words being said," Harrison said.

Before they left the field, Brady tried to get even before Belichick ended the practice. "He was so pissed, he chased me around the field for about thirty seconds trying to throw footballs at me, screaming expletives at me," Harrison said. "He's very competitive. He wants to win. Practice is a game situation. It's not like he practices one way and shows up for a game another way. His personality is the same in practice as it is in the game. He's fiery. He's intense."

He slaps high fives and butts heads in games. He does it in practice, also. He took the approach at Michigan that if he wasn't the best quarterback on Tuesday, Wednesday, and Thursday, he wouldn't be playing on Saturday. Even with Super Bowl titles on his résumé, this mentality hasn't changed. He hates to give up practice reps to his backup, even when his buddy Matt Cassel was behind him and desperate to get on the field. Brady never wants to give Belichick any reason to think he's not the best quarterback for his team. In a 2014 game at Kansas City, one of the worst of his career, Brady was benched early in the fourth quarter of a 41–14 loss. When rookie Jimmy Garoppolo came in and threw the first touchdown pass of his career, he was greeted by high fives on the sidelines, but not one of them came from Brady. Critics say he came off as a spoiled brat. The reality for Brady: nothing personal, but why congratulate somebody who wants your job?

The Michigan experience hardened him. Then he came within fifty-five spots of not even getting drafted.

Brady's career at Michigan ended with his nearly flawless performance against Alabama in the Orange Bowl. He was feeling pretty good about his chances to go relatively high in the 2000 draft. He had recovered from being beaten down and built back up at Michigan, and now the NFL was taking its turn slapping him around. He was taken in the sixth round, the 199th player overall, the 7th quarterback selected in a bad quarterback draft and the 7th player the Patriots selected. He was picked with a supplemental draft choice, the 33rd player taken in the round. Brady was so stressed from the ordeal and so relieved to be picked, his first reaction was just being thankful that he didn't have to be an insurance salesman.

The struggles at Michigan helped mold Brady as a very young man. The motivation provided by the NFL humiliating him on draft day has driven him since the moment he arrived in Patriots training camp at Bryant College in Smithfield, Rhode Island.

"Well, I still carry it," Brady said. "It's always a part of you. There is still a reason why I was drafted that late. I'm still not the biggest guy. I'm not the strongest guy. I don't run the best. I don't throw the ball the hardest."

Peyton Manning arrived in New York two days before the 1998 draft. It was not his first trip to New York. In fact, he had been at the Downtown Athletic Club in December of 1997 for the Heisman Trophy announcement. On the day before the draft, the NFL kept Manning and the other players it brought in for the draft busy making appearances. Brady was not invited to the 2000 draft by the NFL. Those invitations were reserved for players expected to be picked early in the first round. Brady was back home in San Mateo watching the draft on television with his family and waiting for the phone to ring.

It would be a long wait, a long and emotionally draining wait. All these Super Bowls later, Brady is at peace with the indignity of being an afterthought, even by the Patriots. If Belichick had thought Brady was going to be a star, he never would've waited until the sixth round to take him. But then if Brady had been picked by somebody other than Belichick, maybe he never would have become Tom Brady.

"I had the luxury of being under the radar. That's how I look at it," he said. "I also realize that there's people behind you trying to take your job just like I did. You got to prove it every day. That's what I tried to do every day when I was in the position where I wasn't playing. There is no entitlement. I never feel entitled to my position. I feel like I got to earn it every day, I got to earn the respect of my teammates every day. I learned that a lot in college. That was a great lesson for me about competition.

"I actually think it was harder for those guys who are the first-round picks and the top overall pick because the pressure is on right away. You have no time to learn. They throw you in there and you go. 'Okay, let's see how well you do.' Usually it doesn't go well. How could it? There's just too much for you to learn in too short a period of time. That's why I think it's pretty remarkable what Peyton's done, what Eli's done, because you have guys like David Carr, JaMarcus Russell, I'm not putting David Carr in that group, but first overall picks that don't turn out the way the team had hoped."

Ryan Leaf, picked one spot after Manning, is the biggest draft bust in history. Brady is at the opposite end. He was passed over 198 times. Brady's hero, Joe Montana, was the last pick in the third round in 1979, pick number 82. Bill Walsh, the quarterback genius, wanted Phil Simms with the first pick in the second round but his plan was blown up when the New York Giants surprisingly picked him seventh in the first round. Then Walsh had to be talked into taking Montana and out of taking Steve Dils, who had been his quarterback at Stanford, but Walsh's innovative West Coast offense and Montana's football smarts, quick release, and nimble footwork turned out to be the perfect football marriage. Johnny Unitas was a ninth-round pick of the Steelers in 1955, was cut before the season, and then worked in construction for one year and played for the semipro Bloomfield Rams. The next year, the Baltimore Colts signed him, and he went on to win two NFL Championships, one Super Bowl, and three MVP awards. Kurt Warner's rise to Super Bowl champion was even more spectacular. He was undrafted out of Northern Iowa and became a scared rookie free agent cut by the Packers when he was trying to make it as a backup to Brett Favre. He packed groceries at Hy-Vee to make a living, lit up the Arena League, and excelled in NFL Europe. He made it onto the field for one game with the Saint Louis Rams in 1998. He was second on the depth chart in the summer of 1999 behind new starting quarterback Trent Green, a big-money free agent signed from the Redskins, until Rodney Harrison of San Diego crashed into Green's knee in a preseason game. Green suffered a torn ACL and was lost for the season. Dick Vermeil cried at the press conference after the game but expressed full faith in Warner, a complete unknown. He went on that year to win the regular-season MVP and Super Bowl MVP. He played in two more Super Bowls, first losing to Brady and the Patriots, and then, after signing with the Cardinals, losing to the Steelers. Warner, Peyton Manning, and Craig Morton are the only quarterbacks to start for two different teams in the Super Bowl.

Each NFL team invests millions and millions of dollars in scouting. General managers, coaches, and scouts spend countless hours interviewing players at the combine in Indianapolis. They work them out on campus. They bring them into their facility. They watch tape until their eyes can take no more. They still make franchise-altering mistakes. Brady didn't have the measurables that would have predicted success, other than being six foot four. He was skinny, actually scrawny. He was slow, actually turtlelike. His arm wasn't nearly as strong as it is today. He couldn't get on the field for three years at Michigan, and then once he became the starter in his last two years, he had a hard time keeping Drew Henson off the field.

"One of the real troubling parts was the Michigan situation," Belichick said on the *Brady 6* documentary produced by NFL Films. "The fact that really they were trying to replace him as their starting quarterback. You say, 'Okay, they don't really want this guy as their starting quarterback. They want another guy. Well, what's the problem here?' It's a little bit of a red flag there. There was nothing we could really do about the whole Henson situation. We just had to evaluate what we saw. And we saw Tom time and again his senior year start the game off well, and then so many times Tom would come back in and rescue the situation and pull out the win for Michigan against great competition, in the biggest game. He just took his opportunities and tried to make the most out of them."

The one crucial element teams can't measure is a player's heart. As the NFL would find out, Brady played with a lot of heart.

**The 1983 draft** was the Year of the Quarterback. John Elway, Todd Blackledge, Jim Kelly, Tony Eason, Ken O'Brien, and Dan Marino were all taken in the first round—in that order. Marino slipped because of a poor senior year at Pitt and unsubstantiated rumors of drug use. Elway, Kelly, and Marino are in the Pro Football Hall of Fame.

The 2000 draft was not a quarterback draft. Chad Pennington, a game manager with just an average arm, was the only quarterback selected in the first round. The Jets, after trading Keyshawn Johnson to the Bucs for two number-one draft picks, had a record four first-rounders. The other came from the Patriots when the Jets agreed to let Belichick out of his contract so he could coach New England. Pennington won the only two AFC East titles that Brady did not, from the time he took over for Drew Bledsoe in 2001 through the 2014 season. Pennington won the division for the Jets in 2002, the season after the Patriots' first of three Super Bowls in four years, by outplaying Brady in a late-season game. He also won the AFC East with the Miami Dolphins in 2008, but that was the year Brady was lost for the season after tearing his ACL in the first quarter of the first game. Pennington and Brady had a nice rivalry going for a while, but Pennington required four surgeries on his throwing shoulder—he kept blowing out his rotator cuff and labrum—and his career ended with an ACL tear playing basketball in the off-season in 2011.

Pennington was a legitimate NFL starter, and he, not Brady, was the one getting compared to Montana early in his career. But his body betrayed him. Pennington was hurt so often and so severely that he twice earned the Comeback Player of the Year

Award. He completed 66 percent of his passes in his eleven-year career, second best on the all-time list through the 2014 season behind Drew Brees, who was at 66.2 percent.

Giovanni Carmazzi was the next quarterback to be drafted after Pennington, but not until the third round. He played at Hofstra, which no longer has a football program. Two days after Montana was inducted into the Hall of Fame in the summer of 2000, the 49ers played the Patriots in the Hall of Fame preseason game at Fawcett Stadium in Canton. Carmazzi was in totally over his head. The game was too fast for him. "Let it be duly noted that his career begins rather ingloriously with back-to-back sacks," Al Michaels said on the ABC telecast.

Carmazzi was the first quarterback off the bench for the 49ers; he played the entire second quarter and was 3 of 7 for 19 yards. He was outplayed by fellow 49ers rookie quarterback Tim Rattay from Louisiana Tech, the small school that produced Terry Bradshaw, whom Walsh had taken in the seventh round. Brady came in after Drew Bledsoe and Michael Bishop and played the only series the Patriots had the ball in the fourth quarter. He was 3 of 4 for 28 yards and looked as though he belonged. "I think we walked out of that game feeling that we had probably taken the right guy," Belichick said on *Brady 6*.

Walsh and 49ers coach Steve Mariucci must have known after that game that they'd taken the wrong guy. They scouted Brady at a predraft workout in San Francisco held for Bay Area small-college players and for players who went to high school in the Bay Area. Brady did nothing to convince the 49ers to invest a draft pick in him. Walsh had actually said after drafting Carmazzi that he was concerned another team would take him before the 49ers had their chance in the third round. Maybe it was the football gods getting even with Walsh for hitting the lottery with Montana. He passed on Brady, the next Montana, who would have walked the twenty-seven miles from his home to the 49ers office in Santa Clara—that's how badly he wanted to play for the Niners. Carmazzi never got on the field in the regular season in two years in San Francisco; he eventually played in NFL Europe and briefly in the Canadian Football League.

The Ravens took Chris Redman in the third round. Later in his career, he was cut by Belichick when he tried to make the Patriots as a backup to Brady. He had twelve career starts. The Steelers selected Tee Martin from Tennessee in the fifth round. He took over for Manning and won the national championship in his only season as a starter but never started a game in the NFL. The Saints took Marc Bulger in the sixth round but cut him before the season. He then spent time on the Saints practice squad and the Rams practice squad and eventually had a nice career with Saint Louis, taking over for Kurt Warner. Sixteen picks before Brady finally went off the board, the Browns, in their second year as an expansion team, picked Spergon Wynn, who didn't complete even 50 percent of his passes at Southwest Texas State after transferring from Minnesota. Brady had just ripped apart the Alabama defense in the Orange Bowl but had to endure watching Wynn go ahead of him.

Recent Michigan quarterbacks had not become elite players in the NFL. Harbaugh had his moments, but Elvis Grbac, Todd Collins, and Brian Griese, the three most recent Wolverines quarterbacks drafted before Brady, all had backup-type talent.

"At that time, there were three rounds the first day and four rounds the other day," Brady Sr. said. "The first day, Tommy and I played golf in the afternoon. The second day, Sunday, we just kind of hung by the television. At the beginning of the fifth round, Tommy said he had to go upstairs. We were lying on the bed with my wife in the room, and halfway through the sixth round, he said, 'I got to get out of here.' He got up and went downstairs and grabbed a baseball bat and went for a walk."

He was gone for twenty minutes.

The conference table in the Patriots war room at Foxboro Stadium was cluttered with multiple telephones, computers, thick binders, and six water bottles. Scott Pioli, who was Belichick's right-hand man on personnel issues, sat between Patriots owner Robert Kraft and Belichick. Scouts and other members of the personnel department gathered around the table. Belichick had dispatched quarterback coach Dick Rehbein to Ann Arbor in the weeks leading up to the draft to scout Brady, and he came back with a very positive report. He also sent him to Ruston, Louisiana, to work out Rattay. Brady was his guy. That's whom Rehbein wanted.

Bobby Grier, the Patriots vice president of player personnel, also endorsed Brady. He had done his homework, contacting Michigan coach Lloyd Carr. Grier had been at New England for twenty years, first as an assistant coach and then in personnel. But Belichick had been given final say by Kraft when he was hired, three months before the 2000 draft. Belichick then fired Grier after the draft. As early as the third round, Belichick considered Brady. He had inherited an 8–8 team that regressed in each of Pete Carroll's three seasons. Belichick had been a defensive assistant in New England in 1996 when the Patriots lost to the Packers in the Super Bowl, and he developed a strong friendship with Kraft during that year. When Bill Parcells engineered his departure to the Jets, Belichick was Kraft's first choice to replace him. Belichick was a public relations nightmare in his five years as the Cleveland Browns head coach, and Art Modell fired him after the 1995 season. His press conferences were painful. Modell was moving the team to Baltimore and wanted to start off on a positive note in Charm City, but Belichick exuded negativity. Belichick was looking for a job, and Parcells immediately went to Kraft and made a pitch to add his former defensive coordinator, even without any openings on the staff.

As much as Kraft had grown to like Belichick for being in-
clusive, Kraft had such a bitter relationship with Parcells that he
couldn't rationalize keeping such a close ally of the Tuna's. He
believed he needed a clean break and hired Pete Carroll. Belichick
accompanied Parcells to the Jets. Enough time passed by 2000,
and after he fired Carroll, Kraft was ready to reunite with Belichick. But Parcells stepped down as the Jets coach within minutes
after the final game of the 1999 season against Seattle, which by
contract immediately promoted Belichick to head coach. The Jets
knew the Patriots wanted Belichick, but they wanted him also.
Parcells made a preemptive strike by resigning before the Patriots
could request permission to speak with Belichick.

Belichick had been paid a $1 million bonus by Jets owner
Leon Hess in January 1999 as an enticement not to speak with
other teams and to stick around until Parcells quit, whenever that
might be. Hess died four months after making the payment to
Belichick. When Parcells resigned as the Jets coach, the team was
weeks away from being sold for $635 million by the Hess estate to
Woody Johnson.

On the morning after the regular season ended, the Patriots
sent a fax to the Jets requesting permission to speak with Belichick, who had already been named Jets coach. Kraft wanted to
hire him as coach and director of football operations, and Belichick wanted the job. Jets president Steve Gutman denied permission. The next day, Belichick held a rambling press conference. He
read from a handwritten note on loose-leaf paper and resigned as
the "HC of the NYJ." The Patriots and Jets then began a lengthy
fight over Belichick, much as they had over Parcells three years
earlier. Kraft had interviewed former Panthers head coach Dom
Capers and was just about to give up on Belichick and hire Capers
when Parcells called him in his office a few nights before the Rams
were to play the Titans in the Super Bowl. He introduced himself

as "Darth Vader," and they worked out a deal that included sending New England's first-round pick in 2000 to the Jets.

Parcells could have been vindictive and made Belichick sit it out. At the time, however, there was no reason for Parcells or anybody associated with the Jets to believe that allowing Belichick to remain in the AFC East would prevent them from having their own success. Belichick was just 37–45 in five years in Cleveland, then spent four years working as an assistant again for Parcells. If Parcells had thought Belichick would get to six Super Bowls and win four of them in his first fifteen seasons in New England, Kraft would not have been able to offer enough to get Parcells to let Belichick out of his contract.

Once Parcells and Kraft made the deal, Belichick got in his car and drove the four hours from his home on Long Island to Foxboro to sign the contract. "When I hired him, there was an outcry against the move," Kraft said. "I had one media person send me a tape of him doing press conferences in Cleveland. We had to build a new stadium. They said this guy wasn't going to help you, he's not media friendly."

Belichick was taking over a team that was $10.5 million over the $62.172 million salary cap. Belichick and Pioli cut players and restructured the contracts of others to meet the cap requirements. They were left with a roster of forty players. "People don't realize how much of a mess we took over," Pioli said. "What we did have was three quarterbacks, Drew Bledsoe, John Friesz, and Michael Bishop."

Bledsoe was in the prime of his career. Friesz was a capable veteran backup. Bishop, a seventh-round pick in the 1999 draft, was the developmental quarterback. There was no need for another quarterback when the depth chart on the wall was blank at other positions.

"We were completely inactive in free agency," Pioli said. "We didn't sign anyone because we were over the cap."

They didn't have their first-round pick. That went to the Jets for Belichick. After Belichick and Pioli picked Hawaii tackle Adrian Klemm in the second round, the Patriots debated taking Brady in the third round. "He was in the mix of players based on where we evaluated him," Pioli said. "It was a pretty quick conversation."

They had more pressing needs. The Patriots took Arizona State running back J. R. Redmond. They talked about Brady again in the fourth round but took Michigan State tackle Greg Robinson-Randall. They talked about him in the fifth round, when they had two picks. They took Boise State tight end Dave Stachelski and Missouri defensive tackle Jeff Marriott. Belichick needed bodies at positions where he didn't have many bodies. He didn't need bodies at quarterback. Bledsoe had been in the NFL only seven years, had been the first overall pick by Parcells in the 1993 draft, took the Patriots to one Super Bowl, and was durable. He'd started all sixteen games in four of the previous five years.

As Brady went for a walk around the block with the baseball bat in his hands, the Patriots brain trust was trying to replenish a thin roster. They were keeping an eye on him on their draft board, but the waiting around was eating up the Bradys. Team after team was crushing his dream.

"We thought there were several teams that were going to be taking him," Brady Sr. said. They were sure the Chargers would be the team. Leaf was already a bust, and it was a year before they would take Drew Brees in the second round. San Diego coach Mike Riley first came in contact with Brady when he was an assistant coach at Southern Cal; he wanted to recruit him, but coach John Robinson told Riley he was all set at quarterback. Riley saw Brady at the scouting combine in Indianapolis and Brady Sr. said Riley told his son, "I missed you the first time. I won't miss on you again."

Every time the Chargers were on the clock, the Bradys were hoping general manager Bobby Beathard would listen to Riley. If it couldn't be the hometown 49ers, then the Chargers would be a great spot. An easy trip down the California coast for the family to watch him play. The Chargers didn't call Brady's name.

Brady's third start in 2001 after Bledsoe was injured came against San Diego. He led a huge comeback with 10 points in the last 3:31 to send the game into overtime and then brought the Patriots into position for Adam Vinatieri to win it with a 44-yard field goal on the Patriots' first possession of overtime. The Chargers quarterback for that game was Doug Flutie, a folk hero in New England from his days at Boston College. He also played for the Patriots from 1987 to 1989 and would finish his career as Brady's backup in 2005.

By the time the draft entered the sixth round, the grade the Patriots assigned Brady had him all alone on the left side of their board, with lower-rated players in the column to the right. "The conversation came up that we either completely misevaluated this guy or there is something wrong with this guy that we don't know about," Pioli said.

Pioli remembered interviewing Brady at the combine. He had an edge to him, "a rare combination of calm confidence that never even got close to arrogance," he said. "I still see him that way. He has a way about him that is really hard to articulate. He is truly and authentically genuinely humble and not disingenuous."

The pictures from the scouting combine of Brady shirtless, in gym shorts, with his bones sticking out, were not going to get him drafted. They might have gotten him thrown off Cape Cod beach resorts. "Bad body," Pioli said. "Some boys wind up being great high school players who hit full body maturity at age eighteen. Look at what happened to Phil Simms's body from the time he came out of Morehead State to the time he was physically a grown man. Tommy's body hasn't fully matured yet."

Mel Kiper, the well-respected ESPN draft analyst, ranked Brady as only the tenth-best quarterback in the 2000 draft. He wrote some complimentary things about him in his analysis. "Smart, experienced, big-game signal caller getting very high grades in the efficiency department this past season ... He's a straight dropback passer who stands tall in the pocket, doesn't show nervous feet, and does a nice job working through his progressions. He's not going to try to force the action, rarely trying to perform beyond his capability." Kiper was clearly not sold on Brady, however, or he wouldn't have listed him two spots behind Tim Lester, who played at Western Michigan and was not among the eleven quarterbacks drafted in 2000. He summed up Brady by saying, "He doesn't have the total package of skills," but was impressed with his play against big-time opponents in his final season. "At the pro level, his lack of mobility could surface as a problem, and it will be interesting to see how he fares when forced to take more chances down the field," Kiper wrote.

The Patriots had two picks in the sixth round at numbers 187 and 199. They were not worried that another team was about to grab Brady just as they were set to take him. If they lost out on him, so be it. If they were going to take him, it would be only when they had exhausted their list of players who could fill in the depth chart. This was not the 1991 draft, when the Jets, who didn't have a first-round pick, were frantically trying to trade up to get Southern Mississippi quarterback Brett Favre, the top-rated player on their entire board. The Jets had forfeited their first-round pick by selecting Syracuse wide receiver Rob Moore in the first round of the 1990 supplemental draft. Their first turn in 1991 didn't come until the seventh spot in the second round. Unable to make a trade, the Jets cringed when the Falcons took Favre one spot ahead of them. The Jets settled for Browning Nagle. That didn't work out well.

The Jets lost out on Favre in 1991 and potentially lost out on Manning in 1997, but if Parcells had listened to his Midwest scout, Jesse Kaye, he would have drafted Brady for the Jets in the sixth round before Belichick had a chance to take him. Parcells had picked Pennington in the first round, and with veteran Vinny Testaverde expected back as he rehabilitated from a torn Achilles suffered in the first game of the 1999 season, and with Parcells favorite Ray Lucas third on the depth chart, Parcells was not thinking about another quarterback. Kaye all but stood on a table campaigning for Brady, but Parcells didn't listen.

Sometimes, you just have to take the advice of the people around you. Belichick listened to Rehbein.

"He had a strong influence," Pioli said.

Parcells did not listen to Jesse Kaye.

"I don't remember that," Parcells said.

Even so, according to a Jets executive who was in the draft room in 2000, Kaye indeed lobbied Parcells hard to take Brady in the sixth round.

For the eight years that Belichick worked for Parcells with the Giants, the one year they worked together with the Patriots, and their three years with the Jets, Parcells was the mentor, Belichick the protégé. They had a falling-out after Belichick walked out on Parcells and the Jets, reconciled six years later at a Hall of Fame luncheon for Harry Carson, and for many years lived two floors apart in the same building in their winter homes in Jupiter, Florida. Parcells was inducted into the Hall of Fame in 2013—Belichick left Patriots training camp to attend the ceremony—and Belichick is a certainty to join him in Canton one day. His career accomplishments have now exceeded Parcells's and the primary reason is that Belichick took Brady.

Pennington was the first quarterback the Jets had taken in the first round in seventeen years. Instead of Brady in the sixth round, Parcells took North Carolina safety Tony Scott. Brady might never have received an opportunity with the Jets. It's hard to predict how these things turn out, but picking Scott didn't do the Jets much good. He played in twenty-three games in two years, was cut, and never played in a regular-season game again. He was claimed by Belichick in the summer of 2002 and released six weeks later. He was signed by Seattle in 2003 and released in the summer.

Eight picks after the Jets selected Scott, the Patriots passed on Brady for the sixth time. This time, it was for Virginia defensive back Antwan Harris with pick number 187. The picks go quickly at this point in the draft. Teams want to finish up and begin competing for undrafted free agents. It was beginning to look as though that's where Brady was headed as he came in from his walk, 2,692 miles from the Patriots war room. He was on the verge of falling right through the draft. Pioli looked at the Patriots board and the overlooked quarterback from Michigan was by far the highest-rated player remaining. Players are stacked in columns according to their grade, and Brady was not only by himself in the highest-rated column remaining, but the column to his right, which had lower-rated players, was empty. Only one or two remained in the next column.

"Okay, we've got to pull his name," Pioli said.

Brady was coming back into his house, baseball bat in hand. The phone was ringing.

"Coach Belichick would like to talk to you," the voice on the other end said.

Brady was ecstatic. The agony was over. He was on his way to Foxboro.

"It's amazing the number of stories that I hear now of how many people loved Tommy coming out but for whatever reason they weren't in a position to take him," Pioli said. "Revisionist history is amazing, but there are a lot of people that have inserted themselves into Tommy's football life story in order to give themselves credibility."

Bills coach Rex Ryan was a defensive assistant in Baltimore. He said Matt Cavanaugh, the Ravens quarterbacks coach, loved

Brady, but was unable to convince general manager Ozzie Newsome to take him. Ryan was not grading quarterbacks then but says Brady was "Captain Comeback at Michigan." He says he can't imagine, if he'd been making the decision, that Brady would've lasted until the sixth round. "I don't get it," Ryan said. "I swear to God, I always think, if I was coaching, would that guy have lasted? Would I have missed on him? I don't see how the hell I could. He never ran a forty worth a damn? Big deal. The guy is a winner."

Brady developed a sense of humor about the agony of the draft. He posted his college résumé on his Facebook page during the 2014 season. His achievements and job experience were under the heading "Thomas E. Brady, Jr." He graduated with a bachelor's degree in general studies in December 1999 with a GPA of 3.3 out of 4.0 from the College of Literature, Science and the Arts at the University of Michigan.

At the bottom of the résumé on his Facebook page, Brady added a caption: "Found my old résumé! Really thought I was going to need this after the fifth round." Even though he has found a way to joke about it, Brady has never forgotten about the indignity of nearly getting passed over. It still motivates him. When he was told in the locker room after a playoff victory over the Ravens following the 2014 season that he had passed Joe Montana as the all-time leader in playoff touchdown passes, he smiled and said, "That's cool. Not bad for a sixth round pick."

Sadly, the man who loved Brady the most didn't live long enough to watch him develop into a superstar. Dick Rehbein, who had been diagnosed with cardiomyopathy in 1988, died in August 2001. He passed out running on a treadmill at training camp and was taken to the hospital. He lost consciousness after undergoing a stress test and could not be revived. Rehbein's family takes pride in the role he had in bringing Brady to New England.

"I really wish Dick was still here to see this, but my husband's legacy is with Tom, and I feel proud that my girls have something to associate their dad with," Rehbein's wife, Pam, told ESPN.com. "It's an awesome thing for them to have."

**Just as at** Michigan, Brady didn't have a clear path to the starting job in New England, but it was not an impossible journey. Belichick was never a huge fan of Bledsoe, but he was a favorite of Kraft's and the team had a lot invested in him. Kraft was uncomfortable with all the power that had been given to Parcells, who was already with the team when Kraft purchased the club in 1994. After Parcells departed, Kraft overreacted and didn't give Pete Carroll enough input into personnel decisions. He reverted to the power structure that existed with Parcells when he hired Belichick. He went back to the one-voice approach. He trusted Belichick's decisions, even if that eventually would lead to Bledsoe leaving New England.

"We knew we had a good quarterback, not a great quarterback," Pioli said. "Quarterback wasn't our biggest problem."

The first time Kraft met Brady was in the parking lot at Foxboro Stadium a few weeks after he was drafted. The team had its offices in the stadium, and the players, coaches, front-office staff, and owner would exit through the same door. Kraft was parked right in front. As he was getting into his car around eight p.m., Brady walked up to Kraft with a couple of pizza boxes in his arms.

"Hi, I'm Tom Brady," he said.

"I know who you are. You're our sixth-round draft choice from Michigan," Kraft said.

Brady looked Kraft right in the eye. He shook his hand firmly. "I'm the best decision this organization has ever made," Brady said.

Brady had a strong training camp as a rookie and made the roster as the fourth-string quarterback. No team ever keeps four quarterbacks on the active roster, but with salary cap problems preventing the Patriots from keeping a full fifty-three-man roster, there was room for Brady, who came at a nominal price. Belichick could have tried to sneak him through waivers and signed him to the practice squad, but felt it was not worth the risk of another team claiming him. The Patriots could afford to use a roster spot on a player they didn't intend to play all season. Besides, there was something about this kid that Belichick really liked.

Brady didn't look any closer to getting any playing time going into his second training camp. In March, the Patriots signed Bledsoe to a ten-year, $103 million contract, the largest in NFL history. It saved $1.5 million in cap space and reconfirmed New England's commitment to Bledsoe with $24 million in guaranteed money over the first three years of the deal.

"Bledsoe really was the face of the franchise after we bought it," Kraft said. "We had a great coach in Bill [Parcells], but it was always, 'Was he staying or wasn't he staying?'" Kraft sold his brand by selling Bledsoe as the star. He had a special place in his heart for Bledsoe, but Belichick did not endorse Kraft's giving him the new contract, especially with Bledsoe coming off a poor season. "Bill was in transition," Kraft said. "Would he have preferred we wait? Probably."

The Patriots' new privately financed $325 million stadium was under construction and scheduled to open in 2002. There was not a penny of public money going into the building, and Kraft didn't want to sell public seat licenses. Economic times were bad, and after the September 11 terrorist attacks, financing "dried up," Kraft said. He had to personally buy $56 million of blue steel for the stadium because he couldn't get a loan. Waiting would've set back the opening of the stadium until 2003.

When he signed Bledsoe to the deal, he was sending a message to his fan base. The Patriots had finished 5–11 in Belichick's first season, and the fans clearly had not bought in, but at least Kraft was telling them that Bledsoe was not going anywhere. Brady was not going anywhere on the depth chart, either. Belichick signed veteran Damon Huard in March to be Bledsoe's backup, and Bishop was still on the team. Brady is a gym rat and worked on getting stronger and preparing himself to make a run at Bledsoe's job. He might have been the only person in New England who thought he had a chance to beat him out that summer. By early August, Belichick cut Bishop. That moved Brady to third team. By the end of training camp, he had moved ahead of Huard and was closing in on Bledsoe. Belichick admitted that Brady performed at a higher level than Bledsoe in the summer. If Belichick had made his decision based on who played better in training camp and in the preseason games, Brady would have started the opener in Cincinnati.

"We were talking about it. It was an ongoing conversation," Pioli said. "There were a lot of things at play. We had a quarterback under contract that was established in a lot of ways. He was the face of the franchise. His skills hadn't completely deteriorated."

Belichick met with Kraft and told him Brady had a "tremendous" training camp. "But we had a quarterback who had taken us to a Super Bowl who was great," Kraft said.

Belichick never mentioned to Kraft that he even thought about starting Brady to open the season. "All he ever said is he had the most impressive training camp of anyone," Kraft said.

Bledsoe's new contract and Brady's inexperience prevented Brady from winning the job, but now it seemed only a matter of time. Belichick's decision not to bench the franchise quarterback goes back to his tumultuous tenure in Cleveland. Art Modell hired Belichick after the 1990 season, when he was the hottest candidate in the NFL. The Giants had just won their second Super Bowl, and Belichick's defense was responsible. He used a four-three scheme to beat the Chicago Bears in the divisional round, a three-four alignment to eliminate the two-time defending champion 49ers in San Francisco in the NFC title game, and then only two down linemen with nine others flooding the passing lanes to stop Jim Kelly and his high-octane "K-Gun" offense in the Super Bowl.

Belichick arrived in Cleveland, and his quarterback was in place. Bernie Kosar, who was from nearby Boardman, Ohio, had already taken the Browns to three AFC title games in his first five seasons but lost them all to the Denver Broncos. He was the biggest Browns hero since Jim Brown. Belichick was just 6–10 with Kosar in his first season and was 2–5 in 1992 when Kosar broke his ankle. After ten weeks on injured reserve, Kosar returned in the final game of the season and broke his ankle again. The Browns finished 7–9. The following year, Belichick signed Vinny Testaverde, who was Kosar's backup at the University of Miami and the former number-one overall pick by Tampa in the 1987 draft. Belichick was moving away from Kosar, and it wasn't long before he brought Testaverde into a game in relief and then started him. He was forced to go back to Kosar when Testaverde suffered a shoulder injury, but the relationship between Belichick and Kosar was destroyed. Late in a game that was already lost to the Broncos, Kosar changed a play sent in from the sideline, threw a touchdown pass, and boasted that he had drawn the play up in the dirt.

Modell met for three hours after the game with Belichick to discuss Kosar. The next day, Belichick and Modell met with Kosar, and Belichick released him. "Basically, it came down to his production and a diminishing of his physical skills," Belichick said at a press conference.

Kosar went to Modell pleading to keep his job, but Modell sided with his coach. Belichick was vilified for giving up on the local hero. Testaverde was still out with a shoulder injury, and Belichick was forced to start Todd Philcox for the next three weeks. The Browns lost all three games, and their season, which had started 5–2, was washed away. They finished 7–9. The next year, with Testaverde at quarterback, the Browns made the play-offs with an 11–5 record. Belichick and Testaverde then beat Parcells and Bledsoe in the wild-card game in Cleveland before losing in Pittsburgh. Modell announced in the middle of the 1995 season that he was moving the franchise to Baltimore in 1996, sabotaging his team. The Browns were 4–4 at the time but won only one of their last eight games, and Belichick was fired.

Modell was as close to Kosar as Kraft was to Bledsoe, and the two players' popularity in their communities was similar. That weighed on Belichick's mind when he decided to stick with Bledsoe for the start of the 2001 season, even though his instincts told him Brady was ready and better. He didn't want to go through another Kosar situation with the fans, at least not yet. He had admitted he hadn't handled Kosar correctly and was trying to learn from his mistake. Brady had thrown just three passes as a rookie, and Patriots Nation was not ready for Belichick to make the switch to a second-year player they knew little about. Bledsoe was a leader in the locker room, and there was a clique, comprising offensive linemen Bruce Armstrong, Max Lane, and Todd Rucci and tight end Ben Coates, who were known as FOBs, or Friends of Bledsoe. They were his guys and formed a powerful faction. Belichick went for self-preservation over instincts. The job belonged to Bledsoe when the Patriots got on the team plane for Cincinnati.

The Patriots lost to the Bengals, 23–17. Bledsoe's numbers were very good: 22 of 38 for 241 yards with two touchdowns and no interceptions. He was sacked four times. He was now 5–12 as Belichick's starter. Two days after the Patriots returned from Cincinnati, the United States was attacked. It was September 11, 2001. The nation was in shock and in mourning after terrorists hijacked two planes and took down the World Trade Center buildings in New York, slammed a third plane into the Pentagon, and crashed a fourth in Shanksville, Pennsylvania, after the passengers overwhelmed the hijackers, who were targeting the White House or the Capitol.

The nation had no appetite for football. The players had no desire to play. The Jets threatened to boycott their game against the Raiders in Oakland. The World Trade Center had been visible from Giants Stadium, and it would have been insensitive to hold the Giants home game against the Packers so close to ground zero so soon after the tragedy. The Giants and Jets players were too busy visiting fire stations and helping out families of the victims to even think about playing a game. Pete Rozelle's greatest regret as commissioner was playing games the weekend after the assassination of President John F. Kennedy in Dallas on November 22, 1963. Two days after the September 11 attacks, NFL commissioner Paul Tagliabue postponed the games for the weekend of September 16–17 and rescheduled them to be played at the end of the regular season. The Patriots would not be playing in Carolina as planned.

The Patriots' second game would be the third on the original schedule, the home opener against the Jets. The battle between the Jets and Patriots had grown into the so-called Border War, which started when Parcells went from New England to New York in 1997, then signed Patriots restricted free agent running back Curtis Martin, whom he had drafted in 1995, to a poison-pill offer sheet in 1998 that Kraft elected not to match. The Border War culminated with Belichick's drive north on I-95 in 2000. Nevertheless, the animosity between the teams and animosity Boston fans feel for all New York teams was set aside on September 23 at Foxboro Stadium. The Patriots fans greeted the Jets warmly as they ran onto the field. It wasn't just New York that was attacked by terrorists; it was the entire country. The parking lot was filled with American flags. As fans entered the stadium, they were also given American flags. The pregame program was emotional and patriotic.

In the locker room prior to the game, Testaverde, who was now playing for the Jets, had gone over and looked at two posters on the wall with pictures of missing police officers and firefighters from 9/11. Testaverde got a lump in his throat. Ron Kloepfer was among the twenty-three missing police officers. "High school teammates. I know him. It's just sad," Testaverde said. "He was a great guy. Fun to be around."

The Jets won 10–3. It was a victory for the city of New York. It was no coincidence that the Jets, Giants, Mets, and Yankees all won the first game they played after the attacks. The Jets-Patriots game itself was not memorable—except for one play that changed the course of history in the NFL.

On the official play-by-play, it was recorded thus: 3-10-NE 19 (5:11) D.Bledsoe right end to NE 27 for 8 yards (M.Lewis). FUMBLES (M.Lewis), ball out of bounds at NE 27.

Drew Bledsoe dropped back to pass but couldn't find an open receiver. He scrambled to his right, attempting to pick up a first down. He was being chased by defensive end Shaun Ellis. When he neared the Jets sideline, he was met by Mo Lewis, a six-three, 258-pound Pro Bowl linebacker. Lewis led with his right shoulder and hit Bledsoe with tremendous force in the shoulder and chest. It was a brutal hit. The NFL is a game of brutal hits. Bledsoe was briefly knocked unconscious.

"It was third down and I was heading toward the sidelines," Bledsoe said. "It was two yards short of a first down and I tried to turn back, and when I did, I gave Mo Lewis my full chest and he blew me up."

On the previous play, Bledsoe had completed a 17-yard pass to Bert Emanuel that was overturned by a successful instant-replay challenge by Jets coach Herm Edwards. If the play had stood, the Patriots likely would have run the ball on first down. Instead, Bledsoe was forced to scramble on third down.

The Jets went three-and-out on the next series, and when the Patriots took over at their own 39 with 3:36 left in the game, trailing by seven points, it was Bledsoe back under center. Unaware that he had a sheared blood vessel in his chest, he shook off the hit from Lewis and played the next series, which ended with the Patriots losing the ball on a fumble.

The notation on the play-by-play the next time the Patriots had the ball: New England Patriots at 2:16, 1-10-NE 26 (2:16) 12 Brady now at QB (Shotgun) T.Brady pass to P.Pass to NE 30 for 4 yards (M.Lewis, R.Mickens).

"The reason I ended up coming out of the game is because I had a concussion also," Bledsoe said. "I couldn't think straight. I didn't know my plays. I went back in the next series, and I didn't know which way was right and which way was left. That's why I ultimately came out of the game. It wasn't because of the big injury."

Belichick immediately regretted his decision to let Bledsoe return for the one series. "I shouldn't have put him out there," Belichick said. "Watching him play, he wasn't himself. He got his bell rung. When I went over to him he seemed coherent and said he was okay. But after watching him, I didn't think he was. I told him what decision I had made. He understood."

Brady ran onto the field, and it wasn't as though he put any fear into the Jets defense. He had 70 yards to go to get the tying touchdown, and Belichick had used his last two time-outs to stop the clock on the Jets' previous offensive series. Brady quickly completed five of six passes for 46 yards and suddenly the Patriots were on the Jets 29, but only fourteen seconds were left. Brady spiked the ball to stop the clock on first down. He then threw three straight incompletions and the game was over. Nobody was declaring that the Tom Brady era had arrived.

After the game, Bledsoe was walking off the field when he was approached by Ron O'Neill, the Patriots trainer. "Hey, Bub, you need to come with me," O'Neill said.

"Okay, I'm just going to go in for the team prayer," Bledsoe said.

"Nah, I think you need to come with me. You don't look right," O'Neill said.

As Bledsoe started up the tunnel toward the Patriots locker room, his chest really started to hurt. There was a lot of internal pain. He told O'Neill and Dr. Bert Zarins, "I'll just go home, sleep on it, and will see you tomorrow."

Bledsoe knows where he'd be now if he'd gotten his way. "Had they allowed me to do that, I would have died," he said.

Bledsoe said Zarins was aware of the concussion but said "what ultimately concerned him is when you have a concussion, normally your heart rate starts to slow way down. Instead, my heart rate was increasing, was getting faster and faster."

This was now full-scale crisis mode. Bledsoe's uniform was cut off because he couldn't get his arms above his head. He took a quick shower. They had clothes for him to wear in the trainer's room. He was getting groggy. He was taken out of the locker room on a gurney to a waiting ambulance parked in full view of fans and media. He was bleeding out internally at the rate of a liter per hour. "There are seven liters of blood in my body," he said. "Yeah, it was bad."

He was rushed to Massachusetts General Hospital on Fruit Street in Boston. His younger brother, Adam, rode in the ambulance with him. The hospital was thirty miles away, and it took forever as the ambulance tried to maneuver around traffic leaving the stadium on Route 1 North. Adam Bledsoe thought his brother, the quarterback of the New England Patriots, had died as they were nearing the hospital. It took until 2013 for Adam to tell his brother how scared he was.

LEFT Four-and-one-half-year-old Tommy Brady (his family and close friends still call him Tommy) warms up in the parking lot at Candlestick Park before the 49ers beat the Cowboys in the NFC Championship Game on January 10, 1982. The Bradys were longtime season-ticket holders of the 49ers, and Tommy's favorite player was Joe Montana. Who knew this little kid would go on to play in more Super Bowls than his hero? Brady never played an NFL game at Candlestick. *The Brady Family* RIGHT Why is this little boy crying? The Brady family was sitting in end-zone seats right behind where Dwight Clark made "The Catch," in the '81 NFC title game to beat Dallas. Tommy was crying because fans in front of him stood up and he couldn't see Clark's catch. Eighteen years later, the 49ers broke Brady's heart by passing on him in the 2000 draft to take Hofstra's Giovanni Carmazzi. *The Brady Family*

LEFT Archie Manning never made the playoffs in his fourteen-year NFL career and never imagined that Eli (far left) and Peyton (right) would grow up to be Super Bowl champions. The front yard of their house was the scene of their "amazing catches" game, with Archie as the QB and the boys diving for his passes. *The Manning Family* RIGHT The Manning boys may have battled one another as kids, but now they are as close as brothers can be. Cooper (second from left) had his career as a wide receiver cut short by a neck injury before his freshman year at Mississippi, but he has lived his football dreams through the spectacular careers of Eli (far left) and Peyton (second from right). *The Manning Family*

The Brady Bunch is a tight-knit family who have been very supportive of Tom through his early struggles at Michigan to his incredible success in New England. From left: Tom; his aunt Kathy; his father, Tom Sr.; older sisters Julie, Nancy, and Maureen; and mother, Galynn. All the Brady kids played college sports, and Tom Sr. admits they inherited the athletic genes from their mother. *The Brady Family*

LEFT Brady at Michigan. Tom Brady put on an incredible performance against arch-rival Ohio State in 1998 at the Horseshoe in Columbus, Ohio. Although Michigan's eight-game winning streak came to an end in a 31–16 loss, Brady was 31 of 56 for 375 yards. He took a beating from the Ohio State defense with seven sacks, but his coach, Lloyd Carr, said Brady was "bloodied but unbowed." *University of Michigan* RIGHT Peyton at Tennessee. Peyton Manning poses for his senior-year football publicity picture after deciding to return to play his final season rather than enter the NFL draft. Manning loved the college life. Although he lost for the third time in three games against Florida and finished second to Charles Woodson in the Heisman voting, Manning did win his first SEC title and never second-guessed his decision to play his senior year. *University of Tennessee*

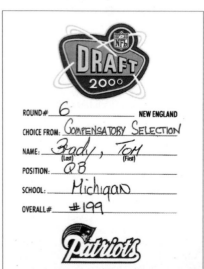

It's the most famous late-round draft card in NFL history. It's so famous that the actual card the New England Patriots used to write down Tom Brady's name as the 199th player selected in the 2000 draft is on display in the Pro Football Hall of Fame in Canton, Ohio. Brady was the seventh quarterback picked and the seventh player drafted by the Patriots. *Pro Football Hall of Fame*

Peyton Manning played the first fourteen years of his record-setting career with the Indianapolis Colts. He was the reason the Colts won at least twelve regular-season games for seven years in a row, making it to two Super Bowls and winning one. It's hard to believe now, but the Colts scouts were split 50/50 between Manning and Ryan Leaf before the 1998 draft. *AP Images*

Tom Brady was just hoping he would be drafted so he didn't have to become an insurance salesman. In his first fifteen seasons, he went to six Super Bowls and won four, tying him with Terry Bradshaw and Joe Montana for most ever by a quarterback. Brady had a good arm at Michigan, but as he became bigger and stronger in the NFL, there wasn't a throw he couldn't make. *AP Images*

Aloha. Peyton Manning and Tom Brady have been good friends for a long time, but the only time they were Pro Bowl teammates came in Honolulu in 2005, the last time Brady played in the all-star game. They could have been together even more, but Brady played only twice out of the ten times he was elected. In the days leading up to the Pro Bowl, Manning would hold court for hours at the outdoor restaurant at the hotel the players stayed in for the week. *AP Images*

Peyton Manning at long last was able to hold the Lombardi Trophy after the Colts beat the Bears in Super Bowl XLI. Two weeks earlier, he beat Tom Brady in the AFC Championship Game, his first playoff victory over his most intense rival, with a late touchdown drive to seal a Colts comeback from an eighteen-point deficit, the largest ever in a conference title game. *AP Images*

Tom Brady and Brazilian supermodel Gisele Bundchen were married in 2009. In the off-season, they spend a lot of time in New York, where they have an apartment near Madison Square Park. She is the world's number one model. He is the greatest quarterback of all time. She makes more money than him. In 2011, Tom and Gisele attended a gala at the Metropolitan Museum of Art in Manhattan. *AP Images*

Tom Brady and Peyton Manning get together after their 2012 game in Foxboro. After playing against each other twelve times when Manning was with the Colts (Brady led 8–4, including 2–1 in the playoffs), this was their first meeting after Manning signed with the Broncos. Brady beat Manning three straight times in the regular season from 2012 through 2014, but Manning beat Brady in the 2013 AFC Championship Game. *Copyright © Gabriel Christus/Denver Broncos*

Peyton Manning added another record to his long resume when he threw the 509th touchdown pass of his career on October 20, 2014, to push Brett Favre into second place. It came on an eight-yard pass to Demaryius Thomas with 3:09 left in the first half of a 42–17 victory over the 49ers. In an entertaining scene, the Broncos receivers played keep-away with the record-setting ball until handing it over to Manning. He helped plan the prank in practice but didn't think his receivers would go through with it. *Pro Football Hall of Fame*

When he was a free agent in 2011, Peyton Manning picked the Broncos over the Titans and 49ers to resume his career after the Colts cut him months after his fourth neck surgery. He made the right choice, and in his second year in Denver, he beat Tom Brady in the AFC Championship Game (he was 1–1 against him in title games when he played for the Colts) and soaked in the adulation from the home crowd while on the podium. *Gary Myers*

Two years after little brother Eli won Super Bowl XLVI by beating Tom Brady on Peyton's home field in Indianapolis, Peyton wasn't so fortunate on Eli's home field against the Seahawks in Super Bowl XLVIII. From the moment the first snap sailed over Manning's head for a safety, the Broncos were overmatched and lost 43–8. On the podium in the interview area after the game, Manning bristled when asked if he was embarrassed. *Gary Myers*

As Deflategate hung over Super Bowl XLIX, Tom Brady had a lot of pressure on him to perform well and eliminate the noise, as the Patriots call distractions. On media day in Phoenix five days before the game, Brady was relaxed and cordial. He threw the winning touchdown pass with just over two minutes remaining to beat Seattle 28–24, tying him with Terry Bradshaw and Joe Montana for most Super Bowl titles, with four. It was Brady's first title in ten years. *Gary Myers*

They have never gone out to dinner or sat down to discuss the great success they've had together—they've been to six Super Bowls and won four—but Bill Belichick and Tom Brady are the best coach-quarterback combination in NFL history. They embraced after beating the Seahawks in one of the best Super Bowls of all time. "Way to go, man. That's tremendous. Great job," an emotional Belichick told Brady, who responded with a huge smile, "What a win, huh?" *AP Images*

Tom Brady has stood the test of time. He raised his fourth Lombardi Trophy on February 2, 2015, which came thirteen years after his first one and ten years after his previous one—the two longest stretches for any quarterback in NFL history. He's won his four Super Bowls by a total of thirteen points. He lost his two by a total of seven points. *AP Images*

"He said we were driving to the hospital and they couldn't give me anything for pain because I'm allergic to morphine and Advil is a blood thinner, and they figured I was bleeding," Bledsoe said. "There was yelling every time there was a bump because it hurt bad. Then we got about ten minutes away and he said I just went out. Just went lights-out. He thought I died in the ambulance. I didn't wake up until the next day."

When he did awake, his wife, Maura, was there. So were Belichick and Brady. Even though he didn't have a great relationship with Belichick, he wasn't surprised to see him by his bedside. "It's different when somebody's life is on the line," he said. "Obviously, you're showing up."

The doctors hooked Bledsoe up to a machine that took the blood that was seeping into his chest, cleaned it, and put it back into his body. They waited for it to clot and for the bleeding to stop. The doctors wanted to give the bleeding a chance to stop on its own. Otherwise they would have to cut Bledsoe's chest open, which could have been career-ending. "There were a couple different times I met double the criteria for opening my chest cavity and they chose not to do it," he said. "They chose to wait, which was very cool."

Bledsoe remained in the hospital four days as Brady prepared to start the first game of his NFL career against Peyton Manning and the Indianapolis Colts. Bledsoe's injury gave Belichick the opening he was looking for to start Brady. "It gave us the chance," Pioli said. "It was more than just Bill that was ready to make that change."

The Patriots beat the Colts, 44–13. Brady threw for just 168 yards with no touchdowns or interceptions. Manning threw three interceptions and the Patriots returned two for touchdowns. Brady threw for only 86 yards the next week in a dreadful 30–10 loss at Miami.

Belichick was now 6–14 in his first twenty games and there

was an uneasiness around the Patriots offices. Pioli said he and Belichick feared Kraft would fire them at the end of the season if they didn't turn things around. "We were in trouble. Me and Bill were in trouble," Pioli said. "We were 1–3 after 5–11. We were in a lot of trouble. We never did talk about it. It was the eight-hundred-pound gorilla in the corner. You know it's there."

Kraft was not happy, and Belichick and Pioli were getting paranoid. Kraft's franchise quarterback had suffered a life-threatening injury, and the anti-Belichick momentum was building in New England. "I remember calling Bill and I said, 'You just keep doing what you are doing. I believe in you,'" Kraft said. "In the NFL you really judge the season, if you are going at a high level, by what happens from Thanksgiving on. It's a great business, but it's a sick business."

Bledsoe was fortunate to be alive. He wouldn't be cleared to play until November 13. The Patriots were 5–2 with Brady and 5–4 overall, but Bledsoe fully expected Belichick to give him back his job, or at least the chance to compete for his job, and that he would start that Sunday against the Saint Louis Rams.

"I'm itching to get back in," Bledsoe said at a news conference he held with his doctors. "I'm going to do everything in my power to be on the field on Sunday. Ultimately, that's not my decision. But I can't wait."

Instead, Belichick made the decision he'd wanted to make in the summer: Brady was his quarterback. It's a teaching point Brady now uses. "I try to express this to the younger players, and it's the attitude I took: You always feel you should be the one in there regardless of whether you should be or shouldn't be," Brady said. "The coach makes the choice. I always wanted to get in there and show them what I could do."

Bledsoe said Belichick never made any promises that when he was healthy, he would have the opportunity to win back his job. It's just something he expected. "There are no promises in professional sports, and anybody who thinks there are, they're just plain foolish," Bledsoe said. "That's no slight on anybody. That's just the way it is. When I came back and my job wasn't waiting there for me, I certainly was really pissed about that. I didn't feel that it was right. I felt like I had been wronged."

He split practice reps with Brady his first week back leading into the Saint Louis game. The Patriots lost to the Rams, the best team in the league, but by only seven points. They were just 5–5 but gained confidence by playing the Rams so tight. Belichick decided splitting the reps was hurting the offense and that this was now officially Brady's team. "Tom started last week against Saint Louis, this week against New Orleans, and he's probably going to start next week against the Jets," Belichick said. "That's the way it was. That's the way it's going to be. I think it's pretty clear-cut."

Brady went out and threw four touchdown passes to beat the Saints, and the Patriots went undefeated the rest of the way, right through the Super Bowl.

The Patriots won their last six regular-season games, then beat the Raiders in the "tuck rule" game in the snow in the divisional round of the playoffs in Foxboro. Oakland cornerback Charles Woodson, who'd played with Brady at Michigan, forced a Brady fumble on a blitz as he began his arm motion to throw; Raiders linebacker Glenn Bickert recovered at the Oakland 42 with 1:47 left. The Raiders led 13–10 and the Patriots were out of time-outs. Oakland merely had to kneel down three times and the game was over. But the play was challenged by the replay assistant in the press box, and referee Walt Coleman reversed the call, citing the little-known and now defunct tuck rule. It was ruled an incomplete pass rather than a fumble. Brady then threw 13 yards to David Patten, missed on two straight passes, and ran for 1 yard, and then Vinatieri drilled a 45-yarder through the blizzard to send the game into overtime. The Patriots won the toss and Brady moved them into position for Vinatieri to win it with a 23-yard field goal after running fourteen plays that took New England from its own 34 to the Raiders 5. The Raiders complained after the game that they got screwed, and that feeling has never changed. They lost to the fine print in the rule book.

The Patriots had truly survived and moved on. The next week, they went into Pittsburgh and beat the Steelers in the AFC championship game. Bledsoe came in late in the second quarter after Brady sprained his ankle; Bledsoe played the rest of the game.

Brady was back for the Super Bowl one week later against the Rams. His legend was born that day in New Orleans. The Rams had just erased a 17–3 deficit with two touchdowns in the fourth quarter, tying the game on Kurt Warner's 26-yard touchdown to Ricky Proehl with 1:30 remaining. The Patriots took over on their 17 with 1:21 remaining. John Madden, the most respected football voice on television, famously told the 86.8 million people watching that Belichick, with no time-outs and poor field position, should run out the clock and play for overtime. The Rams had all the momentum, but Belichick was going for it right then. Brady completed 5 of 7 passes for 53 yards, which helped move the Patriots to the Rams 30-yard line. Vinatieri then kicked a 48-yard field goal to win Super Bowl XXXVI.

"Yeah, baby. Way to go, 12," Bledsoe said as he hugged Brady on the field. "You are the man. You are the man."

Brady, just twenty-four and a half years old, was the youngest quarterback to win the Super Bowl. Less than three months later, Bledsoe was traded to the Buffalo Bills for a first-round draft choice.

# 6

# RESPECT FOR PEYTON

Tedy Bruschi and his defensive teammates entered the Patriots meeting room in the week leading up to a game against the Indianapolis Colts to watch tape of Peyton Manning going through his antics at the line of scrimmage, waving his arms like Leonard Bernstein conducting the New York Philharmonic at Lincoln Center.

Bruschi arrived in New England in 1996 when Bill Parcells picked him in the third round. Manning was drafted by the Colts two years later, and it wasn't long before Colts offensive coordinator Tom Moore realized that Manning was so far ahead of the curve intellectually that he could give him a few run-pass options in the coach-to-quarterback radio helmet and let Manning decide which play to call based on what he saw at the line of scrimmage.

Moore slowly gave Manning the responsibility in his rookie year, and by 2000 the Colts had fully transitioned to a no-huddle attack with Manning running the show at the line.

"Everybody has special talents, and one of your jobs as coaches is to make sure that you give a guy an opportunity to be the very best that he can be," Moore said. "Peyton had a special talent from the standpoint of recognizing defenses, knowing the offense, getting you into the right play, getting you out of the bad play. He had the greatest recall of any player I've ever coached. The whole thing evolved as the years went along. Well, what the heck, if we're going to make audibles and he had the recall and application to get us out of bad plays and get into good plays, then let's just go no-huddle and not waste our time in the huddle."

That was just the beginning. By the time Manning was screaming "Omaha! Omaha!" later in his career, as he worked furiously to get the play calls to his teammates, the league knew that half of what he was doing was real and the other half was dummy calls to throw off the defense.

"It's like one of those things—if I could read Chinese and you didn't," former Colts tight end Dallas Clark recalled. "But you're looking at it thinking, *What in the world is that?* People look at him and go, 'What is he doing?' Peyton loves playing those mind games. I watch it now and go, 'That's what I love.' I just smile. That is awesome. Those guys are having the time of their lives. They might not be thinking it right now, because Peyton is yelling and cussing at them, but it's fun. That's fun football."

Bruschi and the Patriots dominated their games against the Colts once Manning arrived. The Colts and Patriots were in the AFC East and played twice a year until there was a minor realignment in 2002 sending Indianapolis to the AFC South. In the years from Manning's rookie season through 2004, the Patriots won ten out of twelve games, including the 2003 AFC championship game, in which Manning was intercepted four times—Ty Law got him three times in New England's 24–14 victory—and a 2004 divisional-round game in the snow won by the Patriots 20–3, in which the Colts punted or turned the ball over on nine out of their ten possessions.

The Patriots were not confused by Manning at the line of scrimmage. They were amused.

Once the tape was turned on in the meeting room, the players were entertained. They watched him wave his arms, frantically run up to the center, back up, scream to his left, scream to the right, wave his arms some more and call for the ball to be snapped with just seconds remaining on the play clock. In the Patriots' view, the only person he was confusing was himself.

"We didn't respect the Colts at first because they just had a problem beating us," Bruschi said. "We used to laugh at Peyton in the meeting rooms because we used to be able to confuse him so well. And you could see the look on his face and the little gyrations—he let it be known that we'd get to him. Then we would watch film. 'Oh man, look at what I did here. I was supposed to be over there, but I lined up all the way over there and I hopped around, and he's up there gyrating like he's got no control.' Then all of a sudden the play clock winds down."

New England wasn't the only team that made fun of Manning's gestures. Prior to the first of the Manning Bowl games between Peyton and Eli, on the opening Sunday night of the 2006 season, the Giants video staff, on instruction from the defensive coaches, prepared special tapes of Manning's hand signals at the line of scrimmage. The buildup to the game was intense. The Colts were a Super Bowl contender and indeed would go on to win Super Bowl XLI. The Giants were coming off an NFC East championship in Eli's second season and had big expectations.

The Giants players were forced to watch the tapes of Peyton so many times, they were sick of them. "They put together tons of film," said linebacker Antonio Pierce, the leader of the Giants defense. "We were supposed to try and figure out and guess what it was. You will see the shovel. The shovel was a dig route. The pistol. That was a slant. Then he would change it up."

The regular-season schedule had come out in the spring, and the coaches had months to prepare for the first few games. Just as Peyton, Eli, Archie, and the oldest son, Cooper, grew tired of answering questions from the media about the family tree, the Giants defense had reached its limit for watching Peyton tapes during training camp and in the week before the game. To keep themselves from falling asleep and thus getting fined by Tom Coughlin, the defense set Manning's arm-waving to music using an electronic gadget. "It started off as a teaching tape," Pierce said. "The next thing you know, we're watching a music video with Peyton Manning."

Peyton threw for 276 yards with a touchdown and an interception. Eli threw for 247 yards with two touchdowns and an interception. The Colts won the game 26–21.

By the time the Patriots arrived in Indianapolis for the AFC championship game at the end of the 2006 season, Bruschi and his teammates were no longer laughing at Manning. He had defeated them in the regular season in 2005 and 2006 in New England and put up a total of 67 points. Manning never thought it was him against Brady. He knew he had to outscore Brady, but he also had to outsmart Bill Belichick's defense. Belichick won seven of his first eight games against Manning and had gotten deep inside Manning's head. Manning had finally found a way to get him out.

"You get super focused and you can't prepare enough," Manning said. "You know it's going to be a dogfight. I've always felt like it was a pretty good two-headed monster coming at me, between arguably one of the best coaches of all time, certainly a great defensive coach, and then Tom at the quarterback position. It was always tough. You grinded to get ready for that game because you knew you had to be on top of your stuff."

The Patriots and Colts each finished 12–4 in 2006, but San Diego had the best regular season in its history, 14–2, and Baltimore was right behind at 13–3, so New England and Indianapolis were both relegated to the wild-card round with records that in most years would have been good enough to earn the top seed in the conference. The Colts beat the Chiefs and the Patriots beat the Jets in the opening round. The next weekend, the Colts went into Baltimore and beat the Ravens 15–6 in a game without any touchdowns. It was the third time Manning had failed to get his team into the end zone in the playoffs but was the first time he won. Then Brady put up 11 points in the last 4:36 in a wild 24–21 comeback victory in San Diego. The Colts earned home field in the championship game because they'd defeated the Patriots during the regular season.

Colts coach Tony Dungy couldn't say it at the time, but he knew there was tremendous pressure on Manning to beat New England. He knew what Manning's detractors were saying, although he didn't agree with them: "Belichick was in his head, we'd never beat these guys, he's going to choke in the big games," Dungy said.

It was Brady vs. Manning for the third time in the playoffs. Manning needed this game much more than Brady. It was a legacy game. Brady had surpassed Manning and now Manning was trying to close the gap.

"They are great friends, but I don't think either of them likes to lose to the other," said center Dan Koppen, who played with Brady in New England and Manning in Denver.

"They took two different roads," Bruschi said. "It's a kid that had a chip on his shoulder, was the 199th pick, and nobody expected anything out of him, and there was a guy that was given the keys to the kingdom. A lot of credit to Peyton that he's taken those keys and he's still driving. The keys are well deserved, but Brady *made* the keys. He wasn't given them. That's a different approach, a different mentality."

The atmosphere in the RCA Dome was electric for the AFC championship game. This was not Manning's best team. They were better in 2005 when they were 14–2 but lost a tough game to the Steelers in the divisional round. Manning was better in 2004, when he threw forty-nine touchdown passes. This was his second championship game, his first at home, so this was his best chance to get to the Super Bowl. Brady already had three Super Bowl titles.

This was a game the Colts should win. It was a game Manning had to win, or the can't-win-the-big-game label, which haunted him at Tennessee and stuck with him as he didn't win a playoff game in the NFL until his sixth season, might be impossible to shake. "I don't think he would let that dictate his career," Clark said. "Dan Marino is his favorite quarterback, so to have that happen to his hero, to not win one Super Bowl, I don't think he was going to put that pressure on himself." But the pressure was there for the championship game and it was all on Manning.

The Patriots caught a break on their second series. Brady fumbled on a third and 1 from the Colts 4, but guard Logan Mankins fell on the ball in the end zone for a touchdown. New England then scored touchdowns fifty-three seconds apart early in the second quarter to take a commanding 21–3 lead. First, Corey Dillon scored on a 7-yard run, and on the second play of the Colts' next possession, Asante Samuel intercepted Manning's pass intended for Marvin Harrison and returned it 69 yards for a touchdown. There was still 9:25 left in the second quarter, so there was plenty of time, but no team had ever come from 18 points down in a conference championship game, and now Manning had to do it against a defense that had tormented him in two previous playoff games. The doubts about Manning being able to perform in big spots had returned.

He was able to get the Colts 3 points closer at the half at 21–6.

After halftime, Manning scored on a 1-yard run and then threw a 1-yard touchdown pass to Dan Klecko, the former Patriots defensive lineman turned fullback turned pass-catching machine. Manning's two-point conversion pass to Harrison brought the Colts even at 21–21 with four minutes left in the third quarter. Manning had wiped out a 15-point halftime deficit in eleven minutes. This was Manning at his best and finally he was showing it in the playoffs. The Patriots went ahead by 7 on Brady's 6-yard touchdown pass to Jabar Gaffney three minutes later. The Colts tied it when center Jeff Saturday recovered running back Dominic Rhodes's fumble in the end zone. The Patriots went ahead by three. The Colts tied it. The Patriots went ahead 34–31 with 3:49 left on Stephen Gostkowski's 43-yard field goal. The next 3:49 would define Manning's career. The elite quarterbacks *will* their team to victory in game-deciding moments. Amazing Catches with his father and brothers in their front yard in New Orleans was fun. They were playing for bragging rights. This was intense. It was time for Manning to show he was great. It didn't start well. He threw three straight incompletions, and the Colts punted. Brady had the ball on his own 40 with 3:22 left and the Colts down to two time outs. The Patriots were in prime position to run out the clock and make it to another Super Bowl.

On first down, the Patriots were penalized for having twelve men on the field, a crucial 5-yard setback. Brady then completed two passes for 11 yards and was incomplete on third down, forcing the Patriots to punt. They had used only sixty-five seconds. Manning came back on the field with the ball at his own 20 and 2:17 remaining. Dungy saved him one time-out. If Manning ever was going to prove he was a championship quarterback oblivious to the pressure and able to do more than win 12 games in the regular season but come up short in the playoffs, now was the time.

In four plays using only twenty-four seconds, the Colts had

a first down at the New England 11. Manning completed three passes: 11 yards to Reggie Wayne, 32 yards to tight end Bryan Fletcher, and 14 yards to Wayne. New England's Tully Banta-Cain was penalized 12 yards for roughing the passer on the last completion to Wayne, and now the Colts needed to manage the clock, get in the end zone, and not leave Brady enough time to pull off any last-minute playoff heroics. Unless the Colts turned it over, at the very least they would send the game into overtime with a chip-shot field goal by former Patriots hero Adam Vinatieri.

Joseph Addai ran for 5 yards. Then he ran for 3. Belichick called his first time-out with 1:02 left. It was third and 2 on the 3. The Colts could get a first down without getting a touchdown. Manning had numerous options. Play action, rollout, fade pass. He gave it to Addai. He scored. The Colts led 38–34, their first lead of the game, but there was exactly one minute left, and New England still had two time-outs.

Manning took a seat on the Colts bench and prayed. He prayed he had not left Brady too much time. He prayed his defense could get him to his first Super Bowl. "I don't know if you are supposed to pray for stuff like that," he said.

Manning couldn't look as Brady took over at his own 21 after the kickoff with fifty-four seconds remaining. He threw incomplete to Reche Caldwell on first down; forty-nine seconds remaining. Brady then hit tight end Benjamin Watson for 21 yards. Belichick didn't use a time-out. Brady went no huddle out of the shotgun but was taking too much time. He snapped the ball with thirty-one seconds left and completed a 15-yard pass to fullback Heath Evans. Belichick then called his second time-out with twenty-four seconds left and the Patriots at the Colts' 45. Brady could have taken a couple of Hail Mary shots at the end zone but instead threw over the middle on a pass intended for Watson, who was double-covered. Marlin Jackson, the Colts first-round pick in

2005 and a Michigan man like Brady, cut in front of Watson and intercepted his fellow Wolverine.

Jackson's interception was so clean, it left no opening for the replay assistant to even consider issuing a challenge to bail out Brady as the tuck rule had five years earlier. Manning quickly put his helmet on to run off the final sixteen seconds with one kneeldown. He was finally going to the Super Bowl. He had finally beaten Brady in the playoffs. This time it was Brady's heart that was broken. "Even when we were up 21–3, you knew at some point they were going to come back," Brady said.

He said it was "frustrating for all of us when it ends like this, because the expectations are so high." Brady had also become accustomed to pulling out these high-stakes games in the final minutes. He knew it never should have come down to the final drive, and when Jackson picked him off with 16 seconds remaining, he didn't overanalyze things. "It was over; that was my only thought," he said.

Was the monkey off Manning's back? Was there vindication?

"That's been the number-one question I've been asked so far," Manning said after the game. "But I don't get into monkeys and vindication. I don't play that card."

It might not have been a full-size gorilla that had been airlifted off Manning's back, but it sure was bigger than a monkey. He'd lost the first three playoff games of his career before breaking through in 2003 in a 41–10 victory over the Broncos. Now in his ninth season, he had made it to his first Super Bowl. Although Marino never won a Super Bowl and made it to only one in his career, it came in just his second season and his first full year as a starter. Joe Montana was 4–0 in the Super Bowl with eleven TDs and no interceptions, and he made it to his first Super Bowl in his third season. Steve Young won his only Super Bowl as a starter in his fourth season after taking over for Montana; he implored teammates on the sideline to take the monkey off his back in the final moments of the 49ers victory over the Chargers. Brady won three Super Bowls in his first five years in the league, even though he didn't start until the third game of his second year.

Manning downplayed the historical significance of the victory over the Patriots in the moments after the game. He still had a Super Bowl to play against the Bears in two weeks, and the season would be a failure if they didn't beat Chicago. Many years later, at the Broncos facility, Manning opened up about what it meant to beat New England. "We felt pretty good after winning that game," he said. "We thought we'd beaten a really good team. Fact is, we shouldn't have won that game. We were down. Sometimes it's worse to be down at home than away. Everybody is on you. You hear occasional boobirds come out [when you're] down 21–3. It was kind of a symbolic game in many ways. We had been down and gotten over the hump. That was obviously a special win."

Bruschi was not laughing at Manning anymore. He was still trying to disguise defenses, but it was no longer working. Touchdown passes were sailing over his head. It was the 2006 AFC championship game that altered Bruschi's respect for Manning. "At the end of the game, it was important for me to go up to Peyton and say, 'You deserved it. You earned it,'" Bruschi said. "I was, really, it's strange to say, but I was proud of the kid. I was proud of him because we had just beat on them for so long, and they got us. I'm not dead inside. I know the pressure the guy has been going through, everyone calling him a bust, an individual statistical quarterback. For me, finally he got it done. I was proud of him for doing that."

Manning threw for 349 yards, but he completed only 27 of 47 passes with a touchdown and an interception. His quarterback rating was just 79.1. Brady threw for 232 yards, completing 21 of 34 passes with a touchdown and an interception. His quarterback rating was 79.5. Neither quarterback played one of his best games, but it was the most dramatic game they ever played against each other. It was the signature game in the Brady vs. Manning series.

"I think it means something special to win the game when they play against each other," said former Giants quarterback Phil Simms, who did the game for CBS.

**Manning went on** to beat the Bears 29–17 in Super Bowl XLI, a sloppy game in a downpour in Miami, the worst weather ever for a Super Bowl. The game began with Chicago's Devin Hester returning the opening kickoff 92 yards for a touchdown. But the Bears were no match for the Colts. Manning threw for 247 yards and a touchdown and was named Super Bowl MVP. He had never beaten Florida. He had never won the SEC championship. He had never won the national championship. Now he won the Super Bowl, and making it even better, he beat Brady, his nemesis, on the way to getting his ring.

"I think for the nostalgia of the rivalry, the Manning and Brady rivalry, it gained so much more traction by us winning a Super Bowl and by us coming back from that huge deficit to go to the Super Bowl," Clark said. "That's as close to Hollywood writing as you can get."

The AFC championship game victory and Super Bowl victory were significant to Dungy on many levels. He was the first African American coach to win the Super Bowl. He had taken over a joke of a franchise in Tampa in 1996 and by 1999 had them in the NFC championship game in Saint Louis. They were going up against Kurt Warner and the Greatest Show on Turf, which had set a record that season by scoring 526 points. Dungy was a defensive whiz, and the Bucs held the Rams to just eleven points, by far their season low, but Tampa could manage just two field goals in the loss. The next two years, the Bucs lost in the playoffs in Philadelphia without scoring a touchdown.

That made it three straight playoff games the Bucs were unable to get into the end zone. Dungy was fired after the 2001 season. The Bucs were turned down by Bill Parcells as the first choice in their coaching search and eventually sent $8 million, two first-round picks, and two second-round picks to the Oakland Raiders for Jon Gruden, who'd had a falling-out with Al Davis. Gruden inherited a team in Tampa that was stacked on defense but needed a new offensive approach. Gruden supplied it. He took Dungy's players and his quarterback, Brad Johnson, and won the Super Bowl, beating Davis and the Raiders, 48–21. The win was a positive reflection on Dungy's ability to pick the right players, but from a coaching perspective, it accentuated his offensive shortcomings.

Dungy had no trouble finding another job right away. Colts president Bill Polian had fired Jim Mora after a 6–10 season that included two losses to Brady and the Patriots. The Panthers, Polian's former team, had fired George Seifert, who had won two Super Bowls with the 49ers. Dungy was offered jobs in Carolina and Indianapolis. He picked the Colts. He picked Manning. Dungy had met Manning once before on a limousine ride from their hotel in Philadelphia to the Maxwell Club awards dinner after the 1997 season. Dungy had been named coach of the year in the NFL, and Manning was receiving the trophy for college player of the year. Dungy told Manning on the ride over that he wished he could draft him in Tampa, but there was no chance of moving into position to get him. Five years later, they met again, this time in Dungy's office in Indianapolis after he had been hired by the Colts. Dungy was stunned when Manning remembered everything about that night, including the name of Dungy's wife, Lauren, and the name of the hotel they stayed in.

Manning's reputation as a perfectionist, leaning heavily on the overbearing side, was no secret. Dungy's reputation as a coach who couldn't develop an offense was well known as well. Dungy believed he had to win Manning over and convince him he wasn't going to just run the ball and rely on the defense to win games, which had been his formula in Tampa. Dungy had retained Moore as the Colts offensive coordinator. When Dungy played quarterback at the University of Minnesota, Moore was on the offensive staff. "We've got a lot of money spent on offense," Dungy told Manning. "This is an offensive team. We're not going to change what we do."

He was just asking Manning to cut down on the turnovers and let the defense work for him. There was nothing wrong with punting on fourth down and living to see another day. He promised Manning he was going to give him a championship defense, but it would take time. However, in their first year together, Manning and Dungy were humiliated 41–0 by the Jets in the playoffs, making it four playoff games in a row in which Dungy's team had not scored a touchdown. The next two years, they lost to the Patriots, the second time once again not scoring a touchdown. Dungy and Manning didn't lose faith in each other, but the pressure was building on both of them. Manning couldn't win a big game. Dungy literally couldn't get his team across the goal line. Dungy kept preaching to his players what he learned from his mentor Chuck Noll in Pittsburgh. Be consistent. "We don't have to elevate our play to beat the Patriots," Dungy emphasized. "We just have to play our game in the big setting."

As he admitted, "It was a message to Peyton, but that was the way I believe you win."

Dungy and Manning were in this together. Each of them had a reputation he was trying to overcome. Beating the Patriots in the championship game vindicated them. They were winners. The victory over the Bears in the Super Bowl was anticlimactic. Manning had just outdueled Brady. If he couldn't beat Rex Grossman, the worst quarterback ever to start a Super Bowl, that would be trouble.

"It's strange, but I bet Peyton would say the same thing, too—

that game against the Patriots was the satisfying one, that was the big game," Dungy said. "We knew if we were going to get there, it was going to happen that way. We were going to go through New England and finally prove we could beat them in a big game. The way it happened, us scoring all those points in the second half, this defense that supposedly had our number, we finally did the job against them when it counted. That was the biggest game by far. That was our emotional Super Bowl."

Three years earlier, the Patriots defense embarrassed Manning in the AFC championship game by intercepting him four times and sacking him four times. Polian was so incensed at the way the Patriots defensive backs were manhandling his receivers that he helped push through new legislation. It helped that Polian and Dungy were on the competition committee, which presents rule changes for the owners to vote on each spring. Starting with the 2004 season, the officials were told to make illegal contact a point of emphasis. After Manning had brought the Colts to within 21–14 in the 2003 championship game, he missed on 8 of his last 10 throws as New England defenders all but took up residence in the uniforms of the Colts receivers. "We just wanted to pound them and hit them and get those white jerseys dirty in Foxboro," Bruschi said. "That's the mentality we had against those guys."

The Patriots had three penalties assessed by referee Walt Coleman's crew: false start, false start, and delay of game. Not one illegal contact. Not one illegal use of hands. Not one pass interference. Coleman had also been the referee in the tuck-rule game two years earlier.

The new point of emphasis loosened things up in 2004, and Manning broke Dan Marino's touchdown record of forty-eight, which had been set in 1984. Manning threw forty-nine TDs, and his 121.1 quarterback rating was a single-season record, shattering the previous record of 112.8 set by Steve Young in 1994. Manning's previous best was 99.0 in 2003.

The crackdown on the defensive backs, however, didn't help Manning when the Colts returned to Foxboro in the 2004 divisional round. Manning's longest completion was just 18 yards. The Patriots were called for five penalties for 35 yards. There was one defensive holding. The Colts declined an illegal contact and accepted the play instead.

The 2006 AFC championship game was the last time Manning and Brady met in the playoffs before Manning's career in Indianapolis came to an end, but their regular-season rivalry continued. Brady won in the regular season in 2007. Manning won in 2008 against Matt Cassel, with Brady sidelined with a torn ACL. Manning won 35–34 in 2009 when Belichick elected to go for it on a fourth and 2 deep in his own territory with a 34–28 lead rather than punt the ball back to Manning. It backfired and the Patriots lost. The Patriots won in 2010 at home in a 31–28 shootout, the last Brady vs. Manning matchup when it was Patriots vs. Colts. New England held a 31–14 fourth-quarter lead but Manning threw touchdown passes to Blair White with 7:57 and 4:41 remaining to bring the Colts within three points. Then after the Indianapolis defense was able to get Manning the ball on his own 26 with 2:25 left, he drove to the Patriots 24 with 37 seconds on the clock. He went down the right sideline for Pierre Garçon but was intercepted at the 6 by James Sanders.

That would be the last pass Manning would ever throw against the Patriots as a member of the Colts. He missed the next season following neck surgery, and the Patriots beat the Colts 31–24. The rivalry with Brady would resume in 2012 with Manning in a different uniform.

# 7

# GOOD-BYE, INDIANAPOLIS

It didn't end the way it should have for Johnny Unitas in Baltimore, Joe Namath in New York, or Joe Montana in San Francisco. They were the biggest names in the history of their franchises, but they all finished their careers with other teams. It didn't end the way it should have for Peyton Manning in Indianapolis, either.

The problem started in the spring leading into the 2011 season. Manning had neck surgery in May, the NFL players were locked out March 11 by NFL owners in a labor dispute, and Manning was one of the named plaintiffs in an antitrust lawsuit against the league, so the Colts' contact with him was minimal. Team president Bill Polian said he was "barraged" by league counsel and team counsel not to talk to Manning. The league was advising all teams not to speak with any of their players during the shutdown. The lockout lasted 136 days, until July 26.

Polian could not be in touch with his franchise quarterback, even after he had neck surgery. "Dr. [Hank] Feuer, our neurosurgeon, had some contact but not a lot. Our trainer had some contact but not a lot," Polian said. "Only the bare minimum, because the constant refrain was, 'Don't talk to him, don't talk to him, don't talk to him.'"

When the lockout ended, Polian had a lengthy phone conversation with Manning. Manning reported to the training facility the next day and told Polian he was fine and expected to be ready for the start of the season. The Colts then signed Manning, a free agent, to a five-year, $90 million deal.

Polian said Manning told him he didn't need as much money as Brady. "You figure out something that works so we can keep people on the team," Manning said.

"You need to get as much as Brady," Polian said. "There's no reason to do otherwise."

There was a $28 million option inserted for 2012 to protect the Colts in the event Manning's neck was worse than they thought. The minimal contact in the off-season prevented the Colts from getting a precise picture of what was going on, and as a result, Polian left the Colts exposed at backup quarterback. As practices started in early August, Manning was not on the field. There was no indication when he was going to be able to throw.

"Believe me, as training camp went on, we became more and more concerned, because he wasn't coming along the way you wanted him to," Polian said. "He, of course, was becoming more concerned and more irritable about it. I never blame a player who's hurt for feeling that way."

Panic began to set in. Colt owner Jimmy Irsay and Polian had loaded up to make one last run with the core group that had been to the Super Bowl two years earlier, but Curtis Painter was the next man up at quarterback. Painter was best known for coming in for Manning in the third quarter of the fifteenth game of the 2009 season when the Colts had a lead on the Jets. Before the game, Polian had ordered his coach, Jim Caldwell, to take Manning out in the third quarter, because the Colts already had the number-one seed locked up. Polian didn't care that his team was 14–0 and wanted to become the second 16–0 team in NFL history; Brady and the Patriots had done it in 2007. He wanted to protect Manning. Painter came in with a 15–10 lead with 5:36 left in the third period, but on his second series, he was strip-sacked, and the Jets returned the fumble for a touchdown. They desperately needed the game to make the playoffs and went on to win it 29–15. It didn't take a body-language expert to see how upset Manning was after the game.

"No regrets," Polian said.

"Deep down, I wanted to go for the undefeated season, but I didn't stop it, because you can make an argument for either," Irsay said. "I know it gets debated fiercely. I can see why. Personally, I like going for it, and let the chips fall where they may."

The plan was devised to make sure Manning was healthy for the playoffs. He took the Colts to the Super Bowl, but they lost to the Saints.

Considering that there was now so much uncertainty about when Manning would be able to play, Polian was not going to trust the 2011 season to Painter. He convinced Kerry Collins, his number-one pick for the Carolina Panthers in 1995, to come out of retirement on August 24. He signed him to a one-year, $4 million contract. Collins had retired after the 2010 season with the Titans, his fifth NFL team. The Colts were still holding out hope Manning would return in September. At least Collins had a lot of experience, and he had played in a championship game with the Panthers and a Super Bowl with the Giants. He was a leader and gave the Colts a better chance to win than Painter. But he had to take a crash course in the offense to get prepared for the season, which was just fifteen days away.

The Colts played their final preseason game in Cincinnati, and the front office staff gathered the next morning at nine a.m. to cut the roster to fifty-three. "One of the assistant trainers came in and said, 'Dr. Feuer needs you in the back. It's an emergency,'" Polian said. "I excused myself and walked back, and Hank was sitting there. He said, 'I got to show you this MRI.'"

Polian took a look.

"He needs a spinal fusion," Feuer said.

"Wow" was all Polian could think of saying.

Polian stayed for about thirty minutes and walked back into the staff meeting. This was going to be the fourth procedure on Manning's neck. It was the most serious.

"Guys, I've got the worst news possible. Peyton's gone for the year," Polian said.

The May surgery in Chicago was to repair a bulging disc. He subsequently needed follow-up surgery. All during training camp, Chris Polian, Bill's son and right-hand man, stayed in touch with Denver GM John Elway regarding a trade for quarterback Kyle Orton. Now the Colts were desperate. "We were prepared to pay whatever it took, but not a first-round draft choice," Polian said.

Orton stayed put in Denver, started the season, and eventually lost his job to Tim Tebow, who took the Broncos on a magical run to the second round of the playoffs. Manning underwent spinal-fusion surgery in Los Angeles on September 8, and Collins was the starter in the September 11 opener in Houston despite having been on his farm enjoying retirement just two weeks earlier. The Colts lost to the Texans 34–7; Collins was rusty. He was sacked three times and lost two fumbles.

The game ended Manning's streak of consecutive regular-season starts at 208 games. Including the playoffs, he had started 227 consecutive games. Both were the second-longest starting streaks for a quarterback in NFL history, trailing only Brett Favre, who had started 297 consecutive regular-season games, 321 including the playoffs, until missing a game late in his final season in 2010. Manning had started every game of his career, beginning with the first game of his rookie season.

Collins started the second game, a home loss to the Browns.

He suffered a season-ending concussion in the third game against the Steelers in another loss. It was now officially time for the Colts to turn their attention to Stanford quarterback Andrew Luck. The motto of their season became "Suck for Luck." Two years after winning their first fourteen games, the Colts lost their first thirteen. They played the rest of the season with Painter and Dan Orlovsky at quarterback. Painter was 0–8 and Orlovsky was 2–3 after Collins started 0–3.

Polian missed a chance to put himself in a better position to survive Manning's injury by not trusting his instincts in the 2011 draft. He knew it was time to start thinking about a successor to Manning, just as the Packers did with Brett Favre when Aaron Rodgers fell to them in the 2005 draft. Instead, the Colts took Boston College tackle Anthony Costanzo with the twenty-second pick in the first round. "The thing I second guess is, we took Costanzo and not either Andy Dalton or Colin Kaepernick," Polian said. "We might still be there, had we done that. Because if you go 7–9 or 8–8 with one of those guys, even 6–10, you probably survive. That hurts me badly for the coaches and all the other people that got let go largely because we didn't do that in the draft. But we didn't know that Peyton wasn't going to play, believe me. We were as much in the dark as any group has ever been. It was absolutely the perfect storm."

Polian's friends in the league question why he didn't talk to Peyton or his father, Archie, or have a third party call during the lockout to get updates on Manning's status. Polian banged his hand against a table and said, "I can't tell you how strongly it was emphasized to all of us: do not talk to him; you will jeopardize the lockout. It will be a court case, the union will run to court, the lockout will be over, you will ruin the National Football League."

.   .   .

**Manning was such** a dominant personality and such a perfectionist that the organization was often on edge. "Look, he's not a saint. No man is," Irsay said.

His attention to detail could be overwhelming. He made sure all the clocks in the building were set to the same time. "He was so thorough and intense and such a perfectionist, you wanted him to get as comfortable as he could before game time," Irsay said. "He was a thoroughbred. He was wired to do what he does, and his intensity 99 percent of the time was an asset. But even as a rookie, it was kind of like, 'Don't throw your arm out in warm-ups.'"

Polian made a mistake by not placing Manning on season-ending injured reserve after his spinal fusion surgery. It wasn't realistic or in Manning's best interests for him to play in 2011. It also gave him and his teammates false hope that he could get back on the field. Polian knew how much Manning wanted to play. "He played every game as though it were his last game," he said. "I remember telling him during his rookie year, 'Don't play with clenched teeth.'"

By the end of September, it was a lost season in Indianapolis, and Polian could have ended all speculation that Manning would suit up by simply putting him on IR. "We wanted to give him the incentive to come back and it was more psychological than anything else," Polian said. "The doctors said, 'Hey, there is a chance, probably slim, but as long as there is that chance, let's keep him active. It will give him hope that he can come back.' That was the principal reason. The secondary reason is we didn't want to send a message to the team that he's gone for the year and there is no hope."

Manning is so competitive that he was determined to work toward playing again before the end of the season, if only to quiet speculation that his career was over. The atmosphere had changed in the Colts building. They were losing for the first time in forever and Manning was cranky. The losing took its toll on the entire organization.

"It wore down everyone," tight end Dallas Clark said. "We all saw the writing on the wall where, okay, we're oh-and-whatever, we got a lot of big contracts coming up, and if you're running this business, what are you going to do? And you got Andrew Luck coming up, who is the clone of Peyton. We're all aware of the business part of the whole thing. No one was getting along. We all kind of knew we're probably not going to be in this business next year. The reality is, the ride is coming to an end here. We had a heckuva run, and that was pulling at a lot of people."

By late in the year, Manning was pushing to get on the field, but the Colts didn't even know if he could throw the ball to compete at an NFL level. Manning proposed playing only in the red zone in a Thursday night home game against the Texans in the next-to-last game of the season. Once the Colts moved inside the Texans 20, Manning would come in and try to finish off the drive. Back in September, two days before it was determined he needed the spinal fusion surgery, Manning had proposed the same setup.

That arrangement would have been as insane as Dallas coach Tom Landry alternating Craig Morton and Roger Staubach in the Cowboys game in Chicago in 1971 or Michigan coach Lloyd Carr starting Tom Brady in 1999, playing Drew Henson in the second quarter, then deciding at halftime who would start the third quarter. At least then it was Landry and Carr calling the shots. Caldwell was just a figurehead coach taking his orders from Polian. Manning had everybody walking on eggshells. He was an intimidating presence. He had become accustomed to getting his way, and quite frankly, that was often a good thing. If Peyton wanted it, Peyton got it. But he was not a doctor and he couldn't clear himself to play. The first step was proving he could throw.

It was the understanding in the front office that Manning

would go out after practice and throw for a little bit in front of the coaches and Polian. Nothing too complicated, nothing very organized. He was supposed to bring a receiver or two to run short routes. But it turned out to be as scripted as some of the predraft workouts. Caldwell, offensive coordinator Ron Turner, and quarterbacks coach Clyde Christensen were all there. Manning recruited running back Joseph Addai and Clark and others to catch passes. Christensen called the plays. Manning made thirty throws. It was run at game tempo, a seven-on-seven-type drill, only without defenders. Manning maxed out at 20 yards, the ball wobbled, and he was tired at the end. Polian was furious the audition took place. He had no idea it was going to be such a formal affair.

"Obviously, by that time, everything has pretty much hit the fan," Clark said. "If us running routes is going to help Peyton with his rehab, then darn it, I'm going to run routes for him. He's my quarterback. It's a no-brainer. But then you got the politics behind all of it. You hear this person is not happy. As a player, well, if I can help him with his rehab, I'm going to. At the end of the day, isn't that what we all want? Everybody getting better and getting healthy? I don't think anyone was really thinking clearly at that time. It was ugly. The bottom line is, it's the first time facing an injury that stopped Peyton from playing."

This had become Manning's show. It was perceived that Manning was now coach, general manager, and franchise quarterback, and with Irsay away at a league meeting when the audition took place, he was basically the owner, too. Polian's legacy in Indianapolis was drafting Manning and having the success of going to two Super Bowls, being in the playoffs almost every year, and having an incredible seven-season streak from 2003 to 2009 when the Colts won at least twelve regular-season games. He didn't want to confront Manning, especially if it became public.

Manning was not ready to play. It was not worth the risk. The

Colts needed to just say no. The episode caused friction in the organization. Polian denies he was upset with Manning for scripting a workout more involved than he had been led to expect. But the feeling around the Colts at the time was that he felt betrayed by his quarterback. "I wasn't ticked at him," Polian insisted. "I was ticked at the medical people for not letting me know."

Irsay was upset that Polian had not taken control. Manning was upset, knowing his days with the Colts were coming to an end. He did not play in the Houston game. He never got on the field that season. He never would again for the Colts.

**Polian, the Colts** vice chairman; his son Chris, the general manager; Caldwell, the head coach; and his coaching staff were fired once the season ended. Irsay hired Ryan Grigson from the Eagles in early January as the new general manager, and Grigson hired Ravens defensive coordinator Chuck Pagano as the new head coach two weeks later. By the time the football world descended upon Indianapolis for Super Bowl XLVI between the New York Giants and New England Patriots, Irsay had his new management team in place. If Manning had not had four neck procedures in a two-year period, the Colts possibly could have been the first team to play the Super Bowl on their home field. But even before Manning's neck became a major issue, there were signs that the Colts were taking a step backward. They had lost at home in the wild-card round to the New York Jets in 2010, one year after beating Rex Ryan's team at home in the AFC championship game to advance to Manning's second Super Bowl.

**Manning was the** unofficial Super Bowl ambassador. He took care of many of the logistical concerns for his brother Eli, who was playing the game in Peyton's home stadium. On the other side was Tom Brady, Peyton Manning's good friend and most intense rival. Manning did not have split loyalties. Four years earlier, he'd been watching from a private box at University of Phoenix Stadium in Glendale, Arizona, as Eli drove the Giants down the field to beat Brady and the Patriots in Super Bowl XLII. Peyton stood clapping for a long time when Eli threw the winning touchdown pass to Plaxico Burress with thirty-five seconds remaining to end New England's undefeated season. He might have been the most excited person in the stadium. It was a touching scene after the game when Peyton and Eli stood by Eli's locker and dissected the throws that won the game. Peyton was proud of the little brother he used to pick on.

Just two days before the Giants-Patriots rematch, ESPN reported that Peyton Manning had been medically cleared to play by two doctors, including Robert Watkins, the surgeon who'd performed the spinal fusion operation. It was now an issue of the nerves regenerating in his right arm to allow him to get the necessary velocity on his throws.

Archie Manning had gone through his own doubts whether the fourth surgery had ended Peyton's career, but "I never doubted Peyton in his will," he said.

On a visit to the home where he grew up in New Orleans, Manning sat at the foot of Archie and Olivia's bed, just as he had done during the college recruiting process. Instead of being seventeen years old, he was thirty-five. "I knew he wasn't going to go against a neurosurgeon who said, 'Peyton, you don't need to be out on a football field,'" Archie said. "I knew he wasn't going to test that."

He looked his parents in the eye. They had been with him every step of the way in his football career. His wife, Ashley, had given birth to twins in May 2011, giving Peyton a new perspective. "I'm going to do what the doctors tell me to do, so take that out of your worries. But in the meantime, I'm going to try as hard as I can to get well and play," Peyton said.

Archie sometimes thought, *After four neck surgeries, Peyton, this isn't worth it.*

The previous June, during the lockout and after one of his neck surgeries, Manning went to Denver to work out at the facilities of the Colorado Rockies. His college buddy Todd Helton was the Rockies first baseman. The plan was for Manning to throw short passes to Helton, but the football hit the ground before it had even traveled 10 yards. Helton thought Manning was joking. He was not. This was serious.

Once he was cleared by his doctors, around the time of the Super Bowl, Manning put the football part of his rehabilitation in the hands of David Cutcliffe, his offensive coordinator at Tennessee, Eli's head coach at Ole Miss, and now the head coach at Duke. Manning became a regular in Durham, North Carolina. Gradually, the arm strength was coming back, and he was starting to get some zip on the ball. He never had an Elway fastball, and he would never throw the way he did before the neck surgeries, but with his football smarts, he knew there were other ways to get it done.

It just wasn't going to be in Indianapolis.

**Jimmy Irsay boarded** his private Gulfstream jet in Tampa for the quick ride across the peninsula to Miami–Opa Locka Executive Airport. Peyton Manning's limousine driver took him right onto the tarmac; he got out of the car and walked toward Irsay's airplane. The owner of the Indianapolis Colts was standing at the top of the steps to greet him.

It was just the two of them and the pilot and the flight attendant on March 6, 2012, for the two-and-a-half-hour flight to

Indianapolis. Manning had missed the entire 2011 season but still collected the $26.4 million due on his contract. He stayed around the team for much of the year, but was helpless to prevent the Colts' worst season since 1991.

Even before the flight, they both knew Irsay had no choice. He had to cut Manning. Two days after they stepped on the plane, the Colts either had to pick up Manning's $28 million option for 2012, triggering his $7.4 million base salary, or they had to release the most important and popular player in the history of the franchise since Johnny Unitas and by far the most popular player since the team moved to Indianapolis in 1984. Did it make sense to pay $35.4 million to a quarterback who was going to be blowing out thirty-six candles on his birthday cake in two weeks and coming off major neck surgery at a time when Irsay was in rebuilding mode with major salary-cap problems but also with Andrew Luck, the newer and healthier version of Manning, in the draft? The answer had been provided in Jacksonville more than two months earlier with 2:24 remaining in the final game of the season. Jaguars running back Maurice Jones-Drew stretched out and picked up 5 yards on a third and 4 to clinch the 19–13 victory for Jacksonville. The loss was the Colts' fourteenth in sixteen games, and they earned the first pick in the draft in a tiebreaker over the Rams. It ended the Manning Era. The Colts had pulled off their mission statement: Suck for Luck.

"I walked out of the locker room in Jacksonville and tears were rolling down my face," Irsay said. "No one wants to be the person to say the party's over. It sucks."

Luck was Manning with a stronger arm and greater mobility. He was smart, obsessive about preparation, had perfect mechanics, never made anybody worry about post-midnight calls from the police, and was a great leader who held teammates accountable. The Colts had sure sucked enough for Luck, and it was just their luck that after making the playoffs nine years in a row and in eleven of the thirteen years Manning was healthy, the best quarterback prospect since Manning was available for them in the draft. It was like 1998, when the Colts had the first pick by going 3–13 and Manning, the best QB prospect since Elway in '83, was in the draft. The Colts didn't want to "Suck for RG3." They never considered Robert Griffin III but went all-in on Luck. He took them to the playoffs three times in his first three years, including an AFC championship–game loss to Tom Brady after the 2014 season, the Deflategate game.

In his heart, Irsay didn't want to let Manning go. He's an emotional man and has had his own off-the-field personal issues dealing with painkillers that eventually led to his getting arrested for driving while intoxicated. He had a strong bond with Manning and wished it could end differently. He never wanted Manning to play for another team. Lucas Oil Stadium opened in 2008 next to the old RCA Dome, where the Colts used to play; it was "the house that Peyton built." The $450 million retractable-roof facility was funded by a public-private partnership: Irsay put in $100 million, and public money accounted for the rest. The emergence of the Colts brand in Indianapolis once Manning arrived was a major reason the stadium was built, and with it, Indianapolis was awarded Super Bowl XLVI, which brought 116,000 visitors to the city and $361 million to the local economy. Irsay was a good owner. His father, Robert, was not. He traded away the rights to Elway in 1983 and the next year moved the Colts from Baltimore to Indianapolis in the middle of the night, robbing the city of a team that it loved so much.

"'The house that Peyton built' is appropriate. It sounds good, and it's worthy," Irsay said. "He's that sort of figure. He had that kind of influence and presence. He just meant so much to me, the team, city, and state. He's just beloved. I can't say enough about what he means to the franchise and to me."

Manning, who has an off-season home in Miami, boarded the

plane for the conversation he and Irsay didn't want to have but knew was inevitable. The flight attendant remained in the front of the plane with the pilot. No food was served. This was a serious business meeting. Irsay asked Manning to look at it from his perspective. Irsay then looked at it from Manning's perspective. The Colts were going to draft Luck. In the days before the salary cap, it would have been just a matter of whether Irsay wanted to spend the cash on Manning and then also pay big money to Luck to learn sitting behind Manning for a year or two. That was the protocol, but no longer. It just couldn't work. Quarterbacks taken first overall are expected to start from the first game of their rookie year and not be tutored by a veteran making over $30 million. Finances virtually dictate it works that way.

"You could have physically and literally had Andrew and Peyton on the same team, but what you would have done to both players would have been a catastrophe," Irsay said. "It would have been so bad for the National Football League, so bad for Andrew Luck, so bad for Peyton Manning. Peyton would have gone on with a team that was with the likes of the replacement team in 1987 and would have been 2–6 and they would be calling for Andrew Luck to come in. I love history, and I love one guy staying with one team and retiring with one team. Circumstances came that made that impossible."

The salary cap changed the NFL world. If Irsay kept Manning, he wouldn't be able to construct a team around him. The new collective bargaining agreement that followed the 2011 lockout established a rookie wage scale. Luck's deal would come in at $22 million over four years. Getting Manning off the books would allow Irsay to replenish the roster for Luck.

Still, this was Peyton Manning. You can't cut Peyton Manning. But you have to draft Andrew Luck. Manning didn't want to retire. Luck didn't want to sit on the bench. This was not going to be pretty.

You can't have them both, and Manning was not about to take a big pay cut. There was also the health factor—no guarantee Manning would come back at 100 percent or even close. The long incision on the back of his neck was a chilling reminder of what he had endured. He still had a long way to go in his rehabilitation to build back his arm strength.

Polian said if he hadn't been fired, his plan was to keep Manning and draft Luck, clearly not what Irsay had in mind. "The money was not an issue," Polian said. "Keep the guy in the wings. The guy in Green Bay, Aaron Rodgers, stayed in the wings for three years. What better way to have success for the long term than to have Peyton and Andrew Luck ready to succeed him."

Tony Dungy had been gone from the Colts for three years, but if he had still been there, he would have backed Polian's plan. "I thought that is what they were going to do," he said. "You have to draft Andrew Luck. I don't think Peyton would have resisted that, and it would have been the best thing for the franchise in the long run. That's what I would have recommended."

The disconnect between Irsay and Polian on so many issues about Manning led to Polian's getting fired. "It was the most sensitive time of my professional career," Irsay said. "History needs to be recorded."

As the private plane began making its way from Miami to Indianapolis, Irsay updated Manning on where the Colts doctors stood. Irsay revealed confidential salary-cap information to Manning to illustrate the bind the Colts were in. If Manning was paid his $28 million bonus, he could be playing in front of an offensive line of minimum-salary free agents. "There is no way you can construct a fucking football team with what was left," Irsay said. "Absolutely, positively, no way. It was a Rubik's Cube that couldn't be solved. He knew it. I knew it."

Manning and Irsay looked each other in the eye at thirty thousand feet. Manning would never ask Irsay not to draft Luck. He

knew the Colts had to do it. Irsay talks about the "horseshoes"—
that's how he affectionately refers to his franchise—and how he
was the caretaker of the horseshoes. He had to make the right
football and business decision.

"We just had a heart-to-heart," Irsay said. "We concluded in
finality, face-to-face, man-to-man, it wasn't solvable. The best interest of the franchise and for Peyton was to part ways, very unfortunately, because neither of us wanted it. Peyton said it: It wasn't
Jim's decision. It wasn't my decision. It was circumstances."

The plane carrying Manning and Irsay was somewhere over
Kentucky when they conceded that parting was unavoidable.
Manning's contract would be terminated, and he would immediately become a free agent. Tears came to Irsay's eyes "when we
realized we were starting to close the book," he said. "There was a
pause. We both knew we were upon a moment."

Irsay never said to Manning, "I'm letting you go." He couldn't
get the words out of his mouth. It was understood. Five weeks
earlier, the city of Indianapolis was the center of the NFL universe
with Super Bowl XLVI in town. Now that word had spread that
Irsay and Manning were on their way back home for a much less
joyous occasion, all the attention would be on Indianapolis once
again. As the private jet began its descent, they agreed to hold a
news conference the next day. Irsay's plane pulled into its hangar
and was met by a large media contingent. Irsay recalled that Peyton said, "All right, well, maybe I should just say a quick blurb, or
you should."

They were already in Irsay's car. He had offered to drive
Manning home. They opened the window and told the report-
ers, "We'll talk to you tomorrow." Irsay and Manning lived five
minutes apart in Carmel, twenty-three miles outside Indianapolis.
Irsay pulled into Manning's driveway. They both got out of the car.
They hugged in the dark. They said good night and went about
preparing remarks for the press conference.

It had been building to this moment for months. Irsay and Manning had talked about the future when Irsay hosted a party at the Super Bowl. They had a good relationship, going back to the first meeting at the Surf Club at Bal Harbour, Florida, a few weeks before the draft in 1998. On the morning of the farewell press conference, they first met in Irsay's office. "It was very intense," Irsay said. "This was as sensitive as it can get. Peyton casts such a mythic figure. I know I'm no match for that figure, but I have to do my job. So, I mean, it's hard. Peyton was really good. He stood true to really what we both knew. I think, in the end, he will always be reaching for that extra yard and that first down, and in the end, I'm the one who has to turn the lights off in the stadium."

Irsay was behind the podium with Manning to his right as the press conference ended an incredible era in Colts history. "Well, we're here to announce the conclusion of Peyton's playing career with the Colts," Irsay said. "We're here very much as well to honor all the incredible memories and incredible things that he's done for the franchise, for the city, for the state."

Irsay sat down and Manning pulled a piece of paper from his suit pocket. He had jotted down some notes. "I've been a Colt for almost all my adult life," he said. "But I guess in life and in sports, we all know that nothing lasts forever. Times change, circumstances change, and that's the reality of playing in the NFL."

The rivalry with Brady, Colts vs. Patriots, was over. Just twelve days later, a new phase began when Manning signed with the Denver Broncos. Manning vs. Brady would pick up where it had left off.

**The parting with** the Colts in early March allowed Manning to listen to recruiting pitches and offers for the first time since he was a high school senior. This time, the recruiting bothered him. It didn't feel right. But this is life in the NFL. Namath played for the

Rams. Montana finished with the Chiefs. Emmitt Smith spent two years with the Cardinals. Jerry Rice bounced from the Raiders to the Seahawks to training camp with the Broncos before he was willing to admit that his time to call it quits had come. Manning never had to take another snap to be considered a top-five quarterback of all time, but as long as he had the blessing of his doctors, he didn't want his career to end on the sidelines.

Elway, the Broncos general manager, took the early lead in the Manning sweepstakes. He put himself in Manning's situation and knew how he would want to be recruited. He went to the laid-back approach. "If I have somebody selling that hard, they are trying to hide something," Elway said. "That's why I said we're going to show what we are, what we are about, what we have to offer, and then let him go make his own decision. Knowing him and the type of guy he is, he's not going to want to get harassed or pushed or sold."

Elway had been around Manning in Hawaii and Florida, playing golf with Brady and Dan Marino. That was an impressive football foursome. When Manning was ready to embark on his recruiting trip, Elway and Denver coach John Fox were in Stillwater, Oklahoma, scouting Oklahoma State quarterback Brandon Weeden. Elway sent the private plane that took them to Stillwater on to Miami to pick up Manning and then stop back in Stillwater to pick up Elway and Fox and other Broncos staff and return to Denver. Too many people were on the plane for Elway to start talking business with Manning during the flight.

Elway waited for the private dinner he set up in the Palmer Room at the swank Cherry Hills Country Club in Englewood outside Denver to outline why the Broncos were the right fit for him. Fox also had a seat at the table. He's easygoing, a fun guy to be around, and he had pulled off a football miracle by making the playoffs and winning a playoff game the year before with Tim

Tebow. Elway invited former safety John Lynch, who had played the final four years of his career with the Broncos and was tight with Manning. They had become close friends at the Pro Bowl.

Early in the process, Manning called Seattle coach Pete Carroll to express interest in playing for the Seahawks. Carroll never heard back from Manning to set up a visit, but with the football world aware that Manning was now in Denver, Carroll and Seahawks general manager John Schneider arrived unannounced at an airport in Englewood. Word got back to Manning that Carroll and Schneider were in town and would like to meet him on their private plane or accompany him on his next flight, to Phoenix, where he was going to confer with the Cardinals. Manning declined the invitation and Carroll and Schneider left town without seeing him. Six weeks later, the Seahawks drafted Wisconsin quarterback Russell Wilson in the third round, seventy-four spots after the Colts selected Luck. In his second season, Wilson's Seahawks beat Manning's Broncos 43–8 in Super Bowl XLVIII at MetLife Stadium in East Rutherford, New Jersey. In his third season, Wilson lost to Brady and the Patriots 28–24 in Super Bowl XLIX in Glendale.

Manning met with the Cardinals; then as a favor to Marino, his idol, he met with the Dolphins in Indianapolis. He later worked out for the 49ers and Broncos at Duke and met with the Titans and worked out for them in Tennessee. The Jets made one of the first calls to Manning, but he had no desire to play in the same city as Eli. The Jets had had their best chance in 1997, but Bill Parcells wouldn't tell Manning he'd take him if he skipped his senior year at Tennessee. Playing in New York would have been a challenge for Manning, anyway. He reads everything and is sensitive to criticism. He would not have enjoyed the back pages of the New York tabloids.

There were three finalists for Manning: Denver, Tennessee, and San Francisco.

"I really thought it was going to come down to us and Tennessee," Elway said. "Obviously, with the connections he had in Tennessee, I was a little leery of those."

Manning called Elway on a Monday morning to reveal that he had picked Denver. Fox started dancing around the office after Elway gave him the thumbs-up.

Manning's decision to sign with the Broncos kept his rivalry with Brady alive. As long as the Broncos finished first in the AFC West and the Patriots finished first in the AFC East, they were guaranteed to play each other in the years when the AFC East was not scheduled to play the AFC West. Brady vs. Manning would still be an annual event. They hadn't played against each other in 2011 because Manning was injured. They hadn't met in the playoffs since the 2006 AFC championship game.

The first matchup between Brady and Manning's Broncos was in Foxboro, a house of horrors for Manning when he played for the Colts. The game was in early October on a nice 54-degree fall day in New England. Brady threw a touchdown pass to Wes Welker late in the first quarter, and Manning matched that with a 1-yard throw to Joel Dreessen in the first minute of the second quarter. The Patriots then scored 24 consecutive points before Manning made the final score respectable with touchdown passes late in the third quarter and midway through the fourth.

The 31–21 victory raised Brady's lifetime lead over Manning to 9–4. They appeared headed for a showdown in the AFC championship game when the Broncos finished the 2012 season with the number-one seed and the Patriots were number two. But the Ravens took care of both Manning and Brady in the playoffs. Fox called five consecutive runs by Ronnie Hillman, without letting Manning throw the ball once, when the Broncos were trying to eat up the clock and protect a 35–28 lead in the closing minutes. Denver had to punt the ball to the Ravens. Incredibly, the Ravens tied the game on a 70-yard prayer from Joe Flacco to Jacoby Jones with thirty-one seconds remaining.

After a touchback on the kickoff, the Broncos took over at their 20 with two time-outs and still thirty-one seconds on the clock. How many times in his career had Manning directed last-minute drives to win games? All Denver needed was a field goal. Fox had Manning take a knee instead, sending the game into overtime. Manning was then picked off at his own 45-yard line with fifty-one seconds left in the first overtime, setting up Justin Tucker's 47-yard field goal at 1:42 in the second extra period.

It was a devastating loss, one of the toughest of Manning's career. It was just 13 degrees with a wind chill of 2, and Manning looked uncomfortable in the second half. The focus after the game was on the Broncos' blown coverage on Jones's catch rather than Manning's interception or Fox's lack of faith in Manning's ability to pick up a first down at the end of regulation or win it after Baltimore's shocking touchdown.

"When you take a year off from football, you come back for all the enjoyable moments," Manning told the *Denver Post* outside the Broncos locker room after the game. "When you're not playing, you miss out on all the highs, but you also miss these disappointments. But I would rather be in the arena to be excited or be disappointed than not have a chance at all. That's football. That's why everybody plays it. You have to be able to take the good with the bad."

If misery loves company, then Manning could commiserate with Brady the next week. The Patriots suddenly were hosting the AFC title game against the Ravens instead of going to Denver. Not that it did them any good. For the second time in four years, Baltimore went into New England in January and eliminated the Patriots.

Brady vs. Manning in the playoffs would have to wait another year.

They met twice in the 2013 season as Manning was on his way to setting an NFL record with fifty-five touchdown passes. The first meeting was a brutally cold Sunday night in New England on Thanksgiving weekend. The temperature was 22 degrees with a wind chill of 6. The wind was swirling at 22 miles per hour. This was Brady weather.

It turned out to be a strange game. The Broncos went up 7–0 five minutes in when Wesley Woodyard forced a fumble by Patriots running back Stevan Ridley, which linebacker Von Miller scooped up and returned 60 yards for a touchdown. On the Patriots' next series, Miller forced a fumble by Brady, which defensive tackle Terrance "Pot Roast" Knighton picked up and ran 13 yards to the New England 10. Knowshon Moreno ran for 8 yards and then scored from the 2. It was 14–0 and Manning had nothing to do with either touchdown. That was not a good sign for the Patriots. It was 17–0 after one quarter and 24–0 at the half after Manning completed a 10-yard touchdown pass to Jacob Tamme.

Brady came out in the second half and threw three touchdown passes; New England scored 31 straight points to take a 31–24 lead with 7:37 left. The Broncos sent the game into overtime when Manning threw an 11-yard touchdown to Demaryius Thomas with 3:06 remaining.

Four years earlier, Belichick had made the strangest decision of his career when he elected to go for it on fourth and 2 from his own 28 with 2:08 left while holding a 34–28 lead in Indianapolis, rather than give the ball back to Manning. He thought there was a better chance of converting the first down than of stopping Manning, who had led two 79-yard touchdown drives in the fourth quarter.

He called a time-out before fourth down and kept Brady and the offense on the field. It blew up in Belichick's face when Brady's completion to Kevin Faulk was just short of a first down. Manning needed only four plays to get the Colts into the end zone for the winning touchdown on an easy 1-yarder to Reggie Wayne.

On this cold and windy night in New England, Belichick elected to put the ball in Manning's hands to start overtime. He took the wind. The NFL had changed the overtime rules for the playoffs in 2010 and then for the regular season in 2012. No longer could a team win the toss, move down the field, and kick a field goal to win it. The only way the game could end without both teams having at least one possession was if the receiving team in overtime returned the kickoff for a touchdown or moved down the field for a touchdown.

Detroit Lions coach Marty Mornhinweg had been ridiculed when he elected to kick off and take the wind in overtime in a game in Chicago in 2002. The Bears kicked a field goal on their first possession, and the Lions never touched the ball. Mornhin-weg was fired after the season with a 5–27 record in two years.

Belichick, whose lack of confidence in his defense had cost the Patriots the game in 2009, this time trusted his defensive players not to give up a touchdown to Manning that would end the game on the first possession. They rewarded his faith. Manning had the ball twice in overtime: he moved the Broncos to their own 42 and the New England 42 before punting. The first two times Brady had it, he was able to get the ball only to the Patriots 37 and then the Patriots 43. After the second series stalled, New England punted, Broncos returner Tony Carter muffed the catch, and Nate Ebner recovered for the Patriots at the Denver 13.

Brady did two kneel-downs to position the ball in the middle of the field, and the game reached the two-minute warning. Then Stephen Gostkowski ended it with a 31-yard field goal. It was the thirty-eighth game of Brady's career with at least three touchdowns and no interceptions. He was second to Manning, who had forty-two.

This was just the prelude to the number-two Patriots playing at the number-one Broncos in the conference title game. Manning's offense had broken the NFL record for points set by Brady and the Patriots in their undefeated season of 2007. After Brady broke Manning's TD record by one when he threw fifty in '07, Manning took the record back and put it so far out of reach that he dared Brady to try to top it. In the season opener, Manning threw seven touchdowns against the Super Bowl champion Ravens, tying the NFL record. That year, 2013, he threw for a record 5,477 yards, along with his Ruthian fifty-five TD passes.

The Patriots overwhelmed the Colts in the divisional round, and the Broncos struggled but survived against San Diego. When he was asked after the game if an off-season exam on his neck was weighing on his mind, Manning got laughs when he said, "What's weighing on my mind is how soon I can get a Bud Light in my mouth after this win. Priority number one."

On a gorgeous day in Denver in the championship game, there was no stopping Manning. He picked apart Belichick's defense for 400 yards and two touchdowns. Brady was shorthanded without tight end Rob Gronkowski, who had suffered a torn ACL in December, so he had no firepower to keep up with Manning. After he missed Julian Edelman on what would have been a 56-yard touchdown late in the first quarter, the Patriots had nothing going. Brady threw for 277 yards and one touchdown, but New England never threatened to win the game. This Brady-Manning showdown was a dud. Denver led 23–3 early in the fourth quarter on the way to a 26–16 victory.

Manning stood on the podium at midfield as the confetti landed on his head in the celebration after the game. "Empire State of Mind," an acknowledgment that the Super Bowl in two weeks would be in the New York area, blasted out of Mile High Stadium's sound system. It had been seven years and four neck surgeries between confetti showers for Manning, and it felt very nice.

"You realize you still want to win one more game," he said. "Being in my sixteenth season, going to my third Super Bowl, I know how hard it is to get there. It is extremely difficult."

It's too bad the season couldn't end right then. The Broncos never had a chance against Seattle. Center Manny Ramirez's first snap went flying over Manning's right shoulder as he walked toward the line of scrimmage out of the shotgun shouting instructions to his teammates over the loud pro-Seattle crowd. Seattle recovered for a safety just twelve seconds into the game, the quickest score in Super Bowl history, and the 43–8 rout was on. Manning threw two interceptions, the first one setting up Seattle's first touchdown to make it 15–0, and the second returned 69 yards for a touchdown by Super Bowl MVP Malcolm Smith. That return gave Seattle a 22–0 lead in the second quarter. The Broncos played the game in slow motion; the Seahawks were playing at warp speed. Manning was under constant pressure and was throwing a lot of ducks. He had happy feet. The Seattle defense seemed insulted anytime the Broncos ran a play that picked up yardage. Manning did complete a Super Bowl record 34 passes, but it was an empty number.

It wasn't the most lopsided loss of Manning's playoff career. Back in 2002, his fifth year in the NFL, the Colts lost to the Jets 41–0. He was gracious after that game, even asking if a reporter needed more time with him as he walked to the team bus that was waiting for him in the parking lot.

The Super Bowl showed his testy side. The NFL sets up a huge interview room for each Super Bowl team, and Manning was sitting at his podium about ten minutes into his press conference when a reporter for the *New York Daily News* asked him if he was embarrassed. Manning didn't appreciate the question, even though that's the description many of his teammates had already used.

"It's not embarrassing at all," he snapped. "I never use that word. There is a lot of professional football players in that locker room who put a lot of hard work and effort into it, to being here and play in that game. The word *embarrassing* is an insulting word, to tell you the truth."

Manning-Brady XVI, the sweet sixteen of their incredible rivalry, was in Foxboro in 2014 for the third straight time in the regular season. Manning threw for 438 yards with two touchdowns and two interceptions but had a harsh analysis of how he played in the 43–21 loss.

He said he told somebody right after the game that he stunk.

"I never heard you say you stink before," the friend said.

"I don't usually stink, but I stunk today," Manning said.

On a cold and windy day, Manning and Brady combined to throw 110 passes. Manning was 34 of 57. Brady was 33 of 53 for 333 yards with four touchdowns and an interception. It was New England's fifth straight victory after getting ambushed in Kansas City in the fourth game of the year, when for the first time in his career, critics were suggesting Brady was done. It was just noise, as the Patriots like to call outside distractions. "We're on to Cincinnati," Belichick said repeatedly in the days after the loss to the Chiefs, referring to the Patriots' next game.

The victory over Manning eventually earned the Patriots home-field advantage in the AFC playoffs.

"It's a team sport," Brady said after beating the Broncos. "At the end of the day, one person can't do it alone. I've been part of some great teams. I've been very privileged to play with great players and teammates that really work their butts off for each other. That's why you string together five wins in a row like we've done."

Brady-Manning XVII seemed inevitable as the playoffs approached. But Manning suffered a quad injury in Denver's fourteenth game, in San Diego, which clearly compromised his ability to move around in the pocket. Worse, his decreased leg strength made it difficult for him to get much on his throws.

He played poorly in a 24–13 loss at home to the Colts in the divisional round of the playoffs. After the game, Manning was noncommittal about returning for his eighteenth season in 2015, but after reporting to Elway in a meeting one month after the season that he was mentally and physically ready to play, he accepted a $4 million pay cut from his $19 million salary in early March and then passed a team physical to officially signal that he was coming back.

Brady and the Patriots overcame two 14-point deficits to the Ravens in the divisional round and then survived Flacco's Hail Mary attempt into the end zone to eliminate Baltimore 35–31. New England overwhelmed the Colts in the AFC championship game 45–7 and then beat the Seahawks in the Super Bowl 28–24, defeating the two teams that had defeated Manning and the Broncos in the postseason the last two seasons.

Manning's decision to pick the Broncos worked. Elway made it his mission to surround him with enough good players to give him a chance to get that second Super Bowl victory. It was a career-altering decision not only for Manning but for the coaches, executives, and teams he had rejected in March 2012.

After the 2012 season, the Jets fired general manager Mike Tannenbaum, who gave quarterback Mark Sanchez a lucrative contract extension as a make-up call for courting Manning. Rex Ryan was fired as coach two years later. The Cardinals fired coach Ken Whisenhunt and general manager Rod Graves after the 2012 season; the Titans did the same to coach Mike Munchak and senior executive vice president and chief operating officer Mike Reinfeldt. Dolphins GM Jeff Ireland was fired after the 2013 season, and 49ers coach Jim Harbaugh was pushed out after the 2014 season.

Elway and Fox had a falling-out after the 2014 season, Manning's third in Denver. The Broncos had underachieved, and Elway made Fox just another casualty of the Manning sweepstakes.

# 8

# DREW, MEET WALLY

The New York Yankees were struggling in early June of 1925 when first baseman Wally Pipp reported for work at Yankee Stadium for a game against the Washington Senators with a severe headache.

The Yankees were just 15–26, and Pipp, who had knocked in 110 runs the previous season, had not been productive at the plate in his eleventh season with the Bronx Bombers. Miller Huggins, the Yankees manager, was looking to shake up the lineup to get the team untracked. The way the story goes, the Yankees trainers gave Pipp two aspirin on June 2, and Huggins gave him a seat on the bench. "Wally, take the day off," Huggins said. "We'll try that kid Gehrig at first today and get you back in there tomorrow."

Pipp never started another game for the Yankees. He was beaned in batting practice one month later, was hospitalized for seven days, and wasn't used much the rest of the season. He was playing in Cincinnati the next year. Lou Gehrig became known as the Iron Horse. He had pinch-hit the previous day for short-stop Pee-Wee Wanninger and then went 3 for 5 starting for Pipp. Huggins decided to keep the kid in the lineup, and by the time

Gehrig benched himself on May 2, 1939, he had played in a record 2,130 consecutive games.

**The story of** Wally Pipp is why so many of today's players in all sports are reluctant to come out of the lineup when they are banged up or even just to take a day off so they can catch their breath. They don't want to be "Wally-Pipped," the most famous victim of the next-man-up approach.

Drew Bledsoe was Wally-Pipped by Tom Brady. Bledsoe is the Wally Pipp of the NFL.

"I had a little better career than Wally," Bledsoe said.

Pipp was no slouch, though. He played in three World Series for the Yankees and in his career had 90 home runs and 1,004 RBI. He twice led the American League in home runs and led in RBI the season before he lost his job in New York. Gehrig went on to be the greatest first baseman in baseball history, and Pipp supposedly said, "I took the two most expensive aspirin in history."

Drew Bledsoe played fourteen years in the NFL after Bill Parcells picked him over Rick Mirer with the first overall selection in the 1993 draft. He signed a six-year, $14.4 million contract that was replaced two years later by a seven-year, $42 million contract that included a record $11.5 million signing bonus. His parents were both schoolteachers, and Bledsoe found it incomprehensible that "in my first year playing football, I made two hundred years' worth of my dad's salary."

He loved telling the story of calling the automated number for his bank to hear his account balance. "My first signing bonus check went to the same bank account I had all the way through college," he said. "It had the computer voice, and all the way through college I would dial it up and it would say, 'Your balance is negative $8.32.' Then I called it up right after I signed and the same voice said, 'Your balance is $1.3 million.' I thought it was really funny. It was unbelievable. Then my brother called it up. He couldn't believe it either."

Bledsoe threw 251 touchdowns in his career, started in a Super Bowl loss to the Packers, was a backup to Brady in a Super Bowl victory over the Rams, and built a nice reputation in New England for being active in charitable affairs. In 2011, he was voted into the Patriots Hall of Fame. He played nine years with the Patriots, three with the Bills, then reunited with Parcells with the Cowboys for two years. Parcells benched him for Tony Romo at halftime of the sixth game of the 2006 season, and Bledsoe never got back on the field. He retired at the end of the season. He started off his career as though he was going to be the next Dan Marino and ended up losing his job to a sixth-round draft choice in New England and an undrafted free agent in Dallas.

Of course, Bledsoe didn't get Wally-Pipped because of a headache. It was because of the sheared blood vessel from a vicious hit by Jets linebacker Mo Lewis in the second game of the 2001 season, from which he nearly died in the ambulance on the way to the hospital. That gave Brady his chance to start the next game, and other than the fifteen games he missed in 2008 after tearing his ACL in the season opener, he started every game through the 2014 season, including six Super Bowls, a record for a quarterback.

The Patriots had lost their first two games in 2001 with Bledsoe starting, and the feeling in the Patriots organization was that Bill Belichick was getting antsy to make a quarterback change even before Bledsoe was injured. He strongly considered opening the season with Brady but eventually backed off. Bledsoe was a proud player and was not short on self-esteem, so he believes had he not been injured, he would have retained his job as the Patriots franchise quarterback, and Brady would have had a much more difficult path to being known as one of the all-time greats.

"I think Tom would have certainly played a long time in the NFL and would have eventually worked his way into a starting job, but it may not have been with the Patriots, is the honest answer," Bledsoe said. "He demonstrated through two preseasons and through practice that he could play the game. Had I not gotten hurt, he probably would have worked his way into a starting job somewhere. As everybody knows, if you're a starting quarterback for the wrong organization, it doesn't matter what you do. The way it worked, he ended up being the starter for a great organization, one of the all-time great organizations, that won eleven games [in 2008] even without him. He ultimately would have been, in my opinion, a good starting quarterback. But if it had been for one of the bottom-tier teams, it would be probably a different conversation as far as where he fits with quarterbacks."

It was Bledsoe's team when he reported for his eighth training camp in the summer of 2000. Belichick, in his first year as the Patriots head coach, had veteran John Friesz and Michael Bishop, a seventh-round pick in 1999, lined up as the backups. Brady was clearly the highest-rated player on the Patriots draft board when they were picking late in the sixth round a few months earlier, and they had to take him, even though quarterback was not a need position. Bledsoe didn't think much of it. Brady was the third quarterback the Patriots had drafted since taking Bledsoe in 1993. Bishop and seventh-round pick Jay Walker in 1994 were never more than potential backup material. There was no reason for Bledsoe to believe that Belichick had drafted Brady to compete with him or take his job.

"At that point, quarterbacks had come and gone as backup quarterbacks," Bledsoe said. "Okay, he's another kid coming in."

Bledsoe immediately liked Brady. His wife really liked him. They had Brady over to the house a few times for dinner. Brady played with Bledsoe's little kids. "He was just somebody very easy to like and get along with," Bledsoe said. "No, he never babysat the kids. He drove a yellow Jeep, so I wouldn't leave him alone with our kids."

Bledsoe called his financial adviser, who took on only clients he believed in and not just because of their net worth. Bledsoe told his adviser, "I've got a kid here, I'm not sure if he's ever going to be anything, but he's just a good person and you would enjoy the relationship because he's a good guy. He'll probably never be a starter in the NFL, but he will be around ten years."

After two training camps, Bledsoe had formed an impression of Brady: Good. Not great. He threw the ball to the right place, he made the right read, and he did a nice job running the scout team. Great kid. "It wasn't a situation where I thought, *Oh no, this guy is going to beat me out and take my job.* That's never what it felt like," Bledsoe said. "He was tall, super skinny, arm was decent, threw a nice ball, but nothing super special."

Bledsoe is five and a half years older than Brady and thought of him as another little brother. He was happy to help Brady get better. Having a capable backup quarterback would only benefit Bledsoe and the team if he was out for a week or two. That way the Patriots offense wouldn't shut down without him.

Then Bledsoe suffered the sheared blood vessel, and the Patriots started to play well as he recuperated. The offensive line was getting healthy. It wasn't as if Brady was playing lights-out, but other than a loss at Denver at the end of October when he threw four interceptions, he was playing under control. Belichick was easing him in and not asking him to win games on his own. He was a game manager. When Bledsoe was cleared by doctors to return to action in mid-November, the Patriots were 5–4, and Belichick never gave Bledsoe a chance to win his job back. He had been Wally-Pipped.

Bledsoe's injury presented Belichick with an excuse to start Brady. He was never in Bledsoe's corner. "I don't know," Bledsoe said. "That's one I don't really need to comment on."

When Bledsoe went down, Brady hadn't built up enough collateral in the locker room for his teammates to believe he was capable of turning things around. The season was about to slip away.

"We just lost our $100 million quarterback and supposed face of the franchise," linebacker Tedy Bruschi said. "Yes, I was very down on the season. I was frustrated with the whole situation, being 0–2 after we were 5–11 the year before. I didn't know the severity of Bledsoe's injury at the time. I remember being frustrated with him. Just tired of losing at that point. Brady coming in was really an unknown commodity."

Belichick hadn't yet adopted his "Do your job" mantra, which became the rallying cry of the 2014 Super Bowl team, but Bruschi knew the Patriots had to play shutdown defense and hope offensive coordinator Charlie Weis could develop Brady. The players didn't know if Brady had just third-string talent. They certainly didn't think he was going to become Joe Montana. He didn't play very well in his first start against the Colts, but Bruschi realized a difference. Brady got rid of the ball. Bledsoe was a classic dropback passer; he was six five, 238 pounds, and he just stood there and planted his feet, and defenders would often just fall off him. But he took a lot of sacks and threw too many interceptions.

"The offense just had a different pace with Tom," Bruschi said. "That was refreshing to see."

The Patriots started to win with Brady. They knew Belichick was going to be faced with a difficult decision when Bledsoe was healthy. It had the potential to tear apart the team. Bledsoe had a lot of friends in the locker room and in the media. Brady was building relationships and trust. They were friends with each other. Bruschi felt Belichick couldn't go wrong. If he put Bledsoe back in, he would play well because the team had improved in the two months he was out. If he stuck with Brady, they would just keep trying to build on the momentum they were developing.

"There were pro-Bledsoe guys, there were pro-Brady guys,"

said Damien Woody, the starting center on Brady's first Super Bowl team. "I was pro-win."

Bruschi was close to Bledsoe, and Brady was just a young player, but he had no idea what Belichick was going to decide and then had no problem when he announced he was keeping Brady as the starter after Bledsoe was cleared to play. "It took balls for that decision," Bruschi said. "It was a gutsy decision. We all knew what balls it took by Bill, but we knew with either one we would have been fine."

Even after the Patriots went on to win the Super Bowl, Bruschi wasn't convinced about Brady. "We scored a defensive touchdown in the Super Bowl. We won the AFC championship and scored two special-teams touchdowns," he said. "Of course, the quarterbacks get all the credit. The kid was a good role player at that time. And Drew was the one who threw the touchdown in the championship game."

After the 2001 season, the Bills negotiated for one month with the Patriots about making a trade for Bledsoe. On the final day of the 2002 draft, less than three months after Brady's winning drive in the Super Bowl, Bledsoe was sent to Buffalo for a first-round draft pick in 2003. Trades within the division are rare, especially for a thirty-year-old three-time Pro Bowl quarterback who held all the important franchise passing records. It showed how little regard Belichick had for Bledsoe that he wasn't afraid to face him twice a year and was not concerned that he was strengthening a division opponent.

Bruschi believes that even if Bledsoe hadn't been injured, Belichick would have found a way to make the quarterback change. "There's probably no way Brady would have been denied," he said. "Knowing what I know about that kid and the work he would have put in, eventually Drew would be throwing two or three interceptions in a game and eventually Bill would have put in Tom because Drew was having a bad game. Tom would have buckled up his helmet before he went out there and said to himself, *I'm never giving this job back.* And I believe that. Then he'd play the last nine minutes of a game and drive the team down for two touchdowns and a field goal. You know Boston—all the talk would have started, and then Bill probably would have done it then."

Brady's idol, Joe Montana, lost his job to Steve Young with the 49ers when he was injured. He was also Wally-Pipped.

Montana suffered a bruised sternum and broke the little finger on his throwing hand after taking a crunching blind-side hit from defensive end Leonard Marshall late in the 1990 NFC championship game. Young tried to finish off the Giants, but a fumble by Roger Craig set up New York's winning field goal, preventing the 49ers from trying to win their third straight Super Bowl, something no team has ever done. If the 49ers had defeated the Giants, Montana would not have recovered in time to start the Super Bowl the next week against Buffalo. He was back healthy the next summer, but in a training camp practice, he suffered a slightly torn tendon near his right elbow when he was attempting to throw a pass downfield. Montana had been plagued by elbow problems since 1981, his third year in the NFL. Young was now the starting quarterback, as Montana hoped time would heal his elbow. He threw four times in one week in October to test the elbow, but there was too much pain, and he needed surgery to reattach the tendon. He missed the rest of the season and didn't return until making a farewell appearance in the second half of the final game of the 1992 season at Candlestick Park. The 49ers traded him to Kansas City after the season, and he played two years there before retiring.

Brady is so competitive that even before Bledsoe was injured he was telling friends he was going to beat him out. In the offseason between Brady's first and second years, Patriots personnel boss Scott Pioli was working late on a Friday night preparing for the draft. As he pulled out of his parking spot outside Foxboro Stadium, he saw the lights on in the practice bubble. He couldn't imagine why. It was after nine p.m. "I'm a little bit kooky like that," Pioli said. "I'm the guy who turns off all the lights in the office on the way out. It's just how I was raised."

He drove around to the front entrance to the bubble. He saw a yellow Jeep parked outside. He immediately knew Brady was inside. Pioli watched from a distance. Brady was by himself. He had elastic bands around his ankles doing footwork drills, drop-back drills with the football in his hands, and throwing into a net. Pioli and Brady had gotten to know each other in the weight room.

"Tommy and I became real close," Pioli said. "Far closer than probably I should have been. We were always sharing music and stuff. He loved music, but he had bad taste."

"Hey, kid, what are you doing here?" Pioli shouted across the bubble.

Brady was startled.

"I'm just getting a little extra work in," Brady said.

"Tommy, it's Friday night," "Pioli said.

"Yeah, I know, but I got nothing to do," Brady said.

Pioli said he thought to himself, *Here's this guy, he hadn't become Tom Brady yet, he was Tommy Brady, slappy, number-four quarterback of the New England Patriots. But he's still this brutally handsome guy and it's a Friday night, and he's there working out. That's good.*

They talked about family. They talked about the draft. Pioli turned to leave and Brady called after him. "Do me a favor."

"What's that?" Pioli asked.

"Don't tell anyone you saw me here tonight. This is between you and me, all right?"

"Yeah. Why?" Pioli said.

"It's Friday. Seriously, I would appreciate it if you didn't tell anyone," Brady said.

He used to sneak into the team facility and hide out watching tape. "I just fell in love with the guy because he became such a hard worker," Pioli said.

Now that he was starting, there was no way he was going to give Belichick a chance to even think about taking the job away from him. No longer was Brady the kid brother to Bledsoe.

Brady always said Bledsoe was very supportive, but as Bledsoe was in the final stages of his recuperation, some people around the team felt that he was actually disruptive in comments he was making about the Patriots being his team, that he was still the guy, and how he couldn't wait to get back on the field.

Montana despised Young almost from the day Bill Walsh traded to get him from the Bucs in 1987. He considered him a threat. Montana felt Young was working hard behind the scenes to take his job. Bledsoe and Brady were friends, but now Brady had Bledsoe's job and Bledsoe wanted it back.

"It did put a strain on my relationship with Tommy even though I still fully respected him and how hard he worked and what he was trying to do," Bledsoe said. "It certainly was not the same. There is no question about that."

Brady was riding this huge wave as the Patriots won the last six games of the regular season. Bledsoe knew that unless Brady was injured, he had no chance to get back on the field. He could either pout or do all he could to help Brady. "It was just the competition," Brady said. "It wasn't ever anything personal about Drew."

Bledsoe remained stuck to the bench until the second quarter of the AFC championship game in Pittsburgh. Brady first came up limping after a hit by Steelers linebacker Jason Gildon, and then Lee Flowers knocked him out of the game when he rolled into the back of his left ankle as he was completing a 28-yard pass to Troy Brown. Bledsoe entered with 1:40 remaining in the half and the Patriots on the Steelers 40. He had not played since September 23, but Weis didn't ease him back in. He called four straight pass plays, and Bledsoe completed all four, the last one an 11-yard touchdown pass in the corner of the end zone to David Patton. It took Bledsoe 126 days to get back on the field and then just forty-two seconds to get the Patriots into the end zone to take a 14–3 halftime lead on their way to a 24–17 victory. Bledsoe played the rest of the game and completed 10 of 21 passes for 102 yards. He was the most expensive backup in NFL history, but without him the Patriots would not have made it to the Super Bowl. On the podium after the game, as he raised the AFC championship trophy, tears were rolling down Bledsoe's cheeks. He had nearly died back in September. Now when his team needed him most, he was there for them.

The bye week between the conference championship games and the Super Bowl in New Orleans was eliminated when the NFL postponed the games scheduled for the weekend after the September 11 terrorist attacks and placed them at the end of the regular season. The condensed time frame added to the uncertainty as to whether Brady's ankle would allow him to play. The Patriots arrived in New Orleans with the first quarterback controversy in Super Bowl history.

"I want to play," Bledsoe said during Super Bowl week. "I want to play as bad as I ever wanted anything. It's the Super Bowl. It's what you play for. Obviously, I would love to be in there. I'd love to be playing in this game, but ultimately that's Bill's decision. Whoever plays has got to win."

Brady was 11–3 in the regular season and 2–0 in the playoffs, including the Pittsburgh game when he handed Bledsoe a 7–3 lead and Bledsoe won in relief. Bledsoe had been just 7–19 in his last 26 starts.

"Tom has gotten us here—let's get that straight," Bruschi said at the time. "Drew won the game the other day. What do you do? I don't know. That's why I'm not the head coach."

Belichick picked Brady, who had recovered from his ankle

injury. He had already alienated Bledsoe. He was not about to alienate Brady. Contributing to the victory in Pittsburgh made it easier for Bledsoe to handle the disappointment of not starting the Super Bowl. He was amazed how much better the offensive line had become in his absence. He had time to throw the ball. "That was a cool sensation. That's not how it had been before," Bledsoe said. "It was throw the ball, take a hit. Throw the ball, take a hit. I actually was really having fun with it."

Bledsoe knew about the electricity of playing in a Super Bowl. He knew about playing a Super Bowl in New Orleans. He'd been the Patriots' quarterback when they'd lost to Green Bay in the Superdome five years earlier. He prepared for the Rams as if he was going to start, especially with Brady not having much time to recuperate from the sprained ankle. In the tunnel before the Patriots became the first Super Bowl team to run out as a group rather than have their offense or defense introduced, Bledsoe was pounding on Brady's shoulder pads and screaming encouragement to him.

"The one thing I learned from the previous Super Bowl experience is no matter what happens, losing that game feels awful; it's worse than never being there," Bledsoe said. "I just knew that regardless of what happened in that game that we needed to win the game. Tom needed to play well to do that. The simple truth is if I didn't like and respect the guy, it would've been much harder to be supportive. He has always been such a good person, it makes it easier to cheer for him even though he stole my damn job."

Bledsoe stood on the Super Bowl sidelines helping Brady as much as he could. He's never said the Patriots would have had the same success that year or in the years that followed if he'd been the quarterback. "I have no idea whether that is true or not," he said. "That is the honest, honest truth. That's not being politically correct. One thing that did happen that's very real is when your starting quarterback that just signed a big contract goes down, and he was supposed to be your guy and your leader, everybody feels they have to increase their role and they have to support this guy and bring along this young guy. Then, on top of that, Tom played very well."

It took years for the relationship between Brady and Bledsoe to heal and get back to where it had been. They are very good friends again. They text all the time. Their families have spent time together. Bledsoe was coaching high school football for his sons in 2014 in Bend, Oregon, and called on Brady to provide motivational help before a big game. "I asked him to do me a quick favor, and he put together a little video for our high school before we faced our crosstown rivals," Bledsoe said.

Bledsoe's sons have always been great supporters of Brady, and he was happy to make the tape. "I love Drew," Brady said. "Drew has been like a big brother to me. Whenever he calls, I'm there to answer the phone, and whatever he asks, I'll always do anything for him. It's nice that our relationship has come to the point where it is now. We're great friends. We love being together and talking about things. He's still a real great mentor for me."

Bledsoe is proud of what Brady has done on the field and the man he has become off the field. "If you went back and introduced me to the kid that got drafted late out of Michigan and told me that he was going on to this level of success, I would have told you that you were full of crap," Bledsoe said. "Just like everybody else would've."

**Brady and Manning** could walk into any locker room and within fifteen minutes assume a leadership role.

Going into the 2002 season, Bledsoe was in Buffalo, and Brady had established himself, so he was able to assert his leadership skills. He began trash-talking on the field and in practice. "He's not afraid to use profanity," Bruschi said. Brady and linebacker Mike Vrabel incessantly trash-talked each other in practice. Vrabel had a way of getting under Brady's skin. Before one practice, Bruschi bet Brady twenty dollars he would pick him off. He did. Brady was so competitive he couldn't bring himself to hand Bruschi the twenty. "I don't think he had it in him to control himself enough to give me twenty bucks to my face," Bruschi said. "The twenty dollars was in my locker. That's all I needed to see."

Brady was smart enough to become friends with his offensive linemen. When Phil Simms played for the Giants, his best friend was left tackle Brad Benson. It was Benson who had to keep Dexter Manley of the Redskins and Harvey Martin of the Cowboys out of his face.

Brady quickly became one of the guys during his second year and impressed the linemen with his ability to drink beer and show no effect. In the summer, the hangout was Parente's, down the street from training camp at Bryant College. During the season, they would head to a place on Route 1 near Foxboro Stadium.

"Brady can pound the drinks now," Woody said. "I was never the biggest beer drinker, but guys like Joe Andruzzi, Matt Light—those guys could pour it down. We'd go to this establishment and eat and have a couple of drinks. One time Brady came in, and the dude, when I say pound it down, he was just pounding it down. Wow. I never knew he could put them away like that. I had new appreciation for him. This guy right there, he's all right. He wasn't the superstar. He was ascending. We had some great times."

Brady's beer drinking from his younger days in the NFL is still legendary. "He was always one of the guys. No one on the team could beat him chugging a beer," Bruschi said. "Linemen couldn't beat the kid. I remember seeing it for the first time and thinking, *Holy smokes, are you serious?* He was crushing guys."

Manning has a forceful personality and commands respect.

Brady is a nice guy, and players naturally gravitate toward him, regardless of whether they are the long snapper, like Lonie Paxton, who was part of Brady's Kentucky Derby crew, or Darrelle Revis, already a superstar when he arrived in New England for one season in 2014 and helped Brady win a Super Bowl.

John Fox had a routine of giving Manning each Wednesday off from practice in 2013 to rest two sprained ankles. Manning was sitting with his ankles submerged in the cold tub in the Broncos training room watching an opponent's tape on his iPad. Fox was running the practice when his cell phone buzzed. Manning had texted him a selfie. He was in the cold tub wearing his helmet and listening to the coach-quarterback communication from practice. "It was a joke, but still, I don't know how many players I've been around who would have thought about that," Fox said.

Wes Welker is one of five players who have caught passes from both Manning and Brady in the NFL. Tight end Jermaine Wiggins, wide receivers Torrance Small and Austin Collie, and fullback Dan Klecko are the others. Welker had the best years of his career with Brady before he left as a free agent in 2013 following a contract dispute with Belichick. He switched sides in the rivalry and joined Manning in Denver. Brady was upset when Welker left. He was among his best friends and he was his favorite target. Belichick usually doesn't make big personnel mistakes, and he didn't with Welker. Julian Edelman, a former college quarterback at Kent State, assumed Welker's role in the slot and became a more explosive player and a Super Bowl hero in the victory over the Seahawks when he caught the winning touchdown pass with just over two minutes remaining in the game.

As a receiver, if you have to leave Brady, it's not necessarily a bad thing to join up with Manning. Welker wasn't as productive in Denver, and concussion problems slowed him down, but he is the most accomplished receiver to play with both quarterbacks. He has put up Hall of Fame numbers, although he never was able to get a Super Bowl ring with either Brady or Manning. He lost two Super Bowls with Brady and one with Manning.

"There's a lot of similarities as far as making sure everybody is on the same page," Welker said. "The accountability, not only in meetings, but also on the field and in walk-throughs. They are second to none with their decision making. That's a key part of their success."

Kicker Adam Vinatieri had to win over his Colts teammates when he jumped from the Patriots in 2006. He won three rings with Brady with two Super Bowl–winning kicks, and in his first year in Indianapolis, he won his fourth ring. He has a special bond with Manning and Brady.

"When you win a championship, your football team is a fraternity of brothers," Vinatieri said. "It's not your biological family, but it may as well be. There is just as much family feel to a football team as there is to your real family. I got great relationships with those guys, and it's a bond that will never disappear. When you go onto a football field and you're fighting together, especially when you can hoist a Lombardi Trophy, it's something that never goes away."

Brady and Manning are not afraid to show their combustible side on the sidelines in full view of television cameras. Brady got into a heated argument with offensive coordinator Bill O'Brien after throwing a bad interception in a 2011 game against the Redskins. Brady was sitting on the bench and O'Brien was standing over him. O'Brien ripped off his headset and was gesturing wildly. Backup quarterback Brian Hoyer and then Belichick had to push O'Brien away.

The Patriots won 34–27.

Manning's best friend with the Colts was center Jeff Saturday. But that didn't prevent Manning from unloading on him during a 2005 game against the Rams. Manning threw the ball three straight times in the red zone, and the Colts had to settle for a field goal.

"We need to run the ball down there," Saturday shouted to Manning.

Manning got up from his seat on the bench, quickly walked over to Saturday, and screamed, "Hey, quit calling the fucking plays, all right?"

A few minutes later, as Manning sat on the bench next to tight end Dallas Clark and wide receiver Brandon Stokley stood next to him, he broke the news that he was miked up for the game.

"Miked up?" Stokley said. "Shut up."

Manning knew his argument with Saturday would get plenty of airtime.

"It's better than *Desperate Housewives*," he told Clark and Stokley.

The Colts won 45–28.

In Tony Dungy's second-to-last year with the Colts, in 2007, the team drafted Ohio State wide receiver Anthony Gonzalez in the first round. Stokley, a Manning favorite, had been injured, and the plan was for Gonzalez to be the new slot receiver. Ohio State was on trimester, and by NFL rules, Gonzalez was not allowed to participate in minicamps and other off-season workouts until finals were over. Manning was concerned that Gonzalez would not have enough time to learn the Colts offense to make a contribution early in his rookie year. So he got in his car and drove 175 miles to Ohio State.

"Two days a week, Peyton was driving from Indianapolis to Columbus, three hours each way, to throw balls to him for an hour and a half. He would prep him with everything and drive back," Dungy said. "He never spoke about it and nobody knew about it."

Manning had a simple message for Gonzalez. "We need you, so I'm going to get you ready," he said.

Gonzalez caught 37 passes as a rookie and 57 his second year, but injuries shortened his career.

Manning expects everyone to have the same commitment. If you wanted to play with Manning, you had to keep up with him. "You got to be able to function and you can't make mistakes," Dungy said. "As far as driving guys and pushing them, if you were going to play in that offense, you had to keep up that pace. They might say, 'Gee, I wish he'd relax. I wish he would calm down.'"

Dungy suffered an unspeakable tragedy in 2005 when his oldest son, James, committed suicide while at school in a Tampa suburb. After taking time away from the team, Dungy was back in his office when Manning walked in. "Coach, we're here for you," Manning said.

Dungy will never forget the look on Manning's face. "We always talk about family a lot," he said. "What's going on with Eli? I had known Archie for so long. James was there a lot with the Colts. I could tell Peyton was shaken. He's so close with his dad and so close with his brothers, he understood."

Manning spoke to his teammates about being there for Dungy emotionally.

Brady conducted a bedside vigil for Charlie Weis, his offensive coordinator in New England, in June of 2002 after Weis slipped into a coma and nearly died following complications from gastric bypass surgery. "To our family, Tom Brady is a hell of a lot more than a football player," Weis said.

# 9

# THE COACH IN THE GRAY HOODIE

Tom Brady meets Bill Belichick at least every Tuesday and Saturday during the season to prepare for the next game. They talk about plays he likes, go over the game plan, discuss corrections that need to be made from the previous game.

That's around forty meetings per year multiplied by a lot of years to equal hundreds and hundreds of hours, just the two of them in Belichick's office. They will sometimes meet five or six times in a week, adding even more hours to their weekly interaction. They are the most successful coach quarterback combination in NFL history. They've won four Super Bowls together, tying Chuck Noll and Terry Bradshaw and one more than Bill Walsh and Joe Montana. They won 172 regular-season games together through the 2014 season, and that is number one in the NFL since the 1970 merger. Don Shula and Dan Marino are next with 116. They've also been together longer than any coach and quarterback in NFL history.

Nobody knows Brady better than Belichick. But nobody really knows Belichick, not even Brady.

"When it's outside of football, he's a totally different person," Brady said. "As soon as he's in football mode, it's like hitting a switch."

The nonfootball Belichick might be a lot of fun. He might be the life of the party. He might be different from the tortured football genius whom the public sees on the sidelines and in his press conferences. To experience that part of his personality, "it has to be in a nonfootball environment," Brady said.

Surely in all their years together, Brady has been exposed to that side of his coach. "Me? Very rarely, very rarely," he said.

They must have gone out for a pizza and a couple of beers after a long evening meeting before they went home. "I don't think we ever have," Brady said. "We're around each other so much, whenever we have time, nothing ever comes of it."

Belichick once showed up at a team Halloween costume party organized by Randy Moss. But he and Brady keep their distance away from the field.

The NFL has become a game of coaches and quarterbacks. Elite coaches paired with elite quarterbacks win Super Bowls. They need to think alike. Brady is as serious about football as Belichick. They are both heading to the Pro Football Hall of Fame, and there's a good chance one would not have been in position to make it without the other. Belichick coached the Browns into the playoffs just once in five years in Cleveland with Bernie Kosar and then Vinny Testaverde as his quarterback. He was going nowhere in one year plus two games with Drew Bledsoe in New England. Brady came in and went 11–3 the rest of the regular season and then won two playoff games and the Super Bowl.

Tom Brady saved Bill Belichick's job.

Bill Belichick saved Tom Brady's career.

Belichick rescued Brady and threw him a lifeline in the sixth round of the 2000 draft. John Elway was going to be great regardless of where he played. It was the same with Peyton Manning. They were going to play and be given every opportunity to succeed.

If Brady had been picked by the Browns, a quarterback graveyard, he would not have been the same player. What if the Giants had taken the advice of their longtime scout Ray "Whitey" Walsh, who loved Brady? Maybe he would have beaten out Kerry Collins, and then the Giants never would have made the draft-day trade four years later to get Eli Manning. Or maybe he never would have gotten off the bench but just bounced from team to team.

Brady might have succeeded with his hometown 49ers, but they drafted quarterbacks Gio Carmazzi before him and Tim Rattay after him. Steve Young had been forced to retire after the 1999 season because of multiple concussions. Steve Mariucci was the 49ers coach; he had done an excellent job with Young and before that Brett Favre in Green Bay. Walsh was back with the 49ers, running the team from the front office. He was also the best quarterback coach in history. But the 49ers didn't want Brady. Jeff Garcia, coming across the border from the Canadian Football League, took over the job in San Francisco that Brady craved.

He wound up in the perfect situation in New England. The owner loved Drew Bledsoe. The coach didn't. Bledsoe was Bill Parcells's draft pick. Brady was Belichick's. Belichick learned from Parcells to "go by what I see"—production, not reputation, is the ultimate criterion. Belichick takes it a step further in minicamp: no jersey numbers. Offense in blue, defense in gray. That promotes team-building by forcing the players to learn each other by name and not just by number. And when coaches watch the tapes of the practices, they have to learn the players by their movements, not their number.

"I love coaching Tom," Belichick said. "I've been fortunate to have him his whole career. We spend a considerable amount of time together. I think that's important, to have that relationship between the head coach and the quarterback so at least we're on the same page with what we're trying to do. He has great feedback. Nobody works harder or prepares better than Tom does. He's about as good as it gets in that category."

A coach and a quarterback don't have to be best friends, but it helps if they have each other's back. Jimmy Johnson and Troy Aikman had a contentious relationship after Johnson took over in Dallas in 1989 and used the first pick in the draft on Aikman. Just over two months later, Johnson used the first overall pick in the supplemental draft to take Steve Walsh, his quarterback at the University of Miami. Johnson's plan was to immediately trade Walsh and receive more in return than he invested. Walsh was a smart player with an average arm. Aikman was a smart player with a gun. But when Johnson was not able to get a package he liked, he kept Walsh for the entire 1989 season. Aikman was the better quarterback and was clearly the long-term answer for the Cowboys, but Walsh was the quarterback for the Cowboys' lone victory in their 1–15 season, in Washington when Aikman was injured. Early in the 1990 season, Johnson traded Walsh to the Saints for draft picks in the first, second, and third rounds.

The time with Aikman and Walsh together created a cold war between Johnson and Aikman. The quarterback considered asking for a trade. If the Cowboys were going to succeed, Aikman and Johnson needed to be thinking as one. There had to be trust. Johnson was fond of fish and had seven tanks in his house in Valley Ranch, in the same development as the Cowboys headquarters. He discovered that Aikman liked fish, too, and offered to help him set up his saltwater fish tank. Johnson went over to Aikman's house, and they bonded over sea clowns. No joke.

"The relationship was a struggle initially, and there was some conflict," Aikman told the *Dallas Morning News* in 1994. "But I think the reason for that, number one, was because we were losing and we were both frustrated. I think it also took me some time to understand him, and I think now he understands my will to win and the commitment I have to the team. I think Jimmy and I probably have as strong a relationship as any head coach and quarterback in the league. There are still things that I don't necessarily agree with, and I'm sure there are things I do that he probably doesn't like. But that will always happen with two people who are as competitive as we are. We have a relationship now where, if there is a concern, we can sit down and talk about how to resolve the situation."

A few weeks after Aikman expressed warm feelings for Johnson, the Cowboys won the second of their back-to-back Super Bowls. Three months later, the friction between Johnson and Cowboys owner Jerry Jones became unbearable, and Jones paid Johnson $2 million to leave. Aikman was distraught. He had totally bought into Johnson's program of discipline and accountability and was miserable when Jones hired Barry Switzer. Aikman had played for Switzer at Oklahoma before breaking his leg and transferring to UCLA. Aikman had no use for Switzer and his lackadaisical approach to running an NFL team, especially a young team loaded with talent coming off two titles. Switzer won a Super Bowl with Johnson's players in his second year in Dallas, but he and Aikman never developed a strong working relationship.

Dan Reeves and John Elway battled for the ten years Elway played for him. Reeves was so distrusting of Elway that he fired offensive coordinator Mike Shanahan because he felt they were plotting behind his back and changing the game plan.

When Reeves was fired by Denver owner Pat Bowlen after the 1992 season, Elway said playing for Reeves the previous three years had been hell. "Just tell him it wasn't exactly heaven for me, either," Reeves said. "One of these days, I hope he grows up. Maybe he'll mature sometime."

Parcells created so much tension in Giants practice that

quarterback Phil Simms would be mentally fatigued by the time he arrived home. He got nervous before seven-on-seven drills. Parcells picked on him because he knew Simms was thick-skinned, and making him accountable meant making the whole team accountable. Brett Favre would drive Mike Holmgren out of his mind with stupid mistakes; the coach was so fed up, he once considered benching Favre for Mark Brunell. During the 1994 season, Holmgren went as far as polling his coaches about who should start. Enough hands went up for Brunell that Holmgren thought hard about making the change. Holmgren decided to stick with Favre, but when he met with him the next day in his office, he never told him he'd considered benching him. Favre was too carefree to be motivated by the fear of losing his job.

The relationship between Belichick and Brady was never adversarial. Brady cares so much and approaches each practice as if he has to persuade Belichick not to bench him. That has allowed Belichick to give Brady a little bit of the Parcells-Simms treatment. He knows he can yell at him and Brady can take it. The greater message is being delivered to the team. If the coach can yell at the four-time Super Bowl winner, you'd better watch your ass. You're next.

"He knows me as well as anybody. I know what he expects of me," Brady said. "We don't probably talk as much as people may think. He trusts me to do my job and lets me do my job. There's times where I get to express certain things to him, and I think he has a lot of trust in the things that I say and confidence in the things that I say."

Belichick was asked at Super Bowl XLIX in Phoenix about his relationship with Brady. He guards anything regarding his personal life more closely than his game plans. "Tom and I have been together for fifteen years, so I would say our relationship covers a lot of ground," he said. "We played golf together for three days at Pebble Beach."

During a break in the 2014 pro-am tournament at Pebble Beach, Brady told Jim Nantz and Nick Faldo of CBS that he enjoyed the opportunity to play golf with his coach. "He doesn't yell at me out here like he does during the weeks of practice," Brady said. "We haven't had too many chances to do things like this, so this is a really special week for me to be with him."

Peyton Manning was also at Pebble Beach in February 2014, a few days after the Broncos were crushed in the Super Bowl by the Seahawks and a little more than two weeks after he'd played so well beating the Patriots in the AFC championship game. Belichick calls Manning the best quarterback he ever faced, so spending time with Belichick and Brady was good for Manning's state of mind after the Super Bowl loss. "I have great respect for the way they play, the way they approach the game," Manning said. "They're both very similar that way. They are football junkies, if you will. I think that's a compliment. I consider myself that as well, and I think all football players should be, so yeah, I've enjoyed those times."

Manning and Belichick would have been a great combination, too, and chances are, Manning would have more than one Super Bowl ring if he'd played for Belichick and the Patriots.

**Tom Brady has** never spoken much about Spygate, the scandal that resulted when the NFL, acting on a tip from Jets coach Eric Mangini, a former Belichick assistant, caught a member of Belichick's video crew videotaping the defensive play calls from the Jets sideline during the 2007 season opener at Giants Stadium. It was against league rules, a point driven home by a memo from the league office the previous September. Belichick, who claimed he simply misinterpreted the rule, was fined the maximum, $500,000, by Roger Goodell, who also fined the organization $250,000 and took away a first-round draft pick. Goodell considered suspending

Belichick but ultimately decided the fine and the loss of the draft pick were sufficient punishment.

The scandal cast doubt on the integrity of the league and created headlines for months. Goodell said it had to be assumed that Belichick had been taping defensive signals against NFL rules ever since he had been a head coach.

Belichick is such a control freak, he accounts for every minute of the day. If spying wasn't helping him, why would he do it? The idea was to match the coded defensive signals with the play call and then try to use the information to the Patriots' advantage the next time they played that team. It was a time-consuming process. Stealing signals was not against NFL rules, but using video equipment to assist in the process broke the rules.

Once things settled down in New England after Goodell punished Belichick, there was a quiet moment between Patriots owner Robert Kraft and Belichick. Kraft was incensed that his organization and brand had been tarnished, but he never considered firing Belichick. Instead, he asked him, on a scale of one to a hundred, how much the tapes had helped the Patriots.

"One," Belichick said.

"Then you're a real schmuck," Kraft said.

Brady had already won three Super Bowls by the time Belichick was punished, raising the issue of whether their Vince Lombardi Trophies were tainted and deserved an asterisk. Simply because he was the quarterback who would have benefited from knowing what defense was called before the snap, Brady's accomplishments were also questioned.

Did they beat the Colts in those playoff games because Brady was being told in his radio helmet before it was turned off with fifteen seconds left on the play clock whether the Colts were in a man-to-man or a zone or were disguising a blitz? Was he able to move the ball right down the field in the last minute of their Super

Bowl victory against the Rams because the Patriots had played Saint Louis during the regular season and Belichick was able to decode the Rams defensive signals and tell Brady what was coming during the final drive?

Brady is driving through Boston traffic now on his way home from Gillette Stadium many years after the scandal. The question about Spygate doesn't make him drive off the road, but it's clearly a topic that ticks him off. "I haven't thought about that in a long time," he said. "Even when we went through it, I didn't think about it."

How much did the espionage help him? He barely waited to hear the end of the question. "Not one bit. Not one bit," he said. "I'm the quarterback. I go up under center. I'm the one that makes every decision on the field. I didn't benefit from anything other than you go out there and try to do the best you can. You evaluate what the other team is doing and you make a quick decision. I don't think any of that ended up factoring into anything we ever did."

The Patriots played with a chip on their shoulder the rest of the season, winning fifteen straight games after the spying stopped to finish off the first 16–0 regular season since the NFL expanded from fourteen to sixteen games in 1978. They barely missed completing their perfect season when the Giants came from behind to beat them in the last minute of Super Bowl XLII.

"Our team being 18–0 before we lost to the Giants really spoke for itself," Brady said. "But none of that had any influence on me in any game we ever played, you know. It was a whole lot of nothing from my standpoint."

If Brady has one major regret in his career, it's not winning the Super Bowl with that 2007 team. "To me, that was the greatest team that ever played in the NFL," he said. "We won so many games against the toughest competition that year by big margins."

Dungy seemed to relish the idea that Spygate creates doubt about the Patriots dynasty. "Really, a sad day for the NFL," he said at the time. "It's another case of the ninety-nine percent good things that are happening being overshadowed by one percent bad. Again, people aren't talking about our product; they're talking about a negative incident."

Now he's sitting at a hotel coffee shop in midtown Manhattan, but Dungy's feelings haven't changed. He retired from coaching after the 2008 season and joined NBC for its *Football Night in America* studio show preceding *Sunday Night Football*. He believes Belichick's comments to Kraft that signal stealing may have helped the Patriots by only one on a scale of a hundred, but says that was enough to give the Patriots an advantage.

"A 'one' when it's close in a championship game—if you can get one signal, or one time you know a blitz is coming, that's all you need," he said. "Sure, it helps. One play can be the difference between losing a playoff game and going to the Super Bowl."

He said the Patriots always requested extra sideline passes for cameramen. Dungy never knew exactly what was going on, but knew he had to take precautions. Days before the Colts played in Foxboro in the 2003 AFC championship game, word got to him about Belichick's spying. He said that Dave Moore, a tight end who played for him in Tampa, had played that season in Buffalo with former Patriots quarterback Drew Bledsoe and Bledsoe had tipped him off. "He said when they were getting ready to play the Patriots, Bledsoe told their coaches, 'Here is what you have to do. Here is what is going on. You got to change the signals,'" Dungy said. "He said, 'They are taping your signals, so you better change your defensive signals.' It's not like they are the only guys who ever broke any rules. Everybody is trying to get an edge. So you have precautions. You're always worried about that kind of stuff. The league is always one step behind. To me, there's a difference between bending the rules and taking every advantage you can get and breaking the rules."

Dungy never discussed his feelings with Belichick. "No, no," he said.

The anti-Belichick group—and there's a waiting list to get in—points out that in the first seven seasons after the spying ring was disassembled, he didn't win the Super Bowl. To them that proves the cheating paid off. The much smaller pro-Belichick group, which is still accepting applications for membership, says the Patriots won seventeen straight games in 2007 after the cameras were put in storage and Goodell had the tapes destroyed and still made it to three Super Bowls, winning one, in the first eight years after Spygate.

Belichick is a polarizing figure, and some view Brady as part of the Belichick evil empire. The Deflategate fiasco only cemented that feeling.

The Patriots were 9–0 in 2007 after beating the Colts when it became a realistic possibility that they would not lose a game the rest of the season. Don Shula, the coach of the 1972 Dolphins, who were 14–0 and then won three playoff games for the only perfect season in history, told the *New York Daily News* that Belichick's accomplishments that season deserved an asterisk.

"The Spygate thing has diminished what they've accomplished. You would have to have that attached to your accomplishments. They've got it," he said. "Belichick was fined $500,000, the team was fined $250,000, and they lost a first-round draft choice. That tells you the seriousness or significance of what they found. I guess you got the same thing as putting an asterisk by Barry Bonds's home-run record. I guess it will be noted that the Patriots were fined and a number-one draft choice was taken away during that year of accomplishment. The sad thing is, Tom Brady looks so good, it doesn't look like he needs any help."

Belichick and Brady would later become embroiled in the Deflategate controversy before Super Bowl XLIX, when the NFL investigated claims that the Patriots removed air pressure from many of the twelve footballs they supplied for their offense in the AFC championship game against the Colts, which New England won 45–7. Belichick denied any knowledge of the deflations. Brady claimed he would never do anything to break the rules. In the two weeks between the conference championship game and the Super Bowl, the Deflategate story overshadowed the game. On the Thursday before the Patriots left for Phoenix, Brady held a press conference to answer questions about the deflated footballs. He was bombarded with questions. "I didn't alter the ball in any way," he said.

Belichick's history of cheating made the Patriots an easy target. As he was giving an impassioned defense of his team in the deflated-football scandal, Belichick spoke in more detail about Spygate than he had when the incident occurred. He said the signals were "in front of eighty thousand people, okay? So we filmed him taking signals out in front of eighty thousand people, like there were a lot other teams doing at the same time, too. Forget about that. If we were wrong, then we've been disciplined for that."

Brady's image took a big hit as the Super Bowl approached. Many not residing in Patriots Nation viewed him as the mastermind behind deflating the balls. The pendulum started to swing a bit back in Brady's favor, however, after he threw two touchdown passes to overcome a 10-point deficit in the fourth quarter to beat Seattle. Fans related to Brady jumping up and down like a five-year-old after safety Malcolm Butler's end-zone interception in the final seconds of the Super Bowl clinched the title. The postgame pictures of Brady with his wife and two of his children on the field warmed up a country overrun with freezing temperatures.

A new controversy briefly took over for Deflategate: Why

hadn't Seattle coach Pete Carroll just given the ball to the unstoppable Marshawn Lynch at the goal line instead of having Russell Wilson throw a risky pass? Brady came so close to losing his third straight Super Bowl, which could have changed the narrative of his career.

**Tom Brady Sr.** waits in the family area outside the locker room or in the tunnel for his son after games. There have been times when Belichick emerges first but never has Brady Sr. approached him to talk about the game or how his son played. "Are you nuts?" he said, laughing.

Brady Sr. hears a lot about Tom's relationship with Belichick. He agrees with Tom's assessment. "Tommy has said to me different times, Belichick has a perfect soldier with me," Brady Sr. said. "Tommy is the perfect foil for Belichick. When Randy Moss comes in and sees Tommy getting chewed out and not coming back at it and accepting it, the other fifty-two guys fall in line. That is absolutely the ideal military regimen he inherited from his father at Navy. That's exactly what he wants. If you have somebody who doesn't fall in line, like a Wes Welker, you are out the door. Tommy is absolutely the perfect quarterback for Bill Belichick because he understands what Belichick is doing and he has enough pride to know that no matter what Belichick might say to diminish his efforts, it's not going to impact who he is and what he knows he can do."

One Wednesday afternoon in November, it was cold and miserable outside, an early taste of the New England winter. The Patriots were in the middle of another very successful season, but this practice was not crisp. Brady was not sharp. He beat himself up on the way home as usual. He does that even if he practices well but misses one pass that he thinks he should have made. Every second of practice is taped, and the next day at the team meeting, the first play Belichick showed was a bad pass by Brady.

Brady's father said Tom described what Belichick said: "Brady, if you throw a fucking pass like this, it's going to be picked off and run back for a touchdown. You're supposed to be an All-Pro."

Brady had already won three Super Bowls, which made him the perfect target for Belichick. He could have taken the Patriots indoors to practice in their field house, but he liked to make things as difficult as possible in practice, especially with an outdoor game coming up. There was no use practicing in a controlled environment if the ball was going to be wet or cold on game day.

Brady Sr. is astounded at the lack of compliments Belichick has publicly thrown his son's way. It's not the Belichick way. It's not the Patriots way. "They couldn't care less. They are not trying to shine his star," he said. "If Belichick had fifty-three guys named Joe, he would love it."

Manning has been celebrated for his individual accomplishments. When he threw the pass that broke Favre's all-time touchdown record in 2014 with the 509th of his career, it was all the Broncos could do to stop themselves from wheeling a podium out to the middle of the field and having Manning give a speech. They did celebrate with a video presentation on the scoreboard. When Brady surpassed fifty thousand yards for his career, all his father could remember Belichick saying was, "We're not into individual statistics, but I do have to recognize fifty thousand yards."

None of this bothers Brady, because all he wants to do is win. Never once, in a quiet moment, has Belichick initiated a conversation with Brady about all they have accomplished together. Not once has he reflected on winning all those Super Bowls and what a great combination they've been. "Never. Nope," Brady said. 'He's not a look-forward or look-to-the-past kind of guy."

Belichick was sitting at his podium on media day in downtown

Phoenix at Super Bowl XLIX. It's the one place every coach in the NFL wants to be on the last Tuesday in January. They are up there for an hour, and all kinds of questions are asked. Some coaches enjoy it. Belichick showed up in his flip-flops and a sweatshirt with the sleeves cut off, and looked like he was about to get a root canal. Some of the questions are pure Xs and Os. Belichick gives nothing up. Some are about injuries. If a player has a sprained ankle, the Patriots describe it as a leg injury and won't give up top-secret information, such as which leg. Don't even bother asking Belichick about his personal life, other than the fact that he enjoys having his son Stephen on his staff, which allows him to teach him the business and spend more time with him.

Ask him about what he and Brady have accomplished together and he frowns. "We're just focused on this game," he said. "We're not really worried about any of the past games or anything in the future."

The Patriots had twenty rookies on the team in 2000. Brady became the leader of the group. He was invaluable on the scout team. Belichick noticed. When quarterbacks coach Dick Rehbein died during training camp in 2001, Belichick and offensive coordinator Charlie Weis alternated coaching the quarterbacks. That was the start of the daily relationship Belichick had with Brady. "I feel like Tom and I do have a good relationship, and I have a lot of respect for Tom," he said. "No other quarterback I'd rather have quarterbacking our team than Tom Brady. I guess that's the best way I could sum it up."

Belichick provided a little bit of insight into their relationship in an interview with Bill Cowher on CBS in 2013. Brady is so prepared when he meets Belichick that the coach must match his intensity. Even on a Tuesday. "Tom's one of the toughest players that I've ever had to coach because when you walk into the meeting with Tom, he's already seen every game, like the Colts, that the

Colts have played defensively," Belichick told Cowher. "So, you can't go in there unprepared, you can't go in there saying, 'Well, I don't know if they're going to do this.' He'll say, 'Did you see the Tennessee game? That's what they did.' So you got to be as well prepared as he is. That's a good thing, but it's also a hard thing. You can't throw the curveball by him. You better know what you're talking about. He does."

Matt Cassel, the former Brady backup, said Belichick is consistent in his approach to his players. "He wants everybody to feel a little bit uncomfortable," he said.

Belichick and Jimmy Johnson are good friends. Belichick makes a trip down to Johnson's home in the Florida Keys every off-season to spend time fishing and talking football. Johnson didn't treat all players the same. His rules were different, based on importance to the team. He cut fringe linebacker John Roper for falling asleep in a meeting, but he said if he caught Aikman snoozing, he'd whisper in his ear, "Come on, Troy, wake up."

Belichick never has to be concerned about making an example of Brady sleeping in a meeting. Brady likes to be in bed by nine p.m. during the season. He gets his rest. "Bill has such respect for Tom. He knows that Tom knows what he's doing," Cassel said. "Did he yell at Tom? Hell, yes. It kept everybody accountable."

Brady has been coached hard by Belichick, and that's all he's ever known in the NFL. Manning started off with Jim Mora Sr., in Indianapolis, an old-school coach who helped revive Manning's hometown Saints in New Orleans. Mora was hired by the Colts the same year Indianapolis drafted Manning. The Colts were just 3–13 in 1998, then 13–3 in 1999, the best single-season improvement in NFL history, but after a bye in the first round of the playoffs, they lost at home to the Titans. They were struggling again in 2000, and after a 40–21 loss to the 49ers in which Manning threw four interceptions, one returned for a touchdown and the three others setting up seventeen points, the Colts were 4–6. That prompted the famous Mora rant. After he said his team's performance was disgraceful and sucked, he was asked about the Colts' chances to make the playoffs.

"What's that? Playoffs? Don't talk about . . . playoffs! You kidding me? Playoffs? I just hope we can win a game."

Mora was fired after the 2001 season and replaced by Dungy, a mild-mannered man who believed coaches should be home having dinner with their families as often as possible and never sleep in the office or watch tape until two in the morning. Manning was much more high-strung than his coach. It's the coach who usually has trouble putting things in perspective. "He's really a creature of habit and he came to appreciate my consistency," Dungy said. "He was always trying to improve things, reinvent the wheel. That was the hard part for me—to rein him back in."

When Dungy retired after the 2008 season, Polian replaced him with Jim Caldwell, the Colts offensive coordinator. His personality was similar to Dungy's. In their first year together, Manning and Caldwell made it to the Super Bowl against the Saints, back in Miami, where the Colts had defeated the Bears in a downpour four years earlier. This time, the weather was nice.

Manning had once worn a bag on his head at a Saints game as a kid at the urging of his big brother, Cooper, when Archie was the quarterback. Peyton grew up around the Saints. But now the Colts were trailing New Orleans and moving into position for the tying touchdown in the Super Bowl. They had a third and 5 at the New Orleans 31 with 3:24 left. Manning dropped back and looked for Reggie Wayne cutting from left to right. Manning could complete that pass in his sleep. Unfortunately, Wayne cut off his pattern and cornerback Tracy Porter jumped the route and picked off Manning. He returned it 74 yards for a touchdown to clinch the game. The criticism Manning heard before he won the

Super Bowl had returned. He was too classy to assign blame on the interception. It wasn't his fault.

Manning would play only one more playoff game for the Colts, a wild-card loss to the Jets at home the following season. He sat out the 2011 season and went to Denver to play for John Fox, another player-friendly coach. They made it to the Super Bowl their second year together but were blown out by the Seahawks. Fox had a mutual parting with the Broncos after his third season. Gary Kubiak took over, the fifth head coach of Manning's career.

Brady has played for just one, arguably the best of all time.

"It's hard to imagine them not together," Fox said. "I'm not knocking Bill or anybody, but you show me a great coach, I'll show you great players. You could almost say great quarterbacks. Don Shula is the winningest coach ever in professional football. His quarterbacks were Unitas, Griese, and Marino. I'm not slighting Don Shula, but I think he would probably mention that."

The dynamic between Brady and Belichick is much different from the one between Manning and his coaches. Belichick is the producer and director, and although Brady is the star of the show, he's executing Belichick's script. Manning began calling plays at the line of scrimmage early in his career, and as he played for different coaches and different teams, they all adopted Manning's way of doing business. Therefore he has continued operating at peak efficiency as he has transitioned into the later years of his career. Brady appreciates Belichick's attention to every little detail and returns his compliment by saying there's no other coach he would rather play for in his career. "He's a no-nonsense coach," he said. "I think why he's been able to endure is because he has the respect of all the older players, because you believe that what he's telling you and teaching you is the right way to do it. How he prepares our team every week is phenomenal. He's always got his foot on the gas pedal."

He has eased up only four times since he arrived in New England—in the hours after the Patriots have won their four Super Bowls. He's full of hugs on the field, showing the genuine affection he really feels for his players, who have sacrificed so much since the first day of training camp. Belichick drives them, but he also knows how to take care of his players' bodies over the course of the long season. When the Lombardi Trophy was brought onto the field in New Orleans, Houston, Jacksonville, and Phoenix, and Belichick was there to accept it, he's been able to take a deep breath and relax. Even smile.

Brady's father knows why the relationship between Belichick and his son is "100 percent professional." One day Belichick is going to have to cut him or trade him or convince him to retire, and as long as he doesn't establish personal relationships, his feelings won't get in the way of business decisions. "To my knowledge, he and Tommy have never been to dinner, never been to lunch," he said. "That's perfectly fine with Tommy, because he's got a whole bunch of great friends. He doesn't need to be personal friends with the coach. He's got more personal friends than he needs. He just needs to have a coach have the organization going in the right direction."

**Patriots owner Robert** Kraft had four sons with his wife, Myra, the love of his life, who passed away in the summer of 2011. "I always thought my wife was going to outlive me by thirty years, except for that lousy ovarian cancer," Kraft said. "Having my own sons and the players really saved me."

Kraft gets teary-eyed talking about Myra. They met in Boston when he was twenty and she was nineteen. He was attending Columbia University in New York. She was at Brandeis University in Waltham, Massachusetts. He spotted her in a coffee shop, then tracked her down at the Brandeis library the next day, and they started dating. They were married in June 1963, one week after he graduated from college. They were married forty-eight years when she passed away at the age of sixty-eight.

On a quiet morning before the start of the 2014 season, Kraft is having breakfast at the Palm Court at the iconic Plaza Hotel at the corner of Fifth Avenue and Central Park South in New York City. He owns an apartment at the Plaza and stays there on frequent business trips to Manhattan. He is dressed casually in a sport shirt, jeans, and sneakers. In a few months, he will be in a business suit lifting another Lombardi Trophy.

Kraft has been close to many of his players since he purchased the Patriots in 1994. He's been particularly close to Bledsoe, Richard Seymour, Jerod Mayo, and Vince Wilfork but none closer than to Brady. Kraft is a strong supporter of Israel, where he has many business and philanthropic interests. He's brought Seymour and Benjamin Watson on trips to Israel and watched as they were baptized in the Sea of Galilee. "It's just something that turns me on, being able to give them that experience," Kraft said.

Kraft considers his players part of his family. He has a genuine affection for Brady, his wife, Gisele, and their kids. Kraft and Brady text each other and are not afraid to express their feelings. "Mr. Kraft and I have had a very special relationship over the last fifteen years," Brady said. "He has been a part of so many decisions in my life, and I am always grateful for his thoughts on things I am going through and have gone through. I have been very lucky to have someone that has the wisdom and experience to see the big picture of my life."

When the weather gets warm and Brady and his family travel to Cape Cod, they have spent time with Kraft. He hosts an annual pre-training-camp party for his players and their wives and children at his home on the Cape, and when linebacker Brandon

Spikes was celebrating his birthday, Kraft took him out to dinner afterward. He is accommodating and accessible to all his players, but Brady is special to him.

"He is genuine, caring, and sensitive," Kraft said. "He's almost too caring and sensitive. Then he can flick the switch and be a killer on the field. When my wife died, Tommy and a group of players, led by him, were so supportive, they were like my children. They really made a difference in my life. They looked out for me, they were inviting me places. Tommy is like a fifth son. He and his wife, there is no other couple like them in America. Even the movie stars. And they are both so nice. There isn't a mother or father in America who would meet Tom Brady and wouldn't want him to marry their daughter."

Kraft invited Brady to join him on one of his trips to Israel before he met Bundchen. "He knew that spirituality was very important to me," Kraft said. "Every year my wife and I would take a group of people, mainly gentiles who had never been to the Holy Land. Going with Tommy, seeing how he took everything in, being with him at the Wall . . . I explained to him the history of how people put notes in. He put a note in."

In Kraft's office, there is a picture of Brady and him at the Wall. "I know that he and Gi are into spirituality," he said. "This might not be our last trip."

Kraft took Brady to Jerusalem and Bethlehem. "I remember him buying Bibles for his family," he said.

"We spent a memorable holiday together with Mr. Kraft and Mrs. Kraft in Israel," Brady said. "We connected on so many levels spiritually and emotionally and had some experiences I will never forget. I was still a young man but couldn't keep up with RKK's pace. He never slowed down. I won't ever forget it."

Kraft is from Brookline, a Boston suburb, and had been a season ticket holder since 1971, the year Foxboro Stadium opened.

He later bought the stadium and leased it to the Patriots. Before he purchased the team for $172 million, he was offered $75 million by Patriots owner James Orthwein to buy his way out of the lease. Orthwein was planning to move the team to his native Saint Louis, which lost the Cardinals to Arizona in 1988, but Kraft would not let him break the lease. He bought the team from Orthwein instead.

The Pats had been a moribund franchise. The only two things it had going for it were Bill Parcells, a future Hall of Fame coach, and quarterback Drew Bledsoe, both of whom arrived in 1993.

Parcells and Kraft were eventually involved in a power struggle, a fight the owner is always going to win. Kraft was not happy that Parcells would commit to coaching the team only one year at a time. Parcells made Kraft feel like an outsider. Parcells was not happy that Kraft took away his power over the draft. That led to their parting following the Patriots' loss to the Packers in the Super Bowl. The worst-kept secret in the NFL was that Parcells was on his way to the Jets. He didn't even travel on the team plane home from New Orleans. Kraft then hired Pete Carroll, at the time the defensive coordinator of the 49ers, who had been fired as the Jets coach after just one season in 1994.

Carroll inherited a team loaded with the young talent Parcells drafted, and even though he made the playoffs in his first two seasons, each year the team's record regressed, and Kraft fired him after the 1999 season. Carroll developed into an outstanding head coach, winning two national championships at Southern Cal and then leading the Seahawks to the Super Bowl title in 2013 and back to the Super Bowl in 2014, where they lost to Kraft's Patriots. Kraft replaced Carroll with Belichick, giving him three of the highest-profile head coaches of this generation.

In the first twenty-one years of Kraft's ownership, the Patriots went to seven Super Bowls and won four. That's more appearances and victories than any other team in the NFL during that period;

no other team was even close. The Steelers were next with four Super Bowl appearances. The Steelers, Giants, Broncos, Packers, and Ravens were next with two Super Bowl victories. Six of the Patriots' appearances and all four of their victories came in the Belichick-Brady era.

"I've had two quarterbacks start the year," Kraft said of his first two decades as the Patriots' owner. "It's part of a way to do business. You stick with people."

Brady helped out the Patriots when he signed a new deal before the 2013 season. He received a $30 million signing bonus and made a total of $33 million over the next two years. Starting with the 2015 season, his salaries total $27 million for the next three years. The average of $9 million per year is not even half his market value. Brady did that to ease the burden on the Patriots salary cap, allowing them to remain competitive and put a championship-caliber team around him. During the offseason in 2016, Brady reworked his contract again, this time signing a two-year, $41 million extension through the 2019 season that included a $28 million signing bonus. His base salaries for 2016 and 2017 were reduced to $1 million. That meant Brady would make $30 million over the course of the '16 and '17 seasons, an average of $15 million per year, still about $8 million per year below market value. Brady was in a better position than anybody in the NFL to give his team a hometown discount. His wife made nearly $50 million in a recent twelve-month period.

"Would the other player do that? The other person?" Kraft said, referring to Peyton Manning. "I don't know. Think about it: we sat and redid his contract so he could remain with the Patriots for his career."

Manning was due to make $19 million in 2015. After he limped to the finish line with a leg injury and the Broncos lost their only playoff game in 2014, the Broncos asked Manning to take a pay cut to $15 million, which he agreed to do. But he was still making nearly double Brady's $8 million for 2015. Brady's average salary of $9 million was just seventeenth among quarterbacks.

"Tommy does a lot of good, quiet, special things that make a difference, especially with sick children," Kraft said. "I've been a party to it. He's idolized. Peyton is special. He's very, very special. But as a human being, I don't think there is anyone who could be better than Brady. I've met a lot of people. He's off the charts."

Manning also has a big heart. A high school football player from Long Island tragically died after suffering a severe head injury following a collision during a game in 2014. In the eulogy, it was mentioned that Manning was his favorite player. The Broncos were informed by a woman who attended the funeral, and two hours later Manning signed a personal note of condolence on one of his jerseys and it was sent overnight to the family.

Brady and Manning are very giving of their time to charity. In 1999 Manning established the PeyBack Foundation, which assists disadvantaged youth with programs providing leadership and growth opportunities for children at risk. It has provided more than $10 million in grants and programs in Colorado, Indiana, Louisiana, and Tennessee. Manning contributes financially as well. Brady has been involved almost his entire career with the Best Buddies Challenge, which benefits people with intellectual and developmental disabilities. Brady takes part in a flag football game every year as part of the weekend and hosts a big dinner on Cape Cod.

**The Manning Passing** Academy at Nicholls State University in Thibodaux, Louisiana, is one of the most popular football camps in the country. Peyton, Eli, Archie, and Cooper are there, and the four-day camp has become so big that it sells out its 1,200 spots way in advance. Campers get the chance to learn from the Mannings. Campers have included Russell Wilson, Andrew Luck, and Harry Kraft.

Young Harry was named for Robert Kraft's father. Harry's father is Jonathan Kraft, the Patriots president, who is Robert's oldest son. Prior to his senior year in high school, Harry attended the Manning Passing Academy for the fourth time; it's owned, of course, by the family of Tom Brady's number-one rival, Peyton, and his brother Eli, who beat the Patriots twice in the Super Bowl. The first time Jonathan signed Harry up for camp, in 2011, he didn't tell Archie or any of the Mannings in advance. Jonathan arrived in a limousine. That's how they knew the Patriots family had come to Thibodaux.

Harry's grandfather Robert flew in from a conference in Sun Valley, Idaho, in 2014 to observe. His father was also there to watch as the temperature neared 100 degrees. Harry was an excellent high school quarterback with a strong arm, but he was only five nine. Although he was a little taller than his grandfather and father, he inherited their genes for height, which meant an NFL career was not likely. He was recruited by Dartmouth as a quarterback and committed to play at the Ivy League school starting in the fall of 2015. Dartmouth's coach is Buddy Teevens, who got a close-up view of Harry at the camp. He's run the Manning Passing Academy since its inception in 1996, when he was coach at Tulane.

"Harry is super sweet and smart," Archie said.

He then laughs, knowing he's about to say something funny. "I don't think he's ever going to play for the Patriots," he said, "but he's probably going to own them."

Archie keeps an eye on the youngest Kraft at his camp. "We love Harry," Archie said. "People get the wrong idea about our camp. We have 1,200 kids. You're not going to have 1,200 bluechip players. Our goal is to enhance the high school experience; it's not just trying to get you to be a college player or a pro player. Harry's a typical camper, and he's a good little player. He has a good time and he enjoys all the things we do. It really makes me feel good that they make the effort to come all the way to Thibodaux."

Robert Kraft spends time sitting with Archie in his golf cart. One is the patriarch of the First Family of quarterbacks. The other owns the most successful team in the NFL, whose only two losses in the Super Bowl were inflicted by last-minute drives by Archie's youngest son.

"They have been gracious to Harry," Kraft said. "The Manning family has represented the best in excellence. They're a great family and great people, and they've achieved at a high level and kept a sense of humility about them."

When the Krafts and Mannings are together, they represent thirteen of the first forty-nine Super Bowl games and eight championships. It would have been more, but the old man of the Manning family played on lousy teams.

# 10

# BOYS WILL BE BOYS

It was the last day of training camp, and Peyton Manning and Dallas Clark left their dorm room on the basement floor where the Colts veterans reside at Anderson University, about forty-five miles northeast of Indianapolis. They had nothing but mischief on their minds as they walked up one flight of steps.

They commandeered a fifty-five-gallon garbage can and went into the bathroom, put it under a showerhead, and filled it with water. Lots of water. Too much water. The usual protocol for the prank was to fill the can about halfway. Manning never does anything halfway. He and Clark were dragging a garbage can filled nearly to the top.

By the end of training camp, players are tired of being away from home; they are sick of institutional food, bored with endless meetings, worn out by practice, and certainly fed up with looking at each other and being yelled at by coaches. They are a family, or more precisely, frat brothers. They need to find ways to entertain themselves.

"Don't put that much water in," Clark warned Manning.

He didn't listen.

They leaned the can against a dorm-room door with a couple of rookie offensive players inside whose main priority was making the team and not doing anything to piss off Manning.

Manning and Clark pounded on the door and took off. What happened next?

"They opened the door and it just oozed," Clark said.

The dynamic duo went back to their room in the basement pleased they had once again flooded some poor rookies' room. Then they noticed something was terribly wrong. Their ceiling was leaking. The room they had just dumped the water in was directly above theirs, creating an unintended shower. "I think we went too far with this," Clark said. "Man, someone is going to have to clean this up."

The practical joke was the signal that they had survived another training camp. "We're adults, right?" Clark said. "Why are we acting like kids? There is no excuse. But it's one of those things that happen when you're in that environment and around the guys."

Manning and Brady take their jobs on Sunday very seriously. The part of their personality that is reserved for just their teammates is their ability to stoop to childish levels the rest of the week. Brady and Manning are two of the most accomplished practical jokers the NFL has seen in a long time. That's saying something, too, because Brett Favre was one of the best. He used to throw stink bombs in the locker room to make it smell like the residual effect of eating a plate of baked beans.

In the middle of the Green Bay winter, when the weather was appropriate for polar bears, Favre would remove the car keys from a teammate's locker before practice, hand them off to one of the locker-room workers, and request that he move the car to the opposite side of Lambeau Field while they were out on the field and then return the keys to the locker. Of course, when practice was over and the players had showered and dressed and it was pitch black in the dead of another endless Green Bay winter night, the player would hustle out to his car not far from the locker-room exit, but his car would no longer be in the parking spot he'd left it in that morning. Favre was thirty-five years old going on fifteen.

Brady has the impeccable image and the supermodel wife. Jay Feely, his college buddy and longtime NFL kicker, says Brady is so secure in who he is that he often signs off on texts to him by saying, "Love you." Manning is known as an avid letter writer. Not e-mails. Handwritten letters. He will write to players he admired when they retire.

Brady and Manning have the highest character, but it has never been a good idea to mess with either one of them. Part of Manning's standard routine is to change the language on a team-mate's cell phone to Chinese. "That was pretty clever," Clark said. Eli is also known to be quite skilled at changing the settings on cell phones. It must be in their genes. Matt Cassel learned the hard way that being close friends with Brady doesn't earn one an exemption when he feels like screwing around. He became Brady's favorite target.

Brady sat close to the door of the Patriots quarterbacks meeting room. Cassel would come in and swing the door open, nearly nailing him. "Dude, you're going to hit me, you're going to kill me," Brady yelled.

One day, Cassel was coming into the meeting room with a plate of food. Brady was in his usual spot. "So he put his chair close up to the door knowing that I was going to come in," Cassel said. "I spilled my food all over the place."

Cassel couldn't just leave it at that. He had to get even. He found Brady's Nike shoes in his locker and filled them with shaving cream. Naturally, when Brady came in to get dressed after a post-practice shower, he put his sneakers on and his feet were buried. Brady retaliated by throwing a protein shake on Cassel. Brady was willing to call a truce, but first he wanted Cassel to address him with reverence. "He wanted me to call him Daddy," Cassel said. "There is no way I'm calling him Daddy."

Cassel threatened to get back at Brady. "I can call it off," Brady said.

Cassel didn't have a clue what he was talking about. He thought maybe Brady was going to do something to his helmet. It was much worse and much funnier.

"I didn't care at that point," Cassel said.

Yes he did.

"Of course, I come in from practice and there's three of my tires sitting there in front of my locker," Cassel said. "I'm like, 'Son of a bitch!' He hid one of them in the training room. I couldn't get the tires on my car after practice, so I had to get a ride home."

Brady is telling his version of the events and can't stop laughing. Just about everything about his time with Cassel makes him laugh. "He was a fun guy. We were like little brothers together for the years we played together. We had an exchange the previous day. He threw something on me, I threw something on him, he threw something on my car, I threw something on his car. So it just went back and forth," Brady said. "So finally when we went out to practice, I took all four tires off his car, and we left three of them right by his locker and hid his other tire until the next day."

The visual is humorous: Brady with a tire jack in his hands looking over his shoulder to see if Cassel was coming. "God, no," Patriots center Dan Koppen said. "He made a phone call and magically it happened."

Brady again was ready to call a truce. He had one of the locker-room guys put the tires back on Cassel's car. "The offensive linemen thought it was funnier than hell," Cassel said.

Koppen and tackle Matt Light came up with a plan to ostensibly help Cassel get even but it was truly designed because there was so much fun going on and they wanted in. Koppen and Brady are close friends. Brady invited Koppen to be in the audience at 30 Rockefeller Center when he hosted *Saturday Night Live* in 2005 after the Patriots won their third Super Bowl in four years. They socialize and go to dinner with their wives. Their friendship didn't end when Koppen was no longer with the Patriots after the 2011 season. "I think success hit him so hard and early that he didn't know how to handle a lot of that," Koppen said. "He's gotten a lot more comfortable in his skin as he's gotten older. There's some places he stays away from. He can't go to dinner at Chili's on Wednesday night. That doesn't happen. When he goes out, it's probably special. He probably stays in more than he goes out."

One night during the 2007 undefeated season, there was a big get-together for special-team ace Larry Izzo's birthday. "Thankfully, the place was rented out and the public was not in there," Koppen said.

Thankfully because it was a karaoke party, and Brady is just a normal guy who is not afraid to make a fool of himself with his friends. He grabbed the microphone. "I don't remember what he sang, but he sings awful," Koppen said. "He's got an awful singing voice. When he's out in a secured environment, with guys on the team and their wives, he's more laid-back and can have a lot of fun."

Koppen's close relationship with Brady didn't prevent him from messing up his car. He was comfortable pranking him, especially when he was going to blame it on Cassel anyway. The first step was getting into Brady's car. "Stole the keys," Koppen said.

To prepare for the occasion, Koppen went shopping the day before and purchased several extra-large bags of Styrofoam packaging peanuts. Koppen and Light opened the sunroof of Brady's car and poured in peanuts until it was full.

It wouldn't have been any fun if Koppen and Light couldn't observe Brady's reaction. They knew that on the day of the attack

Belichick was holding an indoor walk-through practice on the club level of the stadium. There's a huge window overlooking the players' parking lot. Koppen and Light walked over to get a bird's-eye view of their work. They liked what they saw. They liked it a lot.

"Hey, Tom, come over here and check this out," Koppen said. "Look what Cassel did to you now." Brady came over and looked down. He saw his car overflowing with peanuts. At least they weren't real peanuts in the shell. Koppen thought he was framing Cassel, but Brady was onto him.

"Dan has been hit in the head too many times," Brady said.

By the time practice was over, Brady's car was vacuumed and cleaned out.

"That was kind of a letdown," Koppen said. "We wanted him to go out there and just open the door and all the peanuts fall out."

Brady didn't retaliate. "I wanted them to get the last laugh," he said.

He had gotten a taste of life in the NFL as a rookie when Bledsoe put confetti in the air-conditioning vents in his yellow Jeep. He turned the fan on high. Brady put the key in the ignition and his car suddenly looked like Times Square on New Year's Eve, or as he would soon find out, it was like standing on the podium at midfield after winning the Super Bowl. "He blasted the AC," Brady said. "The whole car got showered with confetti."

Bledsoe was sitting in his car next to Brady enjoying the show. "He thought it was the funniest thing in the world," Brady said.

After the episode with shaving cream and the protein shake and Cassel's tires and Brady's peanut-filled car, word spread around the locker room and right up to Belichick's office. He was not happy. According to Cassel, the coach came into the locker room, rounded up Brady, who was already a three-time Super Bowl winner and two-time Super Bowl MVP, and brought him together with Cassel, a backup trying to make living. He sat them down. Cassel says Belichick was red-hot and told them, "You two assholes are starting World War III. We're going to get somebody hurt. Can we stop this shit?"

It stopped. Brady having Cassel's tires removed made him the winner. "The old adage is, You never mess with anybody that has more money than you," Cassel said.

Brady is proud of his practical joke prowess. "I have my moments," he said. "People don't expect it from me. The guys I've been around a long time know I like to joke around and have fun as much as anyone. It's a little challenging now as an older player. There's so many young guys on our team. You try to find a way to connect. It's hard to be humorous all the time. Sometimes they don't get it. You have to pick the right spot."

Manning and Clark weren't one-hit wonders in Colts training camp, and packaging peanuts weren't limited to Foxboro. They got hold of a few bags. Then they got the keys to the car of one of the assistant coaches who was new to the team. They moved his car to the center of the quad at Anderson University. All the coaches and players had to walk through the quad on the way to breakfast. They also used the sunroof as their port of entry and filled up the car. They went one step further than Koppen and Light. They purchased plastic wrap, using roll after roll and completely enclosing the car.

"It was just sitting right in the middle of this park," Clark said.

Manning was the ideas person. He left most of the dirty work on this job to Clark and Austin Collie. They discussed potential punishment before they executed their plan. "You could look at it as, 'Oh, I'm with Peyton, they won't do anything,' or 'Wait a minute, they wouldn't do anything to Peyton, but they would do something to me,'" Clark said.

Collie feared the second scenario. "He was freaking out," Clark said.

He thought he was going to be cut. He survived. So did Manning and Clark.

If you are going to be a practical joker, then it's useless to complain when the tables are turned.

Koppen finished his career in Denver in Manning's first year with the Broncos in 2012. He has a unique claim to fame. Not only have Manning and Brady both stuffed their hands under his rear end to take the snap from center, but he successfully pulled off practical jokes on both of them that they probably won't mention when they give their speeches after induction into the Pro Football Hall of Fame.

Brady was victim number one. It starts as he's positioning his hands under Koppen's backside as he calls the play at the line of scrimmage in practice.

"All the ladies were jealous because he's touching my ass," Koppen said. "But he came back and said that there were only two butts he would want to touch, his wife's and mine. That made me feel good."

The next step was Koppen passing gas on Brady's hands as he was about to snap him the ball. He feels that's what cemented their friendship. "I think it becomes really special when you're able to fart on him and do all that stuff," he said. "That takes it to a whole new level."

He farted on Brady's hands in practice?

"He did," Brady said, as if he were providing confirmation in testimony in a courtroom. "You get used to it. And sometimes Dan would be chewing tobacco and he would spit on the ball. So when he'd snap it up to me, I would get a handful of his little dip spit. Oh, it was the nastiest thing. He would just laugh, ha, ha, ha. He obviously got the biggest kick out of it. I didn't get the biggest kick out of it all the time. It was funny, like, the first two times, and after that, I said, I don't want to be touching that anymore."

Koppen arrived in New England as a fifth-round pick in 2003.

Brady was already a Super Bowl MVP. How long did it take Koppen to feel secure and comfortable enough to fart on Brady?

"That's a legitimate question," Koppen said. "I think a couple of years."

Brady just didn't stand under center and let Koppen get away with the flatulence. "He will usually come back with hitting you in the nuts the next play," Koppen said. "There is give-and-take."

In a game, it was serious business. No farting. "Maybe accidentally," Koppen said. "In the game, Tom didn't care. The practice ones are the special ones where you actually plan it out. You just save one. You see if you can save one during the team drills. I would tell the guy next to me I was going to fart on Tom the next play."

When Koppen joined Manning, he went from one of the all-time greats to another of the all-time greats. "Pretty good," he said. "Peyton is fun to be around. He's got great stories. He's a great guy to sit down and have a cup of coffee with or have dinner with and just listen."

Koppen was comfortable with Brady. In Denver, he took over as the starter when J. D. Walton was injured early in the season. He quickly developed a rapport with Manning, who could be tough on teammates, but Koppen expected a lot, too. "If they got worn out by Peyton, they were in the wrong business or they were on the wrong team," Koppen said. "Yeah, he was hard on people, he asked a lot of questions, he demanded a lot from his teammates. That's what it takes to win sometimes, especially when people are getting to know each other. I want to know what you are going to do in this situation. All right, this guy blitzes, who has him? So it never really bothered me."

Koppen traveled west to Denver and packed his sense of humor. "I don't think I farted on Peyton," he said. "I only had a year with him, so we never got that far."

One day in practice, however, Koppen did victimize Manning.

Football jersey tops are extremely long, even on these awfully big guys. On cue, as they broke the huddle, Koppen and the Broncos linemen pulled their jerseys out and dropped their pants. The shirts covered their asses, so it was hard to tell their pants were down. "Peyton got under there. He was so focused, he didn't realize it," Koppen said. "Everyone was bare-assed. He got up under there for a little bit. It got a little weird after a while. Does he realize that I'm bare-butt right now?"

Apparently not. "That's an old rival center-quarterback exchange," Manning said. "So, yeah, that's a good one."

Manning has been on the giving end a lot more than he's been on the receiving end. "I don't have a ranking," he said. "I don't have a list."

He does enjoy the camaraderie of his teammates. "In the locker room I think it's important, you spend a lot of time, you are grinding, it's May and we're going from six forty-five in the morning until two o'clock and we haven't had a chance to breathe yet. It's been meetings, treatment, lifting, practice, all that," he said. "So when you have a chance in the locker room to keep things loose, keep the team close together, laughing is a good thing, especially when you are in what I call a grinding profession. That's where that comes from."

The Patriots of Belichick are considered to be about as amusing as a computer infected with a virus. Perception isn't necessarily reality in the NFL. The Cowboys of Tom Landry were supposed to reflect their stone-faced coach. One visit inside their locker room in the 1980s told a vastly different story. They were a loose, trash-talking, fun-loving team. Now, when Landry briskly walked through the room, the players would pretend to be sitting at their lockers studying the playbook. As soon as Landry exited, the clowning resumed. The stories about the Belichick era are similar. The players don't show much of their personality to the public— they answer questions as if reading from a manual prepared by

Belichick—but when the cameras and notepads are out of sight, they love to joke around.

Somehow a pig's head ended up in their locker room, donated by guard Joe Andruzzi. It was moved from locker to locker and then into the coaching room, where it took up residence in the stall of Belichick's trusted assistant Dante Scarnecchia. A live duck was next to make an appearance. "Nate Solder took it home and kept it as a pet for a while," Koppen said.

Belichick was never the target. "Bill's kind of the sacred cow in the group," he said. "No one really goes after him that much."

No cows, sacred or otherwise, have been brought into the locker room for show-and-tell.

Brady marveled at the creativity of the offensive linemen led by Light and Koppen. During practice when the scout team was running plays to give the first-team defense a look at the upcoming opponent, the starting offensive linemen would jog around the perimeter of the field to stay in shape. The Patriots tape their practices with all twenty-two overhead cameras, much like game day, to give the coaches and players a full view. It's a common teaching tool.

"When the scout teams' plays were being filmed, the offensive linemen would run with their pants down," Brady said. "No one would see it because everyone was just watching the practice."

The players then gathered to watch the tape of practice in the team meeting room, and the streaking was there on the screen for all to enjoy. "It was so funny," Brady said. "It takes a lot of personality to do that."

**Peyton Manning takes** even being funny seriously. When he hosted *Saturday Night Live* in 2007 shortly after the Colts beat the Bears in the Super Bowl, he studied as though it was a championship game and was so good that he was invited back when *SNL* held its fortieth-anniversary show in 2015. He and Derek Jeter play-fully argued onstage over who was the best athlete to ever host the show. Manning is so entertaining on television that he was among the celebrities invited to participate in the Top Ten list on David Letterman's final show.

Manning's United Way skit on *SNL* was hilarious. He was in a park in New York playing football with kids. He called the plays and fired the football (they were Nerf balls) at the children, hitting one boy in the back of his head. He was so disgusted that the pass was not caught, he sent the kid to take a time-out in a Porta-Potty and yelled at him to close the door. "Get your head out of your ass!" Manning screamed at the kid. "You suck!"

He then tried to teach the kids how to break into a car on a city street. When a police siren sounded, he yelled, "Cops! Cops! Every man for himself!" The segment ended with this suggestion from United Way: "Spend time with your kids. So Peyton Man-ning doesn't."

He attacked the script as if it was the playbook for a champi-onship game against Brady. "He was the only guy I've ever known to host the show to have a binder with tabs. That preparation cer-tainly came through on Saturday," former *SNL* cast member Seth Meyers said on *Mike and Mike* on ESPN Radio.

Brady enjoyed his turn to host two years before Manning. "He's the coolest person any of us will ever meet," Meyers said. "But he's really nice."

Manning could have owned New York if he had left Tennes-see in 1997 and been drafted first overall by the Jets or had signed with them when he became a free agent in 2012. His brother Eli is laid-back, and he has cashed in by playing in the biggest market in the country. Peyton is so glib and so personable, he might even have been in the running to replace his pal Letterman as host of *The Late Show* when Letterman retired in 2015 if he had been around New York full-time.

Brady was funny on *SNL*, but Manning is a natural in front of the camera. Brady opened his *SNL* monologue with a bit where he sings and dances—a very liberal interpretation of what constitutes singing and dancing. The audience was larger than when he was singing karaoke at Izzo's birthday party.

"I won the Tour de France, and I did it with no pants," Brady croons. "So when I rode by, you saw my sweet behind."

In one skit about sexual harassment in the workplace, Brady fondles one of Amy Poehler's breasts after asking her out to lunch and then arranges a date with Tina Fey when he approaches her in the office dressed in a sport shirt, tie, and underwear.

Brady's parents were in the audience for the show. "He never lets us know he's nervous under any circumstances," Brady Sr. said. "We were nervous because I've never heard him sing before. Oh my god, where did that come from? The opening was pretty darn good. He acted when he was in grammar school when all the kids do school plays, but I've never seen him have any propensity toward acting."

Archie Manning wasn't nervous before Peyton played in his first Super Bowl. "The Colts deserved to play in that Super Bowl," he said. "I didn't have anxiety. I had pride."

But as he sat in the audience for *SNL* at 30 Rockefeller Plaza with Olivia, Eli, and Cooper in studio 8H at NBC headquarters in midtown Manhattan, he was shaking. It was Peyton's thirty-first birthday, and at the end of the show, Eli and Cooper wheeled out a birthday cake during the closing credits. Eli won the Super Bowl the following year, and *SNL* executive producer Lorne Michaels asked him to host. But after Peyton received rave reviews, Eli knew the timing wasn't right to try to one-up his big brother. He has an understated sense of humor and is the best practical joker in the Giants locker room, but following Peyton so quickly was a no-win situation. "Eli is not dumb," Archie said. "He told Lorne, 'Get me the next time.'"

When Eli won his second Super Bowl, beating Brady again following the 2011 season, Michaels called, and this time Eli accepted. Archie wasn't as nervous about Eli hosting, for two reasons. He had already been through it with Peyton, and Eli is so calm he often doesn't register a pulse.

"When Peyton told me he was going to do *Saturday Night Live*—and I don't ever question Peyton—I don't think he really wanted to do it," Archie said. He was getting pressured by his high school friends. "I knew all through the years, there was a certain group of guys telling him, 'Peyton, if you ever get a chance to do *SNL*, you damn well better do it,'" Archie said. "So he was not going to say no."

Peyton brought the news to his parents that he was going to hit the big stage in New York.

"We're going to go, aren't we?" Olivia asked.

"I don't know if I want to be there, Liv. This is not what he does," Archie said.

Peyton had been rehearsing in New York all week. Meyers, who also wrote for the show, and the rest of the writers met every Tuesday night for dinner in the back room at Lattanzi, a classic New York restaurant in the famed Theater District. The creative brains of the show would brainstorm late into the night writing and rewriting. They came up with some clever skits for Manning.

Archie and Olivia left on a flight Friday from New Orleans to New York. They arrived in the evening and were relaxing in their midtown hotel when Archie's cell phone rang.

"Get over here," Peyton said.

"Where?" Archie asked.

"NBC," Peyton said.

Archie walked over to Fiftieth Street, was let through by security, and was brought to the greenroom. Peyton was sitting by himself watching an Elvis Presley concert that the King of Rock 'n' Roll had performed in Las Vegas. The writers had put together a skit in which Peyton was going to play Elvis. Peyton was studying his moves intently.

"I don't seem good enough as Elvis," Peyton told Archie. He watched more tape.

"How is the week?" Archie asked.

"It's good," Peyton said.

He asked Peyton to turn off the video. "I got anxiety about you doing this. How is it going to be? What's it going to be like?" Archie said.

Peyton didn't hesitate. "We're going to kick their ass!"

He was talking about the entire cast. He wasn't talking about himself. He was talking about the *SNL* team. Manning is always about the team and competition. It made Archie relax.

Peyton kicked ass. It helped that the Elvis skit was left in rehearsal. The *SNL* producers had called an audible. Manning could relate.

Brady had a blast doing *SNL*, but he has been more a fixture modeling in print ads, which take advantage of his good looks. Manning's memorable commercials for MasterCard, Papa John's Pizza, and Nationwide Insurance have made him one of television's most popular pitchmen. Brady models for UGGo. He also made a very funny cameo appearance in the movie *Ted 2* and has appeared in *Entourage*, both on television and in the movie.

Manning and Brady came across as very likable on *SNL*. "It was so fun to do that when I finished it, I was almost disappointed that I'll never have a chance to experience that again," Brady said. "It was such a unique thing that I was bummed when it was over. Even if I ever happen to do this again, it will never be like the first one, because I had no expectations going in. You can just go, 'Holy shit!' It was awesome. It was a great experience."

Brady knew Manning would do well when it was his turn. "It was so out of the box for both of us. He was pretty awesome, I got to say it," he said. "He's got a great sense of humor about him. He's very witty, a very funny guy. He's got more of a slapstick humor than I do."

Manning had no problem poking fun at himself when the script called for him to tell a story about visiting eighty-five-year-old Joe O'Malley in a veterans' hospital in Boston.

He said O'Malley asked him, "Peyton, what do Tom Brady and the circus have in common?"

"What's that, Joe?" Manning asked.

"They both have two more rings than you do," O'Malley said.

By the end of the 2014 season, Brady had one more ring than a three-ring circus. Manning was still stuck at one.

**Eric Decker played** two years with Manning in Denver. They became close friends, and along with tight end Jacob Tamme, who also played with Manning in Indianapolis, the three would ride together to games at Mile High Stadium from the Inverness Hotel and Conference Center in Englewood, the team hotel for home games. Manning was behind the wheel and Tamme was in charge of the music, even though Decker is married to country singer Jessie James. The Broncos issued only one parking pass per family, so the players would ride together and the wives would meet them at the game. "We figured it was really good team-building time to just really calm the nerves," Decker said. "Tamme was the DJ and was riding shotgun. He was older than me. I allowed him to sit in the front. I think it was a roundtable discussion of what mixes to play, but Tamme controlled it."

Manning's preference was the Coffee House channel on SiriusXM. The twenty-five-mile drive north from Englewood to Denver is how Decker really got to know Manning. "Everyone looks at him as this iconic football player," Decker said. "He's a family man, a good person who likes to have fun. He's a jokester. I don't know if people know that. He's a lighthearted fun guy. He's a guy's guy."

Manning knows the name of everybody in the building. When a new player arrives, he's the first to introduce himself or play golf with him. "You know that he has your back, which is great," Decker said.

In April 2013, Peyton and Eli invited their receivers to Duke for a passing camp. Peyton throws to the Broncos. Eli throws to the Giants. The players all pay their own way to get to Durham, North Carolina, and then Peyton and Eli take care of the rest. Victor Cruz, Hakeem Nicks, and Louis Murphy from the Giants and Decker, Demaryius Thomas, and Wes Welker from the Broncos were there.

On the last night, the entire group went to dinner at a steak house between Chapel Hill and Raleigh. There was a wine cellar downstairs. Before dinner, Peyton approached all the receivers except for Decker and told them he was going to be handing each an envelope. "Decker is getting pranked," he told them.

Five of the envelopes would have a blank sheet of paper. Decker's would be different. At the appropriate time, Manning handed out the envelopes. Decker looked inside. It was on Duke stationery. Under the letterhead DUKE FOOTBALL was Decker's name and the Broncos address.

To the right was the heading INVOICE. It was an itemized bill:

On-field instruction from Duke Coaching Staff ($500 per session) $2,500

Laundry service from Duke Football Equipment Staff ($20 per session) $100

Taping, treatment, etc. from Duke Football Athletic Training Staff ($50 per session) $200

Facility Fee (use of Pascal Field House, Brooks Building and
    Yoh Center) $300
Airport Shuttle FREE
Total payment due in 30 days
Please include the invoice number on your check
Make all checks payable to Duke University Football
Subtotal $3,000
Tax Rate 7.25%
Tax $217.50
Other $—
TOTAL Due: $3,217.50

*No way,* Decker thought to himself. He didn't even notice that
Manning's math was off. He swallowed hard. He looked at Manning, who just shrugged. "I didn't want to say anything and be
rude," Decker said.

He looked around the table as the rest of the players opened
their envelope. Thomas was sitting next him. He was shaking his
head, commiserating with Decker about the unexpected expense
they had all incurred.

"I know. I know," Thomas said.

Decker was soon to be married, and he was still working on
his rookie contract. He was making $1.323 million for the upcom-
ing season, but it was a year before he cashed in as a free agent
when he signed a five-year, $36.25 million deal with the Jets.

Manning let Decker squirm for a little bit so they all could
enjoy the moment. Then he called it off.

"It probably lasted five minutes," Decker said. "But it felt like
an eternity."

He didn't immediately retaliate. "We still have a relationship,"
he said. "So I am sure down the road I will get the chance."

Colts coach Tony Dungy commanded such respect that Manning never dared mess with him. Manning did once tell a player

that Dungy had gotten word he was out late the night before and was very upset. "I had guys coming to my office to apologize," Dungy said. "I would say, 'What are you talking about?'"

Six games into the 2001 season, Colts star running back Edgerrin James tore his ACL and missed the rest of the season. In the off-season, the Colts had signed Dominic Rhodes, an undrafted rookie free agent from Midwestern State. Rhodes would rush for 113 yards and a touchdown that would give Indianapolis the lead for good in their Super Bowl victory five years later against the Bears. Dungy needed Rhodes to be a quick learner as a rookie, and he stepped up.

On his way to rushing for 1,104 yards his first year, Rhodes passed 1,000 yards—the first undrafted rookie ever to hit that milestone—as he gained 141 yards in the final game of the season, a home game against the Broncos. He needed only 37 yards going in, and Dungy was going to make sure he got them. "The funniest thing I heard Peyton do was tell Dominic, when he gets to 1,000, they're going to stop the game and give him the game ball," Dungy said. "They know how many yards he needs."

Rhodes had a 4 yard run midway through the second quarter and he was up to 1,001 yards. "Dominic doesn't come to the huddle," Dungy said. "He's waiting for the ball. Finally, they get him in the huddle and get the next play going. He's like, 'Where's my game ball? How come they didn't stop the game? Where's my announcement?' Guys were rolling."

Brady had a lot to live up to in New England when he took over for Bledsoe, who not only was popular in the locker room, but pulled off the most legendary practical joke in Patriots history. The removal of Cassel's tires was the equivalent of just getting to the Super Bowl. Bledsoe earned the Lombardi Trophy.

The Patriots landed back at Boston's Logan Airport at four in the morning after playing on the West Coast. There was seven inches of new snow on the ground. The usual routine was, the players rode the team bus for the half-hour trip back to the stadium, where they'd parked their cars. The players were not looking forward to cleaning off the snow and driving home in the middle of the night. Patriots guard Todd Rucci and backup quarterback Scott Zolak were appalled when they found out that Bledsoe was big-timing them by having a car service waiting for him at the airport to take him home. His plan was to have his wife drive him to work the next day. Rucci had other ideas.

Bledsoe and Rucci had been going back and forth embarrassing each other. Rucci once made a collage of nearly naked women and taped the pictures on the passenger side of Bledsoe's Chevy Suburban from the headlights to the taillights. He knew from where Bledsoe was parked he wouldn't see the passenger side as he got in the car. Fans were waiting as usual for players to come out after practice to sign autographs as they drove out of the secured players' parking lot. "They weren't going to wait for Todd Rucci and fat linemen to get autographs," Rucci said. "They were going to wait for Drew Bledsoe."

The fans were allowed to line up and approach the players as they pulled out. They were only allowed on one side of the car. The passenger side. Bledsoe had no idea how Rucci had decorated his car.

Bledsoe headed home from the airport as the Patriots arrived in the snow, and Rucci and Zolak headed right to Bledsoe's car in the parking lot at Foxboro Stadium. They borrowed a couple of shovels from the stadium's maintenance office and spent two hours burying the car. "We make his car into a snowball. We got every available piece of snow within twenty feet piled up, and I made the point to get underneath the car to pack the wheel wells so there was absolutely no airspace whatsoever around his car," Rucci said. "The great thing is, Mother Nature cooperated with us and it started freezing rain a few hours later. His car was literally frozen."

Bledsoe showed up the next day and at first had a hard time even locating his car. It was buried. "He had trouble getting into his car for days," Rucci said. "It was great."

It took one month, but Bledsoe got even. On Christmas Eve day, before practice, Bledsoe stole the keys to Rucci's condominium in Franklin, a Boston suburb, and hired a moving company where friends worked. "I came back home around four p.m., and I found my dog and an autographed picture of Drew Bledsoe on the living-room floor saying, 'Merry Christmas,'" Rucci said.

That's all he could find. The couch was gone. The silverware was out of the drawers. The bed was gone. The pictures were off the walls. It's a good thing he was single at the time. "I don't think my dog was inconvenienced," Rucci said. "He got his bed and bowl."

It was as if no human lived in the apartment. Rucci walked down to the basement and found all his furniture and life's belongings. "At that point, I figured, *Okay, this is a good one, it was a great one, you got me.* I found everything in the basement. I'm trying to get my king-size mattress up a flight of condominium stairs, which is very tight," Rucci said. "It was hot, I'm sweating. I could not do it. I was so irate. I just spent the night in a hotel up the road and completely pissed off he got me so well. It was great, absolutely great."

Rucci knew the owners of the moving company. The apartment was back in order after Christmas. But on Christmas night, Rucci was invited for dinner at the Bledsoes and spent the night. "I couldn't even look him in the eye," Rucci said. "With the unlimited funds a quarterback has, he can play above the rim a lot easier than I can."

Bledsoe wasn't done. He put classified ads in the local paper for each of the two cars Rucci owned. He priced them reasonably. He listed Rucci's home phone number. By the time Rucci returned home from practice, he had seventy-three messages on his answering machine. "It was well deserved what I did to him," he said. "It was pretty well deserved what happened to me."

No hard feelings. Bledsoe was later the best man at Rucci's wedding, and their families spend every July 4 weekend together at Bledsoe's vacation home in Whitefish, Montana. They sit around the campfire and tell their kids stories of how they used to torture each other.

The stories also got passed down to the next generation in the locker room. Bledsoe set the bar awfully high at New England. Brady has tried not to lower it.

"We're in such an intimate environment with each other," Brady said. "You're at work from six in the morning until four in the afternoon. You're in close proximity to these guys for seven months of the year. It's blood, sweat, and tears in everything you're doing. There is a natural camaraderie and bond that probably few professions get to experience. When you're getting the crap knocked out of you and you look to the guy next to you, you got to believe that the guy has got your back. That is what makes football really special."

# 11

# WHO YOU GOT? BRADY OR MANNING?

Rex Ryan had just beaten Peyton Manning and the Colts in the wild-card game in the 2010 playoffs in Indianapolis, and now it was on to Foxboro for a matchup with Tom Brady and the Patriots.

He had once famously declared after the Jets hired him that he didn't take the job to kiss Bill Belichick's rings. He should have added that he wasn't going to kiss Brady's ass, either.

The Jets upset the AFC South champion Colts on a Saturday night at Lucas Oil Stadium. The Patriots had a bye, and Belichick gave his players the weekend off. Brady came to New York, where he and his wife, Gisele, have an apartment, and on Saturday night they went to see *Lombardi*, a hot show on Broadway. It was not quite same as Tony Romo spending the Cowboys' bye week after the 2007 regular season ended vacationing in Cabo San Lucas with then-girlfriend Jessica Simpson and catching grief for a lack of commitment when the Cowboys, the number-one seed, lost in the divisional round to the Giants. Brady is so committed to preparation, he probably had his Belichick playbook tucked inside his *Lombardi* playbill.

If the Colts beat the Jets, they would play in Pittsburgh and the Patriots would meet the winner of the Chiefs-Ravens game being played the next day. If the Jets won, the Patriots would play New York. Prior to the season, Brady declared, "I hate the Jets." The feeling was quite mutual.

Brady was in the Circle in the Square Theatre on Fiftieth Street and Broadway, checking his cell phone at the intermission for Jets-Colts updates. He and Gisele were back in their apartment in time to watch the second half. Even so, when word got back to Ryan that Brady was out on the town, in the Jets' town no less, rather than scouting the entire game on television, he embraced the opportunity to tweak Brady, and he hit him where it hurts.

"Peyton Manning would have been watching our game," Ryan said.

Just a few days earlier, in the run-up to the game with the Colts, Ryan praised Manning's study habits and threw it out there that Brady gets more help from Belichick than Manning receives from his coaches. Ryan loves to agitate Brady. That next weekend, the Jets beat the Patriots, the second most significant victory in team history, after Super Bowl III.

Ryan lasted six years with the Jets. The Patriots won the AFC East six times. Ryan was 3–9 against Brady in the regular season and 1–0 in the playoffs. Years later, he admitted that by trash-talking him, he was just trying to distract him.

"Of course I was," he said. "That's one of those deals—look, the dude is ridiculous. Tom Brady is ridiculous. He studies his fucking ass off and so does Peyton. They are 24/7. Damn near. Maybe they had a little time so they went to Broadway. So I said, 'Oh, I got them,' because I knew it would piss him off. This dude is fricking all football. He's got a life outside of football when the season is over. He's a football junkie. They probably kick his ass out of the building. I was tweaking his ass. I respect the shit out of those two guys. But at the same time, fuck, I got to beat those fuckers. I have to be at my very best to have a chance to beat them. I know they are that good."

Ryan thinks he is that good, too. Ask and he will tell you he and his twin brother, Rob, are the two best defensive minds in the NFL. He senses Brady and Manning don't like facing his defense as much as he doesn't like facing them.

"I don't know if it's the same feeling they get toward me, but I recognize there's like, 'Fuck you, Rex,'" he said. "They have a little bit of that in them to where it's like, 'Yeah, I made you prepare,' and that's why they can't wait to kick my ass. You know what I mean? I sense it because I see it in their faces."

Ryan was fired by the Jets after the 2014 season and hired by the Bills, and by remaining in the AFC East he doomed himself to still facing Brady twice a year. He was 0–2 against him in his first year in Buffalo, in 2015. He is almost reverential talking about whom he fears more if he has to stop one in the last two minutes. "I fear nobody . . . maybe a little bit," he said, laughing. "I've been beaten by both of them in those situations. It's like, *Oh shit, this guy is going to do it to me again.* They are deadly. It's impossible to choose between the two. I just see them as Hall of Fame quarterbacks."

In their seventeen head-to-head battles, Brady tossed 32 touchdowns with 15 interceptions. Manning had 35 touchdowns and 22 interceptions. Brady is 172-51 plus the record 22 playoff victories with 9 losses. Manning finished 186-79, and the 3 playoff victories in his final season allowed him to finish over .500 in the postseason, at 14-13. Brady has the best regular-season winning percentage among quarterbacks, at 77.1 percent. Manning is fourth at 70.2 percent, also trailing Roger Staubach and Joe Montana. Brady has played with the better teams and the better coach. Manning has played with the better skill-position players. He has two rings.

"I hate comparisons, but I'm talking about style," said Ernie Accorsi, the former general manager of the Colts, Browns, and Giants. "Brady is more like Montana. Peyton is more like Unitas."

Brady and Joe Montana each won four Super Bowls. Their styles are very similar. Manning has two Super Bowl championships. Johnny Unitas won two NFL championships and one Super Bowl. Manning wears number 18. Unitas wore number 19. Close your eyes when Manning played with the Colts and he looked just like Unitas on the field. They're the top four quarterbacks in NFL history.

When Unitas died in 2002, Manning wanted to honor him by wearing black high-top cleats, Unitas's trademark. The league threatened Manning with a $25,000 fine if he wore black shoes. The Colts as a team wore white. Manning didn't want to bring anything negative to Unitas's name, so he elected not to wear the black shoes.

**Brady vs. Manning** has been the best argument in the NFL for a long time. It's like asking: Coke or Pepsi? Vanilla or chocolate ice cream? Ginger or Mary Ann? It's a personal choice where you can't go wrong.

The pro-Brady faction has plenty to back up its argument. He's tied with Montana and Terry Bradshaw for the most Super Bowl victories of any quarterback. His six Super Bowl starts are a record for QBs. He won two Super Bowls with last-minute drives and another with just over two minutes remaining. He's been consistently excellent despite a changing cast of players around him, and other than the short time he played with Randy Moss—thirty-seven regular-season games and four playoff games—and the young tight end Rob Gronkowksi, he's never had the benefit of playing with a receiver or running back with Hall of Fame talent.

The pro-Manning faction has plenty of ammunition as well. Most touchdown passes in a season and career. Most passing yards in a season and career. Most career victories including the playoffs. He's been fortunate to play with potential Hall of Fame receivers Marvin Harrison and Reggie Wayne in Indianapolis and a young star in Demaryius Thomas in Denver. He is a surgeon on the field, and considering the influence and power he holds, he is basically a player-coach.

The anti-Brady argument: He has won his four Super Bowls by a combined thirteen points and never by more than four points. He could have lost any or all of those games. The first three titles came in the Spygate era. The fourth came two weeks after Deflategate.

The counterargument: His two Super Bowl losses were by three and four points. He is a couple of plays away from being 6–0. The impact of Belichick's spying was overblown. Deflategate was a farce.

The anti-Manning argument: He won just two Super Bowls, lost two, is barely over .500 in the playoffs, and his team was eliminated in its first playoff game in nine of the fifteen years he made the postseason. It's hard to justify or rationalize his under-achieving in the playoffs. Even in his first Super Bowl championship season, when he was counted on to carry the Colts, his playoff stats were unimpressive: three TDs and seven INTs. In his second Super Bowl title run, following the 2015 season, he had two TDs and one INT, and threw for just 539 yards in three games.

The counterargument: It takes more than a great quarterback to win a championship. Neither of the Super Bowl losses were his fault.

Tim Hasselbeck, a former NFL backup, said prior to Brady's

fourth Super Bowl title that he would rather have Manning. One day after Brady beat the Seahawks, Hasselbeck, an ESPN analyst, went on WEEI radio on Boston and reiterated his position.

"As somebody who played at the quarterback position in the NFL, at a time that both of those guys were playing, nobody's changed the game more than Peyton Manning or changed the way that position is played more than Peyton Manning," he said. "And from my experience as a quarterback in the NFL, that's a fact. Also, what I said was when you look at wins and losses, especially in the postseason, there are so many other factors that dictate who wins and loses the game. It's such a team environment, so . . . I just don't think it does the careers justice for any of these quarterbacks to try to narrow it down to just what happens in these postseason games."

He said Brady is better right now, but he says he would rather have Manning's career. "Peyton Manning has won a Super Bowl; he's achieved things that most quarterbacks aren't able to ever achieve," he said. "He's going to own basically every passing record that exists. So you ask me whose career I would rather have, based on that and how I explained to you he changed the game of football from an offensive perspective, that was my answer."

The last two minutes of a game often tell the true greatness of a quarterback. Right before Eli Manning drove the Giants to the winning touchdown in the final minutes of Super Bowl XLII, Accorsi turned to his son in the stands in Phoenix and said they were about to find out if Manning was all he thought he could be. Accorsi made the biggest trade in Giants history on draft day in 2004 to acquire Manning from the Chargers. Manning then went right down the field and scored to beat New England. He did it again in Super Bowl XLVI.

Seattle cornerback Richard Sherman faced Peyton Manning and Brady in back-to-back Super Bowls. Even though the

Seahawks destroyed Denver, he still holds Manning in high regard. After Brady took a knee to end the game against the Seahawks, Sherman walked over to Brady while he was still on the ground and extended his hand. "You're a great player," Brady said.

"Those two, you really can't go wrong picking either one of them," Sherman said. "They're such computers of this game. You respect every quarterback because you know they work hard, they study it. But those guys go out there and execute what they see. It's harder to do what you practice, to execute when everything is flying around, to know exactly where guys are going to be and hit them on a consistent level. Those two guys have been doing it for years. That's what you respect."

Sherman, a Stanford graduate, is one of the brightest players in the league, and going against Manning and Brady makes him study even more. "You know they're going to find the deficiencies, so you have to find them first," he said. "You have to self-scout, because you have to know when they are going to attack you and what they like to do, as well as scouting them. You probably have another six or seven hours of film on your hands if you're doing it right."

Former Giants defensive end Michael Strahan, inducted into the Pro Football Hall of Fame in 2014, was a big part of the defense that held Brady to just 14 points in the first Giants-Patriots meeting in the Super Bowl. He says he would fear Brady more than Manning with the game on the line in the last couple of minutes.

"I fear Tom Brady more than anybody," he said. "Tom Brady, I don't know, there is just something about Tom, not taking anything away from Peyton at all. I don't want to face him either. But there's just something about Tom. Maybe because we've seen him do it time and time again. Here's a guy who's won quite a few

Super Bowls and been to multiple others. How can you not choose him?"

Montana cast his vote for Brady as well. "He has all the traits that make a great quarterback," he said. "No matter what happens the play before, he's going to fight until the end. That's the thing you got to have. They are both fun to watch. This is a tough one. I think the only reason you go with Tom is, he's proven more in the playoffs down the stretch. I'd take Tom."

Manning and Brady will be in the Hall of Fame as soon as they are retired the required five years. Their legacies are secure. The gaping hole in Manning's résumé is the postseason, and it's why he loses points in the argument against Brady.

"I look at the critical moments in games. I look at the fourth quarter and two-minute ball games," said former Giants linebacker Antonio Pierce, an analyst with ESPN. "The next thing I look at is, how do they perform in the postseason? I would never put Eli as one of the greatest of all time in the regular season, but I'll put him up there in clutch moments and the postseason. He's that guy. Brady is that guy. Peyton has shown he's not that kind of guy in the postseason. For every comeback against the divisional foes that he's had in the regular season, it's a lot different when the lights are brighter and more cameras are on you in the postseason. To me, that is the one glaring difference between Tom and Peyton."

Manning's late-fourth-quarter interception returned for a touchdown in the Super Bowl loss to the Saints was more Wayne's fault than Manning's. Still, the record shows that the Colts were down 7 points and Manning couldn't get them into the end zone. In Brady's first two Super Bowl victories, he drove the Patriots for the winning field goal on the final drives against the Rams and Panthers, and in the first loss to the Giants threw a late TD pass to take the lead, but the New England defense couldn't stop the Giants. In the victory over the Seahawks, Brady threw the winning TD with 2:02 remaining.

Manning's reputation for not being able to win enough big games has followed him from Knoxville to Indianapolis to Denver.

"Completely unfair. Completely unfair," said former Colts president Bill Polian, who drafted Manning in Indianapolis. "We can have a long discussion about this, but the Super Bowl is one game. For the life of me, I can't see how you can take a guy's performance and just isolate it to the playoffs and forget the regular season."

Given the choice of the two, Polian said, "Obviously, I'm going to take my guy. They are without doubt the two preeminent quarterbacks of their time. There's nothing more to say, really, than that. They're both the greatest of their time. To have the good fortune to be associated with either of them is an incredible blessing."

Dungy takes the glass-half-full approach when he evaluates Manning's record in the postseason with the Colts. "I knew the flaws in our team," he said. "For those first few years, the Patriots were just better on defense than we were. They had better people and they probably had a better overall team, but we felt we could beat them if we played our game. I thought, for us, winning twelve or thirteen games every year was more of a tribute to Peyton than the fact that we weren't winning in the playoffs."

Dungy smiled. "Not many people look at it that way," he said. "When I got to the Colts, I'd never coached a team that won twelve games. Now we're winning twelve games every year."

Dungy and former Patriots safety Rodney Harrison work together on NBC's *Football Night in America* studio show on Sunday nights. They argue all the time about which quarterback they would take to win one game.

"I'm taking Peyton," Dungy said.

"Brady is the best closer. I'm taking him," Harrison said.

Dungy said he's been around Manning too many times when he's pulled games out. He was ready to take him out of the game in Dungy's return to Tampa in his second year with the Colts.

Dungy really wanted this game. He had coached the Bucs from 1996 to 2001 but was fired after too many playoff failures. Jon Gruden won the Super Bowl in his first year with Dungy's players and now Dungy was back in town.

"This defense is one of the best defenses that has been put together of all time," Dungy told his players. He would know. He built it.

"We can beat these guys," he told them, "but we can't fall behind. You get behind with that noise, we don't have a chance."

It was a Monday night game. It had a playoff-game intensity and atmosphere to it, but the Colts were letting Dungy down. They were getting embarrassed. Manning had just thrown an interception that Ronde Barber returned 29 yards for a touchdown with 5:09 left in the fourth quarter. Bucs 35, Colts 14.

"I was going to take Peyton out," Dungy said. "We needed to make sure we didn't get anybody hurt."

He was ready to bench the starters. Offensive coordinator Tom Moore convinced Dungy to give them one more series. The Colts got a 90-yard kickoff return from Brad Pyatt.

"Okay, let's go," Dungy said to Moore.

He put Manning and the first-team offense back in.

Four plays later, James Mungro scored from the 3.

Bucs 35, Colts 21, with 3:37 left.

Indianapolis's Idrees Bashir recovered the onside kick, and on the sixth play, Manning completed a 28-yard touchdown pass to Marvin Harrison. Bucs 35, Colts 28, with 2:29 left.

The Bucs went three-and-out. Manning took over at his own 15 with 1:41 remaining. He put together a five-play 85-yard drive with Ricky Williams scoring from the 1. Bucs 35, Colts 35, with 35 seconds left.

The Colts blocked Martín Gramática's 62-yard field goal attempt on the final play of regulation.

Tampa won the toss in overtime and moved to the Colts 41 and punted. Manning took over at his own 13 and moved into position for Mike Vanderjagt's 40-yard field goal. It was blocked, but Tampa's Simeon Rice was penalized for leaping. Given a second chance and 11 more yards, Vanderjagt hit a 29-yard field goal to complete one of the great comebacks in NFL history.

"From then on, no matter what the score was, or how much we were down, I always felt we would win," Dungy said. He says he has "so much respect for Tom," and how he's been able to change his style depending on the personnel around him. But he's still all-in on Peyton in the discussions with Harrison.

"The thing I always tell Rodney is, I can go back and show you Peyton Manning on the last drive beating the Patriots. Not all the time, but he did," Dungy said. "You can never show me Tom Brady on the last drive beating us. Anytime he had the ball and had to score to win, we won the game."

Polian and Dungy remain loyal to Manning, but Colts owner Jimmy Irsay burned some bridges in a 2013 interview with *USA Today*. It was Manning's second year in Denver, and Irsay felt that his departure and the arrival of Andrew Luck had worked out as planned for all concerned. But he lamented that Manning was able to secure only one ring in Indianapolis.

"We changed our model a little bit, because we wanted more than one of these," Irsay said, showing his ring. "Brady never had consistent numbers, but he has three of these. Pittsburgh had two, the Giants had two, Baltimore had two and we had one. That leaves you frustrated. You make the playoffs eleven times, and you're out in the first round seven out of eleven times. You have to love the Star Wars numbers from Peyton and Marvin and Reggie. Mostly, you love this." He again showed off his ring.

Days later, Irsay attempted to backtrack, saying he meant the Colts should have surrounded Manning with a better defense and special teams. Years later he said that if the Colts had won two Super Bowls, he would've said they should've won three.

"That was not a slap at Peyton at all. I know how competitive he is," Irsay said. "I know how all of us feel about not getting more than one. It's not a slap at anyone. It's just a fact. It's just something that we all wish we had the opportunity to have done. In the end, when you sit back and reflect on an era, it doesn't diminish all the incredible things that you've done. There was the championship and there wasn't the sort of bitter pill that Buffalo had to live with."

The 2010 Jets and the 2012 Ravens are the only teams to beat Manning and Brady back-to-back in the playoffs. Veteran safety Bernard Pollard was on the Baltimore team that beat the Broncos in double overtime in the divisional round and then dominated the Patriots the following week in the AFC championship game in Foxboro. Eliminating Brady and Manning one week apart was an impressive accomplishment.

"I don't really like either one of them. On the field, I dislike both of them," Pollard said. "A lot of people might hate me for this, but off the field I'm fans of both of them."

Brady is higher on the fear factor scale for a defense than Manning in Pollard's mind. "Ooh, that's tough, but I would rather see Peyton," he said. "Tom is a guy, he sees things, he understands things. They're both Hall of Famers. Beating the Broncos in the playoffs, that was fun, because we were able to outsmart Peyton. We didn't give up any big plays. Foxboro was a lot of fun, too. Brady is probably the most competitive guy I've ever played against. Between him and Philip Rivers. To beat that guy at home in the championship game, where we lost the year before, that was fun."

Pollard's place in Patriots history runs much deeper than helping the Ravens beat New England in the playoffs. As Brady was dropping back to pass halfway through the first quarter of the first game of the 2008 season against the Chiefs, he had his eyes fixed downfield. Pollard, then playing for Kansas City, was on the ground a few yards from Brady's legs. He lunged forward and hit Brady in his left knee.

Brady stayed down and then limped to the sidelines. It didn't take long for the diagnosis: torn ACL. Out for the season.

"Oh, man, I felt horrible," Pollard said. "Obviously, I heard everything when it popped. I felt it. I went to the sideline and the first thing I told [coach] Herm [Edwards] was, 'Hey, he's done.' I did not mean to do that. Man, I was kind of freaking out. As a player, we don't want to see that. You have some players who actually want to see guys get hurt like that. It was a crazy play."

Seven years earlier, in the second game of the season, Edwards had been the Jets coach when linebacker Mo Lewis crushed Drew Bledsoe as he neared the New York sideline. A sheared blood vessel in Bledsoe's chest nearly killed him. Brady took over and never gave the job back. Matt Cassel stepped in for Brady and led the Patriots to an 11–5 record, but they missed the playoffs. Cassel was traded after the season to the Chiefs, of all teams.

Pollard felt guilty about hurting Brady and some thought it was a dirty play. He indirectly sent get-well wishes to Brady but never apologized. "There was no reason to apologize," he said. "I didn't do anything wrong."

Former Ravens linebacker Ray Lewis created headlines when he told Sirius XM Radio "the only reason we know—I'm just being honest—who Tom Brady is, is because of the tuck rule," referring to the controversial fumble reversal in New England's victory over Oakland in the 2001 playoffs. "So now you've got to ask yourself: When did the legacy really start?"

He said the Patriots wouldn't have gone to the AFC championship without the tuck rule. "That's a fumble," Lewis said.

Brady didn't seem concerned. "Everyone has an opinion," he said. "I think Ray's a great player. He's a first-ballot Hall of Famer. I was fortunate enough to play against him."

Lewis looked foolish claiming Brady would be an unknown without the tuck rule and quickly came back to say his frustration was with the rule, which has since been removed, and he was not being critical of Brady. "I have immense respect for Tom Brady and everything he has achieved in this league," Lewis said. "He will go down as one of the all-time greats."

**Phil Simms, the** lead analyst for the NFL on CBS, meets with Brady and Manning before he does their games. One of them is very open. The other is guarded. Which is which?

"Now, who do you think?" Simms said. "I'll say, 'Peyton, what about so-and-so defense?' And then twenty minutes later, I'll say, 'Peyton, so what else is going on?' He just gets into it. I would say for both of them, being an analyst and being an ex-quarterback, going to talk to them, I would say I'm really conscious of being very prepared when I meet them."

Brady is not as talkative as Manning. As an extension of Belichick, he's not about to give away any secrets. "Not to say he holds back, but I think that's just part of their organization and how they are," Simms said. "It doesn't bother me. I get enough."

Manning was twenty-two when he came into the NFL, but Simms said his greatest attribute was, "He was a thirty-five-year-old man in his head. He was one of those kids that when he was ten years old, when the adults all sat around the table and the kids went and played, he probably sat at the table and wanted to hear what the adults were saying."

He is revered around the league. Players and coaches gravitate toward him. He's held court at the hotel at the Pro Bowl in Honolulu as players and coaches stop by for a chat. One year Simms was there to broadcast the game and sat down for what he intended to be a quick lunch by the pool on the Friday before the game. Manning soon joined him. They began talking and Belichick walked by. Manning invited him to sit down. Then it was Sean Payton. Then Shannon Sharpe. "About eight hours later, we are still there," Simms said. "He kept going down the line of people and had them sit down. It was hilarious."

Manning is not a trash-talker. Brady is one of the best. Sherman says he loves Brady's game and demeanor. "As a competitor, as a player in this league, love him. I relish competitors like that. You love his fire for his team to win games," he said.

Brady was once fined $10,000 for kicking Ravens safety Ed Reed in the thigh as Brady was sliding with his right leg up in a playoff game. He texted Reed to apologize. It's not often quarterbacks get fined for chippy play. Sherman got into some trash-talking with Brady during a regular-season game in Seattle in 2012. Brady told him to come to see him after the Patriots won the game. Seattle scored two fourth-quarter touchdowns to win it, and Sherman got in Brady's face. He then posted a picture of the postgame meeting with the caption "u mad bro?" Brady got even in the Super Bowl two years later, but he stayed away from Sherman's side of the field.

On a December night in 2010, Brady went too far with the New York Jets. After he threw a 1-yard touchdown pass to Aaron Hernandez on the first play of the fourth quarter, making it 38–3 on the way to a 45–3 victory, the Jets felt Brady was a little too excited about a meaningless touchdown. They thought he was pointing to their sideline after the score.

"Just Brady being Brady," Ryan said.

The next day, Ryan grabbed a football—which he claimed was a game ball—and marched his team to the side of the practice field and buried the ball. It's an old trick Belichick once pulled with the Patriots. Ryan was steamed about the 42-point loss.

"That's getting your ass kicked," he would say years later looking back on that game. "I don't expect the guy to feel sorry for me, but trying to rub my nose in it a little bit? That's why I said we are going to get them back. I told the team, 'We're going to get these fuckers back at their place in six weeks.'"

The Jets beat the Colts in the wild-card game, setting up the rematch in Foxboro. Ryan had his players so fired up early in the week, there was a fear they would peak in practice and have nothing left for the game. Five days before kickoff, cornerback Antonio Cromartie was standing by himself at his locker as the media-access period for the day had about ten minutes remaining. Ryan's "Brady being Brady" comment was still in Cromartie's head. His distaste for Brady produced one of the great responses in NFL history. All it took was one question from a columnist from the *New York Daily News:* What do you think of Tom Brady?

"An asshole. Fuck him," Cromartie said.

Brady's response was classic. "I've been called worse," he said. "I'm sure there's a long list of people that feel that way."

The Jets had the last word. They beat the Patriots 28–21, sacked Brady five times, and hit him hard many other times. The cover shot in *Sports Illustrated* pictured Jets linebacker Calvin Pace pummeling Brady. For years, that was prominently displayed on the wall in Ryan's office.


**Brady vs. Manning** has been great for the NFL. It's been great for Brady and Manning. They have pushed each other to the very top of the heap of the all-time best quarterbacks. They have needed each other and been there for each other. They are Magic and Bird, Wilt and Russell, Ali and Frazier, Palmer and Nicklaus, but even better.

They are great rivals. They are great friends.

"I have great respect for him," Manning said.

"It's nice to have a peer that you can really rely on, you know is completely trustworthy," Brady said.

Friends say Manning might own an NFL team one day. Brady is interested in running a franchise. It would be fitting if they can work together and finally stop trying to beat each other.

No introduction will be necessary.

# EPILOGUE

Peyton Manning walked over to Bill Belichick for the usual post-game handshake following the Broncos' 20–18 victory over the Patriots in the AFC Championship Game following the 2015 regular season. He then spent time on the field talking with Tom Brady. It went longer than usual. They embraced not only each other but also the moment, knowing Brady vs. Manning XVII would be the finale in this historic rivalry.

"Hey, listen, this might be my last rodeo," Manning said to Belichick. "So, it sure has been a pleasure."

He relayed a similar message to Brady.

So much happened after *Brady vs Manning* was released—including that fateful final Brady vs. Manning AFC championship in Denver—that I felt it would be important to devote this epilogue to tying it all together and putting a bow on the rivalry that defined this era of the NFL.

Manning had missed the regular-season game against the Patriots in Denver on the Sunday night of Thanksgiving weekend. He was diagnosed with a partially torn plantar fascia in his left foot a few weeks earlier after he had been benched in the third quarter during a dreadful four-interception, five-completion performance in a loss to Kansas City. One week after Manning's backup, Brock Osweiler, beat the Bears in his first career start, he played well against the undefeated Patriots, bringing the Broncos back from a 14-point deficit to win in overtime. There was a strong feeling that Manning could end his career on the bench if Osweiler continued to win.

Osweiler began to regress after his initial hot start, but there was still no Manning sighting. He was going through an extended rehabilitation on his damaged foot, but time was running out for him to get back on the field. The season was nearly over. Once he satisfied coach Gary Kubiak that he was ready to play again, he was designated the backup in the final game of the season against the Chargers. There was no guarantee he would play. But with Osweiler struggling in a game the Broncos needed to win to clinch the number-one seed in the AFC, Kubiak went to the bullpen in the third quarter for Manning, who helped Denver beat San Diego. Kubiak then named Manning to start in the divisional round playoff game two weeks later, even though he had missed seven starts and finished the season with just 9 touchdowns and 17 interceptions.

Now the Patriots were back in the Mile High City for the conference championship game for the second time in three years for what certainly would be the final installment of Brady vs. Manning. The trip to Denver could have been avoided, but Belichick uncharacteristically let up in the final two weeks of the regular season after New England had clinched at least the number-two seed and a first-round bye. The Patriots needed to win only one of their final two games or have Denver lose one of its last two to clinch the top seed and secure home field throughout the playoffs.

Belichick is a brilliant coach, but even brilliant coaches do dumb things.

He elected to kick off after winning the coin toss to start overtime in the fifteenth game of the season, against the Jets, who went right down the field on the New England defense and scored a touchdown to end the game without Brady ever touching the ball. Belichick's postgame answers did little to clarify his convoluted logic in keeping the ball out of Brady's hands, especially since Brady had led the Patriots to their only offensive touchdown to tie the score on their final possession of the fourth quarter. No surprise, but Brady wouldn't second-guess his coach's decision not to give him the ball.

"No, I'm not offended at all," Brady said. "When Coach decided that's what he wants to do, then you go with it."

Even with the lost opportunity against the Jets, the Patriots were still in control of the number-one seed if they beat the Dolphins in Miami to finish the season. But instead of stomping on the Dolphins early and putting a dead team out of its misery, Belichick chose to work on the Patriots' beleaguered running game. In the first half of the 20–10 loss, Brady attempted only 5 passes while the Patriots ran 21 times. Once again, keeping the ball out of Brady's hands cost New England a chance to guarantee it would play all its playoff games at Gillette Stadium.

When the playoffs opened, it was the Broncos who had earned the number-one seed, with the Patriots relegated to the number-two spot. The story line going into the postseason was the anticipation of Brady vs. Manning XVII, but each player had work to do first.

After the wild-card round, the divisional-round matchups were set: Kansas City at New England and Pittsburgh at Denver. It was a favorable matchup for the home teams despite the Chiefs' annihilating the Patriots 41–14 in Kansas City in 2014 and the Broncos losing in late December in Pittsburgh when Osweiler was the quarterback. Kansas City's Andy Reid has been one of the best regular-season coaches of this generation, but just like in his Super Bowl matchup with Belichick following the 2004 season when he was in Philadelphia, Reid's questionable clock management prevented the Chiefs from putting together a late comeback in New England.

The Steelers beat the Bengals in the wild-card game one week earlier in Cincinnati, but paid a huge price in a very violent game that left several key Steelers injured. Despite the Steelers' injury woes, the game was a struggle for the Broncos and Manning. But Manning saved his best for last, hitting wide receiver Bennie Fowler for 31 yards on a crucial third-and-12 on his most important pass of the season. It set up the winning touchdown with three minutes left.

The moment the last second ticked off the clock in Denver, the radio shows, newspapers, websites, and local and national television shows were dominated by talk of Brady vs. Manning. It was clear that Manning, who would turn forty on March 24, was going to retire, even though he deferred all talk until after the season. Not surprisingly, he was also going to be the one to dictate when the final script was turned in. Manning always tried to stay in control of the narrative when it involved him.

It was appropriate that the NFL would be treated to one more Brady vs. Manning matchup, but the road to get there was filled with anger and angst for both of them. The two players who had been the faces of the NFL for the previous fifteen years, players who had impeccable reputations off the field, had been forced to defend their character and integrity.

They had each been accused of cheating, but in very different ways.

By the time the 2015 NFL season began, the biggest story of the off-season was temporarily put to rest: U.S. District Court Judge Richard Berman overturned Brady's four-game suspension for Deflategate, making him available to the Patriots for the season opener against the Steelers at Gillette Stadium on September 10. Exactly one week earlier, Berman had issued his ruling that allowed Brady to get back on the field. Berman didn't comment on the facts of the case, but during the court sessions he clearly seemed perturbed when the NFL admitted it had no direct evidence that Brady had participated in the deflation of footballs used in the 2014 AFC Championship Game against the Colts.

The legal mandate for Berman was to rule on how the NFL handled the case and whether Roger Goodell abused the power granted to him in the collective bargaining agreement. "The court finds that Brady had no notice that he could receive a four-game suspension for general awareness of ball deflation by others," Berman wrote in his forty-page decision.

It was a home run for Brady, Belichick, and Patriots fans and a setback for Goodell.

The commissioner had upheld Brady's suspension one month after an all-day appeals hearing on June 23, 2015, in a basement conference room at the NFL offices at 345 Park Avenue. Brady's decision to destroy his cell phone became a central issue, although he later gave the NFL complete records of his calls and texts and turned over e-mails. The optics were bad. If Brady had nothing to hide, why would he destroy his phone? Goodell clearly didn't buy Brady's argument that it was his standard practice to get rid of all traces of his old phones to protect his privacy when he got a new one.

"I am very disappointed by the NFL's decision to uphold the 4 game suspension against me. I did nothing wrong, and no one in the Patriots organization did either," Brady wrote on his Facebook page. "Despite submitting to hours of testimony over the past 6 months, it is disappointing that the Commissioner upheld my suspension based upon a standard that it was 'probable' that I was 'generally aware' of misconduct. The fact is that neither I, nor any equipment person, did anything of which we have been accused. He dismissed my hours of testimony and it is disappointing that he found it unreliable."

Brady usually speaks to the media once a week during training camp and also following preseason games. But he shut them out all summer as Goodell upheld his suspension right before camp opened and then Brady had nothing to say as he appealed the case. Brady and Goodell sat one row apart in Courtroom 17B at 500 Pearl Street in U.S. District Court in Lower Manhattan for the opening session of the appeal and never made eye contact. Brady looked pretty pissed off. He had to leave training camp twice to be in court. His facial expression gave it away: He would rather face the vicious '85 Bears defense with no offensive line in front of him than be subjected to the indignity of having his integrity dismantled. Seven months earlier, Goodell was posing with Brady after handing him the Super Bowl MVP trophy. Now Brady couldn't stand the sight of him, their relationship irreparably damaged. He hardly took a victory lap when Berman ruled in his favor weeks later.

"While I am pleased to be eligible to play, I am sorry our league had to endure this," Brady said in another statement on his Facebook page. "I don't think it has been good for our sport—to a large degree, we have all lost. I am also sorry to anyone whose feeling I may have hurt as I have tried to work to resolve this situation. I love the NFL. It is a privilege to be a member of the NFL community and I will always try to do my best in representing my team and the league in a way that would make all members of this community proud."

Three thousand miles away, Tom Brady Sr. was thankful Berman had cleared the way for his son to be on the field for the beginning of the season.

"We're very relieved and thankful that Tommy will be able to play football," he said. "It's all he ever wanted to do. Now he's getting on to the season and it's the first time in nine months that he has the burden lifted from his shoulders. He's glad it's over and he's really happy now."

From the moment Brady sprinted the length of the field when the Patriots were introduced as a team before opening the defense of their Super Bowl title against the Steelers, there was a look in his eye. He wanted revenge. If he came into the NFL in 2000 with a huge grudge against a league that forced him to wait until the sixth round to be drafted, then his attitude for the 2015 season was not to prove people of his innocence, it was to make the Patriots opponents pay for how he felt abused by Goodell during a process that took over seven months.

Each time Brady looked over the defense on opening night, it was as if he were peering out at six Ted Wellses and five Roger Goodells. He wanted to burn them on every play. He completed 25 of 32 passes with four touchdowns and no interceptions and a quarterback rating of a nearly perfect 143.8 in New England's 28–14 victory. At one point, Brady completed a franchise record 19 consecutive passes. None of his passes hit the ground from late in the first quarter until early in the fourth quarter, and there were no questions about whether the footballs were properly inflated.

Fans chanted "Brady, Brady, Brady" all night long. In the middle of the fourth quarter with the Patriots up by a comfortable 14 points, the fans derisively sang, "Where is Roger? Where is Roger?" Goodell had wisely opted not to attend the season opener and be present when the Patriots raised their Super Bowl banner. He was not a very popular man in New England.

"It was a pretty special night," Brady said. "I was excited. We haven't had one of these games in a long time. I love to be out there with my teammates playing. It was something I was really looking forward to."

Brady played the 2015 season knowing that Goodell and his team of high-priced lawyers were not going to concede defeat and accept the ruling in Berman's courtroom. The NFL immediately appealed, and a date of March 3, 2016, was set for oral arguments to be heard by the Second Circuit Court of Appeals in downtown Manhattan. Brady and Goodell were not required to attend and were not in attendance as Chief Judge Robert Katzmann and the two other judges assigned to the case, Barrington Parker Jr. and Denny Chin, peppered NFL attorney Paul Clement and NFL Players Association attorney Jeffrey Kessler with questions.

The issue was not Brady's guilt or innocence in Deflategate, but whether Goodell was within his rights outlined in the collective bargaining agreement to suspend Brady and whether he had been fair to Brady in the process. It was a labor-law issue. Not a football issue.

The tone of the questions directed at Kessler, particularly by Parker and Chin, gave a clear indication Brady was in danger of suffering a 2–1 defeat. Parker was not pleased Brady had destroyed his cell phone, which the league's investigator Ted Wells had wanted to inspect for electronic evidence. Brady's explanation that it was his standard procedure to destroy his old phone when he got a new one in order to protect his privacy did not sit well with Parker.

"With all due respect to Mr. Brady, his explanation made no sense whatsoever," Parker said in court.

Chin also wasn't buying Brady's claim that he was unaware of how the footballs lost air pressure in the AFC Championship Game against the Colts. "Evidence of ball tampering is compelling if not overwhelming. How do we second-guess the four-game suspension?" he said in the courtroom.

The Second Circuit usually takes several months to issue its rulings. In this case, it took just fifty-three days. On April 25, the Second Circuit ruled 2–1 in favor of the NFL to overturn Berman's ruling. Katzmann issued the dissenting opinion. Brady's four-game suspension was reinstated, scheduled to be served at the opening of the 2016 season.

The union had signed off on Goodell's power in the CBA, and it would be up to the union to try to rescind it in future labor negotiations. The Second Circuit refused to do it for them.

The next move belonged to the Patriots quarterback. His options were to appeal and request a rehearing before the full thirteen-judge panel of the Second Circuit Court of Appeals or attempt to take the case all the way to the United States Supreme Court. Legal experts believed it would be a long shot that either court would hear the case. Goodell offered no indication he would be willing to negotiate a settlement with Brady after talks failed to produce a compromise prior to Berman's ruling. So, despite the fact that football fans were suffering Deflategate fatigue, the case would not go away.

Given a temporary reprieve from legal proceedings during the 2015 season, Brady played with a chip on his shoulder and cruised with 36 touchdown passes and just 7 interceptions. The Patriots won their first ten games on the way to a 12-4 regular season. It was a letdown when New England was in Denver on November 29 and Manning could not play. His body was not cooperating.

**Peyton Manning was** thirty-nine but seemed to age ten years from the time he injured his thigh in December 2014 until the start of the 2015 season. He had 37 touchdown passes and 11 interceptions in the first 14 games of the '14 season. But then in the final 12 regular-season games of his career—the last two games in 2014 and the 10 he played in during the 2015 season—he had 11 TDs and 21 INTs. His body truly looked like it was being held together by Band-Aids and the next big hit could break him in half.

Manning was a lousy fit in Kubiak's offense. Kubiak wanted him to run it from under center. Manning preferred the shotgun. Manning was accustomed to being the heartbeat of the offense.

Kubiak wanted to emphasize the running game. By the time Kubiak mercifully benched Manning against the Chiefs, he was booed off the field by the Broncos fans.

The frustration of a lost season somehow got worse on December 26, when word leaked of an upcoming report from an Al-Jazeera America documentary called *The Dark Side*, which alleged that HGH was shipped from an anti-aging clinic in Indianapolis to Peyton's wife, Ashley, in 2011 with the insinuation it was actually for Peyton to help him recover from his fourth neck surgery that caused him to miss the entire season.

The veins popped out of Manning's neck and forehead as he denied the allegations, calling them "garbage." The network's informant, Charlie Sly, recanted the information he provided before the report even aired, which assisted Manning in trying to make it go away. Manning hired Ari Fleischer, a former press secretary in the George W. Bush White House, as a crisis manager. The report had a long shelf life, but with no corroborating evidence uncovered by other media outlets, Manning had enough credibility built up that he was able to fight off claims that he was using HGH. At the time, the NFL was not testing for it, but it was a banned substance.

Manning went on ESPN the morning of December 27, the date the documentary was to air, and denied he had ever used HGH. "Absolutely not, absolutely not," Manning said. "What hurts me the most about this, whoever this guy is, this slapstick trying to insinuate that in 2011, when more or less I had a broken neck—I had four neck surgeries. . . . It stings me whoever this guy is to insinuate that I cut corners, I broke NFL rules, in order to get healthy. It's a joke. It's a freaking joke."

Manning had missed only one play in the first thirteen years of his NFL career due to injury before he could not play at all in 2011. He broke his jaw in a game against the Dolphins in 2001.

Backup Mark Rypien came in for one play, and fumbled the snap with Miami recovering. Manning was back in the game the next series. His experience in 2015 was new to him. Never before had he been injured in the middle of a season and then been forced to miss games. There is nothing more lonely than being an injured player in the NFL, even for Peyton Manning. Injured players feel isolated from the team. Manning rehabbed when the Broncos were practicing. When he first resumed throwing, he did it in the Broncos field house at off hours away from the team and with a no-name contingent of receivers.

There really was no reason to believe when Kubiak first put him back in against San Diego that things were going to go well. He was 5-of-9 for 69 yards, but the running game picked up with his being back at quarterback and getting the Broncos into the right play by changing calls before the snap. Brady had said during the 2015 season that he planned to play ten more years, which would put him at close to his fiftieth birthday. At times during the season, Manning didn't look like he could make it ten more minutes.

Kubiak's decision to start Manning in the playoffs not only gave him an opportunity to finish his career with a championship and allow him to go out on top like Broncos boss John Elway had done, but once the Broncos and Patriots won their divisional-round playoff games, it meant Brady and Manning were in each other's way once again.

Manning had been careful not to admit he was going to retire after the season. Even though he was already the story, he didn't want to become a distraction. So, over and over, he kept repeating that he was taking it one step at a time without getting too far ahead of himself.

For the first time since the very first Brady–Manning game, back in 2001, this one appeared to be a mismatch at quarterback— but now it was in Brady's favor. He was coming off one of his best seasons, and until Cam Newton's lights-out stretch that helped the Panthers get to 14-0, it was Brady who was the favorite to be the league's MVP. Manning had played less than six quarters in the previous two months and was coming off a dreadful regular season.

Manning was now a $15 million game manager. He wasn't being asked to win games. He was being asked not to lose them. Denver had a dominant defense, and Manning's job was not to turn the ball over and create a short field for Brady.

The buildup to the AFC title game was intense. One step from the Super Bowl, Brady and Manning were set to meet again for what surely would be the final time.

Manning got off to a nice start throwing a pair of touchdown passes to tight end Owen Daniels to give the Broncos a 14–6 lead less than two minutes into the second quarter. In between, Steven Jackson scored on a short run for the Patriots' first touchdown, but Stephen Gostkowski, the most reliable kicker in the NFL, missed his first extra point in the first season since it was moved back to a 33-yard kick. It was also his first extra-point miss since the final game of his rookie year in 2006. He had made 523 in a row. It turned out to be the most costly mistake of the game.

Ironically, it had been Belichick who was the most vocal proponent of moving the line of scrimmage for extra points from the 2-yard line to the 15-yard line. It had become an automatic play in the NFL, and Belichick favored making it more of a challenge. The success rate dropped from 99.3 percent in 2014 to 94.2 in 2015.

"Philosophically, plays that are non-plays shouldn't be in the game," Belichick said.

Although Manning would not get the Broncos back into the end zone and they managed to score only 3 points in the second half, Denver held a 20–12 lead with ten minutes remaining after

Brandon McManus hit a 31-yard field goal. New England had managed only two field goals by Gostkowski after Jackson's score, and was now in the position of needing a touchdown and 2-point conversion to tie it up. Even so, there was plenty of time remaining for the Patriots to come back without going for it on fourth down in field-goal range.

Belichick, however, outsmarted himself down the stretch. The Patriots had a fourth-and-1 at the Denver 16 with just over six minutes remaining. The right play would have been to go for the field goal to get within 20–15 and then count on the Patriots defense to continuing doing what it had done most of the game: stop Manning.

But Belichick decided to go for it, and Brady's fourth-down pass to Julian Edelman lost one yard.

Manning then went three-and-out, giving the ball back to Brady. He moved the Patriots from their own 29 to the Denver 14, where they faced a fourth-and-6 with 2:25 left. If Belichick had kicked the field goal on the previous series, he could have kicked it again now, cutting the lead to two points with three time-outs and the two-minute warning to help him get the ball back for a winning field goal. He still could have kicked the field goal and then just needed a TD without the two-point conversion to decide the season. He decided to go for it once again on fourth down. Once again, the Patriots failed to convert, this time with Brady throwing incomplete to Rob Gronkowski.

How many chances were the Patriots going to get? As it turned out, one more. Manning once again went three-and-out, and Brady had the ball at his 50 with 1:52 remaining. Belichick had used two of his time-outs on the Broncos' possession. Brady had one left, but would have to navigate 50 yards into the end zone and then convert on the two-point try to send the game into overtime.

If Belichick had shown faith in his defense to stop Manning and kicked the field goal twice, the Pats would have been down 20–18 and needing only 15 yards to give Gostkowski a chance to win. If he went for just one of the field goals, the Patriots would have trailed by five points and not needed to go for two if they scored a touchdown.

But instead, Brady faced the worst-case scenario. He needed a touchdown and then the two-point conversion against a vicious Broncos defense that would finish the day with 2 interceptions, 4 sacks, and 23 hits on Brady, knocking him down 14 times.

"I got hit pretty hard," Brady said. "It's football."

Brady converted two incredible fourth-down throws to Gronkowski on the last drive, a 40-yarder from midfield and a 4-yard touchdown pass. Manning was putting in some mileage pacing on the sidelines, but Brady's two-point conversion to Edelman was tipped by former Patriot Aqib Talib and intercepted by Bradley Roby to send Manning to Super Bowl 50.

"To come down to a two-point conversion is a tough way to end the season," Brady said.

When Brady looked at the film of the failed two-point try, he must have gotten sick. Gronkowski was running free left to right seven yards deep in the end zone, a pass Brady completes in his sleep. It doesn't happen often, but Brady threw to the wrong man.

Broncos 20, Patriots 18.

Brady 11, Manning 6.

That included Manning with a 3–2 lead in playoff meetings. The last three times they met in the postseason were in AFC Championship Games, and Manning won all three. If you include little brother Eli's two Super Bowl victories over the Patriots, then the last five of Brady's losses in playoff games had been to the Manning brothers.

Tom and Peyton met at midfield.

They knew it would be the last time for this must-watch rivalry.

"I have great respect for Tom as a player, as a friend, and as a quarterback for that franchise," Manning said after the game.

He expanded on those thoughts in an interview with Peter King of the MMQB.

"I hope everybody enjoyed that game. I know I enjoyed being there. That's what I told Tom and Bill—that I've enjoyed this game and I've enjoyed all of them. I've enjoyed the rivalry and all the games we've been in. It's been such an honor to play against both of them.

"This is my seventeenth time playing against the Patriots with Tom at quarterback. It's my twenty-fourth against Belichick as head coach or defensive coordinator. I can't shake either one of them. They are always there. They're always standing between me and where our team wants to go. What a rivalry. It's been such a big part of my career. So I wanted to take the time to pass that along to them, with how much respect I have for both of them."

**Brady went home** to Boston, and Manning had two weeks to prepare for the Panthers in Super Bowl 50 at Levi's Stadium in Santa Clara, the home of the 49ers. This was Manning's fourth Super Bowl, and it had arrived unexpectedly. He had gone from potentially ending his career as a backup to Osweiler to having an opportunity to go out a Super Bowl champion. Just two years earlier, the Broncos had set the NFL record for points and Manning had set the record for most touchdown passes in a season, but Denver still lost to Seattle 43–8 in the Super Bowl. Manning was no longer the same player and the Broncos offense was no longer explosive, but the Denver defense was the best in team history and playing at its highest level of the season.

Manning's future dominated the lead-up to Super Bowl 50. He insisted he was keeping the one-week-at-a-time approach he adopted when he was injured and still refused to say that this would be his last game. He had too much respect for his coaches and teammates and too much respect for the NFL to make himself the story by announcing he was hanging it up after the game. Sometimes things are better left unsaid even when they are so obvious.

He was more forthcoming when he spoke first with Belichick and then Brady after the AFC Championship Game.

"It's something I wanted to tell them man-to-man rather than at a banquet or by text. It was important to me they knew it," Manning said a few days before the Super Bowl. "What I said was this could be it. It doesn't mean it will be. I told both of them I really enjoyed these games. These guys have been a part of it. Brady is going to play until he's seventy. Belichick is going to coach until he's ninety. Maybe I'll find the fountain of youth."

Manning and the Broncos were clearly hoping for a better showing in the Super Bowl than the no-show from two years earlier against the Seahawks at MetLife Stadium. It was the AFC's turn to be the home team, and the Broncos had their choice of whether to wear their bright orange home jerseys or the white jerseys they wear on the road. The two previous times the Broncos wore orange in the Super Bowl they lost by 32 points to the Redskins and by 35 points to the Seahawks. Elway decided to change the vibe and opted for the white jerseys.

As part of the festivities to celebrate the 50th Super Bowl, the NFL invited the previous Super Bowl MVPs to take part in a pregame ceremony. Was Brady, a three-time Super Bowl MVP, going to show up at the game, or would he show up Goodell by boycotting the event, even if it was basically down the road from where he grew up in San Mateo? It was the mystery of Super Bowl week. Even those closest to Brady were unsure or even split on whether he would make an appearance. That's how ticked off Brady still was at Goodell for the beating his reputation took in Deflategate.

At mid-week leading up to the Super Bowl, Brady was back in Ann Arbor at the invitation of Michigan coach Jim Harbaugh to take part in a national-signing-day extravaganza. Finally, three days before the game, the NFL confirmed that Brady would be taking his place among the Super Bowl greats. Interestingly, he was booed by the fans at Levi's Stadium. The disenchantment with Brady was most likely from Broncos fans in the house and from fans voicing their displeasure with Brady's alleged role in Deflategate.

This was Manning's fourth Super Bowl, but it was very different from the first three. He was no longer a dominant player. The Broncos would be thrilled if he limited his mistakes and let the defense win it. He led a nice opening drive that resulted in a field goal less than five minutes into the game. The Broncos would never trail. Von Miller, who would be voted Super Bowl MVP, forced a fumble by Newton, which Malik Jackson recovered for a touchdown. Miller would later clinch the game by forcing another Newton fumble in the fourth quarter deep in Carolina territory, which set up a touchdown run by C. J. Anderson to give the Broncos a two-touchdown lead with 3:08 remaining.

Manning played one of the most ineffective games ever for a Super Bowl–winning quarterback. He threw one interception and fumbled twice, losing one of them. His lost fumble set up a Panthers field goal to get them to 16–10 early in the fourth quarter, giving Carolina an opening. Carolina had the ball twice with a chance to take the lead, but they went three-and-out on the first possession and then Miller forced Newton's second fumble.

Manning had an ugly statistical line: 13 of 23 for 141 yards with no touchdowns and one interception. He was sacked five times. Even so, he became the first quarterback to win the Super

Bowl for two different teams. He's also the only quarterback to make it to the Super Bowl playing for four different head coaches.

"Being on two different teams, winning a Super Bowl with each team, I'm proud of that," Manning said. "I'm proud to have been a part of two football teams and organizations that had a chance to win the Lombardi Trophy. Playing a long time, I know how hard it is just to have an opportunity to play in the game. So I do not take it for granted. I'm very grateful and very appreciative."

One hour after the game, he still was deflecting questions about whether he had played his final game. Now, instead of fearing he would be a distraction, he didn't want to take any of the attention away from the Broncos' victory.

But he was not done with controversy. A few days after the game, alleged information on an incident that took place in 1996 between Manning and Dr. Jamie Naughright, a female athletic trainer, when Manning was a twenty-year-old sophomore at Tennessee, surfaced from an old lawsuit. Manning has always maintained it was nothing more than a boys-will-be-boys mooning incident, while the trainer has claimed that while she was examining Manning for a possible stress fracture in his foot, he slid down the training table and pushed his naked testicles and rectum into her face.

According to the document, she reported the incident to the Sexual Assault Crisis Center in Knoxville. There was a settlement with the University of Tennessee, but Naughright sued Manning seven years later for defamation when his version of the story was recounted in Peyton and Archie Manning's book, *Manning*. It was settled out of court.

The story lingered for one month without comment from Manning. He was consumed with deciding his football future. It was assumed he would retire and walk away a champion, but every now and then stories appeared that he indeed wanted to play again, although the Broncos had no interest in bringing him back. The hot rumor was that the Rams, in their first season back in Los Angeles, were interested in him being their quarterback to make a big splash in Hollywood. The Rams would later trade multiple high draft picks to the Tennessee Titans for the first pick in the draft with the plan to get their franchise quarterback. Then old rumors about the Houston Texans started to circulate. Nothing materialized.

Finally, on March 7, one month after the Super Bowl, Manning stood before a packed gathering at the Broncos' headquarters to announce his retirement. Toward the end of the conference, Manning was asked about the Tennessee incident.

"First of all, this is a joyous day and nothing can overtake from this day," he said. "I think it is sad that some people don't understand the truth and the facts. I did not do what has been alleged, and I am not interested in re-litigating something that happened when I was nineteen years old. Kind of like my daddy used to say when I was in trouble, 'I can't say it any plainer than that.' This is a joyous day. It's a special day. Like Forrest Gump said: 'That's all I have to say about that.'"

That was the only deviation from what was otherwise a celebration of Manning's career. He was to turn forty just seventeen days later, and as much as he still loved everything about football, he realized that his body was telling him it was time to go. Even when Osweiler surprisingly signed with the Texans a couple of days later, there was never any indication that Manning would change his mind or that the Broncos wanted him to change his mind.

"When someone thoroughly exhausts an experience they can't help but revere it. I revere football. I love the game. So you don't have to wonder if I'll miss it," Manning said. "Absolutely. Absolutely I will."

He gave an eloquent farewell speech, paying homage to the game, his teammates, and opponents.

"I'll miss that handshake with Tom Brady, and I'll miss the plane rides after a big win with fifty-three teammates standing in the aisles laughing and celebrating during the whole flight," he said. "I'll miss playing in front of so many great fans both at home and on the road. I'll even miss the Patriots fans in Foxborough, and they should miss me because they sure did get a lot of wins off of me."

The day before Manning made his retirement official, King got in touch with Brady after ESPN reported Manning was done.

Brady said, "The way he played football, and the way he was consumed by football, all the mental energy he had to use, and I mean every day of the year you're thinking about it—imagine what he must feel like with all that pressure off."

Brady was asked what it was going to be like for him playing for the first time without Manning in the NFL. "That part sucks," Brady said. "That part really sucks. That part will always suck."

Their rivalry and competition was real. So was their friendship. Manning developed a routine of writing letters to players who retire to let them know how much he enjoyed competing against them. Brady was basically doing the same in his interview with the MMQB.

"Every game he has played, I have watched," Brady said. "I have file folders of his plays, of how he plays. It'd take years for me to watch it all again. But what he's done in Denver has been incredible.

"What just happened, winning the Super Bowl in his last game, is a perfect way to end a career. But what he's accomplished through all these years, what makes it so admirable, is the pressure he's had on him his whole life. He was the highest-rated recruit in high school. He was the biggest quarterback in college football.

He was the first pick in the draft. Who has lived up to the expectations year after year after year as well as Peyton?"

King asked Brady what he learned from Manning.

"A lot," said Brady. "I realized the level of commitment you must have to be great, watching him do it. I know the time I put in, so I knew the time he had to have put in. It's not 9-to-5. It's a lifelong commitment. Football is a sport, it's an art, it's a religion. It's all-encompassing. He mastered it."

Manning's ability to win his second Super Bowl ring not only bolstered his legacy; it allowed him to close the gap on Brady. There are now twelve quarterbacks who have won at least two Super Bowls, and Manning is one of them. Brady finishes the rivalry with a five-game lead on Manning in their seventeen meetings and a 4–2 lead in Super Bowl rings, but when you consider that Manning won the last three playoff meetings over a nine-season period, and all three were with a Super Bowl berth at stake, it doesn't make it appear quite as lopsided.

Their names and careers will be forever linked. They made each other better.

The rivalry lasted sixteen seasons. The friendship might last forever.

# ACKNOWLEDGMENTS

I had known Peyton Manning since the day before he was drafted, covered the first game of his career against his idol Dan Marino in 1998, and, with his brother Eli playing in New York, had seen him quite a bit over the years. He knew me by name. He knows everybody by name. I had been around Tom Brady as well, covering Jets-Patriots games and being at his Super Bowls, but didn't have much luck the first time we tried to meet face-to-face.

It was the summer of 2002, after his first Super Bowl victory. The Patriots set up a lunchtime interview for me to sit down with Brady at training camp at Bryant College in Smithfield, Rhode Island. He was on a tight schedule. Me too. I waited and waited and saw the window to interview him before practice closing and still no Brady. I knew this wasn't going to work.

His meetings ran right through his lunch break between two-a-day practices. I had other commitments and could not stick around until the afternoon practice was over, as the Patriots suggested, but drove back to New York. My phone rang around six p.m. "Hey, this is Tom Brady," he said. "Sorry about what happened today."

We had a long talk. I got what I needed for my column for the *New York Daily News,* and soon after, we had a head-nod relationship. When he saw me in big groups around him at training camp or at the Super Bowl, we would nod at each other. When I wrote the headline-grabbing story about Antonio Cromartie calling Brady an asshole before the Jets played the Patriots in the 2010 playoffs, I knew he wasn't really that way. But then again, I never played against him.

After Brady addressed the New England media at the opening of training camp in 2013, I walked over to speak to him alone. I told him about my book project and asked if we could get together. "No problem," he said. "Set it up with Stacey. Tell him we spoke about it."

Stacey James, the Patriots vice president of media and community relations, is one of the best in the business and a good friend. I left it up to James to let me know when Brady could work me into his schedule. We tried for late in camp but couldn't find a day. The Patriots bye week didn't work either. The next opening came in November.

James wanted me to have as much time with Brady as possible and came up with a plan. He knows Brady very well and was concerned that if we just sat down in a meeting room at the facility, when otherwise Brady would be on his way home to see his kids, he wouldn't be able to give me quality time. He suggested I ride with Brady from Foxboro to downtown Boston, where Brady was living at the time, and with usual Boston traffic, I would probably get close to an hour. I hesitated at first. Would he really be able to give thoughtful answers while he was driving? Yes, James said, he always does his conference calls with the visiting media as he's driving home.

So when Brady exited Gillette Stadium after a quarterbacks meeting into a brutally cold New England mid-November late afternoon and we walked together toward his car in the players' parking lot, my journey to tell the story of Brady vs. Manning was officially under way.

"Ready?" Brady asked as I met him leaving the Patriots facility. "My car is over there."

He told great stories, he was insightful and forthcoming, and the ride went way too fast. When we reached downtown and were stopped at a traffic light, he gave me his cell phone number and e-mail address for any follow-up questions. He asked me questions about the process of writing a book. He always looks you in the eye when he's speaking. Except when he's driving, of course.

The funniest part of the trip came when he dropped me off at a hotel so I could catch a taxi to take me back to my car at the stadium—it was a ninety-dollar ride, by the way. As we pulled up to the hotel, we shook hands as the valet attendant came to the driver's side, asking if Brady needed to have his car parked. He said, "No thanks," and drove away.

I asked the guy if he could help me get a cab. He had a startled look on his face. "Was that . . . ?" he asked.

"Yes."

The meeting with Manning the following June was more routine. Patrick Smyth, the Broncos' excellent vice president of media relations, told Manning that Brady had spoken to me, and he recommended that it would be a good idea to also have his voice in the book. I went to Denver and spent some time with Manning in the Broncos facility after practice. He was typical Manning. His answers had depth and substance. He was thoughtful. He had gotten over being mad at me for asking him minutes after the Super Bowl loss to the Seahawks if he was embarrassed. Oh well, I thought it was a good question.

I want to thank James and Smyth for setting up the most important interviews for the book. Those are what I call two-tape-recorder interviews. "Double fisted," Patriots owner Robert Kraft said when I placed two recorders at the breakfast table when I met him at the Plaza Hotel in Manhattan. There's always the chance my digital recorder will malfunction. The odds that two would fail me at the same time were minimal. The interviews with Brady and Manning would be irreplaceable. I took no chances. They both worked.

I want to thank Tom and Peyton for their cooperation.

Aaron Salkin, the Patriots director of media relations, provided me with key statistics from the Brady-Manning rivalry. He even offered to pick me up after Brady dropped me off at the Boston hotel and take me back to Foxboro and save me the ninety dollars. Of course, by the time he told me this, I was already in the taxi.

Kraft and Colts owner Jimmy Irsay were very gracious with their time. There was one awkward moment with Irsay. I did the interview with him on the phone at the time that he was having legal troubles, in June 2014. We agreed that our conversation would be confined to Manning and football and that I would not ask him about his recent arrest on misdemeanor charges of driving while intoxicated and four felony counts of possession of a controlled substance—prescription pills. I agreed to the ground rules.

Halfway through the interview, an ESPN alert popped up on my cell phone. The state of Indiana had just suspended Irsay's driver's license for one year. The reporter in me wanted to ask him about it. But I had given my word and stuck to it.

My travels took me to a breakfast meeting with Tony Dungy, a trip to Phil Simms's house, and a Starbucks in Rhode Island to meet Dan Koppen. I had several long talks with Archie Manning and Tom Brady Sr., the patriarchs of the families. They provided me with great family photos. I had lunch with Ernie Accorsi, a former NFL general manager and one of the foremost football historians. I met with Scott Pioli when he was working for NBC. I had a long talk with Drew Bledsoe.

I went to Ann Arbor to meet former Michigan coach Lloyd

Carr to ask him to explain how the greatest quarterback in NFL history had such a hard time getting on the field at The Big House. Thanks to Dave Ablauf, the associate athletic director for communications at Michigan, for getting me in touch with Carr. Bill Hofmeier of ESPN and Chris McCloskey of NBC worked hard to set up interviews with their football talent who had Manning-Brady connections. My buddy Drew Kaliski, the producer of *The NFL Today* on CBS, sent me the video of an excellent interview Bill Cowher did with Bill Belichick.

Of course, I want to thank Nate Roberson, my editor at Crown, for his guidance and patience. He was always encouraging and knew deadlines were just a suggestion. He made this book better.

I spent many hours writing at Old Stone Trattoria in Chappaqua, New York, and I appreciate the hospitality of Angelo, who owns the place, and Hector and Marta, who know me so well they didn't even have to ask what I would like to eat. As Peyton sang in the Nationwide commercial, "Chicken parm, you taste so good." It was the perfect place when I needed a change of venue. Risten Clarke, as part of a high school internship, provided valuable research.

My wife, Allison, my best friend, pushed me every step of the way, even when we went to Aruba for one week right after Brady won his fourth Super Bowl. She insisted I write a thousand words every evening after we came off the beach and before we went to dinner. That worked for one day. My oldest daughter, Michelle, a nutritionist, made sure I ate only healthy snacks during the writing process. I got hooked on Skinny Pop, the world's greatest popcorn. Michelle felt strongly both ways in the Brady-Manning comparison. My daughter Emily is incredibly knowledgeable about football, is an excellent writer, and did some editing for me. She cast her ballot, too, in the Brady-Manning debate. It's a secret. My son Andrew was my number-one assistant. He is also a huge Jets fan, and that means he's always hated the Patriots. He's smart, and being a sport management major at Brady's alma mater, he decided the book would be more compelling if the Patriots beat the Seahawks in Super Bowl XLIX. As much as it hurt this kid who bleeds green, he texted me the morning of the Super Bowl, "I'm rooting for Brady."

Finally, I want my parents to always know, even though I can no longer tell them in person, how much I appreciate the tremendous sacrifices they made to put me in the best position to succeed. I miss you both every day.

# INDEX

# ALSO BY

# GARY MYERS

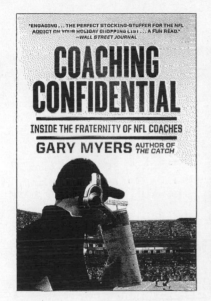

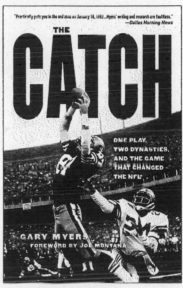

 THREE RIVERS PRESS • NEW YORK

**AVAILABLE EVERYWHERE BOOKS ARE SOLD**